SOCIETY

An Introductory Analysis

SOCIETY

An Introductory Analysis

By

R.M. Maciver

and

Charles H. Page

UNIVERSITY SCIENCE PRESS

(An Imprint of Laxmi Publications Pvt.Ltd.)

An ISO 9001:2015 Company

BENGALURU • CHENNAI • GUWAHATI • HYDERABAD • JALANDHAR

KOCHI • KOLKATA • LUCKNOW • MUMBAI • RANCHI

NEW DELHI

SOCIETY AN INTRODUCTORY ANALYSIS

Printed and bound in India

First Published : 1950, *Reprinted* : 1952-1974 (*thirteen times*),
First Published in India : 1974, *Reprinted* : 1977-2007 (*fifteen times*),
2009, 2011, 2013, 2014, 2015, 2017, 2021, *Edition* : 2023

ISBN : 978-93-5138-081-8

Branches

Bengaluru	080-26 75 69 30
Chennai	044-24 34 47 26
Guwahati	0361-254 36 69
Hyderabad	040-27 55 53 83
Jalandhar	0181-222 12 72
Kochi	0484-405 13 03
Kolkata	033-40 04 77 79
Lucknow	0522-430 36 13
Ranchi	0651-224 24 64

PUBLISHED IN INDIA BY

UNIVERSITY SCIENCE PRESS
(An Imprint of Laxmi Publications Pvt.Ltd.)

An ISO 9001:2015 Company
113, GOLDEN HOUSE, GURUDWARA ROAD,
DARYAGANJ, NEW DELHI-110002, INDIA
Telephone : 91-11-4353 2500, 4353 2501
www.laxmipublications.com
info@laxmipublications.com

C—00000/022/011
Printed at: Ajit Printing Press, Delhi.

A Word about Sociology Itself

In a few academic retreats there may still be those who disparagingly ask: "What is sociology about, anyway?" The question, thus put, is an idle one. Sociology is a field of study. If you want to know what a science is "about", you learn only by studying that science. This book is offered to those who are entering on the study of society.

It may suffice to state here that sociology is "about" social relationships, the network of relationships we call society. No other science takes that subject for its central concern. Cultural anthropology studies man (especially primitive man) in terms of the whole scheme of his activities and his products; it is as much interested in his arts and techniques, his myths and his superstitions, as in his social institutions. Economics studies man as a wealth-getter and wealth-disposer and inquires into the relations of wealth (measured by money) and welfare. History studies the record of man, following the time-order of significant events. Psychology studies man as a behaving individual, or, as some prefer to put it, the interrelation between the organism and the environment to which it responds. Social psychology is, then, a branch of psychology concerned with the ways in which the individual reacts to his social conditions. Sociology alone studies social relationships themselves, society itself. Thus the *focus* of none of these other sciences is identical with that of sociology, and it is always the focus of interest which distinguishes one social science from another. We should not think of the social sciences as dividing between them physically separate areas of reality. What distinguishes each from each is the selective interest.

As sociologists we are interested then in social relationships not because they are economic or political or religious but because they are at the same time *social*. If two people meet in the market place, they are not just two "economic men," but two human beings, and they enter into relationships that are not simply economic. The life of man is many-sided. There is an economic aspect, a legal aspect, an aesthetic aspect, a religious aspect, and so forth, but blending into them all is the social aspect. In all else he does, man relates himself to man. Society is the marvelously intricate and ever-changing pattern of the totality of these relationships.

To find and keep the focus of our subject is, then, of first importance. In particular, we should recognize that in studying society we are not attempting to study everything that happens "in society" or under social conditions, for that includes all human activity and all human learning. We shall be concerned with culture, but only for the light it throws on social relationships. We shall not, for example, study religion as religion or art as art or invention as invention. Unless we find and keep some focus we lose our way in the welter of phenomena, and this danger is always besetting the student of sociology. The only way to avoid this danger is to keep our interest focused upon social relationships themselves.

If we are to deal with social relationships we must discriminate their specific forms, varieties, and patternings. We must observe how they crisscross and how they combine. We must characterize the smaller and the greater systems they build up. We must trace their responsiveness to changing conditions, changing demands or changing needs. It is not enough to be descriptive; we must be *analytic* as well. If this book goes in more thoroughly for social analysis than do most introductions to sociology it is because we believe that such analysis is the first requisite for the intelligent study of society.

R. M. MacIver
Charles H. Page

January, 1949

Acknowledgments

WE ARE DEEPLY appreciative of the numerous suggestions made by teachers and students during the preparation of this volume. For especially generous and helpful comments on its organization and method of presentation we are indebted to Professor Kingsley Davis of Columbia University, Professor Gladys Bryson of Smith College, Professor Wilbert E. Moore of Princeton University, and Professor Robert I. Kutak of the University of Louisville; and for timely aid concerning specific aspects of the book to Mr. Morroe Berger of Columbia University, Professor John C. Thirlwall of City College of New York, and Professor Elsa Siipola and Miss Mary Ellen Bates of Smith College. We have attempted to incorporate a number of these suggestions, including particularly certain of those offered by Professor Davis and Professor Kutak, and regret that we could not take fuller advantage of the constructive proposals given us.

Responsibility for the entire volume rests solely, of course, with the authors.

The junior author must set down his gratitude to his wife, Leonora Page, and his mother, Laura Hunt Page, for their willingness to act as audience for readings of newly completed chapters; for this they have also the sympathy of both authors. The essential but dreary mechanical task of preparing the manuscript for publication has been undertaken by Leonora Page and Donald MacIver.

We wish to record as well our immeasurable indebtedness to the thousands of students who have taught us, as we have tried to teach them, at Columbia University, Barnard College, City College of New York, and Smith College.

Table of Contents

Tables

SOCIETY

An Introductory Analysis

BOOK **I**

Initiation

PART ONE: *Approach to Society*

Foreword:

EACH MEMBER of society is, in his own eyes, something of an authority on society; his participation in society, indeed, requires some knowledge of it. A part of such knowledge is the everyday language with which social living is conducted. Thus such terms as "community," "association," "institution," "custom"—society itself—are not exclusively the tools of social science. The latter, however, faces the task of converting the looseness of popular usage into the precision of scientific reference. Sociology, like every science and discipline, has its own kit of terminological tools. The student of sociology must, then, as a preliminary exercise, grasp and learn to use certain primary concepts which are basic to his field of study.

So in Chapter I we define the terms of root significance in sociological analysis. In Chapter II we proceed to a set of distinctions of a psychological nature which are essential in the study of social phenomena. The most important of these distinctions for our purpose is that between *interests* and *attitudes*, and, among interests themselves, that between the *like* and *common*.

Thus prepared, we make in Chapter III a preliminary attack on the fundamental question on which men have reflected in every age—long before there was a subject called sociology—the question of the individual and the social unity. What does it mean to be a member of a community or a group? What is the nature of the bond that unites us with our fellow men? It would be possible to proceed to our study of society leaving this question aside. But society will mean more to us and our study of it will be more significant if we see the nature of the problem and try to answer it for ourselves.

1

Primary Concepts

The Language of Sociology

The language of everyday speech. **In everyday conversation we employ such terms as "society," "community," "crowd," "institution," "custom," and the like. Throughout this book we shall be employing these same terms. Why, then, should we confront the reader with this preliminary chapter on terminology?**

The reasons have to do with the nature of language and the demands of science. In everyday conversation we do not (and frequently need not) explain in advance what we mean by such terms as community or crowd. If, for example, someone mentions "the community" we generally know the *particular* reference from the context. He may be speaking of his home town or the Italian "community" in Greenwich Village or a particular group of churchgoers or even his nation. But we usually have no trouble in grasping the meaning because we know the object of his reference. Again, if our speaker mentions "the crowd" we may generally be sure that he is referring to, say, "the rush hour crowd" and not "the sporting crowd" or "the crowd at So-and-So's party." Each of these expressions signifies an entirely different kind of social phenomenon but the context of the conversation leads us to the correct choice. In the language of semantics, our "referents" are provided by the circumstances.

When the meanings are not made clear by context, everyday speech itself is apt to be less communication than exchange of familiar sounds. And as Stuart Chase and others[1] have sufficiently stressed, the "big words" frequently reach a high level of use and low level of meaning in the efforts of the platform orator, propagandist, and editorial writer. It is important at the outset that the "big words" of sociology be clarified and rendered precise.

1. See, for example, S. Chase, *The Tyranny of Words* (New York, 1938); S. I. Hayakawa, *Language in Action* (New York, 1941).

The language of sociology. When we approach the study of society we can no longer be content to use the same terms in varying senses. Nor is there available the context of everyday conversation to guide us to the intended objects of speech reference. As sociologists, we are interested in social phenomena in the way in which botanists are interested in plants. We are interested in developing and using concepts which are both *precise* in meaning and *general* in reference. Sociological language, like the language of any other science, is *abstract*. Its useful concepts are *generic*.

For example, when we, as sociologists, speak of "the community" we are referring to a form of social organization which may be distinguished from other forms. We are interested in its common characteristics and in depicting its various types. We are interested again not merely in this crowd or in that crowd, not merely in the description of a particular crowd at a particular time. The sociologist seeks to understand *the* crowd as a certain kind of complex of social relations, to contrast, say, the way men behave in crowds from the way they behave in other kinds of groups.

So we must attach a clear and single and precise meaning to our terms, in spite of the fact that, being terms of ordinary speech, they have many variant uses. This is our starting point. The fullness of meaning, the range of applicability, the richness of content of our concepts will and must vary with the training and experience of each of us. But if we are to study and analyze anything together we must, when we use a word or phrase, be denoting, mentally pointing out, as it were, the same object. This necessity is most imperative for the primary terms, the key words of our study.

The intangibility of sociological phenomena. Beside the fact that our terms are largely those of everyday speech, unlike many terms in the physical sciences, there is a further reason why we must exercise particular care over our definitions. The phenomena dealt with in the study of society are not, for the most part, external tangible things, or kinds of things, that can be identified directly by the senses. We cannot see or touch social relations or social organizations. Institutions cannot be handled and customs cannot be weighed in a balance. We cannot apply to these phenomena a microscope or a spectroscope or other such instruments to aid our senses. We cannot isolate our units in a laboratory. Our laboratory is necessarily the world of everyday living. It is this we must explore. And it is the world of everyday human events that must supply our researches in sociology.

In pointing up the intangibility of certain sociological phenomena we must caution against the assumption of their "unreality." We are not concerned in this book with the age-old philosophical arguments concerning what is "real" and what is not. The fact that we cannot *directly* see or touch or weigh social relations or social organizations does not lessen their significance in social life. Who would deny the importance to human existence of those relations we term "love" or "hate" or "co-operation" or "conflict"? Or who today would dispute the tremendous role in the affairs of men played by such organizations as "the state," "the class," "big business," "the family"? A clearer understanding of these and related phenomena demands that our approach be grounded in common agreement on key terms.

Applying and testing the concepts of sociology. Practice does not make perfect, but it is essential in skill development. So with the language of our science. The student of sociology should not restrict the concepts of his study to the pigeonholed periods of formal class meeting or study hour. We have said that the laboratory of sociology is the world of everyday living. Each of us is a part of this world and should, if we are interested in understanding more of it, be alert to the applicability and usefulness of the language which has been designed for its analysis. The concepts of sociology can seem dull stuff indeed if they are not put to work. But perhaps there is no more rewarding intellectual experience than that which comes from the systematic study of the social life of which we are a part.

Our first task, then, is to ground our primary terms in a brief preliminary account of the objects which these terms signify. In doing so we must remember that in the developing science of modern sociology there is no accepted authority, whether created by scientific tradition or otherwise, to impose a common terminology. True, we now have a *Dictionary of Sociology*,[2] which the student will find useful as a frequent reference. But the definitions of dictionaries are not explanations. Nor is the end of sociological investigation the logical understanding of language symbols. Conceptual understanding is not *the* final objective of our study. But if we form the habit of meaning always the same object when we use these basic concepts, we shall have mastered an essential tool of sociological analysis.

Society

What we mean by society. Our first, the most general of our terms, is *society* itself. Social beings, men, express their nature by creating and re-creating an organization which guides and controls their behavior in myriad ways. This organization, society, liberates and limits the activities of men, sets up standards for them to follow and maintain: whatever the imperfections and tyrannies it has exhibited in human history, it is a necessary condition of every fulfillment of life. Society is a system of usages and procedures, of authority and mutual aid, of many groupings and divisions, of controls of human behavior and of liberties. This ever-changing, complex system we call society. It is the web of social relationships. And it is always changing.

2. H. P. Fairchild, ed. (New York, 1944).

The psychical condition of social relationships. Society, we have said, is the changing pattern of social relationships. What do we mean by social relationship? We may approach the answer by contrasting the social with the physical. There is a relationship between a typewriter and a desk, between the earth and the sun, between fire and smoke, between two chemical constituents. Each of these is affected by the existence of the other, but the relationship is not a social one. The psychical condition is lacking. The typewriter and the desk are in no intelligible sense *aware* of the presence of one another. Their relationship is not in any way determined by mutual awareness. Without this recognition there is no social relationship, no society. Society exists only where social beings "behave" toward one another in ways determined by their recognition of one another. Any relations so determined we may broadly name "social."

The range of social relationships. Social relationships are as varied as society is complex. The relations of voter to candidate, mother to child, employee to employer, friend to friend, are but a few of the varying types. The generality of the concept of "social" is borne out when we note the almost countless terms our language employs to name the many kinds of social relationships between men. Some of them we label "economic," some "political," some "personal," some "impersonal," some "friendly," some "antagonistic," and so on. But they are all *social* relationships when they are grounded in mutual recognition.

Among such relationships there are some which express mere conflict or unmitigated hostility, such as those between two armies in time of war. Armies in the field are certainly aware of nothing so much, and their activities are animated by nothing so much, as the presence of one another. Such relationships are "social." However, the great majority of social relationships involve a principle which the example of the armies expressly denies. This is the sense of community or belonging together. As sociologists, we study both the conditions that unite and those that separate human beings. But if there were no sense of community, if there were no co-operative undertakings by man, there would be no social systems, no society or societies—there would be practically nothing for sociologists to study. Hence the relationships which are central to sociology are those which involve both mutual recognition and the sense of something held or shared in common.

Society not confined to man. From our definition it should be clear that society is not limited to human beings. There are animal societies of many degrees. The remarkable social organizations of the insects, such as the ant, the bee, the hornet, are known to most school children. It has been contended that wherever there is life there is society, because life means heredity and, so far as we know, can arise only out of and in the presence of other life. But in the lowest stages of life, social awareness, if it exists, is extremely dim and the social contact often extremely fleeting. Among all higher animals at least there is a very definite society, arising out of the requirements of their nature and the conditions involved in the perpetuation of their species.

As above defined, there may be society also between animals of different species, as between a man and a horse or dog or, say, between sheep and their shepherd dog. Our concern is with society among the human species.

Society involves both likeness and difference. It is often said that the family, in some form, was the first society. It is certainly true that the sex relationship is a primary and essential type of social relationship. It is clear that this relationship involves *both* likeness and difference in the beings whom it relates. So with society in its various manifestations.

Likeness and difference are *logical* opposites, but as with many *socio*logical (and *psycho*logical) distinctions, their objective manifestations are related to each other. Indeed, the understanding of the one, in this instance *likeness*, depends upon comprehension of its *relation* to the other, in this case *difference*.[3] How is each involved in society?

Without likeness and the sense of likeness there could be no mutual recognition of "belonging together" and therefore no society. Society exists among those who resemble one another in some degree, in body and in mind, and who are near enough or intelligent enough to appreciate the fact. Society, as F. H. Giddings expressed it, rests on "consciousness of kind." In early society and among some of our "primitive contemporaries," the sense of likeness is focused on kin-membership, that is, real or supposed blood relationships. The conditions of social likeness have broadened out in modern societies. But the basic conception of likeness that primitive man identified with the kin remains in even so extensive a principle of union as nationality. And if the struggling principle of "one world" is to win out it must necessarily rest upon the recognition of the fundamental *likeness* of the entire human race.

Society, however, depends on difference as well as on likeness. If people were all exactly alike, merely alike, their social relationships would be as limited, perhaps, as those of the ant or bee. There would be little give-and-take, little reciprocity. They would contribute very little to one another. What we have noted above to be true of the sex relationship is present, in various forms, in all social systems. For they all involve relationships in which differences complement one another, in which exchange takes place. In society each member seeks something and gives something. This is fundamentally the case however "exploitative" or "parasitical" or "unjust" the social system may be. A tyrannical father of a family plays a give-*and*-take role within the family system; so does a tyrannical ruling caste within the class system. At this point we are not concerned with the just or unjust quality of social systems. Rather we are stressing the *reciprocal* role of differences in all patterns of social relationships.

3. "Up," notes Thurman Arnold, only makes sense with relation to its logical opposite, "down." See *The Folklore of Capitalism* (New Haven, 1937), Chap. VII.

[2] *Community sentiment.* Today we find, what never existed in primitive societies, people occupying specific local areas which lack the social coherence necessary to give them a community character. For example, the residents of a ward or district of a large city may lack sufficient contacts or common interests to instill conscious identification with the area. Such a "neighborhood" is not a community because it does not possess a feeling of belonging together —it lacks community sentiment. Later we shall analyze the various elements of community sentiment. Here it is sufficient to stress that locality, though a necessary condition, is not enough to create a community. A community, to repeat, is an area of common living. There must be the common living with its *awareness* of sharing a way of life as well as the common earth.

Examples and borderline cases. We can readily realize that a small town, a metropolis, a vast nation, a primitive tribe, are communities. The members of each may live their whole lives within their respective groups; each is an area of common life. In the modern world, however, the boundaries between communities are not clearcut, and within it are numerous borderline cases. The question of where to draw the line in such examples as the following becomes a difficult though not very important one.

(1) Shall we call a monastery or convent or prison a community in our sense? These establishments are territorially based and they are, indeed, areas of social living. Many, however, would deny them community status because of the restricted range of functions of the inhabitants. But human functions are always limited by the nature of one's community. We should be inclined to answer this query in the affirmative.

(2) Shall we call immigrant groups, which in the midst of large American cities cherish their own customs and speak their own language, communities? Such groups clearly possess the requirements of community, and have very often been studied by sociologists intent upon the analysis of this repeated pattern in American life.[6]

(3) Shall we call a social caste, the members of which exclude their fellow citizens from the more intimate social relationships, a community? Here the negative answer is more appropriate because, in order to satisfy our definition, the community group must by itself occupy a particular location. A social caste, as we shall see, has social coherence, to be sure, but it lacks the community's territorial basis.

The spread of civilization and the world community. The wholly self-contained community belongs to the primitive world. In the modern world the nearest approach to it is found in the huge nation-community included within the

6. See, for example, P. V. Young, *The Pilgrims of Russian Town* (Chicago, 1932); B. B. Wessell, *An Ethnic Survey of Woonsocket, Rhode Island* (Chicago, 1931); W. L. Warner and Leo Srole, *The Social Systems of American Ethnic Groups* (New Haven, 1945).

frontiers of a single state. This has been especially the case when the state has sought to "co-ordinate" the whole national life as did National Socialist Germany, or when, as in Soviet Russia, it establishes a form of economy very different from that of most other nations. But Nazi Germany was never self-sufficient, nor is the U.S.S.R., as American exporters of heavy machinery will testify. Modern civilization, we know, unleashes forces which break down the self-containedness of communities great or small.

These forces are partly *technological*, such as the improvement of the means of communication and transportation; partly *economic*, such as the demand for markets and for wider areas of economic exchange necessitated by the newer processes of industrial production; and partly *cultural*, since the thought and art and science of one country are, whatever the temporary barriers of "ideological" and political construction, inevitably carried on the wings of civilization to others. In the face of these forces, there are no national "secrets," atomic or otherwise, of permanent duration.

Certainly Wendell Willkie's *One World* has been in the making for centuries. We have been approaching a stage where no completely self-contained community can be found on any scale unless we extend the limits of community to include the whole earth. Men's current efforts to develop political agencies of world scope are consistent with the trend of the spread of civilization. In our view, the counterefforts of some men ignore the realities of expanding community itself.

The great and small communities. We have noted the historical expansion of community to the dimensions of the nation and, perhaps, the world. The smaller communities, however, still remain, though only in degree. The nation or the world-state does not eliminate the village or neighborhood, though they may be changed in character. As civilized beings, we need the smaller as well as the larger circles of community. The great community brings us opportunity, stability, economy, the constant stimulus of a richer, more varied culture. But living in the smaller community we find the nearer, more intimate satisfactions. The larger community provides peace and protection, patriotism and sometimes war, automobiles and the radio. The smaller provides friends and friendship, gossip and face-to-face rivalry, local pride and abode. Both are essential to the full life process.

We shall have occasion later to analyze various aspects of community.[7] The significance of the term "community" is more clearly brought out when we contrast it with our next major concept, association.

Associations

Associations as means of pursuing ends. There are three ways in which men seek the fulfillment of their ends. First, they may act independently, each

7. See Chapter XII.

following his own way without thought of his fellows or their actions. However seemingly desirable, this unsocial way has narrow limitations wherever men live together. Second, they may seek them through conflict with one another, each striving to wrest from the others the objects that he prizes. But this method, if not channeled strictly by regulation, is precarious and wasteful and is opposed to the very existence of society. True, as we shall see later, conflict is an ever-present part of social life, but for the most part it is, like economic competition, socially limited and regulated. Finally, men may pursue their ends in company, on some co-operative basis, so that each is in some degree and manner contributing to the ends of his fellows.

This last method, co-operative pursuit, may be spontaneous, such as the offering of a helping hand to a stranger. It may be casual. It may be determined by the customs of a community, as in the case of farmers assisting their neighbors at harvest time. On the other hand, a group may organize itself expressly for the purpose of pursuing certain of its interests together. When this happens, an *association* is born.

We define an association, then, as a group organized for the pursuit of an *interest or group of interests* in common.

Association and community. It follows from our definition that an association is not a community, but an organization within a community. A community is more than any specific organizations that rise within it. Contrast, for example, the business or the church or the club with the village or city or nation. With respect to the business or church or club, we can ask such questions as why they exist and what they stand for. And we can answer in terms of the particular *interests* around which they are organized. But if we ask *why* communities exist, we can expect no such definite answer. (We can ask why a community, say a city, exists *where it is situated*, but this is a different question.)

Another contrast between the community and the association is revealed by considering the interest aspect of associations. Because the association is organized for particular purposes, for the pursuit of specific interests, we belong to it only by virtue of these interests. We belong to an athletic club for purposes of physical recreation or sport, to a business for livelihood or profits, to a social club for fellowship. Membership in an association has a limited significance. It is true that an association may engage our whole devotion. Or the interests of an association may be wider than or different from those officially professed. But we belong to associations only by virtue of some *specific* interests that we possess. Consequently, there can be a multitude of associations within the same community. And the individual, of course, may belong to many. The late President Butler of Columbia University reported membership in twenty clubs in addition to dozens of other associations.[8]

8. W. F. Ogburn and M. F. Nimkoff, *Sociology* (Boston, 1940), pp. 258–260.

Associations may become communities, at least temporarily. There are the examples of seventeenth-century trading company outposts which became communities in every respect, or of military units compelled to create their own communities when isolated for a period of time.[9] And there are borderline cases between community and association, such as the monasteries, convents, and prisons discussed in the previous section. The two major social organizations which may seem to lie on the borderline between associations and communities are the family and the state. We shall consider these two at length later, but each demands brief comment in this introductory treatment of primary concepts.

The family as an association. In some of its forms, especially in some primitive and extremely rural societies, the family has many of the attributes of a community. In these cases, people toil, play, and even worship almost wholly within the orbit of the family. It circumscribes largely or even wholly the lives of its members.

However, in modern society, as in all complex civilizations, the family becomes definitely an association, so far as its adult members are concerned. For the original contracting parties it is an association specifically established with certain ends in view. These interests are vastly important but nevertheless limited. The functions of the family are more and more limited and defined as the social division of labor increases. In a later chapter we shall analyze this process.

But even in the most complex society, the family, for the new lives that arise within it, is more than an association. To the child the family is a preliminary community which prepares him for the greater community. By imperceptible degrees it is transformed for him also, as he grows up, into an association of, often intense, but *limited* interest. Eventually he will normally leave it to establish a new family.

The state as an association. The state is frequently confused with the community. In reality the state is *one* form of social organization, not the whole community in all its aspects. We distinguish, for example, the state from the church, the political from the religious organization. The confusion of community and state is increased by the usage of the same term to indicate either. Thus "United States" refers either to our national state association with its governmental apparatus or to the national community which it governs.

It is highly important, for the understanding of social structure and particularly of the evolution of that structure, that we should realize the associational character of the state. The state is an agency of peculiarly wide range, but nevertheless an agency. The state may assume at times absolutist or

9. See C. H. Page, "Bureaucracy's Other Face," *Social Forces*, XXV (Oct., 1946), 88–94.

"totalitarian" form, claiming to control every aspect of human life. Even if this claim were *fully* realized—which never could be the case—the state would not become the community, but an association controlling the community.

Human beings are, without choice to be sure, citizens or subjects of the state. But they are also members of families and churches and clubs, they are friends or lovers, scientists or laborers or artists associating with their kind. However significant the citizen role may be, it is only *one* of many roles that each man exercises as a social being.

The state, we must recognize, is different in important respects from all other associations. Its peculiarities, its limitations, the interests it can and does pursue, we shall discuss at a later point.[10] We should keep in mind during the intervening discussion that the state as a form of social organization is, like the church or business or club, an association.

Associations as agencies and their corporate character. Associations are means or agencies through which their members seek to realize their similar or shared interests. Such social organizations necessarily act, not merely through leaders, but through officials or representatives, as *agencies*.

Officials may control the organization so that the interests of the majority are subordinated to their own—the problems of "bureaucratic" control and of liberty are involved wherever there is social organization. Or the control may reside in the members. Whichever the case, the association normally acts through agents who are responsible for and to the association. This fact gives the association a distinctive character and its peculiar legal status.

The association actually has no interests that are not the interests of some or all of its members. But it does have *methods* of operation peculiar to it as an association. It may own property which is not simply an aggregation of individual properties; it may own funds which the members cannot at pleasure distribute among themselves; it possesses rights and obligations, powers, and liabilities which the members cannot exercise as individuals. A public utility, a trade-union, a political party, a club, a church, has in virtue of its organization and function certain duties and certain privileges as such, as a unity. It is in this sense, corresponding to its peculiar methods, that the association has a *corporate* character. When legal recognition is made of these conditions and the duties and privileges of the association are legally assigned, it becomes, in the legal language, a *corporation*.

Our use of the term "group." By a group we mean any collection of social beings who enter into distinctive social relationships with one another. A group, then, as we understand it, involves reciprocity between its members. We have defined association as a group expressly organized around a particular

---

10. See Chapter XVIII.

interest. The qualification, *expressly organized*, enables us to distinguish between associations and other social groups. As we shall see, there are many forms and types of social groups, class and crowd, primary and secondary groups, face-to-face groups and great associations.

But a social class, for example, is not—any more than a community itself—an association. Organizations established on class lines such as certain political parties are associations, but a class itself is not a group expressly organized to pursue certain ends or to fulfill certain functions. Nor is the group we term a crowd an association, though certain crowds may become at least temporary associations (and thereby cease to be crowds) if, again, they are organized to pursue specified interests.

Institutions

Institutions defined as established forms of procedure. It is sometimes the practice to refer to anything which is socially established as an institution. This broad usage is illustrated, for example, by H. E. Barnes' comprehensive study[11] in which he describes social institutions as "the social structure and machinery through which human society organizes, directs, and executes the multifarious activities required to satisfy human needs."[12] According to this understanding, the family and the state, no less than marriage and government, are institutions. But we shall gain a clearer view of the social structure if we make a distinction between institutions and associations. In this book we shall always mean by institutions the *established forms or conditions of procedure* characteristic of group activity.[13]

Institutions and associations. When men create associations they must also create rules and procedures for the dispatch of the common business and for the regulation of the members to one another. Such *forms* are distinctively institutions. Every association has, with respect to its particular interest, its characteristic institutions. The church, for example, has its sacraments, its modes of worship, its rituals. The family has marriage, that is, the institution of the mating relationship; it has the home, the family meal, and so forth. The state has its own peculiar institutions, such as representative government and legislative procedures. Chart I provides further illustrations.

We belong to associations but not to institutions. Sometimes a confusion arises between institution and association because the same term, *in a different reference*, may mean either one or the other. There is no difficulty in deciding,

---

11. *Social Institutions* (New York, 1942).
12. *Ibid.*, p. 29.
13. Compare W. H. Hamilton's interpretation, "Institution," *Encyclopaedia of the Social Sciences* (New York, 1935), VIII, 84–89.

according to our definition, that the church is an association and communion an institution, that the trade-union is an association and collective bargaining an institution, that the family is an association and monogamy an institution. But which term shall we apply to a hospital, a parliament, a prison, a college? When we speak of a hospital we may be thinking of a building for the care of the sick, a system of medical service, a provision publicly or privately established to meet certain social needs—in other words we may be thinking of it as an institution. But we may also think of it as a body of physicians, nurses, attendants—in other words as an association. This suggests the simple clue by which we can find an answer to our question. If we are considering something as an organized *group*, it is an association; if as a form of *procedure*, it is an institution. Association denotes membership; institution denotes a mode or means of service. When we regard a college as a body of teachers and students, we are selecting its associational aspect, but when we regard it as an educational system, we are selecting its institutional features. We cannot *belong to* an institution. We do not belong to marriage or property systems or solitary confinement, but we do belong to families, to states, and sometimes to prisons.

Institutions and the community. It should be observed that there are institutions established by communities as well as those that associations set up. Such are, for example, festivals, ceremonies expressive of important occasions, modes of recreation and amusement. Consider in our own urbanized society the quite systematized procedures that have been established for "dating," or the everywhere recognized practices of movie going and radio listening. These forms of procedure, to be sure, are frequently part of the practices of associational groups—thus dating in the college fraternity or radio listening within the family—but they were neither established by associations nor characteristically confined to them.

Communal institutions, unlike many associational institutions, do not result from a deliberate act of establishment. They are, to use Sumner's well-known distinction, *crescive* rather than *enacted*.[14] Communal institutions gradually attain social recognition; they grow into establishment. In the final analysis, as we shall later have occasion to elaborate, *all* institutions, communal or associational, are crescive. "Even if it is deliberately established an institution has neither a definite beginning nor an uncompromised identity."[15]

The ways of studying institutions. The detailed analysis of the established procedures of society has preoccupied students for centuries. In general, three approaches have been used in such investigations, either singly or in combination.

(1) *Historical* analysis has sought to trace the development in time of a single institution. For example, the rise of representative democracy, the

14. W. G. Sumner, *Folkways* (Boston, 1907), p. 54.

15. Hamilton, *op. cit.*, p. 84.

evolution of monogamy, the emergence of capitalistic enterprise have frequently been studied from this viewpoint. As significant as the contributions of such studies have been, they face the difficulty which stems from the *crescive* nature of all institutions. The search for origins is a never-ending pursuit.

(2) *Comparative* analysis involves the study of single institutions in different societies or in different strata of a society. Marriage forms, patterns of sex relationship, property procedures, child-training practices, and so on have been subjected to comparative analysis. Aristotle's *Politics*, which was based upon 158 city-state constitutions, is a famous early example of the comparative approach. Anthropological investigations have especially used this approach, and such studies as those of Westermarck and Briffault in the area of marriage and, more recently, of Ruth Benedict and Margaret Mead, are of major interest to all students of institutional variations.[16]

(3) Institutions may also be studied with respect to the ways in which they are interrelated in society. This approach, with its emphasis upon *functional interrelationships*, frequently involves historical analysis and often utilizes or suggests the comparative study of institutions. We shall be interested in interconnections among institutions throughout this volume, for no institution functions as an entirely "closed system." A realistic study of marriage, to suggest a single example, necessarily involves the relationships between marriage itself and legal institutions, property institutions, kinship institutions, religious institutions, and others.

One note of caution is required in this brief discussion of the study of institutions. These established forms of procedure are clearly methods used by *groups* of men. Whether they are the enacted instruments of associations or the unofficially developed patterns of community practice, institutions *in life* cannot be separated from those who follow their ways. Thus investigation of social reality always includes reference to both human institutions and human groups. However, if the focus is *institutional*, as we have defined it, it centers upon the procedures themselves.

Institutions and interests. There are certain institutions which are found in associations of many types, such as initiation into membership, election of officers, and a form of management. There are others, however, which are peculiar to or characteristic of this or that type of association. The characteristic or peculiar nature of an institution depends upon the nature of the special *interest* the association pursues. The relation between associations, institutions, and interests is exemplified in Chart I.

---

16. See E. Westermarck, *The History of Human Marriage* (London, 1921); R. Briffault, *The Mothers* (New York, 1927); R. Benedict, *Patterns of Culture* (New York, 1934); M. Mead, *Sex and Temperament in Three Primitive Societies* (New York, 1935).

CHART I **Associations, Institutions, and Interests**

Association	*Characteristic Institutions*	*Special Interests*
Family	Marriage, the home, inheritance	Sex, home, parentage
College	Lecture and examination system, graduation	Learning, vocational preparation
Business	Bookkeeping system, incorporation, share capital	Profits
Trade-union	Collective bargaining, strike, picketing	Job security, wage rates, conditions of work
Church	Creed, communion, forms of worship	Religious faith
Political party	Primaries, party "machine," political platform	Office, power, government policy
State	Constitution, legal code, forms of government	General regulation of the social order

Customs, Folkways, and Mores

The nature of customs. Underlying and sustaining the more formal order of institutions and associations there exists an intricate complex of usages or modes of behavior. Thus there are accepted procedures of eating, conversing, meeting folks, wooing, training the young, caring for the aged, almost *ad infinitum.* The socially accredited ways of acting are the *customs* of society.

We conform to the customs of our own society, in a sense, "unconsciously," for they are a strongly imbedded part of our group life. They are so strongly imbedded, indeed, that we frequently make the error of identifying our particular customs with the only correct ways of doing this or that, or even with human nature itself. This situation throws up problems which will demand our careful consideration in later chapters. [17]

Distinction of institution and custom. The difference between a social usage or custom on the one hand and an institution on the other is essentially one of *degree.* Institution implies a more definite recognition. We would call the marriage feast an institution, but various courtship practices are better named customs. Marriage itself is an institution and not a custom. Institutions have external insignia, marks of public recognition, which customs as such do not require. We sometimes hear that our institutions are being "undermined," but this charge is rarely made with reference to our customs.

This suggests another difference. The term "institution" stresses the *impersonal* factor in social relationships. When we speak of customs we think of

17. See Book Two, Part One.

the accepted ways in which people do things together, in *personal* contacts. When we speak of institutions we think rather of the system of controls that extends beyond personal relations. This system of controls is the bond between the past and the present and between the present and the future, linking men to their ancestors, their gods, and their descendents. Thus we do not usually become too seriously concerned with, say, the changing customs of courtship or dress or recreation. But consider how some persons are disturbed by what may appear to be threats to "property" or "marriage" or "free enterprise" —the institutions which ramify into the greater organizations of political, economic, and religious life.

Folkways. Men follow customs and they behave along the lines laid down as institutions. We need a term sufficiently inclusive to encompass the whole array of these socially created usages. So they have come to be called "folkways" or "mores." These names were made familiar by W. G. Sumner through his book entitled *Folkways.* He used the term "folkways" in a very comprehensive sense.

> They are like products of natural forces which men unconsciously set in operation, or they are like the instinctive ways of animals, which are developed out of experience, which reach a final form of maximum adaptation to an interest, which are handed down by tradition and admit of no exception or variation, yet change to meet new conditions, still within the same limited methods, and without rational reflection or purpose. From this it results that all the life of human beings, in all ages and stages of culture, is primarily controlled by a vast mass of folkways handed down from the earliest existence of the race, having the nature of the ways of other animals, only the topmost layers of which are subject to change and control, and have been somewhat modified by human philosophy, ethics, and religion, or by other acts of intelligent reflection.[18]

The folkways, then, are the recognized or accepted ways of behaving in society. They include conventions, forms of etiquette, and the myriad modes of behavior men have evolved and continue to evolve with which to go about the business of social living. They vary, of course, from society to society and from time to time. Wearing a necktie is a folkway of adornment in our community; no less so is the filing of teeth among the Philippine Negritos. Such are the ways of the folk.

The mores as regulators of behavior. If we consider the folkways not merely as norms of behavior but as *regulators*, we are viewing them as *mores.* Every social usage, every folkway, is also in degree a social control. Even the most superficial convention, even the most trivial rule of etiquette, attaches to

18. From *Folkways* by William Graham Sumner. Used by permission of the publishers, Ginn and Company. See also W. G. Sumner and A. C. Keller, *The Science of Society* (New Haven, 1927), I, 20.

itself the quality of being the right or proper way, the prescribed way, of doing things. Hence we should not think of the mores as something different from the folkways. They *are* the folkways, in their capacity as instruments of control. They express the group standards, the group sense of what is fitting, right, and conducive to well-being.

The distinction is sometimes made, following Sumner himself, between folkways and mores. Thus, it is reasoned, that when the folkways have added to them conceptions of group welfare, standards of right and wrong, they are converted into mores. The wearing of clothes of certain style, for example, represents conformity with the folkways, while the wearing of clothes themselves is enforced by the mores. To be sure, there are degrees of compulsion and degrees of conformity—social control is never a steady pressure equal from all directions. But who would deny the regulatory pressure of even such a superficial folkway, in our society, as eating the dessert at the finish of the meal rather than at the start? We find the mores of society in group usages as pressure forces.

The mores represent the living character of a group or community, operative in conscious or unconscious control over its members. They both compel behavior and forbid it; in their forbidding function we know them as *taboos.* They are at once the expression and the limitation of the group life, an omnipresent influence toward conformity. They are forever molding and forever restraining the tendency of every individual. From infancy to old age they mete out to each member the strong medicine of praise and blame, approval to those who follow them and, still more, disapproval to those who seek to defy them. The "nonconformist" is one who fails to abide by some (but never all) of the mores; the "cynic" is sometimes one who belittles their validity; the sociologist should be one who understands their functions and significance in the life of man.

The variety of the mores. The mores are not the result of intelligent contrivance or foreseeing design. In part, no doubt, they incorporate the social experience of the group. But one has only to look at the conflicting mores of different groups to realize that chance and accident also play a large role in their creation. One group uncovers the head to show respect; another the feet. One group prohibits the marriage of its members with outsiders; another prescribes it. One group condemns the remarriage of widows; another commends it. One group has a strict sex code for the married but not for the unmarried; another group follows the opposite system. Such examples could be extended indefinitely.[19] Very little behavior indeed is universally prohibited, with perhaps only mother-son incest a taboo found in all societies. This great variation in the mores as we move from society to society and from group to group is, by

19. Numerous illustrations will be found in W. I. Thomas, ***Primitive Behavior*** (New York, 1937).

itself, sufficient warning to the student of sociology that for purposes of scientific investigation we must strive for an unbiased neutral viewpoint when studying them.

The conservatism of the mores. The mores are always considered "right" by the group that shares them. One reason is that they register a vast amount of the group's experience—mostly forgotten experience. But at most it is experience detoured by the happy or unhappy conjunctures that impress the memory of the group. (Consider, for example, the taboos against healthful and plentiful foods among certain peoples, or our own resistance to the scientific and rational treatment of venereal disease.) It is experience transformed and stereotyped into tradition, distorted by dominant interests, and reinforced by fear or dislike of the untried. The mores are thus generally agents of conservatism. Indeed, legalized efforts to change specific mores, as in the case of the Prohibition experiment in the United States, frequently fail.

On the other hand, the mores have only the appearance of fixity, for they change subtly from age to age—compare the range of approved activities of women of three generations ago with that of today. Sometimes important elements of the mores may be revolutionized in some social upheaval, though, as Sumner stressed, most mores survive the sudden changes of ruling regimes.

The mores and social life. This preliminary chapter may be concluded with a brief statement concerning the general functions of the mores in social life. Why is the student of society always concerned with their study?

(1) The mores *determine much of our individual behavior*. They are the compelling and forbidding apparatus of the social world that constantly exerts pressure on every member. This function of the mores will be of particular interest to us as we consider the complexity and variety of the social codes of our contemporary society.

(2) The mores *identify the individual with the group*. If, on the one hand, the mores exert a pressure upon the individual to conform to the ways of his community or social class or sex, the individual, on the other, gains identification with his fellows by conforming. He thus maintains those social bonds that are clearly essential for satisfactory living.

(3) Finally, the mores are in the last resort the *guardians of solidarity*. Every social unity has its own mores. There are the mores for each sex, for all ages, for all classes, for all groups from the family to the nation and beyond. The mores of each of these function to maintain the solidarity of the group. And any group striving for greater solidarity endeavors to strengthen the hold of its mores on the members.

Since the mores of different communities are widely divergent and often quite contradictory, their force diminishes in those wide-scale societies where diverse groups are brought together. They are more compulsive, more integrated and more integrating, in the rural than in the great urban communities. Furthermore, the multiple sets of mores in the urban centers frequently confront the individual with disturbing choices.

With the evolution of society the mores become more "specialized." They appear as a series of special codes, custom and fashion and law and the codes of variant religious and other cultural groups. As we shall see, their control thus is rendered more flexible and the varieties of social experience are allowed a freer and fuller expression.

2

Interests and Attitudes

Attitudes and Social Life

The social and the psychological. In this chapter our focus will be *psychological.* Our concern remains social relationships, but our attention will be turned from the relationships themselves to the related units. When we study the nature of the behaving individuals, the structure of the individual consciousness which expresses itself in social relationships, we are taking the psychological point of view. When we study the relationships themselves we take the sociological point of view. Both sciences are concerned with different aspects of an indivisible reality. Individuals cannot be understood apart from their relations with one another; the relations cannot be understood apart from the units (or terms) of the relationship. Thus we are *also* students of psychology when we study society; and, as the psychologists themselves are increasingly affirming, we become students of sociology when we study the psychology of the individual being. In the last resort the difference between psychology and sociology is a difference of *focus* of interest in social reality itself.

The sociologist is primarily interested in the way in which beings endowed with consciousness act in relation to one another. Beneath and beyond that consciousness lie such realms as the psychoneural conditions of behavior, the physiology of sensation or perception, the biological processes of inheritance, the functioning of the glands. But the sociologist is concerned with these matters only in so far as they throw light on his own distinctive problems—the problems of conscious behavior. Conscious behavior is always accompanied by neuromuscular activity, but if our focus is directed to this realm and remains there we shall not make much advance in the interpretation and understanding of the processes of consciousness. A student of music may conceivably be aided by an understanding of the physiology of ear and brain, but his focus of attention is music itself. A student of society may be aided by the understanding of, say, neurons and synapses, but his quest remains the analysis of social relationships.

We shall, of course, draw on the conclusions of psychology throughout, as occasion arises. At this early point there is one distinction of a psychological nature that is of particular use in sociological analysis, the distinction between *interests* and *attitudes*.

Interests and attitudes are correlative. Put in one list such terms as "fear," "love," "surprise," "pride," "sympathy," and "veneration"; and in another list such terms as "enemy," "friend," "discovery," "family," "victim of accident," and "God." Terms of the first group connote *attitudes*; those of the second, *interests*. The former signify *subjective* reactions, states of consciousness *within* the individual human being, with relation to *objects*. The latter signify the objects themselves. When we mention love or fear we depict an attitude; when we mention friend or enemy we indicate an interest.

Social relationships always involve *both* attitudes and the interests to which they are related; complete definitions of social relationships must include both attitudes and interests. If we say, for example, that a person is "afraid" we must further identify the situation to which his fear is a response. He may be afraid of snakes or the police or publicity or ill-health or even his own "inner desires." Or, conversely, if we say that a person "is interested in" law or religion or women we must further identify the attitude that attends the interest. The burglar, the policeman, the jurist all have an interest in the law; clearly enough their attitudes are diverse. Religion gains the intense interest of both atheist and worshiper, and women that of both those who offer them devotion and those who profess to be "women-haters." Understanding of actual behavior situations, then, requires knowledge of both *objective* interest and *subjective* attitude.

Our explanation of interests as the objects of subjective attitudes does not mean, of course, that "objects" are necessarily material or external facts. Man's interests are those items to which he devotes his attention. They range from such material phenomena as tools and soil and climate to immaterial beliefs, mythologies, and scientific theories. Take, for example, the authors' immediate interest at this point. It is the definition of concepts needed for the analysis of social reality. Social reality always includes the material and immaterial.

The development of attitudes. The role of attitudes in social life is clarified when we consider the process by which they develop in the life of the individual. The human infant acts as though he were the center of the tiny universe in which he lives and feels, and as he comes to appraise things he does so at first solely in terms of their quality of bringing pleasures or pains to himself. He does not conceive of others as persons, nor relate himself to others as persons.

The mother's breast and the bottle, the hands that tend him and the crib he rests in, the nurse, the carriage, the words spoken by adults, noises, light and darkness—these are all alike construed in terms of their impact on his own being. In short, his attitude is entirely egocentric.[1]

But in the process of mental growth the young child learns to distinguish between persons and things. Only then does he become capable of *social* relationships. For he comes to conceive of himself as bound up with other *persons.* He distinguishes his own folks from other folks, establishing various degrees of nearness or intimacy, with parents and siblings, with playmates and schoolmates, reaching gradually into wider circles. He is distinguished from certain other animals of simpler species who, like the cat, appear to remain egocentric throughout life, by learning to say "we" instead of merely "I." He begins to become socialized.

But generally he invests with a halo of superiority the near circles to which he belongs. His mother is the most wonderful of women, his father the wisest of men, his school the best. Thus arise those attitudes that, directed to still larger circles, support his devotion to clan or tribe, to race or nation or class. That is why the social prejudices of men are so deeply rooted and why they offer such stubborn resistance to change: they have been nurtured and molded in the slow process of socialization characteristic of man alone. The intolerance and prejudice that mark so many of men's relationships with one another are traceable to the same processes of socialization that produce their opposites —tolerance and understanding.

Attitudes and social relations. For sociological purposes a fundamental distinction between classes of attitudes centers about the question whether they tend to *unite* or tend to *separate* those affected by them. In the sociological lens, "the colorful confusion of interhuman life falls into patterns of avoidance and approach."[2] Certain attitudes are in themselves tendencies to approach those toward whom they are directed, while others express tendencies to avoidance. Love seeks to approach, fear or disgust to avoid. Hate separates, socially if not physically, and sympathy unites. Distrust and envy may unite those who share such attitudes, but only in common resistance of those toward whom they are distrustful or envious.

[1] *Attitudes and personal relationships:* Every social relationship involves in fact, an adjustment of attitudes on the part of those who enter the relationship. And the varieties of adjustment are as numerous as the varieties of processes that relate men to one another. Friendliness, for example, may be met by friendliness or by indifference or by enmity. Aggressiveness and sub-

1. On the egocentric character of the child's attitude see Jean Piaget, "Intellectual Evolution," in *Science and Man* (Ruth N. Anshen, ed., New York, 1942), pp. 409–422 and *The Moral Judgment of the Child* (Eng. tr., New York, 1932).

2. L. von Wiese, *Systematic Sociology* (H. Becker, ed., New York, 1932), p. 39.

missiveness form a pair of complementary attitudes that often appear in social relations, like "masochism" and "sadism," in the psychological parlance. Even when we employ the same term for the attitudes exhibited by each of the related persons, these may have a complementary rather than a like quality. The love of a parent for a child, for example, is very different from and is complementary to the love of the child for the parent. Such terms as "love" and "hate" and "fear," in fact, refer to many different kinds of attitudinal complexes involved in both personal relationships and those between groups.

[2] *Attitudes and group relationships:* Attitudinal adjustments are constantly being made in the relations between *individuals*. There is a tendency, however, in every social *group* to develop like attitudes toward interests relevant to the group as a whole. Attitudes are very responsive to the large apparatus of suggestion that is part of the formal and informal educational system of all groups. Consider, for example, the extraordinary changes which were induced in the national attitudes of Italians and Germans by the Fascist and Nazi regimes, or the great alteration of American attitudes toward German and Japanese peoples during the late war. Masses of people quickly came to venerate or to execrate symbols which were formerly largely a matter of indifference, such as the swastika, the lictor's rods or fasces, the hammer and sickle, the rising sun, the "Atlantic Charter." Everywhere we find groups—tribal, local, racial, national, kin, class—displaying characteristic attitudes and attaching them to symbols. In part, these attitudes arise out of common social situations. And in part they depend on the indoctrination the group controls bring to bear on the members. They are sustained and perpetuated within the mores of each group.[3] They are, of course, of vital concern to the student of social reality.

Associative and Dissociative Attitudes

Some difficulties in classifying attitudes. Before suggesting a classification of attitudes for use in sociological study, we must note certain difficulties. In actual experience attitudes are subtle, complex, and changeful modes of consciousness. They are constantly being modified by our training, our reflection, our health, our circumstances of every sort. When we attribute an attitude to a person, we can judge its character only by certain external signs—looks, gestures, words. These signs suggest to us fear or love or pity, but in so naming the attitude we do not fully describe the conscious fact. We are merely judging

3. For an interesting analysis of symbols and attitudes, see H. D. Laswell, *Politics: Who Gets What, When, How* (New York, 1936), Chaps. II and IX; for an excellent discussion of racial beliefs in America, G. Myrdal, *An American Dilemma* (New York, 1944), Vol. I, Chap. 4; and for a lively and sound popular discussion of the subject, M. Halsey, *Color Blind* (New York, 1946); for extensive illustrative material, *One America* (F. J. Brown and J. S. Roucek, eds., New York, 1946).

that the attitude-factor so named is dominant or at least recognizable in the subject. As psychiatry warns, our amateur judgments are frequently in error.

The terms we apply to states of consciousness, to attitudes, shade into one another. Consider, for example, the difference between "respect," "esteem," and "admiration." And the mental realities such terms denote shade still more subtly into one another. The inadequacies of our terms for psychological facts are known to every novelist, and should be realized by every sociologist.

Take, for example, attitudes which seem poles apart, like love and hate. It is an age-old observation that these two may be combined in one perplexing attitude toward a single person or object, and in recent times this observation has been elaborated in the Freudian psychology in terms of the principle of *ambivalence*. Love and hate, deep sorrow and exuberant emotional passion, intense loyalty and repugnance—these and other seemingly contradictory attitudes are frequently interwoven. This creates a complex and often frustrating problem for both the individual who is internally perplexed by such ambivalence and the student of individual psychology.

A further difficulty in classification lies in the fact that the attitude we seek to fix down by a name is itself often variable and inconstant, like a color seen in a changeful light. An attitude is not a static possession of the individual. It is always a *changing valuation:* a way of regarding persons or things, a way of assessing them in relation to ourselves and ourselves in relation to them.

A classification of attitudes. Attitudes, as we have seen, are so complex, so blended, so variant, so individualized that any classification must be, as the logicians say, "artificial," and no classification can be complete. In other words, our classification must depend on our purpose in making it. In Chart II we are considering attitudes from a sociological, rather than a psychological viewpoint. That is to say, our interest is focused upon those classes of attitudes that are of frequently decisive importance in the *relationships* between man and man.

Thus we place attitudes in three main columns according as they tend to prevent, to limit, or to promote social relationships. We name these attitudes *dissociative*, *restrictive*, and *associative*. And we divide the columns horizontally into three groups, according as the attitudes imply, in the relationships of the persons affected by them, *inferiority* feeling or *superiority* feeling or have no such implication.

The classification is merely illustrative and in no sense exhaustive. However, the student will find that if he brings to his study of social relations the distinction between attitudes of *association* and *dissociation* and between those of *superiority* and *inferiority* his task will be simplified. For the attitudes which separate us or bring us together, and those which endow a consciousness of superiority or inferiority are of primary significance in the relationships between individuals and between groups.

CHART II A Classification of Attitudes

(Attitudes of persons exhibited in relations with other persons)

I. *Attitudes implying some present sense of inferiority in the subject with respect to the object of the attitude*

Dissociative	*Restrictive*	*Associative*
Dread	Awe	Gratitude
Fear	Veneration	Emulation
Terror	Worship	Imitativeness[a]
Envy	Devotion	Hero-worship
Bashfulness	Humility	
	Submissiveness[a]	
	Subservience	
	Modesty	
	Snobbishness[b]	

II. *Attitudes implying some present sense of superiority in the subject*

Disgust	Pride	Pity[d]
Abhorrence	Patronage	Protectiveness
Repugnance	Tolerance[c]	
Scorn	Forbearance	
Contempt		
Disdain		
Superciliousness		
Intolerance		
Arrogance		

III. *Attitudes not necessarily implying a difference of plane or status (neutrality)*

Hate	Rivalry	Sympathy
Dislike	Competitiveness	Affection
Aversion	Jealousy[e]	Trust
Distrust		Tenderness
Suspicion		Love
Spitefulness		Friendliness
Malice		Kindliness
Cruelty		Courtesy
		Helpfulness

[a] Imitativeness and submissiveness rather than imitation and submission, since the former are attitudes and the latter processes. But often there is only one term to describe both the attitude and the process.

[b] Snobbishness, looking downward, discourages social relationship; looking upward, seeks to extend it. This attitude is placed in Class I on the assumption that while it involves a sense both of inferiority and of superiority, the former is the stronger element in the complex.

[c] Tolerance not in the sense of open-mindedness, but as the attitude corresponding to the process of toleration.

[d] Pity might seem to fall more appropriately in the restrictive class, but that is because it is so frequently associated with such attitudes as patronage. Pity as such, as for a friend fallen in misfortune, has no such implication.

[e] Jealousy might seem to fall in Class I, since it is so closely associated with a sense of inferiority. But though a sense of inferiority may underlie jealousy, it is not necessarily present in the attitude of the jealous person toward the person for whom he has a jealous regard.

The Statistical Study of Attitudes

"Measuring" attitudes. A considerable part of the sociological literature on attitudes is devoted to the question whether attitudes can be "measured," and if so, how.[4] Many writers, in fact, have in recent years drawn up attitude measurement scales designed to be able to measure by certain techniques the attitudes of different people toward the church, the Negro, birth control, the United Nations, and so forth. Since these attempts illustrate very clearly the problem of the *quantitative* treatment of psychical phenomena, we shall comment on them briefly, as a way of bringing this controversial issue to the attention of the student.

We have already pointed out that attitudes are complex and variable modes of consciousness. They are expressions or aspects of the whole personality of the social being. It is therefore no easy matter for the observer to apprehend their quality from the external signs. As every sensitive student knows, a teacher's "friendliness," for example, may indicate any one of several deeper feelings. This suggests the need for a careful study of attitudes *before* we attempt to apply techniques of measurement.

The attitude-measurers face another *preliminary* task. For they must ask, what *in the attitude* is it that we are undertaking to measure? We do not measure *things*, but only certain *quantitative aspects* of things. We do not measure a table, but its length or height or weight. We do not measure the sun, but its radiation, its apparent motion, its size. What *aspects*, then, of an attitude do we set out to measure? Usually the attitude-measurers are thinking of the degree of favor or disfavor with which the individual regards some object (or interest). He is thinking of the *intensity* of the *attitude*.[5]

We seriously doubt the possibility of *measuring*, in any mathematical sense, degrees of favor and disfavor, of liking or disliking.[6] To be sure, the attitude-measurers are generally concerned with attitudes not in their full significance, as reverence and admiration and respect, and so forth, but in a simplified form

4. For a positive answer to this question, see, for example, L. L. Thurstone and E. J. Chave, *The Measurement of Attitudes* (Chicago, 1929); Read Bain, "Theory and Measurement of Attitudes and Opinions," *Psychological Bulletin*, XXVII (1930), 357-379; G. A. Lundberg, *Social Research* (New York, 1942), Chap. VIII. For balanced and not unsympathetic critiques, see Clifford Kirkpatrick, "Assumptions and Methods in Attitude Measurements," *American Sociological Review*, I (1936), 75-88; R. T. La Piere, "The Sociological Significance of Measurable Attitudes," *ibid.*, III (1938), 175-182. For a digest of the extensive literature on this question, see Daniel Day, "Methods in Attitude Research," *ibid.*, V (1940), 395-410.

5. Two researchers have devised attitude scales which are cleverly designed to indicate levels of intensity as measured from a "zero point." See Louis Guttman and E. A. Suchman, "Intensity and a Zero Point for Attitude Analysis," *American Sociological Review*, XII (1947), 56-67.

6. See, for example, R. M. MacIver, *Society: A Textbook of Sociology* (New York, 1937), pp. 26-27.

as *merely* expressing favor or disfavor of some object. However, we must ask: Has the object itself precisely the same *significance* for the various persons who exhibit attitudes toward it? Does "democracy" or "religion" or "birth control" or "government regulation" *mean* the same thing to them? If not, a measuring scale cannot yield exactly comparable results when applied to the attitudes of different persons.

However, attitude scales do permit us to sort out the favorings and disfavorings, likings and dislikings, of a group of people as exhibited at any one time toward some particular interest, in a series of *grades* or *rates*.[7] (The thing so rated is the degree of approval or disapproval, not the total complex attitude.) Such scales, when carefully constructed and expertly used, often provide us with very useful information about social situations. Thus the attitudes of purchasers in the consumers' market toward various products, of radio listeners toward different radio programs, of college students toward public and local issues of current moment, and the like, are given meaningful ranking through the use of attitude scales and similar statistical devices.[8] The interest in and use made of such devices by the manufacturer of consumers' goods, the radio advertiser, and others suggest the practical utility of grading or ranking the verbal or written responses of individuals. However, we cannot agree with those sociologists and psychologists who equate these controlled responses with the complex changing attitude itself.

Both the utility and the limitations of attitude "measurement" are illustrated by World War II. The United States Army found that its problems of military policy and administration were greatly aided by employing the services of social scientists trained in statistical research methods. These specialists could, by securing verbal responses to carefully constructed questions administered to samples of soldiers, obtain fairly rapidly levels of reactions to such things as new types of equipment, military clothing issues, and civilians living in occupied territories. The immediate utility of such information to the high command can hardly be questioned—though we do not know the extent to which it was in fact used. On the one hand, we realize the usefulness of learning, say, that 80 per cent of a given army "strongly disapproves" of a new type of weapon or that 70 per cent "mildly dislikes" a standard winter overshoe or that 40 per cent regard German women as "more desirable" than French women.[9] But on the other hand, we must emphasize that such data do not tell us the whole story, by any means, of the reactions of soldiers toward the objects of these attitudes. Attitude scales are never adequate substitutes for the

7. For an excellent discussion of the logic of measurement and rating see M. R. Cohen and E. Nagel, *An Introduction to Logic and Scientific Method* (New York, 1934), Chap. XV.

8. See, for example, P. F. Lazarsfeld, *The Technique of Marketing Research* (New York, 1937) and *Radio and the Printed Page* (New York, 1940); G. Murphy and R. Likert, *Public Opinion and the Individual* (New York, 1938).

9. These are fictitious examples, but are illustrative of the kinds of information obtained.

kind of *understanding* of attitude complexities that is revealed, for example, in a psychiatrist's office, in the pages of a sensitive journalist, or even in some of the cartoons of a Bill Mauldin.[10]

Polling public opinion. The use of statistical techniques in the study of levels of attitude intensity is perhaps best illustrated by the numerous polls of public opinion.[11] Newspapers and magazines, politicians themselves, political prognosticators of every kind avail themselves of the sampling of the American public's attitudes undertaken by Gallup, Roper, and many others. These investigators provide us with pictures of the "public's" view on this or that matter by obtaining verbal responses from selected representative samples of the population. The political polls, on a number of occasions, have been able to predict political behavior, particularly election returns, within quite small margins of error. But they are still far from being infallible. While better methods have been developed since the failure of the *Literary Digest* poll of the presidential election of 1936, the complete wrongness of the predictions of practically all the "pollsters" concerning the election of 1948 revealed in a striking manner the inadequacy of current sampling techniques.

In the case of voting expectancies the polls represent, as it were, simply unofficial elections. Individuals are questioned in one way or another as to how they expect to vote. They are asked to predict their own behavior with respect to a definite and anticipated event. Thus the polls seek to register the relative volume of approval and disapproval of parties and their candidates —as indicated by rating expectancies. So much is clear. But what is by no means clear from the poll returns is the precise nature, the constituent elements, or the genuine intensity of political attitudes. These problems require analysis of a kind that may be greatly aided by polls, to be sure, but it must be an analysis that probes social reality more deeply than polling itself can.

The public is polled on many issues other than elections. Thus Americans are asked with what "class" they identify themselves, whether or not they prefer to be employed by government or private business, the extent to which they consider their chances of economic advance good or poor, how they view their children's life chances as compared with their own, and so on.[12] We learn that our "average" fellow citizen regards himself as "middle class," that

---

10. *Up Front* (Cleveland and New York, 1945).

11. For a thorough discussion by a well-known veteran in this field, see G. Gallup and S. F. Roe, *The Pulse of Democracy* (New York, 1940).

12. See "The People of the U. S. A.—A Self-Portrait," *Fortune* (Feb., 1940); for a more detailed consideration of such problems, see A. W. Kornhauser, "Analysis of 'Class' Structure of Contemporary American Society—Psychological Bases of Class Divisions," in *Industrial Conflict: A Psychological Interpretation* (G. W. Hartmann and T. Newcomb, eds., New York, 1939), pp. 199-264.

he calculates his own chances of advancement as "good," that he believes employers' and employees' interests are "essentially the same," and so on.

This kind of polling of attitudes takes us a step, perhaps a large step, along the road of understanding the general pattern—the peaks and depressions of certain attitude complexes. However, when we face such a knotty complex problem as the "class" attitudes of Americans—a problem we must face later in this book—we cannot rest content with the verbal responses made by individuals to questionnaires. For attitudes are expressions of complete human personalities—evaluations of the total social being—and, like personality itself, must be understood as part of the pattern of *relationships* among human beings.

Types of Interest in Social Life

Earlier in this chapter we stated that all social relationships involve both subjective attitudes and objective interests. Every *social* experience may be viewed as a relation, an interaction, between the experiencing person, the subject, and an experienced object, the interest. (The interest itself, of course, is often a person or persons.) If, then, social experiences always involve an adjustment between the attitudes and interests of two or more persons, it is important that we consider those *types* of interest that are of basic significance in social life.

Like and common interests. In our discussion of attitudes we took as the fundamental ground of sociological classification the distinction between associative and dissociative attitudes. No less fundamental is the distinction between *like* and *common* interests. It is a distinction subject to much confusion, partly because of the ambiguity of the words. We say, for example, that people have common capacities or common habits when we really mean that they have like capacities or like habits. The *like* is what we have distributively, privately, each to himself. The *common* is what we have collectively, what we share *without dividing up*. The credits we receive at college represent like interests; the college life in which we participate we share in common. To be sure, the like is often a *source* of common interest, as, for example, in the case of two businessmen whose like interests in profit may lead to the formation of a partnership that becomes a common possession and a common source of pride. One of the great processes of society, as we shall see later, is that whereby the common is built out of the like. Today many of us hope that the like interests of the great nations in maintaining peace may be a source for the development of true common international interests.

The concept of common interest brings into sharper focus a fundamental difference between interests and attitudes. Attitudes, as we have seen, can be harmonious. But they cannot be common in the sense in which we are applying that term to interests. Different people cannot have a common attitude any more than they can feel a common pain. They can have only *like* pains and *like* attitudes, because the subjective element is always individualized. But they can have common interests, just as they can have common possessions. There are two principal forms of common or shared interest that require special mention.

[1] *Attachment to a social group:* The first form is exemplified by loyalty to an "in-group." When men identify themselves with some inclusive indivisible unity of their fellows, common interest reveals itself. When men think of themselves as really *belonging* to a family, to a city, to a nation, to a team, to a friendly clique, they are sharing a common interest with other men. This sense of attachment to a personal unity is found in varying degrees and is manifested in different ways in social groups of many kinds—in communities, in associations, in social classes and castes, in both primary and secondary groups. It is an ingredient of group life that will concern us frequently throughout the volume.

Here we can explain more fully what was said early in the chapter, that intolerance and prejudice are traceable to the same processes of socialization that evoke their opposites—tolerance and understanding. Man becomes socialized as the member of a group, first a very near group, the family or the kinsfolk, and then of a wider group, the local community, the social class, the ethnic group, the nation. He learns to belong, but in learning to belong he learns also to exclude. He divides people into the "we" and the "they," the "in-group" and the "out-group."[13] His devotion to the "we" easily becomes dislike or hostility to the "they." His pride in the "we" is fostered by his contempt for the "they." Thus group prejudice is developed on every scale of belonging, from the family to the nation and perhaps to the "race"—the "race" *we* belong to.

Here is one of the greatest problems of modern civilization. This civilization has become very inclusive, and the parts of it—the groups within the nation, the nations themselves over the narrowing world—have become in vital respects interdependent. Yet within the nation the various groups—ethnic groups, culture groups, interest groups—often gravely damage, through their tensions and their conflicts, the unity and the well-being of the whole. And within the world the inability of nations to set their common interest above their separate interests and their mutual jealousies has been a most formidable danger to the continued existence of our civilization itself. What is clearly needed is a new orientation of our socialization, in such a way that our devotion to group and even to nation will cease to be antagonistic to our membership in a more inclusive community.

---

13. See, for example, W. G. Sumner, *Folkways* (Boston, 1907) pp. 11-16.

[2] ***Attachment to an impersonal goal or endeavor:*** The interest that men show in science, in art, in religion, in tradition, in philosophy, in sport, exemplifies the second form of common interest. When the curiosity, the enthusiasm, the devotion of men is excited we see this form at work. "Causes" of all kinds, from the spread of a religious doctrine or a political creed to an intense interest in, say, antivivisection or prohibition, reveal men seeking ends beyond themselves —*common* ends.

Thus his science is a common interest of the scientist *in so far as* he thinks of it as a worth-while goal, *in so far as* he pursues it not merely for a living or purposes of prestige. As the lives of Roger Bacon, Galileo, and the Curies so vividly illustrate, common interest in the search of truth does in fact motivate much scientific endeavor.[14] Of course, scientists are usually breadwinners and persons seeking recognition in society. But when an individual's *whole* interest in science is determined by the dollars he earns or the kudos it brings him, he is an unsatisfactory scientist. In such a case, and examples may be found without difficulty, he lacks the *common interest* which makes science a value in itself and is often the spur of the most unstinted service.

The omnipresence of self-limited interest in social life. In nearly all human activity *both* common and like or self-limited interests are combined. It is inevitable that men should seek after their private interests. It is equally inevitable that they should find and feel an intrinsic worth-whileness in the groups to which they belong and in the impersonal goals and endeavors for which they strive. Examination of social behavior itself reveals both types of interest operating—in varying degrees and arrangements.

If *all* our interests were self-limited, society could not endure. If other people were merely means to our satisfactions, we would not belong together as social beings. Love and friendship and family affection and group devotion would not sustain us as socialized individuals. We would maintain no relationship with others any longer or any further than it satisfied our egoism. Community, indeed group life of every form, would be rendered impossible.

We have already pointed out in this chapter that the earliest *attitudes* of the human infant appear to be altogether egocentric. But it should not be assumed that in the historical development of social man himself egocentricity of *interests* appears prior to or underlies the common interests. It is sometimes said

14. In his book entitled *Inventors and Money-Makers* (New York, 1915), F. W. Taussig showed that inventors, like workers in pure science, are not actuated simply by the prospect of profit but are often dominated by the interest of discovery itself, as revealed by the happiness they derive from inventing, by their devotion to useless or unprofitable devices, and by the difficulties they have in managing the business end of their inventions. Even the financially successful Edison engaged his whole fortune in a New Jersey ore venture which resulted in remarkable engineering achievements but failed disastrously. When he heard that his losses amounted to four million dollars he said, "Well, it's all gone, but we had a hell of a good time spending it."

that the original driving forces of man are those of self-preservation and self-expression. But social man as he appears in every generation is at once egocentric *and* sociocentric. Both elements are inextricably fused in all man is and does. He lives for himself *and* he lives for his group. He lives for himself *and* he lives for the causes that are dear to him. And however far we pierce back to the earlier stage of human life we find the same ingredients of self-regarding and self-transcending interest.[15] The study of both and of the interaction between them is essential in the analysis of social reality.

Attitudes and Interests as Motivations

The quest for motivations. We are always seeking to discover the motives behind the overt behavior of our fellows. Particularly when someone we know acts in an unexpected manner, we hunt for the explanatory motive. The detective seeks among the potential suspects those with motives for committing the crime, and the judge and jury must inquire concerning the motive for the deed since the same external act, say murder, is legally one or another kind of crime, or even no crime at all, according to the motive which prompted it. On a larger scale, the historian and the biographer are engaged in unearthing the motives behind the doings they record. And the novelist and the playwright make great use of their inside knowledge concerning the motives of the characters they depict.

What is the significance of this endless search for motives? In the first place, our own external behavior is an expression of our own attitudes and interests, and consequently we endeavor to probe to the inner determinants of the behavior of others. Secondly, we generally assume, though this assumption may frequently involve an undue simplification of the truth, that in the complex of an individual's attitudes and interests there is some dominant factor or factors which explain his behavior in a particular situation. Such a dominant factor we call his motive. Sometimes we lay stress on the attitude aspect, as when we attribute an act to envy or jealousy or fear; sometimes on the interest aspect, as when we say the motive of an act was money or prestige. All social behavior, as we have seen, involves *both* attitude and interest.

Motives, then, are the effective incitements to action that lie behind our acts, behind the show of things. And in seeking for motives we may descend, as it were, to various levels of the conscious, subconscious or "unconscious" life. We may look for the immediate motive behind the overt behavior, as when we attribute an activity, say churchgoing, to the desire to be thought

15. Some contemporary psychoanalysts declare that the full realization of "self," generally not possible in our modern society, necessarily would mean at the same time a *harmonious* relationship between the individual and group interests. See, for example, Erich Fromm, *Escape from Freedom* (New York, 1941).

respectable or to considerations of "society" or business connections or to religious devotion. Or we may look for motives behind the mentality associated with the external act, as when we attribute, say, an attitude of respect to a recognition of personal worth or achievement or to an acceptance of authority or to a desire to stand in well with the respected person. Or we may venture still more deeply and undertake the hazardous attempt to discover hidden subconscious urges or tendencies which find their expression in conscious activity under various disguises. Explanations referring to these different levels of motivation are illustrated in a variety of types of investigation.

Types of theories of human motivation. In the following examples we make no attempt to present the details of the elaborate formulations of the writers mentioned. Our concern is rather that the student may recognize certain views to which reference will be made from time to time throughout this book, and that he realize the difficulty of the problem of human motivation and the various avenues which have been followed by those in search of its solution.

[1] *Underlying economic motives:* The historical rise of capitalistic enterprise and the new arrangements of social organization accompanying it have pushed to the forefront of men's thought the significance of the economic factor in human affairs. A century and a half ago Adam Smith and others pictured an "economic man" primarily motivated by a rational calculation of interests in terms of maximum economic gain. Considering the gigantic role played by economic changes in the ensuing period, it is not surprising that many writers have singled out the economic as the underlying and basically important motive of individual behavior as well as the principal motive force of historical change itself. This view of motivation characterizes, for example, the writings of Alexander Hamilton in the famous *Federalist* series, and is no less apparent in the contributions of such modern historians as Charles A. Beard.[16]

The most complex and energetic attempts to discover underlying economic motives have been stimulated by the writings of Karl Marx and his followers. Marx himself was not primarily concerned with the problem of individual motivation, but his analysis of class conflict portrays the individual members of both the owning bourgeoisie and the laboring proletariat as ultimately motivated by their conflicting economic interests. In this view, political, religious, and other "noneconomic" social forms become a "superstructural" complex to be explained in the final analysis by the objective, material interests underlying them. This analytical approach, as we shall emphasize later, is, according to its proponents, essentially a device with which to interpret the historical process, not individual behavior. However, the Marxian emphasis upon the basic function of economic interests has prompted various writers to explain attitudes that are inconsistent with Marxian-defined economic in-

16. See, for example, Charles A. Beard, *The Economic Basis of Politics* (New York, 1934).

terests as "false rationalizations" or "mistaken viewpoints."[17] Such writers seek the key to human conduct in the economic structure itself.

[2] *Constant elements of human nature as motives:* For centuries men have explained the behavior of men by attributing it to "human nature"—to that curiously nonchanging complexity that is assumed to remain a constant in a universe in which all else changes. Such an explanatory device has been a convenient technique for many who have sought the underlying motives of human action. And it remains a convenient, though scarcely revealing, technique for those modern writers, such as McDougall,[18] who postulate four or six or twenty "instincts" as the fundamental forces accounting for man's varied activities. While the instinct approach has fallen into disrepute in recent years largely because of the enormous plasticity of the social being revealed by modern psychology and sociology, constant conditions of human nature continue to be hypothesized as basic needs or drives. These needs range from the physiological necessities of the organism, such as food and oxygen intake and the elimination of waste matter, to the demands for love and affection created by social life itself. Psychologists, sociologists, and anthropologists have recently constructed detailed theories which purport to spell out the motivating needs or "cravings" of individuals as they are shaped by and in turn shape social life.[19] Certain of these theories will concern us in the following chapter.

Perhaps the most famous attempt by a sociologist to deal with the problem of human motivation is that of Vilfredo Pareto.[20] Pareto views human conduct as essentially inspired by certain constant ingredients of human nature which he terms "residues." He classifies the residues under six main groups: residues of combinations (the faculty of associating things or thinking them together), of group persistence (the conservative tendency), of self-expression, of sociability, of individual integrity, and of sex.[21] These, according to Pareto, are the actual motivations of human conduct but are obscured by all sorts of unsound reasonings and misleading explanations which he names "derivations." The derivations are manifestations of the human being's hunger for thinking, constituting a veil of pseudo logic between him and the realities of his nature.

---

17. See, for example, B. Freedman, "Stimulus and Response in Economic Behavior," in *Industrial Conflict: A Psychological Interpretation*, pp. 265–279. For an interesting criticism of what he calls this "pseudo-Marxian" viewpoint see Fromm, *op. cit.*, p. 296.

18. See, for example, W. McDougall, *An Introduction to Social Psychology* (Boston, 1918), Chaps. II and III.

19. Thus, for example, in psychology: A. H. Maslow, "A Theory of Human Motivation," in *Twentieth Century Psychology* (P. L. Harriman, ed., New York, 1946), pp. 22–48; in sociology: R. S. Lynd, *Knowledge For What?* (Princeton, 1939), pp. 193–197; in anthropology: B. Malinowski, *A Scientific Theory of Culture and Other Essays* (Chapel Hill, 1944), pp. 75–131.

20. *The Mind and Society* (*Trattato di Sociologia Generale*, A. Livingston, ed., New York, 1935). For critical estimates of Pareto, see *Journal of Social Philosophy*, I (1935), Nos. 1 and 3; E. Faris, *The Nature of Human Nature* (New York, 1937), pp. 190–201.

21. *The Mind and Society*, II, 888 ff.

It is not in place here to examine the elaborate argument by which Pareto seeks to establish his case. But we may point out his implicit and unwarranted assumption that certain types of motivation (residues) are genuine or fundamental while others (derivations), including the more idealistic motivations, are shallow and protentious. His thousands of illustrations are often suggestive and revealing. It is often the case, for example, that when a politician appeals to the electors on the grounds of his patriotic services to the glorious nation to which they belong, he is not expressing his real sentiments but is using these arguments to further his own ends. But there is another side to the story. Why does the politician appeal in these terms at all? Because he knows that his audience responds to such sentiments—unless his audience is stirred by the idealistic motivations, it is useless for him to use such devices. One might multiply illustrations *ad infinitum* to show that man is motivated thus and so —and as many illustrations would remain over to show that he is motivated otherwise.

[3] *The psychoanalytical quest for motives:* The psychoanalytical explanation of motivation, in its original formulation by Freud and his followers,[22] is essentially a version of the type of analysis we have just considered. For Freud, a physician and psychologist intent upon probing the innermost depths of the human personality, conceived of constant elements of human nature as the principal motivating forces. He named these unconscious forces the "instincts" of Eros and Death—of sex and self-destruction—and saw them in conflict with each other and as standing as the basis of personality formation and human behavior.

The exponent of the psychoanalytic view thus regards the individual's own belief that he is animated by this or that motive as often merely a delusion masking the real determinants of his action. Psychoanalysts find evidences of "complexes" and "fixations" developing very early in the life history of the individual, and likewise find them substantiated by the ritual and taboo practices of primitive peoples. These complexes they regard as active below the conscious level and as symbolically emerging in dreams, daytime reveries, and the forgetfulnesses and "slips" of everyday existence.

This brief statement does little justice to the voluminous theoretical literature and the mass of clinical findings of the Freudian school, but it indicates the direction of its quest. The psychoanalysts attempt to discover the "unconscious motives" standing behind our actions; their search ends with the innermost workings of the human organism. Their interpretations of dreams, of primitive customs, and of adult life histories contain precarious inferences and have been attacked by psychologists and anthropologists, though few would deny the element of truth of their findings. But this element is only a segment

22. *The Basic Writings of Sigmund Freud* (A. A. Brill, trans. and ed., New York, 1938). For a short descriptive article see H. M. Kallen, "Psychoanalysis," *Encyclopaedia of the Social Sciences* (New York, 1935), XII, 580–588.

of the interrelated totality of social behavior which includes the human organism, to be sure, but involves as well the society itself. Men are motivated by many things. Their sex impulses and even their "death-urge" may explain some aspects of their behavior, but, as we shall see in the succeeding chapter, any adequate theory of man's complex activities must be grounded in an understanding of the society of which he is a part.

The complexity of motivation. The theories we have sketched reveal the human tendency to "rationalize"—or perhaps we might say to "socialize"—motives. As social beings, we are disposed to select socially esteemed reasons for our conduct and present them to others, and also to ourselves, as grounds for our action. We form habits of concealing petty and self-seeking motives under high names, like duty and honor and principle and patriotism. We want to stand well in the sight of others and in our own eyes. Thus we "rationalize" our conduct, and this is the more easy and the more convincing—to ourselves at least—because it is always difficult to disentangle the many factors determining our behavior. Historians like Beard and Robinson,[23] political thinkers of the school of Machiavelli, sociologists like Pareto, and psychoanalysts like Freud have done signal service in seeking to penetrate the façade of rationalization which often hides the moving forces of history and the inner springs of conduct. And the same mission is zestfully popularized by novelists, biographers, and today certain movie and radio script writers who expose for us the underlying motives of their characters.

Yet such interpretations may be liable to an opposite simplification to that which their authors assail. For there is always the danger that we simplify the motives of behavior, whether the particular motives we attribute be lofty or petty, altruistic or self-limited. The motives of conduct are indeed as complex as the human personality itself. Medical science each year discovers more of the amazing complexity of our organic structure—it has moved far from Hippocrates' belief that the organism consists of merely blood, phlegm, and the biles. So with personality—as science learns more of its structure and functions its greater complexity is revealed. To be sure, many common and erroneous assumptions are corrected by the "debunkers" of superficial rationalizations, but they, in turn, risk the superficial position of assigning an unwarranted simplicity to motivation. "A history of philosophy and theology," says Robinson, "could be written in terms of grouches, wounded pride, and aversions, and it would be far more instructive than the usual treatment of these themes."[24] Perhaps more instructive, but perhaps also not less one-sided or misleading.

Of all quests, none is more complex than the adequate understanding of motivation. The latter demands that we untangle and reveal human nature itself—human nature conditioned in each variant human being by the unique

23. J. H. Robinson, *The Mind in the Making* (New York, 1921).

24. *Ibid.*, p. 45.

series of experiences which are the history of the individual life, and yet exhibiting in us all the universal traits of humanity. In this respect, however, the task of the sociologist is not so overwhelming as that of the historian who seeks to explain particular events or as that of the psychiatrist in search of the motivations of behavior of this person or that. For the sociologist's interest is primarily in group phenomena where numbers of human beings act in like ways or maintain common institutions. When the same gestures or external signs are employed by many or repeated on many occasions, we can with greater assurance infer their meaning. The hazard of interpretation is somewhat less in reading the motives of a crowd or "public" than in reading those of an individual. This is a theme to which we will return, but is one which must be preceded by the examination of the fundamental relationship in sociological study—the relationship between individual man and society.

3

Individual and Society

In What Sense Man Is a Social Animal

The fundamental question of sociology. In the first chapter, in which the primary terms of sociological analysis were presented, we noted that man's *social nature* is his fundamental attribute. Before proceeding to deal with the various elements and aspects of society we must seek a proper orientation to this largest and most difficult problem that sociology offers. In what sense is man a social animal? In what sense do we belong to society? In what sense does society belong to us? What is the nature of our dependence upon it? How shall we interpret the unity of the whole to which our individual lives are bound? These questions are aspects of one fundamental question—the relation of the unit, the individual, to the group and to the social system. This question is the starting point and the focus of all *sociological* investigation, and, to a great extent, the fruitfulness of any sociological study is measured by its contribution to the problem of the relationship of individual and society.

It is not surprising, then, that men sought answers to this problem long before the term "sociology" was coined. Two misleading and opposing answers have been particularly influential in the history of Western social thought, the "social contract" theory and the "social organism" theory. A brief consideration of these may serve to remove certain false assumptions concerning individual man and the social totality of which he is a part.

Two one-sided approaches. Both of the following theories of the relationship of man and society have been expressed by many writers over many centuries. And both are frequently found today in the folk-thought—the "amateur sociology"—of our fellow citizens. The student of social science, therefore, should be able to recognize expressions of these theories and be prepared to expose their inadequacies.

[1] *The contract theory of society:* Since at least the fifth century before Christ, various philosophers have viewed society as a contrivance deliberately set up by men for certain ends. According to some, such as Thomas Hobbes[1] in the seventeenth century, society is a means for the protection of men against the consequences of their own untrammeled natures. To others, society is an artificial device of mutual economy, a view suggested by the economic philosophy of Adam Smith and his followers. Similarly, the eighteenth-century individualists maintained that man was "born free and equal" in his state of nature and that his establishment of a social contract merely set up social conveniences of order and protection. All such theories view society as based on some kind of original contract between the individuals themselves or between the people and the government. This view has been used as an argument for the "protection" of the individual "from society" and sometimes it has been used for the opposite purpose of enhancing the role of political organization in society.[2]

The belief that society is an artificial invention no longer commands the influence it once possessed, but it has by no means entirely disappeared. Consider, for example, some of the current criticisms of government planning in this sphere or that based upon the argument that planning is an "artificial device" detrimental to the "natural order" of life. Or consider the nostalgic yearnings of some persons to return to nature's ways—ways assumed to have existed before burdensome society was erected by man. Thus certain fads of recent years prescribing diets of uncooked foods or extolling the virtues of nudity have echoed the eighteenth-century conception of man's presocial idyllic state. Or, again, note the present-day tendency of many persons to "blame" the phenomenon of falling birth rates upon the "artificiality" of modern society —here is a problem we shall examine later in this volume. The reader can readily multiply the examples of current thinking that are based upon or imply the theory that society is something men have at some time or other invented and set up.

There is good reason why we should reject this theory. For the theory rests upon the false assumption that human beings are, or could become, human beings outside of or apart from society. It implies that men are individuals *before* they "enter into" society and that they establish a social order to protect their property or their rights or their lives or for some other end which seems good in their eyes. This erroneous assumption is possible only when we overlook the fact that individual man and society are inseparable. Neither has a priority in the history of human development.

[2] *The organismic theory of society:* We must avoid an opposite error to that of the social contract theorists. This error is implicit in the view that regards society (or some area of society, such as the nation) as a kind of organism.

1. See his *Leviathan*, Chaps. XIII and XVII.
2. See G. D. H. Cole's Introduction to *The Social Contract and Discourses by Jean Jacques Rousseau* (London, 1913).

This view, at least as ancient as the contract idea, conceives society as a biological system, a greater organism, alike in its structure and its functions, exhibiting the same kind of unity as the individual organism and subject to similar laws of development, maturation, and decline. Society's cells are individual persons, its organs and systems are associations and institutions. This theory in its extreme form identifies specific structures of society with biological organs and systems, some writers finding in society counterparts of the brains, the lungs, or the limbs of the organism.[3] Less extreme organicists, like the early sociologist Comte, have been more concerned to show that the unity of society and the participation of individuals within it are to be thought of in terms of organism. And others seek to demonstrate that society passes through the organic processes of birth, youth, maturity, old age, and death.[4]

Closely related to the organismic position is the theory that society should be thought of not so much as a greater body but as an inclusive *mind*. This too is both an ancient and a modern doctrine, expressed, for example, in Plato's *Republic*, in the Hegelian school of political philosophy, and upheld by such psychologists as William McDougall, who speaks of the reality of the "group mind."[5] This view would raise no problems if it signified merely that a group exhibits certain traits characteristic of its members generally—that there are, for example, certain attitudes that Englishmen or Americans or Russians are apt to display. But the exponents of this theory mean much more: they insist that society is itself a mind, a mind *common* to its members.

The identification of society with an organism or with a mind, like the social contract theory, finds its way into contemporary thinking on many levels, observed, for example, in the lengthy tome of Oswald Spengler,[6] who claims that societies pass through the organic cycle from birth to death, and in the official doctrines of totalitarian governments, such as the Nazi and Fascist, which envisioned the nation as a living "fatherland" of which the individual citizen is *merely* a manifestation and to which his entire life must be devoted. It is common usage to personify collectivities and say, for example, "England is moving to the left," "America is reaching maturity," "the Russian bear is marching across the world," "Middletown faces both ways," "humanity is

---

3. Thus the Russian sociologist Novicow and the German political scientist Bluntchli. For variants of the theory, see F. W. Coker, *Organismic Theories of the State* (New York, 1910) and P. Sorokin, *Contemporary Sociological Theories* (New York, 1928), pp. 200 ff. For medieval fantasies on this theme, see Otto v. Gierke, *Political Theories of the Middle Age* (F. W. Maitland, tr., Cambridge, 1900), pp. 103 ff.

4. For a discussion of this view and similar ones by a sociologist whose own longer writings are an illustration of semi-organicism, see P. Sorokin, "Sociocultural Dynamics and Evolutionism," in *Twentieth Century Sociology* (G. Gurvitch and W. E. Moore, eds., New York, 1945), pp. 96–120.

5. See Plato, *Republic*, Book II; B. Bosanquet, *Philosophical Theory of the State* (London, 1920), Chap. VII; W. McDougall, *The Group Mind* (Cambridge, 1920), esp. Chap. I.

6. *The Decline of the West* (C. F. Atkinson, tr., New York, 1926).

destroying itself," "the mentality of China (or India or Russia or France) is beyond our understanding." Such statements may imply or suggest the identification of some society with a living being or with a mental entity. On the other hand, they may simply be literary devices. So long, in fact, as we merely compare a group or community to an organism, in order to bring out such aspects of society as the interdependence of individuals within the unity of the social system, we are using a simple and sometimes helpful analogy.[7] But the situation is very different when we describe the social system as actually an organism. For this view fails to do justice to the individuality of the social being, just as the contract theory fails to do justice to his social nature. It is misleading to say that it is *only* society that lives and breathes in its individuals, that our consciousness is *only* an expression of the social consciousness.[8] We must reply that it is only in us, its *individuals*, that society "lives" whatsoever. It is misleading to say that we belong to society as the leaves belong to the trees or the cells to the body. Indeed society can have little meaning unless individuals themselves are real. Whatever literary and suggestive utility the organic analogy possesses, it must not become in our thinking an explanation of the basic relationship in social life, the relationship between society and individual. For organicism, like the opposite theory of individualistic social contract, denies one side of the relationship.

Individual and society: the relationship explored. The inadequacies of the two theories just presented become more apparent when we consider certain factual evidences of the interrelationship between the individual and the social order. Of the several paths that have been followed to explore this interrelationship three are of particular significance to the sociologist.

[1] *The feral cases:* The dependence of man's human nature upon his membership in a society is supported by some evidence of a quasi-experimental kind. It is of course hardly possible to make experiments by isolating infants from all social relationships, though certain absolute monarchs from King Psammetichus of Egypt to James IV of Scotland are reported to have done so. But chance or accident and in one or two instances calculated design have furnished sufficient evidence.[9] Three of these cases which have been studied carefully may be cited.

ONE: The famous case of Kaspar Hauser is peculiarly significant because this ill-starred youth was in all probability bereft of human contacts through political machinations and therefore his condition when found could not be

7. See, for example, the suggestive article by W. B. Cannon, "The Body Physiologic and the Body Politic," in *Science and Man* (R. N. Anshen, ed., New York, 1942), pp. 287-308.

8. A position taken, for example, by the French sociologist A. Fouillée. His *La Science Sociale Contemporaine* (Paris, 1904) attempts to reconcile organicism with the contract theory by naming society a "contractual organism."

9. For collections of such instances see R. Briffault, *The Mothers* (New York, 1937), Chap. I.

attributed to a defect of innate mentality. When Hauser at the age of seventeen wandered into the city of Nuremberg in 1828 he could hardly walk, had the mind of an infant, and could mutter only a meaningless phrase or two. Sociologically it is noteworthy that Kaspar mistook inanimate objects for living beings. And when he was killed five years later a post-mortem revealed the brain development to be subnormal. The denial of society to Kaspar Hauser was a denial to him also of human nature itself.[10]

TWO: One of the most interesting of the feral cases involves two Hindu children who at the ages respectively of about eight and under two, in 1920, were discovered in a wolf den. The younger child died within a few months of discovery, but the elder, Kamala, as she became named, survived until 1929, and her history in human society has been carefully recorded. Kamala brought with her almost none of the traits that we associate with human behavior. She could walk only on all fours, possessed no language save wolflike growls, and was as shy of humans as was any other undomesticated animal. Only as the result of the most careful and apparently sympathetic training was she taught rudimentary social habits—before her death she had slowly learned some simple speech, human eating and dressing habits, and the like. This wolf child's "sense of human selfhood," utterly lacking when she was first found, gradually emerged. But the emergence of individuality was altogether dependent upon her membership in human society.[11]

THREE: More recently sociologists and psychologists have studied the case of Anna, an illegitimate American child who had been placed in a room at the age of six months and isolated there until her discovery five years later in 1938. During her confinement Anna was fed little else than milk, received no ordinary training, and had almost no contacts with other beings. This extreme and cruel social isolation, which provides the scientist one more "laboratory" case, left the child with few of the attributes of the normal five-year-old. When Anna was discovered she could not walk or speak, she was completely apathetic, and indifferent to people around her. As in the case of Kamala, Anna responded to the careful treatment provided after her release, and perhaps because of her younger age and the limited contacts she had experienced while a prisoner she became "humanized" much more rapidly before she died in 1942. Anna's case illustrates once again that human nature develops in man only when he is social man, only when he is one of many men sharing a common life.[12]

---

10. This historical case is the subject of Wassermann's novel so entitled. For the facts of the case see *Meyers Konversationlexicon*, *s.v.*

11. For a brief account of the "wolf children" see K. Young, *Sociology* (New York, 1942), pp. 5-8. The details are recorded in A. Gesell, *Wolf Child and Human Child* (New York, 1939) and J. A. L. Singh and R. M. Zingg, *Wolf Children and Feral Man* (New York, 1942).

12. For the case of Anna, see K. Davis, "Extreme Isolation of a Child," *American Journal of Sociology*, XLV (1940), 554-565; and "Final Note on a Case of Extreme Isolation," *ibid.*, LII (1947), 432-437.

[2] *The growth of self:* Study of the process in which the child develops the capacity for society furnishes us a second body of evidence of the fundamental unit-whole interrelationship. The emergence of the capacity for social life is an aspect of the growth of selfhood, of personality. The child does not merely imitate the social usages of adults, as a parrot might pick up a language. He is certainly imitative, but in the process of imitation his own social nature is gradually revealed. We have already seen that in the earliest stages the child makes no distinction between persons and things—the mother's breast and the nipple of the bottle are equally and solely means of organic satisfaction. Similarly his first conversations are monologues in which the child talks aloud to himself, but these gradually pass into conversations in which *inter*-change of thought takes place.[13] As Jean Piaget has recently expressed it, "egocentric thought" evolves into "rational coordination" in which emerges the "logic of relations" between the individual and the world of which he is a part.[14] As the child becomes a self he discovers thereby that others too are selves. As he advances toward individual autonomy he becomes truly capable of social relations. His first play seems mere imitation and he plays to and for himself, but as he gradually learns to play with others the rules of the game cease to be external restraints imposed by others and become rules for the maintenance of which he feels himself responsible.[15]

Several American sociologists and social psychologists have for many years studied the growth of self. Selfhood develops, as G. H. Mead has shown, as the child in his daydreams and in his play with dolls and with other children assumes the roles of others—of parents or other heroes in his life.[16] More than this, the process of self-emergence involves the child's continual adjustment to the behavior of other persons, a factor considered of central significance in personality formation by some sociologists, including Charles H. Cooley.[17] The fact that the self can come to being only in society—only within the give-and-take of group life—has again been clearly established by more recent investigators.[18]

[3] *Man's peculiar dependence upon the social heritage:* Every individual is the offspring of a social relationship, itself determined by pre-established mores. Further, every person, as man or woman, is essentially a term in a relationship. The individual is neither beginning nor end, but a link in the succession of life.

---

13. See, for example, the admirable study by Jean Piaget, *The Language and Thought of the Child* (New York, 1926), Chap. II.

14. Jean Piaget, "Intellectual Evolution," in *Science and Man*, pp. 409–422.

15. Cf. Jean Piaget, *The Moral Judgment of the Child* (New York, 1932), Chap. I.

16. George H. Mead, *Mind, Self, and Society* (Chicago, 1934), pp. 135–226.

17. See his *Human Nature and the Social Order* (New York, 1922).

18. For an account of the dependence of individuality upon group forces, see E. Faris, *The Nature of Human Nature* (New York, 1937), Part I; and for a report of experimental research in this area, see G. and L. B. Murphy and T. M. Newcomb, *Experimental Social Psychology* (New York, 1937), Part II.

This is a sociological as well as a biological truth. But it does not yet express the depth of our dependence as individuals on society.

For society is more than a necessary environment, more than the soil in which we are nurtured. Our relation to the social heritage is more intimate than that of the seed to the earth in which it grows. We are born to a society the processes of which determine our heredity, and parts of which become in time our internal mental equipment—not merely an external possession. The social heritage, continuously changing because of our social experiences, evokes and directs our personality. Society both liberates and limits our potentialities as individuals, not only by affording definite opportunities and stimulations, not only by placing upon us definite restraints and interferences, but also, subtly and imperceptibly, by molding our attitudes, our beliefs, our morals, and our ideals.

Comprehension of this fundamental and dynamic interdependence of individual and social heritage permits us to appreciate the truth of Aristotle's famous phrase, that man is a social animal. We do not mean that man is a *sociable* animal. Men vary greatly in this respect. We do not mean that man is *altruistic* or other-regarding in his impulse toward society. Nor do we mean that he is social by virtue of some *original* constitution of human nature. But we do mean that without society, without the support of the social heritage, the individual personality does not and cannot come into being.

Individual and society: essential theoretical understanding. We have noted the one-sided individualistic emphasis of the social contract theory and the equally one-sided organicist theory that discounts almost entirely the role of the individual in social life. And we have indicated some of the explorations of the relationship between individual man and society. Realistic understanding of this relationship in general terms requires a final statement before we turn to more detailed considerations. We must seek a general view of the unity of society and of the relations of the members to one another and to the whole.

There are, to be sure, significant resemblances between a social and an organic structure, but there also are very significant differences. Herbert Spencer, though he considered society as an organism, pointed out one great difference when he said that society has no "common sensorium," no central organ of perception or of thought.[19] For it is only *individuals* who think and feel. We can communicate our feelings or thoughts so that others may sympathize with us or understand us. But in fact others cannot *share* our feelings or thoughts. In this sense every self is, as it were, insulated.[20] For feelings and

19. It is significant that Spencer, who used the terminology of organicism, was also one of the most extreme individualists of his day.

20. This fact has been seized upon by the current school of existentialism and erected into a dreary egocentric "philosophy," which enjoys an understandable popularity in France whose people suffered the Nazi rule throughout World War II. It is an unhappy mark of the times that existentialism is gaining adherents here and elsewhere.

thoughts are *like*, not *common;* they are experienced by individuals *as individuals*. Mind communicates with mind, but they do not form a single mind. The same influences often stir a people or a crowd, but only as they pulsate in its several members. If we speak of the "mind of a group" we have no evidence and therefore no right to conceive of it as anything but the minds of its members thinking or feeling in like ways, making like responses, and being moved by *like or common* interests.

Individuals do not belong to society as the cells "belong" to the organism. The only centers of activity, of feeling, of function, of purpose that we know are individual selves. The only society we know is one in which these selves are bound together, through time and space, by the relations of each to each which they themselves create or inherit. The only experience we know is the experience of individuals. It is only in the light of their struggles, their interests, their aspirations, their hopes and their fears, that we can assign any function and any goal to society. And conversely, it is only because they are a part of society that individuals are endowed with interests, with aspirations, with goals. It is only in society that human nature can thrive. The relationship between individual and society is not one-sided: both are essential for the comprehension of either.

The failure to recognize this interdependency characterizes the writings of the individualists of past and present. Thomas Hobbes in the seventeenth century and even John Stuart Mill in the nineteenth wrote as though society were in its very nature inimical to the expression and development of individuality.[21] And today, on the basis of the same misunderstanding of the interrelationship, we hear loud echoes of this "threat" of the social order to the individual in our legislative assemblies or read them in the polemics of those who regard every new measure of social security as a "blow" to liberty.[22]

The same misunderstanding, though from the opposite direction, marks the views of those thinkers who, like Benjamin Kidd, declare that the individual *should* be subordinated to society; or who, like certain followers of the philosopher Hegel, suggest that society itself has a value beyond the service which it renders to its members.[23] Such views imply that in some mysterious way society exists in its own right and that its welfare can be realized apart from or even at the cost of the welfare of its individuals. It is sometimes assumed that it is possible, and even desirable, to sacrifice the welfare of "the individual" (not, observe, of some individuals) to that of society. When the official "phi-

21. See Hobbes, *op. cit.*, Chap. XXI, and Mill, *On Liberty, passim.*

22. We are not here prejudging the issue whether this or that kind or degree of social planning is desirable, but are merely attacking the assumption that social organization is inherently antagonistic to individuality.

23. See B. Kidd, *Social Evolution* (new ed., New York, 1920) and *Principles of Western Civilization* (London, 1902); and, as an example of the Hegelian doctrine, Bosanquet, *op. cit.*, Chaps. V and VII.

losophers" of Mussolini and Hitler spelled out Fascist and Nazi "theory"—elaborate rationalizations purporting to explain the fact and the social worth of dictatorship—it is not surprising that they found certain Hegelian and other similar doctrines congenial to their task.[24]

Our essential theoretical understanding of individual and society, then, is the understanding of a *relationship*—a relationship involving those processes that operate between man and man and between man and group in the constantly changing pattern of social life. Society with all the traditions, the institutions, the equipment it provides is a great changeful order of social life, arising from the psychical as well as the physical needs of the individual, an order wherein human beings are born and fulfill themselves, with whatever limitations, and wherein they transmit to coming generations the requirements of living. We must reject any view of this pattern that sees the relationship between individual and society from merely the one or the other side.

Individuality and Society

The nature of social unity. The unique quality of social unity is revealed when we contrast it with certain other types. Various forms of unity may be distinguished by viewing the nature of the functional relation of the units or parts to the whole.

One type of unity is the ***organism***, to which type, as we have seen, society itself is sometimes mistakenly assigned. In this type we interpret the cells and organs and the various systems that these compose—circulatory, glandular, nervous, and so forth—as deriving their significance *solely* from their utility to the life of the organism as a whole. (Thus the human appendix and coccyx are sometimes described as organically useless vestiges.) Another type of unity is the ***mechanism***, of which the specific form is the humanly contrived machine. The machine is not autonomous or self-sustaining or self-reproducing like the organism, but in it, too, the various parts, the wheels and gears and transmission belts and so forth, are understandable only as contributing to the function of the whole machine. Mechanical unity, like organic, on occasion has been attributed to society or parts of it, as when we speak of a "price mechanism" or of a "political machine."

But a *social* system must be distinguished from these types. For a system of social relationships grows and changes in accordance with the changing attitudes and interests of its members, of some or all of the units or individuals who compose it. Here the system derives its significance from its support of

24. See, for example, G. Gentile, "Philosophical Basis of Fascism," *Foreign Affairs*, VI (1928), 290-304, and A. Kolnai, *The War Against the West* (New York, 1938); and for commentary, R. M. MacIver, *The Web of Government* (New York, 1947), pp. 243-255, and G. Catlin, *The Story of the Political Philosophers* (New York, 1939), Chap. XXI.

and contribution to the ends—the purposes—of individuals themselves. Without these ends social unity cannot be envisaged. This principle makes possible the harmonization of society and individuality. Before developing this principle we must first make clear the meaning we attach to the term "*individuality*."

The meaning of individuality. The sociological meaning of individuality becomes clarified if we consider various references of the term.

[1] *The physical and biological meanings of individuality:* We sometimes use "individuality" in a *physical* reference, as involving the physical detachment of one unit from another. Such usage may prove puzzling, as when applied to plants from which spring new roots—are we to regard these as one or more individuals? There are simple forms of life like the amoeba which reproduce by fission so that what was one individual becomes two. Again, there are some animals that live and move as colonies, in which the individuals are specialized to perform different organic functions—such as reproduction, nutrition, defense—for the whole colony. An example of this kind of colony is the Portuguese man-of-war. Such examples suggest that even physical individuality is a matter of degree, and that individuality is less evident in the simplest than in the more complex forms of life. If we apply the term "individuality" to inanimate objects, another aspect of this truth is seen. Two drops of water or two clouds fuse together so that they become one; the units lose all distinction. Individuality has obviously little meaning as applied to objects so inchoate or formless in themselves that this complete merging is possible.

We may think of individuality not in a physical but in a *biological* reference. In this sense we would say that a living creature is the more individualized the more it is self-determining, the more selectively it responds to stimuli from without, the more it can control or utilize its environment to serve a variety of needs particular to itself. An organism that drifts with the winds or tides, like the jellyfish, is less individualized than one that contrives to move at will with or against the currents. An organism that is capable of only a few simple reactions or that has few and only roughly differentiated organs to serve its various functions is less individualized than one that is organized to finer and more sensitive adjustments as, say, man.

[2] *The sociological meaning of individuality:* When we extend the meaning of individuality to man we find it essential to use the term in its *sociological* reference. Here we say that a social being has more individuality when his conduct is not simply imitative or the result of suggestion, when he is not entirely the slave of custom or even of habit, when his responses to the social environment are not altogether automatic and subservient, when understanding and personal purpose are factors in his life activities. Individuality in the sociological sense is that attribute which reveals the member of a group as more than merely a member. For he is a *self*, a center of activity and response expressive of a nature that is his own. This conception stands behind the ad-

monition we often give to others—or to ourselves—"be yourself." Being oneself need not mean just originality; it certainly does not mean eccentricity. A strong individuality may, in fact, express more fully the spirit or quality of his country or his time, but he does so, not because he is quickly imitative or easily suggestible, but because of his sensitivity to the age itself.

It is true that when members of a group are more individualized they will reveal greater differences and they will express themselves in a greater variety of ways. But the criterion of individuality is not how far each is divergent from the rest. It is rather how far each, in his relations to others, acts autonomously, acts in his own consciousness, and with his own interpretation, of the claims of others upon himself. When the possessor of individuality does as others do, at least in matters he deems important, he does it not *simply* because others do it, but because his own self approves that particular behavior. When he follows authority, except in so far as he is compelled to, he follows it partly because of conviction, not only because it is authority. He does not superficially accept or echo the opinions of others—he has some independence of judgment, some initiative, some discrimination, as we often say, some "strength of character." The degree in which he exhibits these qualities is the degree in which he possesses *individuality*.

A precautionary remark is in order here. Note that we have not claimed that the possessor of individuality exercises a greater *freedom of will* than his fellows. We are not concerned at this point to raise this age-old question as to whether the individual does in fact possess such freedom. Some readers, perhaps, are already convinced one way or the other concerning the individual's ability to exercise freedom of choice. In either case they should be able to agree with our understanding of individuality—as that aspect of personality which sensitizes the social being to his own purposes and to the purposes of others.

The principle of harmony between individuality and society. It is generally admitted that individuality, as we have just defined it, is less developed (but by no means absent) in primitive societies, with their relatively rigid customs and taboos, than in more highly organized ones. It can also be reasonably maintained that in the more complex and more highly organized societies there is both a greater demand and a greater opportunity for the expression of individuality.

There are many evidences that justify this conclusion. Consider, for example, how far the evocation of individuality depends on the flexibility and richness of language, on the fineness of this primary instrument of education and of communication. As one authority puts it, language not only serves as a "uniformizing" force in society but "is at the same time the most potent single known factor for the growth of individuality."[25] We must add to language the numerous other tools of expression which a complex society affords. The more

25. E. Sapir, "Language," *Encyclopaedia of the Social Sciences* (New York, 1935), IX, 160.

highly organized societies also supply a far greater variety and range of contacts, of occupations, of interests, and of opportunities—in short, of the general and specific stimulations to which the differences involved in individuality can appropriately respond. An outstanding sociological treatise, *The Social Division of Labor*, by Émile Durkheim, is written around this theme.[26] Durkheim admirably shows that in primitive societies, with rudimentary division of labor, *likeness*—the belonging to the same kin, the acceptance of the same beliefs and mores—is the dominant condition of social cohesion. But he stresses the point that in the more advanced societies, with more elaborate division of labor, the social structure is built on *difference* as well as on likeness, thus admitting and evoking a greater degree of individuality among the members.

The broad truth underlying Durkheim's formulation is substantiated by the findings of many other sociologists.[27] This truth recognizes that if all men thought alike, felt alike, and acted alike; if they all had the same standards and the same interests; if they all accepted the same customs and echoed the same opinions without questioning and without variation, civilization could never have advanced and culture would have remained rudimentary. There would be little specialization or interdependence—both expressive of some degree of individualization—and what did exist would be of a superficial and rather artificial character. The humanly meaningful aspects of social co-operation would be lost, the fruitful stimulation of social contacts would be lacking. There would be no initiative, enterprise, and experiment, no resistance to regimentation, and thus no hope of development. Life would take on the dreary uniform quality portrayed fictionally by Aldous Huxley's *Brave New World*, the standardized inhabitants of which could make that world tolerable only by recourse to periodic doses of narcotics.

In the real world of man, society and individuality go hand in hand. So far from there being inherent antagonism between them, each is essentially dependent on the other. As we shall see later, one of the best criteria of the evolution of society is the degree in which it can enlist in reciprocal or in common service the variant individualities within it.

Limitations of the principle. But surely, the reader may ask, *all* is not harmonious between individuality and society? Without relinquishing our broad principle of their interdependence, we may answer by considering certain limitations of the principle.

[1] *Social integration is never complete:* Conflicts and clashes, repressions and

26. *De la Division du Travail Social*, translated by G. Simpson as *The Division of Labor in Society* (New York, 1933).

27. See, for example, Herbert Spencer, *Principles of Sociology* (New York, 1916), Vol. I, Part II; G. Simmel, *Uber Soziale Differenzierung* (Leipzig, 1890); F. Tönnies, *Gemeinschaft und Gesellschaft* (Leipzig, 1887); J. M. Baldwin, *The Individual and Society* (Boston, 1911), esp. Chap. I; Cooley, *op. cit.*, Chap. I; R. M. MacIver, *Community* (New York, 1929), Book III, esp. Chap. III.

revolts, are always occurring. Within every group, and between groups, there is an incessant struggle of diverse and opposing interests. There are frictions, maladjustments, competitive jealousies and hindrances, sheer repressions and exploitations—the reader can supply numerous examples, whatever his community—which interfere with the harmony of individual and society and limit the integration of individuals and groups within the social order. And the social order is itself institutionalized in ways that give privilege and dominance to one group or class over another.

Social integration is never complete, is never totally harmonious. The dictatorships of Mussolini and Hitler claimed social integration in the name of "totalitarianism"; their ruthless and bloody records are reminders of the way in which civilized societies can revert to more primitive practices in times of social crisis. And they should be reminders, too, that the integration of society and individuality is not only a mark of man's past development but a goal for which he continues to strive.

[2] *Society's frustration of the individual:* What individual has not at some time or other resented the regulation of society? Who has not at some time resisted and perhaps been defeated by the mores of his community? We are not referring merely to the suppression of antisocial impulses, for that can be more easily reconciled with our general principle, but to the suppression of impulses, of needs, very often even of ideals, which the mere rigor, uniformity, intolerance, or else the inequity and ruthlessness, of the social system impose. Who has not at times yearned for a cloak of invisibility so that he might be liberated from the inquisitiveness of the tyranny of society as from an Argus-eyed and intolerable censorship?

Here the contrast between the less differentiated primitive societies and the more complex society reveals a limitation of our principle as well as its further substantiation. For the complex society of the modern world is characterized by numerous large-scale organizations, vast economic and political associations so marked by division of functions and specialization that each participating person tends to become, as it were, a cog in a large apparatus of social machinery. His task is likely to be a matter of routine, highly specialized, leaving little opportunity for the play of individuality. This "frustrating" aspect of contemporary life frequently is singled out by novelists, cartoonists, and dramatists for bitter or ironic or humorous portrayal; and psychologists and sociologists have in recent years studied the ways in which the individual's inventiveness or "creative impulses" are hampered by the routinized demands of modern occupational life.[28] These institutionally imposed limitations of individuality

28. See, for example, K. Young, *Personality and Problems of Adjustment* (New York, 1940), Chap. XXIII; *Industrial Conflict: A Psychological Interpretation* (G. W. Hartmann and T. Newcomb, eds., New York, 1939), Part II. For somewhat earlier interpretations of occupational frustration of individuality, see T. Veblen, *The Instinct of Workmanship and the State of the Industrial Arts* (New York, 1914); Stuart Chase, *Men and Machines* (New York, 1929).

cannot be ignored, and as a large part of the sequel of this book will recognize, constitute a serious problem of contemporary social life. But we must remember that the very concern with this problem, indeed the very recognition of it by many persons, is possible only in a complex, developed society that has evoked and revealed the possibilities of individuality on a large scale. Routine, sameness, standardization—characteristics largely taken for granted by primitive man—become alarming portents for many representatives of the modern social order.

[3] *The standardization process:* Many persons, too, are alarmed by the extent to which modern man's attitudes and ideas, and even his tastes are being molded in a common pattern. Perhaps there is good reason for this alarm when we view in our own nation the standardizing influences of large-scale advertising, and of the monotonously alike fare served by radio programs and Hollywood productions. The present-day control of these mass media of communication sets narrow limits for producer, writer, and performer, and tends to create in a vast audience expectations and tastes no wider than the limits set.[29] This kind of standardized communication unquestionably limits the range and expression of individuality; all the more so when we realize, as one investigator has recently noted, that the effectiveness of the techniques of "mass persuasion" are often "measured solely by the number of people who can be brought to the desired action or the desired frame of mind."[30]

A century ago a champion of liberty claimed that "society has now fairly got the better of individuality,"[31] and today, more strikingly than in Mill's time, we see revealed the manifold and serious limitations to any complete harmony between individuality and society. Nevertheless the essential facts remain: (1) that society is a fundamental condition for the development of individuality—in fact society is a condition of every satisfaction we find or seek or even dream of; (2) that the more there is of individuality the more it depends on and the more it can give to society.

Individuality is not "individualism." Our discussion throughout this section has centered upon the interrelationship between individuality and society. Note that in this context we have not used the term "individualism." Note also that the formulation of our principle is not meant to imply a defense of those many claims often made in the name of individualism.

To be sure, the history of Western society during the past three centuries or longer has witnessed great social gains that have accompanied individualistic and anti-authoritarian religious, political, and economic movements. Those

29. This problem is discussed from various points of view in *Print, Radio and Film in a Democracy* (D. Waples, ed., Chicago, 1941); and in the report of the Commission on the Freedom of the Press, *A Free and Responsible Press* (Chicago, 1947).

30. R. K. Merton, *Mass Persuasion* (New York, 1946), p. 185.

31. J. S. Mill, *On Liberty*, Chap. III.

struggles with which we associate such names as John Locke and Adam Smith and Jeremy Bentham and Thomas Jefferson have had far-reaching effects—effects that have widened the possibilities of individuality in social life. But individualism, particularly as expressed by many of its present-day exponents, is often a one-sided claim that ignores the fundamental interdependence of individuality and society. The latter consideration leads A. D. Lindsay to remark:

> Individualism thought of as a thoroughgoing and consistent philosophy of social life necessarily breaks down. No one can really be an absolute individualist, any more than anyone can be an absolute socialist. For the individual and society interact on one another and depend on one another. Even religious individualists, who put the worth and value of human personality above all institutions, must recognize the part played by society and institutions in developing and fostering individuality. The history of ideas shows that individualism is infinitely fruitful so long as individuality is regarded as something to be achieved and realized. But if individuality is thought of, as it has been in many "individualist" theories, as something given and to be defended against attack, individualism loses its evocative force and becomes indistinguishable from egoism.[32]

The implications of the principle of harmony between individuality and society and the significance of the limitations of the principle will receive lengthier treatment in later chapters. But while our focus remains the relation of man and the social order, of the unit and the whole, we must view briefly an interesting and important body of research directly relevant to our present considerations.

"Culture" and Personality

The focus of culture-personality study. All over the world there are societies of people we sometimes call our "primitive contemporaries," usually small groups relatively untouched by our own civilization. These peoples, as unlike as the American Hopi Indians and, say, the Andaman Islanders on the other side of the globe, have provided a field of investigation for "the science of man," fortunately one not already claimed by older social science disciplines. The explorers of this field are the "social" and "cultural" anthropologists who have for many years reported in detail the technologies, the social institutions, and the mores and beliefs of a very large number of primitive peoples. All that a given people has created—artifact and taboo, technological system and social institution, implement of work and mode of worship—the anthropologist has named "*a culture*"; and for all that is man-made wherever found he uses the same term generically.[33] For the anthropologist, then, "culture" signifies the

32. From *Encyclopaedia of the Social Sciences*, Vol. 7. Copyright, 1932, by The Macmillan Company and used with their permission.

33. Cf. R. Linton, *The Study of Man* (New York, 1936), p. 78.

total social heritage of mankind, while "a culture" signifies the social heritage of a particular people. Later in this book we shall use this same term in a more restricted sense and as a more precise analytical tool; in the present division of this early chapter our usage is the anthropological one.[34]

In studying primitive peoples and their cultures, anthropologists have become acutely aware of the intimate relation of the individual person and the culture itself. They have come to realize that any adequate understanding of either the personality of the individual being or the social and cultural complex of which the individual is a part demands careful analysis of the ways in which the two are interrelated and, indeed, interdependent. The central problem of many of these investigators has emerged as exactly the fundamental problem faced for many years by sociology itself: the relation of the individual and the social order. One writer, commenting on this development with unqualified approval, has gone so far as to claim that "the precise significance of personality and culture is that it is not an additional field of study but that *it is the field of all the social sciences*."[35] We can certainly agree that the "personality-culture" relationship should be of primary concern to all sociologists, social anthropologists, and social psychologists.[36]

The relationship between culture and personality involves, on the one side, the total social heritage available to the individual and to which he consciously and unconsciously responds, and, on the other, the integral character of the individual being. Personality, as we understand it, is all that an individual is and has experienced so far as this "all" can be comprehended as a unity. Personality is thus a much broader term than individuality, for personality embraces the total "organized aggregate of psychological processes and states pertaining to the individual."[37] The culture-personality focus is one that reminds us that the pattern of any culture basically determines the broad contours of individual personalities, and that these in turn give evidence of the culture pattern and tend to strive for its perpetuation.

The reader should not interpret this emphasis as implying any mechanical or rigidly deterministic relationship between culture and personality. Recall in this connection our discussion of individuality, an aspect of our present problem. And note the words of an anthropologist whose investigations have materially contributed to our understanding of the interplay of culture and personality:

> No anthropologist with a background of experience of other cultures has ever believed that individuals were automatons, mechanically carrying out the decrees of their civilizations. No culture yet observed has been able to eradicate the

34. For a discussion of various uses of "culture," see C. Kluckhohn and W. H. Kelly, "The Concept of Culture," *The Science of Man in the World Crisis* (R. Linton, ed., New York, 1945), pp. 78–106.

35. R. S. Lynd, *Knowledge for What?* (Princeton, 1939), p. 52.

36. Cf. R. Linton, *The Cultural Background of Personality* (New York, 1945), Introduction.

37. *Ibid.*, p. 84.

differences in the temperaments of the persons who compose it. It is always a give-and-take. The problem of the individual is not clarified by stressing the antagonism between culture and the individual, but by stressing their mutual reinforcement. This rapport is so close that it is not possible to discuss patterns of culture without considering specifically their relation to individual psychology.[38]

Studies of culture and personality. It is not surprising that the continual discovery of a close relation between patterns of culture and manifestations of personality—found among the restrained and peaceful and highly socialized Zuñi of the Southwest, the excessive and individualistic and competitive Kwakiutl of the Northwest, the suspicious and quarrelsome Dobu near New Guinea, the enterprising and courageous and democratic Comanche, to name but a few groups—has led certain anthropologists to view that relation as one of immediate importance to psychologists. For here was "laboratory evidence" of the significant role played by culture not only in influencing behavior but in shaping the personality structure itself. Here was a proving ground where there might be tested various psychological principles of supposedly universal application.

[1] *Anthropological evidences:* The investigation of each primitive society provides additional evidence of the ways in which conditioning and imitation and suggestion, incorporated in numerous child-training techniques, produce individuals whose interests and attitudes are consistently in line with cultural demands. Each society, it is shown, "interiorizes" in its new members its standards of right and wrong, its mores and institutional values. Found within each society, too, are some individuals whose personalities and behavior deviate so markedly from the cultural norms that they are considered by their fellows "misfits" of one sort or another (although in some instances extreme departure from conventional standards receives special social recognition, as in the case of the shamans or medicine-men of several primitive groups). The *particular* forms of behavior, in other words, that represent either the normal or the deviational vary widely from society to society, from culture to culture. So manifest is this variation, among the primitive peoples and the more complexly developed societies as well, that cultural relativity has become an essential principle in the study of the organization of social institutions *and* of personality structure.

This principle and the recognition that both culture and personality can be studied "as wholes" and that they must be viewed with relation to each other are characteristic features of a vast amount of anthropological literature, most notably, perhaps, of the investigations of the late Bronislaw Malinowski.[39] In 1937 the anthropologist Ralph Linton and the psychoanalyst Abram Kardiner

---

38. R. Benedict, *Patterns of Culture* (Boston, 1934), pp. 253–254. Reprinted by permission of the publishers, Houghton Mifflin Company.

39. See, for example, *A Scientific Theory of Culture and Other Essays* (Chapel Hill, 1944); and for comment on the significance of Malinowski's studies in the culture-personality area, A. Kardiner, *The Psychological Frontiers of Society* (New York, 1945), Foreword by R. Linton.

began a series of joint explorations of the relationship between culture and personality by subjecting to minute study reports of several primitive societies and one modern American village.[40] These studies have rather convincingly demonstrated—whatever criticisms may be made of the many specific and sometimes questionable interpretations—that each culture tends to create and is supported by a "*basic personality type*" composed of the complex of personality characteristics that are "congenial with the total range of institutions . . . within a given culture." The basic personality type, found among most but not necessarily all of the members of any specific society, is the result of the culturally similar early childhood experiences, and is not in any direct sense the product of instincts or inherent "drives" or fundamental "forces."

Consider, for example, the natives of the Marquesas Islands, where little if any evidence has been discovered of the powerful social role of the sex drive as observed in our own society and as interpreted by Freud and his followers as the basis of neuroses. The Marquesans, we learn, are "exceedingly casual in everything pertaining to sex," possessing no word for virgin and endowing sexual behavior with very little emotional content. On the other hand, the Marquesans display considerable anxiety—are "neurotic" in our language—about scarcity of food and about the danger of being devoured, understandable anxieties among a people who suffer periodic famines and practice cannibalism. "Around these anxieties," Linton comments, "all sorts of taboos and regulations were organized much as they are about sex among ourselves."[41] Or take the case of the Alorese, a small native group in the Dutch East Indies. These little Negroid people are generally suspicious of each other, mistrustful, lacking in enterprise and aspiration, excessively anxious about mutual exploitation, and quite normally manifest violent aggression that in our own society would be found only in psychopathic cases. Such traits, we are told, characterize the basic personality of the Alorese, a configuration, according to Kardiner, induced by the neglect of children by their mothers, who are otherwise occupied tending the fields. This basic personality structure in turn supports the exploitative, essentially non-co-operative, and financially competitive culture of Alor.[42] And so with various other peoples—the Tanala, the Comanche, the citizens of "Plainville, U.S.A."—in each group is observed the give-and-take between culture and personality type. These studies provide a detailed demonstration of the essential unity of individual and society.

---

40. These studies are reported in *The Psychological Frontiers of Society* and earlier, in A. Kardiner, *The Individual and His Society* (New York, 1939).

41. R. Linton, "Potential Contributions of Cultural Anthropology to Teacher Education," in *Culture and Personality* (Washington, D. C., 1941), p. 5.

42. Cora Du Bois reports this group in *The People of Alor* (Minneapolis, 1924) and in *The Psychological Frontiers of Society*, Chap. V. For Kardiner's analysis see the latter volume, Chaps. VI, VII, VIII, IX.

[2] *Studies of culture "via the personality":* We have seen that variations in basic personality types are understandable only with reference to the cultures with which the different types are correlated. Clearly, then, the social scientist faces the possibility of studying a specific culture by concentrating upon the "carriers" of the culture; that is, by using as his primary materials the personality manifestations of the society's individual beings. Put another way, the interrelated and interacting culture-personality complex may be viewed "via the personality." Though employing language somewhat different from the terminology of the present context, sociologists have engaged in this kind of investigation for decades.

The most influential early study of this type was perhaps *The Polish Peasant in Europe and America* by W. I. Thomas and Florian Znaniecki, a remarkable five-volume report and interpretation of peasant family and community life and their changes accompanying modern industrialization and the migration of these people to Germany and the United States. While this research includes lengthy discussions of several broad theoretical and methodological problems of importance to sociology and social psychology, we cite the work of Thomas and Znaniecki here because of the extensive use the authors made of "human documents" in the study of personality and culture. Letters, newspaper accounts, court records, reports of social agencies, and especially life histories including autobiographies (Volume III is a single autobiography, with interpretation, of a peasant immigrant), reveal the attitudes and interests, the prejudices and personal problems, the aspirations and frustrations of numerous individuals. With the support of this material the authors interpreted the organization, disorganization, and reorganization of personality on the one side and of the changing social systems on the other. Whatever shortcomings this ambitious undertaking exhibits in the light of more recent studies, it furnishes us with an imposing example of an attempt to comprehend the configurations of "culture" and the patterns of personality by focusing on the detailed behavior manifestations of the latter.[43] Since the publication of *The Polish Peasant*, sociologists have duplicated this attempt, as we shall often have occasion to note later in this book, in various realms of social life. They have studied the modern city's localities of social and cultural disorganization by utilizing the life histories and case records of disorganized individuals; they have analyzed changing family patterns through examination of personality problems of individual members of families; they have pictured social and cultural conflicts of minority groups by exploring the biographical records of the members of such groups. In these and other areas social scientists have

43. *The Polish Peasant* . . . was originally published in Boston, 1920. For a detailed analysis of this work, see H. Blumer, *Critiques of Research in the Social Sciences I* (New York, 1939); see especially the evaluations by Blumer, G. W. Allport, G. P. Murdock, M. M. Wiley, and R. Bain.

followed for several decades the lead more recently emphasized by the advocates of a culture-personality approach.[44]

Illustrative of the more current efforts to study culture "via the personality" are several investigations of the "caste" division between Negro and White in the United States and of the structure of social classes within each of these groups. The author of one of the earliest of these reports, trained as a psychologist, analyzed life-history materials so as to depict the central features of the community structure of "Southern Town." Through psychoanalytical interviews and other personality exploratory techniques he sought to "grasp and describe the emotional structure which runs parallel to the formal social structure in the community." This work of John Dollard[45] and subsequent investigations marked by the same approach and the same emphasis upon the use of personality materials as data of primary revelatory significance have underscored the close relationship between social structure and personality types. For personality types vary considerably as they are observed in the upper, middle, and lower classes of both the White and Negro populations; and both the rigid barrier of caste and the relatively open lines of class are manifested in and sustained by the personalities of the individuals occupying different social positions in the structure of the community. The interrelationship between social structure and personality is not restricted, of course, to the "Southern Towns" of our national scene, as studies of communities in New England and elsewhere have shown.[46] In a later chapter we shall be concerned with some of the substantial findings of these researches into caste and class. Here they illustrate for us a method of revealing the interdependence of culture and personality.

Some difficulties involved in culture-personality study. When the anthropologist pitches camp in a small, relatively isolated community of Melanesians or Australian aborigines or Eskimo, and after he has carefully observed and

44. For a discussion of some of the methodological problems involved in this type of research and for excellent illustrative material, see L. Gottschalk, C. Kluckhohn, and R. Angell, *The Use of Personal Documents in History, Anthropology and Sociology* (New York, 1945), especially pp. 177-232.

45. *Caste and Class in a Southern Town* (New Haven, 1937), p. 17; See Chap. II for a brief discussion of research method, and the same author's earlier and more extensive considerations of this approach in *Criteria for the Life History* (New Haven, 1935).

46. In addition to Dollard's *Caste and Class in a Southern Town*, see A. Davis and J. Dollard, *Children of Bondage* (Washington, D. C., 1940); E. F. Frazier, *Negro Youth at the Crossways* (Washington, D. C., 1940); C. S. Johnson, *Growing Up in the Black Belt* (Washington, D. C., 1941); W. Lloyd Warner, B. H. Junker, and W. A. Adams, *Color and Human Nature* (Washington, D. C., 1941); R. L. Sutherland, *Color, Class and Personality* (Washington, D. C., 1942); A. Davis, B. B. Gardner, and M. R. Gardner, *Deep South* (Chicago, 1941). And for New England's "Yankee City," see W. Lloyd Warner and P. S. Lunt, *The Social Life of a Modern Community* (New Haven, 1941); W. Lloyd Warner and L. Srole, *The Social Systems of American Ethnic Groups* (New Haven, 1943).

perhaps even shared the social life of the group, he is able, so to say, to see the "culture as a whole." More, he can report more or less objectively the ways in which culture and personality interact and sustain each other in the society he investigates. He has, then, the double advantages of being able to grasp the totality of the group life and of being himself emotionally detached from the compelling values of the primitive culture. But when the anthropologist turns to his own society he loses these advantages. When he joins with the sociologist and social psychologist in the investigation of culture and personality in his own community he is faced with a large and vastly complex social organization, cultural values at least some of which are his own, and a personality type (or types) of which he is himself an example. Yet he and his fellow social scientists are deeply aware of the need of comprehending the complexities of modern society much as they are now able to understand the culture-personality patterns of the Tanala or Comanche or Zuñi. In response to this need, and as we have already indicated, many social scientists are now busily engaged exploring our own and other modern societies.

Conscious of the enormous difficulty of comprehending the culture of the United States, for example, "as a whole," several field investigators have selected fairly small communities for the purpose of studying their cultural configurations and, to a less extent, the characteristics of personality structure. Among the most influential of these are the two studies of "Middletown," published in 1930 and 1937, in which the authors depict the culture of a small city, perhaps representative of many in central United States, by using the conceptual tools of the field anthropologist. In these volumes the culture pattern receives primary emphasis, but in a subsequent work one of the authors, Robert S. Lynd, has analyzed the interaction of culture and personality in broader terms and with reference to larger areas of American life.[47] Indiana's "Middletown" is a city of almost 50,000 persons, a fairly large and complex community. In the interest of limiting the area to more workable proportions and of investigating a "culture" with a developed industry and containing several minority groups—characteristic features of many American cities—the anthropologist W. Lloyd Warner and others have reported in great detail the class and ethnic and status structure of "Yankee City," a New England community of about 17,000 population. These volumes portray the relationships between culture and personality in at least one urban region of the United States,[48] and parallel in approach the previously cited analyses of class and caste. The culture-personality approach of Linton and Kardiner is illustrated

47. See R. S. and H. M. Lynd, *Middletown* (New York, 1930) and *Middletown in Transition* (New York, 1937); and R. S. Lynd, *Knowledge for What?*, especially Chaps. III and V.

48. See Warner and Lunt, *op. cit.*; Warner and Srole, *op. cit.*: also W. Lloyd Warner and P. S. Lunt, *The Status System of a Modern Community* (New Haven, 1942); and for an account of one aspect of "Yankee City," W. Lloyd Warner and J. O. Low, *The Social System of the Modern Factory* (New Haven, 1947).

in a recent description of the culture of "Plainville," a small village of fewer than three hundred residents located in the "North-South border" area of this country. The findings of this teamwork project between anthropology and psychoanalysis are admittedly not conclusive and need not concern us at this point except as an example of one more case of intensive investigation of a local community.[49]

In recommending these sociologically fruitful researches to the reader, we must at the same time direct his attention to certain of their limitations. Note that each of the local communities studied—whether "Middletown" or "Yankee City" or "Southern Town" or "Plainville"—is a part of a much vaster culture complex, one that includes the entire social organization of at least American society. This broader pattern ramifies into and interacts with the social structure of the local town or village in myriad ways. None of the investigators is altogether forgetful of this fact, but the local community approach itself tends to exclude from consideration the interrelations between the local culture and the larger pattern. Understanding the "well-integrated community" of "Yankee City," for example, is not simply a matter of plotting the details of the formal and informal structural organization of that city, for the latter is by no means a closed system of social life such as we sometimes find in primitive groups. Also note that this approach, used primarily to study the "cultures" of smaller communities, similarly tends to neglect the enormously important cultural role of the large-scale urbanization process which is most clearly marked in the great city but which sets the "cultural tone" of much of our entire community life. And note too that preoccupation with the ways in which a given small community "works" as a social system is apt to shade over the dynamic historical processes apart from which no culture-personality structures are possible or, in the final analysis, comprehensible. Whatever their limitations, however, these studies of culture and personality in contemporary life move us considerably forward in the central sociological quest, the relation of individual and society.

Almost all of the writers who have contributed to this area of research have found that the give-and-take between individual and society, between "culture and personality," is not an altogether harmonious relationship. For society breeds discord as well as harmony; society evokes conflict as well as co-operation. Preliminary analysis of these related processes, co-operation and conflict, as they operate in the life of society and in the lives of all individuals, is our final task in this division of the book.

Co-operation and Conflict

Modes of social co-operation. Men cannot associate without co-operating, without working together in the pursuit of like or common interests. The many

49. See, under the pseudonym "James West," *Plainville, U. S. A.* (New York, 1945); and *The Psychological Frontiers of Society*, Chaps. X–XIII.

modes of co-operation in social life may for this preliminary survey be divided into two principal types.

[1] *Direct co-operation:* Under this category we include all those activities in which people do like things together—play together, worship together, till the fields together, labor together in myriad ways. In such activities there may be minor diversities of task—you wash, I'll dry—but their essential character is that people do *in company* the things which they can also do separately or in isolation. They do them together, either because the face-to-face situation is itself a stimulus to the performance of the task or because it brings other social satisfactions. Direct co-operation is exemplified also when people perform together tasks that would be too difficult for one of them to perform alone, as when they pull together on a line or together storm a barricade.

[2] *Indirect co-operation:* Under this category we include all those activities in which people do definitely unlike tasks toward a single end. Here the famous principle of the *division of labor*[50] is introduced, a principle that is imbedded in the nature of social life. The division of labor is revealed in the procreation of life or in the upbringing of a family. It is revealed wherever people *combine their differences* for mutual satisfaction or for a common end. In industry, in government, in scientific research, even in recreational activities, functions tend to become more and more specialized. This process is more manifest in urban than in rural life, but the disappearance of the "husking bees" and "threshing rings" signal the fact that people have to satisfy in other ways the need for social stimulation formerly satisfied through direct co-operation.

The replacement of direct by indirect co-operation has accompanied our great technological advances, which clearly require specialization of skills and functions. But in terms of human needs this is not all gain. It is often claimed that the individual of modern industrialized and urbanized society, increasingly separated from face-to-face co-operative modes of activity and more and more a "specialist" detached from the close ties of intimate community life, tends to take on the highly individualized, "neurotic" characteristics depicted by a growing number of writers.[51] As we shall indicate later, this not altogether unwarranted alarm is based upon additional considerations. It is, we may note here, symptomatic of our times that churches, schools, and numerous social agencies foster direct co-operative programs for their members or clients; that psychologists and psychoanalysts find the impersonal and competitive features of our society significantly related to personality disturbances of various types; even that a growing current trend in general education seeks to turn out

---

50. The *economic* significance of this principle was first fully revealed, of course, by Adam Smith. The classical statement, which every student of sociology should read, is found in *The Wealth of Nations*, Book One. For an admirable recent discussion see W. E. Moore, *Industrial Relations and the Social Order* (New York, 1946), Chap. IV.

51. See, for example, the works of K. Horney, especially *The Neurotic Personality of Our Time* (New York, 1937) and *Our Inner Conflicts* (New York, 1945).

"rounded" useful citizens rather than the trained specialists in this activity or that.

Modes of social conflict. Conflict expresses itself in numerous ways and in various degrees and over every range of human contact. Its modes are always changing with changing social and cultural conditions. Some types disappear, as has dueling in our own society, and new types emerge. It is an error, therefore, to assume, as have some writers, that because struggle is eternal any particular forms of it, such as war or certain modes of economic competition, are also necessarily eternal. "Social conflict" includes all activity in which men contend *against one another* for any objective. Its two fundamental types are *direct* and *indirect* conflict.

[1] *Direct conflict:* When individuals or groups thwart or impede or restrain or injure or destroy one another in the effort to attain some goal, direct conflict occurs. Milder thwarting or frustration of goal attainment is involved in such forms as litigation, polemic, propagandistic activity, and much of the struggle of organized economic groups for larger stakes. More violent forms sometimes mark economic class conflict, as they do more conspicuously in duel, vendetta, revolution, and war.

[2] *Indirect conflict:* When individuals or groups do not actually impede the efforts of one another but nevertheless seek to attain their ends in ways which obstruct the attainment of the same ends by others, indirect conflict occurs. We shall have occasion later in this book to analyze bargaining and competition, which in all their varieties come within this class. *Competition* is impersonal conflict between individuals for attainment of any objects of desire that are limited in supply, whether income or academic honors or beautiful women or social prestige. The competition does not as such directly interfere with the efforts of another to attain such goals, but only indirectly with the other person's success.

In distinguishing these two forms, the reader should note that not all struggle in which man is engaged is *social* conflict of either type. We are struggling to master difficulties, to overcome obstacles, to achieve ends in other ways than through conflict with our fellows. Man's "battle" with the physical environment is a case in point. Social conflict, man against man or group against group, reveals itself wherever there is society. But unless co-operation penetrated deeper than conflict, society could not endure.

The combination of co-operation and conflict in social life. Co-operation and conflict are universal elements in human life. They are present together over a vast range of activities. As in the physical world, where there are forces of attraction and of repulsion simultaneously operative and determinant of the position of bodies in space, so in the social world there is a combination of co-operation and conflict revealed in the relations of men and of groups. "The more one thinks of it," Cooley wrote, "the more he will see that conflict and co-operation are not separable things, but phases of one process which always involves something of both."[52] For when men co-operate their interests are harmonious only up to a point. Even in the most friendly relations, even in the most intimate associations, there is some point where interests diverge, or where attitudes are not in accord. The closest co-operation within the family does not prevent the occurrence of quarrels. The devotion to a common cause does not rule out, among those who espouse it, strong differences of opinion or conflicting ambitions. "It seems that there must always be an element of conflict in our relations with others, as well as one of mutual aid; the whole plan of life calls for it; our very physiognomy reflects it, and love and strife sit side by side upon the brow of man."[53]

Conflict, however, is generally limited in its scope and method by conditions involving some co-operation of the contestants outside *and* within the area of conflict. Indeed there is no form of social conflict, whether face-to-face struggle like dueling or debating or foot-racing or whether more complex group forms as between economic or ethnic or political or religious groups, that does not involve co-operative activity. In fact, the only form of social conflict that is altogether unmitigated, that does not operate within some kind of co-operative framework, is war, for war ultimately is waged without rules. Conversely, there are no examples of co-operative enterprises in society within which conflict in some form is absent. Co-operation crossed by conflict marks society wherever it is revealed—in the "co-operative culture" of the Zuñi among the Pueblo Indians, or in the "competitive culture" of the Kwakiutl among the Northwest tribes, in the collectivized economy of Soviet Russia or the competitive economies of other nations, in the formal debating club or the informal clique of cronies.

Co-operation and types of interest. Recall that in the preceding chapter we distinguished between those interests that are detached or *like* and those that are *common* or shared. These two types of interest characterize two important levels of co-operative activity.

[1] *Co-operation and common interest:* Obviously, when men *recognize* a common interest they tend to co-operate toward its achievement. They co-operate not only from a perception of the greater efficacy of co-operative over isolated action but also because it is of the very essence of a common interest to bring men together, to make them translate their sense of oneness into co-operative activity. Men cannot be united in devotion to a cause, whether the common interest is family or nation or creed or science, without some impulsion to join in its pursuit—to co-operate with one another. It is exactly these social impulses, rooted in common interests, to which leaders appeal when they move men to action on the basis of loyalty to country or class or race or religion.

52. C. H. Cooley, *Social Process* (New York, 1918), p. 39.
53. *Ibid.*, p. 56.

[2] *Co-operation and like interest:* Co-operative activity exists on another level in the pursuit of *harmonious* like or individualized interests. Men combine, for example, to take advantage of the division of labor, to pool their resources in business, to seek favors from a government, or to beat a dangerous competitor. Competitors want to increase the general demand for their goods, they want to keep down costs of materials and labor, even the cost of the competition in which they engage. In these and other respects their like interests are harmonious and lead to a degree of co-operation. Economic organization, as we shall see in a later chapter, is pre-eminently the area of this form of co-operation.

The distinction between these two levels of co-operation has wide sociological implications that can be only suggested at this point. The first, co-operative devotion to a *common* cause, is rooted in a type of interest that is *indivisible* and one cannot pursue it at all without pursuing it for all who share the interest. The *attitude* of co-operation and the interest are therefore inextricably bound together. Hence, on this level, the tendency to co-operate does not altogether depend on success. In fact, defeat or frustration may bind the members more closely than success, as witnessed in the joining together and support of their creed by religious groups in the face of extreme persecution.[54] A member of the persecuted but growing Jehovah's Witnesses has typically declared: "The things that are written and said against the Society I take as personally said about me, because I fully endorse all that is being said and done by the Society."[55] The common interest shared by the Witnesses is reflected in a strong co-operative attitude.

But co-operation on the level of *like*, self-limited interest cannot unite men by such strong ties. For this type, as involved in economic organization, involves a degree of *individual* calculation: the co-operative impulse depends on the fact that the interest of one happens to harmonize with the interest of others. If the harmony is disturbed—as frequently occurs in the co-operation of employers and workers, of competitors, of even business partners—the desire to co-operate is likely to vanish. On this level, the co-operative *attitude* is merely a consequence of the temporary reconciliation of individual considerations. The alliances of competitors for their mutual advantage are forever endangered by the intensity of the competitive struggle and the feelings and suspicions it engenders. Our modern society, with its highly developed division of labor and its large dependence on the harmony of like interests, is marked by an instability that is revealed on the one side in various forms of conflict

54. The history of early Christianity and of early Protestantism, of course, affords large illustrations of this point. So, perhaps, do the recent co-operative developments in Palestine; see, for example, H. F. Infield, *Cooperative Living in Palestine* (New York, 1944) and the novel by A. Koestler, *Thieves in the Night* (New York, 1946).

55 Quoted in H. H. Stroup, *The Jehovah's Witnesses* (New York, 1945), p. 156.

in the social order, and on the other in disturbances of the individual personality.[56]

Conflict, interests, and attitudes. Conflict, like co-operation, is found on different levels, levels that are directly related to our basic types of interest and the closely associated patterns of attitude.

[1] *Conflict and like interests:* There is conflict wherever like interests are *inharmonious*. The simplest case is that of two or more persons or groups who want the same individual thing. "What I want you want" means co-operation where the interest is shared or common, but means conflict when the interest is individualized and exclusive. Anything that is *scarce* relative to the competing desires of people to have and to enjoy, whether it be a commodity, a loved one, an honor, a position of power, is a condition of conflict.

We may note three examples of inharmonious like interests of fundamental importance. First, all *economic* goods, wherever men are in a position to compete or to bargain or to fight for their possession, are spurs to conflict. For economic goods have a scarcity-value; and the desire for them, both for those who have much and for those who have little, is rarely satiated. Secondly, individualized and exclusive *emotional attachments* are apt, under various conditions, to breed rivalries and jealousies and envies and to result in latent or open conflict. Finally, there are interests of *power and distinction* which by their very nature can be neither common nor harmonious. They cannot be harmonized because they are always *relative* to the possession of the power and distinction of others; these intangible goods cannot be apportioned in the same manner as can tangible economic goods. Thus a society can be ordered on the basis of equality of wealth, as in the case of some "utopian" communities in modern times, but never on the basis of equality of power and prestige. There is no power where power is equal. The quest for power and distinction is unending in social life, and is, as we shall see, a perpetual source of social conflict.

[2] *Conflict and unlike attitudes:* So far we have been dealing with conflict as arising out of the disharmony of like interests. The other great type of conflict-situation reduced to its simplest elements takes the form, "What I love, you hate." This is primarily an expression of *unlike and antagonistic attitudes*. These may themselves arise out of discordant like interests, as in economic class warfare, or may be largely independent of such conditions, as in certain religious antagonisms. Frequently a difference in economic interests is translated into a profounder cultural conflict, and frequently the prejudice of race or class justifies itself by appealing to a deep cleavage of interests. Thus attitudes and interests reinforce one another and intensify the spirit of conflict. When men hate one another, they find it necessary to rationalize their

56. The impact of competition on personality formation is explored in the works of K. Horney; see especially *The Neurotic Personality of Our Time*, Chap. XV.

hatred, as is seen in the history of every war. When men have divergent interests, they readily attribute evil motives to their opponents, as is illustrated by the planned and the "unconscious" propaganda of anti-Semitism.

Unlike attitudes may be expressed by *indifference* or by *aversion* or by *positive conflict*. *Indifference* is rare in social life. A man who lives for sport and cares nothing for art may be indifferent to the man with opposite tastes. But such neutrality is unusual, for men are apt to be unfavorably disposed toward those who are cold to the things they value. To hold aloof is itself usually an act of implicit disapprobation. The outsider, the alien, the stranger, the nonconformist usually excite unfavorable prejudice among the members of the in-group, wherever found, because out-groups for most men are objects of suspicion as potential threats to their own systems of values.

Aversion is the repudiation of common interest. This form of emotional hostility denies and disparages the values of the out-group. Thus the elite who despise the vulgar or the vulgar who scorn the "high-brow," or the sophisticated city dwellers who feel superior to the rustic or the ruralists who think the urbanite effete or immoral, are in effect maintaining a resistance to alien values. Cultural differences engender attitudes of aversion, particularly among those who live in relative isolation from other groups than their own or who cherish a strong orthodoxy within their group. By aversion they set up walls of defense against the encroachments of values they reject.[57]

It is only a step from aversion to *active conflict*, from defense to offense. When the conflict is unequal, it takes the form of persecution and suppression; when more equal, it becomes the effort of either party to upset the other by attacking the things it values and frustrating its purposes. Active conflict may take place within a framework of law, as in economic struggle, the strife of political parties, contests for prestige and preferment, the counteractivities of propagandism and proselytism, and the myriad disputes of everyday life. Feuds and vendettas, riots and lynchings, revolutions and other uprisings are partially unrestrained by law, and warfare between states lies outside any legal framework.

The less it is limited by law, the more conflict must rely on physical force and the more destructive it becomes. This is particularly true if the strength of the opposing parties is fairly equal. Conflict is then impartially destructive not only of the interests ostensibly involved in the struggle but also of all the other interests of the parties. This point is illustrated by the history of modern wars between nation-states or between such large groups as the currently contending divisions of China.

[3] *Common interest and conflict:* The common interests of groups are potent spurs to conflict, as war also reveals. For common interest both includes and

57. An example of psychological isolation, self-imposed by the members of an informal group of "sophisticates," and its relation to the attitudes of aversion are well presented in the novel of H. H. Howe, *We Happy Few* (New York, 1946).

excludes, and in the latter process it gives rise to the most significant and the most persistent type of conflict. It is frequently observed that a group becomes most conscious of its unity when it is threatened by another group. Hence it is part of the technique for the stimulation of common interest to present it as being menaced by an opposing interest and to rally all possible prejudices in support of the in-group by heightening the contrast between its values and the alien and aggressive values of other groups. According to such organizations as the Ku Klux Klan and the Black Legion, Negroes and Jews and Catholics are engaged in a vast and dastardly conspiracy against the high ideals of the "true American." To the military patriot the pacifist is a cowardly traitor. The politician paints the program of the opposing party as ruinous folly. And when autocratic rulers are afraid of internal dissensions they are likely to divert attention from them by pointing to the foreign enemy without or to the "menace" within the nation. In the last we observe the well-known "scapegoat" technique, one of several of the propagandist's devices with which he arouses the common interest of this group or that in the arena of group conflict.[58]

Common interest, then, harbors the prejudices as well as the loyalties of men, being sustained at once by their attachment to their own group and by their hate and fear of the outsider. That is why conflicts between religious and other cultural groups, political parties, classes, and nations are so persistent and so significant. The struggles between these groups illustrate, too, the enormously important role of the associative and dissociative attitudes that solidify the members of conflicting groups on the one hand and abet the exclusion of outsiders on the other. Both the uniting and the excluding roles of common interest and related attitudes in group life will concern us throughout this investigation of the social order.

Co-operation and conflict and the changing social order. We have distinguished between direct and indirect forms of co-operation and conflict, stressed the omnipresence of struggle and mutual aid in social life, analyzed the pervasive role of common and individualized interests and related sets of attitudes in both co-operation and conflict, and at several points suggested how these social processes are revealed in the life-patterns of individuals as well as in the group contours of the changing society.[59] Our brief treatment, however, merely sets the stage, as it were, for the more extensive considerations in later chapters.

---

58. There is a large literature on propaganda techniques. See, for example, L. W. Doob, *Propaganda* (New York, 1935); and the Institute for Propaganda Analysis, *The Fine Art of Propaganda* (New York, 1939).

59. Our analysis of co-operation and conflict with reference to types of interest and manifestations of attitudes contrasts with and at some points parallels the more psychologically oriented study of M. A. May and L. W. Doob, *Competition and Cooperation* (New York, 1937); see especially Chap. II.

The complexity of the problems involved in co-operation and conflict is indicated by the fact that in every community these processes assume forms that distinctively reflect the local social and cultural conditions. In the United States, for example, we have an unusual multiplicity of groups and group standards, religious, racial, national; considerable mobility of population physically and socially; an economic organization which expanded rapidly and largely without state controls. The pioneer mentality coexists with the sophisticated mentality of the cosmopolite; expressions of direct co-operative democracy, of, say, the New England town meeting stand side by side with the large-scale "mass democracy" of the urbanized and industrialized world. Our society is to a large extent the result of a fairly recent series of huge immigrations, with many of our present-day social values the reflection of the cultural conflicts involved in the assimilation process. And in spite of our unusual diversity and the many variations in the experience of different groups, we maintain strong barriers of segregation between the "superior" White, Anglo-Saxon, gentile population and the members of other ethnic divisions. These are but some of the features of our own national life that give a special stamp to co-operation and conflict in the United States.[60] So with every social order: these social processes must be viewed with relation to the particular social and cultural circumstances within which they operate.

The manifestations of co-operation and conflict vary in type and detail not only from community to community but from time to time. When we focus our attention on social processes we necessarily recognize the ever-changing order of society. In every case of conflict, for example, as the conflict proceeds, whether between nations or classes or individual competitors, the attitudes and interests of the parties to it undergo change, since their own activities are effectively altering the situation. And in every case of the accommodation of conflict, whether by such temporary expedients as the erection of barriers of segregation or the imposition of the demands of the "victorious" or whether by the resolution of the conflict-situation itself through the discovery of a wider community of interests, the accommodation is a part of an endless historical sequence.

As we study the social processes of co-operation and conflict, the dynamic quality inherent in them leads us to the investigation of the problems of social change. Our concern with omnipresent co-operation and conflict will remain, to be sure, as we explore the characteristics of social structure in Book Two, for always imbedded in social organization are these basic processes. But social change itself is so complex and so significant in the life of individual and of society that all of the final Book Three will be devoted to it.

---

60. For a series of discussions of these matters see *Unity and Difference in American Life* (R. M. MacIver, ed., New York, 1947).

Initiation

PART TWO: *Society and Environment*

Foreword:

Before we study the structure of society and the changes it undergoes we may prepare ourselves further by considering the conditions of the outer world on which social life, as all life, depends, and the nature of that dependence. There are two large questions that here loom before us.

Since every social group, whether racially or nationally or "culturally" defined, distinguished as class or as community or by any other criterion, differs in manifest respects from other groups, we face the question whether these differences are determined mainly by heredity or by the conditions of life. The answer we give to this question has enormously important practical implications and, indeed, colors our whole view of society. This subject we take up in Chapter IV.

The other question concerns the manner and degree in which the various aspects of environment respectively affect the social life of man. In Chapter V we consider this question with particular reference to the geographical conditions to which society and culture are always related in certain ways. And in Chapter VI we face directly the intricate problem of the relationships between man and his total environment.

4

Environment and Life

Environment and Adaptation

The intimate relation of environment and life. When a seed is put into the ground, under appropriate conditions, it germinates, pushes its seed leaves up to the air, and sends its rootlets down into the soil. It enters into a set of relations with its environment so complex that if it were completely detached again, as the seed once was, it would perish. In this complex process the plant develops the potentialities of the particular seed, and no others. It becomes a variety of wheat or of corn, a sunflower or a ragweed, after its kind. But whether it flowers or fruits or withers prematurely, whether it grows strong and full statured or becomes weak and dwarfed, whether it is crowded out by other plants or holds its own, depends essentially on the environment. Different kinds of plants are adapted to different habitats, to marsh or to stony soil, to the dry desert or to the rich humus of well-watered plains, to heat or to cold, to sunlight or to shade. The same kind of plant will exhibit significant differences if the climate changes. This relation of plant to soil is so full of significance that a special branch of botany, called plant *ecology*, is devoted to its study.

Animals are not attached to the soil like plants, but they are no less dependent on and responsive to environment. Human beings are usually capable of passing from one environment to another as well as of changing the conditions of a given environment to suit their own purposes. But they are not on that account more independent of the kind of environment in which they live. The environment is not simply the outside world, thought of as something that surrounds or "environs" us. If we think of it in that way, we underestimate its role. In truth, the relation of life and environment is extremely intimate. The organism itself, the life structure, is the product of past life and past environment. Environment is present from the very beginning of life, even in the germ cells. We think of our organisms as ourselves, and environment as that which lies outside us. But the capacities and attributes of the organism are relative to the whole environment in which they manifest themselves. The environment is more than a "conditioning" factor of a life that can be conceived of apart from it. Imagine, for example, that we were suddenly transported to a much larger planet. Our bodies would instantly become much heavier, and that fact alone would involve a myriad of other differences. We would no longer know ourselves, we would no longer, assuming we could exist at all, *be* ourselves. We never know life except in an appropriate environment, an environment to which it is already adjusted. Life and environment are, in fact, correlates.

So closely interwoven are the two that every variety of life, every species, in fact, every individual living thing, has its own particular environment, in some degree different from that of others. Environment is not one but *infinitely various.* In the American Museum of Natural History in New York City there appeared an exhibit of over one thousand species of insect found in a suburban yard. That little space contained more than a thousand varieties of environment for insect life alone. A curious instance of the specificity of environment is the distinction between the head louse and the body louse, neither of which is found in the environment of the other. The environment is as specialized as the life that is lived within it.

Furthermore, every change in a living creature involves some change in its relation to environment; and every change in the environment, some change in the response of the organic being. Our environment is our habitation in the completest sense. In its totality, as relative to any group (and ultimately to any individual), it is thus a factor of great complexity. Every difference of environment means a difference in our habits, our ways of living. On the other hand, our habits, our ways of living, in so far as they differ, create for us a different environment, a different selection within it, and a different accommodation to it. Through a process of constant selection and constant adaptation, the moving equilibrium of life is maintained.

Environment, life, and human society. The correspondence of life and environment is amply illustrated in the case of social groups. Just as every region of a country is in some respects different from every other, so also are the inhabitants of each region. An inhabitant of the Ozarks or of the Kentucky mountains thinks and feels differently from a New Yorker, just as a New Englander differs from a prairie dweller. The difference in some way is relative to the environment in which they respectively dwell (though, as we shall see, the precise expression of the relationship is fraught with great difficulties). Common observation tells us that as people change from country to city, from agriculture to industry, from mountain to plain, from hot to temperate climates, they become adjusted to the new conditions, undergoing a process of change as their environment changes. It is obvious that a well-to-do group has a different environment from a poor one, a colored urban group from a white one, a professional class from an artisan class. Take the largest effective community we can find, whether that of a nation or of a whole area of civilization, and its character is seen to be in some significant way related to that of the total environment within which it has grown. Or take the smallest group, such as the individual family, and there too the correspondence between life and environment is manifested.

The revelation of the manner in which the environment molds and is itself modified by the life of the group is one of the chief achievements of the social sciences. From ancient times, to be sure, men have observed certain rough correspondences between broad physical conditions and modes of living; for example, that the inhabitants of tropical regions exhibited characteristic differences from those of temperate or of arctic regions, and that the seafarer was typically distinct from the inlander. But more recently these observations have been gradually refined and elaborated into a systematic form. French sociology has been especially prominent in the development of such studies from the time of Montesquieu to the present, inspired by leaders like Le Play, Demolins. and Brunhes.[1]

The relationship between the physical environment and social phenomena has been of particular interest to two groups of American sociologists in recent decades. First, an "ecological school" has developed, stimulated by the investigations of the late R. E. Park and of E. W. Burgess at the University of Chicago. Human or social ecology, finding suggestive analogies in plant and animal ecology, has been particularly interested in the social and cultural phenomena associated with various urban areas. Thus phenomena ranging, for example, from patterns of family organization to the incidence and types of mental disease are regarded as revealing a process of adjustment or accommodation of the life of the group to the special conditions represented by a locality. Focusing upon the social effects of locality, the ecologists have elaborated the operating process—competition and co-operation, centralization and decentralization, specialization and segregation, invasion and succession—that mark the structuring of rural as well as urban communities. Their findings add considerably to our understanding of the "spatial" aspects of social life.[2]

---

1. Frederic Le Play, in his important study of European workers, *Les Ouvriers européens* (Paris, 1855), developed the thesis that *locality* determines *work* and thus has a great influence on the economic organization of the family and the social institutions of the people. Demolins continued the work of Le Play, and in the periodical *La Science Sociale* published various studies showing the social characteristics of particular regions of France. For J. Brunhes, see below, Chapter V.

2. The ecological approach is developed, for example, by three of its outstanding representatives, R. E. Park, E. W. Burgess, and R. D. McKenzie, in *The City* (Chicago, 1925). For sympathetic surveys of the ecological school, see J. A. Quinn, "The Development of Human Ecology in Sociology," *Contemporary Social Theory* (H. E. Barnes and H. Becker, eds., New York, 1940), pp. 212–244, and E. C. Llewellyn and A. Hawthorn, "Human Ecology,"

The positional focus of human ecology is repeated, though with a different emphasis, in the more recent "regional school" of American sociology. The regionalists, under the leadership of Howard W. Odum and his colleagues at the University of North Carolina, have renewed in modern terms the quest of Le Play a century ago—the seeking out of the potential as well as the actual interaction between man's physical environment and man's social life. Thus the United States today is found to be divided into several "natural" regions, each possessing geographical and social conditions that can be integrated, it is claimed, into a balanced way of life. In its search for balance and integration of environmental and social conditions, regionalism sets forth a plan for the development of community life; a plan, however, that stresses the crucial significance of the interaction between man's activities and man's surroundings.[3]

In a subsequent chapter we shall consider some of the substantial findings of social ecology and of regionalism.[4] These studies and others combine to reveal both how complex an environment is and how completely it penetrates the life of a social group. More than this, they raise a deeper question—the question of the extent to which differences between human beings and between social groups can be explained on the basis of environmental differences. The answer to this question, which involves the relationship between the vital factor that we call heredity and environment itself, is fundamental to our understanding of the very nature of society as well as the incessant changes which it undergoes. Before facing it directly we shall seek to clarify some preliminary points.

Three levels of adaptation to the environment. We frequently hear or read the expression "man adapts himself to his environment" used in such a way as to imply that there is one fundamental form or mode of adaptation. This implication often leads to confusion, especially in the study of social life. Therefore, we shall observe that, like the term "individuality," the term "adaptation" may be employed in a physical, a biological, and a social reference.

[1] *Physical adaptation:* Purely physical adaptation occurs whether we will it or not: it is independent of our strivings and our aims. The sun will tan our skin if we expose ourselves to it; that is a form of physical adaptation, whether or not it helps us to live in a sunny climate. Fresh air will stimulate our lungs

---

Twentieth Century Sociology (G. Gurvitch and W. E. Moore, eds., New York, 1945), pp. 466–499; and for a critique of its theoretical aspects, M. A. Alihan, *Social Ecology: A Critical Analysis* (New York, 1938).

3. For a thorough discussion of the regional approach, see H. W. Odum and H. E. Moore, *American Regionalism* (New York, 1938); for an application of this approach in a now defunct federal agency, National Resources Committee, *Regional Factors in National Planning and Development* (Washington, D. C., 1935); and for a vigorous plea for regional planning, L. Mumford, *The Culture of Cities* (New York, 1938), Chaps. V and VI.

4. See below, Chapter XIII.

and poisonous gas will destroy them; physically, the one is no less an adaptation than the other. Strength or weakness, health or sickness is equally an expression of what we term natural law. Nature everywhere makes such demands, death itself being the final statement of physical adaptation. Whatever the conditions are, whether wilderness or city, poverty or prosperity, whether in the eyes of men they are favorable or unfavorable, good or evil, this unconditional physical adaptation remains with all its compulsion.

The examples cited suggest that man is deeply *concerned* with many problems associated with physical adaptation; for example, with death, with health, with bodily changes induced by various conditions of diet and social life. But this concern and man's attempts to prolong life or improve health, sometimes quite successful, should not be confused with the process of physical adaptation itself. Purely physical adjustment is always ongoing, is never "maladjustment."

[2] *Biological adaptation:* By adaptation in the biological sense we mean that a *particular* form of life is fitted to survive or to prosper under the conditions of the environment. We say that fish are adapted to a marine environment or tigers to the conditions of life in the jungle. In this sense we speak also of *maladaptation*. When we say, for example, that a tiger is maladapted to the conditions of the desert or of the polar snows, we mean that the conditions are not such as to permit the adequate functioning of the organism, that in fact the inevitable *physical* adaptation is detrimental to the biological demands. In order that a certain equilibrium, involving the survival or fulfillment of the organism, be attained, the environment, we say, must be such and such. But the *must* here is an imperative, addressed, as it were, to the organism.

[3] *Social adaptation:* The concept of social adaptation reveals an extension of the biological use. Social adaptation, however, always involves some standard of value—it is a conditional adaptation. Various sociologists speak of the process of *adjustment* or of *accommodation*, though the latter term has sometimes been used to stress the adaptation of the social being to the given conditions rather than the adaptation of the conditions to the social being.[5] But *if* we are to live in ways we desire we must find or make an appropriate environment. Man does what every living creature does in proportion to its intelligence: he selects and modifies his environment in such a way that the inevitable adaptation shall admit the greater fulfillment of his wants. In this *social* sense adaptation definitely implies valuation, whereas in purely physical adaptation there is no implication of well-being, no virtue or merit.

Thus when we speak of maladaptation or maladjustment we do not mean that the universal principle of physical adaptation is defeated. We do mean that the existing social adaptation involves a less complete satisfaction of our

5. See, for example, E. W. Burgess, "Accommodation," *Encyclopaedia of the Social Sciences* (New York, 1935), I, 403–404.

wants and of our ideals than would be possible if the environment were altered in a particular direction. In the light of the restless questing nature of social man and the multiplicity of his desires, it is not surprising that he often views every equilibrium of his life with his environment as containing some degree of "maladjustment." In terms of our desires we criticize the adaptation which, considered only as a "natural" or physical phenomenon, is always perfect. What we are really criticizing is the environment to which our lives are adapted, or ourselves because of our failure to control it—to change the conditions of the equilibrium.

The sociologist is necessarily a student of the process of social adaptation, involving man's continuous adjustments to his changing life conditions *and* his evaluations of both his own adjustments and the conditions. Unlike the physical scientist—the biologist, for example—he faces the task of analyzing a complex environment of which his own hopes and wants and criticisms are a vital part.

The outer and the inner environment of social man. In his incessant efforts to modify the conditions of his life, man creates a new type of environment. This man-made environment has a twofold character, an outer and an inner aspect.

[1] *The outer environment:* The outer consists of the physical modifications of nature, including our houses and cities, our means of transportation and communication, our comforts and conveniences, the whole apparatus and machinery of our civilization. It includes what some anthropologists have termed our "material culture." This physicotechnical structure or a part of it would endure for some time if the society itself perished, as is evidenced by the remaining monuments of past civilizations like the Egyptian and the Andean. But this is not true of the other aspect of the social environment.

[2] *The inner environment:* The inner is society itself and endures only so long as the society endures.[6] It consists of the organizations and regulations, the traditions and institutions, the repressions and liberations of social life, of what we collectively name the *social heritage.* For every member of society this system is just as much a part of the environment as are the outer conditions of life, except that his adjustment to it is not of the same inexorable character, not being imposed by natural law. Nevertheless, social man cannot escape its influence, for he is trained within it and habituated to it, and none of his desires can be fulfilled unless he takes it into account.

The total environment, then, of every human being consists of (1) an outer environment in various ways modified by man, in the centers of modern civilization vastly modified, but under all conditions still requiring an unconditional or physical adaptation; and (2) an inner or social environment to which man

6. Cf. E. Rignano, "Sociology, Its Methods and Laws," *American Journal of Sociology,* XXXIV (1928), 429–450.

is adjusted through conscious response and habituation. We shall see that the distinction between these two aspects of the total environment is essential in the analysis of social reality. But we must also remember that the two are always interactive. For man is constantly changing, to satisfy the better his never-satisfied wants, both the outer and the inner environment, both his physical and social worlds.

Civilization and adaptation. During the more recent stages of human history, man's modifications of his outer and inner environment have been vast and peculiarly rapid. It is sometimes claimed that these large environmental changes have furthered some of man's needs at the expense of others, that human nature is not at home in the world of civilization which it has made for itself. One form of this criticism has found a well-known expression in the contention of Graham Wallas that the modern environment balks some of our "instinctive dispositions." "Man is born with a set of dispositions related, clumsily enough but still intelligibly, to the world of tropical or subtropical wood and cave which he inhabitated during millions of years of slow evolution." These dispositions, he maintains, have been through ages adjusted to respond to the stimuli offered by such surroundings, and being thus suddenly (in terms of the span of evolution) dissociated from them, they function uneasily and capriciously.[7] According to this view, man is *biologically* adapted to the life of the fields and the woods, not to the life imposed by the city, the factory, and the office. This claim, that modern technology and social life necessarily frustrate hereditary dispositions, has been widely popularized in recent years. Here we may examine it briefly.

To begin with, there is no evidence that the members of the simpler societies, possessing relatively undeveloped systems of technology and of social organization, are generally more (or less) content with their lots or better adapted to the conditions of their lives than ourselves; the myth of the "happy savage" has been shattered by modern anthropology. Still, it is no doubt true that in modifying our environment to satisfy more fully some of our desires we may make it less favorable for the satisfaction of others. There are, to be sure, many maladjustments created by the conditions of modern life, in the new complex environment that man has made for himself, but they can be explained, we believe, without reference to inherited habituations.

If man inhabited caves for ages we do not find any great yearning on his part to return to that mode of life. Rather, what he most lacks in many modern urban environments is a full share of the universal requirements of a healthy human organism, such as fresh air and sunlight and freedom of movement. For millions of city dwellers the conditions of habitation and work and play are cramped and unhygienic. These conditions, moreover, make demands and

7. Graham Wallas, *The Great Society* (London, 1920), Chap. IX.

offer excitations which induce nervous strain. Particularly to those brought up in the country, the transition to the life of the city, like any other transition from familiar surroundings, often brings a sense of deprivation, of nostalgia; and as in the rapid growth of cities a large proportion of their population is country-bred this malaise has become a widespread phenomenon.

Where the environment has been subject to rapid modification through technological development, there is definite evidence of various forms of maladjustment. There is, for example, as we have noted above, the personal disturbance of the individuals who, habituated to one set of conditions, are confronted with a different set. There is also, as Ogburn has demonstrated, the general "lag" between the social conditions conformable to the new technical order and the social conditions inherited from a past order.[8] Again, in any complex social order there are numerous contradictions between multiple sets of mores and between established mores and behavior practices induced by rapidly changing social conditions. We must reckon with such factors as these in calculating the maladjustments or frustrations or disturbances of the individual. But the more difficult and obviously less demonstrable assumption of a deeper discrepancy, between man's conscious desires as they are active in the remolding of his environment and his organic or "instinctive" dispositions, should be resorted to only if the other and more demonstrable explanations prove inadequate.

The Study of Heredity and Environment

The controversy: heredity "versus" environment. It is an age-old observation, recognized in almost all human groups, that the blood of the parents flows in the children, that like begets like. The difference in heredity, then, might account for the difference in the traits or qualities of individuals or groups, even in very different environments. To this explanation some biologists naturally have leaned (supported by a number of psychologists and a few sociologists), while students of environment have generally stressed the other aspect. Thus a great dispute arose and continues even today as to the relative importance of the two. In explaining the variations of human beings and their societies, some claim that heredity is far the more weighty determinant, while others belittle heredity in the name of environment. Some argue that certain qualities, such as those of health and intelligence, depend mainly on heredity while they admit that other qualities, particularly the social qualities expressed in morals, customs, and beliefs, depend more directly on environment.

8. W. F. Ogburn, *Social Change* (New York, 1922), Part II, Chap. VIII and Part IV, Chap. I. For a large-scale utilization of Ogburn's concept of "lag," see H. E. Barnes, *Society in Transition* (New York, 1939), especially Chaps. XV and XXI; and for our evaluation of this concept see below, Chapter XXVI.

[1] *Earlier studies of the problem:* The whole issue was raised in a definite form by Francis Galton in his pioneer work on *Hereditary Genius* (1869), in which he sought to show that, while there is seeming chance in the appearance of genius, the probability of the occurrence of greatly gifted children is vastly higher when the fathers are of a superior intelligence. Galton's work was carried on by Karl Pearson, who applied his method of correlation to the problem, concluding that the influence of the environment is far less than that of heredity in the determination of important human differences. Pearson claimed that it was even possible to measure the relative efficacy of the two and gave evidences purporting to show that for people of the same race within a given community heredity is more than seven times more important than environment.[9]

Many other researchers have followed the path of Pearson. Some have taken class or occupational categories and have shown that the groups with the higher social or intellectual rating have produced more persons of genius or distinction. This positive correlation has been illustrated, for example, in studies showing that royal families produce in proportion more geniuses than others; that families of the clergy in the United States produce the largest proportion of notable men, followed in order by the other professions, businessmen, farmers, and laborers; that American men of science emanate in largest numbers from the professional classes and in smallest numbers from the agricultural class; and so forth.[10] Others have chosen racial or national categories and by the application of psychological tests, especially "intelligence tests," have brought out considerable differences between them, as in the well-known Army tests of immigrant groups in the United States and more generally of native-born, foreign-born, and Negro sections of the population.[11] Others again have taken selected family groups for comparison, giving us the famous contrast between the prosperous and distinguished lineage of Jonathan Edwards and the wretched descendants of the Jukes and the Kallikaks.[12]

[2] *What these studies do and do not reveal:* From such studies conclusions are frequently drawn that indicate a superficial analysis of the problem of heredity and environment. Most of these earlier researches have given us more precise evidence regarding a common observation: that those who are born in the

---

9. K. Pearson, *Nature and Nurture* (London, 1910), and other papers in the Eugenics Laboratory Lecture Series.

10. F. A. Woods, *Mental and Moral Heredity in Royalty* (New York, 1906); S. S. Visher, "Study of the Type of the Place of Birth etc. of Fathers of Subjects of Sketches in *Who's Who in America*," *American Journal of Sociology*, XXX (1925), 551-557; J. McKeen Cattell, *American Men of Science* (3d ed., New York, 1921), p. 783.

11. For a bibliography of such studies and a careful evaluation of them, see O. Klineberg, *Race Differences* (New York, 1935), Chaps. VIII and IX.

12. A. E. Winship, *Jukes-Edwards* (Harrisburg, Pa., 1900); H. H. Goddard, *The Kallikak Family* (New York, 1912); R. L. Dugdale, *The Jukes* (New York, 1877); and A. H. Estabrook, *The Jukes in 1915* (Washington, D. C., 1916)

families or groups possessing distinction or prestige are more likely to develop intellectual or other attainments. For example, a study cited above calculated that the chances of sons of unskilled laborers to gain eminence (as measured by inclusion in the 1922–1923 edition of *Who's Who in America*) were about 1 in 48,000 as compared with the chances of sons of other occupational groups, which were approximately as follows: skilled laborers, 30; farmers, 70; businessmen, 600; professionals, except clergymen, 1,035; clergymen, 2,400.[13]

Facts of this character are important, but when we deal with them it is essential to distinguish fact from inference. What they tell us *directly* is that, accepting a certain criterion of distinction, certain occupational groups in a particular country (at a particular time) produced eminent persons in varying proportions to their numbers; at this point we need not question the criterion of eminence used. But what we must observe is that such figures tell us nothing directly about either heredity or environment, though they tell us something about *various combinations of the two*. Many of the researchers who have collected such facts as these draw from them the conclusion that heredity is a more potent factor than environment, but the facts themselves might just as well—and just as illegitimately—be used to support the opposite conclusion. Every specific group, we have noted, has a different specific environment. It has been claimed that the resemblances between members of royal families must, in view of the different milieus from which their ancestors came (but they were all alike members of royal courts!), have been brought about "through the germ cells alone."[14] And it has been declared that, as revealed in his lower "intelligence test" rating, the Negro "lacks in his germ-plasm excellence of some qualities which the white race possesses."[15] Again, it is frequently argued that the achievements of the higher social and economic classes are in themselves an index of the concentration in these groups of better heredity—"good stock" is the popular phrase. To establish such conclusions it would not only be necessary to discount the effect of environmental conditions, but, as we shall see, to disregard or shade over the constant *interaction* of environment and life.

[3] *A preliminary word of warning:* Several of the investigations of the type here under review have stressed the varying proportions of achievement—measured by this or that criterion—manifested by the different occupational or "class" groups. We learn that generally the children of the "higher" classes show a greater degree of achievement than those of the "lower." But we must not assume, as some writers have, that the distribution of occupational groups represents the inevitable assortment of the population into levels of "natural" ability. For this assumption ignores certain crucial aspects of the problem. It overlooks the fact that the occupational distribution of people is a complex

13. Visher, *op. cit.*
14. Woods, *op. cit.*
15. P. Popenoe and R. H. Johnson, *Applied Eugenics* (New York, 1926), Chap. XIV.

social phenomenon, not basically determined by or measured by the biological or any other single factor—a point to which we will return much later in this book.[16] Moreover, this assumption greatly oversimplifies the role of *vertical mobility*—movement up and down the occupational divisions—a process especially characteristic of our own society, though probably diminishing in amount in recent decades.[17] Vertical mobility has never operated so freely as to permit all or perhaps even most of the inherently gifted to find their "natural" occupational levels; otherwise we would not find, as we do, that at any given time any large occupational group, no matter what its social standing, contains some gifted individuals.

In the last resort the assumption we have been criticizing rests on our inadequate conception of the relation of heredity and environment, a relation we must now examine in somewhat greater detail.

Heredity "versus" environment: some inconclusive cases examined. Men fall into many serious errors regarding the nature of social classes, of race distinctions, of national unities, and other subjects of great sociological importance because of mistaken views about the relation of heredity and social environment. Therefore we shall use a variety of frequently cited examples of "evidence" to bring out the need for more careful analysis than is often made of them.

[1] *Comparative studies of intelligence scores of Negroes and Whites:* We shall consider first the much-quoted studies of the comparative intelligence of Negroes and Whites in the United States. One of the earliest of these, on the basis of data provided by the psychological tests applied to Army recruits during World War I, reported the average mental age of Negroes as 10.4 years and of the Whites as 13.1 years.[18] Many subsequent investigations of the same comparison have shown similar higher intelligence scores for Whites than for Negroes,[19] although at least two of them, undertaken respectively in Los Angeles and New York, reveal no such contrast.[20] However, the rather con-

---

16. See below, Chapter XXIV.

17. L. Corey has minimized, and in places denied, the existence of vertical mobility in the United States in *The Crisis of the Middle Class* (New York, 1935), p. 222 and *passim*. However, its existence is documented for one American community in P. E. Davidson and H. D. Anderson, *Occupational Mobility in an American Community* (Stanford University, 1937); see also the same authors' *Occupational Trends in the United States* (Stanford University, 1940), especially Chap. I. The economic aspects of the process are discussed in O. Pancoast, Jr., *Occupational Mobility* (New York, 1941). We expand the discussion of vertical mobility in Chapter XIV below.

18. R. M. Yerkes, *Psychological Examining in the U.S. Army, Memoirs*, National Academy of Sciences, XV (1921).

19. These studies are listed and analyzed, for example, in Klineberg, *op. cit.*, and in *Intelligence: Its Nature and Nurture*, The Thirty-ninth Yearbook of the National Society for the Study of Education (Bloomington, Ill., 1940), Vol. I, Chap. IX.

20. W. W. Clark, "Los Angeles Negro Children," *Educational Research bulletin*, Los Angeles City Schools (1923); J. Peterson and L. H. Lanier, "Studies in the Comparative Abilities of Whites and Negroes," *Mental Measurement Monographs*, V (1929).

sistent findings of a lower intelligence score for Negroes in this country require interpretation, and there are two important questions which they immediately raise. (We may disregard the problem of the representativeness of the samples of the populations studied in view of the general consistency of results of many investigations.)

In the first place, how much can we conclude concerning the general level of mentality of the two races from the results of specific tests applied to selected groups? Are the tests valid? There are two difficulties here. One concerns the hypothesis that tests involving degrees of facility in performing particular operations under particular conditions faithfully represent degrees of general intelligence or "mental age." "Intelligence tests," comments one expert, "are to a considerable degree simply knowledge tests scored relatively to the achievement of like-age children"; many of them "are essentially indirect measures of scholastic aptitude."[21] What can we conclude from the results of tests that measure "scholastic aptitude" or similar abilities regarding the general (and hard-to-define) quality we speak of as "native intelligence"? The other and closely related difficulty concerns the cultural background of the two groups. Are the common tests impartial in the sense that they measure equally those aptitudes through which intelligence displays itself under the life conditions of each group? Although in recent years psychologists have greatly improved the impartiality—the "objectivity"—of intelligence tests, few of them would claim that techniques have been devised with which we are able to measure equally the native intelligence of groups of widely ranging backgrounds. The fact that the background of the Negro in general differs from that of the White makes the difficulty here too a serious one.

Let us suppose, however, that these difficulties are surmounted. Then we come face to face with our second main question. We have found, we now assume, adequate indices of the intelligence of the two groups. Shall we then conclude that our indices reveal the hereditary or racial differences in intelligence of the Negroes and Whites? By no means, for we have done nothing so far to eliminate the factor of differential environment. No such tests can discount the influence of differential training, experience, home life, social opportunity. If the Negro comes off worse in these tests, has the environment nothing to do with it, the environment as a whole, including not only such aspects as economic disadvantage and inferior and less schooling, but also the less objective aspects such as the lack of social stimulations and prospects which the White enjoys? In answer, we may note that Negro children in the North make higher scores than do those in the South—about 7 "I.Q." points higher in

21. G. D. Stoddard in *Intelligence: Its Nature and Nurture*, I, 6, who continues: "*Native intelligence*, like *native running ability*, is a postulate; the counters actually employed in mental testing are such school and pre-school familiars as bead stringing, block building, puzzles, animal pictures, conundrums, counting, definitions, and reciting from memory." (Italics are Stoddard's.)

New York City. Professor Klineberg has established that this difference is not due to selective migration, and concludes that the only valid test of race difference would have to be conducted under the ideal conditions of complete absence of discrimination and equality of opportunity. In the absence of such conditions, intelligence tests are measures of accomplishment, to be sure, but *not* of innate racial differences in mental ability.[22]

The environment of our past as well as the environment of the present is written in our lives. Can we ever measure its influence and therefore also the influence of heredity? It is sometimes claimed that we can, and to this claim we must return. All that we here assert is that intelligence tests do not permit us to assess heredity. They are useful as showing differences that exist here and now—differences in specific human performances, jointly the result of environment and life.

[2] *The measurement of physical traits:* Some of the difficulties involved in our first example appear to be absent here. For physical traits are more concrete and certainly more easily measurable than mental traits. The range of variation of physical characteristics for groups of different nationalities can be represented by frequency curves. For example, one study shows the height of Japanese soldiers varying from under 56 to 69 inches and of American soldiers from about 61 to nearly 75 inches; the average stature for the one group is 63.24 and for the other 67.51 inches.[23] We may observe in passing that such figures do not accurately measure the comparative average stature of the males of the two populations, but they are useful indications of difference. The chief danger of this quantitative comparison lies in the assumption that it measures, with any degree of accuracy, a hereditary difference between the two groups. For we do not yet know the effect of continuous subjection to different environments. We cannot assume that the conditions of life, the kind of food, the kind of nurture, the kind of climate, have nothing to do with the differences revealed.

There is, in fact, convincing evidence that when children are subjected to unfavorable conditions, when, for example, the food supply is reduced during a war or severe economic disruption—as is the case today in a large part of the world—their stature, as well as their weight, is affected. On the improvement side, on the other hand, Franz Boas, for example, has shown that American-born children of immigrants, especially among Jewish and Japanese groups, not only grew to an average height of two inches more than their parents but even experienced changes in head formation.[24] In view of the increasing amount

22. Klineberg, *op. cit.*, Chap. IX.
23. Graphs showing these results are presented in R. E. Chaddock, *Principles of Statistics* (New York, 1925), p. 227; see comments in F. H. Hankins, *Racial Basis of Civilization* (New York, 1926), Part II, Chap. II.
24. See F. Boas, "Effect of American Environment on Immigrants and Their Descendants," *Science*, Dec. 11, 1936; and *The Mind of Primitive Man* (Rev. ed., New York, 1938), especially Chap. VII.

of evidence of this type it is mere dogmatism to assert that heredity is *alone* responsible for the physiological differences between national or racial groups.

Note that we are not building a case "in favor of" environment. We are not for a moment denying, for example, that heredity contributes toward measurable physical differences between various groups, but we do deny that the amounts of such differences are accurate measures of the contribution of either heredity or environment. Consider the case of stature as one student of heredity puts it: "From the moment of conception and through puberty, innumerable factors bear upon the action of the 'stature' genes. The mother's health, gland disorders, food habits, climate, living conditions, occupation, exercise, modes of walking and sleeping, all influence the body structure."[25] Given this variety of influences, no wonder that the task of measuring the influences of hereditary differences is far more complicated than many biometricians have realized. We know, through Mendelian and other studies, that offspring inherit in some degree qualities or traits which may be latent in their parents but are revealed in the grandparents or remoter ancestry. In other words, we must think of heredity in terms of at least several generations. If, on the other hand, we think of environment in terms of a single generation we may draw misleading inferences regarding its importance. There is reason to believe that the general stature of European peoples has increased since the days of the armored knights. And there is evidence that American college students today are taller and heavier than those of two or three decades ago, and perhaps that the stature of American males of native stock is about two inches greater than those of half a century ago. If so, then we should not rule out the long-run influence of environment as well as of heredity. And if this is true of physical traits it is more obviously true of mental and social traits, which, as we shall see, bear unquestionable indications of the influence of the *social* heritage.

[3] *Differences between occupational groups:* Our next case bears upon a question we have already raised. How can we explain differences in accomplishment and intelligence that appear to exist between members of different occupational groups? Examination of one or two studies may help us with this question.

One is a study of the social origins of American business leaders, an investigation which, according to its authors, "strongly suggests" that "inequality of earnings between the several occupational classes has its origins in a fundamental inequality of native endowments, rather than in an inequality of opportunities."[26] The evidence for this conclusion was derived from a questionnaire filled out by a large and representative list of business leaders, defined as partners or owners or higher executives of businesses having a volume of sales or gross income exceeding $500,000. Of these, 36 per cent were found to be the sons of "big" businessmen, in all 56.7 per cent were the sons of "busi-

25. A. Scheinfeld, *You and Heredity* (New York, 1939), pp. 81–82. This entire volume is recommended to the student as a highly readable and sound discussion of heredity.

26. F. W. Taussig and C. S. Joslyn, *American Business Leaders* (New York, 1932).

nessmen of one kind or another," whereas only 12.4 per cent were the sons of farmers, 5 per cent of clerks or salesmen, 8 per cent of skilled laborers, and 2.2 per cent of unskilled laborers. Regarding capital and connections as the environmental factors that contribute most toward success in business, the authors asked a series of questions concerning inheritance of funds, aid from relatives or friends, and the like. Of the respondents 11.6 per cent reported "substantial financial aid" from such sources, and almost 36 per cent reported "influential connections" as of benefit in their business success. Of the total number almost 32 per cent were college graduates.

It was from such evidence that the authors drew their conclusion that "lack of native ability rather than lack of opportunity" explains the disproportionate representation of the various occupational groups. In view of our

TABLE I Intelligence and Length of Schooling in Relation to Occupational Levels

Levels of occupation	Number of cases	Average years of school	Average I. Q.
I. Professional, business, executive, etc.	130	17.3	115
II. Semiprofessional, small business, farmers, salesmen, etc.	565	14.0	108
III. Clerical, skilled trades, etc.	228	12.0	104
IV. Semiskilled	12	10.8	99
V. Unskilled labor	10	9.4	97

previous discussion we leave it to the student to consider whether the evidences (even if they had been more one-sided) "strongly" support the conclusion. How is their conclusion reconciled with the fact which they themselves incidentally establish, that "business leaders in the United States are today [circa 1929] being recruited, to a substantially greater extent than was the case thirty or forty years ago, from among the sons of major executives"? On the larger question of the relative roles of heredity and environment can we draw any valid conclusion whatever from figures of this kind?

"Very well," the reader may ask, "but what about the differences in intelligence between the occupational groups?" That the "higher" groups do make higher scores on intelligence tests has been demonstrated in a number of studies that show results generally consistent with those reported in Table I.[27] These

27. W. M. Proctor, "Intelligence and Length of Schooling in Relation to Occupational Levels," *School and Society*, XLII (1935), 783-786. This study and several other similar ones are discussed by A. W. Kornhauser in *Industrial Conflict: A Psychological Interpretation* (G. W. Hartmann and T. Newcomb, eds., New York, 1939), Chap. XI, pp. 203-216.

studies reveal, of course, that the better-paid and more highly esteemed occupations are generally peopled by more "intelligent"—as measured by the various standardized tests—and, significantly, better-schooled individuals. But, we may ask once more, what do they tell us of the respective *amounts* of influence of heredity and environment in determining these "class" differences? To conclude from such data as appear in Table I that the higher economic classes necessarily possess a superior heredity may be a popular and satisfying conviction in certain circles but is not as yet substantiated. A careful student of this problem notes that while considerable research has "demonstrated the contribution of *both* heredity and environmental influences, the whole matter is still too controversial to justify any clear conclusion about the relative importance of the two in accounting for the observed class differences" in intelligence.[28]

[4] *Famous and degenerate family lines:* Our last example will be the well-known contrast between such groups as the Adams, Edwards, and Saltonstall families, on the one side, and the Kallikaks, Nams, and Jukes, on the other. These favorites of "yesterday's sociology books"[29] unfortunately still linger on as "evidence" of good and poor heredity. Take the Jukes. In 1877 there were identified 1,200 descendants of a certain "Juke" who was born in New York in 1720. Of these 440 were physically defective or diseased, 310 were paupers, 300 had died in infirmaries; of the 130 who had been convicted of crimes 7 were murderers, and perhaps more than half of the women were prostitutes. A further investigation in 1915 unearthed 2,820 descendants, and of these 600 then living were mentally defective. Against this dreary picture has been set the bright record of the descendants of Jonathan Edwards, of whom 1,394 were identified in 1900. At least 295 of these were college graduates, and many of them were distinguished members of the professions and business; they included 13 college presidents, a vice-president of the United States, and, so far as the record showed, no convicted criminals.

Such a contrast is striking, but those who immediately claim that it reveals the incontestable supremacy of heredity over environment are ill advised. In the first place we must ask, in what sense are the Jukes and Edwards of the present generation the same families as those of nine or ten generations back? Each generation is a fresh admixture, and the "blood" of countless admixtures flows in each of us. The names of prominent ancestors are borne by many persons who possess none of their chromosomes or hereditary traits in the biological sense. Moreover, the production of every individual involves the loss of one half of the genes from each parent; and these extraordinarily numerous genes rarely, if ever, assume the same combination in two or more individuals. "Consequently the best traits may appear in parents and be lost in their offspring: genius in an ancestor may be replaced by incompetence, imbecility,

28. Kornhauser, *op. cit.*, pp. 215–216. (Italics are Kornhauser's.)

29. Scheinfeld, *op. cit.*, p. 360; see Chap. XXXIX of this volume for an excellent discussion of ancestry.

or insanity in a descendant."[30] Consider the readily observable differences between members of the same family. When we study these differences new environmental factors greatly complicate our search for their causes. We discover, for example, that behavior variations between children are related to such conditions as the order of birth and changes in parental experiences and attitudes. No two Jukes or two Edwards, we should remember, duplicated one another.

This does not mean that we reject the position of the more moderate eugenists, that like *tends* to beget like.[31] We have no more justification for denying the importance of heredity than some eugenists have when they deny the importance of environment. However, two highly significant points are underscored by the above considerations: first, the complexity and uncertainty of heredity itself; and, second, the rashness of imputing solely to the character of some ancestral stock the social virtues or vices of some group of descendants. A well-known student of eugenics asks us to "constantly bear in mind the uniqueness of the individual, whose every cell carries its complement of chromosomes and genes, all alike, yet differing from those of any other living being, so that every part has its own unique reaction to the environmental impacts which condition its growth"[32]—a significant reminder for the student of social life.

The nature of the Juke-Edwards exhibit suggests in other respects the need for caution. About 600 of the Edwards have been marked "eminent." But what is the total number of descendants? No one can state definitely, though it runs into the several thousands—including what characteristics we do not know.[33] Observe also that the more easily identifiable members of the clan are those who have won some kind of distinction, just as in the case of the Jukes it is those who have failed most signally who are most easy to trace.[34] Still,

---

30. E. G. Conklin, *Heredity and Environment* (Princeton, 1923), p. 312. For more recent discussions of this process by students of biology see, for example, F. Osborn, *Preface to Eugenics* (New York, 1940) and S. J. Holmes, *Human Genetics and Its Social Import* (New York, 1936).

31. For example, L. Darwin, in *What Is Eugenics?* (New York, 1928), puts the case for heredity in the following reasonable terms: "We cannot foretell what will be the qualities of a man before he is born. But if we know the qualities of his near relations we can tell a good deal about what his qualities will *probably* be. This means that, though we should make many bad shots, we should be generally far nearer the truth than if we went by chance."

32. Osborn, *op. cit.*, p. 37.

33. Cf. P. A. Witty and H. C. Lehmann, "An Interpretation of the Hereditary Background of Two Groups of Mental Deviates," *American Journal of Sociology*, XXXIV (1928), 28. See also by the same authors, "The Dogma and Biology of Human Inheritance," *ibid.*, XXXV (1930), 548-563.

34. This point is well stated in Scheinfeld, *loc. cit.*, in which appears:

There was a Bostonese
Who searched out pedigrees
Which she stored in the middle of her forehead;
And when they were good, they were very, very good,
But when they were bad—they were horrid!

no doubt, the difference remains: we search for the Jukes in asylums and poorhouses and find some of them there, while for the Edwards we look successfully in the role of distinguished service. But at this point we must not forget that the Jukes had an unfavorable social environment whereas the Edwards had a favorable one. To claim that the group determines the environment more than the environment the group is to prejudge the case: This kind of prejudgment marked these studies of notorious family lines. "They failed to differentiate between the inheritance of bad genes and the effects of a bad environment handed on from one generation to another. As sociological studies they are of interest. As evidence of heredity they are now generally discredited."[35]

Heredity "versus" environment: "controlled" experiments examined. The cases we have thus far examined suggest an incessant interaction between heredity and environment. Those who disparage environment see only one side of it; those who disparage heredity, only the other. Since the character of the environment and the character of the group are always correlates—are never separated in life itself—it is easy to draw opposite conclusions from the same phenomena. The correlations themselves are well established—there is no doubt that the children of successful parents are on the whole more successful than the average. But we must not permit our prior convictions to determine the side of the correlation—heredity or environment—that we choose as the cause of success or failure.

Faced by this constant correlation, various researchers have sought for methods by which either of the factors could be held constant while the other varied. The principle involved here is that differences so revealed can be attributed solely to the variant factor. The botanist can take the seeds of the same plant and grow them under varying conditions of soil and climate. He can then attribute the differences to the environmental factor, or, more exactly, to the combination of the same heredity with different environments. Can the sociologist experiment in this way?

Those who have answered this question in the affirmative have, since the beginning of the scientific study of heredity, given special attention to those cases in which biological inheritance might be regarded as practically identical. For these afford a peculiar opportunity for assessing the role of the variant environmental factor and thus of heredity also. The opportunity is supplied by the occurrence of "identical" twins, derived from the same ovum. Galton initiated these studies during the last century (on the basis of what is now inadequate biological theory); the marked similarity which such twins exhibited under many conditions reinforced his conviction regarding the dominant part heredity plays in the causation of both human resemblances and human dif-

35. Osborn, *op. cit.*, pp. 47-48. The geneticist Lancelot Hogben states flatly, "If social biology ever becomes an exact science, the dreary history of the Jukes will be regarded as we now regard alchemy." Cf. Scheinfeld, *op. cit.*, p. 365.

ferences.[36] Later investigators have endeavored to find the reverse situation, in which children of different heredity have been brought up in practically the same environment. Both these types of situation encourage the hope that we can surmount the difficulties which embarrassed the studies already discussed.

[1] *Studies of identical twins reared together:* For some forty years biologists, psychologists, and statisticians have studied the physical and behavior traits of twins. In recent years researchers have been able to distinguish between fraternal (dizygotic) twins, developed from two different ova, and identical (monozygotic) twins, developed from a single ovum. It has been well established that twins exhibit closer resemblances, physical and mental, than siblings who are not twins; and that, particularly with respect to certain physical traits, identical twins, are more alike than fraternal twins. A few of these studies have found some instances of such exact resemblance, both of mind and of body, as to justify the favorite old plot presented in the *Comedy of Errors*. And again the conclusion has been drawn by some investigators that the influence of environment is feeble as compared with that of heredity.[37]

However, the more recent and more intensive investigations of identical (and other) twins reared together admit no such one-sided conclusion. In recent years numerous observational case analyses, training and learning experiments, and carefully executed statistical studies have been undertaken using the most highly developed techniques for investigating differences of physical traits, intelligence, and personality factors. Close similarities between identical twins have been found, but so have some significant differences. Among these studies should be mentioned the detailed reports of the famous identical quintuplets, the Dionnes, who in spite of their "single-egg" common heredity (and similar but in no sense identical environment) have quite noticeable variations in physical and mental traits and especially personality and temperament.[38]

What are we to conclude from these researches regarding heredity and environment? Again, that *both* factors are important. The close resemblances between identical twins may be attributed in part to their common inheritance and in part to their similar prenatal (even the womb does not offer the *same* environment to its unborn inhabitants) and later environments. Here we have an extraordinary conjuncture of the two factors. Yet differences between iden-

---

36. F. Galton, *Inquiries into the Human Faculty and Its Development* (London, 1883). See G. C. Schwesinger, *Heredity and Environment* (New York, 1933), pp. 175–231, for a review of the series of researches initiated by Galton.

37. Among the earlier studies may be cited E. L. Thorndike, *Measurement of Twins* (New York, 1905) and *Educational Psychology* (New York, 1914), Vol. III; A. Gesell, "Mental and Physical Correspondence in Twins," *Popular Science Monthly*, XIV (1922), 305-331, 415-428; N. D. M. Hirsch, *Twins* (Cambridge, Mass., 1930), a particularly good example of faulty reasoning.

38. The studies of twins reared together are listed and evaluated by H. D. Carter in *Intelligence: Its Nature and Nurture*, Vol. I, Chap. VIII. On the Dionne quintuplets see W. E. Blatz and others, *Collected Studies on the Dionne Quintuplets* (Toronto, 1937).

tical twins develop, as we have seen—differences for which environmental variation must account. And what are we to conclude regarding the relative *amounts* of hereditary and environmental influence? Let one answer who has worked in this area for some time: "The whole array of twin-studies seems to suggest . . . the futility and artificiality of the idea of untangling nature and nurture influences in the sense of ascertaining the percentage contributions of each in any *general* sense."[39]

[2] *Studies of identical twins reared apart:* Here we may, presumably, observe a more revealing test of the nature-nurture controversy. The value of studying identical twins reared in different environments has long been recognized, but the few earlier investigations of single cases of twins produced far from conclusive evidence.[40] More recently H. H. Newman, a biologist, F. N. Freeman, a psychologist, and K. J. Holzinger, a statistician,[41] studied nineteen pairs of identical twins brought up in separate homes. Physical, mental, and personality differences between the twins were analyzed with relation to environmental differences, and comparisons were made with data concerning fifty pairs of identical twins and fifty-two pairs of fraternal twins reared together. The conclusions of the authors of this admirably thorough analysis are cautious but suggestive. While they found considerable differences of many types between identical twins reared apart, they concluded that physical traits are least affected by the environment, that achievement and various skills are somewhat more sensitive to environmental influence, and that personality characteristics are most affected. The majority of their nineteen separated cases revealed fairly similar mental abilities, but in five cases in which the surroundings were markedly different, the intelligence scores also varied widely, a finding consistent with several other recent studies. Their own concluding statement is well worth reproducing:

> If, at the inception of this research project over ten years ago, the authors entertained any hope of reaching any definitive solution of the general nature-nurture problem or even of any large section of the subordinate problems involved, in terms of a simple formula, they were destined to be rather disillusioned. The farther one penetrates into the intricacies of the complex of genetic and environmental factors that *together determine* the development of individuals, the more one is compelled to admit that there is not one problem but a multiplicity of minor problems—that there is no general solution of the major problems

39. Carter, *op. cit.*, p. 248.

40. An earlier study of a pair of identical twins separated from the age of two weeks was made by H. J. Müller, "Mental Traits and Heredity," *The Journal of Heredity*, XVI (1925), 433–448, who concluded that mental ability is genetically determined while variations in "nonintellectual" characteristics are environmentally determined. For a discussion of more recent studies which generally arrive at no such specific conclusions see Carter, *op. cit.*, pp. 248–251.

41. *Twins: A Study of Heredity and Environment* (Chicago: The University of Chicago Press, 1937).

nor even of any one of the minor problems.... We feel in sympathy with Professor H. S. Jennings' dictum that what heredity can do environment can also do.[42]

Investigations of this type, then, discount any theory that claims to measure the exact potency of heredity. And they discount any theory that attributes, in respect of the differences between individuals and groups of the human species, a dominant role to heredity as against environment. It is still possible for the geneticist to argue that even in "identical" twins there are hereditary differences. And it is equally possible for the environmentalists to relate almost all differences which they display to the live situations within which they are expressed. Neither one-sided interpretation is justified by the research to date. Perhaps the really crucial experiment would be one in which from birth the identical twins were reared in vastly different situations. If one were brought up in an American home and the other in the wilds of Africa, or if one of the two suffered the fate of Kaspar Hauser, or if a new set of identical quintuplets like the Dionnes were reared in five greatly different environments, then we might have a conclusive test. And it is reasonable to surmise, from such indications as we shall present in later chapters, that it would justify the claim that environment is a coequal arbiter of our development and our fate.

[3] *Studies of children of different parentage reared together:* These researches follow the alternative quest, which hopes to solve the problem from the study of instances in which environment rather than heredity may be taken as a constant. It is, as we have seen, impossible that any two individuals should have an identical environment in all respects. The best approximations we can find are instances in which children of different heredity have been brought up from infancy or early childhood in the same foster home. A number of studies have been made along these lines and one or two long-range researches are now in process.[43] They differ considerably in their conclusions.

Miss B. S. Burks some years ago, for example, in a study of the resemblance exhibited by foster children and foster parents as contrasted with that of children and parents proper, attempted once more to measure the influences of heredity and environment. She actually concluded that heredity's contribution was about 80 per cent, environment's precisely 17. This statistical result was reached on the false assumption that heredity of the children is definitely knowable and that it is actually measured by the tests applied. By no such

---

42. *Ibid.*, p. 362 (italics ours). For an evaluation of this research and other recent ones of identical twins reared apart see R. S. Woodworth, *Heredity and Environment*, Social Science Research Council Bulletin No. 47 (New York, 1941), pp. 21-32.

43. Earlier studies by F. N. Freeman, K. J. Holzinger, and B. C. Mitchell and by B. S. Burks, referred to in the text, are reported in The Twenty-seventh Yearbook of the National Society for the Study of Education (Bloomington, Ill., 1928). These and more recent studies by A. M. Leahy, by H. M. Skeels and M. Skodak of the famous University of Iowa investigations, and by various others are analyzed by F. L. Goodenough in *Intelligence: Its Nature and Nurture*, I, pp. 331-362, and by Woodworth, *op. cit.*, pp. 33-70.

process can valid measurements of either innate ability or environment (which has never been successfully "measured") be found. In this approach the complexity of environment is not realized, nor is the intricate interaction between the growing life and the changing life conditions. Miss Burks informs us that the best home environment may contribute 20 points to the child's I.Q., and that the worst may depress it by the same amount. This is a comparison within the range of American home life, not between the "best" and "worst" environments. By what logic, then, can she conclude that "the total contribution of heredity . . . is probably not far from 75 or 80 per cent"?

In a contrasting study, conducted about the same time by F. N. Freeman and two others, evidence is offered to show that the character of the foster home definitely affects the degree of intellectual ability attained by the children subjected to its influence, that children admitted to the superior home at an earlier age made greater intellectual progress than those who entered it at a later age, and furthermore that in the superior environment of such a home some children improved in conduct and ability to a greater extent than the character and intelligence of their parents might have led one to predict. These results, which seriously challenge such interpretations as Miss Burks', are not as striking as those of the more recent researches conducted over a several year period at the State University of Iowa.[44] In this investigation over 150 children, mostly illegitimate, were placed in foster homes at the age of six months, and were periodically given intelligence tests, the results being compared with the obtainable information about the intelligence of their blood parents. These and other data which were secured would seem to indicate that "intelligence as commonly defined is much more responsive to environmental changes than had previously been conceived" and that the biologically derived restrictions upon a person's intellectual development are less rigid than frequently described.[45] This last point was given somewhat dramatic support by the discovery in the Iowa researches that 16 of the children, whose mothers were diagnosed as "feeble-minded" with an average I.Q. of 71, after about two years in foster homes scored an average I.Q. of 116 (which, however, two and one half years later fell to 108).

Considerable publicity has been accorded this "proof" of environmental potency—more than the smallness of the sample and other investigatory limitations would warrant. Nevertheless, these results stand in interesting contrast to some we have viewed. But here, too, caution is necessary when we pass from the facts to the interpretation. There is too much of the unpredictable about

---

44. These studies were conducted largely by H. M. Skeels, who summarizes them in *Intelligence: Its Nature and Nurture*, II, Chap. XX, and by M. Skodak, author of *Children in Foster Homes: A Study of Mental Development* (Iowa City, 1939). For a thorough but less environmentally focused study of the same problem see A. M. Leahy, "Nature-Nurture and Intelligence," *Genetic Psychological Monographs*, XVII (1935), 235–308.

45. Skeels, *op. cit.*, p. 305.

individual heredity to justify general conclusions concerning the influence of environment from such indications as these studies have relied upon. The environment is always complex and always changing; the heredity can never be fully known. On the other hand, studies like the Iowa researches at least help us to see more fully that we must always reckon with man's nurture no less than with his nature.

The Inseparability of Heredity and Environment

Right and wrong questions about heredity and environment. We waste our labor if we persist in asking the wrong kind of question. We are asking the wrong kind of question, as our argument to this point shows, if we start with the assumption that we can ever say, as between heredity in general and the environment as a whole, which of the two is the more important or the more potent. Every phenomenon of life is the product of both. Each is as *necessary* to the result as the other. Neither can ever be eliminated and neither can ever be isolated. Both are, in every particular situation, exceedingly complex. Both have been operative, to produce every particular situation, through unimaginable time. For these reasons it seems impossible even to conceive two situations involving precisely the same combination of hereditary and environmental factors. Every situation is in this respect unique, just as every human face is in some way different from every other. Where two or more factors are equally necessary for a given result, it is vain to inquire which in general is the more important. Is food more necessary than air for the sustenance of life? Are the relations between men more essential than men themselves for the creation of a society? Are restraints more or less important than rights in the maintenance of what we call liberty? As unanswerable—and as pointless—as these questions is the quest that so many have pursued, heredity "versus" environment.

Heredity—the germ cells—contains all the potentialities of life, but all its actualities are evoked within and under the conditions of environment. What, then, is the kind of question which we can intelligibly ask and which we may hope to answer? It is never a question regarding the *absolute* contribution of either factor as a whole. But there remain questions of vast significance both to the biologist and to the sociologist. The biologist, for example, is interested in tracing the inheritance of those unit characteristics, such as blue eyes, albinism, hemophilia, and so forth, which suggest separable specific determinants in the hereditary mechanism. He is interested in the manner in which specific organic predispositions, such as the tendency to certain diseases, reveal themselves under varying conditions of environment. The sociologist is interested, for example, in the way in which a group deals with its general environment. He is interested in the way in which a group, brought up in a given environment, is affected by changes occurring within it or by their transference to a different environment. An immigrant group, no matter what its hereditary antecedents, exhibits new like characteristics when transplanted from Italy or Greece or Ireland to North America. One cannot but be impressed by the way in which customs, attitudes, and modes of life change in response to changed economic conditions, to new occupational activities, and so forth. We have numerous examples of how the transition from poverty to wealth or vice versa registers itself in the attitudes and standards of individuals and groups. We have countless historical examples of how the aspect of group life has altered when some change has occurred in the conditions. The proud, vengeful marauding Scottish clans of the seventeenth century were transformed into the settled industrious population of the eighteenth. The mores of pioneer life are transformed as the frontier of civilization moves on. Primitive peoples have shown characteristic reactions when the techniques of Western civilization have been brought to or forced upon them. Agricultural populations all over the earth, in America or Russia or Japan, have revealed significant changes in the process of industrialization. In spite of innumerable variations, we can discover typical responses to typical changes within the environment. Here we have a clew to the understanding of the relation between environment and life.

The study of these changes will not tell us whether heredity or environment is the more "important," but at least it will tell us *why* each is important and in what ways its importance is revealed. When a new element is injected into a situation and a significant change results, we must not attribute the change solely to that new element. A seemingly minor change in a chemical formula may mean all the difference between a food and a poison, but it is the new combination of the constituents which is poisonous, not any one by itself. So likewise in the profound unity of hereditary and environmental factors: a seemingly minor change may induce a definitely new situation, but we must not on that account conclude that environment is more important. The social demand for inventive talents which the industrial age fosters has brought to eminence men who in an earlier age would have remained in obscurity; the modern opportunity to amass wealth through the capitalistic system has brought distinction and power to men brought up in humble surroundings, such as Carnegie and Ford and many of the industrial and financial magnates of America, who in feudal times would in all probabillity have remained clerks or toilers. A new social situation or a happy chance may give a genius the opportunity to reveal his power, but no amount of favorable conjuncture will turn a person of mediocre mentality into a genius. On the other hand, we must not assume, with some protagonists of heredity, that genius will make its way no matter what the environmental impediments may be. If some have triumphed over circumstance, does that entitle us to conclude that all potential greatness must be able to "break its birth's invidious bar"? In this field we must particularly guard our judgment against the subtle forms of bias which are prompted by our nationality, our race or class consciousness, and our degree of success or failure in the struggle for life.

Some broad conclusions. Heredity is potentiality made actual within an environment. All the qualities of life are in the heredity, all the evocation of qualities depends on the environment. It follows from this initial principle that the higher the potentiality, the greater is the demand made on environment. Instead of seeking to exalt the importance of one factor over the other, we should therefore recognize, as one aspect of the correlation on which throughout we have been insisting, that the finer or the greater the heredity the more does the fitness of the environment matter. Thus the more subtle differences in environment may have little effect on beings with low potentialities, while they are vastly significant for beings more responsive to them. A seemingly minor change in a situation, a stimulus to success, an encouragement, a rebuff, may prove decisive to a sensitive nature while scarcely affecting a less sensitive one. Hence the imponderables of the social environment become more important for civilized individuals and groups. These conditions, such as social esteem or disesteem, the presence or absence of incentives to higher efforts, and so forth, are not measurable, but if we neglect them we may have a totally false picture of the difference between one human environment and another.

The more plastic the life the more is it at the mercy of environment save in so far as it learns to control the environment for its purposes. Man, the most plastic of all animals, has therefore been seeking through unknown ages to make his environment more conformable to his growing needs. The quest of the more appropriate environment is for him, alone of all the animals, eternal. For a like reason the fitness of the environment matters most during the most plastic stage, the earlier years, of human life. The stimulations afforded by the milieu in which we live—and likewise its depressing influences—affect us most when we are most impressionable. For this reason if for no other, we should accept the coequal importance of these two ultimate determinants of everything that lives.

5

Geography and People

Geography and Social Life

Geography and its control. As students of society we are necessarily interested in geographical phenomena and in the manner in which they enter our lives as social beings. We make no effort, of course, to cover the large and important field of geography. But we shall attempt to indicate the role of the geographical environment in social life and to point out the necessary precautions against the many loose generalizations often made concerning geography and man.

[1] *The meaning of geography:* Within the total environment of man we can broadly distinguish the geographical conditions from those conditions that are themselves dependent on human activity. The geographical environment consists of those conditions that nature provides for man. It includes the earth's surface with all its physical features and natural resources—the distribution of land and water, mountains and plains, minerals, plants, and animals, the climate and all the cosmic forces, gravitational, electric, radiational, that play upon the earth and affect the life of man. We distinguish this *primary* environment both from the modifications of it introduced by man's *technology*, as when he makes clearings or cultivates the soil or builds roadways and cities or harnesses natural forces, and from the *inner* or *social* environment of folkways and mores and institutions that every human group provides for its members.

The geographical, technological, and social environments, in their influences and their relationships with one another, will concern us frequently in this book. We may view briefly the factors which together make up the geographical environment, for some are seemingly beyond the control of man while others in various degrees bear the imprint of his activity.

[2] *Controllable and uncontrollable factors:* Among the *uncontrollable* factors may be listed the relation of the earth to the sun and to the moon, the area of the earth, the extent and location of its mineral resources, the distribution of

the great land masses and ocean areas, of plains and mountains, the larger rivers and lakes, the seasons, the tides, the ocean currents, the rainfall[1] and the winds, and the electric energies. Most of these man can change only slightly; their larger changes depend on forces beyond his power. Man is not wholly at the mercy of these elemental facts, for, in increasing degree, he can utilize them, seize the advantages which they offer him, overcome some of the barriers which they present to his purposes. He cannot control the winds but he can set his sails to catch them. He cannot as yet remove the larger mountains but he can tunnel through them. He cannot direct the path of the thunderstorm but he can make electricity a conveyor of words and pictures and a source of power for his machines. He cannot alter the seasons but he can protect himself against the heat and the cold.[2]

There are other geographical factors which are in part amenable to the direct control of man and which he can modify, not merely utilize. These are principally the distribution of animal and plant life and the fertility of the soil. He takes those animals and plants which serve his needs, breeds and cultivates them, dispossessing or destroying others to that end. The result is that the "natural"[3] balance of organic life is overthrown by man. Selecting a few species, he breeds varieties of them such as wild nature neither knows nor tolerates. Large areas are characterized by a vegetative life introduced and assiduously maintained by man alone, belts of wheat and cotton and corn and tobacco and rice. These in turn become associated with the culture and the social institutions of the regions where they occur, as any observer knows who has traveled through the "cotton belt" of the South, the great wheat regions of the West, or the rice-growing areas of the Far East. Thus in addition to and often crossing the geographical areas demarcated by natural phenomena arise new areas determined by human exploitation of various forms of organic life.

[3] *"Nature versus man":* Having destroyed the "natural" balance, man has to fight continuously to maintain the "artificial" balance. He struggles against other exploiters which he has not succeeded in conquering, against weeds, insect and other pests, fungi, and microorganisms. The specialized cultivation of the earth by man tends to exhaust its fertility, but he has gradually learned the techniques of restoring and even of enhancing the properties of the soil. The yield from the seed sown in Europe is now about four times what it was five centuries ago; recent advances in crop control in the United States and in the

1. Recently science has made successful experiments to cause precipitation under certain favorable conditions.

2. Julian Huxley, in an address during the winter of 1945–1946, voiced the possibility of the atomic bomb being used as a kind of "industrial dynamite" to blast the arctic ice caps and thus to alter the course and temperature of certain ocean currents and climatic conditions in parts of the earth. However far-fetched this particular notion, the technological potentialities of atomic fission are so great as to qualify within the near future such a listing of "uncontrollable" factors as the above.

3. We should not consider man and his works as *un*natural; hence the quotation marks.

U.S.S.R. are even far greater. Modern biology, chemistry, and other sciences combine today to give man enormous control of soil fertility and crop productivity. And through modern irrigation methods, whole rivers and lakes are harnessed so as to provide water, power, fertilizer, and other necessities of modern agriculture to entire regions like the Tennessee Valley and the rich growing lands of California.

But we should not conclude that man has completely mastered his physical and biological habitat. The forest-buried cities of the Maya civilization witness impressively to the manner in which nature reasserts her ancient sway. The fall of the early Sumerian civilization, it has been claimed, was associated with the spread of malaria; the decline of the ancient cultures of the eastern shores of the Mediterranean, with the impoverishment and desiccation of the soil.[4] The great epidemics of history, still liable to recur, like those after World War I, remind us that man's mastery of biological environment is still insecure.[5] Nor need we elaborate the point that in our own country there are huge areas that, owing to deforestation and soil erosion, are threatened by the invading desert and can be saved only by large-scale methods of scientific conservation; and that several of our "inexhaustible" natural resources, such as oil and high-grade iron ore, are dangerously close to exhaustion.[6] It is not surprising that the relationship between man's physical environment and his social life, suggested by these few examples, has led to a geographical school of sociology.

The geographical school of sociology. From early times men have reflected on the influences of geographical conditions on human society. Perceiving the differences between the modes and exigencies of human life in the mountains, on the plains, and by the seaboard, in the desert and in the forest, in temperate regions and in the tropics, various thinkers attributed a dominant role to geography, regarding it as the primary determinant of the wealth and health, the size and energy, of populations, of their customs and social organizations, of their creeds and philosophies. From such observations arose during the last century a definite school of human or social geography.

[1] *Some representatives of the geographical school:* We may here pass over the geographically focused writings of observers ranging from the ancient Aristotle to Montesquieu in the eighteenth century. One of the pioneers of modern social geography was, like Montesquieu, a Frenchman, Frédéric Le

4. See, for example, V. G. Simkhovitch, "Hay and History," *Political Science Quarterly,* XXVIII (1913), 385–403.

5. Interesting accounts of this struggle are presented in H. Zinsser, *Rats, Lice and History* (Boston, 1935), and H. E. Sigerist, *Civilization and Disease* (Ithaca, N.Y., 1943).

6. Representative studies of waste and conservation of natural resources include S. Chase, *The Tragedy of Waste* (New York, 1925) and *Rich Land, Poor Land* (New York, 1936); K. Glover, *America Begins Again* (New York, 1939); H. R. Muelder and D. M. Delo, *Years of This Land* (New York, 1943); F. Osborn, *Our Plundered Planet* (Boston, 1948); and W. Vogt, *Road to Survival* (New York, 1948).

Play, who was followed in that country by Demolins and others; the study of the region as an area of "human geography" has been a favorite approach of French sociologists and has in recent years been extended to regions outside France.[7] The emphasis of Le Play and his successors upon the relationship between the characteristics of the physical habitat and social developments has influenced, as we noted in the preceding chapter, both the human ecologists and the regional studies of Howard W. Odum and his colleagues. In Germany an important branch of the geographical school was developed by F. Ratzel in his extensive work, *Human Geography.* In England H. T. Buckle wrote a history of civilization along similar lines. Among American representatives of this school may be classed Ellen C. Semple, a follower of Ratzel, E. G. Dexter, and Ellsworth Huntington, who in a series of volumes has sought to depict the impact on human society and culture of racial as well as climatic conditions.[8]

The writers of this school have added tremendously to our knowledge of the role of geography in man's development. They have made us aware of the interplay between climate and topography and the various aspects of the physical environment, on the one side, and political and economic, technological and cultural, phenomena on the other. But their interpretations have sometimes misled us.

[2] *Limitations of the approach:* Much of the work of the geographical school presents the difficulty that it deals exclusively with one aspect of the total environment as though it were a separate and sufficient cause instead of an influence deeply entangled with other influences. The discussion of heredity and environment in the preceding chapter showed the need for great caution in this respect, a caution often lacking in the writings of this school. Thus Le Play tells us that the particular form of the family is caused by the conditions of work, which are determined by the nature of the locality in which the family lives. But what of the fact that several forms of family have developed within the same or similar geographical conditions? Buckle informs us that the growth of wealth depends entirely on soil and climate. But what of the comparatively prosperous history of "bleak and rocky" New England, for example? Huntington in his *Civilization and Climate* seeks to show that favorable climatic conditions are a main determinant of the onward course of civilization. But what, we may ask, of modern Japan, blessed with Huntington's "favorable" conditions, which *borrowed* a large part of its civilization from the Western world?

---

7. See, for example, J. Gottmann, "French Geography in Wartime," *Geographical Review,* XXXVI (1946), 80-91.

8. For accounts of the geographical school see P. Sorokin, *Contemporary Sociological Theories* (New York, 1928), Chap. III; and F. Thomas, "The Role of Anthropogeography in Contemporary Social Theory," in *Contemporary Social Theory* (H. E. Barnes and H. Becker, eds., New York, 1940), Chap. VII. Huntington's most recent and most embracing work is *Mainsprings of Civilization* (New York, 1945).

We have already pointed out that civilization itself modifies the influence of geography. We may add that geography, by and in itself, *never* absolutely determines the course of human events. This is a view held by many contemporary geographers themselves. One of their distinguished representatives puts it simply:

> Contemporary geographical knowledge and thought have abandoned the mechanistic determinism of older schools. Earth facts do not *determine* the form and nature of human society in development. They *condition* it. New earth facts are continually being discovered and old earth facts given new significance as human knowledge, thought, and social action develop. The relations are reciprocal.[9]

[3] *An aside on "geopolitics":* Although not properly of the geographical school of sociology, the recently publicized and now largely discredited "geopolitics" (geographical politics) requires brief comment. For this combination of nationalistic aspiration, military strategy, and geographical study, coming to the fore in Germany between the two world wars, was influenced and partly guided in its early days by one of the writers we have mentioned, F. Ratzel. Ratzel's *Political Geography* (1897) put forward the thesis that the state is a living organism requiring an ever-expanding *Lebensraum* (living space) in order vigorously to survive. This conception appealed, of course, to German expansionists and became a part of the extreme nationalistic-militaristic tradition of that country. During and following World War I geopolitics achieved academic prestige under the leadership of Karl Haushofer, a geographer and former army officer, who established an institute and journal of geopolitics at Munich. Haushofer borrowed extensively from the writings of the British scholar, H. J. MacKinder, whose famous "heartland" theory claimed that the focus of world power lies in the center of that great land mass, the Eurasian continent, and therefore an area of great political concern to all nations. MacKinder used this theory in support of a British alliance with Russia; Haushofer, in support of a German alliance with Russia—a view long held by certain German military men. During World War II many of the findings of geopolitics became a significant part of Axis military strategy; a school of geopolitics developed even in Japan.

The study of geographical facts about friend and foe is, of course, always a concern of military strategists and international policy makers, as our own "geopolitics" during World War II testifies. However, when the characteristics of land masses and bodies of water, and the like are taken as the *basic causes* of national strength, historical destiny, and even as the justification of expansionist policy, we are confronted with perhaps the most extreme form

9. Isaiah Bowman, *Geography in Relation to the Social Sciences* (New York, 1934), p. 225. This view is implicitly and explicitly expressed in the writings of such geographers as R. Hartshorne, J. Russell Smith, V. Stefansson, H. W. Weigert, and D. Whittlesey.

of geographical determinism ever to have gained repute. However skillfully geographical data are gathered and assembled (although Haushofer's researchers were not altogether competent geographers) and however useful such data are to military planners, these data in themselves can justify no theory of geographical determinism. The strength of the two most powerful nations in the world today, the United States and the Soviet Union, rests in part, to be sure, on their locations and available physical resources. But no careful student—geographer, general, statesman, or social scientist—would reckon the power of either of these nations without calculating the state of the industrial arts, the educational levels, the aspirations of the peoples, their unities and disunities, their loyalties and leadership. Whatever the earth facts, they must be viewed with reference to the social heritage of man.[10]

Civilization and geographical conditions. One of the most important aspects of civilization is the control over the external environment which it affords. An important principle is revealed by the relation of man to geographical conditions: as man's control increases he becomes less *directly* and less completely dependent upon and influenced by the immediate environment in which he is situated. We must examine the character and the justification of this principle.

[1] *The stimulus of geography:* The geographical environment alone never explains the rise of a civilization. We can discover no cause inherent in the geographical conditions to account for the birth of a great civilization in the island-center of Crete instead of, say, in the island-center of Sicily, or to explain why the great Maya civilization should have developed in the forest lands of Central America instead of in highlands or in coastal areas. There have been short-lived and long-lived civilizations arising under the same or under similar geographical conditions.

> It is clear that a virtually identical combination of the two elements [nonhuman and human] in the environment may give birth to a civilization in one instance and fail to give birth to a civilization in another instance without our being able to account for this absolute difference in the outcome by detecting any substantial difference in the circumstances, however strictly we may define the terms of our comparison. Conversely, it is clear that civilizations can and do emerge in environments which are utterly diverse. The nonhuman environment may be of "the fluvial type" which has given birth to the Egyptiac and Sumeric

10. Among the several volumes on geopolitics are H. W. Weigert, *Generals and Geographers* (New York, 1942); R. Strauz-Hupe, *Geopolitics* (New York, 1942); A. Gyorgy, *Geopolitics, The New German Science* (Berkeley, Cal., 1944). For briefer statements by various authorities see *Compass of the World* (H. W. Weigert and V. Stefansson, eds., New York, 1944), especially those of E. A. Walsh, I. Bowman, R. E. Harrison and H. W. Weigert, J. Russell Smith, and H. J. MacKinder. Examples of the more moderate American "geopolitics" include D. Whittlesey, *The Earth and the State* (New York, 1939); N. J. Spykman, *America's Strategy in World Politics* (New York, 1942) and *The Geography of the Peace* (New York, 1944).

> civilizations and perhaps to an independent "Indus Culture" as well; or it may be of "the plateau type" which has given birth to the Andean and the Hittite and the Mexic civilizations; or it may be of "the archipelago type" which has given birth to the Minoan and the Hellenic civilizations, and to the Far Eastern Civilization in Japan; or it may be of "the continental type" which has given birth to the Sinic and the Indic and the Western civilizations, and to the Orthodox Christian Civilization in Russia; or it may be of "the jungle type" which has given birth to the Mayan Civilization.[11]

The author of the above statement, Arnold J. Toynbee, has convincingly demonstrated that, however influential the geographical habitat may be in conditioning the character of civilizations, there is no evidence to assign to geography a causal potency in human affairs. More than this, Toynbee seeks to "reject the popular assumption that civilizations emerge when environments offer unusually easy conditions of life and to advance an argument in favor of exactly the opposite view."[12] Thus he compiles case after case, from the Mayan civilization to the Indic in Ceylon, from the Polynesian development in the Pacific to the civilization focused in New England, to illustrate the "virtues of adversity" that nature has offered man as a "challenge" and the way in which he has responded by creating imposing civilizations. However skeptically we view this reversal of the more conventional approach to geographic influence, few readers can leave Toynbee's voluminous work convinced geographical determinists. But we cannot reject the stimulus of geography to human effort. When we account for the achievements of the ancient "river valley cultures" of the Nile and Tigris Euphrates we must refer to the physical characteristics of those rivers and valleys. When we analyze the accomplishments of our own TVA we cannot omit the conditions of terrain and soil and water in the Tennessee Valley.

[2] *Geography and civilization:* It would be a mistake, however, to assume that the role of geography was the *same* in Egypt, Mesopotamia, and the Tennessee Valley. For civilization itself undergoes great changes. Man-made agencies of communication have made possible new foci of civilization. Agricultural fertility has become less determinant of the size or the wealth of a population—perhaps TVA's greatest single technical accomplishment is the restoration of plant-growing soil conditions in the region. Industrial skill, commercial and financial enterprise, and those economic opportunities dependent in part on man's control of nature have caused great shiftings of the centers of population. In England the concentration of people changed after the Industrial Revolution from the agricultural south to the less fertile north,

11. From *A Study of History,* by Arnold J. Toynbee (London, 1934), I, 269. Published by Oxford University Press under the auspices of the Royal Institute of International Affairs. See pp. 249 ff. in this volume or Part II of D. C. Somervell's abridgment of Toynbee's work (New York, 1947) for the latter's discussion of geography and civilization.

12. Somervell abridgment, *op. cit.*, p. 80.

while more recent economic changes have tended to displace it again. Earlier economic conditions established the American textile industry in New England, while later economic factors shifted part of the industry to the Carolinas—but the geographical factors have remained the same. The incessant movement of economic, political, and cultural dominance reveals this *relative* independence of society from the direct influence of the immediate geographical factors. One writer has argued that the march of civilization has been "coldward" since the age of the Sumerian and Egyptian empires.[13] The generalization is doubtful and the implied connection between higher civilization and lower temperature is precarious. What the record of these changes does effectively demonstrate is the way in which forces generated *within society* determine increasingly the habitat of the leading civilizations.

It is not difficult to demonstrate why this should be so. In primitive life man is circumscribed by the limitations of locality. He is dependent on the food products, the building materials, the fabrics for his clothing, provided by the immediate neighborhood. If there is a local drought he may have no recourse against famine. His economic activity is dependent on the products the locality offers freely or yields to his limited techniques. His arts and crafts, his customs and beliefs, are responsive to the local environment. Thus for many years anthropologists were fond of describing whole primitive cultures in terms of some characteristic product of the region, such as the *buffalo culture*, the *maize culture*, the *Eastern Woodlands culture*—names given to the "culture areas" in the pre-Columbian America of the Indians.

The growth of civilization changes and minimizes the direct influence of local geographical conditions. Modern man draws products in great variety from many regions. Many of his occupations have no relation whatever to the geographical environment. His means of communication bring him into contact with the customs and the ways of living of other lands. Indeed the rapid diffusion of cultural influences today is enormously more hampered by the man-made barriers of politics and prejudice than by the natural barriers of terrain and ocean. As these barriers are surmounted and as cultural diffusion is accelerated by modern technology, there develops less local homogeneity on the one hand and less cultural contrast between localities on the other.

Consider the cultural *variation* observable in a community like "Middletown," for example, set in the prairie land of the Midwest, where the most modern technology stands side by side with "hillbilly" folk practices many generations old; then consider the many things in *common*—in economy, religion, political practices, education, and so forth—between Middletown and

13. S. C. Gilfillan, "The Coldward Course of Progress," *Political Science Quarterly*, XXXV (1920), 393 ff. Even Huntington, who has written at great length to establish "a strong relation between climatic efficiency and civilization," now refers to the "basic fact that civilization depends on the combined effect of heredity, physical environment, and cultural history."—*Mainsprings of Civilization*, p. 399.

the New England coastal community of "Yankee City." Or note the complaint of some Europeans that their continent is becoming too "Americanized," too stamped by the marks of our culture. Conversely, note the cultural heterogeneity of the world's great cities—it would be difficult not to be able to find almost any civilizational product one might seek in New York or Paris or San Francisco or Shanghai. Examples could be endlessly multiplied that reveal the increasingly significant role of civilization and the decreasingly direct role of geography in determining man's way of life.

As man learns better to utilize for his own ends the laws of nature, his dependence on the nearer geographical conditions is modified in two primary ways. On the one hand, he gains *geographical mobility* and thus a greater power to select and to change his physical location. He can now move swiftly, without personal exertion, and with decreasing economic cost, from one place to another. The effective limits to migration are set more and more by society, not by geography. On the other hand, he becomes subject to the impact of influences developed in more remote environments. His way of life, his thought, and his social organization are affected by what men do and think thousands of miles away, just as his diet contains items produced in distant lands. In a word, as the social heritage grows, the immediate geographical factors assume a *less determinant* role in the interpretation of society.

This is not to claim, however, that the physical habitat of man assumes less general significance as his technical arts develop.

> As the cultural heritage increases, a larger part of the environment becomes useful and meaningful: *the natural conditions of a region, so far from being nullified by the increase of culture and technical skill, are actually magnified.* The hunter knows the forest only as a home for game; but for modern man the forest is also a source of lumber, a protection against soil erosion, a recreation area, and a field for scientific observation.[14]

Lewis Mumford, the author of this statement and an ardent exponent of regional planning, perhaps overstates his case. But he calls our attention to the give-and-take between geography and civilization.

Specific relations of geography and society. We are not dismissing "earth facts," for they still exercise both an evident and a more subtle influence on the life of society. We may examine some of the relations between the two.

[1] *Direct influences of geography:* Most obviously, geography provides certain conditions which remain of great economic significance. One authority has listed six main types of human activity which take their specific character more directly from geographical facts: (1) habitat and housing, (2) the character

14. From *The Culture of Cities* by Lewis Mumford, copyright, 1938, by Harcourt, Brace and Company, Inc. (Italics are Mumford's.)

and direction of roads, (3) cultivation of plants, (4) breeding of animals, (5) exploitation of minerals, and (6) the devastation of plants and animals.[15]

The significance of geographical facts for these or other human activities, we must remember, varies with technological development and other civilizational changes. For example, the presence of vast coal beds in Europe and later in America was an "earth fact" of no social significance *until* the industrial age began. Similarly, oil fields, sources of hydroelectric energy, and, latterly, deposits of uranium as contained in Arkansas have assumed a *social* importance they did not possess in earlier times. In fact, what we name a "natural resource" is not simply a type of soil or mineral or river; it is the result of the civilizational development—of *how* the earth fact is defined and utilized by the extant society. Take another illustration. Countries have become prosperous and populous with the aid of geographical factors and later, as the technical arts have advanced or spread to other lands, have lost their advantage. Thus changing conditions brought dominance to Venice or to Cadiz or to the Hanse cities or to the early whaling centers of New England, and new changes took their leadership away. Again consider the way in which the presence of waterways, of natural harbors, of topographical "breaks in transportation" as between mountain pass and plateau, or desert edge and fertile plain have influenced the location of such cities as New Orleans, San Francisco, Buffalo, Denver, Cairo, Constantinople, and Antwerp; and how, with new developments in transportation and commerce and industry these cities have blossomed or declined. Or note how the new discoveries in metallurgy, for example, give a sudden significance to areas formerly agrarian, such as the bauxite ore regions essential to aluminum production. These cases show the direct influence upon social life of some geographical factors, but they also should make us aware of the constant *interaction* between the facts of geography and the facts of the social heritage.

[2] *Indirect influences of geography:* When we turn to the more subtle influences of geography, particular caution is necessary. For it is easy to find correlations between climatic or other physiographic conditions and social phenomena. Some writers have pointed out correlations between climate and crime, suicide, insanity, physical and intellectual vigor, and so forth.[16] But correlation is not explanation; it is merely a challenge to further study.

Take the correlation between human energy and a vigorous, variable climate as found in old or New England. This correlation checks with the folk observation that northerners are busy and energetic while southerners are lazy and unproductive. Climate? But an individual's energy and health are the result of

15. Jean Brunhes, *Human Geography* (New York, 1920), Chaps. I and II.

16. Among the earlier works are E. G. Dexter, *Weather Influences* (New York, 1904) and E. Huntington, *Civilization and Climate* (New Haven, 1924). More recent attempts to attribute health and vigor to climate include S. F. Markham, *Climate and the Energy of Nations* (New York, 1944) and C. A. Mills, *Climate Makes the Man* (New York, 1942).

many factors—of diet, hygienic conditions, living standards, and, not least, the "climate" of attitudes and values and incentives in which he lives. "Lazy" southlands are found in the popular thinking even in Ireland and Germany—far to the north of the "vigorous" northlands of France and Italy.[17] And in our own nation, how are we to account for the bustling energy of, say, Atlanta or Dallas as compared with the slower pace of activity of, say, Virginia or Maryland without considering such social factors as industrial and commercial development? Or consider the correlation between summer months and crimes against the person such as homicide and rape. There are some fairly obvious reasons which can be offered in explanation of this fact, such as the opportunity for a greater range of personal contacts which the summer provides in the Temperate Zone. But these explanations must be tested. In South Carolina the highest number of homicides occurs in December, with July in second place. The correlation in this state between the mean monthly temperature and the number of homicides is very low. On the other hand, Christmas Day has the largest number of homicides, a fact which at once suggests a social and not a climatic explanation.[18] Nor does hot weather breed crimes in the way that sun melts the snow.

Here is the crux of the matter: even a perfect correlation does not establish causation. For we must be able to *trace the connection* between the physical and social fact before we can attribute any causal significance to the former. In seeking the indirect influences of geography upon social life we must discover the intermediate links in the chain. We have to discover the relation of the climatic or other geographic fact to the condition of the human organism; we have to relate in turn this condition to the motivations which express themselves in the social phenomena. Since motivations are obviously subject to other than geographical conditions, we are likely, as we have seen, to discover situations in which the initial correlation does not hold.

[3] *An illustration from the study of suicide:* About a half century ago Emile Durkheim investigated the nexus between a climatic factor and a social phenomenon, suicide. His study sought to meet the requirements of a rigorous methodology, often unhappily neglected in the interpretation of environmental influences, and is still well worth the student's careful attention. Many previous researches had shown that in European countries the proportion of suicides in the warmer half (March to August) was always greater than in the colder half of the year. But Durkheim's analysis reveals that the actual temperature level had little to do with the correlation. The monthly variations in temperature did not accord with the variations in the suicide rate. Moreover, there were some very hot countries in which the self-destruction rate was low. Therefore Durkheim examined the correlations between suicide and certain

---

17. Cf. R. T. LaPiere, *Sociology* (New York, 1946), p. 96.
18. See H. C. Brearley, "Homicide in South Carolina," *Social Forces*, VIII (1929), 218-221.

social factors. He noted that the number of suicides increased with the rise in level of civilization, that there were, in proportion, more suicides in the city than in the country, more among the single or widowed than among the married, more among Protestants and nonreligious persons than among Catholics. These facts suggest an explanation of a *social* character—that suicide occurs characteristically where conditions encourage social isolation, where people lack the sense of solidarity created by strong social responsibilities, where they are most apt to be thrown back on their own resources for comfort, companionship, and consolation.

Of course, Durkheim did not attempt to explain all suicide in this way. But he put forward an hypothesis that has a more definite meaning than the hypothesis that high temperature impels to suicide. Returning to the climatic correlation, he noted that, after all, the chief conditioning factor may not be the temperature of the summer months but the longer days—when social life is more active and more intense. Longer days provide greater opportunities for those wider contacts in the very presence of which the sense of social isolation is most apt to develop. With ingenuity Durkheim demonstrated that this theory is in accord with the variations of suicide from season to season, from month to month, and from one day of the week to another.[19]

[4] *The limited role of the physical environment:* Durkheim's study illustrates our thesis that geography provides *an external set of conditions* under which the life of man in society proceeds. These conditions can never be ignored by the sociologist, but his task is to show their relation to the *direct* determinants of social phenomena, the attitudes and interests of men. Man adapts himself to all kinds of geographical conditions, but he is not resourceless in meeting them. He changes when he is subjected to a new environment, but he also puts his imprint upon it. The white man living in the tropics becomes a different white man, but he brings with him his own civilization. The American and the European in the Far East develop differences from those at home. Climatic conditions affect their energies, but they do not usually become followers of Confucius or Buddha. Other factors are obviously present, an alien civilization, races to which they feel alien and over which they may exercise authority. It is not only that the land is different but the whole situation. Many environmental factors conspire wherever human societies exist.

Land and Population

Population and the means of subsistence. We have seen that the territory a group of human beings occupies has an influence on their health and their

19. E. Durkheim, *Le Suicide* (Paris, 1897), especially Book I, Chap. III. M. Halbwachs, in *Les Causes du Suicide* (Paris, 1930), develops and refines the methods of Durkheim, while differing from him on a number of minor points. On the *sociological* validity of this approach, see P. Sorokin, *Society, Culture, and Personality* (New York, 1947), pp. 8–13.

wealth, their work, their opportunities, and their modes of living. Even more significantly, perhaps, geography is an important condition of their very numbers. We have reserved for separate consideration this fundamental question concerning the relation of geography and the size of society.[20]

[1] *The uneven distribution of the world's population:* There are areas of the earth where population is scattered and sparse and others where it is continuous and dense. About three fourths of the world's two billion souls live in Southeastern Asia, Western and Central Europe, and Eastern and Central North America—these are the regions of population density. Asia contains more than half of the world's population, with perhaps 450 million in China and over 380 million in India. More than 900 people per square mile live in Java, only slightly more than 3 per square mile in Canada, to cite extremes. This unevenness of population distribution, clearly, is related to geographical factors. For man is dependent on the productivity of the earth, including not only the fertility of the soil but also the availability of mineral resources, both for his sustenance and for that equipment which turns mere living into a standard of living. Large parts of the land areas of the world are too dry or too cold to support large populations; some 80 per cent of the earth's land has been judged unsuited for crops or grazing, and of the remaining 20 per cent perhaps one third is used for food production. If we think of population in terms of land and basic types of economic production, the earth falls into four broad divisions: (1) the densely populated, industrialized nations of Europe, (2) the overcrowded agricultural Orient, (3) the thinly settled countries such as Canada and Australia, and (4) the United States and the U.S.S.R. "where population, area, and production are in more favorable balance than in any other countries in the world."[21] The size of a particular population or that of the earth as a whole and the level of material advance of these various areas are obviously related to the provisions made by nature as well as to man's own efforts.

[2] *Subsistence populations:* It has long been observed that some human populations tend to grow in size until there is only a sufficient food supply barely to support their numbers, and at this point nature has her way by limiting further population increase. These "checks of nature" include starvation and disease and their secondary effects that raise the mortality rate, especially among the young—a large instance of *physical adaptation* to the environment. Peoples controlled in size primarily by such natural checks have been termed "subsistence populations." They face the unhappy circumstance

20. This section is not presented as a digest—an impossible task here—of the increasingly significant discipline of demography, represented by such textbooks as W. S. Thompson, *Population Problems* (3d ed., New York, 1942) and P. H. Landis, *Population Problems* (New York, 1943). In this chapter we are concerned with *some* aspects of population study, those that are a part of the problem of the relation of geography and society.

21. "Two Billion People," *Fortune* (Feb., 1944).

that increases in food production are soon canceled out by more mouths to feed; material poverty is generally the rule. The vast majority of human beings down through the centuries have been members of subsistence populations, providing at best a high standard of living for small leisure classes. Even the great gains in agricultural production made by various civilizations prior to the nineteenth century improved the situation very little, for they were accompanied by large increases in the population itself.[22]

This is not to say that societies until recently have been simply at the mercy of nature's population checks. In premodern civilizations and among primitive groups we have record of practices limiting the number of people, including socially sanctioned infanticide; destruction of the incompetent and aged, as among the Australian natives; abortion, practiced by almost all peoples; mores restricting sexual relationship; forced emigration; and war. Indeed, the record is an impressive account of man's *attempts* to control his numbers. Whatever the efficacy of these controls in earlier times, nature's brutal checks were a major factor in the limitation of numbers, and a subsistence level of living was the rule for the great majority of people—as it remains today for the many millions who live outside the sphere of civilization's more recent advances.[23]

[3] *The doctrine of Malthus:* The control of population size exercised by geographical conditions greatly impressed Thomas R. Malthus at the start of the nineteenth century. There were prophets of that day who, in the light of the new scientific discoveries and technological advances, predicted a new and happier time in which comfort would be universal and the drudgery of toil abolished—men like Godwin and Condorcet.[24] But Malthus declared that such conjectures "far outstrip the modesty of nature." Science might advance, but the capacity of the land to supply the primary needs of men was limited. The "natural" rate of reproduction, he emphasized, inevitably surpasses the potentiality of the earth to feed the growing population, unless in some way checked by deliberate control.

Malthus said in effect that geography was the limiting factor to the growth of population and, as well, to the advance of society. In his *Essay on Population* he drew a sharp contrast between the fertility of mankind and the potentiality of the food supply.[25] He described the life process of the subsistence population: population multiplying up to, and beyond, the limits of subsistence; nature interposing her checks of starvation and disease; the continuing pressure of constant growth preventing a rise in living standards. Scientific and technological advance, he argued, cannot raise the standard of mankind unless some powerful incentive is introduced to control the "instinct to multiply." To this end

22. Cf. LaPiere, *op. cit.*, pp. 136–138.

23. For population control in premodern times see Thompson, *op. cit.*, Chap. I.

24. W. Godwin, *Political Justice* (1793) and *The Enquirer* (1797); M. J. Condorcet, *Tableau Historique de l'Esprit Humain* (1794).

25. See particularly the first two chapters of the *Essay* (edition of 1803).

Malthus set the preventive check of "moral restraint" against the "positive" checks of nature—but without any confidence that the former would be strong enough seriously to control the urge to reproduction.

Many subsequent investigators have accepted, though in different terms, the rather pessimistic outlook of Malthus. His followers expressed it in the "law of diminishing returns." Later writers have claimed that the extraordinary increase in the population of Europe and America during the last century or two must be regarded as an unprecedented occurrence due to an unusual conjuncture of favorable conditions, and have pointed out that there remain now no virgin agricultural lands to be exploited by modern science. Some have maintained that mankind is at the crossroads, having to choose between lower fertility and lower civilization.[26] Some have calculated the capacity of the earth to produce wheat and corn and cotton and other basic commodities, and have found that the still rising tide of population menaces the future.[27] Several writers stress the international perils which the pressure of population on resources, in the more congested or less favored regions of the earth, has and continues to create.[28]

Other writers have been more optimistic. Certain earlier American economists viewed a concomitance between the growth in population and the growth in comfort. Many writers emphasize the tremendous possibilities of scientific agriculture, one even calculating that its application to Brazil, for example, could supply food for all of Europe. That the larger population of the Western world is far better fed than the smaller population of preindustrial days is often stressed—in the previous chapter we noted the effects on stature and weight. It is commonly observed that the striking scientific advances in food production may only be beginning. The alarms of Malthus seem less formidable today for these and, as we shall see, for other reasons.

The growth of modern populations. It is still true that the increase of the means of subsistence cannot possibly keep pace with the physiological reproductive *capacity* of any population.[29] It is true that a very large part of the fertile areas of the earth is already subject to cultivation. It is true that many lands, like China and India, are so densely peopled that the great mass, under existing methods of cultivation, live on the margin of subsistence. But in the regions of modern civilization new phenomena have developed which are of vast importance and which set the problem of population in a new light altogether.

---

26. E. M. East, *Mankind at the Crossroads* (New York, 1923).

27. W. S. Thompson, *Population: a Study in Malthusianism* (New York, 1915).

28. For example, W. S. Thompson, *Danger Spots in World Civilization* (New York, 1929); H. P. Fairchild, "Postwar Population Problems," *Social Forces*, XXIII (Oct., 1944), 1–6.

29. The physiological reproductive *capacity* of the human female—her fecundity—is something less than 25 children per mother. Actual fertility rates reflect, of course, *socially* determined reproductive capacity. Cf. S. J. Holmes, *Human Genetics and Its Social Import* (New York, 1936), pp. 197–198.

[1] *The growth itself:* Although only the roughest estimates are possible, we know that the gain in Western Europe was from about five million in Roman times to about fifty million in the sixteenth century, and that this increase was in large part the result of improved food production techniques. But during this period and for the following two centuries, though the population made large gains and outright starvation and disease lessened somewhat, until the mid-nineteenth century the great epidemics periodically took their toll and infant mortality declined only slightly.

World population increase from 1650 (the year from which demographers have been able to make their most accurate estimates) has been staggering. Since 1800, as Table II reveals, the earth's less than one billion people have

TABLE II[30] **Estimated World Population and Annual Per Cents of Growth**

Date	Estimated world population (Millions)	Annual per cent growth during preceding period
1650	545	0.29
1750	728	0.44
1800	906	0.51
1850	1,171	0.63
1900	1,608	0.75
1940	2,171	—

much more than doubled. What accounts for this imposing acceleration? What, especially, accounts for the very large reduction of mortality that has almost doubled the average expectation of life at birth since the late seventeenth century? Among the many factors contributing to this reduction, essential for the population growth that has taken place, these must be mentioned: (1) improving agricultural technology and regional specialization of crops that permitted a more plentiful and varied and available food supply; (2) commercial and transportational gains that stimulated the opening of virgin lands and a more adequate distribution of foodstuffs—for example, England became dependent on the importation of grain soon after 1750; (3) after 1850, the development of public sanitation and scientific medicine, which in more recent

30. These figures are presented by K. Davis, "The World Demographic Transition," *The Annals of the American Academy of Political and Social Science*, CCXXXII (1945), 1–3, and are taken from A. M. Carr-Saunders, *World Population* (Oxford, 1936) and, for 1940. *League of Nations Statistical Yearbook for 1941–1942.*

decades has added greatly to the longevity of man; (4) the "intangible" factors —"the growth of democratic institutions, scientific ideals, humanitarian sentiments"—that are perhaps as significant as any others in lowering human mortality.[31] Here we see illustrated, once more, the relationship between geography and population, but a relationship that in recent times has become increasingly *indirect.*

[2] *The falling birth rate:* The enormous decline of the death rate is vividly apparent when we consider that during the recent period, perhaps from as early as 1800 in some European countries, the birth rate has been similarly declining. Table III illustrates this decline of actual fertility by showing the number of

TABLE III[32] **Average Crude Birth Rates, Selected Countries and Years**

Country	1808–1812	1878–1882	1935–1939
United States	—	—	17.1
England and Wales	—	34.4	15.0
France	31.4	24.9	14.9
Germany	—	38.0	19.3 (17.0 in 1930)
Russia	—	48.4 (1876–1880)	44.2 (1933–1935)
Sweden	31.8	29.6	14.5
Australia	—	35.2	17.3

births per thousand population (the "crude birth rate") at selected times during the last century and a half. (Demographically speaking, the population increase in the Western world is attributable to a larger and prior fall in the death rate than in the birth rate.) The birth rate has been falling for all classes and in all civilized countries, but most of all for the more prosperous classes and in the most prosperous countries. Among these groups and in these nations the "instinct to multiply" has been checked, not in the way in which Malthus preached, through "moral restraint," but through the methods of birth control.

As industrialization has grown up and direct dependency upon agriculture has diminished, as urbanization and general education have developed, and as these forces have combined to raise the material standard of human life, more and more families have seized upon the techniques of contraception in order to control the number of mouths to feed. Just as a single family may re-

31. Cf. Davis, *op. cit.*, pp. 3–5.

32. Table constructed from figures presented in Thompson, *Population Problems*, p. 152. See Chap. X of this volume for a detailed discussion of the falling birth rate.

tain a higher standard of living by limiting its numbers, so have large sections of the world's population demonstrated the solution of the old Malthusian problem by limiting their numbers.[33] This is evidenced by the figures in Table IV, where the reader should note especially the contrast between the birth rate, illiteracy, and dependence on agriculture for North America and Europe on the one hand and for Asia and Africa on the other.

TABLE IV[34] **Literacy, Fertility, and Dependence on Agriculture, for the World and the Various Continents, 1930**

Region	Per cent illiterate (Age 10 and over)	Per cent dependent on agriculture	Crude birth rates
World	59	60	39
North America	4	25	20
Oceania	14	30	23
Europe (except U.S.S.R.)	15	36	23
U.S.S.R.	40	67	45
South America	54	65	41
Central America and Caribbean	59	72	44
Asia (except U.S.S.R.)	81	69	44
Africa	88	77	48

[3] *The doctrine of Malthus today:* The higher the standard of living, we have seen, the more effectively it puts in operation forces leading to its preservation and checking the "natural" or biological rate of multiplication. The higher standard of living, in other words, introduces checks on population long before the level is reached at which Malthus's "positive" checks, starvation and disease and the rest, begin to operate. The Malthusian danger has been diminishing, therefore, for the peoples of industrialized and urbanized countries.

However, even today well over a half of mankind, wherever the populations live at or near a subsistence level—as among the billion of Asiatics—unhappily illustrates Malthus's lesson. For Malthus rightly showed what later researches

33. Contraception is not the only birth-preventing technique of significance. The ancient device of abortion, a method of postconception birth-prevention, is practiced in all countries of the world. In the 1930's, according to some estimates, abortion rates were possibly as high as birth rates in certain Western European countries. Abortion rates are perhaps one third as high as birth rates in sections of the United States. See National Committee on Maternal Health, *The Abortion Problem* (Baltimore, 1944).

34. Davis, *op. cit.*, p. 10.

have sufficiently confirmed: that the pressure of population on the means of subsistence has been at all times, save for a few favored classes and a few dominant peoples, ruthless and insistent, revealed in widespread misery and internecine strife, and mitigated only, for the most part, by such alternative evils as abortion and infanticide. True, the Malthusian danger has greatly decreased for the Western peoples. But indirectly it remains for them as well so long as there exist hundreds of millions of men whose multiplication is checked only by the drastic methods that rule the lower organic world. If the standard of living is to be raised in the countries of Asia and Africa and the other "backward" regions, the people of those countries must begin to control their numbers with techniques not as yet at their disposal, for a high level of living and rational control of birth go hand in hand. Only when the two are joined among all peoples will the ghost of Malthus cease plaguing us.[35]

Geography as a limiting condition. In this brief consideration of the numbers of population we see once again that the geographical factors represent limiting conditions rather than immediate determinants of the social situation. On the one hand, the numbers the land can sustain depend on the techniques man has developed. Thus the density of population varies with the manner of making a livelihood. Hunter tribes, for example, require from a few square miles up to two hundred per person, according to the local conditions. The density of pastoral nomads is from two to five persons per square mile; when primitive agriculture is combined with pastoral life, the ratio rises from ten to fifteen persons per square mile. The agricultural peoples, under favorable conditions, can support one to two hundred persons and, with the aid of some industry, as high as five hundred to the square mile. Of course, industrial populations exhibit sometimes a much greater density.[36]

On the other hand, the mere potentiality of subsistence ceases to determine the numbers of a population as people begin effectively to control reproduction itself. Abortion, infanticide, and destruction of the aged—all techniques of *destroying* human life already extant—have been agencies of population control used by man for ages, but their effectiveness has been limited and, in the light of modern values, their desirability is highly questionable. But modern methods of contraception give to man a device which is effectively limiting his numbers. Moreover, modern birth control, in the eyes of increasing millions, meets the demand of our moral principles by permitting the rational planning of the appearance of human life rather than destroying it after it has been conceived. On the other hand, birth control has brought new problems into being, problems to which we must return in later chapters.[37]

35. This point is stressed and perhaps overstated in Vogt's *Road to Survival*.

36. See, for example, E. C. Semple, *Influence of Geographic Environment* (New York, 1927), Chap. III.

37. See Chapters XI and XXIV.

6

The Total Environment and Accommodation

Environment and the Social Heritage

Concept of a total environment. When the geologist or astronomer or physicist views the world outside man as a separate and purely objective reality he does so as a scientist, not as a social being. To the physical scientist this world outside is not what we experience as environment, but is only nature. As students of sociology we are vitally interested in the total environment which social man *experiences*—all the surroundings to which he reacts and renders meaning.

[1] *The physical environment and man:* We may clarify the distinction made above by considering man's physical habitat. The physical world in which man dwells is never, and never has been, a *merely* physical or "natural" one. To the primitive hunter the woods are places where he can seek food and where spirits, no less than animals, wander, places conceived in terms of his hopes and fears, his experiences and his imaginations. The objects that surround him are never mere physical realities; they are the properties of his life colored and interpreted by his mentality. So for the child. The "infant appears in a world where nothing is 'physical' and just that, where nothing appears in the stark skeletal inflexibility that is signalized by science. . . . 'Things' are things that are owned, found, made, aided, feared, loved and sought after, hedged about with prohibitions or colored with possibilities of enjoyment, full of promise if action be aggressive or demanding prudent retreat."[1]

Nor is it otherwise for the civilized adult save that the meaning of things is for him at once socially enriched and scientifically refined. We never stand face

1. A. G. A. Balz, *The Basis of Social Theory* (New York, 1924), Chap. II.

to face with sheer objective nature. Our social heritage always intervenes. In the process we call civilization we increasingly modify the physical environment so that it will respond more nearly to our demands *and* at the same time we modify our conceptions of its character in correspondence with the experience thus gained. But in this more developed correspondence of our thoughts and the outer realities we do not, any more than does the savage or the child, react to the physical environment as a separate object.

[2] *The environment as a complex totality in man's experience:* In the experience of the social being, then, the environment appears as a complex totality of many aspects. He does not separate the geographical environment as one order of things from the social environment as quite another. The fields which we designate as physical environment are for him property, the houses are homes—the social and the physical aspects are blended in every concrete reality. Similarly the institutions and organizations which we classify as the inner environment have external embodiments. The church is revealed in an edifice; the holiday manifests itself in the changed aspect of the world about us; marriage has its physical marks in rings and licenses and shared abodes.

We distinguish the various factors of the total environment for purposes of study, but they are merged together in our experience. When man turns a territory into a country or a plot of earth into a home, he is fusing into one the physical and the social environment. His own activity, as he clears and cultivates the soil, dams rivers, builds roadways, and so on, in time makes it impossible to tell where the geographical or nature-given environment ends and the man-made environment begins. The physical becomes at the same time the symbol of the social. It is charged with human memories, human traditions, human values. Much of it becomes the external aspect of social institutions.

[3] *A classification of the aspects of the total environment:* The total environment, from the point of view of the individual, contains one category in addition to those that constitute the environment of a social group. This category is the group itself, which is a highly important environment for the individual. Thus, keeping in mind both individual and group, we may generalize as follows:

A. Geographical conditions are environmental both for a community or other social groups and for its individual members.

B. The social heritage is environmental both for a community or other social group and for its individual members, since the group itself shares this heritage.

C. The community or other social group is environmental for its individual members.

D. The community or larger group is environmental for the small group which in any degree shares the life of the larger.

Sociologists from Herbert Spencer to the present have divided the environment into what they have considered its major features.[2] In the classification

2. See, for example, Spencer's *Principles of Sociology* (New York, 1880–1896), Vol. 1, Chap. I;

offered in Chart III we are viewing the total environment of the individual within society.

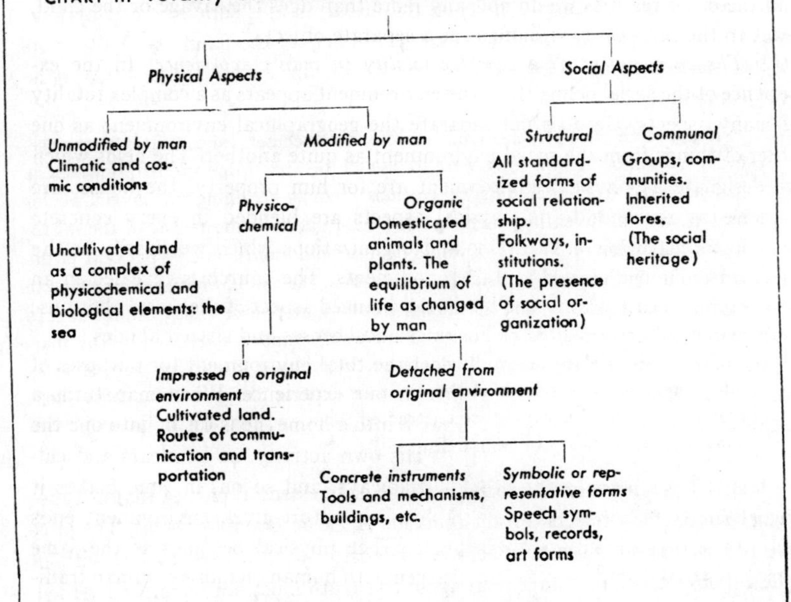

CHART III Totality of Environment of the Individual Life

The social heritage of man. Through unknown ages man has been active in and upon his environment. This process takes on a cumulative character because man is less content than the other animals with mere habituation and adjustment to given conditions and because he acquires thereby a social heritage which is the basis of further acquisitions. The term *social heritage* was used by Graham Wallas to signify "the knowledge and expedients and habits" which are socially, not biologically, transmitted, being handed down from generation to generation through social participation and education.[3] The arts, devices, techniques, lores, myths, traditions, symbols, mores, and institutions of man—all his agencies for the control of the outer environment—are social possessions. (Note several of the categories in Chart III.)

[1] *Man's dependence on the social heritage:* The records of the feral cases,

and for a recent adaptation of Spencer's classification, W. F. Ogburn and M. F. Nimkoff, *Sociology* (Boston, 1940), pp. 6-7. For an extensive classification differing somewhat from the one presented in the text, see L. L. Bernard, "A Classification of Environments," *American Journal of Sociology*, XXXI (1925), 318-332.

3. *Our Social Heritage* (New Haven, 1921), p. 14.

such as that of Kaspar Hauser, indicate the utter dependence of man on socially transmitted powers. Instinct suffices for those orders of life which have no record of achievement, which simply accommodate themselves to the realities among which they live. Man, however, is never satisfied with mere "reality," and his dissatisfaction becomes effective through social rather than biological agencies. Instinct, losing its fixity in the life of man, is supplemented by folkways; the tool and the machine come to the help of the hand. As Wallas puts it, we have become "biologically parasitic on our social heritage." And he conjectures:

> If the earth were struck by one of Mr. Wells' comets, and if, in consequence, every human being now alive were to lose all the knowledge and habits which he had acquired from preceding generations (though retaining unchanged all his own powers of invention, memory, and habituation) nine tenths of the inhabitants of London or New York would be dead in a month, and 99 per cent of the remaining tenth would be dead in six months. They would have no language to express their thoughts, and no thoughts but vague reverie. They could not read notices, or drive motors or horses. They would wander about, led by the inarticulate cries of a few naturally dominant individuals, drowning themselves as thirst came on, in hundreds at the riverside landing places, looting those shops where the smell of decaying food attracted them and perhaps at the end stumbling on the expedient of cannibalism.[4]

Man's dependence on the social heritage is an essential part of that advance which successfully rejects certain demands of the outer environment. The price we pay is that we have become, even biologically, less fitted to live without the aid of our social heritage. But again this truth must not be misunderstood. It does not mean that our life has ceased to be "natural." Why should we call it natural for human beings to live that resourceless and stunted life from which the presence of the social heritage delivers us? The so-called state of nature (recall the misleading social contract doctrine), in which life remained "poor, solitary, nasty, brutish, and short," has no valid claims upon us. Nor does this dependence mean that we are biologically weaker. Perhaps our teeth are weaker than those of earlier peoples; perhaps the process of childbirth is more difficult. But civilized man, with the aid of his own arts, is considerably stronger, healthier, and longer-lived than earlier or primitive man.[5] We do not raise the unanswerable question as to which is the happier, because the kind of happiness attainable is relative to the kind of life, and thus comparisons are impossible. But biological fitness has surely no better measure than that of success in living, maintained throughout the generations.

[2] *Man's acquisition of the social heritage:* Our utter dependence on the social heritage means that education (in the broadest sense) is of fundamental im-

---

4. *Our Social Heritage*, p. 16. Copyright 1921. Reprinted by permission of the publishers, Yale University Press.
5. *Ibid.*, p. 19.

portance in every human society. In modern society with its rapidly growing heritage, education is of ever-increasing significance, as the contrast between, say, our great-grandparents and ourselves illustrates. The social heritage differs in significant ways from a mere economic inheritance. It is not simply handed over to us to enjoy and use. We are only conditional heirs to it, the condition being that we must qualify ourselves to receive it, and make it ours by our own efforts. Social in one sense, it has nevertheless to be *individualized* part by part, in the various members of society.

The process of acquiring the social heritage is therefore of enormous interest to sociologists, psychologists, and others who are concerned with the learning behavior of man. Many of these investigators are studying not only the various behavior mechanisms involved in the acquisition of social habits, points of view, skills, and so on, but as well the findings of comparative anthropology and sociology that reveal the intimate relation between the nature of the particular social heritage and the nature of the behavior manifested by those who share that heritage.[6] Imitation and suggestion and the other processes involved in learning operate wherever human society is found, operate to provide the individual with at least the essentials of the social heritage required for social participation and survival. If at birth any of us had been transferred to a foreign country, we would have as readily acquired the different manners and modes of speech—indeed most if not all of the different way of life—which it exhibits as those we actually practice. We cannot stress too often or too strongly that the civilizational and cultural products are not inherited via the germ plasm, but by means of social machinery. Thus the tools that man uses, the art he creates, the Gods he worships, his courtship and marriage practices, his very ideas, are dependent on his social heritage. Whatever his "race" or inheritance or innate abilities, this dependency remains—notwithstanding some of our folk beliefs to the contrary.

We have discussed earlier (in Chapter III) the manner in which the individual being becomes socialized. Here we may indicate another aspect of this process. Some parts of the social heritage are easily acquired—we soon adapt ourselves to the comforts and amenities of civilization, and with comparative ease we utilize most of the inventions and mechanisms which human ingenuity has devised. Some parts we acquire by simple habituation, such as our speech, our manners, many of our devices and techniques, and most of our customs and folkways. Other parts are more difficult to acquire, demanding of us, in the first place, exacting proof of our ability to receive them. The skill that invents and improves the means of civilization belongs to relatively few, but all of us can enjoy the advantages provided by that skill. Those parts that

6. See, for example, C. L. Hull, *Principles of Behavior* (New York, 1943); N. E. Miller and J. Dollard, *Social Learning and Imitation* (New Haven, 1941); J. Dollard, "The Acquisition of New Social Habits," in *The Science of Man in the World Crisis* (R. Linton, ed., New York, 1945), pp. 442–464.

are easy to acquire have a less intimate relation to personality. They reveal the nature of society in general, rather than of particular individuals within it. The parts of the social heritage that are harder to acquire depend in greater degree on our individual qualities, and are more fully individualized in those who achieve them. They are more selectively interpreted, and assume for each of us a personal aspect. Thus music, art, philosophy, literature, certain aspects of religion—they mean something distinctively different to each of us. At the same time, as every student of the arts knows, they always embody the qualities of the society in which they originate.

The social heritage, then, is unequally possessed by the members of society. No individual, in our complex world, can master more than a fragment of the social heritage. Specialization applies to the process of learning no less than to our economic tasks. A full personal life clearly does not require possession of more than a small part of the social heritage. However, it is highly desirable that certain of its elements be shared as widely as possible. We must postpone discussion of this problem until a later point when we distinguish between two basic aspects of the social heritage, the civilizational and the cultural.[7]

The Process of Adjustment to a Total Environment

Environment and adjustment: some general considerations. We have seen that our environment is not the world about us but rather the world, with all its aspects, as it comes into *relation* to our lives. The more complex the life, the more complex must the environment be and the more complex the adjustment to the total environment.

[1] *From organic to civilizational adjustment:* Thus as we pass from lower to higher forms of life, say, from amoeba to man, direct physiological adjustment becomes a smaller part of the whole process. In the development of man, organic adaptations are more and more supplemented by the devices of civilization. The lower animals have no tools and must adapt their own organs to the performance of new functions—they must develop claws to cut and fangs to tear. But man devises, for such purposes, knives and shears and saws and a great variety of other tools, thus extending vastly his range of operation. Using tools, he does not have to follow a simple scheme of behavior determined by direct *organic* conditioning. When the machine is added to the tool, his range of alternatives becomes still greater. In this way organically determined patterns of conduct lose their rigidity and the more flexible patterns learned through the social heritage become increasingly important. We observe here an important difference between the adjustment of civilized man to his total environment and that of primitive man and, of course, from that of the lower animals.

7. See below, Chapter XXI.

The process of adjustment between modern man and his total environment is consequently so intricate and varied that here we can accord it only the most broad treatment. We shall consider this process under two aspects: first, with respect to the differences between the typical adjustment of civilized man and that of primitive man; and second, with respect to the manner in which civilized man readjusts himself to a new or drastically changed total environment.

[2] *Characteristics of the adjustment of civilized man:* Each of the generalizations that appear below requires careful examination. In the chapters which follow we shall have occasion to return to them, and in the present chapter they may serve as a guide in our discussion of man's adjustment to his environment.

ONE: ADJUSTMENT IS ONLY PARTIAL. In a higher civilization man attains a less complete, a less all-round adjustment to the totality of conditions under which he lives. (The reason for this will become clearer when we discuss the relation of civilization and culture in Chapter XXI.) To his complex changeful world man can achieve only a partial adjustment, a compound of *conflict and accommodation* (accommodation refers to the process in which the person or the group comes to fit into a given situation and to feel "at home" within it).[8] Civilized man rarely feels in perfect harmony with his environment. His wants are so complex and the surrounding conditions are so complex that a perfect sense of equilibrium is hard or impossible to attain, except perhaps for those dulled by the combined influence of age and economic prosperity, and for those mystics who gain a sense of oneness between themselves and the entire universe. This eternal discontent of civilized man is a spur to his incessant endeavor toward new achievement. Each generation is necessarily one of "discontents."

TWO: ADJUSTMENT IS DYNAMIC. The adjustment of civilized man is less stable. He has more controls over his environment, is always changing it and always seeking to change it. The more he modifies the primary nature-given environment, the more he is impelled to modify it still further. The environment of civilized man is forever in flux. His habituations to it, even were they perfect in some hour of unlikely coincidence, are always liable to some disturbance either through external change or through the insurgence of new demands within himself. The citizen of the world today has no greater lesson to learn than this.

THREE: ADJUSTMENT IS SELECTIVE AND VARIANT. The adjustment of civilized man is highly selective and endlessly variant compared with that of primitive man. Suppose a number of modern men went wandering through the same

8. The term "accommodation," as we are using it, refers particularly to the process in which man attains a sense of harmony with his environment. This emphasis is perhaps implied in the use of the term by the "ecological school"; see, for example, E. W. Burgess, "Accommodation" in the *Encyclopaedia of the Social Sciences* (New York, 1935), I, 403–404. The term "adjustment" implies more particularly the process in which man *deliberately* contrives to fit his needs to the environment or the environment to his needs. See R. M. MacIver, "Maladjustment" in the same *Encyclopaedia*. Compare with the definitions of "accommodation" and "social adjustment" in *Dictionary of Sociology* (H. P. Fairchild, ed., New York, 1944).

forest. One might be a hunter, one a bird lover, one an entomologist, one a city-bred artisan; the forest would be a different environment for each of them. Each would be equipped to see and to respond to a different aspect. But the members of an American Indian group whose home was the forest knew it in the light of similar necessities and habituations, similar beliefs and similar lores. Again, in the same urban environment there exists a myriad of different milieus, such that those accommodated to one, say a slum area, would feel themselves alien in many of the others.

FOUR: READJUSTMENT IS RELATIVELY EASY. Finally, the adjustment of civilized man is one which, with all its complexity and partly because of it, permits a remarkable degree of *mobility*, a power of relatively swift readjustment to other and different environments. Civilized man acquires a certain mental versatility in coping with the changing complexity of his situation, and this enables him to adjust more readily to other environments. He can, whatever the reluctance and complaints of some, range from the tropics to the polar snows, move from the conditions of poverty to fame and fortune (or the reverse), adjust to the moderate ways of the Weimar Republic or to the regimentation and bestiality of the Nazi rule. Whatever else the developed complexity of modern civilization brings to man, weal or woe, it gives to him a plasticity unrivaled in the organic world.

Readjustment to a new environment. We have seen that modern man is more capable of readjustment to new conditions than are the members of simpler societies. However, modern man is sometimes confronted with situations in which the readjustment demanded is drastic and difficult.

[1] *The general conditions making readjustment difficult:* Broadly considered, difficulty of readjustment arises in two ways. In the first place, it may be the result of the inherent instability of the *social structure*, culminating in a revolution, peaceful or violent, in which the old order is overthrown. Then men must come to terms with a new order that rejects many of their cherished traditions, their articles of faith, their loyalities, their privileges and prejudices, or their claims. The numerous revolutions in Europe after World War I and the even more widespread upheavals in Europe and Asia and Africa following World War II are examples of the more violent type of transition in which not merely governmental systems but whole schemes of life are drastically altered. These great changes in social structure will concern us especially in Book Three.

Secondly, the problem of sudden readjustment is created also by the increased mobility of modern life which frequently brings people into new environments requiring very different habituations from those they have already acquired. This happens, for example, when the ruralite migrates to the city or the urbanite to the country, when the youth leaves the home environment to work or to study in a very different social atmosphere, and, most conspicuously, when people enter as immigrant aliens into a new community. These situations are, of course, particularly characteristic of the mobile civilization of the United States.[9] We shall examine some of their aspects in the present chapter.

[2] *Typical situations involving the problem of readjustment:* The conditions under which individuals or groups enter an alien social environment are complicated and diverse. There are so many types of situation which arise in the clash of widely different cultures within the environment of either of them that generalization is difficult. Where the newcomers belong to a widely different racial or cultural organization from that into which they enter, the process of accommodation is, of course, usually rendered more difficult.

Consider a few of the type-situations. If the newcomers are the bearers of prestige and of power, they may dominate the native population. They may, when the disparity is very great, be the cause of the extinction of the latter, as have been the white immigrants in Tasmania and in parts of Melanesia. The decline of most American Indian tribes and, in some instances, their outright destruction bear witness to this process. Under other conditions the dominant incomer may build an alien society from which the natives are excluded and to which they may oppose an active or passive resistance as in the case of India; or the two societies may exist relatively peacefully side by side, as in the case of some of the American Indian groups and the "Anglos" in our own Southwest. Under still other conditions miscegenation may take place, involving the gradual dilution of the original native stocks, which in this way acquire some degree of adjustment to the new civilization imposed upon them. This has occurred, for example, in New Zealand, over large parts of Latin America, and, quite conspicuously, in Oklahoma, where the blood of the original Americans and the newcomers is well mixed. Again, larger peoples with highly developed cultures, like the Chinese, may successfully oppose the political and economic domination of the immigrant foreigner, while at the same time the gradual introduction of the technical civilization of the latter tends to undermine the basis of their own culture or assimilate it to that of the alien. Any student of colonial history can list other types of readjustment situations and can multiply at length concrete examples.[10]

The problem of the Negro in North America presents its own distinctive features. In the age of slavery, the status of legal inferiority determined in large part the mode of the Negro's accommodation to the new environment. The formal abolition of that status created a new situation. Social inferiority remained, though subject to limited protest and occasional challenge as educational and economic opportunities were slowly widened. Thus was created the

9. John Gunther in *Inside U.S.A.* (New York, 1947) stresses perhaps more than any other single theme the extreme fluidity of American society. This uneven but voluminous report contains a wealth of illustrative material for the student of sociology.

10. For other illustrations, see G. H. L. F. Pitt-Rivers, *The Clash of Culture and the Contact of Races* (London, 1927), and the excellent collection of readings, *When Peoples Meet* (A. Locke and B. J. Stern, eds., New York, 1942).

present state of uneasy partial accommodation. We may anticipate our later discussion of this problem (in Chapter XV) by noting that so long as the prevailing bar (whether legal or "social") on intermarriage endures and so long as physical and social segregation are maintained by the dominant group, this condition must persist with all its difficulties.[11]

The assimilation of the immigrant in the United States. From almost every country of the earth the immigrant has come to the American continent, and notably to the United States, bringing with him habituations and valuations from civilizations and cultures throughout the world. This movement, including as it has large groups of fellow countrymen, involves the problem of group as well as individual accommodation. Moreover, it is complicated by the presence in this country of a large Negro minority, now about one tenth of the total population. For the Negro as for the immigrant from Europe or elsewhere (*and* for the dominant "native" group), the crux of the problem of accommodation is one of *social* adjustment, not of biological adaptation. Thus the United States offers a unique laboratory for the study, in its endless varieties, of the process by which individuals and groups, transplanted from one social environment to another, learn to live within a society other than that in which they or their fathers were born and bred.

[1] *Variant patterns of adjustment:* There are considerable differences in the ease with which various individuals and groups on similar cultural levels learn to feel at home in a new environment. For a century or more there has been added to our literature the autobiographical testimonials of new arrivals whose reactions to the American scene have ranged from almost immediate wholehearted devotion to an enduring sense of cultural and group antagonism.[12] Groups of different nationality backgrounds reveal quite variant patterns of assimilation and adjustment. For understandable reasons, English and Scottish and, to a less extent, Irish immigrants have lost the feeling of exile more readily than, for example, the French. In general, the "old immigration" coming to the country from Western Europe before 1880 experienced little difficulty in readjustment as compared with the "new immigration" from Southern and Eastern Europe after that year. The alien environment often led immigrant groups to form "colonies" or semicommunities; and within these "cultural islands" they would cling more closely for a time to their own

11. Among the hundreds of volumes on the Negro-White relationship, we note at this point the important two-volume work of G. Myrdal, *An American Dilemma* (New York, 1944); E. R. Embree, *Brown Americans* (New York, 1943); C. S. Johnson, *Patterns of Negro Segregation* (New York, 1943); and the "Segregation" issue of *Survey Graphic* (Jan., 1947).

12. The hundreds of immigrant autobiographies, some written in this century, include M. I. Pupin, *From Immigrant to Inventor* (New York, 1923); L. Lewisohn, *Upstream* (New York, 1923); L. Adamic, *Laughing in the Jungle* (New York, 1932); E. Corsi, *In the Shadow of Liberty* (New York, 1935). For a series of briefer statements by well-known immigrants see *I Am An American* (R. S. Benjamin, ed., New York, 1941).

folkways, sometimes prizing them more highly than they did in their native land. They would feel their unity the more because of their detachment from the conditions which created it.[13]

All of the large cities in the United States and many of the rural areas contain ethnically or culturally distinct semicommunities of this type. Take the French Canadians. Throughout the towns of New England they have for many years lived in districts of partially self-imposed segregation, and their ties with their homeland to the North have been deliberately maintained. Of the approximately 4,000,000 Poles in this country, huge numbers live in "Polish" districts in the larger cities—about 500,000 in Chicago, about 300,000 in Detroit, and about 200,000 in New York. Most of these are workers in plants and mills and foundries. On the other hand, the farms of the Connecticut River Valley have gained a new prosperity under the ownership and skill of the Poles who have settled in that region and who are now "accepted" there as a permanent group. Take the American Chinese. These people, at present fewer than 80,000 came into the United States in fairly large numbers until the 1880's, provided a substantial cheap labor force for Western railroad construction and other enterprises, and between the years 1882 and 1943 experienced not only exclusion legislation but extreme discrimination and, on occasion, even mob violence. Settling for the most part in the larger American cities (especially in San Francisco, New York, Los Angeles, and Chicago), the Chinese have retained their cultural identity more than any other immigrant group.[14] American history provides example after example, each differing in some respects from the others.

[2] *Hinderances and aids to assimilation:* To what extent can we generalize concerning the processes involved in America's "melting pot"? We can point out, of course, that when the newcomer neither possesses in himself nor arouses in others any strong sense of "social distance," of inferiority, or of superiority, the process of accommodation is usually facilitated. But what accounts for the wide variation of feeling between group and group, between the ready acceptance of some Western Europeans, for example, and the relative antagonism toward the Italian or Greek or Russian? Numerous researches in assimilation and a vast literature are available for those who wish to pursue these questions. Here we may indicate certain of the *interrelated* factors that illustrate the complexity and variability of the process.

ONE: THE STAGE OF DEVELOPMENT IN THE SOCIETY ENTERED. The nature of the immigrant's reception in the new land is dependent to a very large extent on the conditions existing at the time he enters. Thus for those millions who

13. There is a large literature on the immigrant in America. Among the studies dealing with several specific groups are E. de S. Brunner, *Immigrant Farmers and Their Children* (New York, 1929); F. J. Brown and J. S. Roucek, *One America* (New York, 1946); C. Wittke, *We Who Built America* (New York, 1940); C. McWilliams, *Brothers under the Skin* (Boston, 1943).

14. These examples and many others are discussed in Brown and Roucek, *op. cit.*

came to the United States when the frontier was still expanding across the continent, and when strength and skill of every kind were needed in the development of new lands and growing industries, differences of language or religion or national background were very apt to be minor barriers to acceptance. We need only to contrast the great advantages of the earlier immigrants in this respect and the disadvantages imposed by a "closing frontier" and a relatively settled society on the "new immigration" during the decades following 1880. The refugees from European countries who entered our country after Hitler's rise to power in 1933 can testify to the way in which they were often viewed as a threat to the economic well-being of native workers and professionals—many Americans considered their arrival as ill-timed.[15] We can observe how this factor continues to operate today by contrasting such relatively undeveloped states as Arizona where outsiders are generally welcome and quickly become "old-timers" with, say, Vermont or Maine, which require residence of perhaps three generations for the acquisition of "native" status.

TWO: BACKGROUND OCCUPATIONAL SKILLS. The immigrant has a great advantage when he has already been trained in a mode of work for which there is need in the new country. The Scandinavians and Germans, for example, who settled in the farming areas of the Middle West were often of rural background and simply applied their agrarian skills to the new land. The fact that many of the Jews from Eastern European countries arriving here thirty to sixty years ago were already trained in clothing and shoe production gave them an economic advantage in those growing industries in the Eastern cities. On the other hand, the more recent refugees from Europe, largely a commercial and professional group, found no immediate market for their specialized skills. Again, the difficulties in assimilation encountered by the Italians and Greeks and Poles, who arrived in such great numbers during the early decades of this century, were in part due to the fact that these largely agrarian people were at once thrust into the unskilled tasks demanded by our growing industries in large urban centers.

THREE: THE NUMBERS INVOLVED. It has long been observed that the attitudes of a group toward the outsider tend to be tolerant until the latter's numbers reach large proportions. *How* large depends upon many interacting factors. From the 1870's for almost half a century expanding American industry demanded and absorbed millions upon millions of the "new immigration" from Southern and Eastern Europe, providing cheap labor for mills and railroads and factories and mines. The "greatest social experiment in human history" was in full beat. But as machines began to replace hands, as technical skills became more in demand, as American workers began to organize into unions, these untrained and unskilled and relatively unorganized newcomers

15. On the recent refugee situation, see G. Saenger, *Today's Refugees, Tomorrow's Citizens* (New York, 1941); M. R. Davie, *The Refugee Immigrant in the United States* (New York, 1946).

more and more encountered discrimination and prejudice—many Americans began to speak of the "melting pot mistake." The relatively few "aliens" in their midst had mattered little in earlier days; now the hordes of "swarthy invaders" became a supposed threat.[16]

FOUR: PHYSICAL DIFFERENCES. The "new immigration" also illustrates the way in which differences in features, complexion of skin, and other physical traits may operate as a hindrance in assimilation. Here caution is necessary. For physical differences in themselves do not produce antagonisms or prejudice between peoples, as evidenced by certain areas in the world, such as parts of Southeastern Asia and of Latin America, where even color distinctions are viewed as socially insignificant. However, when other factors operate to produce group frictions, physical differences are likely to be seized upon as evidence of inferiority and undesirability. It has been calculated by Warner and Srole that in the United States assimilation is generally easiest and most rapid for "light Caucasoids," and harder and slower, in descending order, for "dark Caucasoids," Mongoloids and Caucasoid mixtures with dominant Caucasoid appearance, the same mixtures with Mongoloid appearance, and, finally, Negroes and Negroid mixtures.[17] The evidence seems to bear out this racial "scale of subordination and assimilation." This is to say that generally the adjustment problems are easiest for newcomers who in appearance are supposedly most like the "old Americans."

FIVE: CULTURAL DIFFERENCES. This is by far the most complex and difficult factor to appraise. The investigators cited above have combined their racial scale with a "similar scale for deviation from the dominant American culture" in which they use language and religion as criteria of the latter. In this way they have worked out a ranking of "cultural types" starting from English-speaking Protestants, whose assimilation is most rapid and easy, and including in ascending order of assimilation difficulty, Protestants who do not speak English, English-speaking Catholics and other non-Protestants, non-Protestants who speak allied Indo-European languages, English-speaking non-Christians, and, finally, non-Christians who do not speak English.[18] As in the case of the racial factor, easy adjustment to conditions in the United States is most likely for those who culturally most resemble the "old Americans." There are, of course, many cultural characteristics other than language and religion that aid or hinder assimilation—customs and beliefs and philosophies and so on.

SIX: THE ROLE OF THE SEMICOMMUNITY. The many "colonies" that immigrants have created, whether "natural areas" in the large cities or rural settlements, play an important double role in the assimilation process. On

16. Cf. Brown and Roucek, *op. cit.*, pp. 4–12.

17. W. L. Warner and L. Srole, *The Social Systems of American Ethnic Groups* (New Haven, 1945), Chap. X.

18. *Ibid.*

the one hand, the retention of many features of the traditional way of life and the development of a semiautonomous community meet the immigrant's need for identification with his fellow man and a consequent sense of security. Thus those members of ethnically distinct groups living in the "Ghettos," the Chinatowns, the "Little Italys," and so on, do not experience the drastic "culture shock" of the isolated stranger in a new land. In this way the semi-community of the immigrant serves to ease his readjustment to new conditions. On the other hand, assimilation itself is no doubt retarded by the existence of these "cultural islands." Within them the newcomer, especially the first-generation arrival, achieves a sense of safety, to be sure, but they stand in the eyes of the majority as evidence of the alien and bizarre and distasteful.

[3] *Assimilation and succeeding generations:* To a considerable extent, the Greek still frequents his coffee shop, the German his beer cellar, the southern Italian retains his patriarchal type of household, the Ukrainian and Pole have their native dances, the Irishman celebrates with fervor St. Patrick's Day. But in time, unless as in the case of the Mexicans and Orientals a dividing line of caste is set up between the immigrant and the native born, the influences of the new environment encroach upon and then triumph over the resistances derived from the old. This is revealed in the changed attitudes and behavior of the children and grandchildren of immigrants. One external evidence is the increasing extent of intermarriage.[19] Another is the decline (but by no means the disappearance) of foreign language newspapers. The original speech, the idioms and turns of phrase, the customs of the old land, the reunions and celebrations commemorative of it all lose their appeal.

Often a difficult transitional stage is entered upon. The younger generation, finding the ways of their parents despised in the larger community into which their schooling, their work, and their play initiate them, often revolt from the family traditions and reject the family and neighborhood controls. This is notably the case among some of the ethnic groups in the large cities, such as the Italians and Puerto Ricans (though not the Chinese), but is also found in certain rural immigrant groups, such as the Poles in the Connecticut Valley. A state of disorganization of this kind is evidenced by the prevalence of delinquency and by the growth of substitute social control agencies in the form of gangs in some of the second-generation groups.[20] The child of the immigrant

---

19. Earlier studies of intermarriage include J. H. Drachsler, *Intermarriage in New York City* (New York, 1921); Brunner, *op. cit.;* N. Carpenter, *Immigrants and Their Children*, Census Monograph (Washington, D.C., 1927). For more recent findings, see, for example, I. L. Child, *Italian or American?* (New Haven, 1943); R. J. R. Kennedy, "Single or Triple Melting-Pot? Intermarriage Trends in New Haven, 1870–1940," *American Journal of Sociology*, XLIX (1943), 331–339; L. Nelson, "Intermarriage among Nationality Groups in a Rural Area of Minnesota," *ibid.*, XLVIII (1943), 585–592; J. S. Slotkin, "Jewish-Gentile Intermarriage in Chicago," *American Sociological Review*, VII (1942), 34–39; M. L. Barron, "The Incidence of Jewish Intermarriage in Europe and America," *ibid.*, XI (1946), 6–13.

20. See, for example, F. M. Thrasher, *The Gang* (Chicago, 1927) and W. F. Whyte, *Street Corner Society* (Chicago, 1943).

has a difficult task of accommodation to a total social environment containing the diverse and sometimes conflicting mores of family and community. He must build for himself a new pattern of life.

> The immigrant coming to America was born into customs that were so old that they were no longer questioned. For the first generation these customs have been doctrines of welfare and a guide to correct living. Then in America their children question the desirability of such standards and customs. As the second generation becomes disorganized, the immigrant parents think of the American culture as something pernicious, and Americans think of the disorganization as evidence that the immigrants are undesirable. Neither sees it as a matter of conflict of cultures which inevitably leads to disorganization.[21]

Accommodation: a principle and a distinction. Much has been written regarding the manner and degree in which individuals and groups accommodate themselves to the social conditions of a new environment and the problems and resistances which they encounter in the process. To our example of the immigrant in the United States could be added the grim story of the readjustments made by the many thousands in Europe who were forced into concentration camps before and during World War II, or the accommodation problems and accomplishment of the Japanese-Americans who occupied the American version of the concentration camp—both excellent illustrations of the remarkable plasticity of modern man.[22] Another example of a force-invoked new way of life is observed in the social systems and group patterns worked out by the inmates of prisons and reformatories and other segregated semicommunities.[23] These are extreme and perhaps atypical cases, but again they indicate the ways in which man consciously and unconsciously creates a new scheme of existence when faced by altered conditions. Indeed, the conditions of accommodation are too complex and variable to admit of summary statement. We must here be content to point out one general principle, revealed in the contrast between a more primitive and a more evolved society, and to emphasize one distinction that is basic in the study of social reality.

[1] *Accommodation less rigorous in higher civilization:* In the more evolved and more complex society, because of the differentiation within it, the *complete* assimilation of the newcomer to an entire set of community patterns does not take place. The differences in manners and morals, in customs and beliefs, necessarily make the demands of the community less rigid and less inclusive. The new member has more opportunity of selecting his social relationships,

---

21. L. G. Brown, *Immigration* (New York, 1933), p. 254.

22. For the readjustments made in concentration camps see D. Rousset, *The Other Kingdom* (New York, 1947); A. Koestler, *Scum of the Earth* (New York, 1941); and the novel, A. Maltz, *The Cross and the Arrow* (Boston, 1944). Two excellent studies of the "relocation projects" for American Japanese are A. H. Leighton, *The Governing of Men* (Princeton, 1945) and D. S. Thomas and R. S. Nishimoto, *The Spoilage* (Berkeley, Cal., 1946).

23. See, for example, A. K. Weinberg, "Aspects of the Prison's Social Structure," *American Journal of Sociology*, XLVII (1942), 717-726.

of finding his own place, of expressing under the new conditions his own individuality. In the advanced society, for the immigrant as for the native, there are many mansions. And as we shall see in a later chapter, this is no more strikingly illustrated than in the contrast between the complex and relatively impersonal environment of the great city and the simpler face-to-face world of the rural community.

This principle, of course, admits exceptions. For the readiness with which the entrant into the new society becomes accommodated to its conditions is not wholly dependent, apart from his own adaptability, on the degree of development. For varying reasons, some communities are more tolerant or more receptive than others, less swayed by authoritarianism or by the exclusiveness of religious and national dogma. The Chinese, for example, with a highly developed culture, have historically exhibited these qualities, illustrated by the fact that the Chinese Jews have become, while retaining their religion, completely integrated in Chinese social life.[24]

[2] *Social accommodation versus physical adaptation:* In concluding this chapter, we cite a distinction to which we must frequently return later in this book. The manner in which groups adapt themselves to their *physical* habitat should not be confused with the process in which they accommodate themselves to a pre-existing *social* milieu. The first is a biological process; the second, a social process. When the stature of the children of European immigrants, for example, increases beyond that of their parents, or when they alter in head shape, they are adapting biologically to new conditions. (The *conditions* are physical *and* social.) But when these same children develop aggressive attitudes or form juvenile gangs in city slums they are illustrating the process of social accommodation.

The use of the term "ecology" by both the physical sciences and sociology tends to shade over the distinction we have made. In botany or zoology the term "ecological" is applied to those variations of plant or animal life which are attributable to differences of physical environment reacting on the distribution and the characteristics of the species subjected to them. The social variations exhibited by or within human groups cannot be regarded as "ecological" in this sense. For the total environment of the human being is never merely physical. We may very profitably take local geographical areas as a basis of social investigation, but we must never assume that the conditions we discover are explained by the external characteristics of these areas. The social ecologists have found, for example, that delinquency rates in large cities tend to be highest in the zones immediately beyond the central business districts and to recede progressively as one moves outward. But we cannot assume that the locality as such is in any degree responsible, that the greater frequency of delinquency represents a process of adjustment to the physical factors of the

24. Cf. M. Fishberg, *The Jews* (New York, 1911), pp. 134–136.

area.[25] Geographical distribution in a social environment is in no sense geographical determination. Every social phenomenon is a function of a *total situation*--the search for causes is only begun when we have delimited it in terms of a physical environment.

Moreover, as we have seen, the social environment is very complex, and there are all kinds and degrees of accommodation to its manifold aspects represented in the modes of living characteristic of a social group. The following description of life in an Indiana small city (written almost twenty years ago) admirably illustrates this fact.

> Living moves along in Middletown, as we have seen, at a bewildering variety of gaits. Differential rates of adjustment in the performance of the same function have been observed between elders and their juniors and between people living next door to each other, while the females have exhibited greater conservatism than the males at many points, and the males, with seemingly no more coherence or pattern in their adjustments, are more resistant to adaptation at many other points. In many activities, as has been repeatedly pointed out, the working class today employs the habits of the business class of roughly a generation ago; if it were possible to differentiate clearly the gradations by which each of these two major groups shades into the other, it might appear that many changes are slowly filtered down through various intermediate groups. Shifts sometimes diffuse, however, in the reverse direction, from working class to business class, as has been noted, for example, in the use of commercially baked bread and canned foods.
>
> Not only do these variations, in many cases pronounced enough to affect markedly one's capacity to deal with one's world, appear between individuals and between different age, sex, and other groups within Middletown in the performance of the *same* life-activity, but the city as a whole and groups within the city live in different eras in the performance of *different* life-activities. It is apparent that Middletown is carrying on certain of these habitual pursuits in almost precisely the same manner as a generation ago, while in the performance of others its present methods bear little resemblance to the earlier ones. Among the six major groups of activities a rough hierarchy of rates of change is apparent. Getting a living seemingly exhibits the most pervasive change, particularly in its technological and mechanical aspects; leisure time, again most markedly in material developments such as the automobile and motion picture, is almost as mobile; training the young in schools, community activities, and making a home would come third, fourth, and fifth in varying order depending upon which traits are scrutinized; while, finally, on the whole exhibiting least change, come the formal religious activities.[26]

Such diversity might seem to indicate that the attempt to discover causal

---

25. Illustrative of such studies are C. R. Shaw, *Delinquency Areas* (Chicago, 1927); National Commission on Law Enforcement, *Report on the Causes of Crime*, II (1931), 140–188; C. F. Schmid, *Social Saga of Two Cities* (Minneapolis, 1937), pp. 334–345.

26. From *Middletown* by Robert S. and Helen Merrell Lynd, copyright, 1929, by Harcourt, Brace and Company, Inc.

connections between social developments and the external factors of environment is baffling and hopeless. Certainly we cannot hope to find that any environmental factor is *the* cause of any social phenomenon. Such an hypothesis could be entertained only by those who have an antiquated and erroneous idea of the nature of all causation.[27] What we actually find is that human beings exhibit typical diversities relative to every type of *total environment.* How far these diversities are attributable to *specific* features of that environment is, as we have seen, a very difficult question to answer. The total environment, both in its physical and in its social aspects, is always affecting those who are subject to it. The pursuit of this question and of this relationship carries us from these initial considerations of Book One to the more detailed examination of the social structure and of social change in Books Two and Three.

---

27. Few sociologists in this country have attempted a thorough analysis of the problem of social causation. For one such attempt, see R. M. MacIver, *Social Causation* (Boston, 1942); and for a critique of this volume by F. H. Knight and a rejoinder by the author, see *American Journal of Sociology*, XLIX (1943–1944), 46–58.

BOOK **II**

The Social Structure

PART ONE: *The Sustaining Forces of Code and Custom*

Foreword:

If from an airplane we look down upon a city or village or other area of social living we see buildings and highways and bridges and other evidences of man's works. We may see even the people themselves. But we do not and cannot *see* the social structure. We cannot see society but only its external aspects. For society is the organization of human relationships, built, sustained, and forever being changed by human beings. In Book Two we shall be concerned with the character of the social structure, particularly as it has developed under the conditions of modern Western civilization.

In Part One we face a preliminary but essential task. For while the social structure itself is unstable and changeful, it has a definite character at every stage, and many of its major elements have shown great persistence of type through change. How, then, is this fabric of institutions and associations—the family, the state, and the church, for example—maintained and regulated? How does it endure as a co-ordinated system? What are the forces that bind the structure together? At a later stage we shall study the forces that make for instability and change; here we are concerned with the conservative forces that make for cohesion and stability.

We enter here, once more, a region where sociology and psychology meet. For these regulative principles are of a universal character, and they are as characteristic of human mentality as they are of human society wherever found. Thus we examine the role of the sustaining mores and codes in Chapters VII and VIII. At the same time the mores and codes and other agencies of social control with which we shall deal do not wholly express or invariably regulate the strivings and thoughts of men. So we are brought face to face, especially in Chapter IX, with the question of the adjustment of these principles to the variant individual situations for which the principles themselves never fully account. The consideration of code and custom as a sustaining but ever-changing structure of social relationships will prepare the way for the study of the major forms of group structure in Part Two.

7

The Mores and Social Control

Codes and Sanctions in Social Life

Social control and social structure. A very large part of sociological literature, by whatever name, treats of social control. For by social control is meant the way in which the entire social order coheres and maintains itself—how it operates as a whole, as a changing equilibrium. The concept of social control brings us to the focus of sociology and its perpetual central problem—the relation of the social order and the individual being, the relation of the unit and the whole. To study social control we must seek out the ways in which society patterns and regulates individual behavior and, at the same time, the ways in which patterned and standardized behavior in turn serves to maintain the social organization. This large task will command our attention throughout Book Two, in which we shall consider various parts of that complex order of human relationships that we call the social structure.[1]

Before entering upon a discussion of community and class and family and the other group manifestations of social structure (the subjects of Part Two of Book Two), we must view those sustaining forces of code and custom expressed in the folkways and mores of society. In Chapter I we discussed briefly the nature of the mores and indicated that they function in each society as regulators of behavior and therefore as instruments of social control. We must now consider in greater detail this function and examine those principles along the lines of which the mores operate to sustain the social structure.

1. Of the large literature on social control, books that are written directly around that concept include E. A. Ross, *Social Control* (New York, 1901), the earliest American treatise on the subject and still worth the student's attention; F. E. Lumley, *The Means of Social Control* (New York, 1925); P. H. Landis, *Social Control* (Philadelphia, 1939); L. L. Bernard, *Social Control in Its Sociological Aspects* (New York, 1939); J. S. Roucek, *et al.*, *Social Control* (New York, 1947).

The nature of social law. No order, even the most changeful, exists except as the expression of law. Each thing abides in accordance with the law of its particular being, and the scientific quest, whatever the field, is to seek out the principles or laws that govern in a given area. The physical scientist is interested in the laws of gravity or gases or thermodynamics; the social scientist is no less concerned with the laws manifested by the existence and behavior of social phenomena. But there are some significant differences between the two.

[1] *Social regulations are normative:* Society is distinct from physical reality in that the laws which sustain it are, at least in part, *prescriptive* or *normative.* Unlike the laws of the physical world, they can be disobeyed and they can be changed. They lack the inexorable character of natural laws. It is true that they have their roots in human nature, in man's organic being, in the human need and the abiding awareness of society, in the likeness or conformity to type that characterizes man and therefore his behavior. But the rules themselves are subject to change, since the needs and desires of men are never constant but always seek and find new forms of expression.

The regulative principles of society are standards set up by a group for the control of the conduct of its members, in relation to one another and to the group as a whole. This does not mean that they are merely *imposed* on men, either by their rulers or leaders or by their own past. They are not like the laws that a master makes for a slave or like those an empire makes for a subjugated people. For the most part, they are the ways in which the group as a whole has become accommodated to the necessities and to the amenities of social life, as recognized at its own level of intelligence, education, and opportunity. The regulative principles are, to be sure, inherited from the past, but for the most part only in so far as the group in general accepts the inheritance. They are changed in the present as the group grows conscious of the need for change.

[2] *Social regulations are relative and partial:* Social codes differ from natural laws in another respect. They carry with them a sense of obligation. They are addressed to the feelings and to the reason of those they govern. And they constantly run counter to the inclinations of many individuals. The folkways and mores reveal the solidarity of the group, but the solidarity is never complete. For the self-centered or *like* interest of individuals is always running counter to the general or *common* interest. And the interest of the small group, such as the family or the club, often runs counter to some demands of the larger group, such as the community or class. The social norms of conduct are often too restrictive for the self-seeking. On the other hand, many of the regulations are framed in the interest of dominant groups or classes and are resisted by other groups. The prescriptions of the social codes are never all equally accepted or equally obeyed.

Codes and sanctions. The folkways and mores represent the *norms* or *modes* of procedure in a society or in a group—they present to us the most frequent or most accepted or most standardized ways of doing this or that. They are also, as we have seen, regulative, exerting pressure upon individual and group to conform to the norms. In both of these roles the social regulations fall into certain systems or *codes*. In modern society we are usually most aware of the legal code, but underneath it, and in large measure sustaining it, lie codes of a different order, such as the codes of custom and of religion.

[1] *The relation of codes and sanctions:* The various social codes are all alike in one important respect. For their prescriptions are all subject to violation, and therefore they are all guarded by special provisions, or *sanctions*, calculated to counteract the tendency to disobedience. This is no less true of primitive custom-ruled peoples than of modern ones.[2] In no situation is there unswerving automatic obedience. In every instance the group sustains the code by the exercise of some degree of pressure on the individual violator.

The term "sanction" may be applied to specific rewards attached to conformity. The "praise" mechanism in social control is well known to us all, and is found no less perhaps in the adult world than in child training as a device to elicit behavior in accordance with the social norms. However, "sanction" more generally and more properly refers to the specific penalty attached by society to the violation of the code. Sometimes the sanction is the denial of privileges or the cancellation of rights; sometimes it is the imposition of a fine, or, in the case of the legal code, the loss of liberty or even of life. Each type of code has its own form of sanction, and the major social codes vary considerably from each other in type of prescription, as we shall see in greater detail in the following chapter.

[2] *Social sanctions and individual motives:* Students of sociology should carefully distinguish between the sanction of the social code and the grounds of obedience. For the social sanction is one ground of obedience, one pressure felt by the individual, but it is only one of several. Often it is not even the main ground. The members of a medical or a legal association do not conform to their respective codes *merely* because otherwise they would lose their right to practice. The members of a club do not obey its rules *only* because of fear of expulsion. Nor do people generally obey the legal code *just* because they are afraid of the policeman. People conform to a social code also because they think it right to do so, or because they have become habituated to it so that obedience is the line of least resistance, or because they wish to stand well with their fellows, or because it serves their interests, or for other reasons. The *motives* of the individual are always manifold and mixed and hard to disentangle, as the difficult problems of the psychiatrist indicate. They vary endlessly from person to person, from situation to situation. Sanctions, on the contrary, are definite and relatively simple. Motives are always individualized, sanctions are social. If, for example, people generally in our society feel obliged to prac-

2. B. Malinowski, *Crime and Custom in Savage Society* (New York, 1926), Part I.

tice monogamy, we can attribute this practice to recognizable codes and sanctions that are a part of our social heritage; but the reasons for the particular monogamous choice of any one of us lie in the realm of individual motivation.

This distinction must be kept in mind in any discussion of the regulative principles of society. We shall classify these principles with respect to their social sanctions. But we must always remember that, in the complicated play of motives which underlies human conduct, the sanction is not so much an explanation of conduct as a reinforcement of those promptings to conformity which otherwise would be overborne by the strength of opposing tendencies in an individual situation.

[3] *Types of codes and sanctions:* Every community and every type of organized group or association imposes rules on its members. In a modern complex community these rules are of diverse kinds and their sanctions are highly differentiated.

ONE: ASSOCIATIONAL CODES. The rules of a club are sanctioned by the loss of membership or some privileges of membership or by a fine imposed for violation as a condition of retaining membership or by the loss of esteem or status within the club. These, in fact, are the general sanctions of all "voluntary" organizations, though sometimes the rules of the organization are supported by sanctions of a more absolute nature. The workman who disobeys the regulations of management or of the union in his factory may lose not only his position but his livelihood. The believer who offends against the code of his church may suffer excommunication involving for him the loss of spiritual consolations and perhaps the sense of the displeasure of the deity. The doctor or lawyer who seriously violates the code of his calling may lose his license, though in such instances the additional sanction of the legal code is necessary.

TWO: COMMUNAL CODES. Codes that are generally regulative in the community but are not associated with special-interest groups, communal codes, have less specific but often no less important sanctions. The rule of *custom* is sanctioned only by some degree of social displeasure or ostracism, but this, in its extremer forms, is one of the most powerful sanctions that exists. The rule of *fashion* is guarded by a milder form of the same sanctions, the sense of superiority or contempt felt toward those who do not conform to the code. A very effective safeguard of fashion and generally of *convention* is the ridicule bestowed on the violator, what has been called the "satire sanction,"[3] since the fear of being laughed at is deeply rooted in our reactions. The communal codes also receive strong support, as we all know, from the mechanism of gossip, which generally functions to prevent our deviations from convention from becoming too flagrant or too frequent.

3. R. Maunier, *Introduction à la Sociologie*, Chap. II. For another discussion of ridicule as a social control device, see P. Walters, Jr., "Non-violent Means of Social Control," in Roucek's *Social Control*, pp. 320 ff.

THREE: THE MORAL CODE. This code is in an ambiguous situation as regards sanction, but only because the term "morals," or "moral laws," is used confusedly in two different senses. Sometimes it means those rules of conduct which are held by the group or community to be right and proper and which they impose on deviating members by various degrees of the same sanctions which are the guardians of custom in general. In this sense morals are simply those customs the violation of which is regarded in the community as definitely wrong—in a word, they are the *mores*. But in the stricter sense the moral code is that body of rules which the individual "conscience" upholds as constituting right or good conduct. Here there appears, sometimes in harmony with, and sometimes in opposition to, the social sanction, an inner and personal sanction, the feeling of guilt entailed by violation. The physician who destroys a monstrously deformed baby, for example, may violate the community's moral code and perhaps the legal code, but he remains true to his own moral convictions. There are countless examples of the opposition between the moral code of the group and that of the individual.

It is true, however, that for most of our daily occasions mores are nearly synonymous with morals. Were this not so the concept of group mores would have no application. What we regularly do in conformity with usage—or what usage prescribes even when we disobey it—is felt as the proper or morally right thing to do. If we live in a group where early rising or monogamy is the rule, then early rising or monogamy is *ipso facto* a virtue. But the crucial instances are those in which the individual, as our physician above, feels a moral obligation contrary to the prescriptions of the group. Then we must distinguish the moral code in its stricter sense from the social code in question. Moral codes vary from person to person, but the mores characterize the group or the community.

FOUR: THE LEGAL CODE. Finally there is one code, and in modern countries one only, which has the ultimate sanction of *physical enforcement*, of unconditional fine, imprisonment, or death. This is the legal code of the state. In a quite limited sense the code of the family may be upheld, with respect to the more juvenile offenders against it, by some exercise of force, and similarly the codes of such other groups as the school, the juvenile gang, and the college fraternity. In some countries also there remain vestiges of the right by which the church through its own courts administered and executed its own law. But in modern states these qualified rights, where they exist at all, exist only by the tolerance and permission of the state, within and under the conditions which the state imposes. In the last resort only the law of the state owns the sanction of force, as we shall see when we consider the nature of the political associations in Chapter XVIII.

[4] *The differentiation of codes and sanctions in modern society:* In primitive society the distinctions we have made between types of social code and between code and sanction were not developed. There were no legal codes, no religious

codes, no economic codes, formally set apart from one another, independently instituted and sanctioned, under the guardianship of separate organizations, and generally distinguished from the norms and customs of the kinship group. Developed still less were the distinctions we draw within these various codes, such as that between civil and criminal law.[4]

The number and variety of the social codes generally correspond to the complexity of the society. In modern civilization the code of the state maintains the general framework of social order, but it is supplemented by many other codes of a more flexible nature. There are, for example, many varieties of economic code, from the definite rules of a workshop or a trade-union to the vaguer codes of business ethics. There are codes of professional etiquette and professional honor, codes of family life, codes of informal cliques of cronies and of play groups. There are codes even of the violaters of codes evidenced in the rules of the gang, the rules established by prison inmates, or the standards set up by the "Bohemian" colonies of the Left Bank or Greenwich Village. And all of these have their own sanctions.

Thus the classification of social codes and sanctions we offer in Chart IV is by no means exhaustive. However, the chart suggests not only the developed differentiation of codes in modern society but the complex interrelationships between regulation and sanction and between these and the specific processes of social control that operate in our daily lives. We may now consider these various processes and devices.

Processes and Devices That Perpetuate the Mores

Loyalties: the role of indoctrination and habituation. No social order could long endure if it depended merely on the sanctions of the codes. Unless the codes were more deeply rooted in the group over whom they hold sway they would soon prove unavailing. This we shall see more fully when we consider, in the next section, the question of coercion and the social order. Behind the sanctions and behind the more superficial considerations that may persuade men to conformity there are loyalties and convictions. While these loyalties and convictions are basically a manifestation of the sociality of men wherever human

4. This view, generally held by students of primitive society, has been in part challenged by Malinowski in his *Crime and Custom in Savage Society*, where he shows that the Trobriand Islanders make distinctions between fundamental rules dealing with life, property, and kinship structure, on the one side, and rules of religion, ceremony, and etiquette, on the other. However, nothing approaching the modern differentiation of codes and sanctions exists among the Trobriand Islanders or other primitive groups. For evaluations of Malinowski's findings in this respect, see R. M. MacIver, *Society: A Textbook of Sociology* (New York, 1937), pp. 332–333; and K. N. Llewellyn and E. A. Hoebel, *The Cheyenne Way* (Norman, Okla., 1941), pp. 60, 229, 339.

CHART IV **Codes and Sanctions**

SOCIAL BASIS	CODE	SPECIFIC SANCTIONS
I *Formed in Large-scale Associations*		
State	(a) Criminal Code (b) Civil Code	Physical enforcement through (a) fine, imprisonment, death (b) exaction of damages or restitution
The Church	Religious Code	Excommunication, penance, loss of privileges, fear of displeasure of deity
Professional Organizations	Occupational Codes	Exclusion from membership, denial of right to practice (with aid of legal code)
II *Primary Groups or Face-to-Face Associations*		
The Family	Familial Code	Parental punishment, disinheritance, loss of privileges
The Club	Rules and Regulations	Denial of membership, loss of privileges
The Gang	Code of the "Underworld"	Death and other forms of violence
III *The Community*	Custom, fashion, convention, etiquette	Social ostracism, loss of standing, ridicule
IV *Social Relationships in General*	The Moral Code (individualized)	Sense of guilt or abasement

society is found, they show an extreme range of variation for different groups or for different circumstances. The *particular* loyalties and faiths of men are clearly not inborn, but the result of their social conditioning. They are not like the instinct-bound codes of bees or ants.

No more convincing evidence of this fact can be found than the remarkable diversity of the group codes concerning sex relationships. The powerful impulse of sex, which we have every reason to assume to be basically alike in the physical endowment of different social groups, is nevertheless subjected to the most variant and even the most contradictory codes, each seemingly "natural" to the groups adhering to it though it may be abhorrent to others. As we have already seen, similarly wide variations are found from group to group in the mores governing marriage and courtship, disposal of the dead, property arrangements, child training, and many other institutionalized aspects of social life. Little wonder that a famous ancient Greek traveler and historian summed up the matter by saying that "custom is the king of men."[5]

What concerns us here is to explain why there are such variations in the loyalties and convictions, and consequently in the codes of different peoples. We are considering particularly the manner in which the mores, and thus the social structure, are sustained through all their variations from time to time and from place to place. There are certain molding forces always at work in every society; we shall view first the two great processes of indoctrination and habituation.

[1] *Social indoctrination:* Social indoctrination refers to the inculcation of modes of thought and patterns of belief. Under all conditions this process is the most powerful of all regulative influences. One need think only of the incessant inculcation of "right" modes of conduct made on the child from infancy by parents and by teachers and by comrades. In this formative period the physiological and mental aspects of habit, the ways of acting and the ways of thinking, are most thoroughly and intimately unified. A child may resist the specific commands of his elders, but he cannot resist the system from which they emanate. He knows no other with which to compare it—it fills his whole horizon. It is conveyed in the very language he learns and hears, with its idioms and emotionally charged expressions, so that he cannot speak or think except in the accents of the group approval or disapproval.

In our discussion of "culture and personality" in Chapter III, we noted the manner in which the mores of each culture become "interiorized" in the individual's personality structure, creating in each group common tendencies in disposition and character as well as common beliefs and values. To a very large extent, the indoctrination of the child, whether in primitive or modern complex society, occurs within the circle of the primary family group. The family's role, then, in sustaining the whole social structure can hardly be overestimated.

However, the larger group loyalties are inculcated also by more highly organized means. The church has recognized from of old the great importance of early training in its precepts and beliefs, and for some centuries was the principal agent in the formal education of the young. The state gradually took over this function in modern countries, but there is still here and there (including the United States[6]) a struggle between church and state as to which shall be the dominant influence in the education of youth. For education, especially in the earlier stages, is in large part indoctrination.

This fact is very evident whenever the proponents of a new or different social

5. Herodotus, *Histories*, iii, Chap. 38. Herodotus remarked that "if it were proposed to all nations to choose which of all customs seemed best to them, each would, after examination made, place its own first."

6. As reflected in the current conflict concerning the right of religious denominational schools to share with public schools local state services such as free transportation for school children.

order come to power. They realize quickly that the order they are establishing cannot take root and endure unless, by persistent education and propaganda, they can mold the minds of the people to the desired pattern of loyalty and conviction. Often they try to repress all unfavorable opinions so that all minds, like those of young children, shall be subject to no contrary influences. And they take particular care that the children themselves are thoroughly indoctrinated—the schoolbooks are rewritten, the curriculum is remolded, and the teaching is selected to this end. In the "totalitarian" nations, special organizations outside the school have been created to stir the imagination and further indoctrinate the young, such as the "Young Communists" in Russia and the "Hitler Youth" in the late Nazi Germany and the "Balilla" and "Avanguardisti" in former Fascist Italy.[7] The "new orders" of Italy and Germany have been smashed in military defeat, to be sure, but that the tight educational controls produced sought-for results is evidenced today by the persistence of Fascist values among the youth brought up under those regimes. Soviet Russia, again, has for some thirty years indoctrinated her youth in keeping with the principles of the Communist party, resulting in a general acceptance of the officially espoused values and a relative stability of the entire social structure.

The attempt to control formal education and other agencies of social indoctrination is not confined, of course, to dictatorial regimes. In our own society organizations such as large-scale business associations and local chambers of commerce and veterans' groups and "patriotic" societies have from time to time sought to influence the selection of textbooks or of teaching personnel or even of subjects themselves.[8] However obnoxious such practices may be, they illustrate the significance generally attached to education as a molder of convictions and loyalties and fundamental values.

[2] *Habituation:* Closely allied to and supporting indoctrination is habituation. While indoctrination imposes opinions and beliefs by the direct method of communication and instruction, habituation is the process in which people *unconsciously* adapt their ways of thought to the social conditions under which they live. Men inadvertently take the cast of their surroundings. Apart from what they are expressly taught to believe, they frame ideas of right and wrong in accordance with the use and want of everyday life. What is familiar often comes to appear as both inevitable and good; what is unfamiliar often seems alien or evil. Native impulses are canalized along lines determined by routine. Once habits are formed they tend to breed or to confirm corresponding thoughts. Thus the businessman habituated in the ways of the market may come to

7. Among the many volumes describing the indoctrination process in dictatorial states are H. R. Marraro, *The New Education in Italy* (New York, 1936); F. Brennecke, *The Nazi Primer* (New York, 1938); G. F. Kneller, *The Educational Philosophy of National Socialism* (New Haven, 1941); G. A. Zimmer, *Education for Death* (New York, 1941).

8. The voluminous reports of such activities are discussed in several of the chapters of *Twentieth Century American Education* (P. F. Valentine, ed., New York, 1946).

believe that economic competition is a part of universal human nature; the professional criminal living in a world of suspicion and dishonesty and chicanery may come to assign these qualities fundamental importance in all human motivation; the overprotected child of a family of comfortable means may come to think that all decent folk are mannerly and share the conventions of his own milieu. Habituation works continuously and subtly until belief and opinion are registered in the mental and emotional structure of the human being.

In this way habituation comes to the aid of indoctrination. Through indoctrination and habituation men achieve a sense of solidarity and a feeling of attachment to a particular social order and the codes that regulate it. Indeed, if these processes did not provide men their loyalties and allegiances and convictions there could not exist the great groupings of mankind into communities and classes and that smaller but no less significant group, the family. The attachment to these groups is strengthened by various special factors associated with the interwoven processes of indoctrination and habituation. If a developed social structure is inconceivable without the underlying support of indoctrination and habituation, these processes in turn cannot function save in association with authority and leadership of some kind. At this point we may examine these two phenomena in so far as they bear directly on our main concern, the mores and social control.

The personal techniques of authority and leadership. We draw a distinction here between authority and personal leadership. By *authority* we mean here the right of control attached to *office*, involving the respect, the submission, or the reverence accorded to those who represent the office or are invested with its rights. Here we are not concerned with the authority of a group or of an impersonal principle or ideal or legal code; but rather with authority as it is vested in or focused in a *person*, in his official capacity or field of knowledge or specialization.[9] By *leadership* we mean the capacity to persuade or to direct men that comes from *personal* qualities apart from office. These two types of control are often combined in various degrees. Authority inheres in those who represent or embody the codes, such as the local clergyman or town clerk in the village community, or in those who possess rank or status or any prestige derived from position or wealth; but it is always enhanced if qualities of leadership go along with the prerogatives of station or office. Not infrequently a forceful personal leader consolidates his power by attaining official position. But the two *sources* of power are themselves distinct. A policeman represents authority, not leadership. So does a judge, and so does a king, in so far as his power depends on the reverence or prestige attached to his position. A leader, on the other hand, may be an insurgent against the established order.

9. Simmel classifies the types of personal and group and impersonal authority. See N. J. Spykman, *Social Theory of Georg Simmel* (Chicago, 1925), pp. 97–108. Other writers contrast the authority of the personal sovereign and the impersonal law. We are here speaking of the personal varieties.

[1] *Implications of the authority of office:* Authority takes a multitude of forms and inheres in all social organization. In its crudest and least socialized aspects it acts merely as enforcement. This is the authority of the master over the slave, of the despot over the subject, of the magistrate over the criminal. Here authority may depend solely on the sanction which it controls. But nearly all forms of authority involve in addition an attitude of responsiveness and of deference, an admission of subordination on the part of the subject which in turn helps to create as well as to justify the authority itself.

The grounds of this voluntary subordination are diverse. Acceptance of authority may be the tribute paid to age or to wealth. It reflects certainly the respect for order or station or class, conveyed to the holder or representative of it. Authority may appear as the impersonal embodiment of position, just as the majesty of kingship is personalized in a king apart from whatever attributes of his own he may possess. Tradition and religion may weave a spell about the person who upholds the order to which they belong. Indeed every *system* of authority, whether that of the paterfamilias or of the religious priesthood or of the political order, is rooted in "the myth of authority" itself—a part of the social heritage of all peoples.[10] Authority is also sustained by self-interested motives, submission often being fostered by the anticipation of the rewards which the authority, such as the political officeholder or party boss, can bestow on his friends and followers.

Acceptance is based to a large extent in modern society on the recognition that authority is necessary if the tasks of everyday life are to be performed effectively. For in our complex world of today, with its gigantic structure of economic and political and social service and educational and other agencies, with its elaborate differentiation of tasks and manifold hierarchies of administrative positions and responsibilities, each officeholder fulfills some function, often an essential function, in the business of day-to-day living. And these offices together with their functions and their prerogatives add up to the complex bureaucratic structures that mark the great economic and political and military associations of modern life. Each "bureaucrat"—whether a head of a governmental department or petty official, whether a manager of a large industry or a foreman, whether a general or a sergeant—has his own group of clients whom he serves and for whom his authority seems essential in the whole scheme of daily procedure. A chief mark of our times is the degree to which the disposition of authority is carefully planned and diffused throughout the formalized social organizations. This is both a potent force in maintaining authority itself and a strong support of the mores that sustain the institutional order.[11]

---

10. On "the myth of authority" see R. M. MacIver, *The Web of Government* (New York, 1947), Chap. III.

11. We shall discuss at greater length other aspects of bureaucracy in Chapter X. Max Weber's contribution to this subject is basic in sociological literature; see *From Max Weber: Essays in Sociology* (H. H. Gerth and C. Wright Mills, tr. and ed., New York, 1946), Chap. VIII. See also R. K. Merton, "Bureaucratic Structure and Personality," *Social Forces,*

[2] *Personal leadership:* Unlike the authority of office, personal leadership depends on the prowess, reputation, skill, oratory, or other attributes of the leader. He may be on the side of established authority or he may be opposed to it, seeking to create a new type of authority. He may stand for a definite policy or set of principles or he may be an opportunist, like some party "bosses" or the "strong-man" leaders in certain countries where political parties are named after the leaders they follow and not after the principles they profess. He may be blindly followed, or he may depend on his power to rally men to the banner of some cause. He may be little more than the delegate or simply the mouthpiece of some interest group, though in this case leadership is next to the vanishing point.

When the leader acts within the established system he adds to authority a new appeal; he interprets it afresh and gives it a new vitality—recall the rush of "new blood" to governmental positions and the enormous enthusiasm among the new officeholders in the early days of the "New Deal." And when an established system breaks, the rupture is always immediately caused by a leader who organizes the forces of dissatisfaction and gives them unity and direction. Little wonder that the German sociologist Simmel calls the relation between leaders and followers the most important of all social relationships.[12]

For leadership in some degree and form is present wherever men assemble. Many occupants of office, as we have seen, are also leaders, thereby enhancing their power and decreasing the power of others. But "natural leaders," as the term is generally used, are found throughout the informal organizations of men as well as their formalized groups. Each gang has its leader or leaders, as have each play group and clique and neighborhood. As is known by every alert supervisor of schools, prisons, factories, or military groups, and as certain sociologists today take elaborate pains to demonstrate, there develops in any such organization an "informal structure" of social relationships that pushes upward the natural leaders, whatever their official status, and thrusts into the background the "rejected types," as defined by the attitudes and behavior of their fellows. More often than not, these unofficial group arrangements serve the function of circumventing the formal requirements of the organizations, thereby rendering them more flexible and adjustable and perhaps giving them a permanence they would not otherwise possess. When the sociology of leadership is more complete than it is today, the role of the natural leader of the informal group will very likely have a higher place in its considerations.[13]

XVIII (1940), 561-568; C. H. Page, "Bureaucracy's Other Face," *ibid.*, XXV (1946), 88-94; P. Selznick, "An Approach to a Theory of Bureaucracy," *American Sociological Review*, VIII (1943), 47-54.

12. Spykman, *op. cit.* On this subject see also F. Znaniecki, *Social Actions* (New York, 1936), pp. 182 ff. For an interesting analysis of the role of the leader in social change, a subject we shall reach in Book Three, see S. Hook, *The Hero in History* (New York, 1941)

13. The role of the "informal structure" in industrial organization is a favorite concern of such writers as C. I. Barnard, Elton Mayo, F. J. Roethlisberger, and A. N. Whitehead, whose

[3] *A note on "charismatic leadership":* We are indebted to the German sociologist Max Weber for a penetrating analysis of an extreme but important type of "natural" leadership. Weber used the Greek word, *charisma*, meaning a special gift of power restricted to a select few, to designate that quality of certain leaders whose authority is based on the popular conviction that they are divinely inspired and directed in their public undertakings.[14] He distinguished between the power of the officeholder, the "rational" authority that permeates the large-scale bureaucracies of the modern world, and *charismatic leadership*, which plays a more important role in human affairs "the further we look back in history." "The 'natural' leaders—in times of psychic, physical, economic, ethical, religious, political distress—have been neither officeholders nor incumbents of an 'occupation' in the present sense of the word, that is, men who have acquired expert knowledge and who serve for remuneration."[15] They have been, like many of the great religious leaders and like Julius Caesar and Cromwell and Napoleon, men of "destiny," convinced of their own "right" and ability to lead, and sharing this conviction with their followers—the "deliverers" or "saviors," the "revealers," and usually the exponents par excellence of the mass emotions of group solidarity.

The rise to power in our times of men like Mussolini and Hitler indicates that crisis and historical opportunity continue to bring to the fore leaders of the charismatic type. The charismatic qualities are less pronounced, perhaps, in the case of Stalin, whose person symbolizes the official doctrines of Soviet Communism rather than his own special attributes. Our own country provides examples of charismatic leaders—consider the public career of the late Huey Long or of the relationship between Father Divine and his "Angels."[16] These illustrations suggest that the "natural" leader (whether or not we endow him with "charisma") functions in a dual capacity with respect to the mores of his group. He may lead in the name of traditional values and customs, thereby serving to perpetuate and strengthen parts of the social heritage. But he may also, as in the case of Lenin or of Hitler, use his power of leadership to destroy or vastly alter the mores and institutional structure of his time.

The impersonal techniques of ritual and ceremony. We turn next to the principal *impersonal* influences that bind men to the mores. Each established social order and every subsociety within it is sustained in part by ritual and ceremony.

---

findings we shall examine in Chapter X. See, for example, C. I. Barnard, *The Functions of the Executive* (Cambridge, Mass., 1939); F. J. Roethlisberger, *Management and Morale* (Cambridge, Mass., 1941). For a discussion of informal leadership in an urban, working-class district, see W. F. Whyte, *Street Corner Society* (Chicago, 1943); and in a military organization, Page, *op. cit.*

14. See *From Max Weber: Essays in Sociology*, Chap. IX.

15. *Ibid.*, p. 243.

16. For a discussion of "Recent Types of Charismatic Leadership," see E. Manheim in Roucek's *Social Control*, Chap. XXIX.

[1] *Ritual:* By ritual we mean a formal *rhythmic procedure* controlling a succession of acts directed to the *same end* and *repeated* without variation on the appropriate occasions. Ritual is distinguished from mere habit or routine in that it is accompanied by a peculiar sense of rightness and inevitability. To deviate from it in any way, no matter what the circumstances, is felt to be wrong or undesirable, not on utilitarian grounds, but because deviation breaks the rhythm, disturbing the emotional response, the solemn and often "mystical" rapport between the person and the occasion.

Ritual may be merely personal or it may have a group character. It may, for example, be associated with the act of dressing in the morning or with other routines of daily existence. However, these individualized routines become *ritualized habit* only when the act in question assumes an emotional or compulsive character—I *must* have my coffee immediately upon awakening, or the lawn *must* be mowed Friday. We observe *social rituals* on almost all group levels —the act of public worship, the insistence among a clique of friends that they play "*the* game" at certain gatherings, the solemn business of a college fraternity's formal initiation that usually follows the high jinks of the informal, the singing of the national anthem at various public events, and so on. Ritual is most powerful when the propriety of the procedure is firmly established in the mores of the group. Almost all societies invest those great rhythmic occurrences of the life cycle, birth and marriage and death, with the rhythm of ritual itself. Similarly primitive and ancient peoples have devised rituals with which to observe important yearly events of economic significance, the planting of crops, the harvest, the successful hunt.[17] The observance of these occasions usually takes on a religious character, as illustrated in their modern equivalents such as Christmas and Easter. Every person who as a child searched his stocking on Christmas morning knows that the peculiarly ritualistic significance remains.

Ritual invests an occasion with importance or solemnity and thus combats the process by which often-repeated acts become tedious and commonplace. Hence its significant place in religious usage, and in such public or private celebrations as are thought to demand an attitude of special dignity or reverence. Ritual is thus seen at its best in a church service, in judicial proceedings, at court functions. Hence also its frequent use to maintain a level of dignity in such groups as lodges, fraternities, and clubs, where, without it, the normal familiarity of the members with one another would dissipate the importance they wish to attach to certain occasions.[18] The inviolable rhythm of ritual evokes its own emotional responses, and because each successive act is predetermined and known in advance, each tends to evoke the emotional quality of the whole procedure. To the outsider who does not share the interest or the

---

17. For a study of agricultural rites and rituals among the Trobriand Islanders, see B. Malinowski, *Coral Gardens and Their Magic* (2 vols., New York, 1935).

18. Good illustrations of this function of ritual are contained in N. P. Gist, *Secret Societies: A Cultural Study of Fraternalism in the United States* (Columbia, Mo., 1940), Chap. VII.

belief of the participating group, ritual is apt on that very account to appear ridiculous, because he feels no adequate justification for the solemnity or exaltation which it demands.

[2] *Ceremony:* Ritual, so understood, is the core of and is often identified with *ceremony*. Ceremony, however, is a somewhat more comprehensive concept within which ritual falls. For ceremony means *any* established procedure of a formal and dignified nature designed to make and impress the importance of an event or occasion. It does not necessarily imply the rhythmic precision and undeviating repetition of ritual, though ritual is the distinctive element of most ceremonies. We may ceremonialize once and for all, for example, the return of a hero who has swum the English Channel or flown across the sea, but the ceremony itself may involve the ritualistic procedure of greeting him with paper tossed from the windows of lower Manhattan. From of old, ceremony has been recognized as a powerful means of sustaining the social order. Ceremony is "the bond that holds the multitude together, and if the bond be removed, these multitudes fall into confusion."[19] Ceremony proclaims the elevation and fixity of the social order, establishing distance and priority lest familiarity breed criticism and lack of respect, while the ritual within it works more subtly on the feelings of men, inculcating reverential attitudes toward the principles which it embodies.

Ceremony is the dignified garb with which social functions are invested. It has therefore more influence on the unreflecting than on the critically minded, and thus in an age of criticism is liable to lose its hold. The critic, discerning the disparity between ceremonial appearance and underlying reality is apt to agree with Carlyle that "society is founded upon cloth" and is apt to imagine with him:

> Often in my atrabiliar moods, when I read of pompous ceremonials, Frankfort Coronations, Royal Drawing-rooms, Levees, Couchees: and how the ushers and macers and pursuivants are all in waiting; how Duke this is presented by Archduke that, and Colonel A by General B, and innumerable Bishops, Admirals, and miscellaneous Functionaries are advancing gallantly to the Anointed Presence; and I strive, in my remote privacy, to form a clear picture of that solemnity—the Clothes fly-off the whole dramatic corps; the Dukes, Grandees, Bishops, Generals, Anointed Presence itself, every mother's son of them, stand straddling there, not a shirt on them; and I know not whether to laugh or to weep.[20]

Perhaps profounder speculation, however, distinguishes between the hollow ceremony that seeks to conceal the fraud or pretense within it and the ceremony which gives an essential symbolic and external from to our social valuations. Certainly all established orders ceremonialize their important occasions, whether the celebration welcoming the return of spring among the ancient agrarian peoples

19. Sacred books of the East, *Li Ki*, Book VIII, I, quoted by Ross, *op. cit.*, Chap. XIX.
20. Thomas Carlyle, *Sartor Resartus*, Chaps. VIII and IX.

or that welcoming the return of peace after war among ourselves, whether the meticulous pomp of the Tsarist rulers of old Russia or the equally ritualistic and ceremonious parades and celebrations of the current Soviet regime.

[3] *Some factors sustaining ritual and ceremony:* Why ritual and ceremony should play so important a role in human affairs is an intriguing question of social psychology. Here we may suggest a few of the sustaining factors.

ONE: THE IMPERSONAL FACTOR. In the first place, formal procedure invests an occasion or an event with an impersonal dignity or solemnity, unmarred by the intrusion of the particular and limiting individuality of the performers. This contrast is often noticeable in religious ceremonies when the impersonal ritual ends and the voice of the preacher begins. In the Army and Navy, enlisted men are taught that they salute the uniform or rank, not the individual—a clear case of rendering the ritual as impersonal as possible. Considering that ritual and ceremony permeate the entire social order, their general neutrality with respect to individual personalities tends to support both the formal procedures and the social order itself.

TWO: MAN'S DEPENDENCE ON MYTHS AS A FACTOR. Every social order is held together by a system of *myths*, a term we use to designate "the value-impregnated beliefs and notions that men hold, that they live by or live for."[21] No society can maintain a degree of stability unless the myths upon which it rests —the myth of law, of power, of freedom, and so on—remain as fundamental values for man. Here ritual plays an important role. For in the constantly repeated ritual, the effortless association of ideas instills a sense of rightness as well as of inevitability. The rhythm of the procedure attunes the individual emotionally to the corresponding ideas. Ritual and ceremony impress without explaining, without reasoning. They convey a feeling of larger realities, of faiths, of unities, of social establishments, of the myths themselves, which can never be fully experienced or wholly comprehended by individuals. "The Church," "the State," "the Law," and "God" are distant abstractions, but the rites of the church, the coronation of the king, the inauguration of the president, the protocol of the court of law, the orderly procession at the grave or wedding, seem to bring near to men, even to embody the essence of, these invisible things.

THREE: THE FACTOR OF UTILITY. Apart from the emotional and compulsive aspects of ritual and ceremony, a solution for many of man's everyday problems is provided by these established formalities. What to do when one's daughter becomes married? How to acknowledge a fellow citizen's unusual accomplishments? How to deport oneself at a funeral (whatever the inward feelings toward the deceased or toward funerals themselves)? For these and countless other occasions and events, ceremony and ritual provide the answers. Indeed, however aloof or critical or cynical we may be concerning these processes that per-

21. MacIver, *The Web of Government*, p. 4. See Chap. I of this volume for a discussion of myths.

petuate the mores, we cannot dispense with them. For their persistence is based not only upon utility but upon the very nature of social life.

Symbols and social unity. Indoctrination and habituation could not take place, leadership and authority would be at a loss, ritual and ceremony would be rendered meaningless, were it not that social man has the ability to create and to use *symbols*. A symbol is a representation of a meaning or a value, an external sign or gesture which by association conveys an idea or stimulates a feeling. All communication, whether through language or otherwise, makes use of symbols. Society could scarcely exist without them. Here we can only touch upon certain aspects of the relation between symbols and society, though this problem is implicit in any discussion of social reality.[22]

The unity of a group, like all its cultural values, must find symbolic expression. In many primitive societies the identification of the symbol and the thing symbolized (a common "semantic failing" in *all* societies) is often so complete that the symbol becomes a *totem* and is regarded as an objective embodiment, no mere representation, of the spirit or solidarity of the group. The totem, whether eagle or bull or serpent or whatever it be, *means* the group, thus giving concrete identification to its invisible unity. The symbol is at once a definite focus of interest, a means of communication, and a common ground of understanding. The flag is a symbol of the nation, a visible emblem which is the same for all its members. It has a different significance for the educated and ignorant, for the lover of peace and the militarist, for the conservative and the radical, but it is a common rallying point for all who accept it. This is a peculiar property of the cultural symbol, that it admits of variant interpretations and yet excites in many minds a like devotion.

This fact helps to explain the role of symbolism in the more mystical forms of religion. Their rituals are saturated with symbolism, and the symbols, because their meaning depends essentially on acquired associations, can often be freely reinterpreted to suit the changing demands of the age. This is probably one reason why the Roman Catholic religion, with its strong ritualistic character, does not disrupt into sects as do the Protestant faiths, and why the Catholic, faced with the questions of modern science, is apt to become a "modernist" rather than "unbeliever."[23] The history of the Catholic Church is, in fact, an excellent example of the extent to which a highly ritualized and symbolic creed can retain its unity in the face of quite varying social conditions. In the rural

22. There is a large literature on symbols, semantics, and society. The interested student may consult the bibliography in Roucek's *Social Control*, Chap. XIV; this chapter, "Language and Semantics" by E. T. Arneson, suggests the sociological significance of symbols. For an excellent brief discussion, see E. Sapir, "Symbolism" in the *Encyclopaedia of the Social Sciences* (New York, 1935), XIV, 492–495.

23. Cf. L. S. Cressman, "Ritual the Conserver," *American Journal of Sociology*, XXXV (1930), 564–572.

as well as the urban sections of Europe and America, in Latin America and the Philippines, the objective symbols and rituals of Catholicism are the same, but their interpretations and the manner in which they take on the local traditions and values vary greatly from place to place.[24]

Ritual and symbolism together bring strong reinforcement to the established social codes. Many symbols are, in fact, "morale symbols," suggesting and conveying the sense of group unity or *esprit de corps*.[25] This is the main function of symbols employed in rites of initiation; in the rituals of lodges and fraternal orders and trade-unions; in the badges, ornaments, pins, keys, tokens, pennants, gestures, formulas, and other signs which convey to the "brethren" the sense of exclusive membership in a mystical unity.[26] It is an important part of the business of leadership to make effective use of these symbols, to interpret or reinterpret them, and thus to rally the members in a stronger cohesion and devotion to the common cause of the group. Any organized group, be it a juvenile gang or a political party or a club or a union or an alumni association or a circle of revolutionary conspirators, if it is to develop or maintain unity and strength, must, formally or informally, devise its own symbols and rituals and indoctrinate its members with their meaning and potency. And on a larger scale, throughout the broad social structure, symbols play a vital role (and one that is frequently overlooked) in maintaining the group mores and the social structure itself.[27]

Coercion and the Social Order

Meaning and forms of coercion. In the previous section we dealt with certain conditions that support and consolidate every social system, helping to make men responsive and devoted to it. These conditions were seen to be the more potent determinants of the loyalties and convictions without which the social codes, no matter how sanctioned, could not endure. We may now ask, what part do the sanctions themselves play in social control?

[1] *Coercion defined:* The sanctions bring pressure to bear on men *apart from* their loyalties and convictions. In the last resort, in the form of law, the pressure becomes direct enforcement. In every society there exist many degrees and

24. See, for example, the discussion of Catholicism in Mexico in F. S. C. Northrop, *The Meeting of East and West* (New York, 1946), Chap. II, and his more general discussion in Chap. VII.

25. This is well brought out by Grace Coyle, *The Social Process in Organized Groups* (New York, 1930), Chap. VII.

26. See Gist, *op. cit.*, Chap. VIII, for excellent illustrations in secret societies.

27. The role of symbols in social control is discussed in some of its aspects in the writings of H. D. Lasswell and Thurman Arnold. See, for example, Lasswell's *Politics: Who Gets What, When, How* (New York, 1936), especially Chap. II; and Arnold's *The Symbols of Government* (New Haven, 1935) and *The Folklore of Capitalism* (New Haven, 1937).

forms of coercion. Coercion is felt by the individual either *directly*, as when he faces the force behind the law of the land, or *indirectly*, as when a forceful sanction like a parent's spanking remains dimly in the background only to emerge when crisis occurs. Whenever men act, or refrain from acting, in a manner different from that which they themselves have chosen or would choose in a given situation, *because others deliberately limit the range of their choice* either directly, through present control over it, or indirectly, through the threat of consequences, they may be said to be under *coercion*.[28]

[2] *Forms of coercion:* Our definition indicates that there are as many forms of coercion as there are forms of power. Whoever makes conditions which, when not fulfilled, call forth a penalty is exercising coercion. This is the case whether it be an employer with power to dismiss or a group of employees with the power to strike, whether it be a church with the power to excommunicate or a club with the power to deny its privileges, whether it be even a husband or a wife with the power to make things unpleasant for his or her partner. The fact that society is inconceivable without manifesting various forms of coercion has so impressed certain writers that they have seized upon "power" as the key concept in all sociological analysis.[29] The untenability of this position should become clear in the following discussion.

The ultimate form of coercion involves the exercise of *physical force* to control or prevent action. This is compulsion in its purist unconditional form, or what has often been termed "naked power." In modern communities it is vested, as a *right*, solely in the *state*, whatever usurpations of this right may take place from time to time. This is the form of coercion we shall examine here, seeking to point out the nature and the limits of its social effectiveness and function. This discussion, however, will hold true of the other forms of coercion, in the degree in which, under whatever disguise naked force is cloaked, they constrain the will and the behavior of those subject to them.

The function and limitations of socialized force. The use of force in the social order exhibits curious variations. It is prominent in some primitive communities, but almost nonexistent in others. In primitive society it appears to increase as we pass from the simple to the more complex and highly organized groups, if we may judge from the presence of social ranks or castes.[30] Yet we would be

28. See, for example, H. M. Kallen, "Coercion," *Encyclopaedia of the Social Sciences*, III, 617–619.

29. Among those who have stressed the role of power in this way may be mentioned Thomas Hobbes, who viewed the power of the political sovereign as fundamental to the social order; L. Gumplowicz and G. Ratzenhofer of the "conflict school" of sociology; Treitschke, writing in the German nationalist tradition; and Bertrand Russell, who deplores the role in *Power* (New York, 1938). For a discussion of social power, see MacIver, *The Web of Government*, Chap. V.

30. Cf. L. T. Hobhouse, G. C. Wheeler, and M. Ginsberg, *The Material Culture and Social Institutions of the Simpler Peoples* (London, 1915), Chap. IV, Section 2.

in error to infer that the role of force necessarily increases with the degree of social organization. The vast complex democracies of recent times have been less force-controlled than the simpler feudal economies out of which they rose. On the other hand, Soviet Russia is more complexly developed than the Russia of the Tsars, but whether force has diminished or increased is a debatable question. It is obvious that governmental force is more in evidence in times and under conditions of social crisis, as all of us know who have lived through one or both of the last two world wars; and sometimes it retains a tyrannical form as an aftermath of such crises. It is obvious also that force is a more effective instrument of social control over uneducated or regimented populations than over those which have been brought up in an atmosphere of liberty and criticism. Given these various contrasts, what, then, may we single out as the social function of force?

[1] *Why force is essential in social control:* Physical force cannot, as the anarchists claim, be abolished altogether from the social system. For there must always exist some socialized force to restrain the antisocial manifestations of force itself, whether exerted by individuals or by organized groups. It is necessary to restrain within limits the self-interest, the greed, the lawlessness, the intolerance ever ready to assert its will over others. It is necessary for the maintenance of any system of rights and obligations in a complex society. No rule is secure if the heedless or the unscrupulous or the dissident can transgress it with impunity. It is necessary to settle the disputes that arise eternally among men and that, were there no appeal to a force-invested authority, would issue in the violence of individuals or groups against one another. It is necessary also to curb the encroachments of stronger organizations over weaker ones, or of organizations, such as the economic, over those who are otherwise at the mercy of the powers they wield. There are fundamental forms of order and of security which can be maintained only under laws all must obey. The real service of force is as a safeguard of this order.[31]

Force *alone* cannot protect the social order, but without force as an ally of other safeguards that order could never be secure. Without force law is in danger of being dethroned, though force alone can never keep law on its throne. This truth, long recognized in its application to the legal codes of the state, applies no less to the United Nations or to any other international order that man attempts. If an international body is to be a government of men and nations, it must rest upon generally accepted codes of international welfare, to be sure, but in their support it must also possess the ultimate sanction of force.

---

31. Occasionally it is argued, especially by those dismayed by the frequent violations of the law, *and* by the use of force in social life, that if everyone were taught the tricks of getting around the law, lawbreaking would be eliminated. For example, a blackmailer would have no trade to ply if *all* people were accomplished in his arts. Developing the answer to this seemingly *logical* (but impracticable) proposal is a good way for the student to test his sociological insight.

Essential as are the services of socialized force, however, they have also very decided limits.

[2] *Why force is a limited device in social control:* The nature of these limits appears when we examine the peculiar character of physical enforcement. Two interrelated features are highly significant.

ONE: THE NEGATION OF SOCIALITY. In the first place, the intervention of force substitutes a mechanical for a social relationship. In so far as force is employed it is the denial of the *possibility* of co-operation. It treats the human being as though he were *merely* a physical object. Force by itself admits no expression of human impulses on the part of those against whom it is wielded—there is no give-and-take between a man and a hangman's noose, a prison wall, a rubber truncheon. Force is the end of mutuality and consequently it narrows also to a minimum the expression of the nature of those who wield it. This limitation is also felt in various degrees by all authorities whose task it is to superimpose enforced rules, such as the occupying army in a foreign land, the prison warden and his staff, the colonial rulers of a subjected people, even the parent when relying upon physical force to control or discipline his children. (Even Gestapo agents have deplored the dismal limits of the world to which their occupation condemned them.) For effective social control demands the element of co-operation in the relationship between the ruler and the ruled, as our subsequent illustrations indicate. And co-operation is an element lacking in all situations where sheerly "naked force" is used.

TWO: THE INEFFICIENCY OF FORCE. In the second place, the exercise of force, whenever there is a practicable alternative, is a wasteful operation, for it checks all the ordinary processes of life, all the give-and-take of common living. The more it is used, the more it breeds resistance, thus necessitating still more enforcement—a truth unlearned by the extreme advocates of suppressive measures against "subversive" elements. Consequently any social system that depends mainly on force, whether a "police state" or a tyrannical paterfamilias or a "strong-arm" racket, is in a precarious position, for in the process of change this generated resistance is apt to find some opportunity to overthrow it.

Limits of the efficacy of organized force: some illustrations. The limits of the efficacy of force are best revealed if we consider its operation in those areas of social control where men have generally placed most reliance upon it.

[1] *The case of military preparedness:* "If you wish peace, prepare for war," is an old aphorism which states have followed and continue to follow, in spite of the countless historical evidences that in international relations preparation for war has begotten war. In the light of this experience it would seem expedient to abandon the paradox and accept the more logical alternative, "If you wish peace prepare for peace." One essential difference between the two methods is that war is "prepared" for *nationally*, while peace requires an *international* preparation.

The reason for the failure of the older method, *in so far as* peace and security have been its object, is due to another of the peculiar characteristics of force. For force is effective in so far as there is no opposing force; in other words, in so far as it is centralized and monopolized. If, for example, the United States were forty-eight independent states there would be a vastly greater display of force within its area than there is today, and the greater display would be vastly less effective. Where force is least obtrusive, least in evidence, it is always most successful—as is known both by wise parents and by sage political rulers. There is force behind the police who regulate traffic, but they scarcely need to use it; if it were necessary to have machine guns at the intersections traffic control would be shown to be highly precarious. The greater the show of force, the greater the instability. So long as the nations "prepare for" peace by the display of force, atomic or otherwise, international peace must remain insecure.[32]

[2] *The case of the laws of the state:* Here we turn to another region where reliance on force alone is shown by experience to have been unjustified. It is a well-worn doctrine that the laws of the state are obeyed mainly because of the force behind them. This doctrine is valid only if it is qualified by the acknowledgment that there are other and broader grounds of law-abidingness than submission to force or fear of punishment. If the will to obey is undermined in the people as a whole, no enforcement, as many a revolution has shown, can long prevail. The remedy of more enforcement and stricter penalties has not stood the test of time, as the history of criminal law reveals. And there is considerable evidence that no law can be enforced if a very large minority is permanently and bitterly opposed to it, as illustrated by the flagrant flouting and eventual repeal of the federal prohibition laws in the 1920's and the present widespread violation of statutes outlawing the sale of certain contraceptive devices in such states as Connecticut and Massachusetts. An interesting example of the limits of forceful administration of political regulations is revealed in the successes of the "nonviolent" resistances led by Gandhi, resistances to various decrees of India's former British rulers. The techniques of *Satyagraha*, as this form of nonviolent direct action is termed, call for strict discipline and are themselves forceful, but they illustrate once more both the limits of the "terror of the law" and the fact that naked force tends to breed its kind in opposition to it.[33]

[3] *The case of crime and punishment:* Here we are concerned with the role of force not as a deterrent of lawbreaking but as a punishment of the lawbreaker. If, as criminologists agree, the fear of punishment is a very inadequate

---

32. The two paragraphs above are substantially the same as those written by Professor MacIver several years ago. The authors see no reason to alter them today. For a more extensive treatment of this problem, see Q. Wright, *A Study of War* (2 vols., New York, 1942); R. M. MacIver, *Towards an Abiding Peace* (New York, 1943); L. L. Bernard, *War and Its Causes* (New York, 1944).

33. See K. Shridharani, *War without Violence, A Study of Gandhi's Method and Its Accomplishments* (New York, 1939).

preventive of crime, what of punishment as a method of treatment of the criminal? Until very recent times it was generally taken for granted that the sheer discipline of enforcement, often taking the form of harsh or cruel treatment, was sufficient. The principle of punishment was confused by ideas of retribution, revenge, and expiation, whereas most of us today would agree that the only proper consideration of the state in inflicting punishment is the well-being of society. For society is affected by the manner in which the criminal, himself a member of the community, is treated by it. As this principle has become more accepted, the reliance on force alone has been rendered more and more dubious.

Mere force, being the mechanical treatment of human beings, as we have seen, is ill adapted to be a means of reform and thus, in the long run, of the prevention of crime. Indeed, that the opposite effect is often produced by our penal institutions is attested by a very large amount of evidence that prisons tend to be "crimebreeders." Moreover, mere force is a peculiarly inflexible mode of treatment. Traditionally, the criminal court, in dealing with the endlessly variant cases which come before it, could mete out only fine, imprisonment, or death. Whether the offender were juvenile or adult, man or woman, weak-minded or intelligent, passionate or calculating, sensitive or insensitive; whether the offense were motivated by despair or repression or poverty or greed or sheer ill will—whatever the context of the crime or the environment of the criminal, the court could do nothing but apply some measure of the inflexible legal code. The growing movement for a more scientific adminstration of justice and for a more understanding treatment of the various types of offender—of which the introduction of reformatories, institutions for first offenders, court psychiatrists, psychopathic hospitals, industrial schools and farm colonies, parole systems, juvenile courts, is just a beginning—witnesses to the breaking of one of the traditional strongholds of the faith in sheer, unadulterated force.

Some inferences concerning individuality and society. We have sought to show that force is necessary as the guarantee of political law, but that even where this necessity exists, its service is best rendered under conditions which admit the minimum of its exercise and display. We have seen that a relationship determined by force is the antithesis of a social relationship, and that therefore the function of force can go no further than to preserve social relationships against antisocial tendencies. Where a common rule is deemed necessary or advantageous for the common good, some degree of compulsion is involved, but the compulsion is always a cost to be reckoned in deciding whether the common rule is necessary or advantageous.

[1] *A general principle for the limitation of force:* Society does not need common rules for everything. Fortunately, for the most intimate or personal aspects of conduct, common rules are scarcely needed at all. People cannot run factories

or banks as they please, because if they did so, they would place other people directly at their mercy. But they can hold different religions, express different opinions, cherish different tastes, without preventing others from exercising the same prerogatives. Recalling our discussion in Chapter III of the interaction of individuality and society, we can now add that compulsion is dangerous and usually harmful when applied to matters with respect to which the pursuit by each of his own way does not directly interfere with the equal opportunity of the rest to pursue *their* own ways.

This broad conclusion does not solve many of the practical problems regarding the intervention of society, but it is useful as a limiting principle. It offers a justification of the more fundamental liberties, above all the liberty of thought and of its expression. This is a liberty which all can possess within a social order. The one reasonable exception is when men use this liberty, as in the case of the Ku Klux Klan and the like, to advocate or demand the suppression of like liberty of other men. Since freedom of thought and freedom of expression are vastly more important for the fulfillment of individuality than those rights which some cannot exercise except at the expense of others, we see here once again the fundamental harmony of individuality and society.

[2] *Results of departure from the principle:* When force is not contained within the limits of the principle we have offered, which is to say during most of human history, it strikes at the social bond itself. For it then divides man from man, turning co-operation into slavery and making it harder for the group to feel a common loyalty. When governments, inspired by one of the greatest dividing influences in the history of European civilization, dogmatic religion, excluded "heretics" from social and political rights, they did not heal the "heresy" but they cleft society asunder. When they ceased to take cognizance of religious differences, they made possible a degree of national solidarity unrealized before. "The historical experience of the nineteenth century," says a foremost exponent of the subject, "shows that freedom has the force of a bond, capable of holding men together in associations the more lasting and fertile according as they are more spontaneous in their origin and autonomous in their choice of ends."[34]

Finally the forceful suppression of basic liberties strikes at the processes that give vitality and renewal to society. Different types of personality have different points of resistance to social pressure and the demand for conformity. Such pressure is felt most keenly and is most quickly resisted by the creative members of a society, by its artists and prophets and "intelligentsia." These creative spirits are often critics of the status quo and are apt to deviate in one way or another from the mores of their age.[35] There is much historical evidence

34. G. De Ruggiero, *History of European Liberalism* (Eng. tr., London, 1927), p. 353.

35. Arthur Koestler's clever essay on "The Intelligentsia" is here much to the point; see his *The Yogi and the Commissar* (New York, 1945), pp. 61-76. See also such sociological works as K. Mannheim, *Ideology and Utopia* (L. Wirth and E. Shils, tr., New York, 1936); and F. Znaniecki, *The Social Role of the Man of Knowledge* (New York, 1940).

to show, from the days of Socrates or of Christ to the present that it is on such creators and innovators that force, when given free rein, most heavily descends. Unfortunately, it is hard for the ordinary man, and impossible for the tyrant, to distinguish between the creative individual and the criminal. Only when force is limited so that it becomes the servant of fundamental liberties can those who bear the greatest gifts for society be free to offer them. Only then can the *potential* harmony of individuality and society be most fully achieved.

Social Control in Utopian Communities

Utopian communities as experiments in social control. We have described in the preceding sections the conservative forces that tend to maintain the social structure. In this final section we turn to an illustration that reveals those forces in operation in an extreme degree. For here we are concerned with those communities which follow a distinctive and peculiar mode of life, such as separates them sharply from the greater communities that envelop them. We shall speak of these small-scale experimental groups that establish separate colonies for the pursuit of their own ideals as *utopian communities*.[36] These communities have to defend their mores against the contagion of the mores of the outer world. In order to maintain both their separation and their solidarity, they must resist in an unusually drastic manner the forces of change, whether arising from within or assaulting the group from without. Such communities necessarily exhibit a very extreme development of the agencies of social control. The situation is exemplified by the various utopian societies which exist or have existed in the United States, often on the basis of a religious creed or of some special "revelation," and usually communistic in principle. Among others may be mentioned Ephrata, a long-lived communistic colony established in the eighteenth century; the original Harmony in Pennsylvania; the settlements of the Shakers, Hutterites, Doukhobors, Amanites, and similar religious groups; the famous co-operative Brook Farm associated with such names as Emerson and Hawthorne; and the Perfectionists of Oneida, New York, who uniquely combined economic and sexual communism. Many historical and sociological investigations, as well as numerous biographers of members themselves, enable us to compare the principles exhibited by a considerable variety of these "utopias," and to arrive at certain conclusions touching the conditions under which an intensive and exclusive solidarity is maintained in the face of unusual difficulties.[37]

36. Sir Thomas More meant his title *Utopia* (1516) to suggest an imaginary community, as did Samuel Butler with his *Erewhon* (or "Nowhere") (1872); but we are using the word here to refer to actual communities.

37. An early survey is C. Nordhoff, *Communistic Societies in the United States* (New York, 1875). Among the large number of more recent studies are E. S. Wocster, *Communities of the Present and Past* (Newllano, La., 1924); W. A. Hinds, *American Communities and Co-*

Each of these communities upheld a set of mores sharply divergent from those of the surrounding culture. All of them in one way or another tried to hold in check various activities that were allowed freer scope in the society outside. Consequently each of them deliberately instituted a special system of controls designed to inculcate in the growing generation the habits of work, of thought, and of life which were in harmony with its social order. These small communities were in a very different position from that of the large "communistic" system of Soviet Russia, but it will be observed that some of their principles can be found also in the U.S.S.R.

Characteristic features of the utopian communities. While the communities differed from one another in many respects, they employed similar social devices to maintain solidarity. Four of these devices stand out in particular.

[1] *Isolation and self-sufficiency:* They generally sought to assure their cultural integrity by geographical isolation. They were mostly agricultural communities, especially in their earlier days, essentially self-sufficient, and thus could partly insulate themselves from the rest of the world. When the expansion of neighboring communities threatened their peace, they were apt to move further away. The very name of one of them, the Separatists, indicates a tendency common to them all. There were partial exceptions to this principle, such as the Perfectionists, an industrial community that could not cut itself off as completely as did most of the others. And all of the utopian communities that still exist, such as the Hutterites in South Dakota, have been affected in one way or another by the inroads of modern technology.[38] It is important to notice that though these communities sought to live by themselves, remote from contacts, they were never so remote that malcontents could not leave and join the world outside, thus removing from the group a source of disaffection.

[2] *Special indoctrination:* Each of these communities took special educational measures to inculcate in its members, especially the younger generation, the principles to which the community was attached.[39] The social discipline was thorough and rigorous. And they were under strict leadership, whether of an individual or an oligarchy of elders, whether formally or informally instituted. Each community thought of itself as having "the one right way of life," or as being a "peculiar people" in some sense set apart from the world—the

---

operative Societies (Chicago, 1908); and V. F. Calverton, *Where Angels Dared to Tread* (Indianapolis, 1941). Recent autobiographical accounts include P. Noyes, *My Father's House, An Oneida Boyhood* (New York, 1937); and J. S. Duss, *The Harmonists* (Harrisburg, Pa., 1943). See also the discussion in H. F. Infield, *Cooperative Communities at Work* (New York, 1945), Chaps. I–IV.

38. See, for example, L. E. Deets, *The Hutterites: A Study in Social Cohesion* (Gettysburg, Pa., 1939), Chap. VII.

39. Some aspects of educational methods and goals of "utopias," both imaginary and real, are discussed in G. Masso, *Education in Utopias* (New York, 1927).

Amanites who migrated from Germany to Iowa named itself the "congregation of true inspiration." Some thought of themselves as "the chosen of the Lord"; others as sole possessors of the truth. These convictions called for a strong social pressure toward uniformity of belief and conduct, manners and modes of living in general, even such externals as dress and habitation. This uniformity was strengthened by the custom of doing things together, of coming together, not merely for worship and inspiration but also for meals and other daily occasions. Since the communities were small, everyone was under the eye of his neighbors and deviation in any respect was easily detected and usually discouraged. Among the Perfectionists, a unique group in many ways, an institution of "criticism" was set up for this purpose. Perfectionists offered themselves at regular Sunday sessions for the criticism of their brethren, where their deficiencies of character and of conduct were dealt with faithfully and publicly.[40] The leaders of this community viewed this device as a method of indoctrination and one that would strengthen the cohesion of the group—in much the way that similar group confessionals are reported to function today in such organizations as the Oxford Movement and the Christian Science Church.

[3] *Religious sanctions:* The sense of social uniqueness was in almost all of these communities supported by strong religious sanctions. The religious bond was generally of an exclusive character—a common faith not shared by the world outside. Sometimes it was strengthened by the memory of persecution. It was, moreover, a faith which required a strict orthodoxy, as found among the Hutterites or Shakers or Mennonites today. It is very doubtful whether the unswerving obedience these communities required of their members could have been maintained apart from the fixity of the religious sanction. More than this, the all-inclusive religious code supported by a powerful, supernatural sanction provided "a focalizing center for the social harmony of their personalities."[41] A few groups, to be sure, such as the Icarians who migrated from France to Illinois and other states, professed no religion, but their relatively short duration in this country was perhaps related to the absence of a sustaining sacred creed. It has been observed that communism itself was a "religion" for these people, but without strong leadership the economic doctrine proved insufficient. In any event, "only one of every 33 nonreligious systems survived as long as 25 years, while at least one out of every two religious systems has survived 25 years or longer."[42]

In this respect, Brook Farm, the most distinguished of all American community experiments, occupies a unique place. For its religion was an outgrowth of Unitarianism, the liberal Transcendentalism of Emerson; its economy was a mild co-operative system, in no sense communistic; it numbered among its participants and patrons many of the intellectual leaders of the mid-nineteenth

40. Nordhoff, *op. cit.*, pp. 289–293; see also Calverton, *op. cit.*, pp. 262–266.
41. Deets, *op. cit.*, p. 21.
42. *Ibid.*, pp. 23 ff.

century; and most of its mores, including its sex standards, were those of respectable New England. The failure of Brook Farm, a tragedy to its great leader, George Ripley, was hardly the failure of a unique and isolated way of life.[43]

[4] *Control of sex relationships:* Save for the ill-fated Brook Farm, all these communities found it necessary to take very special precautions for the control of sex relationships. For here lay a great peril to their communistic systems. Unless sex relationships were rigidly controlled, a spirit of individualism could enter through the jealousies and divergent interests which the impulse of sex stimulated. Moreover, the family, with its exclusive possessions, presented a menace to the communistic solidarity. The family remains today, among such groups as the Hutterites, the "point of invasion of capitalism into communism."[44] The resistance to community controls over the intimate life of the members is generated within the family and often inspired by the mating relationship itself.

Consequently we find that various and sometimes curious precautions were taken. Fashion was generally tabooed. Dress was simple, often some kind of uniform. "In Amana and also among the Shakers the intention seems to be to provide for a style (for the women) which shall conceal their beauty and make them less attractive to male eyes. . . . At Oneida the short dress, with trousers, and the clipped locks, though convenient, are certainly ugly."[45] Some of the societies, like the Rappists and the Shakers, were celibate. The latter lived together in small communes instead of in families, the men and women not even eating together, and meeting under only carefully prescribed conditions. The Amanites, though noncelibate, exercised great care "to keep the sexes apart. On Sunday afternoons the boys are permitted to walk in the fields; and so are the girls, but these must go in another direction." When, in spite of these precautions, a marriage takes place, "it is treated with a degree of solemnity which is calculated to make it a day of terror rather than of unmitigated delight."[46]

Even the community which seemed to contradict this rigid principle of sex control, the Perfectionists of Oneida, was in reality seeking an opposite way to avoid the danger which sex presents to communistic solidarity. For this remarkable group, with its practical promiscuity or "sex communism," sought to discourage in every way they could the "exclusive and idolatrous attachment" of two mates for each other. The Perfectionists regarded this attachment as "selfish love" because it formed a rallying point for interests not in accord with the abolition of exclusive possessions on which the community

43. See, for example, Calverton, *op. cit.*, Chap. XIII.
44. Deets, *op. cit.*, Chap. VII.
45. Nordhoff, *op. cit.*, p. 398.
46. *Ibid.*, p. 56. See also Hinds, *op. cit.*, pp. 59–60.

was built. Moreover, their sex mores were strongly supported by their religious doctrines, as worked out by their leader, John H. Noyes.[47]

Utopian communities and individuality: some conclusions. Why, the reader may ask, have we made this brief excursion into these small community experiments, experiments so unrepresentative of the larger social order? One answer, of course, is that they reveal in a vivid way the codes and sanctions and techniques of social control. Another is that they underscore the difficulties of regimenting all or even most of man's social activities. This point has important implications for the greater society.

To all these communities (save, perhaps, the exceptional Brook Farm) the assertion of individuality appeared as "self-seeking" or "selfishness." The social bond assumed for them an inflexible authoritarian character. All divergence was dangerous to their unity. The conditions which generally sustained this unity were religious enthusiasm, strong leadership, simplicity of life, and a relative poverty which made hard work the rule. But when one or more of these conditions failed, disintegrating forces began to operate effectively, dissensions and cleavages developed, and the end of the order was in sight. The high mortality of these societies and the inability of most of them to adapt themselves to changing conditions show the one-sidedness of their systems. They achieved socialization at the cost of individualization: they achieved a human community at the cost of each human being. As we have already seen (in Chapter III), some harmony of society and individuality is a primary condition of every enduring social order and a goal that men inevitably seek.

47. See, for example, Calverton, *op. cit.*, pp. 267–280; and Noyes, *op. cit.*, pp. 8–11, 129–131.

8

The Major Social Codes

Introductory: Social Codes and Their Study

The variety of codes and ethnocentrism. The great variety of cultural norms among different peoples and among different groups in the same society has been of major interest to the students of human life from ancient days to the present. For many years ethnographers have reported the ways of various primitive peoples so that today a large literature reveals the wide range of governing codes that their behavior manifests. And students of contemporary life have similarly compared the codes of different classes, of ethnic groups, of occupational groups, and the like, as well as of different communities. The variety of folkways and mores and their supporting sanctions is so large that the mere task of classifying them into some sort of order is difficult. When we consider that economic procedures, methods of justice, sex relations, family systems, care of the body, belief and worship, techniques of government, food preparation and consumption, education, and technological procedures of all kinds are only some of man's modes of behavior that are prescribed by the codes among almost all peoples, and that there is much variation among them with regard to these matters, the ethnographic interest in description and comparison is understandable.[1]

The cultural variability illustrated by the diversity of folkways and codes

1. Among the numerous studies of specific primitive peoples and their mores are those of the Crow Indians by R. H. Lowie, the Eskimo by K. Rasmussen and V. Stefansson, the Melanesians and Polynesians by B. Malinowski and M. Mead, the Australian natives by W. L, Warner, the Andaman Islanders by A. R. Radcliffe-Brown, the Alorese by Cora Du Bois, the Tanala of Madagascar by R. Linton, and the California Indians by A. L. Kroeber. Ample illustrative material is found in such general studies as W. I. Thomas, *Primitive Behavior* (New York, 1937); A. A. Goldenweiser, *Anthropology, An Introduction to Primitive Culture* (New York, 1937); and G. P. Murdock, *Our Primitive Contemporaries* (New York, 1926).

has an important lesson to teach, as we noted in an earlier chapter. In one society the codes prescribe monogamy, in another they permit polygamy as well; in one they assign spirit to all things in the form of animism, in another they narrowly define the supernatural area; in one parsimony is a virtue, in another it is a vice; in one the female's sex gives her prestige, in another she is subordinated; and so on. These differences not only emphasize the need of viewing social phenomena with relation to their cultural setting; they also warn us against evaluating the ways of other people in terms of the values of our own codes. To this kind of evaluation, which holds one's own group or methods or beliefs to be superior to others, has been given the term *ethnocentrism*, characteristic in some measure of the attitudes of all peoples toward outsiders. The student of social life must be on constant guard against ethnocentric bias in analyzing the ways of different groups; and to this extent he must follow the principle of cultural relativity in his sociological investigations. As we shall see presently, this is a particularly difficult achievement in the study of the social codes.

The variety and types of codes in complex society. In contrast with modern society, such peoples as the Kwakiutl or Alorese or Dobu, or such communities as the semi-isolated rural groups of interior China or Canada's Quebec, possess a simple code of group life, recognized by all members as compelling and "correct," however deviant the behavior of specific individuals. While distinctions are made between various aspects of the code, such as the rules for sharing goods or of eating or of sex behavior or of worship, and while the sanctions of enforcement vary from one area of conduct to another, there is nothing like the complexity of codes that characterize modern society. Modern man, as we have seen, distinguishes between a variety of types of codes and types of sanctions, praises some and condemns others, deliberately plans their alteration, and chooses from among them in conducting himself as a member of society. Unlike the ethnographer's descriptive and comparative task, our purpose here is the analytical one of distinguishing the principal broad *types* of codes, and of indicating their functional role generally in *complex* society.[2]

In modern complex society every social organization has its own code, from the state with its great compulsive system of law and order to the smallest local club or clique or play group. Other codes are upheld not by organizations or associations but by the community. Finally there is one code, that of morals, which, however much the product of the group mores, in the last resort is sustained by the individual himself. How the member of a society finds his relation to these various and sometimes clashing codes will be the subject of

2. For pertinent discussions of the limitations of anthropological materials for sociological study, see A. S. Tomars, "Some Problems in the Sociologist's Use of Anthropology," *American Sociological Review*, VIII (1943), 625-634; R. Bierstedt, "The Limitations of Anthropological Methods in Sociology," *American Journal of Sociology*, LIV (1948), 22-30.

our next chapter. How the codes are or should be distinguished from one another is the theme of the present one.

We take as our five major types religious codes, moral codes, legal codes, the codes of custom, and the codes of fashion. In addition there are various subtypes, as we shall see. The major types of codes are highly interrelated, when we consider them from the viewpoint of their effect on the lives of individuals or from the viewpoint of the operative sanctions which enforce them. The distinctions between the types are therefore frequently overlooked. We shall consider side by side those codes that are most liable to be confused or that are so interdependent or so intimately related that the distinction between them is of particular significance. This is why we pair off religion and morals, custom and law, custom and fashion. Chart V presents the types of codes and symbolizes the close relationship between each of the two types of each pair, and between the codes and the sanctions. The chart is necessarily an oversimplification of a very complex aspect of social life, requiring the discussion that follows in the remaining sections of this chapter.

Religion and Morals

The distinction of the religious from the moral code. Religion and morals are very closely interwoven. If we are to draw a proper distinction between them it must be in terms of the authority and sanction attached to their respective prescriptions rather than in terms of the contents of the codes themselves. (Note "Contrast A" in Chart V.) Religion prescribes rules of conduct, and in so doing tends to identify these with moral conduct. On the other hand, some ethical cults, such as Auguste Comte's creed of "positivism" or the contemporary Ethical Culture Society, claim to be also religious. There are again what we may call "substitute religions," where the emotional characteristic of religious observance is associated with nonreligious or even antireligious elements, as in certain expressions of communism or some other "social gospel." Those who profess no religion have, nonetheless, their own moral codes—indeed amorality is a rare phenomenon. A clear distinction between the two is therefore necessary.

[1] *The suprasocial sanction of religion:* Religion, as we understand the term, implies a relationship not merely between man and man but also between man and some higher power. Hence it normally invokes a sanction which may be called *suprasocial*, whether it be primitive ghost fear or the present "wrath of God" or the penalties of an afterlife of torture in hell or merely the sense of being "out of tune with the infinite" when its supposed laws are disobeyed. Any ordinance is likewise part of a religious code which emanates from an authority accepted on religious grounds as the interpreter of a creed or the deputy or "vice-regent of God." Religion prescribes also the relation of man

CHART V **Dominant Interrelationships of Major Codes and Sanctions**

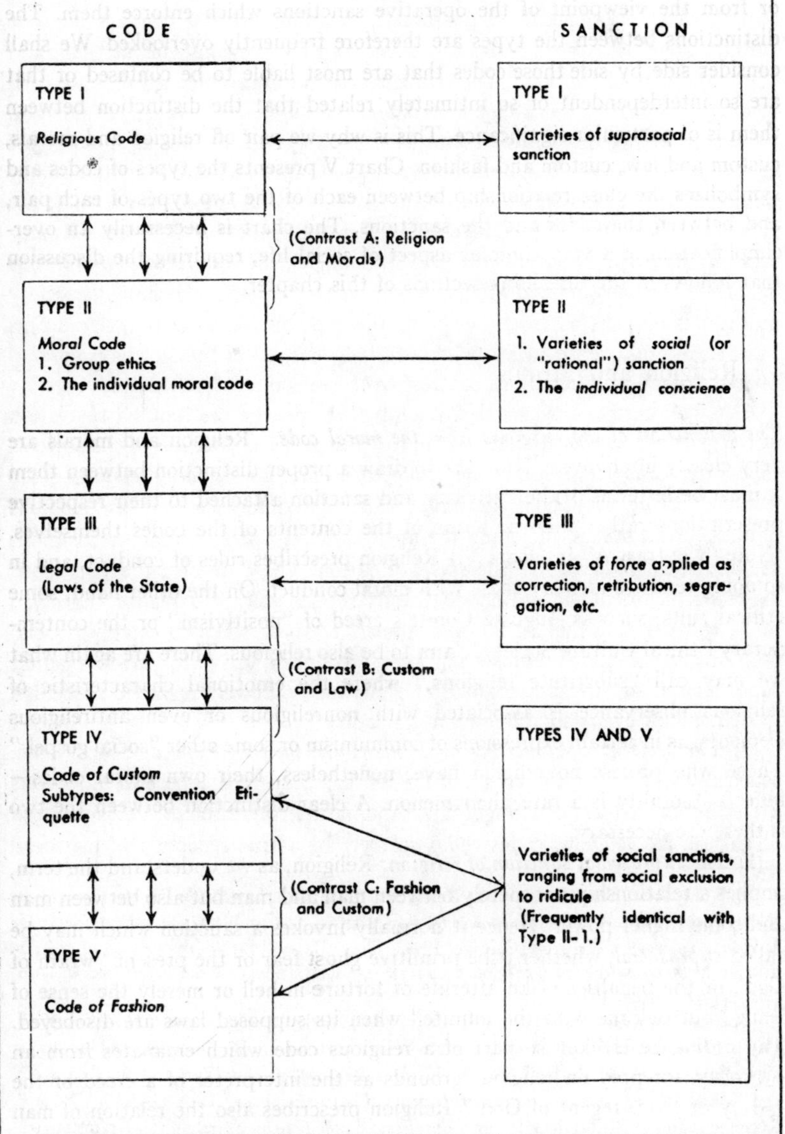

to man, but in so far as the sanction of this prescription is thought of as supra-social, its code is religious rather than strictly moral. It envisages "God's purpose" for man as distinct from man's own purposes, and generally regards the church as an agency for the fulfillment of this "divine end."

[2] *The social sanction of morals, religion, and social relations:* A code cannot strictly be called "moral" except in so far as the sanction comes from the apprehension of evil social results directly accruing from the conduct the code forbids. Here we have the distinction between the religious idea of "sin" and the moral idea of "wrong." The two ideas are naturally blended or associated in many minds, but we cannot understand the difference between religion and morals unless we distinguish them. The one may still remain as the support of the other, and some writers, such as Benjamin Kidd or the contemporary philosopher C. S. Lewis, assume that a moral code cannot endure without the support of religion.[3] Other thinkers, like Herbert Spencer and Thomas Huxley and various modern "naturalists" and "humanists," maintain that a moral code can never become pure and wholly responsive to the needs of a changing society unless it is dissociated from the special sanctions of religion.[4] It is significant, by the way, that representatives of both these schools of thought have characterized the moral sanction, in contrast to the religious, as a "rational" one.

All social norms, however derived, whether they be the reputed revelation of the gods or the inherited wisdom of the past or the ordinances of the present, reveal the ideas prevailing in the group concerning the *social relations* and the *modes of living* they hold desirable. The chief difference between religious norms and all others, including the strictly moral codes, is that the religious are addressed *indirectly* to the social situation. The code of a religious creed expresses an orientation of conduct and attitude toward a reality conceived of as transcending human life and human aims. It seeks to establish social relationships in which human purposes are linked up with, and frequently subordinated to, the assumed will of superhuman powers regarded as benign or demonic or even as indifferent to humanity.

[3] *The problem of reconciling social needs and the religious codes:* Since man, especially in prescientific ages and circles, has conceived supernatural powers according to his fears and in ignorance and misinterpretation of the phenomena of nature, his religious codes could scarcely be a true reflection of his social

---

3. B. Kidd, *Social Evolution* (new ed., New York, 1920); C. S. Lewis, *The Case for Christianity* (New York, 1944). For a more extensive discussion of this problem and related ones, see J. Wach, *Sociology of Religion* (Chicago, 1944), Chap. III; and for an elaboration of the distinction between morals and religion by an outstanding student of the latter, see R. Otto, *Das Heilige* (Gotha, 1927).

4. Spencer, *Principles of Sociology*, III, Chap. XIV; Huxley, *Evolution and Ethics* (New York, 1905). For a discussion of various modern representatives of the humanist and naturalist viewpoints, see E. A. Burtt, *Types of Religious Philosophy* (New York, 1939), Chaps. IX and X; and for two pertinent essays by students of naturalism, see Chaps. II and XV by S. P. Lamprecht and J. H. Randall, Jr., in *Naturalism and the Human Spirit* (Y. H. Krikorian, ed., New York, 1944).

needs. They often perverted social relationships and admitted or inspired conduct detrimental to social interests. To such older and more primitive examples as taboos against useful foods, human sacrifice, religious prostitution, maiming initiation rites, and stultifying superstitions may be added such modern religiously sanctioned prescriptions as that against planned parenthood or against proper medical care of the ill or injured. The religious codes often emerge as powerful engines of control to maintain the interests of the established order against the processes of change, as when the Greek Orthodox Church became a bulwark of the tyranny of the Russian Tsars.[5] Yet in the interpretation and promulgation of religious codes the social ideals of the group inevitably find a place. A *partial* accommodation is made to social needs, though the bias of the interpreters, the medicine men, or the priests, tends to check the process. In any event, the reconciliation of religious code and social need can never be complete so long as the code is based on dogmatically false conceptions of the laws of nature and of society.

Precepts incorporated in a religious code, as in the Ten Commandments, may be inspired more by social than by religious considerations, since in the formative stage it is easy to make the "word of the Lord" the expression of a sense of social need. But the formal distinction between the two types of precept remains. A code is *religious*—no matter whether its precepts are concerned with the relation of man to God, as in the first four commandments, or with the relation of man to man, as in the last six—when its source is presented as divine authority and its sanction is supernatural, or when the penalty is exacted in the name of religion. A code is *moral* when it promulgates standards of conduct that directly derive their sufficient justification from the human interpretation of good and evil.

[4] *The question of priority:* Many writers have discussed the questions as to which of the two codes was the original one and as to which of them was derived from the other. Some have held, like Auguste Comte in his account of the evolution of mankind from the theological to moral or "positivist" conceptions, that religion was the matrix of morals. Others, like Ferdinand Tönnies and Émile Durkheim, have taken the view that religion arose as a projection or sanctification of social or moral ideas. Tönnies held that the mores of the group became gradually reinforced by the religious sanction, gaining through tradition and the authority of the elders that aura of reverence and awe which led on the one hand to the worship of ancestors and on the other to the suprasocial sanction of the established ways. Durkheim regarded religious ideas as arising out of social situations and the religious life as "the concentrated expression of the whole collective life."[6]

The distinction between religion and morals has arisen in the course of social

5. For numerous other examples see Wach, *op. cit.*, Chap. VI. We consider these problems more extensively in Chapter XX below.

6. See Tönnies, *Die Sitte*, and Durkheim, *Elementary Forms of the Religious Life* (J. W. Swaine, tr., New York, 1926).

evolution. As we shall see later, we cannot say that either the religious or the moral code came first. Religion incorporates elements derived from social and moral reflection, and the latter in turn has been greatly influenced by religious conceptions. The distinction of these elements was largely concealed in the primitive outlook upon life, even as it is partially concealed in the outlook of the less educated minds among ourselves. Herbert Spencer thought that the earliest forms of religion contained no moral element, pointing out that they were intended to propitiate evil rather than good spirits and that they were characterized by cruel and atrocious observances.[7] But this situation (not always present among primitive peoples) does not prove his point, since a moral code, too, may be misguided and may make what seems to us atrocious demands. The morals of a primitive tribe are no more the morals of Spencer than its religion is his religion. It would be more correct to say that in primitive religions were contained, in solution, as it were, religious and moral and other elements.

Conflicts between religion and morals. Ever since man has distinguished between moral and religious codes they have had a great influence on each other. Moral codes, with such prescriptions as the duty of humility or obedience or respect for elders, have prepared the way for the perpetuation of religious beliefs. Religious codes have strongly reinforced with their supernatural sanctions the prevailing morals of the group. But the equilibrium of their joint control over conduct has been subject to many strains.

[1] *The conservatism of religion and historical adjustments:* The religious code, as the more conservative of the two, has come into frequent conflict with the moral discernments responsive to changing social needs. And sanctioned by its "higher authority," it has frequently menaced the autonomy of judgment which is the prime condition of an enlightened adult morality. The more conservative religions have resisted the fresh moral insights and the social applications derived from advancing science. They have opposed, for example, the quest for the truth concerning human origins, the first employment of anaesthetics for the alleviation of pain, the admission of divorce where marriage was a living death because of the insanity or cruelty of either partner, and the practice of birth control. At one time witches were burned in the name of the religious code and at another national campaigns against venereal disease were opposed on the same basis—the conservatism of religion has a large and well-known record.[8]

However, this rupture between religion and morals has been partly disguised, and often partly healed, by the consequent transformations of religion itself and the appearance of new religious creeds in response to moral demands. In

7. Spencer, *op. cit.*, III, 152.

8. See, for example, J. M. Yinger, *Religion in the Struggle for Power* (Durham, N. C., 1946), Chap. V.

general terms, religion seeks to confirm established moralities, and new moralities seek to modify religion. In the long run, and particularly in modern societies where the divisions of religion itself prevent any one form from dominating the mores and where the sense of definite and dread types of supernatural sanction has dwindled, both religion and morals tend to be brought into *relative* harmony with social needs.

As a major illustration of the adjustment of religion to changing moral and social conceptions we may cite the development of Protestantism. One acute writer on the subject, Max Weber in his *Sociology of Religion* developed a theory previously suggested by various novelists and historians, that the ethics of Calvinism, in contrast to the religious teachings of the preceding age, were not only in conformity with, but an important preparation for, the growth of capitalism. For the Protestant ethic underscored those virtues of thrift, discipline, personal responsibility, self-help, and unremitting toil which were congenial to the capitalist spirit. While Weber's theory has been subject to certain modifications, he and other writers provide ample evidence of the close relationship between the Protestant and capitalistic developments and of the adjustment of the religious code to the changing moral code.[9]

[2] *The "humanistic" trend today:* When religion is strongly dogmatic, as in the case of pre-Protestant Christianity, there is a serious problem of reconciling the religious and the more changeful moral code. Social welfare, when not made subordinate, is viewed in the light of a suprasocial principle. The conflict is clearly seen in the distinction between "faith" (adherence to a creed) and "works" (social conduct) and in the Protestant controversy as to their relative importance; and it is worth remembering that the *religious* problem is their relative importance in the "sight of God." Another instructive indication is "the system of concessions, tolerances, mitigations and reprieves which the Catholic Church with its official supernatural morality has devised for the multitude," thereby seeking to adjust the rigor of the religious code to the common temper of the age.[10]

Within the major religions of the Western world the growing interest in "works" and in social morality in recent decades has shown itself in a definite trend away from supernaturalism and toward a promulgation of social ethics. The trend has many forms, most of which have certain elements of modern "humanism." "Man's major religious ideas, humanists hold, are everywhere functions of the dominant needs and values of the people holding them. God, far from being the creator of man, is always himself created by man; he is the result of the play of man's idealizing imagination over the quest for the

9. See Weber, *The Protestant Ethic and the Spirit of Capitalism* (T. Parsons, tr., New York, 1930). For appraisals of Weber's thesis, see R. H. Tawney's Introduction, *ibid.*, and his *Religion and the Rise of Capitalism* (New York, 1926); and Yinger, *op. cit.*, Chap. IV.

10. Quoted from the Introduction to John Dewey's *Human Nature and Conduct* (New York, 1922).

appealing goods that life appears to render possible."[11] "Humanism," in this sense, rejects supernaturalistic notions of creation, heaven and hell, inherent sin, and so on, and strives to unite people on the basis of a code of social morality rather than on the basis of creed or denomination or "belief." It generally welcomes the discoveries of science, physical and social.

[3] *Group-centered religion and the larger morality:* A solution of the conflict between religion and morals is found *in so far as* religion comes to transcend the egoisms of tribe and nation and, purified by science of its stubborn misinterpretations of reality, grows world-conscious or cosmos-conscious. Under these conditions it loses the fierce compulsive power which unites the faithful in strong social bonds against the infidel, and sends a nation forth to conquest with the promise, *In hoc signo vinces*—"under this sign thou shalt conquer." It becomes, instead, the emotional integrating sense of the whole, whose range of immensity and power is beyond man's understanding, so that he can only *feel* his communion with it and dimly sense his tiny purposeful life as a moment in its eternal being. Then it no longer divides people from people, and within a people the orthodox from those who "go awhoring after strange gods." It loses that immoral intolerance which only the exclusive visionary possession of an unreasoned faith can inspire.

The great religions that originated in the Western world and have spread in modern times, Judaism and Christianity and Mohammedanism, and at least one of the Oriental religions, Shintoism, have rarely achieved such breadth and tolerance. On the contrary, they have often been associated with tribal and national aspirations, with intolerance of one another, at times with bloody conflict. Perhaps we have much to learn, as one philosopher has recently argued,[12] from the more flexible and more inclusive "religious philosophies" of the East.

Religion, growing world-conscious, may well sustain the nearer sense of our community with one another and thus fall into consistency with a purely moral code. But it can no longer dictate an authoritative morality, since thus sublimated it is no longer capable of defining moral precepts for the particular occasions of life. No longer do most men expect a church, as in the Middle Ages, to lay down precise rules touching the morality of monopoly and usury; and if this limitation is true of the more conservative religions in the modern world, it is still more true of the wider faiths. If in this way morality has lost an anchorage, though one that moored it too fixedly to the past, at least there is the compensation that a freer morality, springing from the consciousness and sheer experience of social good and evil, has become possible.

---

11. Burtt, *op. cit.*, p. 375.
12. F. S. C. Northrop, *The Meeting of East and West* (New York, 1946), especially Chaps. IX and X.

Custom and Law

The meaning of law and custom. We pointed out in previous chapters the peculiar quality of the law that the state upholds, the law that alone in modern society has behind it the authority of unconditional enforcement. All social codes have some attribute of authority, to be sure, as revealed in the sanctions that guard them, but the sanction of the legal code is in this respect unique. This fact enables us to draw a clear line between legal rules and the rules of other associations. The rules of associations other than the state are conditional on membership, and the failure to obey them involves only the loss of membership or of some of the rights or privileges which attach to membership. The legal rules are coercive in a wider sense; their sanction cannot be evaded by the sacrifice of membership. We should not confuse the kind of rules that rest on the authority of the state with those that are maintained by clubs and colleges and churches and economic corporations. Law, a term which throughout this section we shall use to mean the *code upheld by the state*, because of its inclusive applicability, is thus a guardian of society itself.[13]

[1] *The specific character of law:* Law is the body of rules which are recognized, interpreted, and applied to particular situations by the courts of the state. It derives from various sources, including custom, but it becomes law when the state, which means in the last resort the courts, is prepared to enforce it as a rule binding on citizens and residents within its jurisdiction.

Inadequate definitions of law often create confusion on this subject. Law is not simply that which the legislature enacts, or statute law. Law is not an ethical rule, "prescribing what is right and forbidding what is wrong." Law is not any kind of rule that society in some way or other compels individuals to obey—a conception sometimes held by jurists as well as anthropologists. These writers see that certain social codes served in other stages and types of society the function that is now fulfilled by law, and accordingly they define law so as to include these codes. Thus one student of law points out that legal enforcement is a relatively modern phenomenon: "If we look away from such elaborated systems as those of the later Roman Empire and of modern Western governments, we see that not only law but law with a great deal of formality, has existed before the state had any adequate means of compelling its observance—and indeed before there was any regular process of enforcement at all."[14] What this fact really means is that law under such conditions was not fully differentiated from customary and ethical codes. We can define a social phenomenon only as it appears sufficiently differentiated to reveal its distinc-

13. See R. M. MacIver, *The Modern State* (Oxford, 1926), Introduction and Chap. VIII; and the same author's *The Web of Government* (New York, 1947), Chap. IV.

14. F. Pollock, *First Book of Jurisprudence* (London, 1923), Chap. I.

tive nature. The distinctive nature of the legal code in modern society is seen in its coercive and inclusive character as enforced by the association we call the state.[15]

[2] *The specific character of custom:* Custom, too, has its own distinctive nature. Whereas law is often *made*, and is always *applied*, by the definite power of the state, custom is a group procedure that has gradually emerged, without express enactment, without any constituted authority to declare it, to apply it, to safeguard it. Custom is sustained by common acceptance. No special authority prescribes the raising of the hat to ladies or tipping in restaurants or dating on Friday evenings or fireworks on the Fourth of July. Customs are the most spontaneous of all social rules and often the most compelling. But they are sanctioned not like law, by organized coercive authority, but by a wide variety of informal social pressures (see Chart V). Customs are so intimate that, until we reflect on it, we do not realize how they attend nearly every occasion of our lives, how our actions from morning till night, from youth to age, are custom-regulated. In all sorts of ways, through chance, trial and error, experience, particular modes of procedure are devised, are followed and imitated, and unobtrusively are accepted in the social mores. And often just as unobtrusively customs fade and disappear, again without formal abolition and without recognition by any but those who recall the "good (or bad) old ways."

The insufficiency of custom in modern society. Under simple or primitive social conditions there is little need for a separate legal code. Custom serves well enough to regulate the conduct of life. The primitive group is a face-to-face group, every man is a neighbor of all the rest. No one escapes beyond the range of gossip, of group opinion and group control. Seldom does any novel situation arise for which custom cannot provide. With the weight of tradition behind it custom ordains every occasion, assigns to each his rights and duties, adjusts the claims and interests of each to those of the rest.[16] But the further we pass from primitive conditions the more necessary it becomes to supplement the rule of custom by other social codes and especially by law.

[1] *Why custom must be supplemented by law:* There are several reasons why law must supplement custom in modern society.

ONE: THE NEED FOR A SPECIAL AGENCY. Custom, lacking an agency of authoritative jurisdiction in cases of dispute or transgression, frequently must leave to the injured party the right to vindicate his claims against another.

---

15. For various definitions of law and somewhat different conclusions, see N. S. Timasheff, *An Introduction to the Sociology of Law* (Cambridge, Mass., 1939), Chap. XII; and G. Gurvitch, *Sociology of Law* (New York, 1942), pp. 50–60.

16. B. Malinowski in *Crime and Custom in Savage Society* (New York, 1926) argues that there is a "domain of legal rules" in all societies, including the primitive. His evidence, however, shows various levels of *customary* control, not a separate legal code. Cf. Timasheff, *op. cit.*, pp. 275–281.

Custom allows him to retaliate, to take vengeance or retribution; hence the greater proportion of crimes against the person in the simpler rural society than in the large modern city. Personal retaliation and the feuds it engenders cause more serious disturbances to the interests of the rest of the community when in the more developed society these interests grow more complex and interdependent. Special law with its special agency of enforcement is required if interests are to be pursued in peace.[17]

TWO: THE NEED FOR QUICK ADAPTATION TO CHANGING CONDITIONS. Custom cannot quickly adapt itself to changing conditions. Its authority diminishes in the complex society where impersonal relations take the place of personal ones and where individuals are further removed from the direct control of the group as a whole. Custom is a clear guide only where the old ways can be utilized to meet the new situation. When new techniques confound the old ways, as for example in the change to a money economy in England in the sixteenth century, another authority and another kind of code is demanded, a code which does not slowly evolve but one which is made expressly for the situation. The "rule of the road" was formerly a custom, but with the coming of the automobile new conditions arose which required the establishment of traffic laws. Again, in the early days of radio, the airways were "free" but radio's large-scale development required legal regulation. Only the legal code can keep abreast of the rapid changes of modern civilization, and frequently it lags behind.

THREE: THE NEED FOR AN INCLUSIVE AGENCY. In the complex society, different groups—different classes and communities and ethnic groups—have different customs. Thus where a single rule is found convenient or desirable, such as the guarantee of the freedom of speech or of educational opportunity, it is necessary to resort to law.

FOUR: THE NEED FOR AN ARBITER WHEREVER POWER IS ORGANIZED. Custom is most effective when there is no strong organization of social power, whether for military or economic exploitation. Such an organization makes its own rules, thrusting custom aside. Custom has poor means of defense against the conflicts that arise within a power system. Those who dispute for power as well as those who are subject to it call for an arbiter, a judge. And the judge, even though he usually begins as an interpreter of custom, ends as a maker of law. This is the story of the great code makers of the ancient world, such as Moses, Hammurabi, and Solon.

[2] *The functions and limitations of the legal code:* The same conditions which explain the birth of law help to explain its growth into the voluminous codes of modern states. The body of law is always being increased and modified to meet new general situations or new problems of application to special cases.

---

17. See J. Dickinson, "Social Order and Political Authority," *American Political Science Review*, XXIII (1929), 524 ff.

This is done partly by direct legislation, partly by judicial interpretation. Modern industrial developments have occasioned enormous additions to the legal code, and the development of atomic power has already brought into being new laws in our own land with many more forthcoming. Another factor that has added to the bulk of law is the assertiveness of authority which, once established, is urged both by the drive of power and by the pressure of interests to undertake more and more regulation. Indeed, the growth of such a mass of law has brought with it both the bewilderment of the ordinary modern citizen when confronted with its complexity and size and his increasing dependence upon the expert of the code, the lawyer himself.

Gradually, and chiefly through conflict, modern states have been compelled to learn that there are some matters that law is not qualified to control. It cannot be in general an effective substitute for custom or for morality; it cannot, without defeating the values it would preserve, prescribe religious or other forms of belief. Law can command only *external* observance and therefore, where the value of an act depends mainly on the spirit in which it is performed, it is not a proper subject for legal control. Perhaps there is no better illustration of this principle than that presented by the very regimes that denied its validity, the late governments of Germany and Italy, which by decree and with the support of the great power of the state attempted with but limited success to control such intimate and internal matters as propagation and religious belief. And in Soviet Russia, with all of its strict and centralized control, the church, for example, has already emerged in part out of the oblivion imposed on it by the state. Law is an instrument of government, and the nature of the instrument assigns its capacities and its limitations.

The great functions of law may be summed up as being (1) the maintenance of a fundamental order within which men shall find security and the common conditions of opportunity; and (2) the adjustment of those conflicts of interests between individuals or groups which they cannot settle for themselves or in the settlement of which they encroach on the interests of others. Within the territory so marked out there remain debatable areas, for example important regions of economic struggle, where an acceptable legal code is not yet developed. But in our modern societies the range of legal settlement is, and must be, very large indeed.[18]

Clashes of law and custom. When a particular law attacks any widespread custom of a community, it has to depend very largely on the precarious sanction of force. But the custom that is attacked has one element of superiority in that it is obeyed more spontaneously. It does not seem to come to us from without, curtly demanding our obedience. It does not appear to us, as

18. See below, Chapter XVIII, for a more extensive discussion of the functions and limitations of law.

law without its aid tends to do, as involving a control over our desires either for the sake of others or in the name of authority. Therefore a law which attacks a widespread custom, even though a majority support it, both lacks a ground of support that is essential to its effective operation and creates a force of resistance that endangers its authority. If the law in question is not aided by social conditions favorable to the growth of a supporting custom, it cannot succeed.

[1] *Some illustrations:* Consider the Sunday observance laws and the numerous "blue laws" that mark the statute books of various states which are out of accord with the customs of the present. Recall the Volstead Act that attacked the widespread and old-established custom of drinking intoxicating liquors, a custom particularly bound up with many social occasions; in the end the old custom triumphed over it. Certainly a law cannot succeed permanently if it is opposed by strongly resistant and deep-seated customary attitudes. A striking case has been the virtual nullification, for one important area, of the Fourteenth Amendment, the inevitable result, under existing conditions, of the customary attitude of white to colored people not only in the South but in large measure throughout the United States. Until very recently, the judicial "interpretations" of that amendment were mainly subterfuges intended to validate the customs which the amendment denied. Again, consider the more recent legislation of certain states designed to prevent discrimination in employment on the basis of "race" or color or religion. While such laws may well serve to *limit* discrimination, they cannot *by themselves* fully control the customary practices of people whose attitudes are grounded in ignorance and group prejudice. These are significant examples in contemporary life, and they illustrate not only the clash of law and custom, and the limitation of the legal code, but also the fact that effective law itself requires a social support beneath its own formality.

[2] *Both types of code essential in social life:* The fact that custom establishes a social order of its own is often forgotten in discussions of the clash of custom and law. It is an unfortunate situation when law and custom are opposed and men prefer to follow custom rather than obey the law, but the alternatives presented to them in such a situation are not properly expressed as law-abidingness and anarchy. As vividly apparent in the life of the "frontier" communities that have played such a large role in the history of our own country, men must often choose between two codes, between, say, the custom of lynching and the law of trial. Both types of code make a strong claim on our allegiance and, though law has a formal superiority, both are necessary for the maintenance of society. The problem of the individual, compelled to choose between the prescriptions of opposing codes, we will face in the next chapter.

Interdependence of law and custom. We have seen that in the historical process law and custom have grown distinct. But they remain in important respects interdependent. We should remember that customs grow up spontaneously, gradually coming into being, whereas laws are created, emerging at the moment of legislation or of judicial recognition. Thus around law itself customs gather. Laws which are generally approved initiate attitudes as well as procedures out of which new customs evolve, and these in turn become a support of the laws. In fact, unless such customs are in being or arise to strengthen laws, the latter retain a precarious hold on the community.

[1] *Customs as a supplement to law:* Custom not only, under normal conditions, becomes a support of law but also supplements law and prepares the way for its development. Thus business customs, gathering around law, are in time in many cases incorporated within it, as for example the provision of three days of grace on bills of exchange[19] or, more generally, the introduction of standardization or "fair price" usages into the legal code. On the other hand, law establishes conditions which bring new customs into being. Thus industrial legislation, such as acts regulating hours of labor or requiring hygienic conditions or defining the processes of collective bargaining, undermines old customs and prepares the way for new ones. Laws establishing military training induce the customs associated with military life and outlook —as we have witnessed in this country in recent years—while laws abolishing such training destroy the conditions on which these customs rest.[20] To take our earlier example of nondiscriminatory employment legislation, we can surmise that the widespread passage of such laws and their continued enforcement might affect the customs of group discrimination. However, it is *indirectly*, by creating an external order in which the old customs no longer correspond to our desires, that law is most effective in influencing custom, rather than by a frontal attack upon it.

[2] *Constitutional law and custom:* The fundamental or constitutional law is even more intimately related to custom than the type we have so far discussed. Constitutional law, though in part formulated in special documents, lives by usage, and around it a further body of usage grows up which amplifies or modifies or even annuls portions of the written formula. Thus the custom that the President shall not seek a third term of office amplified the American Constitution—a precedent upset by the last two elections of Franklin D. Roosevelt which have been a factor in bringing about a legislative attempt to codify the older custom; the custom by which the Electoral College acts on party lines modifies the Constitution; and the custom of some states of differentiating between the political rights of white and colored in effect

19. J. C. Gray, *Nature and Sources of the Law* (New York, 1927), p. 282.

20. For a good analysis of the relation of law and custom *within* military organization, see the articles by Morroe Berger, "Law and Custom in the Army," *Social Forces*, XXV (1946), 82-87; and "Cultural Enforcement in the American Army," *Journal of Legal and Political Sociology*, IV (1946), 96-103.

annuls some of its provisions. The study of American government, in fact, has become to a considerable extent today the study of the role of customary procedures that supplement the basic law of the land.

Still more apparent is the part played by custom under an "unwritten constitution" such as England possesses, where the old forms are subject at every point to the growth of customary procedures. Formally, the king can refuse his assent to a bill passed by both houses of Parliament, the cabinet can retain office after it has lost support of the Commons, and so forth. But this formal "can" is through custom supplanted by an actual "cannot." One difference between constitutional and ordinary or "municipal" law is that in the former sphere custom is not simply a source and support of the law but is an integral part of the system.[21] This is also true of the developing body of rules which we call international law, where customary practice in international relations and the formal regulations are closely interdependent.

Fashion and Custom

How fashion differs from custom. Various sociologists have contrasted fashion and custom. Herbert Spencer regarded fashion as a leveler of custom and especially of customary distinctions between social classes.[22] He thought of fashion as gaining ground when custom declines, and associated both tendencies with the growth of industrialization. Gabriel Tarde defined fashion as the "imitation of contemporaries" and set it in contrast to custom, which was the "imitation of ancestors."[23] But neither of these views is wholly satisfactory as revealing the relation of custom to fashion, a relationship of significance in the study of both social structure and social change.

[1] *The meaning of fashion:* By fashion we mean *the socially approved sequence of variation on a customary theme.* The variations of fashion occur in a more or less regular sequence—the "cycle of fashion" as it is sometimes called; and fashion specially affects those aspects of the cultural factor which are regarded by the group as being in themselves relatively indifferent to basic values. Fashion applies to such matters as opinion, belief, recreation, dress, adornment of all sorts, house decoration and furniture, manner of speech, popular music, literature, and art. In these areas fashion does not wholly supersede custom, but rather supplements it. Thus there is in every period a *customary* type of dress, such as trousers for men, or of fiction, such as the novel, or of song writing, such as the ballad, on which fashion rings its changes. By its continuous modifications of the type, fashion may, of course, undermine the

21. For the difference between constitutional and municipal law, see MacIver, *The Modern State,* Chap. VIII, Sec. I.

22. Spencer, *op. cit.*, II, 205 ff.

23. *Laws of Imitation* (E. C. Parsons, tr., New York, 1903), Chap. VII.

customary factor and prepare the way for a new one. Moreover, as we shall presently see, the attitude associated with fashion tends to weaken the attitude that clings to custom.

[2] *Traditional custom and changeful fashion:* Custom differs from law in the spontaneity of its origin and the immediacy of its sanction. Custom differs from fashion by reason of the more enduring character of its prescriptions, its closer relations to the intimate life and temperament of the group, and its traditional quality. Fashion is definitely antitraditional. It controls those aspects and expressions of conduct, generally the more superficial aspects, which are apt to escape from custom's hold. The changefulness of fashion is illustrated in the extreme by fads and crazes that bring rapidly to the forefront for a time a certain entertainer or a particular version of "the game" or a special mode of greeting one's friends, only to be forgotten almost as quickly.[24]

In the field of dress there are general types of garments which are prescribed by custom for particular occasions, such as weddings or funerals or sports, or for particular seasons, or for particular times of the day; while within these types the changing modes and styles are regulated by fashion. In recreation, certain games, such as football, basketball, tennis, baseball, and bridge, have become a part of our customs of recreation; but within each of them the fashions change from time to time and from place to place, as is well known to all who are familiar with the history of the "T formation" or the "fast break" or the "Eastern grip" or the "hit-and-run" style of play or the "Culbertson system." So in numerous other areas of social behavior, fashion determines the fugitive varieties of the custom-prescribed general type.

Sometimes, however, the trend of fashion exhibits continuously the same direction. In this case the influence of some underlying factors is revealed, and the fashion may at length undermine the custom which at first it merely variegated Thus the long-range trend in women's fashion in dress has led to the obsolescence or disappearance of certain garments which were previously prescribed by custom—a reflection of major changes in the status of women, the sex mores, and other factors. The same influences have been at work in determining the direction of the fashion in sports apparel, generally from more to less, which in turn has helped to bring about the change from "bathing" to swimming and that from "lawn tennis" to the modern vigorous game. In a similar way fashions in art, in literature, and in music may lead to the disappearance of customary types and to the establishment of new customs.

Fashion, convention, and etiquette. The fact that fashion deals with the changeful variations of an accepted or customary procedure enables us to distinguish fashion from other social phenomena with which it is often confused. Fashion

---

24. On the relation of custom, fashion, and fad, see the excellent article by E. Sapir, "Fashion," *Encyclopaedia of the Social Sciences* (New York, 1935), VI, 139–144.

is apt to be confused particularly with those forms of custom we call *convention* and *etiquette*. (See Chart V.)

[1] *Convention and etiquette as aspects of custom: Convention* prescribes those usages the basis of which is felt to be merely social agreement rather than any significant connection between the usage and the meaning attached to it. Convention has many forms, such as the tacit agreement to ignore aspects of a situation that would breed difficulties if openly expressed, or the tendency to keep relations upon a superficial or arbitrary level, or the acceptance of the assumption that a person is acting from idealistic motives when there is no reason to believe that more egoistic or less noble motives are involved. When the professor is polite to a colleague whom he despises at the faculty tea or when the student sits quietly while the professor offends his intelligence and strains his patience he is following the code of convention. The code thus serves to maintain a superficial but often serviceable type of solidarity.

Etiquette prescribes the detailed formalities to be observed on ceremonious occasions. Whereas convention often serves to cover over social divergences, etiquette is that code of precise discriminations with respect to manners which distinguishes superficially a social class, a professional or other group, and is frequently made a criterion or "shibboleth" of a person's qualification to belong to it. In fact, every group that possesses a tradition of any length develops a protocol of regulations prescribing the norms of behavior for certain events. Thus we can observe the governing etiquette that separates, for example, the warrior or age or sex groups in various primitive societies, the "Hill Street" upper class of "Yankee City," the country club "set" of many American communities, or to mention a conspicuous case, the carefully indoctrinated officers and their wives of the Army and Navy. Etiquette not only serves the utilitarian purpose of prescribing procedure for specific exigencies, but symbolizes significant social distinctions that for more fundamental reasons certain members of the community wish to preserve.

[2] *Convention and etiquette and the range of fashion:* Both convention and etiquette take one of equally possible ways of representing or symbolizing a social attitude and in a seemingly arbitrary manner rule out other ways. Handshaking and kissing are examples, since alternative forms of greeting and affection, such as saluting and nose rubbing, can, and in some cultures do, serve the purposes equally well. Any variation within the practice itself, such as a different mode of handshaking, may properly be called a *fashion*, but a change from handshaking to saluting or from kissing to nose rubbing would be a change in the customary convention. This line is often hard to draw, of course, but we can discern the nature of fashion if we think of it as concerned with the *transient styles* within a custom or convention or any cultural form. Where almost no variation or modification of the type is permissible, as in the case of military uniforms or girls' bloomers for sports during an earlier era, then fashion is almost entirely ruled out.

This distinction also enables us to understand the significance of fashion as applied to artistic and other cultural changes. For every true artist his style is his own, but when any such style is followed widely by others, then the element of fashion enters in. Thus in one cultural field the host of "little Hemingways"; in jazz music the many emulators of, say, Louis Armstrong; in movie direction the wide adoption of the Hitchcock techniques. Among the followers the style is culturally a matter of indifference. The range of fashion is, in short, the limit of variation made possible by *cultural indifference.* It should be remembered that fashion is not the cultural current of a period—not the more deeply rooted tendencies of any age—but only the more detachable manifestations and mannerisms which are capable of easy imitation. A fashion is not to be explained by imitation, for reasons that will presently appear, but part of the nature of fashion is that it is an external form of observance capable of being easily imitated.

The social role of fashion. Though fashion plays from moment to moment on the surface of social life, behind its seemingly inconsequent changes there are often deeper forces at work. Fashion deals with the externals and superfluities of social life which can be changed without affecting the more basic procedures and values which we cherish. Fashion promises no utility; it makes no direct appeal to our reason. Yet it exercises a strong tyranny over us. Why is this the case?

[1] *The need for conformity and for novelty:* Fashion regulates those aspects of life concerning which we are, on the whole, individually indifferent and therefore socially susceptible. Within this region it harmonizes the satisfaction of two strong demands of social man which in other areas often come into conflict—the demand for novelty and the demand for conformity. Psychologically these logically opposite needs go hand in hand, and fashion meets the demands of both.[25] For fashion turns the desire for novelty into social practice: it makes novelty the right and proper thing for the group. "The slight changes from the established in dress or other forms of behavior seem for the moment to give the victory to the individual, while the fact that one's fellows revolt in the same direction gives one a feeling of adventurous safety."[26]

Fashion may limit the range of innovation at any one time but it compensates for this by accelerating the tempo of innovation for the group. With the desire for novelty there is associated also the desire for distinction, and fashion also succeeds in accommodating this desire to the rule of conformity. Moreover, fashion prescribes a style, not a uniform. Within it there is room for minor,

25. See R. S. Lynd, *Knowledge for What?* (Princeton, 1939), pp. 195-197, for a discussion of the needs for conformity and for novelty.

26. Sapir, *loc. cit.*

but for the purpose of individual distinction, important variations. People can still conform to fashion "with a difference."[27]

[2] *Fashion and social class:* Fashion generally, though not always, radiates from the elite, the prestige-owning groups. The "leisure class" especially, having both the time and the material means, tends to set the style in dress, the niceties within etiquette, styles in sport and recreation in general, and so forth. Even when a specific fashion originates within other groups, as in the case of modern jazz music, which first appeared among the Negroes of New Orleans, or the "work-shirt" type of sport garment which was first used for manual work itself, it is "taken up" by the elite before the fashion is more widely diffused throughout the population. In modern society, fashion spreads rapidly from class to class so that the Paris-designed gown, for example, is soon the model for almost all pocketbooks, differing from price to price only in quality of workmanship and material. Thorstein Veblen, in his well-known and caustic analysis of the leisure class,[28] noting the role of that group in providing the models of fashion for general emulation, even goes so far as to claim that the two criteria of fashion are expensiveness and "ineptitude" or ugliness. Veblen was stressing the conspicuous expenditure of leisure and of "valuable goods" as a device by which upper classes and those imitating them, in such primitive groups as the Kwakiutl as well as in our own society, maintain and enhance their prestige. In Chapter XIV we shall examine Veblen's claims more carefully, including the question of the relation of class and fashion.

Although fashion tends to affect all groups within a community, it is always an item in the cost of living. Some forms of fashion, such as polo playing or frequenting certain night clubs or visiting "fashionable" resorts, are limited to those who can afford their expense. Few, in fact, can actually "keep up with the Joneses," though many in their striving to do so engage in expenditures unwarranted by their means, and all can "enjoy" the vicarious experience of reading and gossiping about the fashionable activities of the more affluent. This situation is especially characteristic of large-scale democratic societies, which are marked by a wide prevalence of the same fashion types, the differences within the type expressing standards of income and of taste. Long-established aristocratic societies, on the other hand, tend to develop distinctive types of fashion for different social classes.

The spread of fashion in modern times. The area over which the same rule of fashion extends and the speed with which it makes and abrogates its laws have both greatly increased within our modern civilization. We may consider briefly the conditions of our age that have given a freer play to fashion than it ever possessed before.

---

27. For the social psychology of fashion, see K. Young, *Social Psychology* (New York, 1944), Chap. XVII; R. T. LaPiere, *Collective Behavior* (New York, 1938), Chap. IX.

28. *The Theory of the Leisure Class* (New York, 1922), Chap. I. For Veblen's comments on fashion, see also Chaps. III, IV, and VII of this volume.

[1] *Economic and class factors:* One important consideration is the change in the character of our class structure. The development of greater mobility of people from class to class which, as we shall see later, accompanied the growth of capitalism, has broken down an important social barrier of fashion. Spencer was probably right in correlating the growth of fashion with the transition from a "military" to an "industrial" society.[29] The former is bound up with the insistence on rank, ceremonial, and status, with an inflexible order of subordination which checks the democratizing reign of fashion. Another factor which has increased the range of fashion has been the increase of prosperity and leisure. This is not only due to the fact that a larger group is able to emulate the style of living of the aristocracy, but also because, as we have indicated, fashion is chiefly concerned with the superfluities of life or with the superfluous decoration of life's necessities. We do not think of fashion in overalls until they are adopted as a playsuit or as a "smart" mode of garb. There is more of fashion in the body of an automobile than in its chassis; there are changes but no fashions in steam shovels or other devices that are strictly tools. The higher the standard of living—the more playsuits and automobiles and the like—the more material there is for fashion to operate upon.

[2] *Factors of communication and invention:* The modern spread of fashion is also in part the result of the enormous development of the means of communication, which has broken down the barriers of time and distance, and the related acceleration of invention. In the numerous and complex contacts which our civilization produces, especially in the more populous centers, the area assigned to custom has diminished. For custom is always most powerful and far reaching in the regions remote from communications. Contacts bring alien customs together and diminish the sanctity of many of the established ways. Moreover, the cumulative inventions of the industrial age, as applied both to modes of work and to modes of living, are inimical to the older customs and introduce a continuous process of change which limits the formation of new ones. Thus there is an increase in that area of moral indifference which is controlled by fashion. Where custom loses hold, fashion gains new ground. The increase of fashion's hold today, taken by certain critics of our age as a portent of social decadence, is traceable in part, then, to the civilizational accomplishments that have increased men's contacts with one another.

[3] *Fashion in diversified society:* In complex society, fashion may be viewed from either of two quite opposite sides. On the one hand, among frivolous or very sophisticated groups, fashion may become the main guide of life. In decadent civilizations it may usurp the place of morals. Thus Tacitus, in deploring the decline of moral standards in the Rome of his day, declared that "to corrupt and to be corrupted is called the fashion."[30] And in many subsequent

---

29. Spencer, *op. cit.*, II, 213–214.

30. Tacitus, *Germania*, p. 19.

ages, not least so our own, devotion to the whims of fashion and indifference to more fundamental aspects of life, whether on the part of the Italian aristocracy of the late Renaissance or the disappearing "bobby-soxers" of recent years, have been hailed as certain evidence of social decay. We may note that many such transitory and superficial developments are not significant "evidence" whatsoever, but that when any individual or group is exclusively concerned with the code of fashion he or it, however temporarily, is in a decadent stage.

On the other hand, within its sphere fashion serves a useful social function. It introduces a common pattern into the area of indifference, an appearance or sense of likeness which enables people of very diverse interests and dispositions to meet on common ground and which makes it easier for them to retain, in harmony with one another, their essential individual and group characters. Fashion has on that account a special significance in the extensive range of a diversified democratic civilization. But when its control passes beyond the superficialities of life, so that it becomes "fashionable" to frequently change one's wives or political affiliations or friends, it offers a poor substitute for the more established sanctions. For its rule is shallow and inconsequent, concerned with the form and not with the substance of living, devoid of conviction and of stability.

How fashion is prescribed. We have suggested some reasons why fashion holds such sway over the minds of men. What is perhaps less obvious is whence its commands proceed, who the leaders are, and why they should be so authoritative. The explanation that fashion is the "imitation of contemporaries" does not suffice. For the fashion must exist and be recognized before it is "imitated." It is followed because it is the fashion. It has leaders as well as followers, and the leaders, as we have seen, are those who have prestige in their particular field. They also must have a flair for the prevailing mood or temper of the time, whether in matters of dress or of art, of language or of thought. Even the most reputed leaders may fail at times to divine this mood and lose prestige for the moment, as the Paris fashion experts have done more than once. Nor can fashion be explained in simple terms of economic interests. It is quite capable of dealing ruthlessly with any particular economic interests which do not serve its purposes, as the woolen and other textile industries have known to their cost. It is true that important economic agencies are at work to stimulate the growth of fashion and above all to accelerate the change of fashion. When once the new mode is sensed, vast publicity is applied by these to persuade the community that a fashion has arrived and to urge its adoption. The claim that a book is a "best seller" or that a new song is the "rage" or a new play the "hit of the season" or that some particular color or material is being worn in the "best circles," provided it has a modicum of truth, helps to substantiate itself. But economic interests do not create the appeal of fashion; they merely reinforce it.

However, fashion is not purely wayward, equally ready to move in any direction that the leaders choose. Fashion in the long run may be allied with profounder forms of social control, adapting its prescriptions to moral, religious, or economic changes. While from season to season it seems to move forward and backward, in the larger perspective, fashion exhibits distinct trends.[31] These trends are sometimes indications of more important changes within the community. It is no accident, as we have seen, that with the change in the economic and social status of women there should have gradually come about certain permanent modifications of feminine dress. (In fact, the somewhat longer skirts called for by 1947 styles induced protest demonstrations, for example, in Dallas, Texas, on the basis of modern woman's "emancipation.") It is no accident that in war and postwar periods the dress of women more closely approximates that of men.

Fashion, playing at the surface where resistance is least, responding to the social whim of the moment, discovers on this level a compensation for the restraints of custom and habit and the routine of life. Through its passing conformities it helps to bridge the greater transitions of the process of social change. It often creates a series of seemingly inconsequent steps leading from one custom to another, thereby playing a part in both the maintenance and the alterations of the social structure.

We have in this chapter depicted the principal types of social codes by contrasting religion and morals, custom and law, and custom and fashion. We have discussed each of these with special reference to their functions, significance, and limitations in modern complex society. Throughout Part Two of Book Two, in considering the various kinds of groups in the social structure, and also throughout Book Three, in the analysis of social change, we shall have frequent occasion to recall this discussion of the social codes. One final task remains before us, however: to view the codes with relation to the life of the individual person, a task we face in the following chapter.

31. See A. L. Kroeber, "On the Principle of Order in Civilization as Exemplified by Changes of Fashion," *American Anthropologist*, N. S., XXI, No. 3 (1919), 235-263.

9

Social Codes and the Individual Life

Custom and Habit

The problem before us. **Our study of the social codes raises again the fundamental question, already discussed in Chapter II and in Chapter VI as well as in various passages elsewhere, of the relation of the individual to his society. In this chapter we shall discuss it from the standpoint of the individual as he faces the demands and the sanctions of the variant and sometimes conflicting codes which bear upon his conduct. The nature of this problem will appear more clearly if we first consider how the social principle of custom is related to the individual principle of habit.**

Custom and the nature of habit. **Few distinctions throw more light on the character of society than that of custom and habit, a distinction which is often clouded by ambiguities. It is true that custom is a *social* and habit is an *individual* phenomenon, but this distinction requires interpretation. It is not enough to regard customs as the habits of the group or as "widespread uniformities of habit."[1] Of course, any particular habit that, growing out of a common situation, characterizes many of the members of a group is likely to become a custom. A custom is then formed on the basis of habit, gaining the sanction and the influence, and therefore the social significance, which is peculiar to custom. Wherever there is a widespread habit there is probably a corresponding custom *as well*. Habits create customs and customs create habits. But the two, though intricately related, are distinct. Customs could not exist unless the corresponding habits were inculcated into the rising generations, but**

1. So defined by John Dewey in *Human Nature and Conduct* (New York, 1922), Chap. IV. On this point we differ from Dewey's account of custom and habit in that chapter, although it presents a penetrating and very suggestive analysis.

habits can exist without the support of custom. Feral beings, such as Kaspar Hauser or the "Wolf Children," must live without customs but they cannot live without habits.

Habits are behavior modes which through repetition have grown canalized. Man's tendency to respond in a similar way to a similar situation is confirmed and defined—grooved, as it were—by physical and psychical modifications. The acquisition of habit renders a specific action, brushing the teeth or feeding the baby or going to church, easy and familiar, relatively effortless and congenial. Habit means an *acquired* facility to act in a certain manner without resort to deliberation or thought.

When we form a habit we make it easier for ourselves, both *psychologically* and *physiologically*, to act in a certain way, and more difficult to act in ways alternative to that which has become habitual. In this sense habit is "second nature," or, more strictly, our realized nature, the established, rooted, and often almost indelible modes of response for which we have exchanged the unformed potentialities of our heredity. Since human nature is so adaptable, so rich in potentialities, so accommodating, since the young life can be trained in any of so many diverse ways, indoctrinated in any of so many diverse skills and capacities, the formation of habits is of supreme importance in the process of education. For habit realizes one alternative by shutting out many others. Habit closes countless avenues of life in order that a few may be more easy for us to tread. Without habits we could not achieve anything, but *which* habits we form and perhaps still more *how* we form them is of decisive moment.

Automatic habit and controlled habit. How we form habits determines whether habit shall be a tyrant or an instrument of our lives. In this determination the varying limitations of heredity play a part, but particularly important is the manner of our education.

[1] *Learning and automatic habit:* All learning, no matter what it is we learn, involves to some extent the acquisition of habits. We may learn to do things by the authoritative imposition of a routine, in which the process of learning is denuded of immediate meaning and only the mechanical result is counted. This method of learning characterizes many of the routines inculcated in the very young of all societies, involved in such basic activities as nursing, weaning, elimination, sleeping, and walking. Cultural variability in these matters is very great, and in each society the particular training techniques used to induce automatic habits play a role in determining broad personality types—a situation of considerable interest to many anthropologists and psychologists, as we pointed out in Chapter III.

This type of habit formation is not confined to the training of infants. An extreme example is the average Army sergeant or Navy "boot school" method of drilling recruits, based upon the questionable learning theory that the inculcation of automatic obedience in one activity will carry over into others. "Theirs not to reason why" unfortunately also finds frequent illustrations in the classroom when teaching becomes dictation, and knowledge, instead of being the exploration of a world of endless interest, becomes a task of memory.

Another type of automatic habit is that imposed by the technology and urbanization of modern society. The machine, for example, with its endless cycle of unvarying repetitions, calls for a similar routine in those who feed and tend it—a favorite subject of cartoons and one brilliantly portrayed by Chaplin's *Modern Times*. But this imposed routine is so limited and specialized that, unless it is accompanied by other conditions which rob life of interest and dignity, it does not bite so deeply into character as the enslavement of habits which impose themselves primarily in the name of authority. Nor is this authoritarian element present in those automatic habits induced by the congestion and facilities of city life, the habit of pushing to make the subway door, of walking on the right of the sidewalk, of depending for lunch on the same corner drugstore, and so forth. These are mostly habits of necessity, routinizing much of our behavior, to be sure, but essential if we are to adjust to the conditions of modern life.

[2] *The positive function of controlled habit:* Habit as the instrument of life economizes energy, reduces drudgery, and saves the needless expenditure of thought. Wherever there are purely repetitive acts to be performed, such as shaving in the morning or walking to one's work or typing letters or punching holes in steel, it is a vast gain to be able to entrust the *process* to the semiconscious operations of habit. We could never learn to do things easily or well if we had to think afresh each step of the process. This applies not only to mechanical tasks but to the finest and most creative arts. In the mechanical tasks, thought, liberated from the conscious superintendence of the process, must divorce itself from an activity which offers no scope for its free play. In the creative arts the artist seeks to express himself through the habit-controlled technique, subordinates it to the thing he is seeking to express, and thereby prevents it from hardening into mere mechanism. His satisfaction, his achievement, is not merely an end result of the process but also a concomitant of it. When, for example, the musician is able to relegate to habit the technique underlying his art he is then free to devote himself to the interpretation of the music, so that he can both enjoy it himself and communicate to others what it means to him.

This illustration from the arts permits us to view another important aspect of habit. Where an operation is performed solely for the end result, where there is no interest sustained and developed within the process which leads to it, habit is *mechanical* and becomes drudgery or tyranny. Mechanical habit is most frequently the result of economic necessity and was as characteristic of most preindustrial toil as of our own forms of labor. Men ordinarily seek relief from the burden of mechanical habit in sport or excitement or hobby or creative employment of leisure or perhaps in alcohol or drugs or daydreams. But we should not for this reason regard such devitalized habit as revealing the inherent nature of a phenomenon the essential function of which is to save and thus to liberate our energies.

Habit as a conservative agent in social life. Most of us at one time or another have condemned the habits of others or of ourselves on the ground that they have prevented new or alternative ways of doing this or that. In other words, we have complained about the role of habit in maintaining the status quo of some situation, about habit as a conservative force in social life. This function of habit has various aspects.

[1] *The "power" of habit and its limitations:* We often speak of the "power" of habit. In an eloquent and famous passage William James described it thus:

> Habit is thus the enormous fly-wheel of society, its most precious conservative agent. It alone is what keeps us all within the bounds of ordinance, and saves the children of fortune from the envious uprisings of the poor. It alone prevents the hardest and most repulsive walks of life from being deserted by those brought up to tread therein. It keeps the fisherman and the deck-hand at sea through the winter; it holds the miner in his darkness, and nails the countryman to his log-cabin and his lonely farm through all the months of snow; it protects us from invasion by the natives of the desert and the frozen zone. It dooms us all to fight out the battle of life upon the lines of our nurture or our early choice, and to make the best of a pursuit that disagrees, because there is no other for which we are fitted, and it is too late to begin again. It keeps different social strata from mixing. Already at the age of twenty-five you see the professional mannerism settling down on the young commercial traveller, on the young doctor, on the young minister, on the young counsellor-at-law. You see the little lines of cleavage running through the character, the tricks of thought, the prejudices, the ways of the "shop," in a word, from which the man can by-and-by no more escape than his coat-sleeve can suddenly fall into a new set of folds. On the whole, it is best he should not escape. It is well for the world that in most of us, by the age of thirty, the character has set like plaster, and will never soften again.[2]

Whether this hardening of character is "well for the world" is questionable. In the instances here presented habit should be thought of as making more easy and tolerable, rather than as dictating, the persistent activities of men. Habit makes necessity tolerable, but it does not make the necessity. Habit accommodates us to the necessity, so that it seems so no longer, so that once we are habituated it may shut out even from our imaginations the alternative experiences and goals which once seemed more appealing.

2. William James, *Principles of Psychology* (New York, 1890), I, 121. Reprinted by permission of the publishers, Henry Holt and Company.

The conservative quality of this accommodating function of habit is sharply illustrated in those people who for years have dreamed of new home surroundings or a new way of life only to discover upon its acquisition a longing for the old habitual surroundings or ways—a situation often depicted in novels and movies. What from one viewpoint may seem the dreariest type of existence, through the force of habituation, takes on a value of its own to which men often cling when confronted with the opportunity for change. In time even the prisoner may come to love his chains.

But there is another side to this picture. The energies economized by habit, if they find no outlet in or beyond the activity, the potentialities unutilized or obstructed by it, may break the dams and channels of habit, seeking in new ways a hitherto denied satisfaction. This is the phenomenon which in a particular religious manifestation is named "conversion." Another form of it is seen in the conquest of addictions, such as those created by drugs. It is often thought of as the revulsion from "bad" habits, but it also occurs as the sudden rejection of "good habits," imposed by past authority or by social pressure. These sudden revolts from conventional habituations are frequently portrayed in cartoon and fiction, for example by the violent explosions of a "Dagwood" or the "secret vices" of an otherwise model of propriety. This abrupt habit-defying change of the personal life is like the social phenomenon of revolution, the sudden rejection of custom and institution which have grown repressive beyond endurance, though this parallel is not complete since the custom against which we rebel is felt to be external and alien while the habit has become incorporated in our personalities.

When therefore we speak of the power or the "slavery" of habit we should remember that habit is not some all-powerful master ruling us against our will. This conception has, to be sure, a limited application to the abnormal group of drug-induced habits with their peculiar psychological character, though even here we should remember that the addict wants both the drug and freedom from it. But, in general, habit is the accommodation of the individual life to the conditions under which it must carry on its existence. Man can live in the snows or in the tropics, in the city or in the country, under the conditions of almost any social and physical environment; he can enter on any one of a thousand occupations, and there are a multitude of interests and diversions which many claim his leisure. From these a choice has to be made, and it is made under the influences of the nearer environment, of education and training, of temperament and capacity, of economic opportunity. Once made, habits begin to confirm the choice, to counter its disadvantages and disappointments, to close the alternatives. In the earlier stages they are more subject to revision and readaptation, but once fully established, especially as we grow older, they weave themselves into our personalities, habit joining with habit to form the pattern of our lives. Then only the strongest eruptive influences, such as the shift from civilian to military life or from a free community to the life of a prison or a concentration camp, can prevail against them, and only with profound disturbance to the human personality.[3]

[2] *The case of emotionally rooted habits:* Habit's function, its advantage, its sacrifice of alternatives are seen with peculiar clearness in the case of those habits which, unlike more technical aptitudes, become closely associated with our basic emotions. Such are pre-eminently our moral and religious habits, and include also our ways of thinking and acting on those political and economic issues which closely affect our interests. The endless diversity of moral codes and practices exhibited by different peoples or groups, while each nevertheless regards with strong revulsion the divergent practices of others, has been the subject of wondering comment since ancient times. And the hotly defended habituations in morals, sex behavior, religion, politics, and business practice are a constant source of modern speculation.

Consider sex relations. It is an obvious anthropological fact that even in this vital area different peoples can successfully accommodate themselves to a great variety of different systems. The universally shared drive of sex can adapt itself to various forms of expression so much so that "perversions" are a matter of cultural definition. However, the various possible alternatives of sex behavior do not all remain open in any society. Some dominant system is evolved under the prevailing circumstances of each group, suited to the modes of living resulting from its geographical and economic environment, to the fixations arising from its gradual translation into law of the accidents and inevitabilities of experience, and to the whole complex of customs of which the sex code is a part. Under each system custom becomes the ground of habit, and through their combined influence the deep emotions of sex convey a profound moral import to the accepted ways. The strong deviational tendencies of an urge so imperative as sex means that there is always present the possibility of its breaking loose from the prescribed channel of custom and habit, and this no doubt helps to generate the strength of sex taboos and prohibitions. Again we may note that the habits imposed by the latter are not complete masters of our inclinations, as evidenced by the presence of sexual deviation from the prescribed norms in almost all societies.[4]

Similar considerations apply to the other habits of work and industry in our own society that have become linked with religious and moral values, with habits of political behavior that have been built into the traditions of families and other groups, even with habits of everyday convention, departure from

3. On this point see, for example, the excellent study by two Army psychiatrists, R. R Grinker and J. F. Spiegel, *Men under Stress* (Philadelphia, 1945), especially Chaps. XIX and XX.

4. For anthropological evidence in this field, see B. Malinowski, *Sex and Repression in Savage Society* (New York, 1927); M. Mead, *Sex and Temperament in Three Primitive Societies* (New York, 1935); and for the United States, A. C. Kinsey, W. B. Pomeroy, and C. E. Martin, *Sexual Behavior in the Human Male* (Philadelphia, 1948).

which sometimes causes intense personal or group disturbance. With respect to them all, the danger is that the very necessity which imposes them tends to wrap them in a shroud of blind emotion, thus precluding the possibility of growth, of flexibility, and of intelligent redirection. Here as well as elsewhere, here perhaps more than elsewhere, the only assurance against needless limitation, against stagnation, or against equally blind revolt, lies in the constant association of habit and reflection. When either habit or custom grows sacrosanct, beyond the range of scrutiny and critical evaluation, the welfare of both individual and group is threatened.

Social organization and the relation of custom and habit. We can now draw certain conclusions concerning the distinction between habit and custom that was suggested at the outset of our discussion. If we are content to identify customs, as is commonly done, with "the habits of the group," then there is either no distinction at all, or a merely quantitative one, between the two concepts. The psychiatrist's interest in the habits of an individual would be identical with the sociologist's concern with the ways of a society. The two interests are necessarily related, are even interdependent, as we shall see, but they are not the same.

[1] *The social character of custom:* The identification of custom and habit ignores the social quality, the social sanction, of custom, a quality which is in no sense part of the meaning of habit. Habits formed in isolation, as by the hermit, or through personal idiosyncrasy, are just as truly habits as those formed under the influence of and in conformity with the conduct of the group. A custom, on the contrary, exists only as a *social relationship*. If, for example, I go to church because it is the thing to do, because it is the practice of the group to which I belong, because if I fail to do so I am subject to some degree of social disapprobation, or because by doing so I establish some useful business or social connections, then I am conforming to a custom. If when I am away from my group I have no prompting to attend church, then my former conduct, even if habitual, is to be attributed to custom rather than to habit.

Custom has for the individual an *external sanction*. It is a mode of conduct of the group itself, as a group, and every custom is in consequence adjusted to the others which the group observes. It is part of a complex of determinate relationships sustained and guarded by the group. Each individual sustains it, even though it gains also the support of habit, in the consciousness of his membership in the group. We would not give the name of custom to those habits of technical aptitude which we acquire in learning a trade or a profession. It is true that we owe these also to our social heritage, but they need no social sanction because they are direct objective means to the ends we seek. Thus the professional skill of the surgeon is habit, not custom, but his professional etiquette is custom though it may also be habit.

The peculiar social character of custom is revealed by the one great class of customs which cannot be practiced except collectively. Nearly all celebrations, rituals, and ceremonies fall within this class. They derive their significance from the fact that people come together and by participating in a common occasion stimulate the social consciousness of one another. There are many emotions for whose full satisfaction a social setting and the participation of others are requisite, and a whole range of customs, the ritual of worship, the dance, the reunion, social games, and so forth, arises to meet this need. Such customs are in no sense merely uniformities of habit, and many of them in fact involve a diversity of role on the part of the various performers.

[2] *The causal relation of habit and custom:* If custom and habit are distinct, they are at the sar : time causally related in social life. The customs of the group, impressed on the plastic natures of the young, shape and direct, focus and limit, their native potentialities. Undirected potentiality is also sprawling helplessness. Education is rendered both possible and necessary by the pressure of alternatives. The customs of the group are translated through education, in the broadest sense, into the habits of each generation, and the habits thus formed perpetuate the customs. In this educative process customs may be thought of as preceding habits, but if this were the whole story the weight of the past would repress all innovation, all readjustment, all development. Man is assertive as well as plastic; he refuses to take on the perfect mold of the past.

One aspect of this truth is that *habits also precede customs*. Our habits are a more intimate part of our personality than are our customs, and they arise not only from social education but also as our personal response to the immediate conditions of our lives. Thus they exhibit a greater variability, and as they impinge on customs they make these in turn more flexible and subject to modification. When personal habits are sufficiently similar, such as those induced by the discovery of new techniques, they are apt not only to modify old customs but also to stimulate new ones. Thus new habits induced by the telephone and automobile and radio have undermined old customs and have helped to bring about others. Many of the customs of our industrial age, such as the recreational custom of attending "mass spectacles" like movies and sports events or the custom of eating tinned or frozen foods or that of frequently changing one's automobile model, may be attributed in part to the habits necessitated by machinecraft and urbanization or the opportunities released by invention.[5]

The process we have been describing—custom determining the general direction of habituations, and habits in turn sustaining and sometimes altering customs—is a significant aspect of all social organization. As we go on to explore in later chapters the features of the social structure we should keep in mind a lesson that the understanding of habit and custom and their interrelationship teaches, namely that all social phenomena ultimately involve the strivings and dispositions and attitudes of individual human beings as well as the customs and institutions and other characteristic ways of human groups.

5. For numerous illustrations, see *Recent Social Trends* (New York, 1933), Chap. III.

The Individual Confronting the Mores

Opposing aspects of the mores and the individual. From the standpoint of the individual the mores have two aspects. In the first place, as we have seen, through indoctrination and habituation, they are incorporated into his very nature. Secondly, they confront him as socially sanctioned demands, bringing pressure to bear on his native inclinations, on his personal desires and personal calculations. Thus they arouse resistance and create conflict within him.

[1] *The intensification of the problem in modern society:* The conflict between the individual's desires and the mores is more apparent in complex society than in the simpler types. In all societies, as the growing child is indoctrinated in the mores, he tends, under their prompting, to rationalize his first unreasoning acceptance. The mores appear to him as the eternal, the sacred, the adult-given, the God-given. But when the child or the adolescent comes into contact with new groups and new situations, when he enters a world in which the authority of the family or the discipline of the school or the tradition of the local group no longer holds, this attitude of acceptance is subject to challenge. The presence of new mores raises questions regarding the basis of acceptance of the old. The conflict of mores and codes may shake the sense of the inevitable rightness of the hitherto established, may disturb the psychological security of the narrower social world of the young child.[6]

This challenge and this kind of disturbance are more frequent and more formidable in modern complex society. In primitive society, generally, adolescence means initiation into the old tribal ways. In modern society it often means initiation into new ways, frequently incomprehensible to the elders, and into some degree of liberation from former indoctrinations. The consequent widespread uncertainty and conflict represent a phenomenon characteristic of modern life which is found to a much less extent in primitive life. This situation is intensified by the very complexity of modern social organization, with its numerous and often conflicting codes.

[2] *The individual's problem of selecting a code:* The number and variety of codes in modern society confront the individual as a great social pressure, often as an overbearing but inconsistent demand for conformity. The individual is faced with the problem of charting his way through the claims of family tradition, of business practices, of political loyalties, of sex standards, of religious prescriptions, of humanitarian considerations, for example, and ultimately of his own conscience. This situation, imposed by the complexities and inconsistencies of contemporary life, has increasingly in recent years occupied the attention of psychoanalysts and psychiatrists. For many of the problems of

---

6. This process is admirably revealed in J. Piaget, *The Moral Judgment of the Child*, (New York, 1932). See also the analysis of G. H. Mead, *Mind, Self and Society* (Chicago, 1934), Part III.

personality maladjustment, the neuroses and some psychoses, and various physical maladies as well, according to "psychosomatic" medicine, cannot be understood without reference to this sociological characteristic of our era.[7] This is a problem to which we shall return.

However, the majority conform to the codes. Although at times everyone feels an inner resistance to some of their aspects, most of us accept them most of the time and nearly all of the time approve the conformity of others. The individual, faced by the necessity of selecting from among the number and variety of the codes, acquires a code of his own. This personal code is compounded of many elements, selective within the limits imposed by the sanctions of law and custom, deeply responsive to the influences of education and of the social environment, but nevertheless expressive of the whole of the particular personality.

There are important implications of the individual's selection of his own code. On the one hand, this liberty of choice is an essential mark of adult selfhood in our culture. The process necessarily requires the mitigation of such drastic external sanctions as those of a compulsory fear-inspired religion, typical of an earlier period in Western society, and cannot take place in a "totalitarian" environment in which the ruling authority seeks to close all avenues of choice but one. On the other hand, the freedom of the individual to select his own code may take place within social conditions that provide no guarantees of life's material requirements and few or no strong group values that are essential for psychological security. This situation, according to some writers, characterized much of Western society during the period preceding the recent European dictatorships, themselves attributable in part to the modern individual's longing, albeit unconscious, to "escape from freedom."[8] In any event, if the individual is to retain this highest mark of cultural development, the ability and desire to select his own standards, he must at the same time strive to maintain a kind of social order in which choice itself is protected and guaranteed.

[3] *Contrast of the social and individual codes:* The *social codes* are standards, but they are not, in the full sense, ideals of conduct. They are essentially workaday rules, deriving in part from tradition and in part from the necessities of group life. As we shall see in a later chapter, the social codes reveal also the dominant interests of the power holders in all societies. They constitute at best a rough translation into formulas or norms of the limited experience and reflection of the average mentality of the group.

7. See, for example, T. Burrow, *The Social Basis of Consciousness* (New York, 1927); K. Horney, *The Neurotic Personality of Our Time* (New York, 1937), especially Chap. XV, and *New Ways in Psychoanalysis* (New York, 1939) especially Chap. X; A. Kardiner, *The Psychological Frontiers of Society* (New York, 1945), Chap. XIV; and the articles by F. Alexander, T. Burrow, E. Mayo, P. Schilder, H. S. Sullivan, and E. Sapir in *The American Journal of Sociology*, Vol. XLII, No. 6 (1937). The problem is well stated by K. Mannheim in *Diagnosis of Our Time* (London, 1943), Chaps. II and V.

8. See E. Fromm, *Escape from Freedom* (New York, 1941).

In contrast, the *selective code of the individual* expresses, in proportion to the strength of his character and the clarity of his intelligence, a more definite and vivid and intimate set of valuations. These individual codes could not exist without the support of the social codes, but they exceed the latter in substance, vitality, and detail. The mainspring of the individual's life is in fact the inner set of valuations he cherishes. Within these valuations there are often conflict and contradiction, involving in normal cases a sometimes painful adjustment to new experiences, but in extreme cases going so far as to disrupt the personality. At the same time, there is also a degree of conflict between the individual code and some dominant social code, a conflict that is most apt to show itself in relation to the sex code, to the economic code, and in many communities to the religious code of the group to which the individual belongs.

Two general types of conflict between the individual and the code. There are, then, two main types of conflict: (1) that in which personal interest or personal valuation is opposed to a prevailing code, and (2) that in which the individual is pulled opposite ways by the prescriptions of different codes, when two or more are applicable within the same situation. In the individual life the two types are sometimes found in combination. The most significant variety of the first type is that where the individual conscience denies the rightness or validity of the code, as when, for example, the citizen who abhors war is called by the state to military training or service.[9] At times closely related to this variety of conflict is an example of the second type, the situation, once so frequent and still by no means obsolete, in which the religion of the citizen prescribes a course of conduct contrary to that which is commanded by the state.

[1] *An illustration from drama:* These two types of conflict provide, because of their intrinsic interest and their consequences, the supreme subjects of literature, especially of the novel and of the drama. One of the famous dramatic presentations of the clash between two social codes is Sophocles' *Antigone*, where the heroine has to choose between the prescriptions of her religion, involving her sacred duty to her dead brother, and the edict of the king. The drama, as life itself, frequently combines the two types of conflict, as in *Hamlet*. In drama's whole range from the Orestean trilogy to the plays of more modern authors like Ibsen, Shaw, Galsworthy, O'Neill, Anderson, and Odets, its main theme has been the predicament of the "hero," incarnating some social or personal code and beset by the sanctions of an opposing social code. It is of sociological significance that when, as in *Agamemnon*, *Macbeth*, *Hamlet*, *Ghosts*, *The Emperor Jones*, the social sanctions triumphed over the "hero," the drama takes the form of tragedy; but often when, as in the Falstaff plays, *Peer Gynt*, *Arms and the Man*, and many others with a "happy ending" including such

9. On the general subject, see R. M. MacIver, *Community* (New York, 1920), Book III, Chap. V. For various aspects of the problem, see K. Young, *Social Psychology* (New York, 1944), Chap. XV.

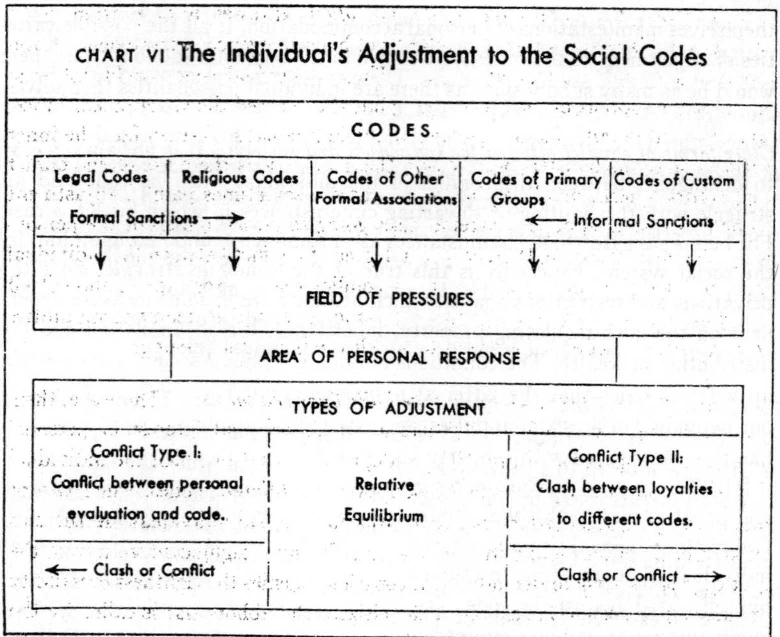

farces as *Arsenic and Old Lace*, the "hero" outwits, triumphs over, or achieves some form of reconciliation with the social code, the result is technically a comedy. The keen dramatist recognizes and exploits the high value we generally place on the individual's selective code.

[2] *The conflict in contemporary life:* Consider the problems that face us in everyday life. Shall I vote for the candidate who seems best qualified for office or shall I follow the party of my family, my employer, my closest associates? Shall I take a position with the type of business firm in the family tradition or shall I seek one more suited to my own nature? Shall I obey the legal code and employ workers on the basis of their qualifications to do the job or shall I follow the code of custom, giving preference to Whites, "Anglos," "Gentiles"? Shall I marry the person I love who happens to be Jewish or Catholic or whatever it may be or shall I marry the "nice" girl or boy whose social credentials meet the prescriptions of my own group? Shall I remain sexually faithful to my husband or wife or shall I seek affection or diversion more in keeping with my inner desires? And so on.

Such are the questions that confront each of us as we go about the business of selecting between the social codes or between the latter and our own codes. The range of pressures and the range of accommodation to them are suggested in Chart VI. The accommodations, as we have seen, can take many forms, including those types our culture defines as "neurotic" and "maladjusted"—

themselves manifestations of personal accommodation. If all the possible varieties of adjustment to the codes were shown in the bottom box of our chart there would be as many subdivisions as there are individual personalities themselves.

Other forms of conflict between the individual and society. It is not always easy to distinguish between the conflict of the individual with the code and his struggle with the limiting or thwarting circumstances in which his lot is cast. For he may regard these circumstances as in some sense imposed upon him by the social system. Especially is this true of the economic struggle, since the privations and restrictions against which he fights are in some measure dependent on the laws regulating property, inheritance, the accumulation and the distribution of wealth. The conditions obtaining within a society are so linked up with its codes that the latter at numerous points come into conflict with our individual desires and impulses, and especially with our strongest impulses, like those associated with property and with sex.

[1] *Three types of pressure on the individual:* The unequal conditions of power and privilege and wealth that obtain in all societies—no less, so far as the first two of these inequalities are concerned, in communistic societies than in more individualistic ones—lead to frequent situations in which the individual finds himself pitted against the code. The different types of dominance which bring about this result will be examined in greater detail in Part Two of this Book. Here three types may be distinguished.

ONE: THE PRESSURE OF DOMINANT GROUPS. In the first place, there are dominant groups which impose their will on other groups, bringing to bear strong social pressures under which the less dominant suffer. This is the case whatever the form of society, whether a "utopian community" such as Oneida or a huge modern nation. In one sphere the pressure takes the form of social ostracism, in another of economic exploitation, in another of arbitrary or tyrannical laws.

TWO: THE PRESSURE OF AUTHORITY. Within every group, no matter how small, no matter how united by common purpose, there is the tendency of authority and prestige to seek its own ends and to express its power at the cost of the variant individualities subject to it. To secure any common end there must be common rules, but the drive of authority, fostered by lack of understanding as well as by pride of position, goes beyond the degree of regulation which the common end requires. Even in the circle of the family this tendency is displayed. The divergent viewpoints of the older and the younger lead often to bitter compulsions and revolts and sometimes to tragic sacrifices. It is the sensitive, the imaginative, the original minds on whom the pressure bears most heavily. It is these, too, who feel most bitterly the tyrannies which are often imposed by officials and bureaucrats, "clothed in a little brief authority." The resulting sense of frustration may be expressed in a bitterness against the particular organization or even against society itself.

There are, of course, beneficent and needful restrictions. All organizations involve some restriction, some rules. There must be a common policy for common ends, for common discipline. If wisely devised and maintained, this is a means of strength. Without order there is no direction and no achievement in a common cause. But there are many restrictions which are due to the failure to understand individual differences, to the ambition or narrow-mindedness of power, to the willingness of men to exploit others without consideration of the cost.

THREE: THE PRESSURE OF INSTITUTIONS. A third source of social restriction arises from the almost impersonal control exercised through institutions. The social structure rests on a social heritage. It has been built through many generations. Its institutions express the prejudice and superstition as well as the intelligence of their countless builders. Although it is constantly being rebuilt according to the standards of each age, the process is never complete. Some of its institutions may be harmful survivals, repressive of the individuality of its present members. Conventions and mores, especially of the prohibitive type, may derive authority from the mere fact of long establishment. They are apt to grow sacrosanct and thus resistant to change, all the more because they fail to justify themselves by the only legitimate test, the service they render to the members of the society. The demand for conformity is often unreasoning, and history is strewn with instances of the suppression of those less gregarious and more original minds whose insight proved in the retrospect to be greater than that of the mass of their fellows.

[2] *The sense in which conflict is inevitable:* Beyond these difficulties there lies another, in the very nature of society. Every social situation or environment, even the most intimate, is one each individual shares with others. Each must adjust himself not only to these others but also to the *common situation.* Hence certain uniformities of conduct are demanded of him. The common situation and the variant individual, the situation and the code demanding conformity and the individual seeking to be himself—these are the terms of countless conflicts.

The more extreme manifestations of these conflicts are, on the one hand, the ruthlessness of power crushing individuality in the name of social authority. They are, on the other hand, the fear, distraction, revolt, and psychological instability of those who from the standpoint of the prevailing code are "abnormal" and in the eyes of authority are "antisocial." This clash of conformity and individuality reveals itself most vividly, perhaps, in the sensitive protestations or critical evaluations of a society's "intellectuals" or "intelligentsia" who, as one writer has expressed it, seem to most people and sometimes to themselves, by virtue of their critical function, to be "queer" or even "neurotic."[10] When authority, whether in the garb of a dictatorial political party or,

10. Cf. A. Koestler, "The Intelligentsia," in *The Yogi and the Commissar* (New York, 1945), pp. 61–76.

say, Boston's Watch and Ward Society, forces the artist to abide by this or that code, the latter loses his "neurotic" status, to be sure, but society also is deprived of an essential contribution to its own progress.

[3] *Social utopias as a reflection of the conflict:* Confronted with the obstacles that material and social circumstances oppose to the fulfillment of personal ideals, men have in all ages either longed for or striven for a social order "nearer to the heart's desire." The striving is in the form of group activity, working for "reform" or for revolution, processes we shall examine in Book Three. The longing finds individual expression in visions of social "utopias."

These utopias are the individual's substitute for reform or revolution, his private dream or myth of a new society. Though imaginary, they nevertheless reveal the conflict between individual ideals and social realities. In all times, from the earliest conceptions of the "golden age" to more recent expressions such as Edward Bellamy's *Looking Backward* or H. G. Wells's *Modern Utopia*, men have given literary form to these visions. They serve both as an escape from the world of reality and as an inspiration toward a possible future. In this sense, as Lewis Mumford has pointed out, the utopia exercises a double function. On the one hand, "it seeks an immediate release from the difficulties or frustrations of our lot." On the other, it "attempts to provide a condition for our release in future." There are thus "utopias of escape" and "utopias of reconstruction," as one or the other function dominates. "In one we build impossible castles in the air; in the other we consult a surveyor and an architect and a mason and proceed to build a house which meets our essential needs; as well as houses made of stone and mortar are capable of meeting them."[11] Only a few individuals create utopias in literary form, but the "utopian mentality" that envisions a different and improved social order is a widespread phenomenon. Those who share this mentality are often labeled "dreamers" by the defenders of the status quo, but the latter dream also when they fail to recognize that the utopian visions of men as well as their time-honored codes and authorities are an important part of ever-changing social reality.[12]

The social codes embody at best only the standards acceptable to the group in general. They can never meet the demands of every particular situation or fully regulate the attitude and the behavior of the individual toward his group. This consideration brings us to our final question, that of the reconciliation of two things equally necessary for the conduct of life, the social code and the individual judgment.

11. L. Mumford, *The Story of Utopias* (New York, 1922), Chap. I. In addition to this excellent analysis, see also J. O. Hertzler, *The History of Utopian Thought* (New York, 1926), especially Part Two.

12. For an analysis of the utopian mentality, various of its forms, and its social functions, see K. Mannheim, *Ideology and Utopia* (New York, 1936), Part IV.

Social Codes and Individual Judgment: the Problem of Moral Liberty

The social code and the particular situation. In this final section we pose a question that has puzzled philosophers and others for many centuries. This is the question of the moral liberty of the individual member of society. It is a "philosophical" question, to be sure, but the answer to it, as we shall see, rests upon an adequate sociological understanding.

[1] *The limits of the code:* An ancient student of social life once contrasted law and equity, the former being like a rigid rod that can measure only flat surfaces and the latter a flexible rule that can be fitted into the flutings and cornices of actual buildings.[13] A similar distinction may be drawn between social norms and the determinants of individual conduct in each concrete situation. The social norms never envisage the full particular situation in view of which conduct is always directed. They cannot descend from their high altitude of generality to prescribe in detail the course of action befitting the immediate occasion. In the infinitely varied texture of life no two occasions are exactly alike. Social norms are limiting principles within a zone of conduct, and even the most docile and subservient of individuals could not regulate his life by their aid alone. They are not schoolmasters which assign the definite task for the present hour. Seldom can they say, Do this here and now, and even when they go thus far, as political law in some degree does, the reference is then only to the external aspect of conduct.

Consider various situations. Our moral code calls for truthfulness, but it would be absurd to hold that it insists upon the telling of the whole truth about everything to everyone on every occasion. Should one tell the truth to a madman who is seeking one's friend to kill him? Should the doctor tell the truth to a nervous patient who would thereby be made worse? The code calls for fair dealing between man and man but who beside the individuals concerned can decide what fairness is in the hour of action? Who can decide which of the various codes and which of their various precepts is the most relevant to the situation? In the final analysis, the decision must be made by the individual who finds himself in it and who in one way or another must interpret both the situation and the code.

[2] *How the code is applied to the particular situation:* There are two closely associated ways in which the social codes bear on human behavior and therefore on the specific situation itself. Both are highly important in social life but neither, as we shall see, can in itself fully explain the relation of code to practice.

ONE: INDOCTRINATION. Through indoctrination, the codes form the basis of individual habits. In the process of education the code is continually trans-

13. Aristotle, *Ethics*, 1137c.

lated to the young in the form of specific injunction, who gradually come to recognize a situation as one in which such and such conduct is expected of them. The similar elements in successive situations become the stimuli of the growing habit. To the youth trained to churchgoing, for example, Sunday morning, with the changes in the household routine, the cessation of regular work, the discarding of workaday clothes, the ringing of church bells, and so on, constitutes a *total stimulus* that readily evokes, as a step in a habitual series, the act of church attendance. So in situation after situation the codes enter the process of indoctrination so that the individual's habituations tend toward conformity with the ways of the group.

However, in this process human beings do not react simply as insects or as the mere products of "conditioned response," as they are sometimes described by the extreme behaviorists. The functioning of habit involves response to similar elements and situational patterns which are recognized and selected for attention in constantly varying circumstances. Every conscious act involves the *total* personality of the individual, including his intelligence, and the *total* situation to which it is a response.[14] The individual cannot help forming habits of his own, but if they prove out of harmony with his developing personality he may modify or reject altogether many of those habits inculcated by authority or impressed by training in his earlier years. The codes become incorporated into habits, not simply because the younger generation is plastic to the teaching of the older, but also because it finds these ways of life in keeping with and serviceable to its own desires. In the long run, when the old ways cease to be serviceable, because of growing knowledge or changing life conditions, no amount of inculcation will assure their survival. Thus as modern technology or new value-systems such as democracy or communism have spread from people to people they have initiated vast transformations in the social codes.

TWO: THE PRESSURE OF OPINION. There is a second way, distinct from its translation into specific habit, in which the code exercises influence over conduct. Man is a social being, sensitive to the opinions of his fellows. The proud motto of a Scottish family—"They say. What say they? Let them say."—may express a group attitude to outsiders, but no man is completely indifferent to, or unaffected by, the views of his neighbors. As we have seen, the principal sanction of such codes as custom and fashion is the pressure of public opinion, while this same pressure forms an additional sanction of other codes, such as those of religion and law. The omnipresent sense of what others will think of us, expressing itself on the one hand in the positive satisfaction of conformity, and on the other in the aversion from the direct and indirect consequences of nonconformity, sustains and perpetuates the codes against many of the tempta-

14. Our position here is similar to the learning theory of the *Gestalt* school of psychology, which, in contrast to extreme behaviorism, seems sociologically valid. See, for example, K. Koffka, *Principles of Gestalt Psychology* (New York, 1935) and W. Koehler, *Gestalt Psychology* (New York, 1929).

tions of private rebellion. We are uneasy if we fail to do what our associates expect of us and this uneasiness readily assumes a moral significance.

[3] *The particular situation and the question of morals:* Indoctrination and the pressure of opinion lead us to select for attention in each concrete situation those common aspects which are of significance also to our group and to conduct ourselves accordingly. However, the complexity of the particular situation cannot be disregarded nor can it be met in terms of social expectancy or by a simple appeal to a common code. The code prescribes a typical or standardized conduct. There is, moreover, the frequent situation wherein more than one precept or more than one code claims equal validity. How, for example, can the code solve the problem of the youth who has to choose between doing lip service to a creed he disbelieves or causing grave distress to an invalid parent, or of the girl who has to choose between her lover and her religion, or of the writer who must sacrifice his literary ideals to ensure a decent living, or of the businessman who has to decide between bankruptcy or the adoption of competitive methods of which he disapproves, or of the workman who is asked to participate in a strike which he believes is justified but which would bring his family to want? These are a few obvious illustrations of the problems of conduct which, in far more specialized and difficult forms, occur continually in everyday life.

It is apparent that each of these illustrations involves a *moral* problem for the individual, and one which for him transcends the standardized prescriptions of the codes. Therefore when it is claimed that "for practical purposes morals mean customs"[15] this problem is being oversimplified. Morality, of course, historically for the group and psychologically for the individual, can only be derived from the experience of social relationships. But the developed significance of moral questions, especially in complex society with its multiplicity and inconsistency of codes, is the burden of judgment and decision carried by each human being. In this sense moral liberty for the individual exists as a fact of social life.[16]

The inadequacy and the necessity of codes in social life. The question of moral liberty, then, has important sociological aspects. In fact, its real significance cannot be understood unless we perceive that the social codes are quite essential and at the same time quite inadequate for the conduct of individual life.

[1] *Why the code cannot be a substitute for individual judgment:* Even in the simplest situations the code has to be selected, accepted, interpreted, and applied. How large an element of personal discretion enters in can be seen if we consider the analogy of the judge, whose business it is to apply to a particular case the most explicit, detailed, and objective of all the codes, that of the law

15. Dewey, *op. cit.*, Part One, V. See also Part Four, IV.

16. For a pertinent discussion of this problem in somewhat different language but with a similar conclusion, see P. W. Bridgman, "Freedom and the Individual," in *Freedom Its Meaning* (R. N. Anshen, ed., New York, 1940), pp. 525–537.

of the land, to a case which he knows only from the outside and without the distraction of personal interest. Yet even here with his books of recorded precedents before him, the judge has to rely largely on his own sense of what justice *should* be, and the issue is often doubtful until the decision is delivered. This applies to the interpretation of the Constitution no less than to the application of statute law, as the record of the Supreme Court of the United States abundantly reveals. Clearly, from that record, there is no infallible way of deciding whether the "commerce clause" has been violated, whether "due process of law" has been adhered to, whether a business is "affected with a public interest," whether competition has been "lessened," and so forth. Substitute for the professional judge the individual arbiter of his own case, who has to determine the course of action to be taken and not merely to assess it afterward, who has no single authoritative code which it is incumbent on him to apply, who is immersed in the situation by personal interest and familiar engrossment and does not sit, like the judge, in cool and ample reflection over it. The conclusion is surely clear that the mere acceptance of the social codes is quite inadequate for the guidance of conduct, apart altogether from the fact that such acceptance, were it feasible, would denude the individual of initiative and all the quality of character.

[2] *The necessity of the code:* Yet if we deny the adequacy for conduct of the social codes, we must no less insist on their necessity. Without them the individual would be utterly distracted and helpless. Ingrained in him through indoctrination and habit, and continually impinging on him from his social environment, the codes reduce the limits of individual judgment to practicable proportions. Without them the burden of decision would be intolerable and the vagaries of conduct utterly distracting. The dream of absolute anarchism, were it realizable, would in fact be a horrible nightmare. The social codes afford a solid foundation on which man can deal with man. They reveal to him both his likeness to and his unity with his fellows. They bring home to him his membership in the group, his present hour of participation in the continuity of the past and future of the human race, and his unit of contribution to the life of the whole society.

The final problem of reconciling the code and individual judgment. In earlier chapters we discussed other pairs of logical opposites such as individual "versus" society, conflict "versus" co-operation, and heredity "versus" environment, finding them to be not in fundamental opposition in social life itself. Here we have a similar case. How far and in what way, then, can the necessity of the social code be reconciled with the antithetical necessity of individual judgment?

A partial reconciliation, varying in adequacy with the personality of the individual and with the character of the social order, is certainly attainable. We saw in Chapter III that individuality cannot develop apart from society, or society if it suppresses individuality. Recall that through both his *common* interests and his *harmonious* like interests, the individual can be in full accord with the social order—the same point now pertains. *In so far as* the social order reflects the common interests of men, which must be shared in order to be realized, the individual is both free within, and sustained in his individuality by society. In this situation, he is able to say "we" instead of merely "I," and thereby to liberate important elements of his socially dependent personality. For he finds *himself* also in that which he shares with others, in identifying himself with a common cause, in the exercise of his individuality through devotion to his family or community or nation or political party or business or trade-union or cultural group. In this devotion he loses his isolation and finds his individuality. Were it otherwise the group could not evoke as it does man's greater loyalties and enthusiasms and aspirations.

The deeper loyalty, therefore, is not that which slavishly follows the social code—"my country, right or wrong"—but that which responds to it in the spirit and the obligation of the common cause for which it, however imperfectly, stands. The individual who slavishly follows the code of nation or class or religion or other group is unconscious of or unfitted for a greater social obligation. Within him society has, paradoxically, no deep roots. He is bound to the code by the superficial and uncreative bonds of imitation and compliance: he reflects but does not express society. Those regimes, it may be pointed out, that through coercion and strict control suppress the manifestations of individuality, however unaware they may be of the fact, build among their followers what in the long run are the weakest rather than the strongest of group loyalties.[17]

No human being is, in fact, a kind of automaton reflecting in his conduct only the prescriptions of the group codes. Primitive man was once so pictured by various writers, but modern anthropology has undermined "the assumption that in primitive societies the individual is completely dominated by the group —the horde, the clan or the tribe—that he obeys the commands of his community, its tradition, its public opinion, its decrees, with a slavish, fascinated, passive obedience."[18] What needs further to be observed is that this spirit of passive obedience, to which of course we find approximations both in civilized and in primitive society, especially in matters of belief, is the least and not the most fully developed expression of social-mindedness. To be fully social is to be socially *responsible*, to bring the whole social situation, as it affects and is affected by one's conduct, into the focus of one's consciousness and act accordingly. This, however, is a statement of the ideal, to which in actuality we find only various degrees of approximation.

This chapter brings to a close Part One of this Book. In it we have indicated the way in which the relations between men are patterned by the mores, by the

17. For a scathing evaluation of the ruling regime of Soviet Russia in the form of a fable, which incorporates the point made above, see G. Orwell, *Animal Farm* (New York) 1946.
18. Cf. B. Malinowski, *Crime and Custom in Savage Society* (New York, 1926).

social codes and sanctions. We have distinguished the major types of codes and sanctions and discussed their general functional significance in social life. And we have considered the various processes that operate to make the individual a part of a structure of social relationships. At the same time, we have seen, once more, that social life cannot be completely understood without taking into account the individual's own role, his attitudes and judgments and decisions. The even larger task lies ahead of examining the principal forms of group structures into some of which we are born and within which we find work and recreation, rewards and penalties, struggle and mutual aid.

The Social Structure

PART TWO: *The Major Forms of Social Structure*

Foreword: WE ARE now prepared to consider the various modes of grouping that together comprise the complex pattern of the social structure. In Chapter X we sketch the major types of social groups, emphasizing the general characteristics of the more intimate primary associations, and the large-scale, relatively impersonal organizations. This preliminary discussion of contrasting types of groups should be a guide through the succeeding chapters. Thus in Chapter XI we view the family, the most significant and pervasive of the primary groups; in Chapters XII and XIII the community, the most inclusive spontaneous grouping in the social structure; and in Chapters XIV, XV, and XVI we consider respectively the enduring phenomenon of class, the ethnic or "racial" in-group, and the temporary grouping of crowd, all being more or less spontaneous configurations responsive to various interests that develop within the community. Chapters XVII through XX deal with the principal forms of organizations deliberately established for specific ends, the associations—the group manifestations of the pursuit of like and common interests. The associations constitute the most conspicuous part of the social structure, and they gain in coherence, definition, number, and efficacy as the conditions of the society grow more complex. They combine into elaborate functional systems and institutional complexes, as we show in Chapter XXI.

In the analysis of the social structure the role of the diverse attitudes and interests of social beings is revealed. In particular, associations, being definitely functional, correspond closely to interests. A classification of interests therefore provides a basis for the study of associations. This classification rests on the broad distinction between *cultural* and *utilitarian* interests, a distinction that assumes major importance for the interpretation of social change in the final Book of this volume.

10

Types of Social Groups

Introductory: Groups in Social Life

The group and its many manifestations. Man's life is to an enormous extent a group life. He not only lives in groups and continuously creates with his fellows new groups, but he also develops a variety of verbal symbols with which to identify them. The result is a series of group terms in the language of every society, terms essential for everyday communication. In our own society we often use the word "group" itself to refer to such diverse collectivities as the family or the crowd or the social class, to informal cliques or vast communities, or to the members of races or religions or occupations, or to this or that division of sex or age or intelligence or temperament. Little wonder, then, that sociologists have set about the task of rendering more precise the language of group analysis.[1]

[1] *The meaning of group:* As we explained in Chapter I, by *group* we mean *any collection of human beings who are brought into social relationships with one another*. Social relationships involve, as we have seen, some degree of reciprocity between those related, some measure of mutual awareness as reflected in the attitudes of the members of the group. On the basis of this criterion, many of those divisions of a population that are sometimes named social groups, such

1. Among the earlier ambitious attempts to systematize the classification of groups are those of G. Simmel in *Soziologie* (Leipzig, 1908); see also N. J. Spykman, *The Social Theory of Georg Simmel* (Chicago, 1925), Book II; and of L. von Wiese and H. Becker in *Systematic Sociology* (New York, 1932). For more recent attempts see D. Sanderson, "Group Description," *Social Forces*, XVI (1938), 309–319, and "A Preliminary Structural Classification of Groups," *ibid.*, XVII (1938), 1–6; G. Lundberg, *Foundations of Sociology* (New York, 1939), Chap. IX; E. T. Hiller, *Social Relations and Structures* (New York, 1947), Chaps. XVII–XIX. For a summary and critique of various group classifications, see L. Wilson, "Sociography of Groups," in *Twentieth Century Sociology* (G. Gurvitch and W. E. Moore, eds., New York, 1945), Chap. VII.

as the people of a certain age or income level or intelligence range, are more properly thought of as statistical aggregates. However, the young or the old-aged, for example, may become social groups if they are set apart by institutional arrangements as in some primitive societies or if they develop similar attitudes and interests as in "Youth" movements, or "Age" movements such as that represented by the Townsend Plan. Again, those in different income brackets may at the same time possess an awareness of their differences and the contrasting attitudes that mark them as different social classes. Class and community and crowd are among the significant types of groups we shall investigate, but these categories by no means exhaust the varieties of this most general sociological concept.

[2] *Classifying types of groups:* We may classify from a variety of viewpoints the types of groups in which men participate. Consider size as a criterion. The German sociologist Simmel, being interested in the way in which the numbers of a group affect its organization and the social interaction within it, began with the "monad"—the single person as a focus of group relationships—and pursued his analysis through the "dyad," the "triad," and the other smaller collectivities on the one hand and the large-scale groups on the other.[2] Consider the degree of quality of social interaction that operates within groups. Several sociologists have used as their basic division that between the more intimate face-to-face groupings, such as the family and neighborhood and village, and the more impersonal larger collectivities, such as the large city or corporation or state.[3] This distribution has been further refined by some writers who have classified groups into degrees of intimacy of contact between the members.[4] We shall see shortly that size and the nature of social contact within the group are interrelated and that both are important considerations in the study of groups. Consider the range of group interests. Some groups, such as the community, are inclusive territorial units having no specialized interests; others, such as the varieties of association, are organized in order to fulfill specific interests of their members. The members of all groups, of course, are in some degree conscious of their collective interests whether they are specialized or not. Consider the duration of interests. Those of some groups like the crowd are short-lived while those of such groups as the class and community are relatively permanent. Finally, consider the degree of organization. Groups range from such highly developed organizations as the modern factory or governmental hierarchy to the largely unorganized temporary crowd and permanent class.

2. Simmel, *op. cit.* This type of analysis was further developed by von Wiese and Becker in *Systematic Sociology*.

3. This is the distinction developed by F. Tönnies in *Gemeinschaft und Gesellschaft* (Leipzig, 1887), which has been translated and supplemented by C. P. Loomis in *Fundamental Concepts of Sociology* (New York, 1940).

4. See, for example, F. Stuart Chapin, *Contemporary American Institutions* (New York, 1935), p. 162; and Lundberg, *op. cit.*

CHART VII Schematic View of Major Types of Groups in the Social Structure

GROUPINGS OR ORGANIZATIONS (*Persons in relationship*)	BASIS OF GROUPINGS
I. *Major category: Inclusive territorial unities* Generic type: *Community* Specific types: Tribe, Nation, Region, City, Village, Neighborhood (See Chapters XII and XIII)	I. *Major criteria*: (1) most inclusive range of interests; (2) occupation of a definite territory
II. *Major category: Interest-conscious unities without definite organization*	II. *Major criteria*: (1) like attitudes of group members; (2) indefinite social organization
Generic type (a): *Social class* Specific types: Caste, Elite, Competitive class, Corporate class (See Chapter XIV)	Additional criteria for specific types: (1) ability to move from one group to another; (2) distinctions of status, prestige, opportunity, economic rank
Generic type (b): *Ethnic and "racial" groups* Specific types: Color groups, Immigrant groups, Nationality groups (See Chapter XV)	Additional criteria for specific types: group origin, "stock," length of residence, physical characteristics
Generic type (c): *Crowd* Specific types: Like-interest crowd, Common-interest crowd (See Chapter XVI)	Additional criteria for specific types: (1) transitory (like or common) interest; (2) temporary group
III. *Major category: Interest-conscious unities with definite organization: Associations*	III. *Major criteria*: (1) limited range of interests; (2) definite social organization
Generic type (a): *Primary group* Specific types: Family, Play group, Clique, Club (See Chapters X, XI, XVII)	Additional criteria for specific types: (1) limited size of membership; (2) personal contact between members (3) degree of formal recognition; (4) type of interest pursued
Generic type (b): *Large association* Specific types: State, Church, Economic corporation, Labor union, etc. (See Chapters X, XVII–XX)	Additional criteria for specific types: (1) relatively unlimited size of membership; (2) formal social organization; (3) prevalence of impersonal relationships; (4) type of interest pursued

Our basis for the classification of groups, then, may be *size*, or some quality of *group interaction*, or some quality of *group interest*, or the degree of *organization*, or some combination of these. The classification of major types of groupings in Chart VII is based primarily upon the range and nature of interests and the degree of group organization, while other criteria, as examination of the chart will reveal, enter into the distinctions between the subtypes.

The group and the individual. The discussion of the relation of the individual to society in Chapter III and to the social codes in Chapter IX guards us against certain fallacies concerning the individual and the group. We should not, for example, think of the social group as standing in opposition to the individual life—we have seen that both can be understood only with reference to the relationship between them. This understanding will prevent us from regarding certain types of group, such as the public or the crowd, as necessarily a threat to individual welfare.[5] Neither should we attribute the inevitable presence of groups in social life to an instinctual organic disposition of man, as if his myriad collectivities were a reflection of his physiology rather than of his life with other men.[6] Nor should we fall into the opposite error, made by certain extreme behavioristic and individualistic writers and by others who would semantically "purify" us, of viewing group concepts as a "fallacy" and of insisting therefore that all social phenomena must be "reduced to" or understood as the behavior of specific individuals.[7] These are varieties of a mistaken conception of the interaction of individual and group, a relationship we shall keep in view as we consider the different types of social groups.

[1] *The group viewed from the individual's viewpoint:* The member of a primitive or simpler society belongs to relatively few social groups, though the latter are more numerous than early anthropologists sometimes believed. Among the primitive's groups are those based upon kinship, age, sex, and often upon fundamental occupational differences. Each group membership gives to its possessor a certain status or prestige in accordance with the customs and institutions of the society, and the memberships themselves are to a large extent, as in the case of the age or sex divisions, nonvoluntary. In modern complex society, however, the individual ordinarily belongs to a large number of groups. Belonging to some of them can no more be avoided by the individual than it can be in primitive life. Thus whether he wishes it or not, he belongs, for example, to his sex division, to his race, to the citizen body. But many of our affiliations are "voluntary," such as membership in club or party or business. The degree to which the individual elects his group affiliations is a striking feature of contemporary life, and thus from the individual's viewpoint

5. This view characterized the writings of G. Le Bon and his followers; see, for example, Le Bon, *The Crowd* (Eng. tr., London, 1925) and E. D. Martin, *The Behavior of Crowds* (New York, 1920).

6. For the development of this view, see H. A. Miller, "The Group as an Instinct," *American Journal of Sociology*, XXVII (1921), 334–343.

7. See, for example, F. H. Allport, "The Group Fallacy in Relation to Social Science," *American Journal of Sociology*, XXIX (1924), 688–706, and *Institutional Behavior* (Chapel Hill, N. C., 1933), Chap. I; A. Korzybski, *Science and Sanity* (Lancaster, Pa., 1941); S. Chase, *The Tyranny of Words* (New York, 1938).

groups range from strictly compulsory attachments, such as sex and color, to the free associations of club and clique. There are other distinctions of significance to the individual. One is whether or not his more intimate activities are involved in the group membership. He may contrast the near groups like those of friendship and family and neighborhood with the more inclusive attachments to nation or great corporation or denomination. Again he may distinguish between the groups that appear to have an immediate significance in his life such as his *own* business or *own* town and those in which his affiliations seem a casual matter as, for example, his "paper memberships."

The individual is always a focus of group affiliations. His interpretations of the many collectivities that impinge upon his life constitute, however "mistaken" or "biased" they may be from the outsider's viewpoint, a vitally significant aspect of our study of society. If we think of the group as an objective reality in the life of the individual, we must also think of the individual's conceptions and attitudes concerning the group as a subjective reality essential to our understanding of collective phenomena. As a major illustration of this point we take the distinction between in-group and out-group.

[2] *In-group and out-group:* In Chapter II we pointed out that man in the process of socialization learns to divide people into the "we" and the "they," that the common interests of a group and the attitudes that support the interests are reflected in the group distinctions made by the individual. The groups with which the individual identifies himself are *his* in-groups, his family or tribe or sex or college or occupation or religion, by virtue of his awareness of likeness or "consciousness of kind."[8] Thus the subjective attitudes of the individual person reveal his in-group memberships. They, in turn, are always relative to particular social circumstances.

It follows that the out-group is defined by the individual with relation to the in-group, usually expressed in the contrast between "we" and "they" or "other"—we are sophomores, they are juniors; we are Christians, they are heathens; we are humanitarian democrats, they are ruthless red communists; and so on. In-group attitudes, as we have seen, usually contain some element of sympathy and always a sense of attachment to the other members of the group. Out-group attitudes are always marked by a sense of difference and frequently, though not always, by some degree of antagonism. The latter varies from the mild antipathy of, say, fraternity members toward the "unorganized" college students to such powerful aversions as those engendered by the culturally imposed Negro-White caste line in a theoretically democratic society. In subsequent chapters of this book we shall have numerous occasions to examine the principal types of group antagonisms and conflicts of contemporary life.[9]

---

8. The term "in-group" was used by W. G. Sumner in *Folkways* (Boston, 1907); see pp. 11-16. "In-group" or "we-group" and the contrasting "out-group" or "they-group" or "others-group" have become a regular feature of modern sociological literature.

9. For a series of discussions of group relationships today, edited by R. M. MacIver, see

In-groups and out-groups are found in all societies, though the interests around which they develop vary with differing conditions of life. In primitive communities they are not as numerous as in modern "multigroup society," but members of the former make many group distinctions that are sometimes not apparent to an outsider. Thus the early explorer, in lumping together all "savages" or "natives" in a given tribe or region, frequently failed to detect the niceties of group distinction that formed an important part of the lives of such people—much in the same way that many American soldiers during the recent war viewed all Chinese as "Slopies" or all Filipinos as "Flips." To the member of any in-group his own distinctiveness is, of course, unmistakable, and the outsider's inability to recognize his group credentials may be construed as a lamentable lack of social intelligence.

This situation becomes exceedingly complicated in a society as group-marked as our own, where the finest shades of distinction exist to separate, for example, among the dock workers the stevedores from the "banana fiends," or among jazz musicians the renderers of "New Orleans" from those of the "Chicago style." Not only is there a vast number of in-groups and out-groups in modern social life but they are greatly overlapping, often confronting the individual with contradictions and confusion. For the individual is a member of many in-groups. Each exerts its pressure to conform to its ways and beliefs however inconsistent these may be with those of the others. There thus develops for the individual the problems of selection and code making that we discussed in Chapter IX.

The task before us in this chapter. Every social group is an in-group for its members—the concept applies equally to the smallest clique and the largest aggregation of men so long as they are aware of their identity. This enormously wide applicability of the concept limits its usefulness. Systematic study requires that we distinguish between the broad types of grouping that permeate the social structure. One such type is the *primary group*, the intimate face-to-face collectivity. A contrasting type is the large-scale *association*, the great impersonal organizations of man. These two types to which we devote the remainder of this chapter are found in all complex societies, though their concrete manifestations assume a variety of forms. We may begin with the primary group.

The Primary Group

The primary group as the nucleus of all social organization. The simplest, the first, the most universal of all forms of association is that in which a small number of persons meet "face to face" for companionship, mutual aid, the

Group Relations and Group Antagonisms (New York, 1944), *Civilization and Group Relationships* (New York, 1945), *Unity and Difference in American Life* (New York, 1947).

discussion of some question that concerns them all, or the discovery and execution of some common policy. The face-to-face group is the nucleus of all organization, and, as we shall see, is found in some form within the most complex systems—it is the unit cell of the social structure. The primary group, in the form of the family, initiates us into the secrets of society. It is the group through which, as playmates and comrades, we first give creative expression to our social impulses. It is the breeding ground of our mores, the nurse of our loyalties. It is the first and generally remains the chief focus of our social satisfactions. In these respects the face-to-face group is *primary* in our lives.[10]

[1] *Examples of primary groups and the quality of spontaneity:* The primary group as a free-functioning unit is illustrated by the play group, the group of friends, the gossip group, the partnership, the local brotherhood, the study group, the gang, the tribal council. From this free form we may distinguish groups which are a part of a larger organization. These may be loosely affiliated, such as those clubs, recreational groups, teams, and so on, whose members are connected with some business firm, church, college, or other large-scale organization. Or they may be functioning units of the larger whole, such as a committee, departmental organization, or college class.

The nature of the face-to-face group, however, is revealed most adequately in the detached form where the members come freely together, not as representatives or delegates constituted, defined, and limited to allotted tasks by predetermined arrangements, but spontaneously and apart from executive direction. A group which of its own initiative comes together for debate or study or conference meets this requirement more fully than, say, the class that assembles in a college lecture room; so do the informal cliques of workers in a factory more fully represent the primary group principle than the formal divisions established by the factory's organizational plan. In the former instances *spontaneity* is more directly and convincingly revealed and the basic group process more untrammeled.

[2] *Primary groups within formal social structures:* The spontaneous development of face-to-face groups is illustrated, as we have seen, by the play group, the family, the gang, relatively unattached social unities. But the process through which primary groups arise is by no means confined to these areas of human activity; in fact, it continually takes place within the most highly organized, the largest, and the most complex structures that man has devised. Sociologists (and others) have noted this fact for many years, but only recently have the students of specific fields of organization grasped its implications.

Consider industrial organization. The formal structure of the factory is indicated by its "blueprint" plan that outlines the divisions of function and responsibility and the lines of authority from top-management through "staff" offices and superintendents and foremen to the individual workers. However,

10. The expression "face-to-face group" is taken from C. H. Cooley, whose *Social Organization* (New York, 1909) remains a keen analysis; see especially Chaps. III and IV.

this plan—a functional necessity for the industrial engineer or manager—does not reveal the informal groupings, the cliques, the "grapevine" channels of communication that invariably develop within a factory and that disclose an area of spontaneity characteristic of the primary group. The presence of these informal face-to-face groups and the role they play in production efficiency, workers' "morale," union activity, and the like, have become major considerations to the growing field of "industrial sociology." Contributors to this field document the fact that the factory may be viewed as a social system within which primary groups are generated and of which they are a highly significant part.[11]

The factors that give rise to primary groups in industrial organization are present in all formalized social structures. Thus in governmental bureaus, military organizations, political parties, prisons, schools, labor unions, and many others the complete organizational picture includes the *formal* "blueprint" arrangements on the one hand and the *informal* spontaneous groupings on the other. The latter are evidence of the basic nuclear nature of the face-to-face group in social life. For in these unplanned little circles we confront each other as total personalities, not as categorically defined foremen or skilled workers, sergeants or privates, professors or students, ward leaders or precinct workers. In them we are less restrained by the impersonal systems of the rational designers; in them we can "be ourselves." We often resort to the informal arrangements that we may more effectively express our aspirations and resentments; within them we may circumvent or frustrate the methods or goals of the formal group itself. It is small wonder, then, that the "human engineers" of industry, of government, of military organization, are being urged to take into account the functions of the primary groups that inevitably develop wherever men are brought together.[12]

Primary and secondary relations. The small face-to-face collectivity is not only a basic type of group, but a focus of a fundamental form of *social relationship*.

[1] *The relative intimacy of primary relations:* In primary group life our

11. The most detailed study in this field is F. J. Roethlisberger and W. J. Dickson, *Management and the Worker* (Cambridge, Mass., 1939), a full report of the researches at the Western Electric plant, the conclusions of which appear in brief form in Roethlisberger's *Management and Morale* (Cambridge, Mass., 1941). This study may be compared with W. L. Warner and J. O. Low, *The Social System of the Modern Factory* (New Haven, 1947). For other treatments, see B. B. Gardner, *Human Relations in Industry* (Chicago, 1945); *Industry and Society* (W. F. Whyte, ed., New York, 1946); W. E. Moore, *Industrial Relations and the Social Order* (New York, 1946).

12. For a discussion of the informal, primary-group factor in governmental organization, see R. K. Merton, "Role of the Intellectual in Public Bureaucracy," *Social Forces*, XXIII (1945), 405–515; and in military organization, C. H. Page, "Bureaucracy's Other Face," *ibid.*, XXV (1946), 88–94.

relations with the others are always, to some extent, *personal*. Here we *feel* sympathy or antipathy, we often love or hate. In any event we face our fellows as total human beings and with them we *directly* co-operate and directly conflict. These sympathetic or "sentimental" relationships may be distinguished from those that are characteristic of the larger and more formally organized groups. The relations within which people confront one another in such specialized group roles as buyers and sellers, voters and candidates, officials and citizens, teachers and students, practitioners and clients, are *secondary*, involving categoric or "rational" attitudes.[13]

We contrast, then, the type of relationship between friends or between lovers or within cliques or gangs or families with the type that permeates the large-scale groups. The line between the two types is not always sharply drawn in group life, a fact illustrated by the "vicarious" primary attachments we form with remote individuals—with celebrities of sport or screen or even politics. Yet the distinction concerns an important aspect of social reality. The fundamental basis for the distinction is the quality of the *attitudes* surrounding the social relationship itself rather than mere physical proximity. Thus even the relation of prostitute to client is usually of the secondary type, for whatever the degree of physical intimacy the attitudes of both parties in the relationship tend to be categoric, devoid of the sentiment characteristic of primary bonds.

[2] *Primary and secondary relations in contemporary society:* Among primitive peoples and in village and small town communities individuals are linked together for the most part by primary bonds—the other members of the group are known as persons, not merely as representatives of positions in the formal order. Thus for his apprentices the member of the medieval guild was more than a "boss": he was counselor, disciplinarian, teacher, friend (or enemy), and so on. The early guild was itself a primary group. But today an increasingly large number of our relationships are secondary. Today the "boss," like the "politician" or "bureaucrat" or "expert," is apt to seem to us a stereotyped symbol, a category, not a living being one sees and works with and learns to know. This categorization of individuals into functionally defined roles is particularly characteristic of those highly organized groups, such as military hierarchies and governmental bureaus, that endow each office with specific duties and prescriptions so that the office and not its human occupant becomes the entity to which we react.[14] As the complexity of society has increased and as the accomplishment of more of its tasks has required the development of bureaucratized large-scale organizations, a greater number of secondary ties have evolved and many of the older primary relations and the groups within which they were expressed have been disturbed or displaced.

It is not surprising that this trend has alarmed a number of students of social

13. The distinction between personal and categoric relations is systematically developed by Hiller, *op. cit.*, Chap. XXXVIII.

14. See above, Chapter VII.

change. For they are aware that the primary values of social life—love, friendship, family sentiment, fellowship—are revealed within the face-to-face groups and the primary relations. These are the values that define the ultimate goals of the social being, goals threatened, according to some critics, by an increasing dominance of secondary attachments. In later chapters we shall discuss this claim more extensively. But in the present context the significant point is that however formalized and systematized and "rationalized" an organization may become, the basic primary group process continues to operate, erecting its informal collectivities both within and without the large-scale associations.

[3] *Primary and secondary relations from the individual's viewpoint:* In Chart VIII we schematize some of the principal types of group affiliation of the individual member of contemporary society. Of course, no individual divides his group life as clearly as the chart's divisions are shown. But, generally, taking the individual as the focus of many memberships in a variety of social organizations, we can agree that the individual lives most intimately, closest to the dictates of his own personality, in the area of primary relations (Area II), and that the remoter aspects of *his* life, from [illegible], are found in the zone of secondary relations (Area III).

The primary group and interests. Why do pr[illegible] groups form throughout the social structure? What do their members gain from association which they could not achieve by independent action? We have suggested part of the answer in our discussion of the nature of primary relations—within the face-to-face groups is realized the human need for spontaneous living. But these questions require a further consideration, the relation of the primary group and interests.

Let us take an independent study group as an illustration. Certain external advantages are sometimes an inducement in bringing the members together. For example, the group as a whole can afford to hire a teacher whom each member might not be able to hire for himself. But obviously there are other advantages of a different sort. The presence of the others is, within limits, a stimulus to each. Most pursuits are enhanced, more keenly appreciated, more ardently followed, when they are shared by a congenial group. This is one reason why the true university can never be, as one sage claimed, a "collection of books." Association affects alike the nature of our interests and the manner in which we pursue them.

[1] *How the primary group affects the quality of our interests:* Association changes the quality of our interests. We see them as they appear to others, from new angles. Through participation the interest gains a new objectivity. We see it through the eyes of others and thus it is in some measure freed from irrelevant personal implications. It is defined more closely for each of us, for being now both mine and yours it must have a common meaning for us. Before

CHART VIII The Individual and Types of Group Affiliation

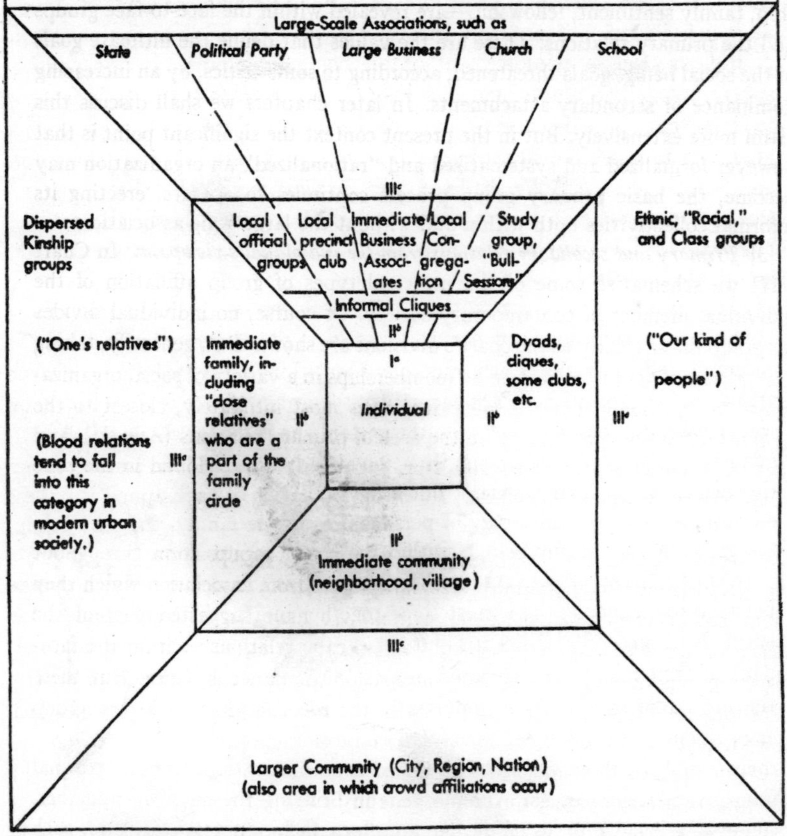

[a] I. The individual as a focus of group affiliations.
[b] II. Area of primary relations.
[c] III. Area of secondary relations.

we can effectively pursue it together we must learn to perceive it together. Each seeing it from his own viewpoint seeks to convey that aspect to his associates. Thus the character of the interest is enlarged and enriched, as each contributes something different to the understanding of it. Our study group, for example, soon discovers that the problem being discussed holds unexpected potentialities which gradually come to light as the play of different minds is directed upon it. But there are decided limits to this process of definition, concentration, and enrichment of interests. These limits throw into sharper focus the essential attributes of the primary group process.

ONE: SIZE. Effective and full participation is possible only for quite limited numbers. There is always a point, though varying for different kinds of groups, at which increase of numbers means dispersion instead of concentration, dilution instead of reinforcement of the common interest. In the political sphere, recognition of this limitation has led various writers, such as Rousseau, to claim that "pure democracy" can take place only in the smaller face-to-face groupings in which the citizens are full participants and not merely spectators and occasional voters. We shall see later (in Chapter XVIII) that there is a small element of truth in this claim, though it confuses the special political interest with the many diverse interests that are fulfilled within the primary groups themselves.[15]

TWO: SIMILARITY OF BACKGROUND. The members of a primary group must be not only to some extent congenial but also on approximate levels of experience and understanding. Each must have something to contribute, to give as well as to take, or his presence encumbers the group. There is thus a level on which every group must dwell, and the person who is too far above or below it, disturbs the process of group participation already described. In a study group this limitation is clearly evident, but some similarity of background is no less essential for the easy interplay of personalities in the family, the play group, the gang, or the informal clique within the larger organization.

THREE: LIMITED SELF-INTEREST. If the group is to achieve a give-and-take between its members, these must come together in a participant co-operative spirit. In other words, the central interest of the group as such must be dominant in their minds. The common interest must be strong enough to control the inevitable self-assertive impulses which are exhibited in all face-to-face association. If people meet merely to confirm their prejudices or to bolster their own egos, they will probably succeed in doing precisely that. If, on the other hand, they meet, for example, to study a subject together or to correct a common grievance or to enjoy one another's fellowship they will more fully express the nature of the primary group.

The fulfillment of these conditions is promoted (and sometimes hampered) by the ease and extent of communication which modern society provides. The freedom of association and the improved means of communication make possible more selective and more specialized groupings. Groups dependent merely on locality or neighborhood tend to give place to groups brought together from a wider area on the basis of a common interest. People devoted to, say, modern music or ancient philosophy or international affairs or mystic cults or culinary innovations or philately or any of a myriad of human interests come together, not from the same street—unless the street itself is highly selective—but from the whole area of a city and its borders. The passing of neighbor-

15. For discussions of "pure democracy," see R. M. MacIver, *The Web of Government* (New York, 1947), Chap. VII; K. Mannheim, *Man and Society in an Age of Reconstruction* (New York, 1940), pp. 327 ff.

hood life, a process we shall examine in Chapter XII, brings at least this compensation.

FOUR: INTENSITY OF SHARED INTEREST. Under the conditions just described, any interest becomes focused and enriched in the group process. Not only does the presence of others contribute directly to the interpretation of the common interest which each shares; it contributes also indirectly, since through association each acquires a stimulation, a heightening of the emotional significance of the interest. Each is spurred on in his pursuit by the fact that others are pursuing with him. When his own energy and devotion flag, for there is ebb and flow in all human endeavor, he is sustained by the energy and devotion of his fellows. The interest, by being shared, acquires a new significance, a new emphasis, a new valuation. It has a breadth of support which it formerly lacked. The interest is thus maintained for the group more nearly at one level of intensity than would be possible for the isolated individual. That it is generally a higher level is seen in the fact that people are ready to pursue interests in association which they would find too arduous or too uninspiring to pursue in isolation.[16]

The sustaining power of companionship on the face-to-face level is evidenced by the growing emphasis of industry and of research upon small "team" units of workers, by the political party's use of district "clubs" or small "cells," by the insistence of numerous large-scale organizations that their strength depends upon the condition of their local "grass-roots" units. These are examples of the recognition of the fact that men can endure in company privations and perils and boredoms that would be utterly insufferable in isolation. Side by side, sustained by the sense of a common lot and a common cause, they will face the horrors of warfare or the threat of imprisonment, they will live cheerfully through the winter darkness of the polar wastes, they will engage in unremitting and drearily monotonous toils. The primary group does more than sustain this interest or that; it sustains the interest of living itself.

[2] *How the primary group affects the pursuit of our interests:* Not only the character of an interest, but also the method of its pursuit, is changed by association. In the face-to-face group we have the clearest illustration of simple or direct co-operation, where men do the same thing together, in contrast with complex or indirect co-operation, where men do different things interdependently—in other words, specialize. Direct co-operation is as characteristic of the face-to-face group asspecialization is of the large-scale association. The members of a group discussing the same problem make different contributions, but they do not have separate functions; all participate in the same *process.* In complex co-operation, the so-called division of labor, all contribute to the same result, but not in the same process. On the other hand, the face-to-face group, though

16. An excellent and currently significant illustration of the effect of common interest on the Committee on Atomic Energy, a face-to-face group called into being by the U.S. Secretary of State, appears in the Introduction to the Committee's *Report on the International Control of Atomic Energy* (Washington, D.C., 1946).

it admits of subsidiary and preparatory division of labor, is essentially a mode of sharing a common experience. A play group involves a certain division of "labor," but the pitcher, the batter, and the fielders must all play together if they play at all. The members of a study group may undertake separate tasks in preparation for the activity of the group, but they must bring their results into a common process at the point where the group activity begins. They cannot, if they are engaged, say, in learning a foreign tongue, so specialize that one learns the nouns, another the adjectives, a third the irregular verbs, and so forth. In short, the group is a *unity* in the performance of its function.

Being thus united in the process and not merely in the product, the face-to-face group has a peculiar social significance. It serves a function which no other kind of organization can fulfill, a function additional to, and in the last resort more necessary than, the increment of economy, convenience, and efficacy which comes from co-operation. It satisfies most fully the essential need of man for man, the need of man for society.

Primary group decisions and the problem of integration. We have said that the process of the face-to-face group is a sharing or communicating of experience. How then is experience shared? How from being mine or yours does it become ours? We shall examine but one aspect, though a crucial one, of this intricate and searching question. How does a group achieve a consensus, a harmony, with respect to the differences of opinion which appear within it? To what extent are the differences which the members bring to the group harmonized within it? If we assume that the degree in which consensus is attained is a measure of the degree in which experience is shared, here would be a test question. Let us then examine it.

[1] *Types of group agreement:* We should first observe that all groups do not need to seek consensus. There are some which can function as well, perhaps better, when the members do not agree on the issues raised by the group. Debating societies and discussion groups are obvious examples, but the statement holds also, in degree, for groups of neighborly gossips or cliques of all sorts. The salt of friendly difference gives to such groups their savor. But groups faced with the problem of determining, officially or informally, a common policy are compelled by this function to reach a group decision. This decision may be arrived at in various ways and may represent various degrees or levels of agreement.

ONE: AUTHORITY. The minimum of group participation is found where the decision comes from the dominance of authority, involving no more than the acquiescence or assent of the subordinate members. In this case the potential contributions of these members to the process of decision are wholly or largely suppressed. This mode of group agreement is illustrated in various types of face-to-face units, obviously so in the small military unit or "disciplined" revolutionary party cell, but also in the older paterfamilias household or the boss-ruled gang.

TWO: COMPROMISE. The group decision may represent a compromise, in which, while the agreement is formally unanimous, the contending parties yield some portion of their respective claims or waive in part their differing opinions in order that a unified policy, giving all some measure of what they desire, may be carried through. This type of decision is distinct from the authoritarian one, both in the mode and in the content. The differences of the members here affect the decision, but the process is one of bargaining, of give-and-take, and therefore they remain unreconciled. Compromise characterizes not only many of the decisions of legislative committees in the form of "compromise" bills and of such groups as the United Nations Council but is frequently found in the group agreements reached by modern "democratic" families, juvenile gangs, clubs, and other face-to-face assemblies.

THREE: ENUMERATION. Voting differs from the first two types of decision-making in that there is not even formal unanimity in the registration of policy. It is determination by majority (whether of persons, of voting shares, or other units). The differences of the members remain in stark opposition. The necessary basis of agreement is not found on the level of the particular issue determined by voting, but lies in the willingness of the members of the group to abide by the result of the poll. This type is, of course, of central significance in modern democratic political procedure, which extends far beyond the range of the primary group.

FOUR: INTEGRATION. No one of the three types of determination just described is the expression of a complete harmony within the group. No one reveals the group as a unity with one mind and one will. If, then, we conceive of a group as potentially such a unity we must seek for a further type of decision, in which the differences of the members are neither suppressed nor compromised but instead harmonized or synthesized, transmuted without loss but rather with gain, into a group idea or group policy. Some writers put this principle forward as expressing the only effective and finally desirable type of agreement. Its relation to the others can be most briefly presented if we classify them as in Chart IX.

[2] *Integration: ideal and intragroup process:* Integration, Type IV of our chart, raises a question of peculiar importance for our understanding of group life. Should we regard integration as an ideal to which the reality of group agreement never fully attains, or is it as verifiable in experience as any of the other three types? Do our varied interests and individual differences admit of comprehensive integration? Is it, in short, a dream or an actuality? One exponent of the integration principle claims that the group idea is not compromise, for "just in so far as people think that the basis of working together is compromise, just so far they do not understand the first principles of working

CHART IX **Types of Group Agreement**

Basis	Process	Nature of Decision	Treatment of Differences
I. Authority	Acquiescence and assent	Formal unanimity	Suppressed or held in abeyance
II. Compromise	Give and take	Formal unanimity	Registered in the result but not reconciled
III. Enumeration	Inconclusive discussion	Majority determination	Registered in the process but not in the result
IV. Integration	Conclusive discussion	Real unanimity	Expressed in the process and conserved in the result

together." Nor is it, so runs the claim, the majority idea, or even the consensus derived from the persuasion of some by others, for "we have no more right to get our own way by persuading people than by bullying or bribing them." The group idea is a "composite idea," evolved through the free admission of difference. In fact, "the only use for my difference is to join it with other differences." We begin with individual thinking and we end with "joint thinking."[17]

This conception of integration may be regarded either as an *ethical ideal* or as a *social-psychological process*. If taken as an ideal, we cannot claim that it expresses the actuality of group life. It is not, as such, a principle we can demonstrate. All we could demonstrate would be the consequences which follow from its acceptance, as revealed in such approximations to its realization as we can find. We might claim on such grounds, as do its exponents, that its acceptance would create a new harmony of society, a new joy of co-operative living. We might claim that it is a principle of peculiar importance in the complex societies of our age, where people of very diverse types must get along together and to do so must overcome the prejudices of class, religion, and race. We might claim that it has a special appeal in a democratic society, where the ground of authoritarian decision is undermined so that another basis of solidarity must be found.

But an ideal can be realized only as it is brought into relation to the experience of living. We must therefore consider integration as a social-psychological process operating within the group. How far, under what conditions, with what limitations does this process actually occur? When scientists meet to discuss a problem, their primary aim is truth, not harmony—in so far as they

17. The above quotations are taken from M. P. Follett, *The New State* (New York, 1926). The principle of integration has many advocates, and is promulgated by such organizations as the publishers of the bulletin, *The Inquiry* (New York).

remain scientists. People in all kinds of groups have interests other than the attainment of harmony. Moreover, the demand of open-mindedness does not imply that we should hold every belief as merely provisional. If all the evidences point a certain way for us, we should be poor group members not to hold to it, not to try to persuade others of its validity, not to prefer difference to agreement which did not accept it. The integrationists too often demand a degree of plasticity which is not attainable and which is not even desirable. For sometimes it is because of the higher loyalty to both himself and to the group that a man stands firmly on his conviction—a principle unrecognized by those superintegrationists, the "totalitarians." We all know that even unanimity is no criterion of truth or of wisdom.

In conclusion we may suggest that the principle of integration combines and even confuses two quite different forms of group unity.[18] There is a difference between the subjective harmony of the attitudes of group members toward one another and the harmony of ideas. We can observe in many groups a social unity within which people feel at one though their opinions still differ. To many, "integration" demands a unity on the intellectual level, so that people come together thinking differently and end thinking alike. The different viewpoints of the group members are supposedly harmonized in a kind of composite—as though the group itself became a mind with an idea of its own, comprehending the desires of all. However desirable integration may seem as an ideal, we should not in its name blunder into this "group-mind" fallacy. "Mind" is a possession of individual human beings, whatever the group ties that bind them together.[19] The history of the many attempts to secure unanimity on the level of extreme "integration," including our present-day jury systems and numerous group "harmony" movements, reveals the impossibility of the demand. In our various face-to-face groups, our families or clubs or committees or assemblies, we may reasonably and realistically seek the harmony of group attitudes, the sense of community with our fellows. But any quest for a "group-oneness," in which we lose sight of the individuality of the person, is based on a miscomprehension of the relationship between the group and the individual—the very starting point of sociological understanding.

The Great Associations

The nature and significance of the great associations. We now turn to a type of social group of such special significance in modern society that three later

18. The same criticism applies to Rousseau's concept of the "general will," from which the principle of integration is historically derived. (From Rousseau's writings stemmed *both* democratic and "totalitarian" notions.) See R. M. MacIver, *The Modern State* (Oxford, 1926), pp. 444 ff.

19. For an extreme criticism of the "group-mind" fallacy, see G. A. Lundberg, *Foundations of Sociology* (New York, 1939), pp. 163–173.

chapters (Chapters XVIII, XIX, and XX) are devoted to its principal manifestations. In this chapter we may consider the more general features of the large-scale association.

[1] *The growth of large-scale organization:* Where life is relatively simple, as in a primitive community or in a frontier settlement, or where for any reason the area of effective communication is small, the face-to-face group suffices for most purposes. But where society expands, another kind of association grows necessary, the large-scale organization with its impersonal or secondary relationships and its specialization of functions. Interests become differentiated. The service of experts is required. Techniques are elaborated, and the average member has neither the time nor the energy nor the skill to attend to them. The new range of the interest demands a complex organization. It is no longer localized and no longer controllable by the local group. The members are too numerous and too scattered to conduct their business through face-to-face relationships. Specially selected persons must act on behalf of the whole, a hierarchy of officials arises ("bureaucracy"), and the executive or controlling groups become distinct from the mass of the members. These features mark the rise of the modern state, the great corporation, the international cartel, the large church, the nation-wide political party, and the labor union. There are, of course, significant differences between these groups, but there are equally significant similarities.

[2] *The individual's roles in large-scale organization:* Within these multicellular organizations, with their various departments, informal primary groups develop, as we have seen. Other face-to-face groups remain as part of the formal structure—directorates, committees, and so forth—but their character and function have changed. Their members have become agents, delegates, officials, or experts. The lay members are now reduced to a more passive role, and while their relationship to one another and to the whole may become more complicated, they are, for the most part, less engrossing. In this way the great state tends to develop its spectator-citizens, the church its spectator-worshipers, the large corporation its passive stockholders, the political party its exploitable "rank and file," the union its "paper" dues-paying members.

The large-scale organization is marked by formality and mechanical regulation. There is concentration of direction as well as division of labor. The average member occupies both an *active* and a *passive* role, and the two are not easy to reconcile. As in the state he is *both* citizen and subject, so in degree he is in every great association. The passive role bulks more largely the greater the association grows, and thus the members are apt to feel that its elaborate machinery lies wholly outside themselves, beyond the area of their control. This feeling exists particularly among the members of the great state and even more among the shareholders of large economic corporations. But it is widespread also in all organizations where the participation of the "rank-and-file" member seems limited to the payment of dues, an occasional election, an infrequent convention—where his relations with most of the others are secondary.[20]

[3] *Large-scale organizations and the primary group:* Some sociologists have taken the position that with the growth of complex society the primary group gradually loses its character and binding strength. The primary group is an expression of *communal* relations, involving a sense of collective participation, and these, it is held, are in a large measure superseded by more superficial relations. This view was stated a century ago by Tönnies and today is frequently expressed by the students of rural-urban and regional sociology.[21] Certainly the increase and functional dominance of the less intimate and less personal relationships are characteristic of every more advanced civilization. But whether the communal life that flowed into primary group relations actually declines and degenerates is a more debatable question. Possibly it is expressed in other ways and is attached to larger unities like the nation or the large region. In any event the question itself suggests significant differences between the primary group and the large-scale association. The latter type is marked by three distinguishing characteristics.

ONE: INDIRECT CO-OPERATION. As the group grows in size, indirect co-operation dominates over direct. In the small group the members work together, listen together, play together, worship together, discuss together, decide together. In the large organization it is only the group's objective—to maintain order, to produce goods (or profits), to create bargaining strength, and so on—no longer the intragroup process, that binds the members together. One person works *for* the other, not with him; they do different tasks toward a common product; they have not only different functions but different powers, different degrees of participation, different rights and obligations.

TWO: DOMINANCE OF CONTRACTUAL RELATIONS. As a consequence of this division of labor and authority, the transition from the small to the large association involves a movement from "status to contract," the phrase used by one writer to characterize the trend of "progressive societies."[22] If we substitute the word "complex" for "progressive," this characterization of modern developments is valid. For in the larger organizations the duties and functions of the various members must be defined, made specific, and thus explicitly or implicitly *contractual.* The working of a complex system cannot be entrusted to the spontanenous adjustments which occur in the face-to-face group.

Another aspect of the same principle is the substitution of *formal* for in-

---

20. See Area III, "Large-Scale Associations," on Chart VIII, p. 223.

21. For Tönnies' distinction between *gemeinschaft* (traditional communal grouping) and *gesellschaft* (large-scale associational grouping), see Loomis, *op. cit.* The view under discussion appears, for example, in O. Spengler's analysis of urban life in *The Decline of the West* (C. F. Atkinson, tr., New York, 1926), and in L. Mumford's study of the city and his plea for regional decentralization in *The Culture of Cities* (New York, 1938).

22. Sir Henry Maine, *Ancient Law* (London, 1907).

formal regulation—a substitution, as we have pointed out, that never completely succeeds. But every large-scale organization becomes an administrative mechanism, whether in government, business, labor, education, religion, social service, or even criminal enterprise. Not only is the structure of this mechanism intricate in itself, but it must be fitted into a complex social order. This adjustment demands formal rules, a formal authority with designated powers, a precise delimitation of interests and benefits, a clear-cut division of labor in which the function of each unit is specified in relation to the functions of all the rest—in a word, a carefully worked-out organizational "blueprint."[23]

THREE: IMPERSONALITY. Formal regulation means that there is a substitution of impersonal or secondary for personal relationships. The face-to-face group depends upon the congeniality of the members. The large association puts other requirements first. The face-to-face group demands a social qualification for membership, for it must satisfy—or otherwise balk—the need of its members for group life. The large association is detached from this interest and therefore generally makes no such demand. It is an *agency* and as such is more indifferent to the personal qualities of its members, provided they contribute to the associational interest—perform their jobs, pay their dues, vote the ticket, carry out the orders, and so on. This is a main reason why, in a complex society, the members are more liberated or more detached from group control over their intimate life; why, for example, there is a greater area of personal freedom for the members of large business firms or governmental agencies or universities than for those of smaller, more intimate groups. At the same time, however, the former in their associational roles are subject to a system of meticulous regulation proceeding from sources felt to be remote from themselves.

The organization of authority in the great association. In the large association, the age-old problem of liberty and authority presents new and significant aspects. Four of these are particularly important in the study of complex contemporary society.

[1] *Formal authority and the problem of inflexibility:* If the forms of control in the large-scale association are less intimate, less definite, perhaps less arbitrary, they are also less spontaneous, less visible, less personal. In the small group, such as the patriarchal family, the custom-sustained authority is expressed by *commands;* in the large association, such as the state or corporation, the "legal" authority operates through *formal regulations* or laws.[24] Each kind

23. This aspect of large-scale organization is ably analyzed in the writings of Max Weber. See, for example, *From Max Weber: Essays in Sociology* (H. Gerth and C. W. Mills, tr. and ed., New York, 1946), pp. 196-244; and *The Theory of Social and Economic Organization* (T. Parsons and A. M. Henderson, tr. and ed., New York, 1947), pp. 329-341.

24. See Weber's distinction between "traditional" and "legal" authority in *The Theory of Social and Economic Organization*, pp. 328-329.

of authority is necessary in social life but each has its dangers. The danger of the first kind lies in the omnipresence of personal authority, from which, when it is harsh or overbearing, the subordinated individuals cannot hide any aspect of their lives. The danger of the second kind arises particularly from the separation of the authority from the subject of it, so that its impersonal inner working is hidden from him.

Explicit standing rules are necessary in every complex organization. Without them it could not achieve its peculiar services of order, efficiency, and economy. But an established system of regulations may stand in the way of that flexibility which responds both to changing situations and to individual needs. The official is apt to prefer the routine, the uniformity—indeed the "security"—of the smooth-running machine. This is a basic reason why vested interests that are opposed to adaptive changes grow within all large-scale organizations. The power of the top official or of his petty underling lies in his enforcement of the rules—often very complicated rules that permit the masters of "red-tape" to become "bureaucratic virtuosos." The rules tend to grow sacrosanct in the official's mind, as if the regulations, functionally merely instruments, carried in themselves an end value.[25] As the institutionalized rules take on the sanctity of age, a sentiment similar to the official's is apt to spread throughout the lay members of the organization. In short, the danger of elaborate organization is that it tends to grow stereotyped. Examples of this tendency include the historical bureaucratization of the Christian churches, an organizational development quite contrary to their initial principles. The tendency is exhibited in governmental bureaus, industrial plants, university administrations, large social service agencies, political parties, and all associations of sufficient age and size to have developed institutional hardening and resistance to change in the organizational structure.

Faced with this problem of retaining some degree of liberty and flexibility while securing order and efficiency, of making authority an agent instead of an exploiter, large-scale associations have experimented with two principles of organization, federation and official responsibility.

[2] *The federative principle:* This principle seeks to build up an organization on the basis of *local* or *regional* units, each possessing as much autonomy as is compatible with the ends of the association. In the political sphere the principle is revealed not only in the contrast between a federal and a unitary government, but also in the widespread devolution of authority to municipalities, counties, and other administrative areas. In the sphere of industry the principle finds expression in the decentralization and geographical distribution of specialized productive functions that characterize a considerable proportion of our nation's industrial activities.[26] Similarly political parties, professional associations,

25. Cf. R. K. Merton, "Bureaucratic Structure and Personality," *Social Forces*, XVIII (1940), 561-568; and Page, *op. cit.*

26. See, for example, C. Goodrich, *et al.*, *Migration and Economic Opportunity* (Philadelphia, 1936), Chap. VII.

fraternal societies, and other large organized groups assign various degrees of autonomy to their local units.

In so far as the federative principle means that local interests are determined locally, it is workable and salutary. Its range, however, is limited by the fact that in a complex society few interests remain purely local, though they retain peculiar local aspects. Facing large-scale associations, therefore, is the constant problem of adjusting local to wider interests, of achieving a balance of centralization and decentralization. In a pioneer economy people drew water from their own wells; in a metropolitan area they depend on an elaborate common system by which their water supply is furnished from a large area. In an earlier period, blacksmiths, for example, were independent artisans and were often paid in produce. Today workers in a local plant perform perhaps one function in an elaborate productive process and are paid according to wage scales worked out by special agencies. These are simple examples of the growing complexity of civilization in which the interests of a locality cease to be entirely localized. This is why local *representation* must supplement local control.

It should be noted also that the degree of effective localization varies with the type of group *interest*. Interests pursued by certain organizations can be fulfilled only by means of face-to-face contact and personal communication. This is why colleges, for example, must be in essentials localized, and why fellowship organizations, such as Rotary or Kiwanis or the myriad fraternal orders, must be composed of local groups. A church, no matter how highly centralized its government may be, depends for its life on the local assembling of its members. Technical advances may change the size or the location of the local unit. Thus radio has tended to move the local musical assembly from the concert hall to the home; even the religious assembly has been affected similarly. With this type of organization, however, no technical advances can effectively substitute the central organization for the local unit. The direct activity of the participant members is a requirement for the satisfactory fulfillment of those interests that we shall later call the *cultural*. Consequently, in this area, the federative principle has greater play.

We pursue other interests, especially in connection with our economic and technological and political activities, the fulfillment of which does not demand localization. A central organization can make treaties or tariffs or currency regulations for a whole country—or for a whole civilization. Agencies for economic production or for regulation of commercial practices or for control of the seaways or airways or for the application of the legal code are often highly centralized, and sometimes effectively so. There are certain aspects of order and efficiency which are best provided by centralized control. But even in these areas (which we shall later call the *civilizational*[27]) the local unit often has an important role, especially when the service which the organization

27. For the distinction between *cultural* and *civilizational* see below, Chap. XXI.

renders is more *personal.* A steel or aluminum factory can from one center provide effective service for the whole country. A retail store has a much narrower range, and therefore a combination of units takes the form, not of a single central plant, but of a chain-store system. The less standardized the service, the more the local unit resists absorption; thus luxury shops, fashionable tailors, millinery establishments, and so on, flourish as local concerns. The same principle may be illustrated from political organization—we can do without local legislatures, but we cannot do without local courts or party units.

[3] *The principle of official responsibility:* All the great associations must achieve some equilibrium of centralization and decentralization, varying in accordance with the nature of their functions. Since some of the most important organizations, those which supply the more uniform or standardized services, such as insurance or electricity or political order, lend themselves to a high degree of centralization, we must resort to some other principle than the federative in the attempt to solve the problem of control, to save efficiency while resisting domination. Here is where our second principle, that of *responsibility*, enters in.

It is of peculiar importance with respect to the most powerful and comprehensive of all organizations, the *state.* For the state in which the principle of responsibility is assured can thereby prevent the undue encroachments of other organizations. It is the essential principle of the democratic state, though its full realization is beset by many difficulties. In so far as it is achieved, arbitrary authority, authority acting in its own right, yields to functional authority. In other words, it turns governments into public agencies and officials into delegates or representatives, acting on behalf of and subject to the control of those whom they govern. The earlier champions of democracy too readily concluded that in our complex and heterogeneous societies this end could be achieved merely by the mechanics of popular election, but we have realized through experience that it is possible only in so far as a people is enlightened and public-spirited. The business of government, like all other large-scale business, needs the service of experts. The people in general cannot understand its intricacies or adjudge the qualities requisite for the conduct of this business. The relics of direct popular administration, such as the jury system, are cumbrous and perhaps moribund. But experience also shows us that a politically intelligent people can establish and maintain a system of government which on the whole is subservient to the wishes of the majority. In spite of the practical difficulties and problems involved, the principle of responsibility is formally and to a considerable extent substantially attained in many modern states, and is liable to be overthrown only in time of grave crisis.

[4] *The principle of automatic control:* In addition to the principles of federation and responsibility, there is another factor operating in large-scale organizations which tends to keep them in some measure flexible and subject to the interests of those whom they serve. This factor, which we term "automatic

control," has but a limited application to the compulsive organization of the state or to monopolistic corporations. But it powerfully affects the more competitive associations. A department store, for example, is obviously not maintained merely to serve the public, but unless the public's desires are at least partially met, the store will cease to exist. Likewise, any organization whose members may leave it at will is bound to consult, in one way or another, the wishes of the members. The free associations which are characteristic of modern complex society, such as clubs or labor unions or churches, when they are not responsible to their membership, tend to suffer a decline. The effectiveness of this "automatic control" in modern societies has increased with respect to *cultural* organizations, since these have been so largely liberated from the compulsions of a political and religious authority. However, the principle has serious limitations in the economic sphere, owing to the growth of vast combinations restricting the play of competition.[28]

The sense in which the great association is always a limited agency. We have already shown that smaller primary groups inevitably come into being within the large-scale associations. This is one evidence of the fact that the increase of large organizations does not and cannot involve the substitution of these for the face-to-face groups. For the latter render one essential service to man which the former can never satisfy—the satisfaction of the need for fellowship, the need for society itself. This satisfaction demands personal participation within a small group; it demands the opportunity for spontaneous and unrestricted expression of the individual's personality. Even under the most favorable conditions the specialization and routine of the great association involve some degree of impersonal constraint, against which human beings chafe and from which they seek refuge in more spontaneous groupings. This is one reason why there are so many clubs and cliques—and so many "joiners"—in our large-scale civilization. For in it, as we shall see, the traditional face-to-face groups, those of family and kin and church and neighborhood, are less inclusive and less absorbing, and men are impelled to devise others through which they seek to save, against the pressure of organization, the ever-present impulse toward unhampered personal relations.[29]

---

28. The frustration of "automatic control" in economic activities by monopoly and combination is, of course, a major problem today and one to which we shall return in Chapter XIX. Among the many pertinent studies of it are A. A. Berle and G. C. Means, *The Modern Corporation and Private Property* (New York, 1932); T. W. Arnold, *The Bottlenecks of Business* (New York, 1940) and *Democracy and Free Enterprise* (Norman, Okla., 1942); W. Berge, *Cartels: Challenge to a Free World* (Washington, D.C., 1944); and from the Temporary National Economic Committee, Monographs Nos. 21, 26, and 35 (Washington, D.C., 1940-1941).

29. The failure of large-scale associations to provide opportunity for the sociality and spontaneity characteristic of primary groups is a concern of many writers, including Charles H. Cooley. Cooley believed, however, that these qualities could and should be re-created within

Our world of large-scale organizations is inevitably a mechanized impersonal world. Within it each man has his specialized function, his delimited calling. His work confines him within the routines and techniques of a smaller and smaller portion of the social order within which he lives. For the greater that order the smaller is the part which a man's work directly reveals to him. The engrossment in this limited task, imposed in the first instance by economic necessity, is often thought of as a peril to the realization of the fuller life of man, of his essential humanity. Doubtless the danger exists, and it is probably impossible to balance gain and loss. But specialism is only one aspect of this greater order, and the same conditions which impose it bring also certain means of possible deliverance from its perils—vastly greater intercommunication, a much extended period of general education in which the foundations of a broader culture may be laid, and new potentialities of leisure which, wisely directed, may liberate the mind from the dominance of the narrow task.

---

the larger groups. See C. H. Cooley, "A Primary Culture for Democracy," *Publications of the American Sociological Society*, XIII (1918); and *Social Organization* (New York, 1909), pp. 25, 53, 178.

11

The Family

Sociological Significance of the Family

The family in general. The family is by far the most important primary group in society. Historically it has been transformed from a more or less self-contained unity into a definite and limited organization of minimum size, consisting primarily of the original contracting parties. On the other hand, it continues to serve as a total community for the lives born within it, gradually relinquishing this character as they grow toward adulthood. The family, more profoundly than any other organization, exists only as a process. We can understand it only through a study of its changes, the changes it has undergone in human history and the changes within it in the life history of each individual example. In this chapter we must therefore anticipate the subject of the last division of the book, where we consider the theme of social change.

[1] *The meaning and general characteristics of the family:* At the outset, in view not only of the varying forms which the family assumes but also of its varying degrees of attachment to some larger kin-group, the sib or clan, it is important to explain the sense in which we use the term "family." *The family is a group defined by a sex relationship sufficiently precise and enduring to provide for the procreation and upbringing of children.* It may include collateral or subsidiary relationships, but it is constituted by the living together of mates, forming with their offspring a distinctive unity. This unity has certain common characteristics everywhere in human society, of which the following five are particularly significant: (1) a mating relationship, (2) a form of marriage or other institutional arrangement in accordance with which the mating relation is established and maintained, (3) a system of nomenclature, involving also a mode of reckoning descent, (4) some economic provision shared by the members of the group but having especial reference to the economic needs associated with childbearing and child rearing, and, generally, (5) a common habitation,

home, or household, which, however, may not be exclusive to the family group. While these five conditions are so universal as to seem essential to the very nature of the family, they may be met in extremely different ways.

[2] *Cultural variability of family forms:* Seemingly every possible variety of family arrangement is found somewhere in human society, and hundreds of volumes describing mans' devious family-ways attest to our interest in the subject. Consider some of the contrasts.

ONE: FORMS OF THE MATING RELATIONSHIP. The mating relation may be lifelong or of shorter duration. It may, as with us, take the institutional form of *monogamy*, which may be strict or modified by subsidiary sex relationships It may be *polygamous*, involving either *polygyny*, the most highly regarded arrangement in many communities, or *polyandry*, an infrequent and unpopular variety. Even what seems a form of *group marriage* has been found in one or two primitive societies.[1] A society may, in fact, recognize more than one of these varieties, as among the Tibetans, where the economically depressed practice polyandry; the better off, monogamy; and some of the wealthy nobles, polygyny.[2]

TWO: SELECTION OF MATES. Wives (or husbands) may be selected by parents or by the elders, or the choice may be left to the wishes of the individuals concerned. It may be socially compulsory to marry within a group to which one belongs (*endogamy*) or else to marry into another group (*exogamy*). Some forms of both barriers are everywhere found. But there are widely differing prescriptions as to the prohibited degrees of relationship within which one may not marry.

THREE: RECKONING DESCENT. Descent may be reckoned through the male line (*patrilineal*) or through the female line (*matrilineal*). Both systems have been used successfully, and though there is more difficulty in establishing the fact of biological paternity, many groups have shifted from the matrilineal to the patrilineal form. On the other hand, a few peoples have shifted in the opposite direction.

FOUR: FORM OF THE FAMILY CIRCLE. Among some peoples the husband joins his wife's relatives and among others the wife joins her husband's, the residence in the former case being termed *matrilocal* and in the latter *patrilocal*. There are even instances where there are annual alternations between the patrilocal and the matrilocal abodes.[3] Not only the place of residence but the structure of the family circle varies. Thus the *consanguine* arrangement has been pictured as "a nucleus of blood relatives surrounded by a fringe of spouses," the brothers and sisters representing the core of the family unit. This arrangement stands in contrast with the type with which we are mainly concerned, the

1. As among the Marquesas and the Toda. It is not clear as to whether these are actual examples of group marriage. Cf. R. Linton, *The Study of Man* (New York, 1936), pp. 181-182.
2. *Ibid.*, p. 183.
3. R. F. Fortune, *The Sorcerers of Dobu* (New York, 1932).

conjugal, "a nucleus of spouses and their offspring surrounded by a fringe of relatives."[4]

Various customs qualify these main distinctions, such as the admission of concubines in some forms of the monogamous family or the practice of wife-lending in guest hospitality as found in various tribes. Moreover, the different types of institutional arrangements are brought together in different combinations. The varieties of the family are endless, and the range of its functions, no less than the mode in which it performs them, varies enormously.

Distinctive features of the family organization. Of all the organizations, large or small, which society unfolds, none transcends the family in the intensity of its sociological significance. It influences the whole life of society in innumerable ways, and its changes, as we shall see, reverberate through the whole social structure. It is capable of endless variation and yet reveals a remarkable continuity and persistence through change. It is in many respects unlike any other association, having besides those already suggested several distinctive features.

[1] *Universality:* It is the most nearly universal of all social forms. It is found in all societies, at all stages of social development, and exists far below the human level, among a myriad species of animal. Almost every human being is or has been a member of some family.

[2] *Emotional basis:* It is based on a complex of the most profound impulses of our organic nature, those of mating, procreation, maternal devotion, and parental care. These are fortified in man by a highly significant and close-knit group of secondary emotions, from romantic love to the pride of race, from the affection of mates to the desire for the economic security of a home, from the jealousy of personal possession to the baffled yearning for perpetuity.

[3] *Formative influence:* It is the earliest social environment of all the higher forms of life, including man, and the profoundest formative influence in the awakening lives of which it is the source. In particular it molds the character of the individual by the impression both of organic and of mental habits. In order to recognize its lasting influence we need not subscribe to the view that family influence in infancy determines once and for all the personality structure of the individual.

[4] *Limited size:* It is of necessity a group very limited in size, for it is defined by biological conditions which it cannot transcend without losing its identity. Hence it is the smallest in scale of all the formalized organizations that make up the social structure, and especially so in civilized society, where it is most completely detached from the kin-group.

[5] *Nuclear position in the social structure:* It is the nucleus of other social organizations. Frequently in the simpler societies, as well as in the more advanced types of patriarchal society, the whole social structure is built of family

4. Linton, *op. cit.*, p. 159.

units. Only in the higher complex civilizations does the family cease to fulfill this function, but even in them the local community, as well as its divisions of social classes, tends to remain unions of families. One of the first definitions ever given of a community made it "a union of families," and for the local community the definition, with some qualification, still holds today.[5]

[6] *Responsibility of the members:* It makes more continuous and greater demands on its members than any other association is wont to do. In times of crisis men may work and fight and die for their country, but they toil for their families all their lives. The family leads men—and women still more—to perform for others than themselves the most exacting tasks and to undertake the heaviest responsibilities. We do not mean that the family makes its members to a high degree altruistic, or, on the other hand, that these toils are undertaken as being a condition of the satisfactions that the family affords. The life of the family is too deeply rooted in basic impulses to be interpreted in this way. These impulses lead men into the increasing responsibilities of the family and sustain them in the fulfillment of tasks which they did not foresee.

[7] *Social regulation:* It is peculiarly guarded both by social taboos and by legal regulations which rigidly prescribe its form. In the first place, the marriage contract is more strictly defined than other contracts, the partners not being free to decide its terms or to change them by mutual agreement. While the form of the marriage contract is very different in different types of society, in each there is a prevailing form zealously insisted upon. In modern society the family is one of the few associations which the consenting parties may freely enter but may not, even by mutual consent, freely leave or dissolve.

[8] *Its permanent and temporary nature:* While the *institution* of the family is so permanent and universal, the family as an *association* is the most temporary and the most transitional of all important organizations within society. The contrast between these two aspects of the family is so significant, and throws so much light on many of the perplexing social problems that cluster about the family, that it demands our special attention.

The life history of the individual family. Each individual family is, in part, the story of the life together of the original partners, a story that ends with their life (if it lasts this long). What we often speak of as an old-established family is really a succession of families bearing the same name and in some degree (often slight) perpetuating the same stock. During this life history the family is recruited from within itself, and in this process the association undergoes the greatest, most inevitable, and most difficult transitions. It involves a continuous change alike in its interests and in its emotional foundations, a constant transformation in the relations of its members, old and new, to one another.

[1] *The major stages in the life history:* So far as the original partners are con-

5. Aristotle, *Politics*, iii, p. 9, 1280b.

cerned we can distinguish in the history of the representative family four stages, among others not so clearly marked by external signs.

ONE: THE FORMATIVE PRENUPTIAL STAGE. The first or preparatory stage is marked by an increasing intimacy of man and woman, an exploration or revelation by each of the personality of the other, or at least of those aspects of personality which a growing sex attraction emphasizes and heightens. This is less the case where marriages are prearranged by the elders, though this characteristic is generally found even where economic and other social considerations are determinants of marriage. In our own culture, which so highly values the sentiment of romantic love, this stage has, as we shall see, a large significance in the course of the family history.

TWO: THE NUPTIAL STAGE. The second stage, before the offspring arrive, is the beginning of the family proper. It involves the living together of the mates, creating the environment of the home, evoking new experiences, initiating new attitudes of the partners toward each other, and toward society and of society toward the partnership, subtly establishing new habituations between the man and the woman. The high value with which this stage is regarded in our society is suggested by the emphasis we give to the "honeymoon" and by the connotations of the word itself.

THREE: THE CHILD-REARING STAGE. The third stage fulfills the family proper, linking the partners to one another by the vital link of their own children, the fruits of the sex union. It introduces new sentiments which can (but do not in all cases) fortify and in a measure replace the initial ones, bringing new interests and also growing responsibilities.

FOUR: THE MATURITY STAGE. The final stage emerges when the biological functions of the parents have been fulfilled and when the children no longer require parental care. The partners are liberated from this responsibility so that again, especially in these days of the limited family, new interests and new activities must take the place of old ones, more particularly on the part of the wife, on whom the heavier tasks of childbearing and child rearing had fallen.

All families do not, of course, pass through all these stages. Among one large group in this country, for example, almost one in five families are childless.[6] The progression is interrupted by death or separation or divorce before the final stage is reached—divorce alone affects almost one third of all marriages in the United States today. But these stages form an inevitable time-succession wherever the family endures and fulfills its primary social function of perpetuating the race. The length of each stage varies with the social conditions. Thus in our own society the maturity and increasingly the nuptial stages tend to be lengthened, while the child-rearing stage tends to become a shorter span.

[2] *The significance of the family stages:* It would take volumes to describe

6. Namely, Midwestern white couples. See C. V. Kiser and P. K. Whelpton, "Social and Psychological Factors Affecting Families," *The Millbank Memorial Fund Quarterly* (Jan. 1944).

the significant variations of human relationship which occur during this endlessly repeated process. In fact, a very large part of modern literature is devoted to this subject, which in its detailed interest seems inexhaustible. The psychological adjustment of the members of the family to one another in the course of its inexorable changes creates perhaps the most important series of the numerous problems, personal and social, engendered by an association which affects so intimately and in such incalculable ways, which more than any other engrosses, expresses, and circumscribes, the personality of man. Men and women are generically like in certain respects, but they are also unlike and they are complementary.[7] Thus the stage is set by nature for the innumerable complex situations, so rich in the possibilities of harmony and disharmony, which, according to the surrounding circumstances and to their individual personalities, unfold for the members of the family partnership from its initiation to its close.

Early Forms of the Family

The problem of the origin of the family. It seems established that so far back as we can penetrate into the conditions of the primitive human world we nowhere find a group in which some form of the family does not exist. Always we discover some form of mating, some degree of social regulation over sex relationships. It is, in fact, hard to conceive any order of society, and especially of primitive society, in which such regulation could be entirely absent.

[1] *The theory of early sex communism:* Some authors have put forward the theory that the "original state of mankind" was one of sexual promiscuity. But that doctrine has been weakened by the weight of anthropological evidence; in fact, among the primates and other nonhuman species, family life is often highly developed.[8] The advocates of the theory noted the survival among primitive peoples of customs assumed to point back to a state of promiscuity, such as sex license at festivals, exchange of wives, and the offering of wives as a form of hospitality. They were impressed by *classificatory systems* according to which all the members of one age-group are indiscriminately called "fathers" or "mothers"; of another, "brothers" and "sisters"; and of the child age-group, "sons" and "daughters." Again, they cited the ignorance of biological paternity which has been reported as existing among certain groups, such as the Central Australians and the Trobriand Islanders.

7. For excellent studies of the implications of this fact see, for example, Havelock Ellis, *Man and Woman* (new ed., New York, 1929); and the highly readable volume of A. Scheinfeld, *Women and Men* (New York, 1943).

8. The theory of primeval promiscuity appears, for example, in L. H. Morgan, *Ancient Society* (New York, 1907) and R. Briffault, *The Mothers* (New York, 1927). Contrary anthropological evidence is presented in many volumes, such as Linton, *op. cit.* and B. Malinowski, *Sex and Repression in Savage Society* (New York, 1927). For family systems among nonhuman species see, for example, G. H. Seward, *Sex and the Social Order* (New York, 1946), Chaps. VI and VII.

But these "evidences" can be explained on other grounds, and cannot outweigh the fact that even in the simplest societies known the family is thoroughly established. The classificatory system may be explained as a conventional device for social purposes, particularly for the regulation of exogamy. Thus a man will distinguish his actual wife (or wives in a polygynous system) by a term signifying "own" while still applying the equivalent of "wife" to all the women from whom it is permissible to choose a wife, in contrast to those women, his "sisters," with whom marriage is prohibited under the rules of exogamy. This naming system is perfectly intelligible without any assumption of a prior promiscuity—even today we use a form of it as when we speak of fellow members of an organization as "brothers" or "sisters" or "dames." Ignorance of the biological paternal role of the father does not negate the fact that where such ignorance exists the family as an important social group *also* exists, or the fact that most primitive peoples are less troubled about physical paternity than they are about *social* paternity. Finally, periodic license is not incompatible with some forms of a marriage system, nor is there any necessity to assume that license is a survival. There are many primitive peoples among which practical promiscuity exists prior to mating—should our age be surprised?—but there is always a mating or marriage *system* and often its rigorous regulation stands in sharp contrast to the premating license. We can agree with a modern anthropologist: "The old concept of a promiscuous horde as the starting point for family development was required by the type of logic which made the Victorian family the last step in social evolution, but there is nothing else to support it."[9]

[2] *Theories of the original form of family:* Students of primitive life have sometimes thought that an answer to this question would throw light not only on the evolution of the family but also on its essential characteristics and its roots in "human nature." Consideration of certain attempts to answer it should suggest the difficulties involved here and perhaps the inadequacy of tne question itself.

ONE: THE CLAIM FOR MONOGAMY. In his *History of Human Marriage* Westermarck supported the theory of Darwin that the family took shape from the operation of male possessiveness and jealousy, the dominant male claiming monopolistic rights and guarding them by force until they were secured by custom. Hence he regarded pair-marriage as the normal form which the jealous assertion of property rights took and traced the origin of monogamous marriage back to the subhuman world, maintaining that it prevails among the higher apes. While the traits to which Westermarck points have certainly been important factors, any theory which lays exclusive stress upon them is inadepuate.

TWO: THE CLAIM FOR MATRIARCHY. Among others, Briffault in *The Mothers* has challenged Westermarck's position.[10] This volume illustrates at length the

9. Linton, *op. cit.*, p. 147.

10. Briffault, *op. cit.*, especially Vol. II, Chap. XIII. See also Westermarck's reply in his "On Primitive Marriage," *American Journal of Sociology*, XLI (1936), 565-584.

prevalence of matrilocal and matrilineal institutions in primitive communities and the fact that in some of them women hold a social position equal to and sometimes superior to that of men.[11] He notes the ignorance of the fact of paternity among some primitive peoples. He shows the absence of jealousy and the absence of the love sentiment, from which it often springs, under primitive social conditions, maintaining that these and other feelings, such as sexual modesty and the esteem for chastity, are not instinctive but *acquired* in the course of social development. He points out that certain relations between the sexes characteristic of our society are reversed in primitive communities, in such matters as coquetry and personal adornment for sex attraction. Thus "the American squaw is a drab peahen by the side of her gorgeously decorated male, decked in all the glory of feathers and war paint."[12] Briffault concludes that the family arose out of the insistent need of the *mother* for the economic and social protection of herself and her children, that in following her basic instincts she won out against the more casual and merely sexual interest of the male. Consequently he argues that the earliest form of the family was *matriarchal* and that only with the development of higher agriculture and the economic dominance of men could the patriarchal type emerge.

While acknowledging the importance of the role of maternal need in family development, we must emphasize that as an explanation of origins it is open to the same objection as that of Westermarck. The assumption that any deep-rooted social arrangement is the expression of some one particular human attribute or "instinct" is not borne out by the evidence. Nor is Briffault's argument established that mankind has passed from a system of "mother-right" to one of "father-right." Some of the simplest groups have complex patrilineal institutions, such as the Central Australians and the Philippine Negritos, while some highly developed societies, such as the American Iroquois and Pueblo, are matrilineal. Again, there is no clear correlation between matrilineal institutions and a high social status of women.[13] Few would deny the significance of the factors emphasized by Westermarck and by Briffault, but neither explains the origins of the human family.

[3] *Is there one explanation?* The older quest for a single explanation of the form of the original family has been largely forsaken today, for modern anthropological evidence reveals the inadequacy of the question. The family has no origin in the sense that there ever existed a stage of human life from which the family was absent or another stage in which it emerged. "Societies have not followed a single consistent line of evolution, but a multitude of diverging lines."[14] The family has no one origin in the sense that it is explained by one

11. Briffault, *op. cit.*, I, pp. 316 ff.
12. *Ibid.*, Vol. II, Chap. XV.
13. See, for example, W. H. R. Rivers, *Social Organization* (New York, 1924), Chap. V; and R. H. Lowie, *Primitive Society* (New York, 1920), Chap. VIII.
14. Linton, *loc. cit.*, pp. 147.

single human trait or instinct. It has no one original form in the sense of a specific primal type of which all the others are later varieties. Rather, a complex of human desires and conscious needs, finding different expression in different environments, everywhere gave birth to some form of family system.

The conditions of family growth. While we cannot find a single answer to the question of origins, we can, on the other hand, indicate the role of the various conditions that everywhere combine to produce a definite family pattern. We consider first the conditions on which the family institutions have depended and still depend.

[1] *Sex—reproduction—economy:* There is, in the first place, the *sex drive.* It motivates man to seek an established basis for its satisfaction, to find some safeguard against the precariousness of unlimited competition. It reveals various degrees of sensitiveness and discrimination, gradually becoming attached to a number of secondary sentiments, and thereby is woven into the folkways and mores that define its expression and limit its range. Secondly, there is the *reproductive* (or philoprogenitive) *urge,* strongly manifested in the mother. But this urge is developed and reinforced in the male as well by such social considerations as the pride of race, the desire to transmit property or prowess or name to his descendents, the desire to have offspring to work with or for him and to support his old age, and so forth. Even apart from such considerations, the consequences of the sexual act create a problem of which a solution is the family. There is, in the third place, the *economic need* or group of needs which in the life of the sexes together combine with the biological and psychological factors to create a system of sex relationships. Beyond the functions directly dependent on sex are economic functions which the woman fulfills in relation to the man and to the family group, within or outside the household itself, just as there are economic functions which the man similarly undertakes. These three factors, sex and reproduction and economy, are the chief variables that in interaction with one another are found in all forms of family life.

[2] *The life conditions of the group and variations of family form:* While all forms of the family somehow combine the three basic factors, the pattern that arises in a particular society is a product, in a broader sense, of the socioeconomic conditions of the group to which the mating combination belongs. Even if we call the sexual and the reproductive impulses "instincts," it does not follow that they have uniform, unvarying manifestations. Moreover, the biological conditions under which they operate, such as the "natural" proportions of the two sexes, are themselves affected and changed by some social practices, such as infanticide and war. Still more variable are the economic conditions surrounding family life. The life of the hunter or of the nomad gives the woman (and the man) different duties and functions, and consequently a different status from that allotted to her in an agricultural or in a modern economy. The position of each sex is affected by such other conditions

as the presence of inferior slave classes (a significant factor, for example, in determining the role and status of the white woman in our own Southern states), the warlike or pacific character of the group, the vicissitudes of conflict and conquest, the contact of peoples and the mingling of traditions. Customs and institutions controlling sex and family relationships, as anthropologists have demonstrated at length, are not the sheer expression of original "instincts" or needs, but grow out of the accommodation of man's desires to the particular conditions that impinge upon his life.

Thus it is not surprising that in Tibet, for example, where most of the usable land has become the possession of a few owners, leaving tiny holdings barely sufficient to support a "normal" family, the arrangement has evolved whereby several brothers marry a single woman. This system provides a degree of economic security for the polyandrous family and permits the holding to be passed along to the children intact. Here we observe the influence of rigorous economic conditions upon the form of the family, an influence even more clearly evident when we learn that only the lower economic classes practice polyandry, while those somewhat better off are monogamous and the wealthy nobility are sometimes polygynous.[15] Polygyny is clearly an expensive practice for the husband, and, though it is not everywhere correlated with specific economic conditions, very few men among such groups as the Greenland Eskimo and Mohammedans can afford the luxury of more than one wife. These observations should not lead us to assume that the prevailing economic conditions *determine* the family form. Their influence is clearly apparent, but like all patterns of social organization, the form of the family is the result of a combination of life's many conditions and man's diverse needs.

The maternal and the patriarchal types. Among the various forms of the family we can distinguish two broad types, the patriarchal and the maternal Not all early forms of the family represented one or another of these types; and even in primitive society we find varieties that resemble the unitary detached families of modern days. But a very large number of family systems are examples of one or the other pattern or some combination of the two.

[1] *The maternal family:* "Matriarchy," strictly defined, means a form of family in which the control is centered in the wife or mother. There are grave doubts whether such a *system* ever existed in primitive society, though the women in some groups, such as the American Iroquois and Wyandots, the Eskimos, and certain African tribes, often exercised considerable authority.[16] However, the fact that women appear in positions of authority is not evidence of a matriarchate—Queen Elizabeth ruled in patriarchal sixteenth-century

15. *Ibid.*, p. 183.

16. Briffault and some earlier writers used such evidence as indication of an early matriarchial system. See *The Mothers*, pp. 316 ff. Modern anthropologists have not been able to substantiate this view.

England, and many women have occupied high offices before and since. Therefore, rather than "matriarchal," we use the term "maternal family" to apply to the system under which status, name, and sometimes inheritance are transmitted through the female line. The chief characteristics of this type are the following.

ONE: Descent is traced through the mother, not the father—this is the *matrilineal* system.

TWO: In most cases, though not always, matrilineal descent is associated with *matrilocal* residence, the children being raised in the home of the wife's relatives. The husband, sometimes merely a privileged visitor, has in this respect a secondary position in the home where his own children live. (He may have the *dominant* position in the family of his sister.)

THREE: Authority within the family group belongs primarily not to the husband but to some male representative of the wife's kin. Often, as in the Malay Islands and among the Omaha Indians, the mother's eldest brother has authority over the children; sometimes the mother's father, as among the Labrador Indians.

FOUR: The maternal system tends to weld the *kin-group* (or "consanguine family") together, but to lessen the cohesiveness of the "conjugal" family itself. It is usually associated with the principle of exogamy, the tribe being separated into separate intermarrying groups.

The maternal family prevails in many parts of the earth.[17] Since under this system the husband has a less important role, some authors have connected it with an original ignorance of the physiological fact of paternity. Among the Trobriand Islanders, for example, it is believed that although a virgin cannot conceive, pregnancy is caused by "spirits."[18] But the matrilineal system, which exists in this group, is found among other peoples who are perfectly aware of the fact of paternity; in fact some groups have replaced the patrilineal with the matrilineal system of reckoning descent. The latter is widespread among primitive peoples, but it is only a guess that it goes back to an earlier stage when physiological paternity was unknown.

[2] *The patriarchal family:* The patriarchal family was the prevailing type not only in the greater civilizations of antiquity but also in the feudal society from which our own has evolved. Therefore it demands more detailed consideration. The growth of property, the development of agriculture, the concentration of authority, and the specialization of function, which characterize the more modern societies, were more in harmony with the patriarchal principle. In many cases they no doubt led to its victory over the maternal system. More-

---

17. For descriptions of American Indian examples, see M. E. Opler, *An Apache Life-Way* (Chicago, 1941); and D. Eggan, "Hopi Marriage and Family Relations," *Marriage and Family Living*, Vol. VI (1944).

18. B. Malinowski, *The Sexual Life of Savages in North-Western Melanesia* (New York, 1929), I, pp. 5 ff.

over, the patriarchal principle permitted the family to serve as a compact unit of society, for here there is no division of functions between the father and some relative by marriage, as the maternal system involved. Under the latter a society is usually divided into exogamous groups; but under the patriarchal system it becomes a system of family units consolidated into larger kin-groups.

The patriarchal family assumes a number of forms, but it is a type realized in various degrees throughout the history of civilization. Under the patriarchate the family is a closely knit, inclusive system in which all authority (in principle) belongs to the paternal side. Sometimes it is part of a "joint-family," the father and mother and their sons' families forming one household. Sometimes the household includes concubines as well as the official wife, as in the more prosperous families of old China. Sometimes it is part of a "stem-family," with only one of the sons bringing his family within the paternal household. Sometimes these "extended" forms are associated with the communal ownership and use of property and facilities, as among the Kabyli, where the individual family households are ranged around a common courtyard, use the same well, and have common property, and where at the same time the whole group is subject in certain respects to the patriarchal authority of the grandfather or eldest male.[19]

The term "patriarchate" suggests the inclusive powers of the family's father. Generally he presides over the religious rites of the household, he is guardian of the "family gods," of the sacred hearth. Where, as in traditional China, the ancestors of the family are themselves the object of religious devotion, the entire maintenance of the religion is under the charge of the paterfamilias. Under the ancient law of China the woman was subject to three successive obediences, first to her father and mother, next to her husband, and last, if a widow, to her son. In the developed patriarchal system the head of the household is also a representative of the state, and the political council is often composed of the fathers, the *patres*. Thus in our language the word "senate" means the meeting of the old men; in some regions we still speak of the "town fathers." The power of the patriarch over his children, young or adult, was often almost unlimited. In ancient Palestine he could sell his daughter into servitude; in ancient Rome the *patria potestas* meant the power of life and death. In principle, almost complete social subordination marked the position of the wife. She could not own property in her own right; she had no standing before the law over against her husband. Among the Jews, the early Romans, and the Chinese, for example, she could be divorced on certain grounds at the will of her husband, though, of course, she had no reciprocal right.

In most of the highly developed communities in which the patriarchate flourished, occasionally an individual woman would achieve great fame, usually

19. R. Maunier, *La Construction Collective de la Maison en Kabylie* (Paris, 1926).

as ruler or artist. But this was the exception, for women seldom participated directly in public life and received no general education aside from training—often rigorous training—in the arts of the household. At Athens the wife and daughters were secluded in the "women's apartments" and not expected to leave without the husband's permission—they could well envy the greater freedom of the hetairai or "companions," who were frequently foreigners and as such were not subject to the moral restrictions of the patriarchal system. In China, the ancient practice of binding the feet had two important aspects, the aesthetic and, significantly, the fact that this custom prevented the woman from leaving the household unaided.[20] The patriarchal regime of ancient Greece broke down in the later period of classical civilization, just as it is breaking down in China today. What influences are significant in this transition? We can best answer by examining the forces at work in the rise of our own type of modern family.

From the Patriarchal to the Modern Family

The patriarchate and family attitudes in the eighteenth century. In our Western civilization the patriarchal family, descending from the feudal age, has succumbed to the onset of new social and economic forces. Many features of it survived into the nineteenth century, traces of it still remain, and individual families, especially in the less-developed regions, occasionally conform to the older pattern, the features of which we may briefly note.

[1] *The patriarchal family in England and America:* In eighteenth-century England scarcely any career or any public position was open to women—unless they were queens. A woman had few property rights, beyond a dower which went to her at her husband's death. On her marriage her property vested in her husband, and even such earnings as she might acquire by her own labors belonged to her husband. At law she was treated as a "minor" or a "ward." The family was still an economic unit owned and managed by the husband. In the households of poor and rich alike the women co-operated in economic tasks that have now almost everywhere been transferred to other agencies.

In America the same conditions generally prevailed. The law of colonial days enforced the principle that it was the duty of women to serve and obey their husbands. While in the South the position of women was rather higher, because of their scarcity in the earlier settlements and because of the relegation of household work to the slaves, in Puritan New England the rigor of the Mosaic law was reaffirmed. The codes of Connecticut and Massachusetts contained enactments which recalled the *patria potestas* of Rome or the stern judgment

20. Cf. Olga Lang, *Chinese Family and Society* (New Haven, 1946), pp. 45–46. This volume is a detailed study of the modern changes being wrought in the patriarchal family of China.

of Palestine, a statute of Connecticut even going so far as to decree death for the "stubborn and rebellious son."[21] The elders of the church, as in the Geneva of Calvin, exercised a formidable inquisition over the life of the family, and the penalty of adultery might be death. While no doubt a study of the letter of the law may lead to an exaggeration of the severity of the prevailing mores, it is still indicative of the general temper of the age. There were significant mitigations of that severity long before the end of the eighteenth century, and New England in particular sought to protect the wife against ill-usage by the husband. But patriarchal rule, with its subordination of women, still flourished until the nineteenth century felt the impact of the new economic forces which the eighteenth had brought to birth.

[2] *The woman's place in society:* The remarkable transformation which the family has undergone since the end of the eighteenth century is no better illustrated than by the contrast between the attitudes toward the place of women in society current then and now. The scientist Erasmus Darwin summed up the older patriarchal attitude in the characteristic words:

> The female character should possess the mild and retiring virtues rather than the bold and dazzling ones; great eminence in almost everything is sometimes injurious to a young lady; whose temper and disposition should appear to be pliant rather than robust; to be ready to take impressions rather than to be decidedly marked, as great apparent strength of character, however excellent, is liable to alarm both her own and the other sex, and to create admiration rather than affection.[22]

Mary Wollstonecraft's *A Vindication of the Rights of Woman*, published in 1791, a work regarded at that time as bold or even dangerous, contained demands now accepted as commonplace. She argued that women be given a broader education for the business of life, and attacked Rousseau, who had written that "the education of women should always be relative to that of men," for they "are specially made to please men." That this conclusion should have satisfied Rousseau, the great radical theorist of the eighteenth century, is itself a revelation of the change which the following century was to accomplish.

The crumbling of the patriarchal foundations. But while these patriarchal attitudes still flourished at the end of the eighteenth century in Western Europe and in America, the foundations of the system to which they adhered had long before begun to crumble. On the one hand, the *economic* conditions which tended to focalize work and authority within the household were giving place to others which broke down the toilsome and inadequate self-sufficiency of the individual

---

21. Quoted in W. Goodsell, *Problems of the Family* (New York, 1928), Chap. V.

22. Quoted in W. Goodsell, *A History of the Family as a Social and Educational Institution* (New York, 1927), Chap. IX.

family. On the other hand, the *cultural* conditions grew less in harmony with the attitudes and the prerogatives of the patriarchal system. Let us consider the latter first.

[1] *The decline of the authoritarian mores:* The authoritarian mores of feudalism and the religious conceptions that accompanied them were congenial to the close-knit hierarchical unity of the patriarchate. The dynastic order penetrated down from the king to the householder. The insistence of the church on family discipline, its conception of the nature and purpose of marriage, its doctrine of the subordinate place of women, as seen, for example, in the use of the word "obey" in the marriage service, its glorification of chastity, and its utter condemnation of all sex relations outside marriage, all worked strongly in the same direction. At the same time the feudal-militarist principle, with its designation of the clergy, the landowners, and the warriors as the three honorific occupations, placed the life and the service of women in a much inferior category to that of men.

The decline of these authoritarian mores, alike in religion and in politics, undermined the cultural foundations of the feudal-patriarchal family. The family lost some of its control over its members. The more democratic trends were detaching citizenship from family connections and at the same time making it a right no longer exclusive to the established or "patrician" families.[23] The changing state curbed the domination of the paterfamilias over his wife and children and appointed its own courts to decide issues over which the head of the family had once been supreme. The right to vote, which at first belonged to a man by virtue of his being a propertied householder, became by degrees an individual right. The religious functions of the family diminished. The idea that the family was of divine ordinance, and its laws divinely appointed became less prevalent. Words which had given a religious connotation to familial loyality or obedience—like the word "pious"—changed their meaning.

The choice of the marriage partners of the children came to be less determined by the head of the family or by family considerations. In the eighteenth century there became manifest the attitude which created the main theme of the popular novel—the conception of *individualized romantic love* as the great adventure of life culminating in marriage. By romantic love we understand an engrossing emotional attachment between a man and a woman, exclusive and individualized, transcending at need all sorts of obstacles, involving some kind of idealization, and enveloping the sex relationship in an aura of tender sentiment for the personality of the loved one. In its idealizing quality and in its tendency to ignore or sublimate the sexual aspect, it resembles the older chivalry; in its concentration upon an exclusive object of devotion and particularly in its implication that marriage is the adventurous goal of the attachment, it is far apart from that older principle. We shall return to this conception of romantic love shortly in considering the problems of the modern family.

---

23. See R. M. MacIver's *The Modern State* (Oxford, 1926), Chap. I.

[2] *The impact of economic and technological changes:* These cultural changes were associated with economic changes and received at length a vast impetus from the eighteenth-century inventions which substituted the power machine for the manual tool. More and more, as the development and the application of the new techniques advanced, they stripped the family of its economic functions and in so doing profoundly affected the whole character and the social significance of the family. They increasingly took both the work and the workers out of the home. Above all, they drew ever larger numbers of women into workshops and factories and offices. They broke down the age-old doctrine—"man for the field and woman for the hearth." They gave wives and daughters some earning power independent of the jurisdiction of husbands and fathers. For the first time in modern history the work of women began to be specialized like that of men instead of being devoted to the promiscuous tasks of the household. The family changed from a production to a consumption unit.

TABLE V **Data on Gainfully Employed Married Women in the United States, 1890–1940**[24]

Year	Number of married working women	Per cent increase over previous decade		Per cent all married working women are of	
		Married working women	All married women	All married women	All working women
1890	515,260	—	—	4.6	13.9
1900	769,477	49.3	24.1	5.6	15.4
1910	1,890,661	145.7	28.1	10.7	24.7
1920	1,920,281	15.7	20.6	9.0	23.0
1930	3,071,302	59.9	22.8	11.7	28.9
1940	4,560,835	48.5	15.0	15.2	35.5

At the same time the results of industrial discovery began to penetrate within the home, not only in the substitution of bought for homemade commodities but also in the application of laborsaving devices. The net consequence was the gradual reduction of the amount of energy and time involved in the economic tasks of the family, in the business of homekeeping.

[3] *The continuation of the trend today:* These processes are still going on. The transference of women from domestic to "gainful" employments has advanced rapidly during the last sixty years. In the United States in 1890 about half a million *married* women were in the labor force; by 1940 the figure had

24. E. W. Burgess and H. J. Locke, *The Family* (New York, 1945), p. 504; adapted from the U. S. Bureau of the Census, *Fifteenth Census of the United States* (1930), *Population*, Vol. V, *General Report on Occupations*, p. 272; *Sixteenth Census of the United States* (1940), *Population*, Vol. III, *The Labor Force*, Part I, p. 22.

increased to four and one half millions. "These were the most daring pioneers of all," remark two students of the American family, "since the traditional mores had even less place for married women outside the home than for their unmarried sisters."[25] Yet the percentage of married women employed outside the home and, even more consistently, the percentage of all working women who are married have steadily increased since the beginning of this century. Thus in 1940 about one of every seven married women were "breadwinners," and about one of every three job-holding women were married. These trends are presented in Table V.

An important aspect of these trends is the very large proportion of young women, married and single, drawn *temporarily* into industry, especially during periods of war and labor shortage. In the spring of 1945, for example, about 37 per cent of American women were serving in our "labor force," and two years latter only about 29 per cent—the reduction coming about in large part because many of the younger women left their jobs to return to their husbands or to school or to marry.[26] This temporary employment of the younger women is rather a condition of than an alternative to marriage and family life. Moreover, it suggests that the woman's relation to the family is, as in some respects it must always remain, different from that of the man, and that the difference places her at a competitive disadvantage in the economic field. For very good reason we often bestow kudos on the successful wife and mother who has also achieved distinction in the professions or business or some other field where she is competing with the male.

[4] *What the trend cannot change:* Economic change has deeply affected the form and character of the family, but it does not affect the basic biological facts and the social needs which create the essential functions of the family. We may in fact look upon these changes as an aspect of the great evolutionary process of society, later to be discussed, in which its organizations have become specialized to perform more limited and more exclusive functions. In this process the family has been gradually stripped of functions irrelevant to its peculiar character as a system of more or less enduring social relationships based on the fact of sex. Let us see how these changes have affected the mode in which the family is today fulfilling its essential functions.

Changes in the central social function of the family. Here we shall consider one primary function of the family, the perpetuation of the race. This function includes, of course, the procreation of children. But it also includes inducting the children into the basic social heritage and superintending their initial adjustments to the world in which they must live. What are the chief changes that have occurred in recent times in this central activity of the family?

[1] *The role of outside agencies:* Various social organizations have been de-

25. A. G. Truxal and F. E. Merrill, *The Family in American Culture* (New York, 1947), p. 340.
26. U. S. Bureau of the Census, *Monthly Report on the Labor Force, Population*, MRLF-No. 58 (April 4, 1947), p. 3.

veloped to aid the family in the fulfillment of its principal function. These include the maternity hospital and out-patient clinics for mothers, the baby clinic, the crèche, the kindergarten, and other preschool agencies, including the modern organization of "baby sitters." Here the problem to be met has been twofold. On the one hand, there are more and more mothers whose employment lies outside the home and who can neither leave the children behind nor bring them to the factory or office. On the other hand, there is the more general problem of bringing to the home the benefits of modern hygiene, sanitation, preventive medicine, and the techniques of child welfare and training. We should include here also the increasingly accepted agencies of "planned parenthood," urging mothers to guard their own and their children's welfare by spacing or limiting births in keeping with the health of the mother and the means of the family.

[2] *The role of public aid:* Various systems of economic aid from public or private funds have been devised in order that the family, no longer upheld by the larger kin-group, may be able to fulfill its central function in the competitive life of large-scale society. The necessarily limited contribution of child welfare and other philanthropic associations is today far outweighed by that of governmental agencies of several kinds. A plan for mothers' pensions was one of the earlier aids to the family, and was developed in New Zealand, Denmark, Canada, and many of our own states. National systems of social insurance were put into effect in several European countries after World War I and have been extensively developed in more recent years. Economic aid to and protection of the family were largely left to private agencies and to the local states in the United States until, with the passage of the Social Security Act in 1935, the federal government devised a method of bringing assistance to dependent and needy children, the unemployed, the aged, and the blind.

Several European countries, including France and Italy, largely because of their governments' concern with the declining rate of population growth, adopted family allowance programs, involving either cash subsidies to parents in proportion to their number of dependent children or direct payments of services and goods needed for family life and child development. Several of these programs were brought to a close by World War II, but in 1944, Soviet Russia's "Marriage Law" established cash grants and monthly allowances for families with three or more children, increasing in each case with the number of offspring (up to eleven!).[27] Except for Russia, perhaps the largest degree of economic aid is provided the individual family by the program undertaken in Sweden which, though planned in part to increase the birth rate, is designed to guarantee each family not cash but the housing, goods, and services essential to its needs.[28]

---

27. See "Text of Decree Issued July 8, 1944, by Presidium of the Supreme Soviet," *The American Review of the Soviet Union*, VI (1944), 69–76.

28. The European programs are comprehensively analyzed in D. V. Glass, *Population Policies*

We should note that *none* of these policies aims to take away from the family its primary function but, on the contrary, all of them seek to make it more capable of performing that function efficiently. Nor is Soviet Russia an exception. Quite the contrary, for in that country, where day nurseries for the children of factory and farm workers and other similar services have been highly developed, the idea of the substitution of a public institution for the private family has been wholly rejected.[29] The family in *all* societies is recognized as the legitimate and necessary agency through which society itself is perpetuated.

[3] *The decreasing rate of procreation:* This third change, the lessening of the fertility of marriage, is of a very different order from the other two and has a more profound significance for the future of the family. Since the 1870's the birth rate has been falling in the countries of Western civilization. The decline has been more marked and more rapid in some countries, especially in Northern and Western Europe, than in others, but they have all, sooner or later, revealed it. It has been more conspicuous in some classes than in others, being greatest for the most prosperous economic groups, for the more highly educated, for city dwellers, and for those occupational groups in which the largest percentage of married women are "gainfully employed." These group differences in fertility have been lessening in recent years, and the trend of fewer births is exhibited so widely throughout the population as to be a phenomenon of our civilization itself. In Chapter V we examined certain aspects of this phenomenon and later (in Chapter XXIV) we shall consider its significance with respect to broader social changes.

Here we must emphasize that the decreasing rate of procreation does not involve the substitution for the family of any other agency to undertake its primary task. Births outside the family, except in certain groups and during periods of wartime relaxation of the mores, have probably been reduced.[30] Moreover, the decline of the birth rate has been preceded by a decline of the death rate, and especially of the infant death rate. The concomitance of the two trends has meant a vital social economy. The prior decline of the death rate brought about an enormous *increase* in population, while the corresponding decline of the two rates has diminished the waste and sacrifice of human life, health, energy, and efficiency in the family's task of perpetuating the race.

This result is in harmony with the increase of aid to the family from outside

and Movements in Europe (London, 1940); and more briefly in W. S. Thompson, *Population Problems* (New York, 1942), Chaps. XXV and XXVI. For the Swedish plan, see G. Myrdal, *Population: A Problem for Democracy* (Cambridge, Mass., 1940).

29. See Burgess and Locke, *op. cit.*, Chap. VI (which presents a good bibliography) for the Russian family.

30. We are aware that illegitimacy has been reported as "increasing" in the United States from 1917 to 1940. But such reports are calculated on the basis of the number of illegitimate births per 1,000 total live births rather than in their ratio to the total population. This shortcoming and others lead Burgess and Locke to describe the conclusion of an increasing trend as "exceedingly uncritical and questionable."—*Ibid.*, p. 498.

agencies and from the government. Together they have reduced the expenditure of energy by the members of the family in the sheer task of its maintenance. The resulting social economy means the liberation of the family, especially the wives and mothers, for other activities. This new liberty, like every other, creates new problems which, as we shall see, men must seek to solve.

Changes in the structure of the family. Along with the changes affecting the principal function of the family have gone changes in its form. Institutional alterations have greatly influenced the marriage contract and the relations of the members to one another. Three closely interrelated changes are particularly significant.

[1] *Decreased control of the marriage contract:* The marriage contract today is entered into more autonomously by both men and women. People are less subject to parental control and other forms of social pressure concerning whom and when they shall marry—the pressure is lightened especially for women, on whom it had weighed most heavily. The term "old maid" has fallen into relative disuse and has lost much of its older connotation of contempt. Women have attained a new legal status and, more recently, a new political status, in which there is much less discrimination between them and men.

The character of the marriage contract has changed even more in fact than in outward form. The traditional marriage ceremony in Western civilization was based on the principle of male dominance and female obedience. But when the wife promises to "obey," where this word remains in the marriage ritual, she and her husband alike are aware of the fact that this aspect of the ceremony is for the most part a relic of the past. Choice of mate *by* mate and *mutual* determination of the relationship that binds them have replaced the older external and one-sided controls.

[2] *Changing economic role of women:* An important factor in bringing about the new character of the marriage contract is the increasing degree of economic independence attained by women. In the more prosperous classes they have become property owners, and in the general population they are actual or potential wage earners or professional workers. They are, of course, still far from possessing an equal economic status to that of men. For, in addition to the persistence of the mores of male domination, women are handicapped by sex disabilities in certain fields and, above all, by the heavier claims of the family on them, increasing their competitive disadvantage before as well as after marriage. Nevertheless the movement has been toward equality and it will no doubt advance, whether under capitalistic or more collectivistic regimes.

The degree of economic independence already achieved has had significant results. Formerly the young woman had no alternatives beyond an early marriage or continued dependence upon and subjection to the parental home. Now she can earn her own living and thus gain a sense of immediate independence which affects her whole attitude, gives her more power to choose when and whom she shall marry, and even to decide in terms of her own life whether she shall marry or not. There are relatively few women who regard an economic occupation as a permanent alternative to marriage, but the fact that it is a temporary alternative is enough to alter greatly a situation which was bound up with her economic helplessness.

[3] *Decline of religious control:* Marriage has become today essentially a civil contract, though it is often attended by religious rites. In early colonial New England the civil character of the marriage contract was insisted upon, to be sure, but this insistence was due, as in other Calvinistic communities at that time, to the struggle of nonconformist religion against an established church and did not prevent a strong religious determination of the whole system of marriage. But in our times, for a large portion of the population, religious rites, when not omitted altogether, assume a secondary importance. In any event, they are not necessary for the validity of marriage in the eyes of the law. Outside the Catholic Church, the authority of organized religion over the conditions of marriage, and over the conditions of divorce, has markedly declined.

This fact has considerable importance for the present situation. For the church has always been deeply concerned with marriage and with sex. The emphasis of the Christian church in particular was upon sexual asceticism, based on the notion that sex itself was "impure."[31] This conception was easily tied in with the "impurity" of women as such and with the consequent desirability of their control and subjection. It is not surprising that various denominations have in recent years adjusted their religious doctrines to the realities of sex, of the new position of women, and of family life.

Not only economic and religious changes but the whole process of modern civilization within which they fall has worked toward giving women a new position in society and especially in their relations to men. The reduction of the functions of the family, the lightening of the tasks of the home, bringing more leisure to large numbers of women, the shortening of the period of child-bearing or the lengthening of the interval between the arrival of successive children, these and other conditions presently to be discussed have transformed the family into a new kind of partnership and created new problems for the family of the present and of the future.

Increasing divorce and its interpretation. One evidence of the freer or less authoritarian character of marriage is found in the increasing frequency of divorce. In many primitive communities, custom permitted the husband to divorce the wife on stated grounds—it might be for witchcraft or even for bad cooking—though the wife much more rarely had a similar privilege. Among the ancient Hebrews the husband could likewise give his wife a "bill of divorcement," and the *patria potestas* of the Romans of the earlier republican times

---

31. See the explicit teaching of St. Paul on this subject, I Cor. 7.

included also this right, while the later Roman law extended it rather liberally to the wife. But the patriarchal family of Christendom rested on social and religious beliefs and was bound up with economic conditions which made divorce a rare phenomenon when it was admitted at all. It is only in recent decades that the question of divorce has become one of serious practical importance.

[1] *National and regional variations in divorce:* Not only has the divorce rate greatly increased in general during the last fifty years, but it has shown remarkable differences from country to country. Table VI indicates both its general increase and the marked variations for different nations.

TABLE VI **Divorce Rate per 1,000 Population in 1900 and 1938 for Selected Countries**[32]

Country	Divorce rate in or about 1900	Divorce rate in or about 1938	Ratio of 1938 to 1900 rates
Australia	.10	.44	4.4
Canada	.00[a]	.20	—
England and Wales	.02	.15	7.5
France	.25	.58	2.3
Germany	.15	.72	4.8
Japan	1.42	.62	.4
Russia (European)	—	2.81 (1928)	—
Sweden	.08	.55	6.9
United States	.73	1.88	2.6

[a] In 1903 only 21 divorces in population of 5,651,000.

The situation in Japan and in Russia is unique. The higher Japanese rate for 1900 (1.42 per thousand population) than for 1938 (.62 per thousand population) is a reflection of the fact that the "old" Japanese family—still a predominant type in the *rural* areas of Japan—incorporated father- or husband-determined divorce as a regular feature; the more recent rate corresponds quite closely with that of such countries as France and Sweden. Divorce in the older patriarchal family of Tsarist Russia, on the other hand, occurred infrequently, while in the early days of the Soviet regime it was obtainable upon the demand of either husband or wife. However, in 1936 and again in 1944 much more strict divorce laws were put into effect that both increased the cost of divorce and, as a result of an intense antidivorce educational campaign, caused it to be

32. Adapted from Burgess and Locke, *op. cit.*, p. 628.

viewed as an undesirable mode of adjusting family affairs. Thus in the Soviet Union, where since 1944 divorce is perhaps more difficult than in most of our states,[33] the rate has lowered considerably in recent years.

One interesting aspect of these differences is that countries with fairly similar cultural traditions, such as England and the United States, have remarkable divergences in the divorce rate. Frequency of divorce does not conform to the degree of industrial and urban growth, and thus it presents a different problem of interpretation from that involved in most of the changes we have so far been considering. The differences are seen still more clearly when we compare the rates for various regions of the United States, as in Table VII. Why should

TABLE VII **Estimated Divorce Rate per 1,000 Population by Geographic Division in the United States for 1940**[34]

Geographic division	Rate per 1,000 population
United States	2.0
New England	1.2
Middle Atlantic	0.9
East North Central	2.0
West North Central	2.0
South Atlantic	1.8
East South Central	1.8
West South Central	3.5
Mountain	4.1
Pacific	3.5

the West South Central, the Mountain, and the Pacific regions be so much more prolific in divorces than the Middle Atlantic and New England? Why should such sparsely settled states as Oregon and Wyoming have much higher rates of divorce than, for example, New York and Pennsylvania? On a larger scale, why should divorce in the United States as a whole occur so much more frequently than, say, in Canada or England or Japan?

[2] *Inadequate explanations of the differences in divorce rates:* We cannot explain these differences as merely the result of religious or legal factors. Religious differences, such as the proportion of Catholics, are no doubt involved. But some non-Catholic countries, like England, have a very low rate; on the other hand, New England with a larger proportion of Catholics, has more divorce than the heavily non-Catholic Middle Atlantic states. In the United States racial differences complicate the problem, but the rate is higher for native Whites than for foreign-born Whites, so that it is essentially an indigenous development.

33. Cf. *ibid.*, p. 191.

34. Truxal and Merrill, *op. cit.*, p. 692, based on U.S. Bureau of the Census, Vital Statistics—Special Reports, *Estimated Number of Divorces by State: United States, 1937–1940*, Vol. XV, No. 18 (March 20, 1942).

Differences in state laws in our country afford *secondary* explanations: South Carolina actually outlaws divorce; Nevada, contrastingly, and Florida, with their liberal legislation, are havens of divorce seekers. About one fifth of divorces over a several years' period have been granted in states other than those in which the parties were married, but this proportion is related fairly closely to the general physical mobility of the population, so that migratory divorces are, perhaps, only about 3 per cent of the total number.[35] Moreover, the state laws themselves presumably reflect in some degree the temper of the different communities. In any event the laws cannot explain the fact that divorces throughout the whole country have increased 500 per cent since 1890, especially as the tendency has been toward greater stringency in legislation since that date.[36] The inadequacy of the legal explanation is further revealed when we look at the situation in other lands.

In general, there are three broad legal attitudes toward divorce. First is the attitude expressed in the saying "whom God hath joined together let no man put asunder," as this is interpreted by the Catholic Church (though on occasion it discovers grounds for *nullification* of marriage). This principle was written into the law of Fascist Italy as it is in that of South Carolina. Second is the attitude that marriage is normally indissoluble, but that divorce is permissible on the suit of either partner when certain grave offenses are committed by the other. This conception is the basis of the laws of many European countries and of almost all English-speaking countries. Lastly, there is the attitude that, with certain safeguards, marriage should be regarded like any other contractual partnership and should be terminable by mutual consent. This is in one respect the exact counterpart of the second attitude. In the United States or in England if both parties contrive together to seek a divorce, they thereby commit the crime of collusion. But in the Scandinavian and a few other European countries, including Soviet Russia (in principle), and in China and Japan, the mutual consent of the two partners is a valid and sufficient ground. Here we again see the danger of a legalistic interpretation of divorce, for there is no correlation between the liberality of the legal attitude and the divorce rate itself. (See Table VI.)

[3] *Some sociologically significant factors in differential divorce rates:* In the absence of sociologically oriented investigations of the causation of national and regional divorce differences,[37] we present the following suggestions to explain why its increase does not conform to the main trends of the changing family, why it is most prevalent in the United States, and why as we proceed westward in the United States we encounter higher rates.

35. So concludes A. Cahen in *Statistical Analysis of American Divorce* (New York, 1932).

36. Cf. J. P. Lichtenberger, *Divorce* (New York, 1931), p. 137. For a good analysis of the long-range divorce trend, see K. Davis, "Sociological Analysis," in "Children of Divorced Parents," *Law and Contemporary Problems*, Vol. X (1944).

37. See R. M. MacIver, *Social Causation* (Boston, 1942), pp. 335–339, for a brief statement on the causation of differential divorce rates.

ONE: SOCIAL CONTINUITY AND MOBILITY. A sudden rise in divorce rates has taken place in the modern world wherever the entrance of women into the economic life has been associated with an abrupt break in old traditions, as in Soviet Russia between 1917 and 1936, or with an individualistic trend in which old traditions lose their hold, as in the United States. The family has been the rallying point for the sense of *social continuity*—of group tradition and of name from generation to generation. Indicative of the situation in our own country is the fact that European studies of the family generally lay far more stress on social continuity than do American studies.[38] The mobility of life so characteristic of the United States, and particularly of the West, has weakened this sense of continuity. It weakens also the external pressure of public opinion. Physical mobility, such as movement from one residence to another within a city or between communities, tends to release individuals from group control. Various studies indicate that when the family as a whole or one or the other of the married partners moves about a good deal for occupational or other reasons a strain is placed upon the group, with a tendency toward its breakup.[39] Under these circumstances difficulties between the partners which in other countries, such as England or France, would be adjusted or tolerated are sufficient to disrupt the family.

TWO: INFIDELITY AS A REASON FOR DIVORCE. Another factor that may contribute to the greater frequency of divorce in the United States is our legacy of puritanism, with its insistence that any infidelity is destructive of the marriage partnership. In this respect our cultural values differ considerably from those of certain European countries as well as Oriental countries, where extrafamilial sexual relationships, especially for men, are openly or implicitly sanctioned.

THREE: ROMANTIC LOVE AS A FACTOR. The significance we give to infidelity is closely associated with the idea that romantic love is the only proper foundation of marriage. This is a modern development which was alien to the spirit of the patriarchal family. That it is in harmony with the character of American culture is evidenced by the great stress placed upon it in the modern novel, drama, the films, even much of our advertising. If, as some observers maintain, "in America the romantic view of marriage has been taken more seriously than anywhere else," it no doubt helps to explain the prevalence of divorce.[40] For romantic love, which is so individualized and so responsive to the unpre-

---

38. Contrast, for example, the space devoted to this subject in the English text, *The Family*, by Helen Bosanquet (London, 1915), with the omission or sparing reference to it in American texts.

39. See, for example, E. R. Mowrer, *Disorganization, Personal and Social* (Philadelphia, 1942), Chap. XVII. The effects of the mobility associated with the American frontier are discussed by Truxal and Merrill, *op. cit.*, Chap. V; and of that associated with more recent migration by J. N. Webb and M. Brown, *Migrant Families* (Washington, D. C., 1938).

40. Bertrand Russell, *Marriage and Morals* (New York, 1929), Chap. VI.

dictable conjuncture of the harmony of moods between men and women in a changeful world, is more apt to bring periodic stimulation to the individual life than to be the successful basis of a permanent institution. Many of the divorce and marriage "repeaters," therefore, are understandably individuals who are striving once more to establish a marriage on the dubious single ground of romantic attachment. This factor has even larger implications for family instability today, as we shall shortly point out.

The evolutionary emergence of a new family type. The important changes in the family with which we have dealt have a decidedly evolutionary character. We conclude this section by considering the emergence of this new type of family in the Western world.

[1] *The separation of nonessential functions from the family:* The family in the course of modern history has parted with a great many functions which are not essential to its emerging nature. These functions have been taken over by other social agencies, which in turn have become specialized to perform them, and which perform them with more economy and with greater efficiency. The factory and the office can fulfill their economic tasks in a complex world more effectively than the family ever could. The school can provide many kinds of education which the home could never furnish. The hospital and clinic can offer medical service which the family has neither the skill nor the equipment to maintain for itself. And so with a large number of other agencies. In the cities, and increasingly on the farms as well, many traditional tasks of the household, such as laundering (even of diapers), preserving and baking, and in some measure even cooking and cleaning, are becoming specialized. The process advances still further as more and more families rely upon common heating plants in our huge multiple dwellings, upon prepared and manufactured goods consumed by the family, upon textbooks and teachers and social workers for guidance and education, and so on. But as extensive as these changes in family function have been or as much as they may continue in the foreseeable future, the family remains as a permanent feature of human life.

[2] *Main features of the modern family:* What, then, are the *essential* functions of the family? What are the functions it is peculiarly fitted to perform which give it its justification in a world of specialized agencies and institutions? The sex partnership of the family has a different basis and has different purposes and different consequences from those of other partnerships. Its social claims and social responsibilities are correspondingly different.

The process in which irrelevant activities are being stripped from the family makes clear its essential functions. The peculiar claim of the family is not that it alone fulfills any one function, but rather that *it alone provides a way of combining and harmonizing certain closely related functions.* There are at least three of these for which it provides this common basis. They are shown to the right on Chart X:

CHART X Emergence of the Modern Family Type[41]

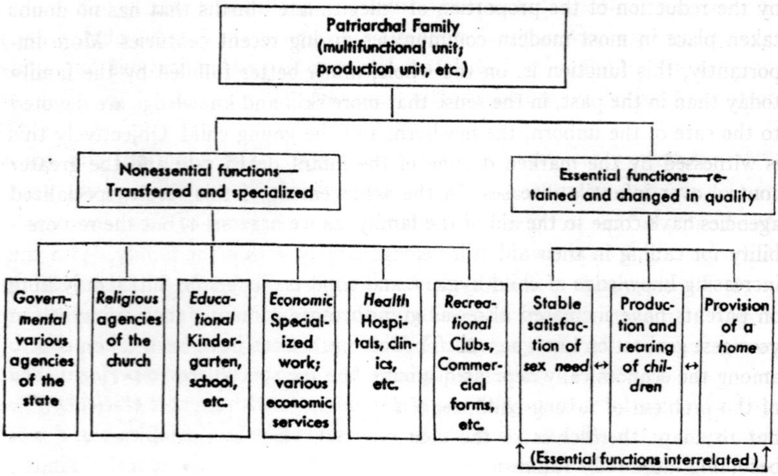

The primary functions of the modern family, then, include (1) the procreation and the care and nurture of the young, (2) the more stable satisfaction of the sex needs of the partners, and (3) the sharing of a home, with its combination of material, cultural, and affectional satisfactions.

Only in a *successful* family are these three functions so united that each of them reinforces and enriches the satisfaction of the others. Sex becomes not a detached phenomenon—as it tends to be in extramarital relations and usually is in prostitution—but part of a larger experience of meeting common problems. And the nurture of the children takes place within the focus of the home which, as considerable evidence seems to indicate, is a more favorable environment for them than that of the state nursery or other public or private agencies. The modern family, increasingly denuded of its older socioeconomic activities, stands—*or falls*—on its ability to harmonize the needs and satisfactions involved in its three essential functions.

[3] *Changing aspects of the family functions:* The evolution of the modern family means more than the process that tends to limit it to certain specific functions. There is also in some degree an evolution of these functions themselves, and it is with respect to these that further changes are likely to take place. The shedding of irrelevant functions prepares the way for the development of relevant ones. From this standpoint we may consider each of the three central activities of the family.

41. This chart is based upon a suggestion of Professor R. J. Kutak of the University of Louisville.

ONE: PROCREATION AND CHILD REARING. The task of race perpetuation is today as much the function of the family as it ever was.[42] That it is more exclusively a family task than it has been in most periods of history is suggested by the reduction of the proportion of "illegitimate" births that has no doubt taken place in most modern communities during recent centuries. More importantly, this function is, on the whole, much better fulfilled by the family today than in the past, in the sense that more skill and knowledge are devoted to the care of the unborn, the newborn, and the young child. Objectively this is witnessed by the marked decline of the infant death rate and the greater control over infantile diseases. In the achievement of this result, specialized agencies have come to the aid of the family, as we have seen, but the responsibility for calling in their aid still belongs largely within the family. With the increasing knowledge of child hygiene and child training, the duties devolving on parents have increased also—as grandparents watching the raising of the youngest generation know so well. Though much remains to be done, especially among the economically depressed groups, the importance and the complexity of the problem of raising children, of fitting them not only to survive within but to adapt themselves to the changing conditions of modern society, are becoming more fully realized.

It is frequently claimed that an offset to this advance is that through the practice of birth control married people are enabled as never before to avoid having children. It is conceivable, of course, that this tendency might proceed so far as to threaten the very existence of society. But we should remember, in the first place, that birth control is also a beneficent form of human control permitting us to enhance the lot of mothers and the care of children; and, secondly, that the degree to which married people practice it is not primarily the result of the availability of contraceptive information but rather a reflection of existing social values. In any event, the prophetic fear that the human race is committing "suicide" through birth control may well be vain, since mankind over the long run usually learns to adapt its new discoveries to the general necessities of its continued existence.

TWO: THE SEX NEED. The degree in which marriage suffices to satisfy the sex need is, when we think in terms of human experience and not of ethical dictates, highly variable and subject to perplexing differences of personality. The satisfaction involved may vary from the mere release of physical appetite to the sense of total renewal in mutual love. This problem has so many aspects that dogmatic and sweeping assertions on the subject, so common in modern literature, are peculiarly futile.

But this much is clear: in contrast with the patriarchal family the modern

42. The Nazis' official sanctioning of extrafamilial production of "Aryans" was a short-lived and relatively unimportant program; so with the sanctioning of illegitimacy as a *normal* child-production process by the Soviet government. The *treatment* of illegitimate children is another matter.

family is built on a more intimate sense of personal relationship. The choice of partners is more free, and thus personal qualities and personal attraction of each partner for the other count for more. This personal basis for marriage, while it carries the danger of the instability we have already noted, permits, so long as it lasts, a more complete satisfaction of the sex need within the family. When the economic bonds of the family were weakened under the onset of industrialism, the demand that it should satisfy the personal life of the partners grew stronger. The modern family is therefore called upon to fulfill a more difficult task, and one that requires a maturity and understanding that many newlyweds do not possess.

This task has been partly aided, but also complicated, by the modern practice of birth control, which has introduced *within the family* the distinction between the sexual and reproductive functions. In the unlimited patriarchal family the two were necessarily combined, and the independent satisfaction of sexual desire was commonly associated with extramarital practices. Within the limited family of the present the wife is better able to assume the role once reserved for the "lady of love"—the concubine or prostitute—and thus within it a greater reconciliation of sex and reproduction may take place. This is but one of the implications of the development of modern birth control. The use of contraceptives removes one important support of the mores relating to sex in our society, the fear of pregnancy as a result of intercourse between the unmarried. It is evident that with this powerful incentive already greatly weakened, the sex mores for large groups are undergoing an extreme change.[43]

THREE: PROVISION OF A HOME. In most societies, for men as well as for women, the desire for a home, a personally created and congenial "hearth," a setting for life's activities within an enduring relationship, is a powerful incentive to marriage. In all complex civilizations, other agencies, such as the club and hotel in our own, compete with the family in offering these satisfactions. But the family generally wins out in this competition, for it provides them in a more intimate form and within the congenial circle of man and woman and of parents and children. Here again the change from the patriarchal to the modern family has liberated its potentialities for the fulfillment of its primary functions. For the patriarchal family the household was both home and workshop, within which the wife was often confined to the drudgery of incessant toil in addition to the continual bearing of children. If the home has lost some of its former unity because other agencies compete with it, it has also gained in that it has become more liberated from conditions, both of drudgery and of male dominance, which prevented it from being, in a finer sense, a home. Now

43. The implications of birth control for family life are well stated by W. Lippmann in *A Preface to Morals* (New York, 1929), Chap. XIV. The most extensive evidence thus far compiled concerning actual sex behavior in this country, showing large changes in the basic sex mores, appears in A. C. Kinsey, W. B. Pomeroy, and C. E. Martin, *Sexual Behavior in the Human Male* (Philadelphia, 1948); see especially Chaps. XII, XIII, and XIX.

that the members of the family pursue many of their leisure-time interests as well as their economic tasks outside its walls, the demands they make on the home are different but no less essential. The demands are in some aspects narrower, but they are more exclusively directed to those satisfactions associated with its emerging central functions.

The position of the family today is both a result and a *stage* of the evolutionary process we have been tracing. We must keep this process in mind as we examine certain aspects of its present character and especially some of the social problems it creates.

Family Problems of Today

The relative instability of the modern family. Throughout the whole range of Western civilization the patriarchal family system has dissolved. A century ago Le Play could stress the contrast between the evolving family of Western Europe and the rigid patriarchate of Russia and Eastern Europe.[44] But the latter also has crumbled. The patriarchal family was upheld by authority, buttressed by the religious and political traditions conformable to an agricultural economy. The authority has departed, the traditions have been eclipsed, and the old economy has been undermined or revolutionized. The modern family has emerged, itself no doubt transitional but in its stage presenting problems of great sociological significance.

Undoubtedly the frequently cited contrast between the stability of the patriarchal family and the instability of its modern successor exists. The patriarchal system was so deeply imbedded in the social structure of feudal times that the voluntary dissolution of the individual family was rarely thought of and was rarely possible. For the woman particularly there was little refuge outside the family except the nunnery or prostitution. Social mobility was slight. The relatively fixed social status of the times was essentially the status of the whole family, confirmed by such legal-economic principles as primogeniture and entail and, for the poorer classes, the inherited craft or the rights of the peasant family in the land it cultivated. The family faced the world as a unit, toiled and enjoyed and suffered as a unit.

Today the economic division of labor and the parallel increase of specific social agencies have greatly diminished common participation in the various interests of life, whether in work or in play. The process is still going on, as evidenced by the continuing decrease of "whole family" gatherings and the increase of special activities for the different age groups and the different sexes conducted outside the home. There are a multitude of these, including school programs, juvenile gangs, sanctuaries for the male like clubs and bars, and for

44. P. G. F. Le Play, *Les Ouvriers Européens* (Tours, 1877–1879), Vol. II, *init.*

the female like bridge cliques and cocktail counters, hobby groups, and so on. Moreover, the claim that inventions such as the phonograph and radio have tended to reunite the family within the home is doubtful, for records and air programs alike are largely designed not for the family as such but for special age or sex levels, for the young, for example, or for the housewife. And whatever the short-range effect of depression or war periods in bringing the members of the family more closely together, there is overwhelming evidence that the urban family of today is a less inclusive system of social relationships than perhaps it ever has been before.[45] This fact has made possible the instability charged against it.

Two main causes of family instability. The modern instability of the family is revealed by the frequency of divorce, separation, desertion, and other evidences of disharmony or lack of cohesion which come to light particularly in the courts, in social work, and in "marriage clinics." The degree of instability varies considerably from place to place, being relatively low in England, for example, as compared with many other European countries, as it is in some areas of the southern United States as compared with the Far West. But on the whole the evidences of instability are increasing.[46] Our survey of the evolution of the family suggests two main causes of this situation.

[1] *Less social protection of family crises:* In the first section of this chapter we pointed out that the individual family passes through more drastic psychological transitions than any other social grouping. In the patriarchal family the adjustment of the partners to one another through the tensions and crises of the family cycle was imposed, if not otherwise obtained, by economic necessity and by social pressure supported by the rigid mores and manifested in the various sanctions of social control, from law to gossip. Today the necessity and the pressure are lessened, and the family, no longer strongly if rudely cemented by extraneous functions, must rely much more upon its own strength (or weakness), *by itself*, to survive the crises of its own life history. It is frequently not successful, a situation intensified by the second main cause affecting the stability of the family.

[2] *Replacement of domination by co-operation:* The family has become not only a more limited union, but one that depends more and more on the cooperation of two or more individuals and no longer on the dominance of one.

45. Among the many researches in this area may be cited such studies of the family in specific communities as R. S. and H. M. Lynd, *Middletown* (New York, 1930), Parts II and IV, and *Middletown in Transition* (New York, 1937), Chaps. V and VII; W. L. Warner and P. S. Lunt, *The Social Life of a Modern Community* (New Haven, 1941), Chaps. XII and XVI. For extensive statistical confirmation of extrafamilial activities, see W. F. Ogburn and C. Tibbitts, "The Family and Its Functions," in *Recent Social Trends* (New York, 1933), Chap. XVII.

46. These evidences are well presented in Burgess and Locke, *op. cit.*, Part IV; Truxal and Merrill, *op. cit.*, Part IV; and M. F. Nimkoff, *Marriage and Family* (Boston, 1947), Chap. XVIII.

In this regard the greater personal and social independence of women plays a crucial role, for it has developed new attitudes that stand in marked contrast to those engendered by the patriarchal regime. No doubt the unquestioning acceptance of the doctrine of male dominance made for a more stable family in that earlier age. But the modern family, like any "equal" partnership that demands reciprocity, give-and-take, some degree of harmony between the partners, is apt to be less "stable" than an autocracy of one. This is peculiarly the case in the intensely personal and subtly changeful relationship of sex. This relationship is more experimental, more variable, and more liable to easy disturbance.

These two causes of family instability go hand in hand. The less inclusive and less onerous the tasks which the family performs as a unit, the more possible it becomes for the members to develop and express their individual personalities, each in relation to the others. Economic conditions in the past made of the family, for the most part, a forced union, especially for the woman. For the great majority of women, even today, their condition of at least partial economic dependence is a determining factor in their attitudes toward the family. But this dependence is more relative, more mitigated, than it formerly was, and for the women members of the more prosperous classes it often does not exist. It seems very likely that the process that has increased the economic independence of women will advance further. This trend, together with other factors we must now consider, suggests that the problem of family instability will become even more urgent than it is today.

The need for perspective in the study of family instability. Family instability is not a phenomenon which can be detached (and perhaps evaluated) apart from the whole complex of social and cultural conditions within which it occurs. It is therefore misleading to express the contrast between the patriarchal and modern family as simply or mainly a contrast between stability and instability. For it is *also* a contrast between a more coercive and a freer union. It is not a contrast between a type of family which presented no social problems and one which presents many. Rather it is one of different ideals and values, different advantages and disadvantages. This essential point becomes clearer when we consider some of those activities closely associated with or affected by the new type of family.

[1] *The sexual relationship:* While the sex life of our age reveals a grave array of problems and maladjustments, it also provides an approach toward the solution of some of the most serious problems which the patriarchal system either created or could not solve. The modern attitude toward sex is more intelligent and realistic, less clouded by those taboos and dogmas and fears which forbid any rational endeavor to adjust social systems to human needs. Perhaps the greatest gain springing from this new attitude is the dispersal of socially and psychologically harmful supersition of the uncleanness of sex.

The greater enlightenment in sexual matters among an ever-growing percentage of the population has not, of course, automatically brought about the disappearance of sexual maladjustments. It may be, as is sometimes claimed, that our present-day preoccupation with the topic—manifested in much of our literature, including those "scientific" writings that interpret all social life in sexual terms[47]—actually induces some maladjustments. But this claim itself illustrates the possibility of seeking, rationally and scientifically, the causes of and the remedies for the disturbances that so frequently mar the relationship between the sexes.[48]

[2] *Prostitution and venereal disease:* The rigor of the patriarchal system has generally been associated with prostitution, an institution which brought peculiar degradation to an economically largely defenseless class of women, and which plays a large role in the spread of venereal disease. It can at least be said for the freer sex relations of the present age that where they exist, prostitution has a serious rival and tends to diminish, though it does not and probably will not disappear.[49] But prostitution's legacy of veneral disease persistently remains with us, and is in fact guarded by another inheritance of patriarchal days. This is the refusal to apply in this area the medical and sociological knowledge of prevention which has abolished almost all other forms of contagious disease from the more developed world regions. The modern attitudes toward the facts of sex, however, have permitted a start in the direction of coping rationally with veneral disease rather than regarding it, after the fashion of our forebears, as a punishment for "sin."[50]

[3] *Illegitimacy:* Another legacy of the patriarchal family has been its lack of consideration for the unmarried woman, reaching its extreme in the social stigmatization of the unmarried mother. The latter attitude might be socially justified in so far as its basis was solicitude for the parental care of children, but this interpretation cannot be reconciled with the facts. For the comparatively inadequate treatment afforded the 75,000 to 100,000 "bastard" children

47. An extreme manifestation of this type of interpretation appears in the writings of Wilhelm Reich, editor and leading contributor to the publications of the Orgone Institute Press. Reich's influence is apparent in the popular and, in our view, gravely misleading volume by F. Lundberg and M. F. Farnham, *Modern Woman, The Lost Sex* (New York, 1947), in which, as an illustration of "this phallic world," appears among many similar statements, "What but the greatest orgasm ever seen on earth was the atomic bomb explosion . . . ." (p. 84)—What *but* indeed!

48. Among many studies of marital adjustment, the more penetrating include L. Terman, *et al., Psychological Factors in Marital Happiness* (New York, 1939); E. W. Burgess and L. Cottrell, Jr., *Predicting Success or Failure in Marriage* (New York, 1938); G. V. Hamilton, *A Research in Marriage* (New York, 1929); and H. R. Mowrer, *Personality Adjustment and Domestic Discord* (New York, 1935).

49. On this point see the able analysis of Kingsley Davis, "The Sociology of Prostitution," *American Sociological Review*, II (1937), 744-755.

50. See, for example, H. J. Locke, "Changing Attitudes toward Venereal Diseases," *American Sociological Review*, IV (1939), 836-843.

born each year in the United States (a very small fraction of the number of births *within* families) is attested by the much higher mortality and disease rates in this group. The practice of birth control, a cardinal fact within the modern family, is also tending to lower the proportion of illegitimate births, which, even during the war years from 1940 to 1943, fell from 41 to 36.5 per 1,000 live births.[51] Birth control is no doubt similarly affecting the resort to abortion which, made more perilous because practiced under the ban of the criminal code, and used perhaps ten times more frequently as a method of birth-prevention by married than by single women, has nevertheless been far more common than is usually realized.[52]

[4] *The new economy in reproduction and its implications:* One extremely significant aspect of the situation which has brought with it the instability of the family is the manner in which it tends to reconcile the older opposition between the expression of individuality and the perpetuation of the race. Generally, the costs of reproduction are heavier when the birth rate and the death rate are high, and they fall when the death rate is lowered or when they decrease together. The emergence of the modern family has brought close to its limit a process which is operative throughout organic evolution. In the lowest forms of life the excess of reproduction over survival is enormous—the fecundity (not fertility) rate of the housefly, for example, is about 6,000 *billion*. This excess diminishes as we mount the scale of evolution, and is least in the societies of civilized man. A point has now been reached in countries with a very low death rate, in New Zealand for example, such that an average of less than two and one-half children per marriage may be sufficient to maintain the level of population, although under more typical conditions the figure is perhaps four or over.[53]

Although there are serious problems connected with this development which we shall examine later, it is hard to exaggerate the gain in social economy, the reduction of the waste and the suffering of human life, and the emancipation of the personality of women which it represents. The life of woman need no longer be exhausted in the toils of child-bearing, suckling, and the inadequate care of numerous offspring, with its attendant mortality, with the perpetual poverty which accompanied it. The responsibility and devotion of the family in the upbringing of children is more fully compensated by the satisfactions which they add to the life of the parents. Thus the demands of sex and the demands of procreation are both more fully harmonized with the whole complex of interests and needs which make up the existence of civilized man.

---

51. U.S. Bureau of the Census, Vital Statistics—Special Reports, *Illegitimate Live Births By Race: United States, 1943*, Vol. XXI, No. 15 (Nov. 15, 1945). For further statistics on illegitimacy, see Truxall and Merrill, *op. cit.*, pp. 385-390.

52. Cf. Nimkoff, *op. cit.*, pp. 557-560.

53. Cf. F. Lorimer, E. Winston, and L. K. Kiser, *Foundations of American Population Policy* (New York, 1940), pp. 20-21.

[5] *Is the family breaking down?* It is sometimes claimed that the development of the situation wherein the family is no longer the inclusive focus of the interests of its members, and wherein their familial common interests are increasingly defined by its more limited functions, means the breakdown or even the disappearance of the family. The evidences give little support to this prediction. To begin with, the long-range trend indicates the rising frequency of marriage, not a decline.[54] Moreover, the frequency of divorce, though increasing, is not, as we have shown, strongly correlated with the trends of industrialization and urbanization. We have shown also that the reproductive process probably is being more exclusively fulfilled within the family than before. As the fulfillment of the reproductive function is the first condition of the survival of society, it seems very unlikely, apart from a complete revolution of the present mores, that the family will disappear. Within the life of the family develop the chief motives for offspring and the chief compensations for the responsibilities they entail. Even if the taboo against illegitimacy were removed, modern birth control knowledge would tend to make it more rare. This fact occasionally becomes an argument for the breaking of that taboo, but the woman with strong maternal desires still has important inducements, economic and otherwise, to seek their satisfaction through marriage.

To be sure, the instability of the modern family, as measured by divorce and separation and domestic discord, will continue to increase for some time. For, viewed in terms of the longer historical process, these are the by-products of man's attempt to evolve a new type of pattern of human relationships. The functions, tasks, and interests of the modern family have become more delimited. In this process many new problems of intrafamily relationships, as between husband and wife and between parents and children, have arisen or at least have come to light. The instability we have been discussing arises from the rapid transitions which inevitably characterize family relationships but which are no longer disguised by the social and economic conditions that sustained the unity of the patriarchal family.

New problems and the need for new mores. Many books on the modern family devote half or more of their space to the *problems* of the family, and a large number are entirely concerned with these. Underlying these specific problems is one of a general nature, that of the development of new mores to meet the challenge of the new conditions. We conclude this section by illustrating this need of new values in closely interrelated spheres that impinge on family life.

[1] *Sex adjustment and sex values:* If a greater degree of stability of the family is to be achieved, we must frankly recognize that every disturbance of the

54. There were about 37,500,000 families in the United States in 1945; it is estimated that this figure will rise to 44,775,000 by 1960. Cf. U.S. Bureau of the Census, Population—Special Reports, *Estimates of Number of Families in the United States: 1940 to 1960*, Series P-46, No. 4 (June 1, 1946).

marital relation, especially of its sexual aspect, is not a reasonable ground for the dissolution of the family. This recognition is already more apparent in some countries, such as the Scandinavian and France, than in others, especially our own. The family exists, as we have shown, for other purposes than the mere satisfaction of sexual desires, and in no stage of civilization has the monogamous family been able to persuade all men and women to seek that satisfaction always within its bounds. The desire for varied sexual experience—one that is no doubt abetted by the emphasis placed upon sex in our culture—characterizes at least a considerable portion of mankind, a factor, incidentally, that possibly guarantees a continuation of prostitution in some form.[55] Conditions which tended to suppress the expression of this desire, such as strong religious beliefs or the fear of gossip or of pregnancy or of disease, have lost some of their power, permitting an increase in premarital and extramarital sexual relationships.

This is a situation which must be admitted and faced if the family is not to suffer disorganization. How it should be met cannot be answered by any hard-and-fast prescription. The evidence of social work, psychiatry, and marriage "clinics" indicates the necessity for greater general understanding of the realities of sex life if disillusion, frustration, and marital discord are to be avoided; it also indicates that the adjustment to one another of two personalities admits of endless variations in individual cases. The point stressed here is simply that divorce should not be viewed as an easy and automatic solution for every instance of "unfaithfulness" or for every sexual disharmony between the married partners.

[2] *The stress upon romantic love:* Romantic love involves an integration of sex with the whole personality of the individual. The flowering of this sentiment has been recognized for ages, by the troubadours for example, as one of the great experiences of life. But the modern family, significantly and uniquely, has assigned this sentiment to itself, and, particularly in America, has come to view romantic love as the true bond of marriage and has thereby complicated its own problems. For *by itself* romantic love cannot normally sustain the individual family through the inevitable stages of its growth. In the course of time it has to be supplemented in part, and in part replaced, by other sentiments. The relation of lovers to one another is one thing, the relations of parents to children is another; and from the standpoint of the society at large the latter is the more important.

The portrayal of romantic love in much of our literature, in some of our advertising, and especially on the screen, is concerned almost exclusively with the initial stages of the family and inculcates the "perpetual honeymoon" idea that the later stages are merely a continuation of these into the future. This simplification is seriously misleading and underlies a share of the inadequate

---

55. Cf. K. Davis, "The Sociology of Prostitution," *loc. cit.*

preparation for family life. Understandably, romance often turns into illusion and marriage partners embark on experiences that might enrich their lives in new ways but for which they are unprepared and untrained. They stumble, for example, against differences in the emotional nature of man and woman and against biologically determined differences in their parental responsibilities which the glow of romantic love tends to conceal. Formerly social and economic pressures made it imperative for the family to hold together in spite of such difficulties. But today it must depend much more on its intrinsic strength.

[3] *Education for and the benefits of family life:* The considerations we have discussed indicate the importance of education based on facts and not on illusions, the significance of a new set of mores adapted to the conditions of the age, and the need of an approach reflecting the discipline of knowledge. This education should include not only adequate information concerning the facts of sex, but also an understanding of the role of the family in society. Though we have a long way to go in the development and particularly in the diffusion of such knowledge, many recent publications, courses in marriage and the family, and adult educational services are welcome signs of the growing recognition of the need for informed and realistic discussion of these matters.[56]

Educating for marriage is a service to society and to the individual. Numerous studies reveal the significant fact that for men, and for women over the age of thirty, the death rate for single adults is about twice that of the married, and that deaths caused by tuberculosis, accidents, suicide, alcoholism, and syphilis are considerably lower among the married group. These correlations admit various interpretations, to be sure. They do "not imply that marriage is the panacea for the ills of the flesh and the discouragement of the spirit or that marriage will automatically solve all the perplexities of the modern world." But they suggest "that mutual affection guards against many of the mental and physical tribulations of a complex society."[57] If this be the case, it would indicate that, beyond its direct services, the family is one of the conditions of social solidarity and social strength.

The Family and the State

How and why the state controls the family. One peculiarity of the marriage partnership is that the state exercises over it a more stringent control than it

56. Among the many recent books of this type are J. F. Fowler, *Marriages Are Not Made in Heaven* (New York, 1944); E. M. Duvall and R. Hill, *When You Marry* (New York, 1945); and T. B. Rice, *Sex, Marriage, and Family* (Philadelphia, 1946). For briefer presentations see the Public Affairs Pamphlets, E. M. Duvall, *Building Your Marriage* (New York, 1946); and B. C. Gruenberg, *How Can We Teach about Sex* (New York, 1947).

57. Truxall and Merrill, *op. cit.*, p. 395. For statistical verification of these correlations, see Metropolitan Life Insurance Company, "The Married Live Longer," *Statistical Bulletin* (July, 1943), and "Why Married People Live Longer," *ibid.* (November, 1941).

generally exercises over any other partnership or association. It does not leave the form of the contract to the will of the members. They cannot prescribe for themselves its conditions or its duration. It fixes a minimum age of marriage. It determines degrees of relationship within which people must not marry. It treats certain violations of the contract (bigamy, for example) as criminal offenses. It defines the economic and other responsibilities of the husband toward his wife and of the parents toward the children. It treats the property of the partners as, in some degree, not individual but family possessions, limiting in the name of the family the freedom of bequest. These regulations vary considerably in different states of this country, but everywhere the state is an important determinant of the form and character of the family. When, for example, the French government after the Revolution prescribed, with certain limitations, the equal division of the patrimony among the children of the family, abrogating thereby such old customs as primogeniture, it accelerated the breakup of the joint family and gave an impetus to the process of family limitation.[58]

On what grounds does the state control the family so much more rigorously than it does many other associations? One answer at least is evident, for the family's function of perpetuating the race is of extreme importance to society. The function of procreating and rearing children involves responsibilities utterly unlike, and more significant socially than, those of any other voluntary relationships. Therefore the marriage contract, though the most intimate of all contracts, is not simply the personal concern of the contracting parties. The state, as the agent of society, is also deeply interested. The relation of marriage to procreation is sufficient, and, as we shall see, alone sufficient to justify a a peculiar control of the state over the family.

State policy: its limitations and trends. The state has in fact regulated the family on various grounds other than its procreative function. Sociologically considered, certain of these reasons put forward as justifications of state action in this sphere are of doubtful validity.

[1] *A principle of legitimate state control:* In many countries the state long exercised control of the family on religious grounds which modern political theory regards as beyond the state's competence.[59] Nor can the coercion of the state be justified by the claim—even if the claim could be established—that it is for the good of the partners themselves that they should remain married against their wishes. This is a claim that only social experience and education, not political or religious compulsion, can ratify. It has been argued that married persons cannot derive the ultimate satisfaction of marriage, "the consciousness of a permanent and unbreakable friendship," unless marriage itself is made a normally unbreakable contract.[60] But such an argument cannot without

58. Bosanquet, *op. cit.*, Chap. V.
59. See MacIver, *The Modern State*, Chap. V, Section I.
60. E. J. Urwick, *The Social Good* (London, 1927), Chap. VII.

grave danger be made a basis for legal coercion. The claim may be attacked on psychological grounds, and we may show, for example, that there are relatively few divorces under the mutual consent system of countries like Norway and Sweden. A more important criticism is that enforcement in matters where personality is intimately involved is often a means of destroying the very good it seeks to enforce.

But there is a broader objection. History shows how perilous it is to force people to do or endure what others believe to be for their good. If the state says, addressing its adult citizens, "You must do this because a majority thinks it is good for you," it is asserting a principle which would justify any tyranny, over morals, over religion, even over opinion. It is quite a different affair when the state says, "You must do this because if you fail others will suffer a definite hurt." Hence we conclude that the protection of child life, the safeguarding of its future citizens, affords the only clear ground on which the state can reasonably claim to regulate marriage beyond all other contracts.

[2] *The principle applied: helpful and harmful policies:* If the principle we have forwarded is applied, it leads to important conclusions regarding the policy of the state. It follows, for example, that the state has no particular concern with childless marriages (which in some primitive societies are automatically declared dissolved), and among which, in fact, divorce is most frequent. It has very little concern with the period of marriage after it has fulfilled its primary function, when the children no longer need the special guardianship of the family. In so far as the welfare of the race is the state's chief interest, it should provide most protection for those children, including the offspring of the unmarried and of the poverty-stricken, who most need its aid. Generally, it should regulate marriage to the extent that regulation can serve the cause of the young and helpless. When a marriage fails to realize its primary interests, the state should not, on moralistic grounds, insist on its maintenance unless it has good reason to believe, in each particular case, that the continuance of the marriage is demanded by the needs of the children. Where the failure is deep-seated, where the probability is that, because of extreme or long-established incompatibility or because of cruelty, insanity, venereal disease, or other serious ill, the marriage is actually harmful to the welfare of the partners or of the children, the duty of the state is rather to dissolve the partnership than blindly to insist that it be maintained.

No other environment has proved as favorable for the upbringing of children as the home which the parents create, if that home is relatively harmonious; but if the home is utterly inharmonious or positively harmful, the state cannot by compulsion end the trouble, and it must seek to protect the children in some other way. The future of the family does not depend on state coercion but on human experience of its benefits. In the last resort it depends on the recognition of its superiority, as a means of satisfying certain human needs, over any alternative system.

[3] *The trend of state policy and experimentation in family life:* On the whole, the trend of state policy has been in the direction of our principle.[61] Experience shows that there are some matters the state is competent to control and others over which its control fails. As social conditions change, the character of state control must correspondingly change. For example, adultery has sometimes been made a crime, but even where such a law remains on the statute book its enforcement has proved so impracticable that the law is generally a dead letter. The state has tried to prohibit the knowledge of birth control by law, as it still does, for example, in Massachusetts and Connecticut, but has succeeded only in keeping it from a decreasingly small group of the very poor and very ignorant. On the whole, the traditional policy of the state, which is now breaking down, has aimed at the preservation of the *status quo ante*. But no social institution can remain remote from change in a changing age. And no institution can or should stand in its own time-established sanctity, immune from the process of experiment. In a complex society force cannot prevent experiment, though force may pervert it—a principle that holds in the area of sex relationships where considerable experimentation exists in fact.

The advocates of "companionate marriage," for example, have proposed for many years that the state sanction one form of experiment, but such action is also, on our principle, beyond the competence of the state. Since "companionate marriage" does not contemplate offspring, there is no good reason why the state should either recognize it or, directly or indirectly, prevent it. It is rather a question of *social* approval or disapproval, according to the standards of different groups. It is meant to solve, without hypocrisy and without disguise, some of the problems of sex life under the conditions of modern society—to make possible an honorable sex relationship for those who are not in an economic position to establish a family, or to institute a period of trial and adjustment before the partners are committed to the bonds and parental responsibilities of marriage proper. As such, it has advantages and disadvantages. Its chief disadvantage—that instead of being a preparation for marriage it might tend to reduce the social significance of that institution and the sense of social responsibility which it demands—would be increased by legal recognition. We see no reason here to make an exception to the general principle which is becoming in several respects accepted by the modern state. The state's right to control marriage, it is increasingly recognized, rests upon the fact that marriage is the avenue to the life of the family, to the procreation of children, whose welfare, being the welfare of the race, must always remain a primary consideration of the state.

Co-operative and regulative functions of the state. Our discussion so far of state

61. For a conspectus of laws regulating the family, see S. P. Breckenridge, *The Family and the State* (Chicago, 1934); and for the various state regulations in this country as of 1945, Nimkoff, *op. cit.*, pp. 423–431.

policy affecting the family has illustrated its regulative or coercive function. The state has another and more constructive function, that of bringing positive aid and support to the family.

[1] *The co-operative function:* The state can, apart from compulsion, uphold the family in many ways. This is in large measure a growing task for the state, and one which does not oppose the processes of social change but rather endeavors to make fruitful application of them. In modern society the welfare of the child requires the provision of many services which the state can stimulate or guarantee. Above all it can make them available to those families which through poverty or unemployment are unable to supply for themselves or through ignorance are unaware of the need for them. The equipment of the child to take his place in society, the equipment of mind and body through appropriate training in an environment made healthful on *both* counts, is an immense task that cannot today be performed without extensive state aid. In a previous section we mentioned the various programs of modern nations, developed most extensively perhaps in Soviet Russia and the Scandinavian countries, including public housing, social security legislation, financial support of parenthood and of old age, education, and other direct and indirect supports of family life. The extension of this type of program in all modern countries points up the increasingly significant role of the state in making available to the majority of families the vast social heritage.

A further co-operative function, still in an experimental stage, is illustrated by the juvenile courts, child-welfare clinics, and similar agencies designed to meet the maladjustments of child life that arise under the conditions of modern society and are not solved by the family itself.[62] Another experiment is the court of domestic relations, found in a number of cities in this country. These courts, when presided over by persons of wide social experience and sociological understanding, can prevent temporary discord from leading to permanent family disruption. However, the over-all record of successful reconciliations of domestic relations courts has not been impressive. They handle but a small fraction of the family cases, cases which usually come to them long after adjustment is possible, and to a large extent their concern is merely with the economic responsibilities of the family members.[63] Nevertheless this is one more illustration of an entirely different service from the traditional coercive function of the state.

[2] *The regulative function today:* If the state is to fulfill its function as we have defined it, there remains an area for coercive control. The prevention of

62. For an earlier but illuminating statement of this subject, see W. I. and D. S. Thomas, *The Child and America* (New York, 1928), Part II. More recent appraisals appear, for example, in G. Abbott, *The Child and the State* (Chicago, 1938); and J. K. Folsom, *Youth, Family, and Education* (Washington, D. C., 1941).
63. Cf. Nimkoff, *op. cit.*, p. 701.

controllable conditions that are clearly a threat to the welfare of the society becomes a definite obligation of the state.

For example, in the United States in 1945 the legal minimum age of marriage for girls ranged between twleve and eighteen years, with four states setting the lower figure (for common-law marriages) and only one (Colorado) the higher, while nineteen states prescribed fifteen or below.[64] There is physiological evidence and, more importantly, sociological evidence indicating that these minima are too low for women in our society. Again, the state still sanctions marriages which, because of some grave ailment, hereditary or acquired, in either partner are beyond doubt a great risk for one of them and especially for the children. The duty of the state here is to discourage and, if possible, prevent such marriages. In recent years, our local states have advanced considerably in this direction, with respect to venereal disease, so that, in 1941, thirty states required blood tests for syphilis of both partners, three states required medical examination of the man only, three prohibited infected persons from marrying; but twelve granted licenses without regard to infection.[65] These laws are handicapped, of course, by difficult problems of administration and are often evaded. But there should be no objection in principle to legislation of this type, though it can achieve its end only if backed up with social education. If the state is in earnest in its attempt to combat venereal disease, it must not only permit but encourage, as a few communities are demonstrating today, the application of medical and sociological knowledge for prevention as well as for treatment.[66]

The danger of confusing moral and medical problems is seen again in another type of regulation. A large number of our state laws permit or compel the sterilization of feeble-minded, mentally diseased, epileptics, habitual criminals, sex delinquents, and even "perverts." There is perhaps reasonable biological evidence to justify a cautiously administered sterilization program in the first of these groups, though the problem of detecting hereditary feeble-mindedness is by no means solved and, in any event, the genetic improvements anticipated through such regulations are slight. But to include habitual criminals, as did ten states in 1944, and sex delinquents as in eight states, and even "nervous diseases" as in Georgia and North Carolina, is clearly to ignore the significant social basis of these conditions. As Bertrand Russell observes, "the law of Idaho would have justified the sterilization of Socrates, Plato, Julius Caesar, and St. Paul."[67] It is perhaps in part a reflection of the wisdom of administra-

64. *Ibid.*, pp. 424–425.

65. *Ibid.*, p. 428.

66. The publications of the American Social Hygiene Association provide much information on various phases of this problem. See also T. Parran and R. A. Vonderlehr, *Plain Words about Venereal Disease* (New York, 1941).

67. *Marriage and Morals*, Chap. VIII. For discussions of these regulations see Nimkoff, *op. cit.*, pp. 674–681; and M. S. Olden, *Your Questions about Sterilization Answered* (Princeton, N. J., 1944).

tors that only about 14,000 sterilizations have been performed under the laws, some two fifths of which have taken place in California. For compulsion cannot, without risking the kind of abuse that reached its extreme in the "race purification" program of the Nazis, do more than obviate the more extreme social dangers. Beyond that, we must rely on social education.

We should remember that marriage itself is the most significant of all forms of social selection. It is one that has become intensely personal, but that fact makes it all the more important that the younger generation should receive a realistic training for the responsibilities of marriage and of parenthood. The state by its policy, if it is based upon knowledge, rather than folklore or mere tradition or prejudice, can here lead the way.

We have discussed at some length the significance and the forms of the family, the evolution of its modern type, and some of the more crucial problems reflected in its life today. Yet our exploration has been brief in one sense. For upon this small but ever-present association of human beings are impressed the tone, the changes, the stresses of the greater society and of the community within which the family dwells. Therefore in shifting our attention to the larger inclusive grouping of the community in the next two chapters, we shall be confronted with a number of considerations of importance in the understanding of the family itself.

12

The Community

The Community as Place: Its Physical Configuration

The task of this and the following chapter. Very few, if any, aspects of social life can be dealt with realistically without a consideration of the community setting within which they are revealed. Thus, in the preceding chapters, we have frequently suggested the significance of the community—of the tribe or village or city or nation. This is one reason why, in the first chapter of this book, we included *community* among the concepts the meaning of which required clarification at the outset.

In Chapter I we depicted the community as the most inclusive grouping of man, marked by the possibility for the individual member to live his life wholly within it. We explained that the community need not be self-sufficient, and in fact is decreasingly so as civilization becomes more interdependent. And we briefly examined the two bases of all communities, the occupation of a *territorial area* and the shared possession of a *community sentiment*. In this chapter we face the task, first, of considering more fully the community's bases of locality and common feeling, secondly, of analyzing some of the more significant aspects of the national community, and, finally, of depicting the unifying and the diversifying roles of social differentiations within the community. We shall shift our attention, in the following chapter, from the community as such to the contrasting types of social arrangements found in urban and rural areas and in various regions within the nation.

The community as concentration. If we study a population map, whether of a countryside or a whole country or the entire world, we observe curious configurations. The irregular massing and thinning of habitation is apparent, and, generally, the concentration points of greatest density shade off into more sparsely settled areas. Our density map shows us, of course, ranges and types of *community*.

[1] *Variations in population density:* Areas of higher congestion of population in some degree, but by no means wholly, correspond with regions of the earth marked by certain physiographic conditions. In some regions, such as the prairie plains, it seems geographically accidental that there should be stray settlements of people, here a village and here a town. Even when we examine the variations in soil conditions or other natural resources and the natural facilities for communication and for the amenities of living, we fail to find a consistent correlation between geographical conditions and human habitation. On the other hand, the location of concentrated populations at certain places is clearly responsive to naturally determined advantages, apparent in the site of most great cities, for example, or in the rural settlements of the grain-growing "breadbaskets" of North America and the Ukraine. But in these examples, too, the natural advantages of the localities must be understood in the light of the existent state of the civilization. Thus the density of urban centers and that of the hinterland areas as well require explanation in terms of the historical process, including the mere conjunctures of history, and in terms of the level of social and technological development. These considerations would be of essential significance were we to pursue the study of relative population densities. Here our concern is rather with the community itself.

[2] *Concentration and specialization:* In some regions of the earth there are areas of scattered homesteads that possess no visible focus, amorphous communities with no communal division of labor and therefore with no centers of economic and administrative functions.[1] But most communities have some center of their social activities. In particular, wherever human habitation is congested in an area too small to contain within itself enough land for its basic needs, there a community center exists, in rudimentary or developed form, since this condition implies *exchange* and *specialization*. The center provides some common meeting place, such as the market square of the small town or the general store of the village. If the community is small, the center is undifferentiated; if large, it is more elaborate and specialized. In the great city there may be one dominant focus of its pulsing life, but it has also distinctive foci of business, of finance, of retail trade, of recreation, and so forth. The center is itself relative to the community; a market place may be the center of the town-community, but the town itself is a center for a region and the metropolis for a country. What distinguishes externally the center from the periphery is the fact that there the lines of communication meet. Without communication there can be no community, and the life of the community revolves around the points where communication is most intense.

The community and communications. The relation of community to communications is illustrated in various ways. A community frequently arises at a

1. N. S. B. Gras, *Introduction to Economic History* (New York, 1922), pp. 50 ff.

terminal of transportation, where topographical conditions combine with economic and technological advantages so as to create a settlement. Thus many cities throughout the world have grown at topographically strategic points, at river fords or river mouths, around natural harbors or on conveniently situated islands. For centuries European cities arose not only at river and harbor sites, but at the places where man's own highways crossed and converged. With the development of railways in Europe, but much more conspicuously in the United States, the railroad junction became a predominant site of community expansion. Today the airport is exerting a similar but much less extensive influence. The size of the community that flowers at these points of "breaks in transportation" varies from the village to the metropolis, according to the natural facilities of the site, the economic resources of the region it serves, the state of the technological arts, and the general level of civilization.[2]

The large community is both a terminal and a starting point, but it has especially the quality of a destination, both in a geographical and a psychological sense. For it is the end of the road more than the beginning, a fact often emphasized by its position beside some natural barrier, the sea or a lake or a mountain range, a forest or a desert. Hence large urban communities have hinterlands, regions that "lie behind" them and on which they always depend, to some extent, for their economic necessities, resources of wealth, and population. These are attracted to the city not only by facilities for trade and finance but also by opportunities for cultural stimulation and for the more elaborate and exciting forms of living and spending. A large city, unless it is unusually specialized around one central economic function, such as mining or a single industry, is a "culture center" where a great variety of the surrounding civilization is available to its old and to its new inhabitants, as well as a focus of human communication.

The relation of community to locality. As we have seen, the community possesses a distinctively territorial character. It implies a common soil as well as a shared way of life. The relation of communities to the regions in which they appear has been a subject of keen interest and intensive study for a number of years.

[1] *The ecological and regional approaches:* In the discussion of the physical environment and its relation to the social life of man in earlier chapters (Chapters IV and V), we took account of the fact that geography sets broad limits within which may develop a wide variety of civilizational complexes. More specifically, in the present context, we may point out that the local area is not only a basic condition of the social relationships that weld a group together and

2. See C. H. Cooley, "The Theory of Transportation," in *Sociological Theory and Social Research* (New York, 1930) for an early but able analysis of this point. For a comparison of European and American community development with relation to transportation, see M. Jefferson, "Distribution of the World's City Folks," *Geographical Review*, Vol. XXI, No. 3 (1931).

give it distinctive social form, but is also a specific common environment to the peculiar characteristics of which the local group must make appropriate responses. For this reason we call attention, once more, to the ecological and regional approaches with their stress upon the relationship between locality and cultural development. The literature of human ecology reveals the accommodation patterns of man as he builds a community existence in the different types of environment found within the city or the country. It contrasts, for example, the ways of community life of the immigrant slum dwellers with those of the suburban middle class, or those of the industrial town with those of the rural village. Similarly the regionalists, since the time of Le Play, have indicated the significance to community formation of such local factors as natural vegetation, types of soil cultivation and animal domestication favored by the region, and climatic conditions. These studies conclusively indicate, as we shall see more fully in the following chapter, what has long been claimed: that the character of the local physical environment, whether a rocky New England hillside or the wide spaces of the Southwest or the zone of deterioration within a city, places its stamp on local social life.[3]

This is not to say, of course, that there is any full correspondence between the process of physical adaptation, say of plants to new soil or of animal life to new surroundings, and the vastly more complex process of social accommodation to a locality. We saw in Chapter VI that every social group adapts itself to a total environment of which the physical environment is but one aspect. Every group creates, for all its members, an environment of its own. The process by which a group, as each younger generation grows up, accommodates itself *to itself* is thus different from the process by which it adjusts itself, at any given time, to the external environment.

[2] *The relative and changing significance of local factors:* The significant differences, both obvious and subtle, between groups living in different localities are the result of a changing complex of many factors. These combine to bring a group together and to hold it together in a given area, and it is exceedingly difficult to isolate the influence of any one, since they are all interactive in determining the community character.

Consider the simplest community, the *neighborhood*, the "first grouping beyond the family which has social significance and which is conscious of some local unity." Study of the rural neighborhood shows a variety of factors: the interwoven conditions of its solidarity, "such as topography and original vegetation, nationality bonds, religious purpose, the migration from a common place of residence and economic and social purposes."[4] The *relative* importance of these factors, once the community is formed, is always changing. Some factors grow more prominent, as have the educational and sometimes the

3. For citations of various discussions of human ecology and regionalism, see Chapter IV above, footnotes, 2 and 3.

4. J. H. Kolb, *Rural Primary Groups*, in Research Bulletin 51, Agricultural Experimental Station, University of Wisconsin.

religious in some Midwestern rural groups, while others, such as kinship-consciousness, dwindle. Shifting of population, changes in communication and transportation, changes in leadership, rising or declining economic opportunities, the impact of new influences from without—these and other forces are always at work.[5]

A vivid and currently significant example of both the direct and the indirect influence of new conditions upon the structure, the attitudes, indeed the entire way of life, of the small community is afforded by the changes already wrought and continuing throughout the Tennessee Valley in the United States. Here the new availability of electric power, fertilizer, transportation facilities, and so on, is reflected in various co-operative programs, educational advances, and the rise of new cultural values as well as technological improvements and a higher material standard of living. The quality of community life has already greatly changed in this region, but is destined to alter still more as the rising generation comes to maturity surrounded by social conditions which to its parents have been innovations but which to it will be among the "normal" requirements of living.[6]

A final and much broader case serves to illustrate the relative and changing significance of local factors in community growth. Consider our own national community. The United States today indubitably reflects the character of its physical locality—the lengthy coast lines, the vast plains and the prairie lands, the great topographical and climatic variation, the numerous river valleys that mark its surface, and so forth. But no social scientist attempts to explain the characteristics peculiar to "modern America" as merely the result of these factors. If the frontier, for example, has played an important part in shaping our national community life, its changing aspects and its final closure have been no less, perhaps even more, significant. And how could we conceivably understand America's "cultural pluralism," its diversities and contradictions, without examining its changing political values and economic processes, the history of its immigration and of its legislation, its external as well as its internal accommodations and conflicts? We should, therefore, while insisting on the importance of locality as a basis of community study, be careful to avoid the assumption that the basis of study is also the basis of *interpretation*. But the reader who has followed the argument of the preceding chapters will need no further warning on this point.

The external structure of the community. Every community reveals an external structural character. A country is not simply a number of towns and cities

5. For detailed descriptions of changing small communities in Asia, England, Canada, New England, the South, and the Middle West, see C. C. Zimmerman, *The Changing Community* (New York, 1938); and for a good analysis of "the variability of social adaptation to space," see W. Firey, *Land Use in Central Boston* (Cambridge, Mass., 1947), Chap. II.

6. On the TVA, see D. E. Lilienthal, *TVA—Democracy on the March* (New York, 1944); R. L. Duffus and C. Krutch, *The Valley and Its People* (New York, 1944).

scattered over a delimited territory: it has its metropolis, its capital, its functionally specialized regions and cities, and the network of connections between them. The city is not simply an aggregate of households or families, but a *system* or *pattern* into which the units—families, occupations, specializations of all kinds—are fitted. So with the smallest and the largest of communities.

[1] *Specialization and changing types of community structure:* Even the smallest village has some rudimentary form of structural system, evidenced, for example, by the location of the store or church or some locally important home, and by the particular configuration centering at or near the intersection of main and secondary lines of transportation and communication. The variety of spatial patterns of small communities is almost endless. Perhaps of major significance during recent years in altering the character of the local village structure is the "conquest of space by automobiles" for it "has broken the chief bond that held people together in communities, and this, together with economic conditions, has brought about a dispersal of institutions," lessening the orientation toward a specific village center.[7]

With the growth of the city the single focus of the village becomes differentiated into a number of foci for different activities, centers of finance, administration, fashion, recreation, and so forth. The various trades and other functional activities aggregate in special areas, "automobile rows," "garment districts," even specialized areas of prostitution and "night life." Some of the centers of dominance, such as the administrative and the financial, tend to be relatively fixed; others, such as shopping and recreational districts, tend to move away from the central business zones toward the residential parts of the city. The latter are also subject to change and to the encroachments of the one on the other, some locations rising and others falling with respect to social estimation and to its reflection in land values. Changing means of transportation, changing business conditions, the increase or decrease of population, the arrival of new groups from the rural hinterland or from foreign countries, even changing fashions that render "smart" one residential area and then another, are constantly interacting to modify the physical pattern of the city.[8]

7. E. H. Bell, *Culture of a Contemporary Rural Community—Sublette, Kansas.* This is No. 2 of the series of excellent studies of small communities in this country made by C. P. Loomis, C. G. Taylor, K. Young, and others, U.S. Department of Agriculture, *Rural Life Series*, 1-5 (1941-1942). See also C. P. Loomis, *Studies of Rural Social Organization in the United States, Latin America and Germany* (East Lansing, Mich., 1945).

8. A large literature exists concerning the variant and complex forces determining the city's physical structure. An early influential study is R. M. Hurd, *Principles of City Land Values* (New York, 1903); for a more recent consideration of the same factors, see A. M. Weimer and H. Hoyt, *Principles of Urban Real Estate* (New York, 1939). The many ecological studies of specific cities include, for Chicago, E. W. Burgess, "The Growth of the City" in *The City* (R. E. Park, E. W. Burgess, and R. D. McKenzie, eds., Chicago, 1925); for St. Louis, S. A. Queen and L. F. Thomas, *The City* (New York, 1939), Chap. XIII; for Rochester, R. V.

[2] *Community structure as a "natural" development:* Unlike that of an association, the pattern of the community is usually unplanned. It is determined by forces generated wherever people in any numbers are thrown into close relationship—forces of competition, attraction, struggle for dominance, co-operation for the sake of economy, and so forth. Thus the city takes spatial form. Here there is the financial center, perhaps overtopping all the rest with the skyscrapers that rise from narrow, crowded thoroughfares; here the political center, broadly architectural; here the fashionable shopping center, its locale changing from time to time; here the brightly lit center of night life, often somewhat tawdry by day; here the drab industrial areas with their tall chimneys; and filling the interstices and flowing out to the periphery are the myriad homes of human beings, where economic and cultural forces bring groups together in areas that range through all degrees of "highly desirable" locations down to the congested slums. The pattern changes somewhat as the city continues to expand or as the greater forces shaping man's civilization bear upon it. But always there is the physical configuration, the distinctive form of a community.[9]

No long-range preconceived plan stands behind the areas of specialization within the city, its variety of zones of residence, its extreme of haphazard and crowded growth, on the one hand, and splendidly designed sections, on the other. It is in this sense that the physical structure of the large city, especially as it has been influenced by the impact of economic and technological developments of modern times, may be understood, in part, as a "natural" emergence.[10]

Planning the physical structure of the community. The largely unplanned character of the modern community—of the town, the region, and especially of the large city—has brought with it congestion and use of and dependence upon physically deteriorated habitations and other buildings, unbalanced development of various areas of living and of business activity—in short a widespread neglect of man's own needs. This situation, long recognized and decried by a few writers, has in recent years provoked a number of proposals for planning the community, some of which have been put into operation, particularly in certain localities of Scandinavia, Great Britain, Soviet Russia, and, more limitedly, in the United States. Here we can indicate only certain general features of this trend.

[1] *Some types of community planning:* Men have gone about the task of building their communities according to some preconceived arrangement in

Bowers, "Ecological Patterning of Rochester, N. Y.," *American Sociological Review*, Vol. IV (1939); for New Haven, M. R. Davie, "The Pattern of Urban Growth," in *Studies in the Science of Society* (G. P. Murdock, ed., New Haven, 1937); for Minneapolis and St. Paul, C. F. Schmid, *Social Saga of Two Cities* (Minneapolis, 1937); for Boston, Firey, *op. cit.*

9. For characteristic physical patterns assumed by the modern city see Chart XI on page 325.

10. For extensive elaboration of this point and a sharply critical portrayal of the results of this "natural" process, see L. Mumford, *The Culture of Cities* (New York, 1938), Chap. III.

many societies and in many different ages of civilization; we still study the planning schemes used, for example in primitive communities, in various ancient civilizations, in medieval town building. However, we are at present more immediately concerned with the varieties of programs inaugurated by members of modern complex society. Most of these are outgrowths of surveys of local communities, especially of the working-class areas, and of the findings of neighborhood settlement agencies in London, New York, Chicago, and other large cities. Both trends began during the nineteenth century, gaining scope and public attention in the twentieth. The drive for community reform was thus spearheaded by social surveys such as Charles Booth's *Life and Labour of the People of London* (1892) and Paul Kellogg's Pittsburg Survey (1909–1914), and by such opponents of the city slum as Jane Addams of Hull House in Chicago, the leaders of Toynbee Hall in London, Jacob Riis, the author of *How the Other Half Lives*, and others. At first only a few individuals, most notably the Englishman Patrick Geddes, matched the zeal of this reformistic activity with considered plans for community reconstruction, but in recent decades not only have many concrete remedies been proposed but several have been put into effect.[11]

ONE: REHABILITATING THE COMMUNITY. Numerous programs have been undertaken, and many more are in the "paper stage," for the purpose of using more adequately the space available in congested communities. The overcrowded urban dwelling area especially has been redesigned to provide more ample space for the family unit, more sunlight and air, less ugliness and discord for the eye and ear. While the accomplishment of such projects is a limited one to date, housing projects in many European and American cities, under both public and private auspices, testify to the positive results that are possible when architect, economist, and sociologist join forces to provide a physical setting for community life in keeping with modern technological facilities. These programs, applied primarily to localities inhabited by members of the lower and middle income groups, are hampered by factors varying in significance from country to country and from city to city, including general opposition to "planning" of any type, economic "stakes in congestion," absence of enabling legislation, scarcity of materials, technical architectural design difficulties, and many others. Moreover, some of the finest of the large-scale housing projects are in the midst of areas so physically deteriorated as to take on the "slum" characteristics themselves. Nevertheless they represent an important example of man's effort to change certain features of his physical community.

Other features of planning are zoning ordinances, parks and playgrounds,

11. For discussions of the sources of community planning, see, for example, Queen and Thomas, *op. cit.*, Chaps. XXIII–XXIV; G. A. Lundberg, *et al.*, *Trends of American Sociology* (New York, 1929), Chap. VI; N. P. Gist and L. A. Halbert, *Urban Society* (New York, 1941), Chap. XXIII.

community center buildings, and facilities of transportation, especially highways and main arteries. These programs have introduced in the modern city a degree of orderly development far greater than existed in the nineteenth-century town, which often "just grew," and are responsible, most conspicuously when integrated within a metropolitan regional plan, such as that of New York or St. Louis or Manila, for important changes in the physical configuration of the urban center.[12]

TWO: PLANNING THE LOCAL COMMUNITY FROM THE "GROUND UP." In the discussion of "utopian communities" in Chapter VII we considered an example of the occasional attempts of relatively small groups to erect and to maintain communities on the basis of particular value-systems. Had we pursued this topic we would have witnessed considerable evidence of the extent to which these groups planned the physical aspects of their settlements, the design of the individual homes, their location to one another, the street layout, the construction and position of the communal buildings, and so forth. The effort of the utopian experiments in this respect finds a parallel in a number of programs, worked out in various localities in Europe and in the United States, to build entire residential communities according to preconceived plans.

Illustrative are the several "garden cities" of England, the first one founded early in this century, initiating a program that has been fairly extensively expanded in more recent years. "Garden cities" are planned to incorporate the more desirable features of urban and rural life, providing space for parks and playgrounds as well as private gardens, restricting certain activities to designated zones, and placing the control of rents with the community instead of the "market." They range in size from a few thousand to 100,000 or more inhabitants. And they compare in design with such American developments as Radburn, New Jersey, a planned community of some 25,000 with its characteristic features of arterial highways, "super-blocks," home fronts facing upon a common park, and closed-end streets. Also planned from the "ground up" are a few resettlement suburbs, the small "greenbelt" communities sponsored by the federal government during the years preceding World War II, and located within commuting distance of large cities, but protected from "natural" encroachments by surrounding areas of forest, park, and farm land.[13] We may add as examples of planning of this type the numerous communities, some temporary and some relatively permanent, erected during the war for civilian workers or for military personnel and their families, located near training fields, shipyards, special projects, and so forth. We should remember that, in each of the cases involving the careful creation of a physical pattern, with its

12. For this type of planning see the Public Administration Service's *Action for Cities, A Guide for Community Planning* (Chicago, 1945), which includes extensive bibliographical references.

13. For a discussion of "garden cities" and resettlement suburbs see, for example, Gist and Halbert, *op. cit.*, pp. 594–600.

streets and stores and homes and recreational spaces and the rest, when the plan becomes embodied in the life and activities of community existence, developments take place unforeseen by the planners themselves. This is a point to which we shall return.

THREE: BROAD REGIONAL PLANNING. Here we anticipate a problem to be more fully considered in Chapter XIII. Regional planning is a type that is not focused upon the local community or some area within it, but upon a larger expanse of human habitation. The area of interest to the regionalist is one that affords the physical basis of the community life of a more or less wide territory, one that may be viewed as a unit because of a combination of geographical and social and cultural circumstances. The "region" may be the Northeastern, the Southeastern, the Southwestern division of the United States; it may be the valley area of the Tennessee River or that of the Missouri or the Colorado; it may be an area of Eastern Europe or Southeastern Asia; or it may be a smaller "subregion." Here we are not concerned with the bases of the world's many regions except to note that there must always be some conjunction of factors, including the geographical, providing the regionalist a "natural" framework for his plan.

The plan itself may take the form of the Tennessee Valley Authority, or of the proposed Missouri Valley Authority, cutting across state boundaries and emphasizing the controlled and long-range exploitation of the whole region's natural resources. Or it may be, as is more frequently the case in our country, a series of "piecemeal" projects involving interstate agreements concerning the control of waterways, highways, irrigation developments, sanitation programs, and the like. The regional plan, whatever its particular manifestations, always in some degree reshapes the physical contours of the whole area and affects the relationships between the smaller communities within it.[14]

[2] *The complexity of the problem of planning*: When we set about the task of designing the shape of a new community or of redesigning one already established we are confronted with a problem that outreaches the difficulties of physical design itself, one caused by the very nature of the community. For this most inclusive grouping in society encompasses the whole range of man's activities in a specific area and is, therefore, sensitive to all that takes place within it and to any impacts upon its life from without. This complicates enormously the planner's task, for planning means prediction, and to predict the responses of a whole community to a new design, whether of a town or a city or a region or a larger area, is fraught with difficulties. We lay out new streets and new parks and playgrounds, for example, sometimes to learn that the streets are usurped for the very purposes for which the recreation areas were conceived; we put up a new building as a center of community activity and

---

14. See Chapter XIII below, pages 341 ff. for a more extensive discussion of the regional basis of community life.

find its halls deserted by those for whom it was created; we hedge off tracts of woodlands and mountains so that nature may be observed and preserved, but men often seem to prefer to ignore it or to destroy it; we plan a "greenbelt" town so as to prevent the formation within it of rigid division of status groups only to witness their emergence within a few years after the town's establishment.[15] Failure to anticipate the effects of a new plan and the uses to which it may be put does not, of course, justify the condemnation of planning. But it suggests, if it does not demonstrate, that community is more than the place it occupies, more than territory, more than any physical configuration man can devise. Community is also sentiment.

Community Sentiment: Its Psychological Configuration

The nature and basis of community sentiment. Wherever human beings are thrown together, separated in whole or in part from the world outside so that they must live their lives in one another's company, we can observe the effects of those social impulses which bring men all over the earth into communities. We observe, in other words, the formation of *community sentiment.*

[1] *Some "laboratory" examples:* All of us at one time or another have participated in the process that tends to pull together those who live in the same place. This process often is instigated even when the residence is quite temporary, as among the passengers on shipboard.

> Every slightest action betrayed their inordinate consciousness of one another. Those who walked, walked either more emphatically than was their wont, or more sheepishly, aware of the scrutiny, more or less veiled, of the row of sitters. Those who sat in deck chairs were conscious of their extended feet, their plaid rugs and shawls, and the slight physical and moral discomfort of having to look "up" at the walkers. The extraordinary feeling of kinship, of unity, of a solidarity far closer and more binding than that of nations or cities or villages, was swiftly uniting them; the ship was making them a community.[16]

Perhaps this novelist's statement is an exaggeration of the intensity of community sentiment created in such circumstances. But wherever people are set apart and must turn in upon themselves for any length of time, common values appear, rooted in the common place.

Thus to our shipboard illustration we may add other "laboratory" cases of community sentiment in the making, such as summer camps and vacation "colonies," mobile groups like the earlier wagon trains pushing westward in America and northward in South Africa, and even the unisexual "institutions for the care of segregated persons"[17] including, for example, monasteries,

15. Cf. W. H. Form, "Status Stratification in a Planned Community," *American Sociological Review*, X (1945), 605-613.

16. From *Blue Voyage*, by Conrad Aiken, Copyright, 1927, by Conrad Aiken.

17. The expression is the late Professor Willard Waller's.

prisons, and young ladies' finishing schools. The persistence of community as a cohesive framework within which people organize their ways is manifested even in the concentration camp, where the most heterogeneous elements, deprived of all their previous relationships, of their status and normal activities, and under the most extreme pressures and intense hardships, nevertheless re-establish some kind of community life. Here, as in the other cases, whether short-lived or relatively permanent, new groups and statuses and relationships form. The new or temporary community becomes differentiated, but over all there is a sense of participation in a common enterprise.

[2] *Formation of community sentiment:* In the more permanent communities the same influences work more profoundly, rooted in the historical conditions which have created the cultural values of every territorial group. The land the members occupy together is for them much more than a portion of the earth's surface—it is their "home," enriched by past association and present experience. The sense of what they have in *common*—memories and traditions, customs and institutions—shapes and defines the general need of men to live together. The community becomes the permanent background of their lives, and, in a degree, the projection of their individualities. Other attachments are sometimes more intense, but no other is so broad based as that which binds men to their community.

Community sentiment is developed by the socialization process itself, by education in the largest sense, working through prescription and authority, social esteem or disfavor, until habits and conformities become the ground of loyalties and convictions. No human being can grow up within a community—except congenital idiots incapable of normal experience—without having this sense of community impressed in the depths of his personality. For the individual, then, once his early training period is passed, community sentiment is not an outer compulsion but an inner necessity, always a part of his own individuality. Even when he revolts against some of its codes, as he often does in fact, he still belongs *in feeling* to some community. He cannot escape the impact of a socializing experience found wherever man has built a common life.

Analysis of community sentiment. It must not be assumed that we are implying that community sentiment is *altruistic* or *other-regarding*. Such terms, like their contraries, *egoistic* or *self-regarding*, are misleading when applied to group attachments. Self-interest and unselfishness are individual *motivations*, group attachments are *attitudes*, and, as we pointed out in Chapter II, we should not confuse the two. In analyzing community sentiment, then, we are undertaking the sociological, not the psychological, task of depicting the characteristics of a highly significant example of *group* attitudes.

[1] *The elements of community sentiment:* Community sentiment combines various elements, various types of attitudes, which are subtly compounded. Three of these, though closely interrelated, are clearly distinguishable.

ONE: WE-FEELING. Most evident is the sense of communion itself, of collective participation in an indivisible unity. This is the feeling that leads men to identify themselves with others so that when they say "we" there is no thought of distinction and when they say "ours" there is no thought of division. This "we-sentiment" is found wherever men have a common interest, and thus throughout group life, but is nowhere revealed more clearly than where the interest is the territorial community. It is the sentiment we feel rising within us when our town or city or region, and especially when our nation, is criticized or threatened. In the latter instance we are often ready to sacrifice our private interests for its protection. Yet, again, we should avoid confusing the we-feeling with altruism. Rather the interest of the individual is identified with or merged in the larger interest of the group, so that he feels indissolubly bound up with it, so that to him the community is "home of his home and flesh of his flesh."

TWO: ROLE-FEELING. Another ingredient in community sentiment is the sense of place or station, so that each person feels he has a role to play, his own function to fulfill in the reciprocal exchanges of the social scene. This feeling, involving subordination to the whole on the part of the individual, is fostered by training and habituation in the daily discipline of life. In the individual, thus socialized, it expresses the mode in which he normally realizes his membership in the whole community. As we shall see, other group attachments, such as those of class or ethnic membership, often conflict and sometimes are integrated with the feeling of place in the broader community.

THREE: DEPENDENCY-FEELING. Closely associated with role-feeling is the individual's sense of dependence upon the community as a necessary condition of his own life. This involves both a physical dependence, since his material wants are satisfied within it, and a psychological dependence, since the community is the greater "home" that sustains him, embodying all that is familiar at least, if not all that is congenial to his life. The community is a refuge from the solitude and fears that accompany that individual isolation so characteristic of our modern life.

These three elements, the feeling of identification, of role, and of dependency, are manifested in different degrees and in different combinations within man's many communities. And whereas they develop automatically, as we have seen, whenever men live together, numerous examples can be found of deliberate attempts to build up one or more of them, or, as more frequently is the case, of attempts to channel community sentiment itself into avenues deemed desirable by this group or that. An illustration is seen in the various "morale" programs during World War II which for patriotic purposes sought to enhance the individual's sense of participation, his sense of role, in the national life, as well as his feeling of attachment to and dependence on the nation. Shortly we shall be concerned with nationality, the most significant type of community sentiment in the modern world, and shall consider certain aspects of the effort so often evoked to direct, to increase, or to control its power.

[2] *The complexity of community sentiment:* So far we have been considering community sentiment as it stimulates a *common* interest among the members of a locality. The peculiarity of this common interest is its broad or inclusive character, for it is not attached to specific objects but to the whole background of daily life, to place and people together. It embraces both *what belongs to us,* the heritage of tradition, the position we occupy in the community, the familiar features and our possessions, and *what we belong to,* the obligations and responsibilities that hold us within the accepted social order. These strands are variously interwoven into the community sentiment. Common interest here as elsewhere combines with self-limited interest in various proportions, that is, with individual perception of private benefits and advantages, and with the sense of prestige or privilege or power that the particular community bestows upon its members. In so far as the common interest extends among them, however, it represents an attachment to the complex *unity* of place and group.

Community sentiment is no simple bond. In the primitive group, for example, social cohesion is often highly developed, but it is not based on mere kinship. Rather it is the kin occupying a specific terrain, and without this qualification we can understand neither the nature nor the limits of the group attachment. Anthropologists have pointed out that among various primitive peoples in the administration of justice and the prevention of conflict the principle of the territorial unity of the group is at work. "Not only do local ties coexist with those of blood kinship, but it may be contended that the bond of relationship when defined in sociological rather than biological terms is itself in no small part a derivative of local contiguity."[18] The significance of the relationship between place and group life found in primitive society remains and is vastly more complex in the modern community.

Indications of community sentiment. Common living on a common soil engenders distinctive likenesses in the members of a group. The recognition of these in turn reinforces community sentiment.

[1] *Community folkways:* The most clearly revealed evidence of attachment to the community is that of the folkways, the modes of behavior that characterize a locality. Of these, perhaps none is a more subtle index of the distinctiveness of the group than the peculiarities of speech of different regions. Through turns of phrase, idioms, manners of pronunciation, special words, and the uses of words, we can identify localities, although the more extreme distinctions of speech are being diminished by the extension of communication between communities. But every community, village or city or larger region, has its own marks of some sort, its local customs, its local spots of interest, often its peculiar beliefs and superstitions, its own folk tales and myths.

That distinctive local folkways have become an important ingredient of

18. R. H. Lowie, *The Origin of the State* (New York, 1927), Chap. IV.

American community life, as they are so clearly in the older countries, is brought out in the almost inexhaustible literature of recent years devoted to this subject.[19] In Chapter XIII we shall examine certain of the more outstanding differences setting off one type of community from another. Here their significance is seen in the extent to which they identify the individual with his own locale and thus both sustain and reveal community sentiment.

[2] *Interest in the local life:* The members of a community are likely to be, not only physically but psychically, nearer to one another than to those outside. One indication is the love of gossip—always a certain sign of communal sentiment in any group. We find it more interesting generally to talk about those who belong to our community; what they do excites a more intimate emotion than even the more intrinsically important acts of outsiders. In the modern local community this interest is supported by a local press, which gives far more space to the daily life of the community than to the events of the outside world; and even in the greater cities the "gossip columns" reflect "the general truth that some adequate vehicle for circulating gossip is found wherever there is a populace emerging into a world wider than the area of oral distribution."[20] Similar signs of community sentiment include the belief in the excellence of local products and pride in the success or prestige, particularly outside the community, of a local resident.

These attitudes do not imply that the members necessarily feel a strong devotion to one another. Gossip, for example, is often malicious, and we often condemn conduct in our neighbors which we would condone in strangers. Again, the local officeholder or business leader or professional person is subjected to the sharpest kind of criticism by his immediate fellow citizens of town or state who are often his staunchest defenders against *outside* attack. Rather than illustrating "Love thy neighbor," these attitudes reveal that the members of a community feel a peculiar interest in one another, that they contrast themselves with the members of other communities, and that they appreciate more vividly and with a warmer imagination what anyone in their own group does or suffers.

The changing character of community sentiment in the modern world. There are many ranges and degrees of community in modern society. Today none of us belongs to one inclusive community, but to nearer and wider communities at the same time. Moreover, our sense of attachment to our different communities varies from one to another and from time to time.

[1] *The impact of multigroup society:* The member of the large-scale society, as we saw in Chapter X, belongs to various associations and other groups, so that his social interests become specialized. Part of the allegiance that formerly

19. For example, G. Hutton, *Midwest at Noon* (Chicago, 1946); H. W. Odum, *The Way of the South* (New York, 1947); G. Hicks, *Small Town* (New York, 1946); and the lengthy excursion into regionalism by the journalist John Gunther, *Inside U.S.A.* (New York, 1947).

20. H. M. Hughes, *News and the Human Interest Story* (Chicago, 1940), Chap. VI.

men gave to their local communities is transferred to specific interest-groups. The development of communications enables them more and more to transcend the limits of any one community, resulting in a loss of its former coherence. This is most evident in the large city. The newcomer, for example, does not enter into the community "as a whole," but affiliates himself with those organizations within it to which his previously developed interests attract him—he joins a club, a labor union, a nationality group, a church, and so forth. These interests are not, for the most part, focused in the particular neighborhood in which he settles. For him, as well as for the established city dwellers, the neighborhood as a community may not exist at all. There seems little doubt that community sentiment in the great urban centers has been replaced to a fairly large extent by attachment to other and less inclusive groups.

[2] *Changes in the smaller community:* Another evidence of the lessening of the coherence and intensity of local community sentiment is seen in many rural districts, as they come within the orbit of an urban center. The automobile and modern highway, the radio, the invasion of the urban newspaper and of the chain store, and generally the increasing dominance of the city which we shall shortly examine, weaken the attachment to the locality and reduce the number of interests which depend upon it. Contacts with the city become more numerous and more important.[21] The decreasing dependence upon the local community center indicates not only a change in its physical configuration, as we noted earlier, but a diffusion of community sentiment itself.

But this sentiment is deeply imbedded in the social life of man, and when it loses one outlet it seeks another. Under modern conditions, man, in his search for unity, has tended to find it in the appeal of larger groups, especially in that of nationality. This relatively modern form of community sentiment is of such importance in the study of the social structure and raises such weighty problems concerning its future development that we must examine it more closely.

The Nation as a Type of Community

The community bases of the nation. In our present-day civilization the nation remains the largest effective community. By this we mean that the nation is the largest group which is permeated by a consciousness of comprehensive solidarity. There are interests extending far beyond national frontiers, including, perhaps, those most vital to man's own welfare; and there are international associations of many kinds, the United Nations and many less comprehensive. But as yet there is no international *community* in any effective degree, a point that becomes clear when we remind ourselves of the fundamental bases of all communities.

21. See, for example, J. H. Kolb and E. de S. Brunner, *A Study of Rural Society* (Boston, 1946), especially Chap. XVI.

Like other communities, the nation rests upon locality and community sentiment. Every nation, whether it exists in legal fact or merely in the hopes and aspirations of a people, views some geographical area as its own. But the boundaries setting off one national area from another are not so easy to plot as might be suggested by a political map of the world. We need only to cite the enormous problems in this connection faced by the designers of the new Europe at Versailles after World War I, and the equally complicated difficulties of the treaty makers following World War II. The complexity of these difficulties is in large part the result, to be sure, of the conflict of interests of the great powers, but there remains, especially in such regions of the world as Eastern Europe and India, the question of determining the proper or appropriate boundaries of national areas with relation to national sentiment. We shall explore, then, the nature of this sentiment.

The distinctive features of nationality. That the nation has all the earmarks of a community is borne out when we examine nationality as a type of community sentiment. It shares the characteristics of other community attachments, and it also has distinctive marks of its own.

[1] *Its democratic nature:* Like all *communal* sentiments—as contrasted, for example, with class consciousness or ethnic group attitudes—nationality feeling is essentially democratic. In other words, it admits no grades, no hierarchy of membership. It does not exclude the poor or the wealthy, it does not distinguish between the intelligent and the stupid or between the learned and the ignorant. It claims alike the allegiance of reactionary and conservative and liberal and radical, and these groups in turn, whatever their degree of special interest or of control from outside the nation, promote their programs in patriotism's name. This fact alone suggests the breadth and the significance of its appeal.

Hence the sentiment of nationality does not depend on peculiar interests or specific attributes of all the members of a nation. It does not depend on common speech or culture or economic interest or religion or physical type or even on a long historical tradition. The Swiss are a nation but they have no common speech. So are the citizens of Soviet Russia, with their many tongues and their wide cultural diversity. Differences of economic interest and of religious belief have obviously characterized most European nations as well as the United States in modern times. Physical type or race, for large communities, is never an exclusive common possession, and even the consciousness of a common race, delusive as it is, is a bond of union which nations such as the United States and Russia, for example, do not possess and do not need. "In modern times, it has been the power of an idea, not the call of blood, that has constituted and molded nationalities."[22] What conditions, then, does the sentiment of nationality demand? What distinguishes it from the felt unity of the tribe, of the village, or

22. Hans Kohn, *World Order in Historical Perspective* (Cambridge, Mass., 1942), p. 93.

of the region which may be located within the nation or may extend beyond its frontiers?

[2] *The basic criterion of nationality:* These questions are answered when we examine the relation of the nation to the *state*, which has developed in the history of nation making. Thus a foremost student of the subject explains:

> The most important outward factor in the formation of nationalities is ... the state. Political frontiers tend to establish nationalities. Many new nationalities, like the Canadian, were formed entirely because they comprised a political and geographic entity. Generally ... statehood or nationhood (in the generally accepted sense of common citizenship under one territorial government) is a constitutive element in the life of a nationality. The condition of statehood need not be present when a nationality originates, but in such a case (as with the Czechs in the late eighteenth century) it is always the memory of a past state and the aspiration toward statehood that characterizes nationalities in the age of nationalism.[23]

There are nations, then, that do not rule themselves politically, but we call them nations if they seek political autonomy. This is the basic criterion enabling us to distinguish the nation from other groups. Thus we define nationality as a type of community sentiment, created by historical circumstances and supported by common psychological factors, *of such an extent and so strong that those who feel it desire to have a common government peculiarly or exclusively their own.*

We are here defining the nation in terms of the sentiment the members share, a nonobjective criterion. In this, too, the nation resembles other types of communities. For while common territory and common living are the basic conditions of *any* community, they do not of themselves demarcate it. How much common territory, how much common living? At what point does the persistent desire—and it must be *persistent*—for statehood indicate the existence of a nation?

Our answer to these questions cannot be a rigid one, for modern nations are not born at a moment in time, but emerge. And the conditions surrounding their emergence are complex, involving various interrelationships. For example, the evocation of nationality in one people often influences its development in others, as illustrated at length by the history of Latin America and by present-day events in Southeastern Asia. Our answer, then, must be of a general type, allowing for the variety of possible historical conditions—these must be of such a nature as to inspire nationality sentiment. "In the last resort, we can only

---

23. Reprinted by permission of the publishers from Hans Kohn, *World Order in Historical Perspective.* Cambridge, Mass.: Harvard University Press, 1942, pp. 90-91.

This book of Professor Kohn's, especially Chap. II, and *The Idea of Nationalism* (New York, 1946), especially Chap. I, include useful discussions of the sentiment of nationality. See also R. M. MacIver, *The Web of Government* (New York, 1947), pp. 162 ff.

say that a nation is a nation because its members . . . believe it to be so."[24] Communities, for all their external marks, are not merely objective entities, they are sociopsychological realities. The limits of community are psychological limits, and its expansion beyond the nation-state, in the modern world provided with the physical means of communication, is fundamentally a question of the expansion of attitudes.

The ground of the sentiment of nationality. On the scale of the nation, community sentiment must be reconciled with the fact that millions of persons of different rank and class and ethnic status are equally entitled to share it, and together constitute the social reality to which the sentiment is devoted. On such a scale it is not easy to find like qualities characteristic of the group as a whole.

[1] *National likenesses and national stereotypes:* The feeling of the in-group permeating the nation involves, of course, a sense of its distinctive qualities, traditions, and achievements. But when we seek specific *likenesses* that characterize the members of any one nation in contrast to all others, we are faced on a larger scale with a difficulty inherent in the nature of all community feeling. Fundamentally, the sense of solidarity rests upon what the members have in *common* rather than upon what they have alike.

There are, to be sure, characteristic expressions of a nation, revealed in art, literature, folklore, and historical event. But they are elusive, subtle, and variable. Many of the attempts to state them are marred by the ethnocentrism of the devotee who disparages other nations in exalting his own, or by the overemphasis of certain cultural characteristics, thereby neglecting others just as significant.[25] Dozens of writers from abroad, for example, have described, with varying success, the distinctive features of "Americanism," highlighted by such studies as that of De Tocqueville a century ago and those of André Siegfried and D. W. Brogan in more recent years. And reporting the uniqueness of specific nationalities has been and is a preoccupation of social scientists and of journalists, as well as of certain novelists whose efforts often seem more incisive than the "objective" accounts.[26]

---

24. Ramsay Muir, *Nationalism and Internationalism* (London, 1916), Chap. II. For a recent analysis of this point, see MacIver, *The Web of Government*, pp. 168 ff.

25. An example of such overemphasis is the analysis of G. Gore, "The American Character," *Life Magazine*, Aug. 18, 1947, which, we believe, overplays the role of "second-generation consciousness" in American society.

26. Among the more penetrating studies of the United States is A. de Tocqueville's classic, *Democracy in America*, 2 vols. (P. Bradley, ed., New York, 1945); A. Siegfried, *America Comes of Age* (New York, 1927); and D. W. Brogan, *The American Character* (New York, 1944). And of other countries see, for example, S. Madariaga, *Englishmen, Frenchmen, Spaniards* (London, 1928); A. Siegfried, *France, A Study in Nationality* (London, 1930); D. W. Brogan, *The English People* (New York, 1943) and *French Personalities and Problems* (London, 1946); Lin Yutang, *My Country and My People* (New York, 1939); and K. J. Shridharani, *My India, My America* (New York, 1941).

Most concrete representations of national type are exaggerations or stereotyped caricatures, such as the figures of Uncle Sam or John Bull or the Russian Bear. The Latin is thought of as logical and volatile, the Englishman as stolid and unemotional and a lover of sport, the German as heavy and disciplined and thorough, the Oriental as an unworldly "mystic," the American as standardized, mechanistic, and engrossed in the pursuit of the dollar—though closer acquaintance in every case reveals countless exceptions to the popular judgment.

[2] *Manipulating nationality symbols and "crowd mentality":* The symbols of nationality sentiment become attached to the cultural, economic, and political achievements of the group taken *as a whole.* Therefore, for lack of a specific object the sentiment is apt to take a traditional or mystical form, as seen in the adoration of the flag, the national anthem, or similar symbol. It is difficult for most individuals to grasp the content of the nation-idea; hence the importance of terms like "fatherland" and "mother country" and "homeland," for they suggest the recognized intimacy of the primary group. Attachment to these symbols is normally ingrained early in the socialization process. This is one reason why men are readily susceptible, especially in a crisis, to propagandistic teaching. In time of war or preparation for it, even many of the most educated and scientifically trained are swayed by utterly misleading ideas about their own and other nations. An important characteristic of the simple national stereotype is that, in the hands of the propagandist, it is fairly easy to manipulate—the kindly and generous Uncle Sam, for example, becomes dangerous and selfish, or the friendly Bear turns angry and ruthless.[27]

Its manipulable nature means that nation-sentiment has distinct affinities with the crowd psychology with which we shall be concerned in Chapter XVI. It exhibits, in periods of crisis, a characteristic emotional tone, an enlarged egoism, irrational love and hate, a de-individualizing sense of absorption, and the thrill of a vaguely conceived common purpose, which are the recognized attributes of one important type of crowd behavior. These features of nationality are particularly apparent in certain of its more extreme forms.

Forms of nationality sentiment and some broader implications. We have seen that nationality, wherever found, rests upon the sense of sharing some common values, usually expressed with relatively simple symbols. But the sentiment itself assumes many diverse forms.

[1] *Patriotism:* In one form nationality coheres about the idea of the fatherland or the homeland. When this thought inspires altruistic devotion it is properly named *patriotism.* The profession of patriotism may indeed be and

27. Among the many studies of the manipulation of nationality symbols are H. Lavine and J. Wechsler, *War Propaganda and the United States* (New Haven, 1940); K. London, *Backgrounds of Conflict: Ideas and Forms in World Politics* (New York, 1945); and *Propaganda by Short Wave* (H. L. Childs and J. B. Whitton, eds., Princeton, N.J., 1942). For an interesting collection, see A. A. Roback, *A Dictionary of International Slurs* (Cambridge, Mass., 1944).

often is a cloak for selfish interest or narrow conservatism or class pride or the hatred of other nations, but *in itself* patriotism is a deep communal feeling, capable of inspiring the most devoted and disinterested service, in peace no less than in war. Nor is it reasonable or accurate to argue that any one group or viewpoint is *necessarily* "more patriotic" than another. Was the radical Thomas Paine less patriotic than the conservative George Washington? Was Lenin less devoted to his nation than the Tsar who preceded him in power? Are the Democrats more or less patriotic than the Republicans? It should be clear that to answer such questions as these is exceedingly difficult if not impossible.

[2] *Nationalism:* In another form the sentiment of nationality turns into *nationalism*, a group attitude of profound significance in the modern world. Nationalism as the "state of mind" that seeks not only to make the nation an effective unity, but to make it the object of man's supreme loyalty,[28] has developed remarkably in the Western world since the eighteenth century, and is growing today in the Eastern world. Historically, this movement has demanded the unity and integrity of the nation, its political autonomy, its liberation from the domination of alien powers. At this level it has been a powerful influence in the breakup of feudalism and in the making of modern territorial states. It has prepared the way for modern democracies, since the demand for self-government expanded into the demand that the nation really govern itself—having assaulted the feudal dynastic order it assaulted in turn the class-dominated state. Thus the spirit of nationalism helped to broaden the community basis of the state.

But nationalism, having performed this function, tends, like every other sentiment of group solidarity, to become *exclusive.* And here lies its greatest danger, since the agency of exclusiveness is the armed might of the state, a danger brought home to us by two world wars and by what often appear as preparations for a third. Nationalism, to be sure, serves as a source of integration within the state, but it is dangerous when it denies the common interest that binds nation to nation, thereby defeating the true national interest itself. In this form it becomes *chauvinism*, which is intolerant and boastful, or *imperialism*, which seeks economic or political domination over others. The positive services of nationality to the community are as a basis for the pursuit of common interests, not as a line of demarcation cutting off the interests of one nation from those of another.

[3] *Positive and negative aspects of nationality:* Nationality, it follows, may express a beneficial ideal of unity or it may be a cause of serious division between man and man. Consequently it has been as much denounced by some as it has been extolled by others. The prophets of nationality, like Mazzini, have regarded it as the very breath of life stirring in the people, while those of an opposite view have declared it an evil whose course "will be marked by material and

28. Cf. Kohn, *The Idea of Nationalism*, p. 18. Professor Kohn writes: "The fixation of man's supreme loyalty upon his nationality marks the beginning of the age of nationalism."

moral ruin, in order that a new invention may prevail over . . . the interests of mankind."[29] Justification of either opinion can be found, if we cite only the constructive or only the destructive work of nationality. Its accomplishments are beneficial so long as the nation is itself in the making, and so far as, once the nation is born, it helps to create harmony within it. But it is too easily turned into fear and hate or contempt of other nations, too often made a front for selfish economic exploitation and political aggrandizement, too readily inflated, especially today with the aid of controlled media of communication, with the pride and vainglory of the mob.

In the modern world, as a *limit* to the range of community, nationalism is disastrous. Nationalism first became a potent force in Europe, but there is no better area in which to observe its harmful aspects, not only among the "troublesome" smaller nations of Eastern Europe but also among the greater nations. European nationalism has disrupted the economic interest that might be shared, and has fostered the deadly mutual distrust leading to war. It was available, in Japan as well as in Europe, for the most ruthless utilization by the dictatorial regimes that maintained power until defeated in a conflict which threatened the existence of civilization itself. And nationalism continues to play a vital part in the struggling role of new countries, such as Korea and Pakistan and Israel and the Philippines, and continues to thwart the understanding of one nation by another and the international co-operation the world so desperately needs.[30]

An international community? Perhaps we should not, within this brief context, pose the question of the possibility of an international community. The justification, however, lies not only with its enormous significance to the future of humanity but with the possibility of clarification of the question itself by making use of certain principles already developed. We have seen that all communities—the neighborhood, the complex city, the region, the nation—have two interrelated bases, the territorial and the sociopsychological. We may face the present question, therefore, by examining these essential conditions of community with relation to the world society.

[1] *The territorial basis of international community:* We need not labor the point that the physical barriers separating the larger groups of peoples have been rendered less and less significant by the modern developments of communication and transportation. Geographically, as compared with even a decade ago, the inhabited areas of the earth are approaching the "one world" condition. This condition has been brought about, in the first place, through the growth

29. Lord Acton, *History of Freedom and Other Essays* (London, 1907).

30. Among recent studies of nationalism two of the more thorough are Royal Institute of International Affairs, *Nationalism* (London, 1939) and F. Hertz, *Nationality in History and Politics* (New York, 1944). The story of the role of nationalism since 1945 has not been carefully recorded as yet.

of modern agencies of intercourse, especially aviation and radio, and, most dramatically, through the development of atomic fission. Technologically viewed, these advances have set the world itself as the only geographical locality appropriate for the large-scale community. On this level, the earth could be fairly rapidly knit together, as it already has become in part, as closely as modern technology binds the various areas *within* the modern nation. Thus it may be claimed that the territorial basis of an international community is in large part already established.[31] But community, we know, is more than place.

[2] *International community sentiment:* The desire for some kind of international governing agencies has slowly increased among many peoples for perhaps several centuries, culminating in such associations as the ill-fated League of Nations and the burdened United Nations. But these organizations, however vital their role in preventing international conflict, do not reflect a widespread *international* community feeling among the peoples of the world. An increasing number of persons, to be sure, especially in the more educated groups, are active proponents of this or that type of "World State" or "World Federation," and view the United Nations as, at best, a step in the needed direction. However, the vast majority of the earth's two billion inhabitants in their conception of community are limited to the nation, or, at most, hold a vague hope for an internationalized world. This hope is no doubt sharper among the members of certain of the smaller and weaker nations, for understandable reasons. The great powers, more "secure" in their strength and in their pride, to a large extent continue to rely upon the international bargaining practices of the nineteenth century, following their own interpretations of national interests, rather than being guided by any clear recognition of world interests as such.

We see, then, an international situation wherein territorial unity is increasingly achieved, but is far in advance of whatever small degree of psychological unity is so far accomplished. Upon the closing of this gap may depend whether or not the world itself is to continue as a habitation for man.

[3] *Nationality and international order:* While extreme nationalism, as we have seen, is a major obstacle to the further advance of internationalism, nationality itself is a necessary condition of this advance. The extension of effective community beyond the limits of the state requires a system of units if the larger unity is to be secured. The growth of nationality has led to the conviction of each nation that each is a true community. This conviction has brought and continues to bring the countries of the world into autonomous being as national entities. The process has meant, and still means, in such areas as India and China, a serious disturbance of the former equilibrium; any further

31. For the significance of modern communication and transportation techniques see, for example, W. F. Ogburn, *The Social Effects of Aviation* (Boston, 1946), especially Chaps. XXXIV and XXXV; and the same author's "Sociology and the Atom," *American Journal of Sociology*, LI (1946), 267–275.

advances face grave practical difficulties. Nevertheless the practical necessities are far more urgent than the difficulties. Technology makes the world one, and if our sentiments do not ultimately adjust themselves to this fact, as they have to others in other ages, we face the possibility of destruction heretofore undreamed.

There are, of course, serious obstacles to the establishment of an international order in which national communities will be effectively united. The most serious is the atmosphere of emotional prejudice that is so all-pervading, the product of excessive nationalism abetted by the narrower interests of various economic and political groups. Even after the several demonstrations of the atomic bomb, the statesmen of the great nations appear often not to realize the necessities imposed upon them by the growth of a world civilization. The expansion of civilization—the accomplishments of modern technology and of physical science—continues as an irresistible process, whether under the banner of socialism or of individualism. But the expansion of scientific statesmanship, based upon the understanding of human needs and human foibles, lags far behind. Nor is it enough that statesmen become students of social science. For social science, concerned with the goals of man as well as with the means of their attainment, unlike physical science, must be the possession of the *many* if its fruits are to be attained.[32]

Community and Intracommunal Differences

Types of intracommunal differences and their roles. Every community is marked by a consciousness of solidarity among its members. But the solidarity always admits, even in the smallest groups and most obviously in the larger ones, the presence of differences. Certain differences do not disrupt the sense of community and some even support it; others weaken, threaten, and may at length destroy it.

[1] *Nondisruptive differences:* Among the many intracommunal differences are three broad types which by and in themselves do not disrupt community cohesion and may, in fact, serve to increase it.

ONE: FUNCTIONAL DIFFERENCES. Some degree of division of labor is required in all community life, even the simplest. The differences which assign to the members a recognized and accepted place in the social economy, ranging from the most primitive organization where sex or age may determine function, to complex society with its thousands of specialized occupations, do not interfere with the group solidarity. Indeed these differences may serve as an objective basis for role-feeling, an essential ingredient of community sentiment.

32. Concrete proposals for the establishment of an international order, incorporating some of the principles developed in this section, are put forward in R. M. MacIver, *Towards an Abiding Peace* (New York, 1943); see also *The Web of Government*, Chap. XII.

TWO: STABLE CLASS AND CASTE. The same situation characterizes those class differences that are rooted in a system of authority the belief in which is shared alike by the subordinated and superior groups, as in the feudal system. Caste itself, though it prevents the free participation in the affairs of the community or large sections within it, may, provided it conforms to the beliefs and the indoctrinations of the great majority, be a strong social bond. For example, the reverence in which the Brahman has been held by the lower caste orders in India has been an important element in the cohesion of Indian society. Note that we do not include here as a nondisruptive difference the mobile social class, nor do we include the "caste" separating White and Negro and other groups in our own society.[33]

THREE: FREE POLITICAL DIFFERENCES. In a mobile modern society the differences between political parties, to the degree that they are issues determined freely and fully by resort to the vote, are quite compatible with communal solidarity. For the implied agreement that all will accept the majority verdict involves a deeper sense of the whole. This system, unlike that of caste or of single-party dictatorship, allows differences to be expressed freely, but is practicable only *in so far as* the differences themselves are held subordinate to a fundamental unity, *in so far as* they are differences of policy with respect to commonly accepted ends. Given this basic agreement, there is room for countless minor differences on the political level.

[2] *Disruptive differences:* In contrast with these differences that need not, and by themselves normally do not, impair the feeling of community are others that are prejudicial and may even prove fatal to it. Again, we may consider three types.

ONE: ACCENTUATED ECONOMIC DIFFERENCES AND CLASS WAR. In the days of classical Greece it was said that every city was two cities at war with each other, a city of the rich and a city of the poor.[34] Economic disparity may prove a dividing issue of great significance, especially when associated with class distinctions no longer tolerable to the subject groups. This type of dissension is aggravated by the realization of the possibility of improvement, and by conditions involving rapid change when a feeling of instability is combined with a sense of social injustice.

The crisis of war frequently precipitates economic cleavage. While the immediate effect of war often is to stimulate intense solidarity within the belligerent community, obliterating or overwhelming conflict over domestic issues, as the war continues or after it is finished, the strains and pressures it creates and the attitudes bred by the resort to force are apt to accentuate old differences and to breed new ones. It has been observed from ancient times that an aftermath of war is class war. This old principle is amply illustrated by the intensification of class struggle after World War I, culminating in Russia and

33. See Chapter XIV below for a discussion of class and caste.

34. Plato, *Republic*, iv, p. 422.

Italy and Germany and Spain in the complete suppression of one or the other of the contending sides; and by the bitter internal strife in most countries after World War II, marked by intranational unsettlement made the more extreme by the development of an international "cold war" between former allies.

TWO: RACE CONSCIOUSNESS. A type of difference that always *threatens* community solidarity is that between race-*conscious* groups (not between biological races as such). The subjective nature of these antagonisms, whereby a group is identified as a "race" by the in-group and out-group attitudes alike, means that they are easily inflamed and are very apt to blind men to a reasoning consideration of their common interest. There are such obvious and unhappy examples of this as the conflict between the Arabs and Jews in Palestine, and between the latter group and others in many countries. And in long-established communities this type of antagonism often remains half submerged, ready to intensify other disturbances, as in the situation of the Swedes and the Finns in Finland or of the Flemish and the Walloons in Belgium. Differences in speech, as in these latter instances, help to perpetuate the fissures between race-conscious groups. So do marked external signs of psychological difference, or what has been termed "racial visibility." The most conspicuous of these signs is color, which frequently, as in the United States or in South Africa, becomes a formidable barrier to solidarity where groups of different color meet. However, we should not attribute intergroup conflict to physiological differences themselves, for these become significant only when they are associated with antagonistic attitudes.[35]

THREE: RELIGIOUS DIFFERENCES. Another important danger to solidarity arises from the contact within a community of strongly dogmatic religions. "How can we live at peace," asked Rousseau, "with those we believe to be damned?" As we saw in Chapter VIII, a partial answer to this question has been found in many modern communities, though the history of the Western religions, of Christianity, Judaism, and Mohammedanism, has been marked by intolerance and frequently by violence. In some areas, with modern India affording tne most significant example with its clash between Mussulmans and Hindus, religious difference remains a grave cause of division. And so it does where differences of religion combine with differences of race consciousness, as in Palestine or, more generally, in communities where anti-Semitism flourishes.

These three types of difference—economic, "racial," and religious—sometimes separately, but often combined in various degrees, have been throughout history the great precipitants of civil war and revolution. Such convulsions are relatively rare, but the differences themselves generally operate to limit or thwart community sentiment. Of the three, the economic is the most universal breeder of dissension—the conflict of the "haves" and the "have-nots" is everywhere latent or active. In "classless" Soviet Russia there are few signs

---

35. See Chapter XV below for a discussion of "race" differences.

of the conflict but economic differences are evident and are possibly increasing,[36] while throughout most other countries in this postwar era economic struggle is conspicuous. There seems no prospect that it will wholly disappear. Its revolutionary forms are fundamentally the product of sheer destitution and ruthless exploitation, and if we are to avoid the extreme and desperate manifestations of class conflict we must abolish the conditions which breed it.

Communal solidarity and cultural differences. We have already seen, in the case of the nation, that the sense of community is often shared by peoples of different cultures. Cultural differences need not but may be a hindrance to communal solidarity, a point that becomes clarified when we consider the following two cases.

[1] *Immigrant groups and communal solidarity:* In Chapter VI we discussed the accommodation of the immigrant when faced by new conditions in his new land. The American continent similarly offers peculiar opportunities for the study of the manner in which the growth of communal solidarity embracing groups of diverse origins and national characteristics is advanced or retarded. Immigrant groups, entering a social environment which at first is alien to them, tend to cherish their old customs and seek, through the establishment of clubs, institutions, newspapers, and other agencies of intercommunication, to guard their group traditions and group individuality. By such means they mitigate the abruptness of the transition to the new life, provide themselves with a temporary status and with a self-respect which the sudden impact of an alien environment might otherwise endanger. But gradually, unless strong social discriminations are roused by economic or racial or religious prejudice, these groups become integrated within the larger community.[37]

This process affords a large illustration of the principle that communal solidarity does not demand uniformity. Assimilation is not a one-way process, and differences are by no means simply eliminated; in fact, difference itself may become a symbol of national or of metropolitan unity. Least of all is unity achieved by coercive suppression of differences, as myriad historical instances, from the fate of the Israelites in Egypt to the subjection of German-speaking groups in the former Austro-Italian Tyrol, sufficiently reveal. The requisite is rather the maintenance of conditions under which diverse groups can learn to feel "at home" in the new land, thus spontaneously establishing habituations that assure a sufficient *sense* of familiarity to permit them to participate freely in the community life.

---

36. See, for example, N. S. Timasheff, "Vertical Social Mobility in Communist Society," *American Journal of Sociology*, L (1944), 9-21; R. S. Lynd, "Planned Social Solidarity in the Soviet Union," *ibid.*, LI (1945), 183-197; M. Fairchild, "Social-Economic Classes in Soviet Russia," *American Sociological Review*, IX (1944), 236-241.

37. For bibliographical references on this process, see footnotes 12, 13, and 15, Chapter VI above.

[2] *Disintegration of community through the clash of cultures:* A different and far less soluble problem is presented when groups representing peoples of markedly different cultural levels live together in the same area. One of the broad social tragedies of world history is the destruction of the community feeling of primitive peoples under the impact of alien civilizations. Representatives of Western civilization have imposed upon the primitive their laws and morals, their industrial methods and mechanisms, bringing also their unwanted services, their vices, and their diseases, destroying the old sense of unity and the ancestral customs. This process is sometimes the result of the misguided zeal of ignorant missionary enterprise, but more often of the greed of economic exploitation. Thus have perished the Tasmanian, the Andamanese, the ancient peoples of South America, and many other groups; and thus have dwindled to insignificance such groups as the Fijis, the Hawaiians, and several American Indian tribes. A few examples of careful restraint relieve the dark picture of communal disintegration presented so frequently in Africa and Asia and the Pacific Islands, but the economic and military power and scornful superiority of the Western peoples have made mutual accommodation difficult and often impossible. Communal solidarity in the strict sense is ruled out because of the enormous differences in power, a situation complicated by the fear of the dominant group that the admission of the native to equal participation in communal rights would lower or imperil their own cultural standards.[38]

Another scarcely less difficult, if less tragic, case is the meeting of alien cultures each of which asserts its own superiority while one is politically dominant over the other—a situation, like the former, for which modern imperialism provides many examples. The "classic" illustration is that of India. Certainly Britain could not have maintained so long its Indian suzerainty if it had not been in some measure respectful of the custom, of the community life, of the politically subject culture; in fact, Indian administrators for many years felt "a nervous fear of altering native custom."[39] But while respect for native usage is a basis of comparative harmony when the subject people is on a distinctly different cultural level, it proves quite inadequate when nationalism awakens within that people. India's recently achieved political independence illustrates the point, as does that of the Philippines and the drive for political autonomy throughout the peoples of Southeastern Asia.

[3] *Some conclusions:* Fuller consideration of these problems is beyond our present scope. What we have sought in general to show is that the solidarity of a community depends not on the absence of differences within it but rather

---

38. *When Peoples Meet* (A. Locke and B. J. Stern, eds., New York, 1942) provides an excellent collection of readings on the impact of Western civilization on primitive community life; see especially Chap. III. For an appraisal of the American program in the Pacific islands, see J. Useem, "The American Pattern of Military Government in Micronesia," *American Journal of Sociology*, LI (1945), 93-102.

39. Sir H. Maine, *Village Communities* (New York, 1889).

on the absence of certain barriers to the liberation and the consequent modification or adjustment of these differences. In this respect, the chief barriers to solidarity are two: (1) *Coercion of group by group within the community.* This need not be physical coercion but may be social and economic pressure or discrimination directed against politically disfranchised groups, economic classes, racial or religious minorities. (2) *Lack of free contacts which mitigate both cultural and physical aloofness.* Cultural aloofness is expressed in the contempt of group for group, a feeling which often means the failure of one to comprehend the life of another, and physical aloofness prevents the expansion of any community sentiment, as exemplified in certain ethnic blocks of the Western prairies and particularly in extreme separatist groups such as the Mennonites, Doukhobors, Hutterites, and similar bodies. Often these settlements have an intensely communal life of their own, but under conditions which prohibit their participation in the wider community.

Perhaps the reader has noted that in this chapter we have in several instances referred to other chapters, especially to those dealing with such intracommunal phenomena as class and caste, ethnic groupings, and the like. The community, because of its inclusive nature, provides the general but essential setting within which these more specialized social developments take place, and thus serves as a transitional "topic" toward their consideration. But it is not a subject from which we shall now, in any fundamental sense, depart. For community, as we have seen, exists in some degree wherever men live together. How their common living varies from country to city and from region to region is the problem we next face.

13

City, Country, and Region

Comparing the City and the Country

The problem of contrasting "ways of life." One of the broadest and most revealing of all social contrasts is exhibited by the differences of urban and rural life. This contrast is one of social environment. It is also one that permits us to distinguish between two broad types of community organization. The city is an environment created by society, in which for the purposes of community living many aspects of the natural environment are modified or entirely eliminated. Under rural conditions social attitudes and social institutions present characteristic differences from those developed within the city.

[1] *A reminder on environmental influence:* In Chapter VI we discussed the total environment within which man lives and of which he and his accomplishments are a significant part. We now return to this problem, but with particular reference to the contrasting modes of common life in the city and in the country. To describe these differences is itself no simple task; to interpret them is even more difficult.

However, when we push our analysis back into the problem of causes; when in seeking to discover the pure influence of environment we are forced to discover once more that environments select and attract as well as influence those who live in them; when we remember also the incessant process in which man modifies as well as readjusts himself to an environment so that conditions found at one stage of city growth, say certain health conditions, will not be found at another; when lastly we reflect on the interplay and unequal exchange of influences that radiate from one environment to another; it is then that the deeper interest and the greater difficulty of the comparison appears.

[2] *How contrasts may be misleading:* We are apt to draw false inferences from comparisons of social groups, whether of communities or classes or oc-

cupations, unless we realize these complicating factors. The sociologically untrained person is constantly being misled, even when his observations are accurate and even when he does not generalize rashly from a few examples, because he imputes the differences between two total situations to some one element in each. He compares, for example, the English and the French, the Jew and the non-Jew, the immigrants to the United States from Western and from Eastern European countries, and attributes the observed differences, usually themselves grossly simplified and exaggerated, simply to "race" or to "national character." He compares the social characteristics of Protestants and Catholics and attributes the differences solely to religion. He compares the politician and the businessman, the inventor and the money-maker, the artist and the executive, the professional soldier and the civilian officeholder, and makes their respective occupations entirely responsible for the differences they display. He contrasts those of different regions, say the New Englander and the Southerner, and the outcome is explained as due to climate or terrain or some other single factor.

We shall best avoid these simplifications if, in the comparisons before us, we examine the historical process in which the different situations have developed to their present forms, and if, furthermore, we analyze the various factors which enter into the complex of each contrasted situation as it now appears. We shall seek briefly to satisfy these general requirements of proper comparison in the present chapter. In this section and the following two we shall restrict our discussion, for the most part, to the contrast and the interrelationships between the rural and urban social systems, while in the final section we shall consider the development and potentialities of the region within which both city and country are essential elements.

Difficulties of comparing the urban and rural. As we shall see, most of the writers of the regionalist school have as an important goal the integration of and balance between urban and rural life. Before examining the work of this school, therefore, we must clarify this contrast. The comparison itself is beset with difficulties.

[1] *Urban and rural a matter of degree:* For many centuries city and country have been the two most recognizable general types of human habitation. But between the two there is no sharp demarcation to tell where city ends and country begins. Scattered farmsteads pass imperceptibly into villages, villages into towns. A mansion set in the forest or a suburban home in the country or a hotel on the mountaintop is usually essentially urban in character. *Rural* and *urban* depict modes of community life, not simply geographical location.

For statistical convenience, the census takers of different nations decide that every area with a density of population to the square mile of, say, 1,000, or every cluster of habitations containing 2,000 (as in France) or 2,500 (as in the United States) or 30,000 (as in Japan) shall be regarded as urban. Differences in the method of reckoning are often a source of confusion, whether the basic criterion used is specific size or density or legal status of the community or dominant mode of occupation (a criterion combined with size in Soviet Russia). Differences within the groups respectively accounted urban and rural complicate the problem of comparison. In this country, for example, were we to use the Census Bureau figure of 2,500 as our only guide, we should discover over 43 per cent of the population to be "rural" (as of 1940), yet more refined examination by that agency shows that less than one quarter of our 140,000,000 people fall within the "farm" category. The social characteristics of a town of 2,500 inhabitants, moreover, are obviously unlike those of a great metropolis.[1]

The contrast between city and country, then, breaks down into a series of contrasts. We may think of a spectrum with the rural community standing at one extreme and the large-scale metropolis at the other. Between are all degrees of urbanization, reported by sociologists at one level as "small-town stuff" and "Plainville," at another as "Yankee City" (17,000) and "Middletown" (50,000), at another the large city like St. Louis or Chicago or Detroit. But even in the last group there are significant distinctions. In 1940 there were 140 "metropolitan districts" in the United States, each made up of one or more cities of 50,000 inhabitants together with the immediately adjacent areas. Yet here and in almost all other countries of the world there is one "primate" city, larger two or three times over than any others in the national territory, and thereby occupying a distinct position in terms of cultural influence as well as size—for example, Vienna, Copenhagen, Helsinki, London, Buenos Aires, Manila, New York.[2]

[2] *The manifold environments within the city:* There is the further complication that the city, especially the large city, is not only a single community for all its inhabitants but also a series of extremely different social environments for the different groups within it. While rural communities differ considerably from one another, each one exerts in far greater measure than does the city a common influence on its inhabitants. In the city the ways of life are legion, and the diversities of its man-made scene admit extreme variations of equipment and opportunity. There is no sense of a common and vital dependence on the aspects of the seasons and the vagaries of the weather. There is no sense of a common earth, a common fortune, and a common fate. There are few common tasks, few incidents in which all men share. There are few impressive signs to call out at the same moment those universal comments and reflections which make man feel kin to man—the devastation of the storm, the flow of

1. On the problem of determining the urban on the basis of size and other statistically suitable criteria, see, for example, N. P. Gist and L. A. Halbert, *Urban Society* (New York, 1941), Chap. I.

2. Cf. Mark Jefferson, "The Law of the Primate City," *Geographical Review*, XXIX (1939), 226–232.

the sap, the fall of the leaf. There are no common hours of work and rest, no common occasions of meeting for personal gossip or public discussion. And among the events of man's own making only extraordinary happenings or catastrophes or extreme threats to safety inspire like responses among the inhabitants of the large city.[3]

The heterogeneity of city life is enormous. Within a few blocks of one another its dwellers live alien and utterly disparate lives. Concerning vital statistics alone, we find striking differences in birth rates and death rates, in conditions favorable to health or disease, for different groups and different districts. A "primate" city, like London or New York, exhibits within it extremes of healthiness and unhealthiness, no less than of wealth and poverty, surpassing those found elsewhere in the whole countries to which they belong. The city is the home of opposites, and therefore it is often misleading to contrast the average figures for city and country, or to treat as unities for the purpose of comparison the less homogeneous and the more homogeneous. These difficulties can be met, however, by the adequate statistical analysis we find in a growing body of research in this field.[4]

[3] *The changing character of city and country:* A comparison of city and country faces the further difficulty that the phenomena compared do not stay constant. On the one hand, the country itself becomes increasingly urbanized under the impact of the city and, on the other, cities tend to grow at the expense of the country, in large measure through migration from the country—both of these processes marking especially our own civilization. In the latter process the city comes to include a much larger proportion of country-bred residents than the country does of those bred in the city. Here two factors are significant.

One is the greater comparative fertility of rural populations. In 1940 the rural net reproduction rate in the United States was about 166 (100 representing the "replacement" level), the urban only about 73.[5] The difference suggests the extent to which the country must supply population for the cities if they are to continue to grow in size. The other factor consists in the technical-economic conditions which have made the city a source of livelihood for an increasing proportion of the total population. Although our growing urbanization has slowed down considerably in recent years, it remains true that the joint operation of differential fertility and urban migration means that the city

3. For a study of one such event, the reaction to an unusual radio broadcast, see H. Cantril, *The Invasion from Mars* (Princeton, N. J., 1940).

4. Still a useful source is P. Sorokin and C. C. Zimmerman, *Principles of Rural-Urban Sociology* (New York, 1929). For further statistics on the rural-urban comparison and for cities of different sizes, see, for example, W. F. Ogburn, *Social Characteristics of Cities* (Chicago, 1937); National Resources Committee, *Our Cities* (Washington, D.C., 1937) and *Better Cities* (Washington, D.C., 1942), and *The Annals of the American Academy of Political and Social Science*, Vol. CCXLII (Nov., 1945), various articles.

5. A. J. Jaffe, "Population Trends and City Growth," in the issue of *The Annals* cited above.

must readapt to its own changing conditions large numbers who were born in and habituated to a very different community life.

One aspect of this situation is that many phenomena sometimes attributed to the city as such are in part the result of cityward migration rather than of urbanization proper. The loneliness and unfriendliness of city life of which we often hear, for example, may well be predominantly a part of the experience of the newcomer as distinct from the experience of those brought up within the city. Or again, the personal and family disorganization found in such groups as the American Negro in large Northern cities is no doubt closely related to the fact that the great majority of these people have, since 1910, undergone the psychologically difficult transition involved in moving from the largely rural South to the great industrial and commercial cities of the North. As we have seen in an earlier chapter, "culture shock" resulting in deviational behavior of various types is inevitably manifested in large-scale migrations of human beings from one mode of community life to another.

Why cities grow. Migration from the country to the city and city growth have been witnessed in the course of every great civilization. In fact, the original meaning of the word "civilization" is urbanization. In earlier civilizations—Mesopotamian, Egyptian, Cretan, Greek, Roman—as their cities rose in power and influence, so did the corresponding civilizations; as their cities declined, so did the civilizations decline. We must postpone the question of urban decline. But what are the conditions of city growth?

[1] *Surplus resources as the fundamental factor:* Cities grow wherever a society, or a group within it, gains control over resources greater than are necessary for the mere sustenance of life. In ancient civilizations these resources were mainly acquired through the power of man over man. The growth of city life rested on the precarious foundations of slavery, forced labor, and taxation by the conquering or ruling class; and in some modern civilizations, such as the Chinese and Indian, the exploitative factor remains highly significant in the maintenance of large cities. However, a surer basis has been found in modern times in the power of man over nature. The extension of this power, especially in Western society during the past two centuries, an extension the limits of which are not as yet discernible, has been the primary condition of the unprecedented growth of cities and the ever-growing proportion of city dwellers in the total population.

Basic to this growth has been the revolution of agriculture. This transformation has witnessed a huge development of new "energy crops," such as the potato and maize. It has seen the specialization of agriculture on a regional and national and particularly on an international basis, permitting England, for example, to employ well over 90 per cent of her population in nonfarming occupations. The agricultural revolution has encompassed—and we cannot yet guess the limits of this trend—technological improvements resulting in vast increases in quantity and quality of crops and cattle and other sustenance items, the growth of "agrobiology," improvements in preservation and transportation of foodstuffs. In brief, the modern agricultural revolution has enabled relatively few people to supply the basic food necessities of many.[6]

[2] *Industrialization and commercialization:* If a surplus of resources is a basic condition of urban growth, the growth itself, in modern times, has been enormously stimulated by the new techniques of production associated with the industrial revolution. Of early importance was the development of steam power which, in Western countries, effectively brought about the mobility of traditionally immobile groups of workers, hastening their concentration around the new centers of factory production—thus the boom of textile cities in England between 1820 and 1830 and of coal and iron towns during the following decade. On the European continent and in the United States we witness in the succeeding years hundreds of cities rapidly increasing in size as they become headquarters for the industrialism of the modern era. And more recently in Russia and in the Orient, as illustrated by India's steel center Jamshedpur, the continuing influence of industrialization on city growth is clearly evident.[7]

While industrialization is predominantly a modern phenomenon, trade and commerce have played an important role in urban expansion in ancient civilizations as well. In Greek and Roman days and earlier, and again in medieval times, centers developed wherein goods were distributed and commercial transactions were accomplished. But the rise of modern marketing institutions, the development of methods of exchange and rationalized bookkeeping, the enormous increase in efficient techniques of communication and transportation, all interrelated with industrialization itself, have greatly abetted the growth of the small and the large cities of the world today. And the fact that a large percentage of their residents are engaged in commercial occupations—the "paper" enterprises—is, as we shall see, a significant characteristic of the large-scale city.

[3] *The economic pull of the city:* These advances have been associated both with an increase in the population and with a higher standard of living. The latter tendency has, as we explained in an earlier chapter, operated to restrict the former, and has thus still further encouraged the growth of cities. For as the standard of living rises for a whole country or for any group within it, there is an increasing demand for the kinds of commodities and services which are supplied in and by cities, as contrasted with the relatively inelastic demand for agricultural products. This increased demand means that a larger percentage of people can win a livelihood in the cities.

The proportion of urban to rural inhabitants is thus not a matter of choice, but is, on the whole, determined by economic conditions. If, for example, more

6. For figures on agricultural surplus, see *Our Cities*, p. 29.

7. For a graphic description of this growth see L. Mumford, *The Culture of Cities* (New York, 1938), pp. 143–160.

females than males migrate to cities like New York or Washington, D.C., or to centers of light industry like Fall River, Massachusetts, or Patterson, New Jersey, while more males go to Seattle, Washington, or Akron, Ohio, the obvious explanation is economic. Migration within a country is determined, except that political barriers do not interpose, by much the same principles as international migration. It moves in the direction in which economic opportunity presents itself.[8] We must not make the mistake, therefore, of regarding country and city as equally competing attractions, between which people can decide at will. The city is selective with respect to the types rather than to the numbers it attracts, and because the numbers are determined mainly by the possibilities of making a living, more imperative considerations than personal preferences are operative in cityward migration. This also should be kept in mind in our comparison of city and country, especially as the "rush" to the cities and the "depopulation" of the rural areas are frequently deplored.

We shall return to the problem of urban growth in connection with the dominance of this form of community life over the rural. We must first examine their contrasting features.

Contrasts of Urban and Rural Life

The distinctive social features of rural life. We should not think of the rural community as simply the way of life of the American farmer. The countryside in the United States, in fact, has changed considerably under the strong impact of urban civilization, a point to which we shall shortly return. But still in this country, as in Europe, and much more extensively among the many millions of residents of the Far Eastern countries, the rural community remains as a distinctive mode of common life. In spite of the many cross-differences of race and climate, of location and of resources, there is a marked and general contrast found everywhere between the social life of the country and that of the city. There must be, therefore, factors that belong exclusively or predominantly, under all conditions, to one or the other type of social environment. We shall consider first the distinctive features of the rural type, keeping in mind especially the country life that has remained relatively undisturbed by urbanization.

[1] *Semi-isolation of the family and the predominance of primary relationships:* The most obvious feature is the relative isolation of the country life. It is not an isolation of the individual, but usually of the homestead or group of homesteads—to a great extent, it is the semi-isolation of the family.[9] The family

8. On internal migration see C. Goodrich, *et al., Migration and Economic Opportunity* (Philadelphia, 1936); for more recent figures see *Statistical Abstract of the United States*, 1946, pp. 30–33.

9. The case of the occasional solitary trappers, hunters, and prospectors is one of isolation of the individual, but is hardly characteristic of *rural* living.

circle must supply the greater part of the economic and social needs of its members. The necessities of common toil and reciprocal services strongly corroborate the ties of family relationship. And the unity of the family itself is emphasized by the physical separation of the homestead. It is often observed that in sparsely settled areas families are frequently at strife with one another, a consequence of the intense and exclusive cohesion of the rural family. Its attitudes and its morals are apt to be predominantly familial. It tends to grow self-centered and, to a large extent, psychologically self-sufficient.

Family customs, undisturbed by the constant succession of new contacts and new stimuli characteristic of the urban world, grow more deeply rooted. The rarer contacts with the outside community tend to sharpen in the mind of the country dweller the contrast between his ways and those of others and to confirm him in his own. He has neither the opportunity to cultivate an attitude of broad-mindedness nor the temptation to become a busy seeker after new things. Custom rules over him, and for fashion he has little use. His ways are fixed for him, and his vicissitudes are mainly those associated with the natural sequence of the seasons and with the stages of his own life span.

If the contacts of the semi-isolated country dweller with the outsider are infrequent and impersonal, those with the members of his immediate household and rural neighborhood reveal the intimacy and noncategoric characteristics of primary relationships. His social existence consists predominantly of face-to-face situations, and his associates are whole persons with whom he directly co-operates or directly conflicts. His limited rural community, the details of which and the members of which he knows so well, is often itself a primary group.

[2] *The impact of a predominant mode of occupation:* The principal occupation of the countryman may be hunting or fishing, as in many primitive communities. But pre-eminently it is farming, involving the raising of crops and of stock. In any event, the central mode of work usually determines the geographical basis of the rural community—fixes it within access to the game-providing forest or to the fish-infested stream or ocean, or, more commonly, within regions in which the soil may be made to yield.

Whether the ruralite is farmer or hunter or fisherman, he is in constant contact with nature. He sees nature not as the artist who observes her moods in the detachment of aesthetic appreciation nor as the scientist who seeks to know her secrets for their own sake, but as the practical worker who must wrest a living from the soil. He sees nature as friend and as enemy, as the ripener of crops and the sender of weeds, as the bringer of drought and moisture, of storm and sunshine. He must win her rewards through struggle and endure her caprices with resignation. It is the reproductive forces of animate nature on which his livelihood depends and to which his main effort is directed. He is thus inclined to view all nature as *animate.* The forces which he must utilize are largely beyond his control and often beyond his reckoning. In their presence the countryman grows imbued with religion and with superstition. He must come to terms with inscrutable powers, and the limits of his own power make him susceptible to traditional beliefs.

This predominant occupation of agriculture has other attributes which impress themselves on the mentality of the countryman and are reflected in his social life. He is not, like the urban wage earner, an employee working under immediate supervision at a task specifically assigned to him. Whether he is a tenant or a freeholder, even where he is a serf, his times and seasons, his varying tasks and his alternations of work and rest, are set for him not by the commands of a master but by the exigencies of nature.

The ruralite tends to view the land itself as the most substantial of all heritages and the primary source of all other wealth. When he does not own the soil he cultivates, or when his ownership is threatened by oppressive taxes or other measures, he may align himself with radical movements that promise him protected ownership of his most prized possession—thus the Russian peasant thirty years ago and the Chinese peasant farmer today. But when he has traditionally owned or partly owned the land, without grave oppression, he usually has a strong sense of the rights of property, with a consequent tendency to believe in the fixity of the social order. This conservatism differs, however, from the more nervous conservatism of the capitalist-employer, for it is not dependent on the unstable distinction of economic class.[10] The countryman is not, typically, a professional employer of labor. He normally has no permanent helpers beyond his own family, and when he does hire one or, at most, a few workers, he still engages in the same tasks as his help. He remains both artisan and employer in one.

[3] *The variety of rural tasks:* While the rural community is marked by a predominant type of occupation, the occupation itself involves a large variety of tasks. As compared with that of the city dweller, the work of the countryman is conspicuously unspecialized. The direct operations of agriculture are themselves diverse, and beyond them the farmer must be conversant with many other crafts, as woodsman and veterinary and smith and carpenter, and so forth. He is incessantly turning from one kind of task to another, including that of teaching his sons to be Jacks-of-all-trades. If modern invention has lightened the labors of some farmers, it has also made new crafts imperative, those of the mechanic and electrician. The round of daily duties for the farmer's wife is at least as variegated. She helps in the farm work, gardening, feeding animals, milking; she adds to her household tasks the preparation of many commodities, their number varying with the accessibility of retail stores; she is cook, laundress, seamstress, and tailor in the intervals of bearing and caring for the several children of the usual rural home.

Many of these tasks are eliminated or lightened, of course, as communication

10. See Chapter XIV below for an analysis of class.

improves and as modern technology and outlets for consumption goods increasingly penetrate rural regions, as they have so markedly in the United States.[11] But even here the typical contrast remains between the countryman's diversity of work and the specialized and concentrated labor of the city dweller. The toil of the former is generally more arduous and unremitting, and this, too, finds expression in his social attitudes, in his moral code, and in his philosophy of life. Nor does he have the hope, so long as he remains a farmer, which even the most exploited urban wage earner can cherish, of promotion or at least a change of occupation. His role in social life is more deeply fixed, and so are his ways and thoughts and aspirations.

[4] *Simplicity and frugality of living:* The rewards of the farmer's toil are rarely bountiful, especially of the small-scale farmer. If the rewards are somewhat speculative, it is usually between the limits of penury and a modest livelihood. In bad years he falls into debt; in good years he does little more than recover. If he is a proprietor he is still a manual worker and his income is nearer to the average income of manual workers than to that of property owners. In the United States, even in a farm "prosperity" year, 1944, the average cash income per farm in the five lowest states was $1,400 or less; in 1940 it had ranged between $433 and $630.[12] Agriculturists with large investments fare much better, of course; on the other hand, small, family-type farms with an investment of under $3.000 were earning less than $500 net cash income in 1941.[13] These figures suggest merely the comparative frugality of living of the ruralite in our own nation, where the material standards are generally high: they do not reveal the greatly lower levels that typify rural communities in many other regions of the earth.[14]

The frugal and simple mode of living of the farmer is not, after the manner of the city, competitive—until the city ways become in part his own. Traditionally the countryman has felt less the spur to keep up appearances, for the range of wealth in the country neighborhood is narrower, contacts are fewer, and in the closer ties of his family life he is less tempted to set a pace for his neighbors or to keep one set by others. He is less subject to the stimulations that come from social proximity, sharp social contrasts, and social mobility. Where, as in certain primitive and feudal and Oriental civilizations, a relatively

11. For the large improvement in this respect of the life of the American farmer in 1947 as compared with his situation in 1940, see *Fortune Magazine*, Oct., 1947, "The Farmer Goes to Town." Basic to the improvement in this period was the farm family's increase of cash income.
12. For comparative figures on cash income per farm for the forty-eight states for the years 1920–31, 1940, and 1944, see J. H. Kolb and E. de S. Brunner, *A Study of Rural Society* (Boston, 1946), p. 111.
13. C. McWilliams, *Small Farm and Big Farm*, Public Affairs Pamphlet No. 100 (New York, 1945), p. 6.
14. For the economic conditions of the farmer in various countries see, for example, K. Brandt, *The Reconstruction of World Agriculture* (New York, 1945); and E. de S. Brunner, I. T. Sanders, and D. Ensminger, *Farmers of the World* (New York, 1945).

fixed class system pervades the rural community, there is even less incentive to the ambitions of the countryman than where competitive values have spread and the possibility of individual advancement has emerged, as in our own society.[15]

These, then, are the elementary factors that distinguish in general rural from urban life. Together they form a community environment which profoundly influences the social responses of the countryman. In the city, roughly in proportion to its size, opposite conditions are found: aggregation instead of physical isolation; associations of many kinds supplementing or supplanting the functions of the family and rural neighborhood; a predominance of secondary or categoric relationships; contacts with human beings and civilizational diversity superseding contacts with nature; differentiation of economic classes and specialization of economic tasks ranking and grading men in ways often unknown in the country; limited and intensified work, with its endless varieties and disparities of opportunity and of fortune creating an intricate design of competitive living traditionally alien to the rural scene—here we have the basis for the social contrasts that follow.

The contrast in terms of social control and family solidarity. We shall consider first the fundamental sociological aspect of the contrast, the manner in which the individual belongs to his society. In general the force of the traditional mores and the bonds of family solidarity are more dominant in the rural community than in the urban. Let us view the two types in terms of these factors.

[1] *The rural community:* In rural life, where the family is relatively dominant and self-contained, a group responsibility prevails that tends to be more and more dissolved in the growth of the city. In the comparative absence of other forms of relationships, the patriarchal type of family tends to persist, imposing greater control over its members. The status of the individual is likely to be the status of his family. Property is likely to be thought of as a family possession. Family opinion develops about most matters of interest and is apt to permeate all its members. Generally there is less individual questioning and rebellion. Marriage itself is a duty to the family, a responsibility of the individual for the maintenance of its name and property, often determined by the family for its members, as to whether and whom the individual should marry.

Not only marriage, but also religion, occupation, mode of living, recreation, and politics are far more strongly influenced by family tradition in the rural community than in the city. The morals are, to a large extent, the morals of family cohesion. Deviation from the established code, especially in sex relations, is less tolerated since this is an offense against the unity and function of the family. Prohibited sex relationships occur, to be sure, but more often in the

15. For the class system of a small rural community in the Middlewest see James West (pseudonym), *Plainville, U.S.A.* (New York, 1945), Chap. III.

form of outbursts of repressed desires, with little semblance of romantic love. Divorce is generally less frequent than in the city. There is little place for the man, and still less for the woman, whose life is not rooted in some family circle.

The dominance of the family explains, in large measure, why social control in the rural community is exercised with a minimum of formality and a maximum of command. The group mores, reflecting a commonly shared system of values, are themselves effective as social pressures, in little need of the support of specialized control agencies. Gossip and the other informal devices of social regulation tend to prevent wide departures from the code. When departures are committed, the punishment is apt to be directly administered by those offended—both the family feud and the "shotgun wedding" are essentially rural customs.[16]

[2] *The urban community:* Social control in the city, especially when the community reaches the dimensions of the modern metropolis, reflects the multiplicity of social contacts, the diversity of social codes, and the predominance of secondary relationships that mark the complex society. Regulation itself becomes in large part the activity of specialized associations, including the agencies of the impersonal law. Police and courts and teachers and social workers tend to take over the regulatory functions of the family head or the family circle. If the city dweller's rights are trespassed or if his child is criminally delinquent or if he has offended the legal code, most likely the judge and the law will decide the issue. On the other hand, his deviations from the norms of conduct, sexual and otherwise, may pass unnoticed, relatively unchecked by gossip or opinion, in the impersonalized urban world.

Although there is great diversity here as elsewhere, the city family is typically less engrossing. Urbanization denudes the household of economic functions, as we have seen, and throws the individual into associational relations determined by specific interests of work and temperament. In drawing the contrast, however, between the self-determination of the urbanite and the subjection to family and communal mores of the country dweller, we must avoid the bias of personal predilection. The city dweller is no less a socialized being because his family relationships are less inclusive and because many of his contacts are more impersonal. The scale and variety of his relationships are extended so that they can range from the most superficial to the most intimate and binding. If relationships in rural life gain in quality because they are more persistent, they gain similarly in the city because they are the more definite choice of the individual.

There is no evidence that the countryman is more stupid or that the city

16. These general characteristics are borne out by all important studies of the social life of rural people, where they live in relative isolation. They are well illustrated by Le Play and his successors, and in such studies as W. I. Thomas and F. Znaniecki, *The Polish Peasant* (New York, 1918); C. M. Arensberg, *The Irish Countryman* (New York, 1937); and C. C. Zimmerman, *The Changing Community* (New York, 1938).

dweller is more superficial because the latter faces a greater variety of possible social stimulations.[17] The urban community leaves the choice of activity and of interest more to the individual, but his is no less a socialized personality and the choice is no less a social choice. Country and city are both society, one no more "natural" or "artificial" than the other. But the city as a more differentiated form presents a variegated pattern in which a myriad of individualities seek and find a common life. It has become a dominant type in Western society today, and, therefore, we must examine in greater detail some of its principal features.

Specialization and the urban social structure. We have already indicated certain differences between the social structure of the rural and the urban community, particularly the contrast between the modes of occupation. The most conspicuous difference, in fact, and the source of many minor contrasts, is the specialization that urban concentration develops.

[1] *Occupational specialization and the competitive emphasis:* One condition of specialization is the size of the economic market, a condition guaranteed in the large-scale urban society. The country, as we have seen, calls for the "all-round" man; the city, for the semiskilled worker, the skilled artisan, the technician, the "paper expert," the "white-collar" employee, the professional, the business administrator, the politician, the financier, the artist, and many others. The trades directory of any large city shows a bewildering variety of the most curious and unsuspected types of work. Even unskilled labor has its work specialized in the city, by limitation to a single type of task, while skilled labor grows more specialized both by limitation of tasks and by differentiation of skill—the trend in the urban world, in fact, is clearly in the direction of a larger percentage of specialized *semi*skilled work.[18]

This economic differentiation of the urban community is the source of social groupings, both *vertical*, involving occupational divisions on the same social level, and *horizontal*, or in terms of social status. But these divisions should not be confused with the immobile class or caste divisions that characterized the older types of rural life. For the modern city is essentially *competitive*, with at least some of its members moving up or down the social scale according to their ability and eagerness to seize the opportunities afforded. This vertical mobility together with an even greater amount of horizontal mobility, from occupation to occupation, is a characteristic feature of urban social structure.

Competitiveness is, in part, a concomitant of high specialization. The process of selection is keener, the chances of quick promotion for the owner of special

17. For a discussion of these misconceptions and of the research in this area see, for example, Kolb and Brunner, *op. cit.*, Chap. V.

18. In the United States in 1910 the percentage of semiskilled workers in the labor force was 14.7 as compared with 21.0 in 1940, while the percentage of unskilled workers during the same period dropped from 36.0 to 25.9. See *Statistical Abstract of the United States, 1944–45*, Table No. 144.

ability are greater. Business is keyed to a higher pitch, and management selects employees more rigorously and is more ruthless in discharging those who fall below the competitive standard—hiring and firing are on a more impersonal and rational basis. The able have more incentive to utilize and improve their special talents, for they are usually pitted against their equals or superiors. In this mobile society the individual is rated more in terms of his accomplishments than he is in the relatively static countryside. The city sifts and segregates all of its members, finding a particular place for each, according to the economic and cultural standards of the community.[19]

Consider the example of education. The city provides separate schools for the wealthy, the moderately well to do, and the poor. But it also provides distinctive schools for different forms of education, elementary and advanced, cultural and technical, professional and artistic; and frequently today it provides separate training designed for different grades of intelligence, for the mentally defective, for the backward, for the "average," for the exceptionally bright. In the more isolated rural community these would likely all be thrown together. This illustration suggests that while social status is, to be sure, a determinant and limit of opportunity in the city, its dividing lines are often being crossed and broken by the lines of individual choice and of sheer competitive advantage.

[2] *Social mobility and chance opportunity:* With specialization and competition the speculative element enters strongly into the life of the city. With greater mobility comes greater uncertainty as to the future. Where so many possibilities of individual enterprise exist, the mere vagaries of fortune, good and ill, have increased play. An individual's career is not so much, as in the country, foreordained. An accident, a lucky contact, a sudden opportunity seized or missed, a change of style or fad, a happy or unhappy forecast of some event far beyond his control, may revolutionize his prospects in a day. This maximization of chance opportunity is reflected in the degree to which various forms of gambling, including the "rackets" of the slot machine and "numbers" game, penetrate urban life.[20] The sense of chance is always present in the city, and although it does not essentially diminish the intensity of the competitive struggle, it frequently affects the rewards.

[3] *Areas of specialization in the city:* Another aspect of urban specialization is the blocking out of distinctive areas within the city, each with marked social and cultural peculiarities.

> There are regions in the city in which there are almost no children, areas occupied by the residential hotels, for example. There are regions where the number of children is relatively very high: in the slums, in the middle-class residential

19. On urban social structure see, for example, H. Speier, "Social Stratification in the Urban Community," *American Sociological Review*, I (1936), 193–202. See Chapter XIV below for a more extensive treatment of class stratification.

20. On "policy" or "numbers" in Chicago, see St. C. Drake and H. R. Cayton, *Black Metropolis* (New York, 1945), Chap. XVII.

suburbs, to which the newly married usually graduate from their first honeymoon apartments in the city. There are other areas occupied almost wholly by young unmarried people, boy and girl bachelors. There are regions where people almost never vote, except at national elections; regions where the divorce rate is higher than it is for any state in the Union, and other regions in the same city where there are almost no divorces. There are areas infested by boy gangs and the athletic and political clubs into which the members of these gangs or the gangs themselves frequently graduate. There are regions in which the suicide rate is excessive; regions in which there is . . . an excessive amount of juvenile delinquency, and other regions in which there is almost none.[21]

The larger the city, especially among those of the Western world, the greater is the specialization. This makes of the city, as the ecologists have demonstrated at length, a complex pattern of specialized areas within the more general "ecological structure" of the urban community. The structure varies from city to city, in accordance with differences of size and site and historical development and dominant functions, but in almost every case there is a clearly evident division of space into zones of business activity, of low rentals and residential congestion, of transitory abode, of "middle-class" residence, of expensive dwellings, of industrial concentration, and so forth. This spatial specialization of land use, particularly as revealed in rental differences and those of social prestige between residential areas, is in itself an important index of the urban social structure.[22] Among the innumerable variations of spatial pattern the modern city assumes are those indicated in Chart XI.

[4] *The city and the social position of the sexes:* A further aspect of the urban social structure that has been considerably affected by the industrialization, commercialization, and specialization of city life is the relationship between the sexes. In recent years the increasing "feminization" of many large cities is indicated by the proportion of males to females in the population. In 1940 the number of men per 100 women in Chicago was 98, in New York 97.3, in Philadelphia 95.3, in St. Louis 92.4, and in Kansas City slightly under 91—each of these figures representing a decrease from the more "normal" ratios of 1930.[23] Here we have an indication of the fact that the city becomes more and more a place of opportunity for women, especially the unmarried. Moreover, a growing percentage of the urban population of both sexes belongs to the unmarried group, a situation reflected in the city's larger preoccupation with nonfamilial activities and in its greater degree of social isolation of the

21. R. E. Park, in *The Urban Community* (E. W. Burgess, ed., Chicago: The University of Chicago Press, 1926), pp. 11–12.

22. For an excellent discussion of various aspects of urban social structure, see L. Wirth, "Urbanism as a Way of Life," *American Journal of Sociology*, XLIV (1938), 1–24.

23. *Statistical Abstract of the United States, 1946*, Table No. 21.

CHART XI Generalizations of Area Specialization of Cities[24]

(The following diagrammatical generalizations are only three of the possible patterns of area development of large cities. The concentric-zone theory has sometimes been put forward as a generalization applicable to all cities, but there seem to be many exceptions. The arrangement of sectors in the sector pattern varies from city to city. The multiple nuclei diagram represents one possible pattern among innumerable variations.)

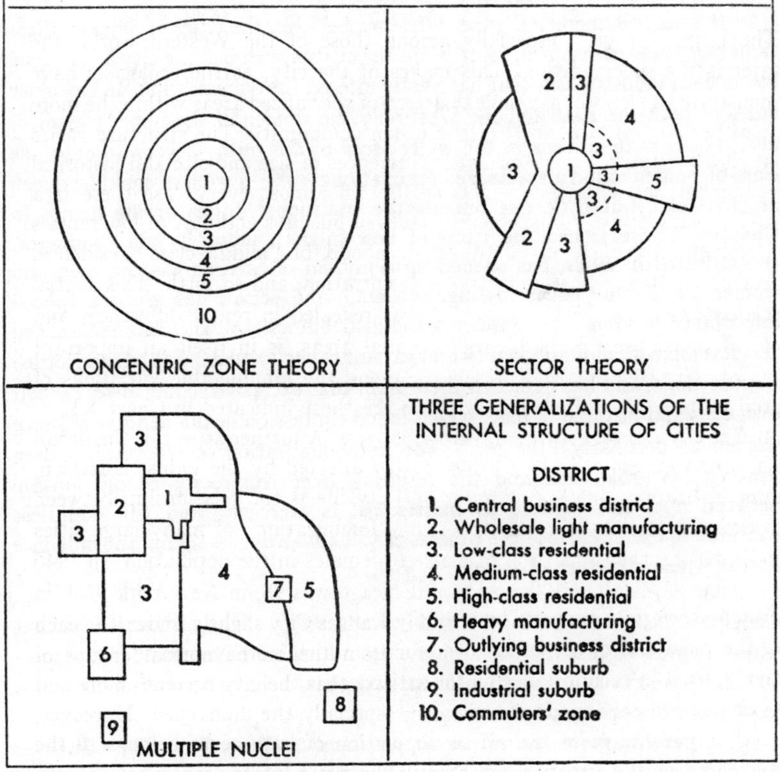

24. Reproduced, by permission, from C. D. Harris and E. L. Ullman, "The Nature of Cities," *The Annals of the American Academy of Political and Social Science*, CCXLII (Nov., 1945), 13. For a detailed study of a different pattern of area specialization in terms of "nonrational" and "rational" adaptation to space, see W. Firey, *Land Use in Central Boston* (Cambridge, Mass., 1947).

individual without primary group ties—a point to which we shall shortly return.[25]

The influence of the urban environment on the social life and attitudes of women has not been explored thoroughly, but certain trends are clear. The changing functions of the family which the city encourages have been of peculiar significance to woman, in her role as mother, wife, housekeeper, and economic producer. Her tasks have been limited and she has been greatly liberated from the exclusiveness of domesticity, though this gain in freedom has not yet removed her from the ambivalent position in which she is often placed by lingering patriarchal attitudes.

In this respect there is a great difference between the cities of older civilizations and those of our own, for it is not the city as such but the city as changed by modern industrialism that has vastly altered the woman's life. In the older cities of both the East and the West only the women of the upper classes, if even these, were citizens in the wider sense of the term. Otherwise only one class of women found a specialized occupational role—a woman could be queen or courtesan, but little else outside the traditional duties of the home. In Chapter XI we traced the story of how modern industry and commerce, concentrated in cities, has opened up a myriad of careers, has put men and women on a more equal footing, economic and social, has given a special importance to women as consumers and distributors of wealth, has encouraged the development of individuality and variant capacity which was once accorded to men alone, and has detached them from that exclusive significance, in their own eyes and in those of men, which found expression in the denomination of women as peculiarly "the sex." The individualization of women has been fostered by urban life, and the resulting freer reciprocity of relationship between men and women, as *individuals*, is exercising and will doubtless continue to exercise, since the process is still advancing, a significant influence on the whole structure of society.[26]

Sociopsychological contrasts between city and country. The distinctive features of the rural and of the urban community, which we have considered respectively, react in each instance on the attitudes and behavior patterns that come to characterize the mode of life.

[1] *Associative individualism versus persistent traditionalism:* The combined influences of the urban scene stimulate what may be called an *associative*

25. The percentage of one-person "families" of all families in the urban population of the United States in 1930 was 8.0 and in 1940 it had grown to 11.1, as contrasted with the rural-farm percentages of 5.2 and 6.3 for the same years. *Statistical Abstract of the United States*, Table No. 48.

26. For a discussion of current trends in this area, see E. K. Nottingham, "Toward an Analysis of the Effects of Two World Wars on the Role and Status of Middle-Class Women in the English-Speaking World," *American Sociological Review*, XII (1947), 666–675; for an interpretation of the modern woman's social situation, M. Mead, "What Women Want," *Fortune Magazine*, Dec., 1946.

individualism. In the thronging presence of his fellow men, and more immediately dependent on their specialized services than is the ruralite, the city dweller must *selectively* organize his social relationships. He is accepted by his fellows more in terms of his own specific qualities. His social needs are fulfilled, not in one familial or neighborhood close-knit group, but in a series of more or less independent memberships. He faces the problem of co-ordinating these into his own social life—here too he has greater chances of success or failure. As a personality he must, more than the countryman, make his own terms with society: he is *detached* except for the stronger or weaker attachments of his own choice. This condition, involving the predominance of secondary over primary relationships, distinguishes the wide range of social attitudes characteristic of the city.[27]

The constant initiative demanded in the social relationships of the urban community evokes qualities standing in marked contrast with those demanded by rural life. The country calls for persistence, a more stern and dogged fidelity to the way of life. The city requires more alertness, quicker responses to changing situations; and satisfactory personal adjustment in the large city may even require the urbanite's adoption of a veneer of protective unawareness against the myriad stimulations surrounding him. This contrast, shown superficially in manners, is revealed more significantly in morals. "Urbanity" belongs to the city, the polite—"How do you do"—but often disinterested manner that makes casual contacts easy and smoothly accommodates one to the diversities of personality and of situation. Similarly, in the diversity of moral codes, of religions, of modes of life, of tastes, and of opinions, the city dweller is more likely to learn tolerance and to make allowances. The rural communities are more apt to ban socially or legally those doctrines and ways of living that the majority disapprove. The countryman is less subject to the comparative criticism leading to the refinement or to the limitation of belief. In their traditional character the rural moral codes tend to be as strict as rural political or economic doctrines. Consequently violations of the code, which of course occur in every rural community, lead to more bitter estrangements and to greater personal tragedies. Yet the countryman, in so far as he remains unaffected by the impact of urban culture, is generally more secure from the questioning quality of city life, which often undermines weak convictions and distracts the lives of many people in our predominantly urban civilization.

[2] *The intensity of community sentiment in city and country:* Community sentiment in the large-scale city has characteristics that clearly distinguish it from the attitudes which bind the countryman to his locality. The contrast is evident when we consider the three predominant aspects of this sociopsychological phenomenon. The *we-feeling* of the city dweller is weakened

27. See, for example, Mirra Komarovsky, "The Voluntary Associations of Urban Dwellers," *American Sociological Review*, XI (1946), 686–698.

by the very complexity of urban society, with its developed division of labor and its multitude of specialized activities—there are many rivals for the allegiance of the individual. The absence of a dominant mode of occupation and the greater impersonality of city life narrow the urbanite's attachments and detract from his feeling of identification with the whole community. His *role-feeling* is similarly affected, for he has little awareness of the roles of most of his fellows, and his own role is very apt to become less significant and meaningful in his own eyes. Thus his *dependency-feeling* is likewise lessened. Note, for example, the relative psychological ease with which the city dweller can detach himself from the community when he moves to another—his feeling of loss is usually much less intense than that of the countryman when he is uprooted from his traditional surroundings.

Here we have once more a significant illustration of sociology's central concern, the interdependent relationship between the personality of the individual being and the social and cultural pattern within which the former is expressed. Our contrast between city and country is necessarily a contrast between two distinguishable forms of this fundamental relationship.

The cultural contrast and relationship between city and country. We may conclude this brief survey by referring to certain cultural contrasts, as these are affected by and in turn influence the two broad types of community organization. It may be true, as some writers maintain, that all great cultures of the past, in the general forms of creative imagination and world outlook which inspired them, have originated in the country and have been developed in the city. We can agree, at least, that a purely urban culture, divorced from the types of stimulation found in the rural community, would be fundamentally unbalanced and creatively handicapped. The country reveals the significance of permanence. It leads man beyond himself, to a consideration of nature's great forces, to the larger interdependent life of earth and plant and animal, to the more inclusive pattern of which his own life, whatever the level of his civilization, is but a part. It offers the ageless wonders of life, beside which man's own accomplishments often seem puny and temporary. It reveals for some an infinitude of forms and colors and harmonies and rhythms that repeatedly bring fresh inspiration to the arts. To this extent the country provides the raw materials of the cultural as well as the economic life of man.

Cultural expression in the countryside tends to retain a relatively simple form, as folk lore, folk legends, folk songs, folk dances. These are taken up into the arts of the city and reshaped to its specialized and variant demands. The urbanite, in his more changeful and heterogeneous community, wants, among other things, novelty and excitation. In the city these cultural materials are used in distinctively urban ways. Sometimes they are merely embroidered into sophisticated and transient forms, and occasionally they are transformed into rich and new cultural expressions. Both the symphonies of Beethoven, which are vastly more than mere variations of the simple folk airs on which they are based, and the more recent, if possibly less significant, development from its folk origins of jazz music in New Orleans and Kansas City and Chicago illustrate this cultural process.[28]

There are numerous detailed contrasts between the culture of the countryside and that of the city, contrasts that are discernible in spite of the many diversities exhibited within the latter. They are discussed in detail in a large number of demographic studies and social surveys that have been undertaken during the past century.[29] These contrasts are often revealed in the works of novelists depicting urban or rural life. The countryside is vividly portrayed, for example, by writers like Hardy and Hamsun and Rölvaag, the "classical" rural novelists, and by such moderns as Dreiser and Caldwell and Steinbeck. Less comprehensive treatment of various aspects of city life, understandable in view of its greater complexity, is seen in such novels as those of Dickens and Proust and, more recently, of Dos Passos, Farrell, and Halper.

The social structure of the city is necessarily as complex as its culture, presenting a variety of extremes and modulations. It stands in contrast to the countryside with its forms of accentuation, intensification, or sophistication. The difference in the last resort is one of contrasting types of social organization, of the nature, kind, and number of social relationships to which the members of the two groups are exposed.

Interaction and Dominance

The city as a center of dominance. In the preceding section we sought to portray characteristic differences between the urban and rural communities. To a considerable extent we had to rely on common observation rather than on specific indices of a quantitative character. Moreover, since our purpose was to emphasize a broad contrast, we tended to treat each type of common life as though it were self-contained, as though no influences emanating from either of them greatly affected the character of the other. In this section we shall qualify our picture by considering the process of interaction between city and country, presenting objective evidences of the changing relationship between the two.

In the process of interaction, the attitudes, the modes of life, and the institutions of the city tend to become predominant over those of the country.

28. Jazz music, usually viewed as a fad in the 1920's and even later, has persisted and expanded in a variety of forms; there is a growing body of sociological literature in this area. See, for example, M. Berger, "Jazz: Resistance to the Diffusion of a Culture Pattern," *The Journal of Negro History*, XXXII (1947), 461–494.

29. This cultural contrast was explored by Le Play and his school and by many others. See, for example, Sorokin and Zimmerman, *Principles of Rural-Urban Sociology*, Chap. XXI.

The reasons are not difficult to trace. The city has the prestige of power and wealth and specialized knowledge. It holds the keys of finance. It is the market to which the ruralite must turn in order to buy and sell and borrow. Its people, habituated to many contacts, have the advantage, when city and country meet, of being more articulate, more expansive, and, superficially at least, more alert. The products the city sends to the country, unlike those it receives from it, carry with them something of the urban culture, of its way of life and its techniques. Consequently, in the intercourse of city and country, the former tends to dominate. In all the great civilizations of the past, where to be sure the vast majority of the population remained peasants, the influence of the urban centers has overshadowed any other. In our own civilization the dominance of the city has been greatly intensified by two new phenomena. On the one hand, the contacts of city and country are far closer and more numerous than ever before. On the other hand, the urban population has been increasing in proportion to the rural so that now, in almost all countries where industrialism is well advanced, an actual majority of the total population is in some sense *urban*.

The growth of cities in recent times. The distinctive rise of these two related phenomena, the multiplication of rural-urban contacts and the increasing proportion of urban population, belongs to the history of the last century and a half. The rapidity and size of urban growth during this period have been significant factors in determining the nature of modern social organization.

[1] *The growth itself:* By the close of the eighteenth century the growth of cities was already manifest in England, the home of the industrial revolution. But while at this date England had 21 per cent of its population inhabitating cities of 10,000 or over, France had less than 10, Prussia about 7, and Russia and the United States were close together with less than 4 per cent. The proportion of the rural population of these and other countries has been declining ever since with considerable regularity, though the speed of urbanization has varied from country to country as indicated by the figures in Table VIII.

The percentage of urban population steadily rose in the United States from its earliest days; between 1910 and 1920 it exceeded the rural for the first time, as reckoned in terms of the Census Bureau's definition of "urban" as an aggregation of 2,500 or more. By 1920 the rural population had fallen to 48.6 per cent, and by 1930 to 43.8 per cent of the total. The most recent official figures, for 1940, show a further slight decline of the rural group to 43.5 per cent, suggesting a significant retardation of urban growth in this country. While it is true that the rate of growth of large-scale cities has been slowing down in recent years, the urbanization process itself has not lost its force, a view supported by a breakdown of rural-urban data. In 1946, for example, sample studies indicated that 60 per cent of the civilian population lived in

TABLE VIII **Percentages of Total Populations of Different Countries Living in Urban Areas of 20,000 or More**[30]

Year	United States	England and Wales	France	Germany
1800	—	20.0	—	—
1860	—	54.6	28.9	—
1890	35.4	72.0	37.4	47.0
1930	56.2	80.0	49.1	67.1

urban places, and of the remaining 40 per cent almost half were residents of rural *nonfarm* sections of the country, showing that only about 20 per cent of our total population could be classified as *rural-farm.*[31] In any event, probably no more than one quarter of our people today are associated with the distinctly rural mode of life that was followed by the overwhelming majority a century ago. The long-range trends reflecting this change in the American social structure are evidenced by the figures in Table IX.

TABLE IX **Distribution of the Population, by Size of Community, United States: 1850–1940**[32]

Area	1850		1900		1940	
	No. of places	Per cent	No. of places	Per cent	No. of places	Per cent
Urban	236	15.3	1,737	39.7	3,464	56.5
100,00 and over	6	5.0	38	18.8	92	28.8
25,000–100,000	20	3.8	122	7.3	320	11.2
10,000– 25,000	36	2.4	280	5.7	665	7.6
2,500– 10,000	174	4.0	1,297	8.0	2,387	8.9
Rural (including farm and nonfarm)	—	84.7	—	60.3	—	43.5

[2] *The metropolis:* During the process of urban growth cities have been increasing in size and differentiating from one another. Moreover, the concentra-

30. For more extensive comparative figures see, for example, Gist and Halbert, *Urban Society*, Chap. II; *Our Cities*, pp. 25 ff.
31. *Statistical Abstract of the United States, 1947*, Table No. 12; for further figures see Table Nos. 13, 14, and 15.
32. Adapted from W. S. Thompson, in *Cities Are Abnormal* (E. T. Peterson, ed., Norman, Okla., 1946), p. 56.

tion of population has been increasing in the areas of higher density. In the United States the percentage of population living in cities of 100,000 and over rose from 5 in 1850 to almost 29 in 1940 (see Table IX). This concentration appears to have been greatly retarded since 1930, with cities of 500,000 and larger having exactly the same percentage of total population, 17, for the years 1930 and 1940. However, cities differ from one another in the rapidity of their growth with some, such as Los Angeles and Washington, showing huge gains during this ten-year period and others, such as Philadelphia and Boston and Cleveland, indicating an actual loss of population.

While there is, in most countries, a metropolis outtopping all the rest in its intense concentration of power and influence as well as population, other great cities have arisen, diverse in quality and in form, each a distinctive embodiment of the urban community. Chicago has a different character from Philadelphia, Philadelphia from Detroit or from Los Angeles. Beside them flourish smaller cities of all ranges, mediating between the metropolis and the countryside and often more alien to the former than to the latter. At the top of the list tower a few cosmopolitan centers, such as New York, London, Moscow, Paris, Shanghai, and Buenos Aires, whose power and influence radiate far beyond the boundaries of their own countries.[33]

Technological and organizational aspects of urban dominance. If most of the great civilizations of the past were city-fostered and, at least in their later stages, city-dominated, they still on the whole left the rural community life little changed. The cities could tax the countryman for their luxury or devastate his lands for their wars, but they could not greatly alter its social characteristics. The peasant, as Spengler has said, was, in a sense, "beyond history." The situation today is vastly different.

[1] *The impact of technical advance:* In modern society, it is not simply that the techniques of our civilization are inexorably making city dwellers of the majority of the population, but rather that the very techniques that draw people to the cities carry the influence and quality of urban life to all but the remotest recesses of the countryside. One of the chief manifestations of this process is the annihilation of physical distance as a barrier to intercommunication, to the contagion of ideas and modes of living. Of the factors we enumerated in the previous section as characteristic features of the rural community, one in particular, its cultural isolation, is being eliminated. With its elimination the influence of the other factors—the relative social isolation, the direct contact with nature, the predominant mode of occupation, the absence of specialization, the comparative frugality of living—is inevitably reduced.

---

33. In the late 1930's there were 17 cities of a million or more in Europe, 12 in North America, 11 in Asia, 3 in South America, 2 in Australia, and 1 in Africa.

It is a commonplace sociological observation that social influences radiate from centers of prestige and wealth and power. Modern techniques have enormously influenced this process. If the automobile, the airplane, the telephone, the radio, and the press play the major role in linking the remotest sections to the urban foci, such agencies as the chain store with its array of prepared foods, the devices purveying "canned music," the ubiquitous motion-picture theatre, and especially the mail-order catalogue enhance the urban impact upon rural life. The mass media of communication are particularly the carriers of culture, though we do not imply that the culture carried by radio and newspaper and film is "higher" or "lower." The significant point is that they almost always bring the more urban culture to the country, and not vice versa. For in the dominating position are the giant broadcasting companies with their outlets in the large and small cities, the centrally located and controlled movie producers, the offices of the great urban newspaper and magazine companies which supply the rural press with cheap "boiler plate" or the rural store with standardized news and feature weeklies.

[2] *The spread of urban types of organization:* Besides the social prestige and the technical advantages of the city, another factor operates to increase its growing dominance. We have seen that wherever the opportunity is present there is a tendency in social life for specific interests to become articulate and to form the basis of *associations*. The small isolated community holds these interests under restraint. Its foci of organization, its meeting places, from the corner grocery store to the church, necessarily take on a general character and involve the activities of most of the community members—in a "rural society it is generally possible to predict on the basis of a few known factors who will belong to what and who will associate with whom in almost every relationship."[34] The rural community's social occasions, its feasts, funerals, parades, the village entertainment, can make little provision for the varying specific interests of different individuals. Where locality is the most important basis of social activity the sense of community is pervasive but undifferentiated. This means a certain repression—often unrecognized, especially among the older members—of those specific interests that cannot easily be accommodated to the more homogeneous life.

However, these special interests are given an opportunity for expression in the form of associational development whenever communications and contacts are facilitated. The locality basis of organization gradually yields to the demands of specific interests. The rural community tends to assume more closely the type of social structure characteristic of the city. When the countryside becomes differentiated along the lines of particular activities and interests, economic and educational and recreational and according to age or sex, the primary type of community rooted in locality gives way, in some degree, to

34. Wirth, "Urbanism as a Way of Life," 22.

the multigroup, complex social organization of the urban center. This change is brought out graphically in Chart XII.

The city is the center of innovation, and its constant impact not only changes the social organization but undermines the social conservatism and established custom of the rural community. The results are evident in many directions.

CHART XII **Figure Suggesting the Relation of Interest Groups to Locality Groups in Rural Life**[35]

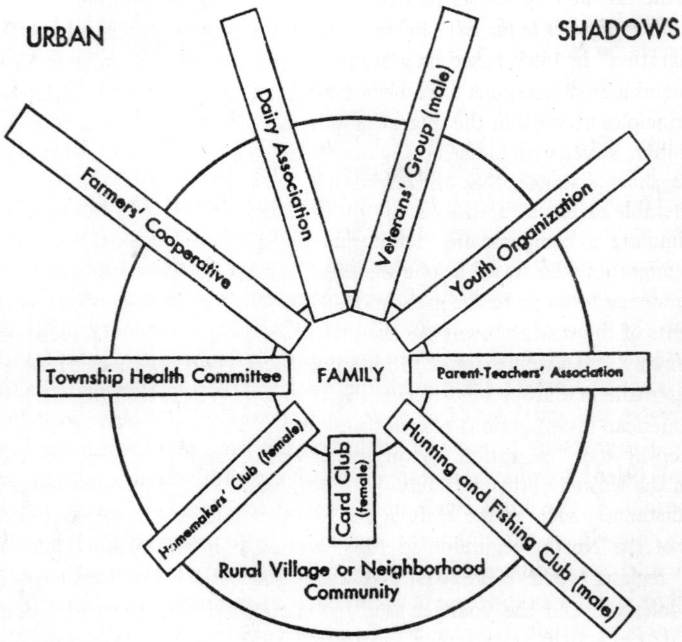

Statistics of many lands, viewed over a period of from thirty to seventy years, show that, with respect to birth rate, death rate, age of marriage, infant mortality, divorce, suicide, church affiliation, and so forth, rural indices are moving nearer to urban indices. These changes could not take place unless the more subtle and less measurable characteristics of urban life—its competi-

35. This chart is suggested by the similar one of J. H. Kolb in "Family and Rural Organization," *Proceedings* of the American Sociological Society, XXIII (1928), 147. However, the organizations depicted are among those investigated by C. H. Page in a small village of southern Vermont in the spring of 1948.

tive emphasis, its varied and less rigid codes, its more questioning attitudes, its greater specialization—were filtering into rural organization.[36]

The problem of dominance in selective migration to the city. We have seen that a large proportion of the increasing urban population of recent times has been supplied by migration from the countryside. It is sometimes held that this movement has brought to the urban community the characteristics of the rural people and their way of life. However, the migrants, dispersed within the urban environment and subject to its many influences, sooner or later become adjusted to city conditions and lose their rural customs and habituations. Nevertheless the city selects its newcomers in one way or another.

[1] *Who migrates to the city and why?* Since Ravenstein published his "Laws of Migration" in 1885, based on a study of the population of cities in Britain, innumerable investigations have been undertaken in an attempt to determine the principles at work in the migration of people from one type of community to another. Ravenstein himself came to the conclusion that most migrants move only a short distance, that the moves to the large cities are therefore to a considerable extent a "step-by-step" process, that each large movement tends to stimulate a compensating countermovement of population, that among those migrants who travel a long distance from their own communities there is a tendency to move to the great industrial and commercial centers, that the residents of the smaller towns are less migratory than those of the countryside, and, finally, that women tend to be more migratory than men. More recent studies made in Europe tend to confirm most of these conclusions, while various American investigations bear out some of them but qualify or alter others.[37]

"Step-by-step" migration, characteristic of European countries, takes place also in the United States, but here there have been large-scale movements over long distances, such as the shift of the Negroes from the rural South to the cities of the North, beginning in 1910, and the migrations from the "dust-bowl" regions to the West coast. We know, moreover, that the city attracts the adolescent and the younger adult people rather than the very young or the old; since 1920 at least one third of the total migration to cities in the United States has been made up of persons between fifteen and twenty-five years of age. Again, there is considerable evidence that the city attracts young women even more than it does young men, for the country offers less economic opportunity to the former than to the latter. These two selective factors have definitely influenced the population structure of the urban community, swelling

36. For evidence of these changes see, for example, Kolb and Brunner, *op. cit.*, Chap. XVI; and for a detailed study of one rural community, West, *Plainville, U. S. A.*, especially Chap. VI.

37. Cf. E. G. Ravenstein, "The Laws of Migration," *Journal of the Royal Statistical Society*, XLVIII (1885), 167–235; this study is discussed in the light of more recent investigations in Gist and Halbert, *Urban Society*, pp. 263 ff.

the proportion of its members of the most vigorous years, and tending, as we have already seen, to unbalance the sex ratio; they have also operated to remove from the country its "excess" of young persons.

Some studies indicate a tendency of members of the less successful farm families to migrate to the cities, a situation we might expect. For there are many who are urged to the urban centers by sheer economic pressure, since the rural birth rate is higher and its occupational opportunities have been diminishing. On the other hand, some individuals find their capacities repressed and their ambitions thwarted in the rural environment and turn to the avenues of advance the city offers. Among the latter group there is very likely a high proportion of the more gifted among the country-born. The larger cities provide better schools and more specialized training, both cultural and professional, and they offer greater hope to talent. But these observations are concerned primarily with *opportunity*, and should not lead us to any easy generalizations about the *quality* of the migrants as compared with those who remain in the rural areas.[38]

The growth of cities in the United States has been greatly abetted by the influx of two groups, immigrants from abroad and Negroes from our own countryside. The former, as we pointed out in an earlier chapter, came into this country in a series of migrations that have taken place during the last hundred years; the latter have entered the larger urban centers in great numbers since the early 1900's. In 1910 the population of Chicago, for example, was almost 36 per cent foreign-born and 2 per cent Negro; in 1920 the corresponding percentages were 29.8 and 4.1; and by 1944 they were 17.1 and 9.3.[39] The city's principal appeal to both of these migrations, as to most others, has been the promise, though not always the fulfillment, of greater economic and social opportunity for their members.

There are many, of course, whom the city attracts on other grounds—the restless, the seekers of amusement or excitement, the exploiters, the nonconformists, the lovers of crowds. To these, including the genius and the criminal, the sensitive and the superficial, the contributors to civilization and those who prey upon it, the atmosphere of the great city is more congenial than that of either the small town or the countryside. The city is a complex selective agency, even though the rapid expansion of the urban population has lessened the discrimination of its selection. There seems little doubt, however, that its promise of opportunity and its emphasis on youth have served to enhance the dominance of the city.

[2] *Does the city select "better types"*? Various studies have sought to discover

38. For detailed statistical data on migrations see, for example, C. Goodrich, *et al.*, *Migration and Economic Opportunity;* and U.S. Bureau of the Census, *Sixteenth Census of the United States: 1940*, Special Reports, *Internal Migration, 1935-1940*, 4 vols. (Washington, D.C., 1943 and 1946).

39. Drake and Cayton, *op. cit.*, p. 9.

whether or not the city robs the countryside of its finer human resources. The problem here is extremely difficult, and the investigations of rural-urban differences of physical type, susceptibility to various diseases, "emotional instability," and the like, throw little light on the selective process itself. How far "urban" characteristics, such as minor physical traits, lower rates in the case of certain physical maladies (and higher in others), and psychological disturbance, are due to the fact that the city attracts particular types, and how far the urban environment works selectively on all within its influence, we cannot tell. We find, as we might expect, that city children display in health and in intelligence a greater range of deviation from the mean than do country children. Certain researches show that among some groups young people tend to migrate to the cities whose intelligence-test scores are slightly higher than the scores of the youth remaining in the country. On the other hand, some studies indicate that no such differences exist in certain rural groups, for example the Negroes, and that performance on these tests tends to improve as children become accommodated to the urban environment. The tests themselves, as we saw in Chapter IV, not only tend to be "urban" in their orientation, but tell us little or nothing about the relative significance of heredity and environment or, to put it otherwise, about the "natural types" that are drawn to the city.[40]

Nor should it be forgotten that within the city itself a further selective process takes place. There is migration from as well as to it. There are types of temperament and of constitution, perhaps also of nationality or of race, which adapt themselves more quickly or more thoroughly to its conditions. Here we are making no assumption that such types are "better" or "fitter" in any broad moral or biological significance, for there is adaptation to city slums as well as to its "residential areas," there is adaptation to the privations which the city, with its congestion and its high cost of living, enforces on the poor, no less than adaptation to the luxuries which it opens to the wealthy. The principle of social selection, as will be shown in a later part of this volume, is far too intricate and many-sided to be reduced to the delusively simple dichotomy of better and worse. Every environment is selective in numerous ways, by its attraction for certain types and groups and by its operation on those who live within it, sorting and segregating, affecting grade and station, success and failure, even life and death. It appeals to some types more than to others, calling them from without, but it also modifies all types within its range. Here our only valid conclusion is that the selective action of the city upon its membership combines with its attractive action to produce those types that enhance its cultural and social dominance.

Pessimistic interpretations of urban dominance. The dominance of the city is

40. For a discussion of several of these studies see, for example, Gist and Halbert, *op. cit.*, pp. 278–293.

regarded by several students of social life as offering an explanation not only of the development but also of the decay of civilizations. This interpretation, though expressed in quite different ways and with varying degrees of emphasis, can be found in the writings of such "historical sociologists" as Oswald Spengler, Werner Sombart, Alfred J. Toynbee, P. A. Sorokin, Patrick Geddes, and Lewis Mumford. The views of the first and the last of these writers illustrate vividly the pessimistic interpretation of urban dominance.

[1] *Examples of "urbanism as social decay"*: The most extreme statement of this view is Spengler's treatment of "the soul of the city."[41] For him the great cosmopolitan center represents a stage in the history of each major civilization, a stage that prepares its dissolution. Not only does the city as such drain into itself the vitality of the countryside, but the world-city fulfills a tendency inherent in all urban life. It stimulates to the full the intellectual activity of man and at the same time undermines his "instinct" activity. Its artificiality is contrasted with the native simplicity of the country; its tension with the "animal harmony" of peasant life. The city destroys the solidarity of the kin, the family, the "blood," the nation, and with its competitive stress fosters the disintegrating attitudes, as Spengler regards them, of individualism, socialism, rationalism, and cosmopolitanism. Finally the meaning of these attitudes is revealed in the sterility of civilized man, the failure of the group will to live, and depopulation results. "The wheel of destiny rolls on to its end; the birth of the city entails its death." The chief difference between Spengler's doctrine and those of other proponents of the decadent role of the city is that while Spengler writes as though the city were the *cause* of these phenomena of decay, he in fact views the cosmopolis as only a symptom of an inevitable process. He is dominated, as were many earlier writers, by the misleading organic analogy. For him the great city is merely the type of community appropriate to a late stage in the fated life history of every civilization

Lewis Mumford, our second example, not only is strongly critical of Spengler's organicism as well as of other aspects of his works but is a representative of an entirely different tradition of social thought. Following the lead of the earlier studies of Patrick Geddes, who viewed the development of urbanization as a cyclical growth, Mumford outlines several stages of that process.[42] *Eopolis* is the collective village community, a type that remains in all societies notwithstanding the presence of cities, while *polis*, the second stage, involves the association of villages or kin-groups and the growth of a distinct division of labor. Great agricultural advances and the extension of trade permit the rise of the third stage, *metropolis*, and with it marked separation of classes and the rise of social criticism—Dantean Florence, Shakespearean London, and Emersonian Boston are among Mumford's illustrations. He sees the beginning

41. O. Spengler, *Decline of the West* (C. F. Atkinson, tr., New York, 1926), Vol. II, Chap. IV.
42. Mumford, *The Culture of Cities*, Chap. IV.

of civilizational decline when "the city under the influence of a capitalistic mythos concentrates upon bigness and power"; this *megalopolis* stage is marked by the dominance of the profit motive, display, speculation, the "triumph of mechanism," passivity, the predominance of large cities over small—Alexandria in the third century B.C., Rome in the second century A.D., Paris in the eighteenth century, early twentieth-century New York. His final stages, *tyrannopolis* and *nekropolis*, represent the crumbling of urban civilization through dictatorial control, destruction of the arts and sciences, the spread of war and famine and disease. This portrayal, similar to Spengler's in many respects, is not, however, defended by Mumford as an inevitable historical process. To him the large-scale urban community contains cataclysmic potentialities, to be sure, but it contains also, if man chooses to plan and to decentralize his cities, if man chooses to use them, the possibilities for a finer common life.

[2] *Is the pessimism justified?* We need not read a gloomy Spengler or a more hopeful Mumford in order to recognize the undesirable aspects of city life. But the conclusion of the former that all great civilizations end in an "appalling depopulation" after the cities have absorbed and "sterilized" the best blood of the country is an unjustified generalization. We may cite certain factors that are generally overlooked by those who hold extreme views regarding the destructive role of the city.

In the first place, it should be noted that, so far as healthful living is concerned, man is gradually making the urban environment more adjusted to his needs, and perhaps at the same time is himself becoming adjusted more adequately to its conditions. In the more favorable areas of the city healthfulness and length of life show a better record than that of the country, and in recent years the infant-mortality rate, though not the mortality rate for older age groups, has been considerably lower in metropolitan areas as a whole than in rural communities. These trends are emphasized by two of our outstanding rural sociologists:

> There was a time when rural leaders boasted, with justification, of the natural advantages of rural life—fresh air, sunshine, and direct access to food. They pointed to lower disease and death rates in the country . . . , to a longer life expectancy, and to smaller chances of contracting diseases spread by personal contacts.
>
> Recently many of these trends have been reversed . . . . the rates are decreasing in both the rural and urban [areas], but the health of city people has been improving rapidly, while progress in rural areas has been relatively slow. . . . In 1900, the rural death rate was 50 per cent under the urban, but in 1940, it was only 10 per cent lower. . . . Of even greater significance was the fact that death rates from preventable diseases tended to be higher in rural than in urban areas.[43]

43. J. H. Kolb and E. de S. Brunner, *A Study of Rural Society* (Boston: Houghton Mifflin Company, 1946), p. 573.

The increased health of cities has been brought about largely by improved sanitation and the development of preventive medicine. That much further improvement is possible and greatly needed is clear to all who are aware of the evils of urban congestion, who appreciate how relatively little has yet been done to abate such health menaces as city smoke and lack of light and air and living space in its crowded tenements, who know how the growth of most cities has been haphazard and uncontrolled and exploitative, and with how little care for the health and convenience of the poorer citizens they have generally been administered. But this knowledge is not a ground for the condemnation of cities as such, but is rather an important reason to seek a more intelligent and planned control over the urban environment. As we pointed out in the preceding chapter, only in quite recent years have most urban communities begun to realize that city planning is something vastly more important than laying out a checkerboard design.[44]

Beyond the question of health and life expectancy, there is that of the maintenance of population numbers in the urban community. The growth of cities could not have taken place save for the influx from the country. Moreover, the urban birth rate has fallen to such low levels in all but a few centers of Western civilization that the continued maintenance of their existing population depends in large part upon continued migration from the rural areas. This situation, however, should not be interpreted as involving the inevitable collapse of the large-scale city. There is no convincing evidence of Spengler's claim that the biological fecundity of man is affected by urban conditions. Nor is there ground to assume that the lower fertility rates of the city must necessarily continue to decline; in fact some groups, such as the Jews, long habituated to urban life, have shown under favorable conditions relatively higher birth rates than others less experienced in city living. But even the assumption of a future population decline, as predicted, for example, for the United States in the next twenty or thirty years, is not sufficient reason for gloomy pessimism, unless we are more concerned with the quantity of human beings than with their quality. Furthermore, if the city depends upon the country for a proportion of its numbers, it is no less true that the country could not maintain its higher fertility and avoid the poverty of previous centuries without the economic opportunities the city affords to its surplus. The remarkable process revealed in the growth of cities is one to which both city and country make equally important but very different contributions—a point of particular significance in our consideration of the region.

44. On planning for better health see, for example, E. C. Potter, "Health and Welfare Services," *The Annals of the American Academy of Political and Social Science*, CCXLII (1945). 139-148.

The Region and Regionalism

The breakdown of the country-city division. The influence of the city continues to be dominant in our civilization. But the urban and rural communities cannot be viewed as always standing apart, in relative isolation and frequently in antagonism. For there is a tendency for these two types of social organization and human environment to coalesce, a trend according to one sociologist "in which the specifically urban and rural traits are merged together, preserving the plusses of both and decreasing the shortcomings of each of these agglomerations. This new trend is emerging in only a few regions and countries, but it is bound to develop more and more, creating thus a new form of sociocultural world."[45]

This "rurbanization" process, as it is sometimes called, shows itself in the fact that the country is becoming, in many respects, urbanized, just as a new community environment is being shaped for large numbers of city dwellers that includes an element of rural life. The city throws its suburbs further and further into the country. With improved means of communication and transportation it is increasingly possible for many to live in the country and work in the city, and for others to spend their week-ends and their holidays in rural surroundings. The development of electrical power is decreasing the economic advantage of industrial congestion, and the possibilities of atomic energy in this respect may be tremendous. The city is creating a great hinterland that is gradually forming one community with the urban nucleus—the metropolitan region. Just as the dwellers of city and country are being brought nearer to one another in the process of interaction and dominance, as we have seen, so, though in less degree, the environments of city and country are tending to become the common possession of all those who inhabit certain large areas. These areas, the home of city and country alike, are the *regions* we must briefly examine in this final section.

The regional approach to community study. In previous chapters we have had occasion to discuss the regional approach. Here we are less concerned with the detailed techniques and findings of this "higher ecology," as a foremost regionalist has termed it, than to indicate its general significance in the study of community life.

[1] *The development of regionalism:* Investigation of the relationship between place and social life, as we know, has been of major interest to European and and American sociologists for at least a century. The development of the "new regionalism" in recent years has been principally associated with the researches of Professor H. W. Odum and his colleagues at the University of North Carolina

---

45. P. A. Sorokin, *Society, Culture, and Personality* (New York, 1947), p. 302.

and with the related efforts of certain governmental agencies to discover the larger areas of community life that are emerging as more or less unified, though not independent, divisions of our nation. Significantly, regionalism as we know it today grew out of the concern with and the investigation of rural social life and rural folk culture, especially that of the Southern area of the United States. The unique qualities of the rural community together with the impact upon it of urban civilization became for the regionalists principal reasons for their studies, and have greatly stimulated their search for an approach that would somehow bring together scientific methods of investigation, a recognition and delineation of regional differences, and an adequate basis for the planning of a more balanced and satisfactory way of life for those living in the socially and culturally distinct geographical areas of the larger nation.

Its leading exponent has described regionalism as a science, an "American frontier," a tool for governmental use, and a goal.[46] Its claim of being a science is based upon its use of acceptable research methods in bringing together a unified body of historical, geographical, and social data that permits us to understand more realistically the life of man. As a "frontier," it views the "conservation and development of the resources in relation to the people in each of these great regions" as a central problem as challenging as that faced by the frontiersmen themselves. Moreover, if governmental policy making and planning are to be geared to the realities of the geographical distribution of culture and modes of life, it is claimed that regionalism must become a technique employed by the state. Finally, its advocates recognize regionalism as "a great purpose or motivation," a goal to be sought by those who are trying to achieve a more finely integrated community.

[2] *The integrated region and decentralization:* A fundamental aim of regionalism is the closer integration of the traditional rural society and the modern urban civilization. The former, as we have seen, gives man a sense of permanence, a feeling of oneness with his fellows and with the earth they share. The city, with its developed technology and its concentrated harnessing of power facilities, with its cultural variations and modifications, whatever problems it creates for man, enormously enriches the social heritage. But we have not yet discovered or, at any rate, have not made effective those methods that permit the common sharing of the cultural heritage by city dwellers and countrymen alike, or those that foster the creation of a balanced way of life for both groups. The regionalist, therefore, seeks to bring about the elimination of isolation and of economic and cultural backwardness in rural life, and at the same time to eradicate the congestion and impersonality and what amounts to the urban

46. H. W. Odum in *In Search of the Regional Balance in America* (Odum and K. Jocher, eds., Chapel Hill, N.C., 1945), pp. 11–13. This is a useful volume for the history, point of view, and techniques of regionalism; see especially chapters by Odum, R. P. Vance, E. W. Williams, and C. H. Pritchett.

ethnocentrism of city life. His aim is the development of an integrated large community within which city and country each has its place and makes its contribution.

What, then, are the areas of human habitation that constitute the unit of the regionalist's interest and within which he envisions the potentiality for a better integration? Each region, to begin with, is a locality having a "specific geographic character: certain common properties of soil, climate, vegetation, agriculture and technical exploitation."[47] This geographical requirement suggests, for example, the "lowlands" of Western Europe, most of Southeastern Asia, the great river-valley areas of China, or, within the United States, the Deep South or the Northwest or the New England states. In each of these the natural setting has its own peculiar qualities that necessarily affect and are affected by the social and cultural ways of the inhabitants. Secondly, a region, in so far as it has become an integrated area of social life, exhibits "a balance, a state of dynamic equilibrium, between its various parts." This requirement has various aspects. It means that technological or social changes introduced in any part of the region will, directly or indirectly, bring about changes in the entire region. And it means that a region must be large enough to encompass a variety of interests and activities, urban and rural and industrial and agricultural, to ensure balance, though not economic or political self-sufficiency. On the other hand, the region must be small enough "to keep these interests in focus and to make them a subject of direct collective concern." Finally, the region is not a political area with sharply drawn boundaries—indeed political lines are often a major hindrance to "proper" regional development. Regions merge into one another, forming interdependent units of the larger community, and their margins are shifting areas or "intermediate zones."[48]

A partial justification, at least, of this conception of the balanced and integrated region is found, as we shall see, in certain clearly evident trends in modern social life. One of these and one of central significance to the regionalist is the tendency toward *decentralization* of the concentrated urban civilization. Not only must cities be encouraged to disperse further their habitations over wider areas, but modern technology must be utilized to break up large-scale industries into smaller and more scattered units so that the rural-urban balance may be developed throughout the larger regions. As several of the regionalists see it, decentralization provides the possibility of the re-establishment of smaller, more intimate communities, making these more effective units in the political and economic life of the greater society, and even stimulates a generally richer cultural production. "Thus, regionalism becomes the tool for decentralization . . . and if there is any way to prevent totalitarianism in a great complex, urban and industrial civilization of standardized tendency and to retain a

47. Mumford, *The Culture of Cities*, p. 312.

48. *Ibid.*, pp. 312–315.

quality civilization in a quantity world, it is through regionalism that it must be effected."[49]

The emergence of regions in the United States. We need not defend, nor need we dispute, these large claims of regionalism's advocates in order to recognize the actuality of the region as a significant intranational (and international) focus of community life. Let us consider, as an important example, the case of the United States.

[1] *Marks of regional division:* There are many ways in which this nation has been and continues to be broken into subareas other than those imposed by the political divisions between states. Much of our country's history, in fact, as several of its foremost students have explained at length, has been one of conflict between opposing interests of different sections, between North and South, between East and West, between subsections of these larger areas. Sectionalism in the United States is often the regionalist's starting point, for his own approach is one that aims to supplant the "divisive power of self-seeking *sections*" with the "integrating power of co-ordinate *regions* fabricated into a united whole."[50] But the older sections themselves—the business and industrial dominated East, the agrarian West, the plantation and slaveowning South—were significant marks of broad regional variation, however harmful were their conflicts to the larger national interest.

Today there are several indications of regional division, or, more exactly, several types of regions in the United States. First, and most easily depicted, are the country's "natural regions," the large areas set apart from one another by geographical characteristics, by conditions of climate and soil and topography, and by the linkage imposed on this or that locality by a great river or chain of lakes or some other natural phenomena. Here we have a basis for the corn belt, for example, and for the northeastern dairy region, the cotton belt running through the South, and other areas marked by distinctive occupational specialization. Secondly, there are the "cultural regions," the localities possessing their own folkways, "regional" literature and other forms of aesthetic expression. Finally, there are the innumerable "service regions," those divisions of the nation set up for purposes of governmental or business administration. An exceedingly large body of literature exists dealing with each of these three types of regional growth and with the many subtypes found within each. Geographers, economists, political scientists, sociologists, students of literature

49. Odum, *In Search of the Regional Balance . . .*, p. 11. For characteristic statements on the economic, political, and cultural advantages of decentralization see the chapters by P. L. Vogt, J. J. Rhyne, S. C. McConahey, H. C. Nixon, and R. L. Smith in *Cities Are Abnormal.*

50. H. W. Odum and H. E. Moore, *American Regionalism* (New York, 1938), p. 39. See Chap. II of this volume for a full discussion of the distinction between sectionalism and regionalism.

have contributed to the investigation of these regional differences long recognized in our society.[51]

These various manifestations of regional differentiation tend to combine or correlate so as to reveal a pattern of more or less distinct major social regions. Each of these "composite regions," as they are termed, is rooted in the community bases of place and sentiment, and each has its distinguishing geographic, economic, cultural, and social characteristics.

[2] *Composite regions in the United States:* Since the publication of Professor Odum's exhaustive statistical study of *Southern Regions of the United States*, in 1936, writers in this field have generally accepted the national regional pattern outlined in that volume. While no claim is made, of course, that any rigid boundaries set them apart, six distinct composite regions are described—the Northeast, Southeast, Middle states, Southwest, Northwest, and Far West. Chart XIII indicates these regions, as well as the marginal bands between them.

CHART XIII **Regional Divisions in the United States**[52]

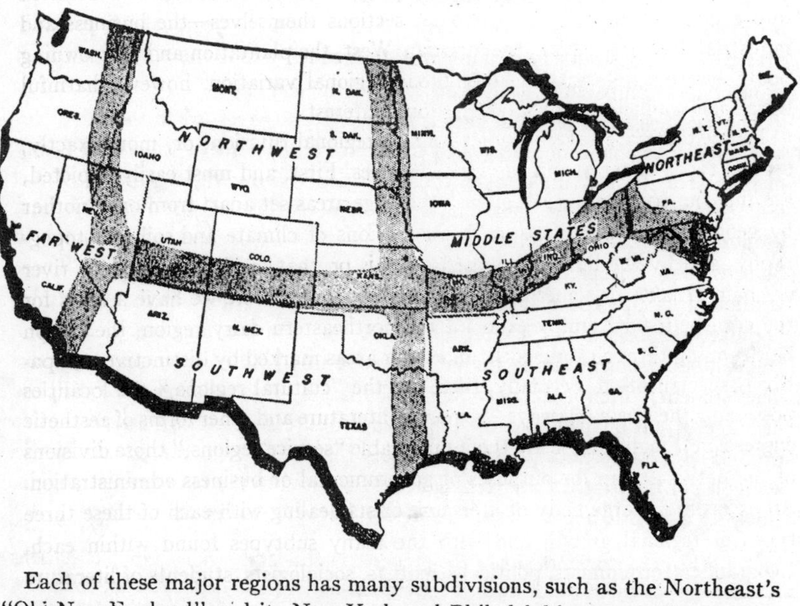

Each of these major regions has many subdivisions, such as the Northeast's "Old New England" and its New York and Philadelphia metropolitan areas;

51. See Odum and Moore, *American Regionalism*, Parts I and II, for the most complete discussion of types of regions and regional investigation in the United States.

52. From H. Odum: *Understanding Society*. Copyright, 1947 by The Macmillan Company and used with their permission.

the Middle states' focal Chicago, to which the whole region is in many ways a hinterland; the Northwest's division between plain and mountain, a social as well as a geographical distinction; the Southwest's contrast between its new great cities like Dallas and its vast stretches of thinly settled lands; and many others. But each of the six regions has its own quality, its own traditions and economic emphases, its own social problems. Each, too, has at least the potentiality of balance and integration, with its rural lands and urban centers, its exploitable rivers and preservable soil. Each in some degree is a unit of community life, not self-sufficient, to be sure, but a distinctive area within the greater national—and world—interdependency.[53]

Implications for the larger society. One of the principal difficulties in furthering the development of integrated regions in the United States is the existence of political divisions between the local states. These lines, many of them fixed long ago when quite different political and economic conditions were present, frequently become, from the regionalist's viewpoint, unrealistic and arbitrary barriers standing between regional subdivisions that demand a more complete unification. Hence the significance of such interstate arrangements as those involved in the Tennessee Valley Authority—often the regionalist's primary example of the desirable type of integrating agency—and in the growing number of interstate compacts in various sections of the country.

The significance of political lines is far greater, however, when the principles and aims of regionalism are applied to certain other parts of the earth. Many of the "area studies" undertaken today are concerned with large geographical segments wherein there is a "natural" combination of physiographic and economic and cultural factors, evidenced, in varying degrees, for example, in Southeastern Europe, in Southeastern Asia, in most of Latin America. These studies often propose planned regional programs for these areas, sometimes popularly expressed as "TVA's for China" or "for the Balkans." Clearly a tremendous problem facing the advocates of this kind of large-scale regional development, often seemingly unsurmountable, is that presented by the heritage of nationalism and by the zealous desire to maintain rigidly—or to expand—the sacrosanct political frontiers that have been carved out in the struggles of the past. In a searching article devoted to the many recent suggestions for a "world regionalism," Professor Hertzler makes this point:

> When one examines any of the proposed continental regions, group-of-nations regions, or those which might be groups-of-nations-and-dependencies, one notes only infinite differences and antagonisms. There are the variations within the proposed regions of geographic factors, industrial and agricultural techniques and

53. See Odum and Moore, *op. cit.*, Part III, for a detailed description of these six regions. The Southeast has received the most extensive study; see, for example, R. P. Vance, *All These People* (Chapel Hill, N.C., 1945). John Gunther's journalistic exploration, *Inside U.S.A.* (New York, 1947), follows, in large part, these regional divisions.

levels, consumption habits and standards, racial and nationality differences, often aggravated by long historical antagonisms, variant but tenaciously adhered to cultural features such as language, religion, customs, traditions . . . , uneven cultural levels, variously satisfied aspirations for national status, long-existing intra- and inter-national superiority-inferiority situations, varying degrees of political independence and experience. The very fact that there are everywhere separate nations and people implies a long-standing conditioning under the sway of rivalry and antagonism in order to achieve unique identity and self-preservation.[54]

However great the difficulties, few of us would quarrel with the goals of regionalism, within our own nation or throughout the world. Fundamental to its position is the ever-present relationship between social life and the particular territory where it thrives—or is frustrated. Regionalists seek to make the region itself the guiding configuration of the larger communal life, through planning based on geographic and on social fact and inspired by socialized aim, to guarantee the conditions of a finer human existence.

In this and the preceding chapter we have been concerned with the community, with its general sociological characteristics, and with its more significant specific manifestations. This aspect of the social structure, as we have noted earlier, is one that must always be a part of any thorough or realistic study of social life. Study of the community provides us with the general but essential framework of the more particularized features of the social structure. None of the latter is more important in the life of man than those barriers that separate one part of the community from another, producing the cleavages of class and caste and ethnic division—the subjects which we shall explore in the following two chapters.

54. J. O. Hertzler, "Some Basic Queries Respecting World Regionalism," *Social Forces*, XXII (1944), 373. This article cites many of the proposals for international regionalism; see especially note 3, p. 371.

14

Social Class and Caste

Principles of Class and Caste

The meaning of social class. Communities are socially stratified in various ways. The sex division is always of major sociological significance, and division into age groups may be, as is often the case in primitive society, a predominant characteristic of the internal structure of the community. But the principal type of social stratification, especially in the more developed civilizations, is seen in the phenomenon of *class*. Social classes, like the community itself, are more or less spontaneous formations expressive of social attitudes. They are not, like associations or like "political classes,"[1] simply instrumentalities for the furtherance of particular interests. The class system, as we shall see, emanates from and profoundly influences the whole mode of life and thought within the community.

[1] *Status as the criterion of social class:* A "class" may mean any category or type within which individuals or units fall. We may speak, for example, of bachelors or novel readers or theatergoers or social reformers as constituting a "class." Here, as a rule, we are not even dealing with a group, in the sociological sense. We may think of artists and physicians and engineers and mechanics as classes. But these are occupational categories, not necessarily coherent groups definitely related to one another in a social structure. The various occupations make up *vertical* divisions of the community, whereas the divisions that reflect the principle of social class are the *horizontal* strata, always a graded order. Wherever social intercourse is limited by considerations of status, by distinctions between "higher" and "lower," there *social* class exists. A *social class*, then, is *any portion of a community marked off from the rest by social status.* A *system* or *structure* of social classes involves, first, a hierarchy of status

1. The concept of "political class" has been recently elaborated by O. C. Cox in *Caste, Class, and Race* (New York, 1948); see especially Chap. X.

groups, second, the recognition of the superior-inferior stratification, and, finally, some degree of permanency of the structure.[2]

This understanding of social class as a distinct status group provides us with a precise concept, and one generally applicable to any system of class stratification, wherever found. It regards those social differentiations arising out of language, locality, function, or specialization as significant *class* phenomena only when they become closely associated with a status hierarchy. The subjective factor of social status, a manifestation of group attitudes, is always related to such objective differences in the society as income levels, occupational distinctions, distinctions of birth, race, education, and so forth. But these objective differences, *apart from a recognized order of superiority and of inferiority,* do not establish cohesive groups. It is the sense of status, sustained by economic, political, or ecclesiastical power, and by the distinctive modes of life and cultural expressions corresponding to them, that draws class apart from class, gives cohesion to each class, and stratifies a whole society.

[2] *Class as economic division:* The reader should note that our definition of *social* class is not formulated in economic terms. This alternative approach to class is presented by the Marxian school and by others. Certain of these writers have used the term "estate" to refer to status divisions, maintaining that "class" is always a manifestation of economic differentiation. The economic factor is commonly associated with status distinctions, to be sure, and no more markedly than in modern capitalistic society.

But the identification of social class with economic division is inadequate sociologically for two important reasons. In the first place, this view greatly limits the area of applicability of the concept. There are status-class differences that do not correspond to economic differences. In the Hindu caste system, for example, members of the highest or Brahman caste, without diminishing their "social distance," may be the employees or servants of members of a lower caste and very inferior to the latter with respect to wealth. Again, an old-established landed class frequently regards itself, and is generally regarded, as socially superior to a wealthier and more powerful industrial or commercial class of *nouveaux riches*, a situation found not only in Europe but in the older American communities and in some regions of Asia. In the second place, the concept of class loses its *sociological* significance if it is defined by any purely objective criterion, such as income level or occupational function or ownership and nonownership of productive means. Economic division does not unite people and separate them from others unless they *feel* their unity or separation.

2. Cf. T. H. Marshall, "Social Class—A Preliminary Analysis," *Sociological Review*, XXVI (1934), 55-76. The view that status is the basic criterion of *social* class, rejected by writers of Marxist persuasion, is well presented in this article. See also T. Parsons, "Analytical Approach to the Theory of Social Stratification," *American Journal of Sociology*, XLV (1940), 841-862; and K. Davis and W. E. Moore, "Some Principles of Stratification," *American Sociological Review*, X (1945), 242-249.

Whatever objective criterion we use, we do not have a *social* class unless class consciousness is present. If white-collar workers, for example, do not regard themselves as belonging to the same class as industrial workers, then they do not together form one social class. The members of all social groups, as we have seen, share some sentiment of what they have in common, and we cannot, without departing from the sociological approach developed in this volume, make class an exception to this rule.

[3] *Social class versus economic class:* Our criticism of the strictly economic view of class should not be taken as a dismissal of the importance of economic divisions in social life. Economic cleavages, especially those that have risen during the "age of capitalism," are of real concern to the sociologist, as well as to the economist—a point we shall develop shortly. A few students of modern social organization, recognizing the divergence between the economic interpretation of class and the sociological concept, have retained both approaches in their studies. Thus the great German sociologist Max Weber emphasized that "the social and the economic order are not identical. The economic order is . . . merely the way in which economic goods and services are distributed and used. The social order is of course conditioned by the economic order to a high degree, and in its turn reacts upon it."[3] Weber's conception of *class*, however, was essentially economic, for he viewed such a group as one having the same "life chances" or social opportunities as determined typically by economic conditions. He contrasted class in this sense with communal "status groups," which may but frequently do not parallel the economic class lines.[4] We shall find it necessary to use this type of distinction in treating the American class structure later in this chapter. In keeping with our initial definition, however, we shall refer to status-marked and group-conscious strata as *social classes*, and shall designate as *economic classes* segments of the community determined strictly by some economic criterion.[5]

Social status and occupation. Status is the social position that determines for its possessor, *apart from* his personal attributes or social service, a degree of respect, prestige, and influence. There is an intimate historical association between social class, as we have defined it, and type of *occupation*. But the two should not be identified, for class distinctions basically rest not on function but on *status*.

[1] *Functional versus class divisions:* The distinction between social class and status on the one hand and occupational function on the other is illustrated by

---

3. *From Max Weber: Essays in Sociology* (H. Gerth and C. W. Mills, tr. and ed., New York, 1946), p. 181.

4. *Ibid.*, pp. 180–188.

5. The distinction between social and economic class is used, for example, by R. H. Tawney in *Equality* (London, 1929), Chap. III; and by C. H. Page in *Class and American Sociology* (New York, 1940), Chaps. I and VIII.

our official statistical reports on "socioeconomic groups." The United States Bureau of the Census has classified the working population according to the six major categories presented in Table X, and a number of students of social stratification in this country have used this classification as a description of the class structure itself.

TABLE X **Socioeconomic Groups in the Labor Force in the United States, 1940**[6]

(Persons 14 years old and over, and excluding new workers.)

Socioeconomic group	Number		Percentage	
I. Professional persons	3,381,993		6.5	
II. Proprietors, managers, and officials	9,233,643		17.8	
(a) Farmers (owners and tenants)		5,274,706		10.1
(b) Wholesale and retail dealers		2,037,900		3.9
(c) Other proprietors, etc.		1,921,037		3.7
III. Clerks and kindred workers	8,923,939		17.2	
IV. Skilled workers and foremen	6,104,985		11.7	
V. Semiskilled workers	10,918,312		21.0	
VI. Unskilled workers	13,457,151		25.9	
(a) Farm laborers		3,708,191		7.1
(b) Laborers, except farm		5,566,493		10.7
(c) Servant classes		4,182,467		8.0

The six principal categories in Table X may be viewed as constituting a class hierarchy or status system, but only with important qualifications. If we take only the broad divisions, such as that between Groups I and II or between Groups II and those below, the factor of status is obviously present. But *within* some of the major divisions, particularly in Groups I and II, there are numerous differences of status that depend only in part, if at all, on mode of occupation. Moreover, the multitude of subclassifications that go to make up these broad groups in the original census report are occupational-functional categories, and are not status designations. Status, unlike function, is a *subjective variable*, and must be sought in the attitudes groups hold one to another. Therefore, to equate function with social class is apt to be misleading. If the student asks himself how far the classes from I to VI in Table X correspond with status levels in present-day Soviet Russia, for example, he will see that the relation of function and social class varies enormously with the social conditions.

6. Data from U.S. Bureau of the Census, *Comparative Occupation Statistics for the United States, 1870 to 1940* (Washington, D.C., 1943), Chap. XIV.

[2] *Occupation as an index of class in modern society:* In modern complex society many factors enter into the determination of status, including material possessions, achievement, lineage, social affiliations, authority and power, and function—we shall consider these various criteria later. But here it should be noted that the type of occupation, while never an altogether accurate indication of status, is a particularly useful *general* index of social class in such countries as the United States. In this country occupation "combines to a fairly high degree a number of the more important criteria of class membership," such as wealth, consumption habits, social affiliations, even intermarriage.[7]

Consider the case of the farmers, included under Group II in Table X, intermediate in position between the professional and "white-collar" categories. This American group reveals in a very interesting way the nexus between occupation and status. In earlier times there were two great classes associated with the soil, the landowner (or controller) and the land-cultivator or peasant. But in our modern industrialized nation, with its money economy and other far-reaching social changes, and particularly through the parceling out of the land into homesteads or small farms, a class of owner-cultivators rose into prominence. They differ from the "free" husbandmen and yeomen of earlier days in that they have not been dominated by a landowning aristocracy, and this difference has been accentuated by the greater mobility of the farmers, a point we considered in the previous chapter. Thus the land has lost some of its old character as a family inheritance and has become more nearly an investment of capital, like any other. But these farmers employ relatively few laborers (see Group VI [a], Table X) outside their own families, and their relation to the hired worker, who is often a temporary or occasional helper, is not the same as that of the landlord to the peasant. Consequently the social and economic difference between the owner-farmer and the tenant-farmer has diminished, and the two together form an agricultural class with common interests and common problems, with common characteristics arising from the nature of their occupation, with a more or less common standard of living, and a common group consciousness. They form a social class as we have defined it (though not a completely solidified "political class"), for the factor of status is bound up with their mode of living, their relatively low and inelastic income, their comparative economic solidarity set over against that of other groups, and their relative, though diminishing, segregation from the cultural influences that play upon urban populations.[8]

Yet even in this fairly clear example of a social class, the farmers in the United States, the status pattern is a complicated one. In recent years, as we saw in Chapter XIII, the type of social organization characteristic of urban society, with its economic and social specializations and gradations, has greatly in-

7. Cf. W. E. Moore, *Industrial Relations and the Social Order* (New York, 1946), Chap. XXII; see also Parsons, *op. cit.*, 856–862.

8. For a criticism of this view, see Cox, *op. cit.*, p. 288.

fluenced the agricultural communities—as is manifested in new alignments and social divisions—so that *within* the latter social stratification is developing. In the industrialized and commercialized urban world itself status sometimes becomes attached to specialized types of work, such as the "white-collar" occupations, so that both the horizontal and vertical divisions are at times bound up with the status arrangements. Add to this situation the various degrees of prestige of different racial and nationality and religious groups, and we see how enormously complicated is the problem of depicting the status structure of contemporary society.[9]

The criteria of class distinctions. The commonest and the oldest type of social classification is expressed as a dichotomy. Its various forms distinguish the few and the many, the gentry and the commonality, the elite and the masses, the free and the servile, the rich and the poor, the rulers and the ruled, the educated and the uneducated, the productive and the unproductive (the leisure class), and, in the Marxist formula, the *bourgeoisie* and the proletariat. Tripartite divisions are also commonly employed, such as the feudal distinction of noble, burgher, and serf, and the present-day conventional designation of "upper," "middle," and "lower" classes. We may now ask: What principles are involved in these various modes of social classification? How do the different criteria of class distinction affect the character of the social structure?

[1] *The bases of status:* The grounds of status vary greatly from society to society and from one historical period to another within the same society. In a few primitive communities where class lines have not formed, prestige is gained by personal achievement, while in others it rests upon some group-recognized, status-giving factor.[10] Status may be based upon differences of birth, wealth, occupation, political power, race, or, as in the case of traditional China, intellectual attainment. Frequently status is determined by a combination of two or more of these factors. When the attitudes of the members of a community become firmly attached to specific marks of status, when they become a part of the social heritage, they form the pattern of the community's system of social classes. There are, of course, many such systems. Yet the character of the class structure is most clearly revealed when status is associated with a *single* controlling factor around which the others cohere. We may illustrate this principle by contrasting the type of class system that assigns status on the basis of birth with the type that gives primary importance to wealth.

[2] *The criteria of birth and wealth:* When status is fixed by birth, as in the

9. For the complications of status see, for example, E. C. Hughes, "Dilemmas and Contradictions of Status," *American Journal of Sociology*, L (1945), 353–359; and E. Benoit-Smullyan, "Status, Status Types, and Status Interrelations," *American Sociological Review*, IX (1944), 151–161.

10. For status in primitive society see G. Landtman, *The Origin of the Inequality of the Social Classes* (Chicago, 1938), especially Chap. I.

traditional Indian caste system or in feudal society, the class structure tends to be compact or "integrated" and rigidly stratified at the same time. Structural changes take place, to be sure, but slowly and usually imperceptibly from the viewpoint of the members of such a static system. In feudal and early medieval life, for example, not only did birth determine status for the overwhelming majority but the values incorporated in the mores and sanctioned by the teachings of the church sustained the universally recognized three-class structure of noble, burgher, and serf. Political power and wealth in the form of land-control were, of course, closely bound up with birth as marks of status, but the latter remained the predominant controlling factor of social position until the system itself became undermined by new social and economic developments. So long as birth defined status, vertical social mobility was impossible for all but the few who could move upward within the ranks of the army or the church hierarchies, on the one side, or, on the other, within the historically increasing mobile group of burghers, the artisans and merchants.

The latter groups, the "middle class," were historically responsible for revolutionizing the feudal class system, for they fought for and eventually gained, first in northern Italy and later throughout most of Western Europe and America, a new definition of social status in terms of *wealth*. Here we need not consider the details of this vast historical movement, climaxed by the "bourgeois revolutions," except to note two of its features that came to be of central significance in the class structure of modern Western society.

ONE: THE REDEFINITION OF WEALTH. Under the feudal system land was the principal form of wealth; in fact, the whole feudal structure has been described as an institutionalized system of land control. But with the growth of commercial, financial, and factory-production enterprise, wealth became redefined so that land, though remaining as an important type of wealth, was increasingly subordinated to the new forms of money and credit. This was a crucial development in that wealth was "detached" from its feudal institutional setting, from the traditional distinctions of birth, land-control, and status. The evolution of wealth as an "independent" social value greatly weakened birth as the determinant of status and thereby upset the older integrated class system. It permitted not only the rise of wealthy individuals, whatever their birthrights, the new *bourgeoisie*, but influenced the development of a "detached" science of wealth, the "classical" economics of the nineteenth century.[11] Expanding capitalism, detaching and "freeing" wealth, necessarily stimulated social mobility.

TWO: THE RISE OF VERTICAL MOBILITY. As status came to be more and more defined in terms of the new forms of mobile wealth, and as birth and tradition lost their hold as criteria of prestige and power, an *open-class* structure evolved.

11. The "detachment" of economic matters from their social setting was inconceivable to medieval thinkers. Various present-day economists are adopting this earlier viewpoint.

The "cake of custom" was broken. A class system came into being that in some degree permitted persons to rise, and to fall, on the basis of their *individual* achievements. Members of the feudal upper class either entered the new system sometimes through marriage, and often indirectly by concealing their contacts with the "vulgar" world of trade, or joined the "decadent aristocracy," a class without function in the new capitalistic age. In the mobile capitalistic societies, therefore, the traditional class demarcations were blurred, and eventually became of only secondary importance.

In feudal times the class structure was a series of demarcated stages. The different classes were marked off by different modes of living, different recreation, dress, and so forth. This *closed-class* system stands in contrast to the relatively open system of modern times. In the latter, a sharply demarcated hierarchy is replaced by a gradient arrangement, wherein the various ranks, though differentially because of their differences of economic means, follow the same fashions, view the same spectacles and entertainments, and, generally, share the same values. Only in the open-class system, as we shall see, do worker and banker alike strive to "keep up with the Joneses."

[3] *Competing criteria of status:* Under the conditions of modern capitalism, wealth, then, takes on a more determinative role, and wealth, though in degree associated with mode of living, cultural opportunity, occupational advantage, and political power, is of all attributes the most detachable from personality and from cultural attainment. In democracies particularly the bulwarks of the older class system have been undermined, so that whatever cohesion the new system possesses depends mainly on the role of wealth. Yet the older determinants of status still modify and limit it, and new criteria are often introduced.

In the United States, for example, the "old-line" families, especially in the Eastern and Southeastern states, assert counterclaims of class distinction, and lineage is, in fact, an important status-bearing factor in such cities as Boston and Philadelphia and Richmond. Broader class distinctions are asserted in the name of the pride of "race," such as that between the West European peoples and the "new immigration" from Southern and Eastern Europe, or that between Gentile and Jew. These barriers, however, do not create clearly defined social classes, and some of them are already shown to be transitional lines, becoming less determinative of status in the degree in which cultural differences are merged and group discrimination is broken down. The situation is more complicated in the case of the Negro-White division, a conspicuous status demarcation in this country.[12] Lineage, national origin, religion, and color are criteria of status that compete, at times quite effectively, with wealth. But the more decisive significance of wealth in our society is revealed by the extent to which this value penetrates *all* social divisions and provides a common standard of social distinction.

---

12. See Chapter XV below for a discussion of ethnic and racial groups.

Caste as unchangeable status. The closed feudal order came close to being a caste system. When status is wholly predetermined, so that men are born to their lot in life without any hope of changing it, then class takes the extreme form of caste.

[1] *The Hindu caste system:* By far the most significant example of a caste system is the one incorporated in Hindu society. "Every Hindu necessarily belongs to the caste of his parents and in that caste he inevitably remains. No accumulation of wealth and no exercise of talents can alter his caste status; and marriage outside his caste is prohibited or severely discouraged."[13] Although there are some exceptions to the fixity of this order based on heredity and exogamy, and although whole castes sometimes shift position in the social structure, caste remains an almost complete barrier to individual mobility, except within the caste itself. In principle there is an absolute and permanent stratification of the community. The strata are kept apart by the exclusion of the lower from the more intimate forms of social intercourse with the higher, and especially by the ban on intermarriage, by the observances of obeisance due from the lower to the higher, and by the reservation of honorific ceremonies, functions, and occupations to the higher while certain despised offices are relegated to the lower. In India, with the multitudinous caste compartments in the Hindu system, the higher caste groups—at the top the Brahman and next in order the Kshatriya and Vaisya—are thought of as beings of different clay from the low-caste group of the Sudras, while still further beyond these are the "outcastes" or "untouchables," whose very presence has been traditionally considered a defilement to the rest, who are still thought to pollute food and water by their touch, and who in some regions are not permitted to approach the neighborhood of the high-caste Hindu. The idea of defilement is common in every caste system and reveals most clearly how caste prevents common participation of the various groups in the communal life. While some of the more strict barriers have been relaxed in recent years in India, particularly the rules governing the former "untouchables," the stratification system is so strongly imbedded in Indian life that only tremendous upheavals or the long processes of deep-working technological and cultural change can greatly alter it.[14]

[2] *Caste, occupation, and status:* It has sometimes been claimed that the Hindu caste system is basically a fixed order of occupations. The sacred literature suggests this interpretation; thus Manu, describing man's creation, states: "But for the sake of the prosperity of the world, he caused the Brahana, the Kshatriya, the Vaisya, and the Sudra to proceed from his mouth, his arms, his thighs, and his feet. . . . But in order to protect this universe he . . . assigned

---

13. *Report of the Indian Statutory Commission*, 1930 (Cmd. 3568), Vol. I, Chap. IV.

14. See Cox, *op. cit.*, Part I, for detailed description of and extensive bibliography on the Indian caste structure.

separate duties and occupations to those who sprang from his mouth, arms, thighs, and feet."[15] In principle, it is true that each of the many subcastes and some of the outcaste groups have a specifically assigned and regularly inherited occupation, illustrated most clearly in the artisan crafts. However, not only do different castes that are otherwise set apart often engage in the same type of work, but some economic functions, such as agriculture and trading, both highly important activities in the social life, seem to be open to the members of all caste groups. Moreover, shifts in occupation, though usually involving whole castes, have been necessitated by changing economic and technological conditions, without disturbing the basic caste structure itself. The methods of Western production introduced here and there in India in recent years have brought about important breaks with traditional occupational practice on the part of some groups, and the potential repercussions of this alteration are very large.

A solidified caste structure, such as India's, involves the most extreme form of status hierarchy. The horizontal stratification, with the distinctions of privileges and immunities and duties, affects almost every phase of the social life, including work and worship and recreation and marriage. The separation of caste from caste, however, does not prevent significant status differences from developing *within* the major divisions. "Castes of any size always have their superior and privileged families. Individuals within the caste may differ in wealth, in occupational efficiency, in physical attainments, in choice of vocation among those to which the caste is limited, in political position, in number of Vedas read, or in number of knots in the sacred cord, and so on."[16] In short, social classes may form within the broader caste divisions, a phenomenon we shall observe in our own soceity's "castes," such as the Negro and other groups set apart by strong barriers to social intercourse.

[3] *The religious reinforcement of caste:* The rigid demarcation of caste could scarcely be maintained were it not for strong religious persuasions. The hold of religious belief, with its supernatural explanation of caste itself, its doctrine of the elect and the "pale," its attribution of a mystic cleanness and uncleanness, its instillation of reverence and awe, and its overruling conception of the sacred and the profane, is essential to the continuance of the system. The Hindu caste structure may have arisen out of the subjection or enslavement incidental to conquest and perhaps also out of the subordination of one endogamous community to another. But the power, prestige, and pride of race thus engendered could give rise to a caste system, with its social separation of groups that are not in fact set apart by any clear racial signs, only as the resulting situation was rationalized and made "eternal" by religious myth.

Caste signifies the enhancement and transformation of social distance into

---

15. Manu, I, 31, 87, quoted in *ibid.*, p. 60.
16. Cox, *op. cit.*, p. 10.

a religious or, more strictly, a magical principle.[17] In the Hindu system the religious doctrine even permits caste mobility for the individual—in a reincarnated life. And it is the magical aspect of the doctrine that made the shadow of an "untouchable" or even his unseen presence in the vicinity a source of pollution, that forbade him to enter the same temples as the higher castes, and that attributed to the latter, as "twice-born men," an exclusive virtue and sanctity.

"Caste" in an open-class society. The caste system we have described involves a sizable percentage of the earth's population. But this is not the only reason that it warrants our attention. For the caste principle, assigning status strictly in terms of birth, enforcing endogamous marriage, vastly limiting social contacts between groups, and restricting certain occupations to the "right-born," is one that, in some degree, is manifested in all societies, including our own. Whenever status is predetermined by birth, whenever one's color or ethnic origin or religion or "name" automatically assigns one special prestige or privilege, or special social handicaps, the *principle* of caste is at work. The two principles, open-class and closed-caste, may operate together in the same community, and, according to some sociologists,[18] both are always present. In any event, as we shall make clear in Chapter XV, many modern societies in the Western world, where the open-class system has developed most extensively, are marked by social fissures that display some of the elements of caste.

Class Attitudes and Class Consciousness

The nature and types of class sentiment. We must now consider the socio-psychological aspect of class, the sentiment that characterizes the relations of men toward the members of their own and other classes. This is the aspect that establishes *social distance*, an essential feature of class distinction. "Social distance," as applied to class attitudes, should not be confused with personal liking or aversion; the concept rather refers to that bar to free intercourse between individuals that arises from their belonging to groups rated as superior or inferior in status.[19]

[1] *Class attitudes contrasted with community sentiment:* Class feeling, as we suggested in Chapter XII, exhibits striking contrasts with community sentiment. If the latter admits no grades, the former is rooted in the principle of hierarchy—the sentiment of class is essentially a sentiment of disparity.

17. Cf. M. Weber, *Gesammelte Aufsätze zur Religionssoziologie* (Tubingen, 1923), II, 44.
18. For example, C. H. Cooley; see Page, *op. cit.*, pp. 189–201.
19. Cf. P. Sorokin, *Social Mobility* (New York, 1927), Chap. I. "Superior" and "inferior" are here used, of course, with no implications of differences of intellect, character, or similar qualities.

Although it unites those who feel distinct from other classes, it unites them primarily because they feel distinct. Above all, it unites the "superior" against the "inferior." It emanates from the belief in superiority, however unfounded, so that class division is really imposed on the lower by the higher classes. Hence class sentiment involves entirely different attitudes, with respect to one another, of the various groups within the hierarchical system.

In so far as tradition rules, the attitude of the lower classes to the higher is one of respect and subservience, while the higher exhibits condescension and patronage toward the lower.[20] Since intermediate classes look both ways, class feeling under such conditions differs most markedly at the two ends of the social scale. If, on the other hand, tradition is weakened by social changes and class struggle emerges, the attitudes of the opposing classes—one conservative and striving to maintain, the other radical and striving to overthrow, an order—cease to be complementary and become as different as the social values for which they respectively struggle. Class sentiment, therefore, has no inclusive quality comparable to that of community feeling. Moreover, class attitudes and community sentiment operate to limit and restrain one another. The one divides those whom the other integrates. In less mobile societies, communal tradition, religion, and custom are usually so strong and pervasive that the dividing influences of class or caste cannot prevail against them. In more mobile societies the counteractive roles of the two types of sentiment are particularly noticeable. For example, as we have seen in an earlier chapter, the competitive quality of class sentiment expresses itself in the restlessness of fashion as against the stability of the communal codes of custom. Class feeling itself, however, assumes quite different forms.

[2] *Two main types of class sentiment:* Some kind or degree of class sentiment is almost universal in human society. The communist ideal of a "classless society," with respect to *social* classes, is by no means realized in Soviet Russia, where there are conspicuously different degrees of prestige attached to occupation, party membership, and political position. There are sharp class distinctions in Negro Harlem no less than on Park Avenue. There are distinctions between social classes, based upon different criteria of status to be sure, between the inmates of prisons, between the members of "utopian" communities, even between those who perform slightly different types of work in the same occupation, among the dock workers, for example.

But while class sentiment is so pervasive, its range, character, and social implications are very different under different conditions. In particular, a distinction should be drawn between *corporate class consciousness* and *competitive class feeling*. Corporate class consciousness is a sentiment uniting a whole group sharing a similar social status. But there is a more personal form of class sentiment that frequently determines the conduct of individuals toward one

---

20. For a fuller list of upward looking and downward looking attitudes see Chapter II.

another without involving on their part any express recognition of the whole groups to which they respectively belong. Class feeling in this sense is one thing, the corporate consciousness of class solidarity is quite another. When Mr. A blackballs Mr. B from membership in his club, he does not necessarily think of himself as thereby upholding the standards or the interest of a whole class of Mr. A's; when Mrs. A patronizes Mrs. B or refuses to call on her, she does not on that account necessarily feel her solidarity with a whole order of the "superiors" of Mrs. B. Here the response is immediate, specific, personalized, an expression of competitive class feeling.

This type of class sentiment is characteristic of the competitive system that developed in modern Western society. Corporate class consciousness, an obvious feature of the closed or caste-divided structure, has developed in modern society chiefly under the spur of strong economic incentives, and has gained most strength at the extreme ends of the economic scale, in the struggle to maintain or destroy a predetermined status. "Society," on the one hand, and low-paid wage-earning groups, on the other, most clearly exhibit corporate class consciousness.

[3] *Social implications of the two types of class sentiment:* Class sentiment takes a different range as well as quality according to the degree in which the element of *caste* is present. When a man's lot in life is fixed by anterior social conditions, he more readily identifies himself with the whole group of his fellows subject to the same conditions. If the mores of an authoritative religion hold sway, so that the members of the group accept, in the language of the English Book of Common Prayer, the "duty to order themselves lowly and reverently to all their betters," then the class consciousness of the subject class is a conservative influence. If the old mores break, as they do in the process of industrialization and urbanization, then this class consciousness becomes a powerful engine of social change. In either event the solidarity of class consciousness depends on the sense of a sharp cleavage and on the recognition of an unsurmountable barrier under existing conditions.

The situation changes considerably where vertical mobility develops. Where the belief prevails, supported by at least some factual instances, that a higher status may be individually acquired or that a present status may be lost, the solidarity of at least the socially subordinated classes tends to be broken. In the United States, the industrial worker or the clerk has before him the examples of those, whether few or many in number, who from the same position have risen to social power and economic affluence; and the more ambitious and energetic members of these groups are buoyed by the prospects of a like success. In the presence of vertical mobility, the lower-class members do not feel so strongly the permanence of status that creates solidarity and stimulates class organization.

In a mobile system, class sentiment may be *even stronger* than among groups with rigidly determined status, though it now becomes localized and competitive. The class system is no longer tier above tier, but a continuous incline. Class struggle tends to take the form of the striving of individuals and families to maintain their place and still more to "rise in the world." Appearances consequently count for more, since class is judged by external signs. The standards and modes of living of the higher prestige groups are imitated by those below them: an inclusive set of competitive values tends to motivate the members of all groups. The phenomena so caustically described by Veblen mark the social scene—emulation, competition, display, and the "conspicuous consumption of valuable goods" that signalize a class order dominated by the principle of wealth.[21] Somewhat similar characteristics may be observed in certain simpler societies, such as those involved in the institution of the potlatch found among the Northwest Kwakiutl, wherein status is maintained or gained by competitive gift-giving and by the conspicuous destruction of material goods. However, Veblen's principles of emulation, competition, and conspicuous display are revealed as clearly, as we shall see, in the class attitudes that have grown up in the "free enterprise" society of the United States.

The Marxist view of class consciousness and its limitations. Competitive class feeling is so distinct from corporate class consciousness that the two are fundamentally antagonistic. The former expresses in greater measure the individual or *self-limited* interest, the latter is a manifestation of the *common* interest of the class. The contrast is excellently illustrated by the position taken by Karl Marx and his followers in their endeavor to accentuate in the working classes the consciousness of their corporate unity.

[1] *The Marxist interpretation:* While the followers of Marxism profess as their final goal the abolition of classes altogether, their immediate objective in capitalistic countries is the solidarity and consequent organization of the whole class of the proletariat, that is, the "propertyless wage earners." In seeking this objective, they have not only subordinated those sentiments that unite classes, but have also necessarily minimized the distinctions that exist within each of the "basic" classes, the capitalists and the workers. They have generally insisted on the common conditions and hence the common interests and the common subjection of the working class, and on its economic, social, and even cultural separation from the other main class, the *bourgeoisie.* To them, the wage-earning class is essentially homogeneous because of its nonowning and exploited economic position in the capitalistic order. Therefore the competitive struggle for position between its members, associated with competitive class feeling, is inimical alike to their general interest and to their solidarity. Hence the program summed up in the famous words of the *Communist Manifesto:* "Proletarians of the world, unite."

Marxian theory, materialistic and economically oriented, views class attitudes

21. Of T. Veblen's writings, see especially *The Theory of the Leisure Class* (New York, 1922), Chap. IV.

and class consciousness as fundamentally a reflection of economic conditions, and teaches that the sentiment of corporate unity inevitably emerges within each of the basic economic classes. Yet its exponents recognize that the growth of corporate class consciousness does not take place automatically or according to any definite time-schedule—thus the organizational efforts to solidify the working class. Marx himself, noting the absence of corporate feeling in large sections of the European working class of his day, explained this lack by attributing it to the first "stage" of working-class development, when the economic conditions are appropriate, to be sure, to the existence of a "class," but when its members do not as yet rid themselves of competitive attitudes. This stage, that of the class "in itself," is followed in the course of historical growth—and especially with the aid of history's instrument, the Marxists themselves—by the stage of the class "for itself," marked by unity, common interest, and, most importantly, by concerted class action.[22] This theoretical prognosis of the rise of class consciousness has, in *some* parts of Western society, been substantiated by subsequent events. But the problem is by no means as simple as this analysis suggests.

[2] *The complexity of the problem:* In the countries of Western civilization the Marxist dichotomy of *bourgeoisie* and proletariat is too simple and sweeping to fit the facts of the system of *social* classes. So broad a division and so sharp a cleavage is more applicable to a feudal order, such as that of prerevolutionary Russia, than to a complex industrialized society. The Marxist class philosophy itself became a historical fact of vast significance, the full outcome of which we cannot foresee but the tremendous results of which we are daily witnessing. But it became so because it gives a vision and a policy to propertyless and frequently exploited workers as well as an opportunity to power-seeking groups. In Tsarist Russia, a country industrially undeveloped and lacking the "middle classes" of industrial and urban civilization, the chaos and disaffection created by an incompetent aristocracy and a disastrous war gave to a small group of very remarkable men, led by Lenin, the opportunity to rebuild a whole society on Marxist principles. In certain respects similar conditions existed in the Eastern European countries of the "Soviet zone" following World War II. But even under such conditions the sudden application of Marxist principles meant and still means the rigorous suppression of the spontaneous forces that in every social order generate major and minor class distinctions. Under the more complex conditions of Western Europe and America, the Marxist system, however significant *politically*, reveals its inadequacy as an *interpretation* of the social facts. On the one hand, there are many influences uniting the classes which this system sets in stark opposition to one another. On the other hand, there

22. For "orthodox" statements of the Marxist interpretation of class division and class consciousness, see, for example, K. Marx, *Wage-Labour and Capital* (New York, 1933), Chap. IX; F. Engels, *Anti-Duehring* (New York, 1935), III, Chap. II; N. Bukharin, *Historical Materialism* (New York, 1925), especially Chap. VIII.

are many variant and intermediate forms of class sentiment that cannot be fitted into the system without fundamentally altering it.[23]

The cultural resemblances of social classes, for example, vary greatly in extent and intensity according to the conditions. We saw that caste itself generally exists only on the basis of common cultural values, serving as a unifying force, especially as incorporated in a dominant religion. Again, in feudal society we can trace the expansion of common beliefs, such as the official Christian conception of marriage and the family, over all classes. In the modern world, the facilities of communication have greatly increased the cultural homogeneity of classes, a fact indicated in many ways. Even when cultural influences appear at first in the higher economic classes, such as the influences leading to the decline of the birth rate, they permeate rather quickly to the lower economic classes. Given the conditions of modern open-class society, most cultural influences radiate from the prestige groups, but the whole society tends to be leavened by them.[24] The attempts, therefore, of the Marxist advocates to distinguish a "bourgeois" from a "proletarian" culture—in music, art, drama, fiction, even in the physical sciences—may be effective propaganda but cannot be described as objective interpretation.

[3] *The special problem of the "middle classes"*: The Marxist scheme as an interpretive theory is unsatisfactory on another count, for it shades over the class sentiment as well as the social importance of those various groups that make up the "middle classes." In the Marxian view, the development of capitalism, or rather the process of its inevitable decay, reduces the middle class to proletarianism. With the expansion of large-scale capitalism the members of the old lower middle class, the small tradespeople, the artisans, and the working farmers, are drawn within its orbit as dependent wage earners. A similar lot awaits the professionals, technicians, "white-collar" workers, civil servants, and other categories created by the demands of a more complex society. This latter group of middle-class elements may or may not align themselves with the capitalists, but in either event their status for the most part becomes, in effect, identical with that of the proletariat. In this reasoning there is no place for the existence of a middle class because there is no economic basis for its continued existence. As a modern one-time exponent of the Marxist thesis states, "There *must* be disunity, for the middle class is not a class. It has no identity of *class* economic interests in terms of a definite mode of production, or economic order."[25]

Justification for this interpretation can be found only if we disregard a sociologically essential aspect of class, namely class sentiment. It is a misleading

23. G. A. Briefs, in his suggestive analysis of *The Proletariat* (New York, 1937), describes several alternative patterns of class attitudes that develop among working-class groups; see especially Chap. VI.

24. Cf. E. A. Ross, *Social Control* (New York, 1901), Chap. XXVI.

25. L Corey, *The Crisis of the Middle Class* (New York, 1935), p. 168.

simplification of the social facts to group together, over against the "proletariat," all of those whose incomes are derived from "salaries" or from individual enterprise and who are not working-class conscious, to think of them as necessarily belonging *with* the large capitalists and financiers. If many of them sometimes become united, it is only in a negative position, as being generally antisocialistic, but this is hardly enough to constitute them a social class. Similarly, an unjustified simplification is made when large elements of nonowning "workers," including "white-collar" groups, some parts of the "petty *bourgeoisie*," and many "intellectuals," are defined as essentially "proletarian." These various groups differ widely in their social stations and ambitions; and even their economic interests are diverse and often conflicting. Marx, centering his interest in one *economic* class, was prone to group all of the population into two opposing classes, ignoring the fact that several of the "intermediate" and "mixed class types" lacked the like attributes and common status that *social* class requires.[26]

Marx's "law of the accumulation of capital," as he saw it, would reduce an ever-larger portion of the population to proletarian status. The "middle classes," in other words, could be only a temporary obstacle to the two-class system and, eventually, to revolutionary seizure of power by the workers.[27] On the economic level, the greater concentration of the *control* of capital has worked out much as he foresaw it. But his prediction of the inevitable growth of an order of two antagonistic social classes, the members of each motivated by a focused common consciousness, has not been borne out by the historical events of the last century. Rather there is considerable evidence that groups marked by middle-class sentiment, with their competitive attitudes and their refusal to become identified with either the "ruling class" or the exploited industrial workers, have grown in size during the period of expanding capitalism and have often played a crucial role in the important social changes of that era. We are afforded no better illustration of this situation than in the case of the United States.

Class in the United States

The economic structure and social mobility. All complex civilizations, as we have seen, are marked by some system of social classes. This is true of our own traditionally open-class society, a fact sometimes denied, but one long recognized by many of its students, including such earlier sociologists as L. F. Ward,

26. Bukharin, *op. cit.*, Chap. VIII, discusses these "intermediary" and "mixed" groups, but, in keeping with Marx's formula, insists that their *class* position must be understood *with relation to* the two basic classes in capitalistic society.

27. This "law" is stated by Marx in *Capital* (New York, 1906), I, Part VII, Chap. XXV. It is applied by L. Corey to the United States; see *The Crisis of the Middle Class*, and *The Decline of American Capitalism* (New York, 1934), especially Parts IV, VI, and VIII.

W. G. Sumner, and C. H. Cooley.[28] In spite of this recognition, the detailed characteristics of the class structure of the United States and of its changing features have not been studied carefully by American sociologists until very recent years. Today, however, we have considerable information concerning various interrelated aspects of our class system, including its economic divisions and the social mobility of individuals from one division to another, the peculiarities of class sentiment in this country, and especially the structure of social classes and of "castes" found in different types of local communities. We shall consider the economic divisions at the outset.

[1] *Lines of economic division:* The economic divisions of a community may not, as we have seen, correspond with its *social* strata. This is clearly the case in the United States. A preliminary consideration of the general features of this nation's economic classes may serve to illustrate this fact. Ours is a society in which the forces of capitalism have enjoyed maximum scope, in which the distribution of economic rewards, the concentration of wealth, and the determination of status on the basis of wealth have operated with a minimum of restraint. It is, unlike the societies of Western Europe, a society without deep roots in an older and more tightly closed class system. It is one, too, in which the belief in economic opportunity for all has played and continues to play a significant role. Finally, it is a society in which the shifting pattern of economic divisions suggests important aspects of the social class system itself.

There are economic divisions of different kinds, several of which are revealed in the statistics gathered by the governmental agencies. We can discover, for example, the contours of our economic structure on the basis of income or of occupation or of spending, or in terms of the kinds and amounts of ownership of different types of wealth, or we can see the way in which our total national income is allocated to profits, wages, farm income, and so on. Each of these alternatives represents a possible criterion of *economic* class. Here we shall consider three interrelated types.

ONE: INCOME DISTRIBUTION. The distribution of income, both cash and real income, among individuals or among families or consuming units in the United States, takes the form of a gradient, with a relatively small group at the top receiving huge amounts and, at the other extreme, a somewhat larger but still a small number of persons in the "negative income" bracket. In 1945, for example, it has been estimated that slightly over 2½ per cent of families and single individuals received incomes of $7,500 or more, less than 27 per cent had incomes ranging between $3,000 and $7,500, almost 22½ per cent received between $2,000 and $3,000, 27 per cent between $1,000 and $2,000, and over 20 per cent less than $1,000.[29] Were lines to be drawn between, say, "upper,"

---

28. For the views on class of these three and of those of A. W. Small, F. H. Giddings, and E. A. Ross, see Page, *Class and American Sociology*, Chaps. II–VII.

29. Figures based upon reports of the Office of Price Administration and the United States Bureau of Agricultural Economics, and presented in *Information Please Almanac 1947*

"middle," and "lower" income classes, they would necessarily be based upon arbitrarily selected points of division, and would, of course, disregard the variation in the *social* significance of amount of income that exists between city and small town, between different regions, even between different ethnic groups. Nevertheless this index of the distribution of economic rewards throws into sharp relief its uneveness in American life.

TWO: DISTRIBUTION OF ECONOMIC POWER. A still greater unevenness is apparent when we view the structure of economic power. In their extensive investigation of corporation ownership, undertaken several years ago, A. A. Berle and G. C. Means concluded that, in spite of a fairly wide distribution of some corporation stock, almost half of industry was actually controlled by a few hundred persons. The replacement of many small economic units by relatively few vast organizations, the limitation of "free" competition by monopolies and semimonopolies, especially associated with the growth of large-scale corporations, and the transition in which capital more and more takes the form of economic *organization* itself rather than tangible goods, are among the forces bringing about a society "in which production is carried out under the ultimate control of a handful of individuals."[30] Subsequent studies, most notably, perhaps, the reports of the Temporary National Economic Committee, have documented the trend toward the concentration of economic power, particularly in such fields as transportation, power, mining, and manufacturing. There is still a large area for the "little" business enterprises that offer a more personal type of good or service, but the trends clearly indicate that an economic power structure has been evolving that encompasses an increasing amount of our total enterprise, drives competition more and more into "monopolistic competition" for huge market areas, separates the management and production function from the ownership and financial function, and, generally, represents the solidification of an *economic* class standing at the apex of the total economic organization.[31]

THREE: OCCUPATIONAL LINES. This growing concentration of economic power affords a measure of contrast with the complicated pattern of occupations which is directly related to the status structure in the national community. We may take the major categories used in Table X on page 351 as a classifica-

(J. Kieran, ed., New York, 1947), p. 282. For a careful study of income in the United States, with estimates for 1950, see J. Dewhurst, *et al.*, *America's Needs and Resources* (New York, 1947), Chap. IV.

30. A. A. Berle and G. C. Means, *The Modern Corporation and Private Property* (New York, 1933), pp. 45–46.

31. For a summary and evaluation of the reports of the Temporary National Economic Committee, see D. Lynch, *The Concentration of Economic Power* (New York, 1946). Various aspects of this concentration are treated, for example, in Berle and Means, *op. cit.;* H. G. Moulton, *Income and Economic Progress* (Washington, D.C., 1935); E. Chamberlin, *The Theory of Monopolistic Competition* (Cambridge, Mass., 1938); U.S. National Resources Committee, *The Structure of American Economy* (Washington, D.C., 1939), Parts I and II.

tion of broad occupational types and consider the shifts in these groups during recent decades, as shown in Table XI.

TABLE XI **Occupational Classes in the United States, 1910–1940**[32]

(Persons 14 years old and over, and excluding new workers in 1940.)

Occupational class (Socioeconomic group)	Percentage Distribution			
	1910	1920	1930	1940
I. Professional persons	4.4	5.0	6.1	6.5
II. Proprietors, managers, and officials	23.0	22.3	19.9	17.8
III. Clerks and kindred workers	10.2	13.8	16.3	17.2
IV. Skilled workers and foremen	11.7	13.5	12.9	11.7
V. Semiskilled workers	14.7	16.1	16.4	21.0
VI. Unskilled workers	36.0	29.4	28.4	25.9

Note first that Class II, within which are the great majority of persons who exercise the largest degree of economic power and who enjoy the maximum incomes, has been declining proportionately; on the other hand Class I, the professionals, has somewhat expanded. The largest gains have been made in Classes III and IV, the "white-collar" and semiskilled workers, while the skilled workers reached a peak in 1920. Finally, the unskilled, Class VI, have shown a steady relative decrease since the beginning of the thirty-year period. If we divide the entire working population into "manual workers" (farmers, farm laborers, industrial wage earners, servants) and "brain workers" (professionals, lower-salaried workers, proprietors, officials), and follow the trends from as far back as 1870, we discover that the first group included over 80 per cent of the working population in that year in comparison with only slightly more than 60 per cent today, whereas the second group has risen from about 10½ per cent to over 31 per cent in recent years.[33] These trends reflect a more complex division of labor, a more developed machine technology that demands a larger proportion of *semi*skilled as distinct from unskilled or skilled workers, an expanded area of commercial activity in which the service and "paper" or "white-collar" occupations play a greater role, and a growing concentration of the control functions in the economy. Moreover, these trends have considerably increased the proportion of the population most likely to seek and gain "middle-class"

32. Data from Bureau of the Census, *Comparative Occupational Statistics*, Chap. XV.
33. T. M. Sogge, "Industrial Classes in the United States," *Journal of the American Statistical Association* (June, 1933), 199–200.

status, and, therefore, are significantly related, as we shall see, to a predominant type of class sentiment in the United States.

[2] *Vertical and horizontal mobility:* There is no necessary inconsistency, of course, between the existence of economic strata, whether divisions of wealth or of power or of occupation, and a system that guarantees to the individual the opportunity to rise in the social order. To a far greater extent in the United States, in fact, than in any other large modern nation, individuals have been able to improve their social position. Expansion, geographical and economic, through much of the country's history has meant a sizable degree of vertical mobility essential to the maintenance of an open-class system. Expanding frontiers, a growing industrial and commercial economy, and a constant replenishment of the labor force, by immigration for many years, thereby thrusting upward many of the older residents, provided evidence of and gave strength to the conception of a land of opportunity for the enterprising, the industrious, and the lucky. But now that the geographical frontiers have closed and immigration has almost ceased, and now that the area of free competition has narrowed and vastly larger economic units have grown up, what, we may ask, is the actual mobility pattern?

In answering this question we must rely upon general statistical information concerning the shifting occupational divisions and upon a few studies of selected groups. Of the latter, the most detailed investigation available reports the moves, both vertical and horizontal, of a representative sample of the residents of San Jose, California.[34] The authors of this study, utilizing the occupational categories shown in Table XI as an index of class position, discovered that between 60 and 73 per cent of the occupations of sons are on the same class level as those of their fathers or on an adjacent level, with the largest amount of occupational "inheritance" in the three lowest groups and the least amount in the professional class. Of the sons of the unskilled workers, about 42 per cent were also unskilled, while almost 72 per cent remained in the wage-earning categories.[35] In this Western community, located in a region of maximum economic growth, it is not surprising that on every occupational level there are some persons who "have worked on each of the other levels." We see here considerable vertical mobility, to be sure, though for most of the individuals involved the range of movement is limited. "Three-quarters of all moves are confined to the same level or the levels immediately adjacent to it," and about one half of all the shifts are *horizontal*, involving no change in occupational-class position. Very rare indeed are moves from the bottom of the scale to the top or from the highest positions to the lowest.[36]

---

34. P. E. Davidson and H. D. Anderson, *Occupational Mobility in an American Community* (Stanford University, 1937).

35. *Ibid.*, Chap. II.

36. *Ibid.*, pp. 184–185. For a discussion of these results by a foremost student of occupational statistics, see W. S. Woytinsky, *Labor in the United States* (Washington, D.C., 1938), pp.

While there is some evidence of a decrease in vertical mobility, this has not been accompanied by a comparable decrease in the attitudes that are characteristic of an open-class society, or by a large-scale growth of corporate class consciousness among those groups showing an increasing degree of occupational inheritance. This may be explained on the grounds that a not inconsiderable number do still rise in the occupational scale and that *some* individuals do actually move from the ranks below to peak positions in our society, thereby providing objective evidence of the possibility and support for the aspirations of many. Furthermore, the relatively undiminished amount of *horizontal* mobility, shifts from one type of work to another in the same occupational "class," tends to bolster mobility consciousness, especially among that great majority of individuals who stand between the two economic extremes. The existence in an urban-industrial society of thousands of occupational specializations, including the many different "white-collar" tasks, with each tending to take on its own status and offering a particular opportunity, provides the individual with at least the chance and clearly the hope of proving the validity of the "American dream."

Class attitudes in the United States. A well-known trait of American people is the extent to which they profess to belong to the "middle class." Various opinion polls, conducted during the last ten years, indicate that few persons, usually less than 6 per cent of the population, describe themselves as "upper class," and that a minority, varying between 10 and 25 per cent, place themselves in the "lower class." Yet the three fourths or more who speak of themselves as "middle class" by no means represent a group-conscious division of the national community.[37]

[1] *Characteristics of middle-class sentiment:* The attitudes that make up the predominant "middle-class" emphasis in American life, are, in the first place, a reflection of the type of sentiment we have named *competitive class feeling.* This attitudinal complex is essentially individualistic, as we have seen, and basically in conflict with the growth of a corporate consciousness in any group. Middle-class sentiment, then, is less a feeling of group attachment than a feeling of rejection of hierarchical attitudes as such, less an attitude of identification with any particular group than of identification with the whole community or with the unidentified "common man" or "everyday citizen."

266-268. A more recent study tending to confirm the findings of Davidson and Anderson for a larger area is R. Canters, "Occupational Mobility of Urban Occupational Strata," *American Sociological Review*, XIII (1948), 197-203.

37. For poll studies of class attitudes see, for example, E. Roper's "Fortune Surveys," *Fortune*, Feb., 1940, and Jan., 1947; G. Gallup and S. F. Rae, *The Pulse of Democracy* (New York, 1940), Chap. XIV; and for a detailed discussion of various studies, A. W. Kornhauser, "Analysis of 'Class' Structure of Contemporary American Society—Psychological Bases of Class Divisions," in *Industrial Conflict: A Psychological Interpretation* (G. W. Hartmann and T. Newcomb, eds., New York, 1939), Chap. XI.

These latter symbols, once associated especially with the rise of the *bourgeoisie* in Europe, in this country are tied to no one segment of the population. A large proportion of the people on almost all economic and occupational levels and possessing almost all degrees of social prestige say that they are "middle class." This claim, at bottom, is a denial of the existence of any recognizable social stratification in the United States.

Wherever middle-class attitudes are dominant we are apt to find the values that Veblen portrayed so vividly, competitiveness and emulation and display, governing behavior in various ways. The semiannual scramble for "better" addresses (if not curtailed by a housing shortage), the seemingly constant desire to possess the latest models of clothing and cars and radios and the innumerable gadgets our technology provides, the eagerness to display overt evidence of "cultural" attainment such as shelves of books (or merely empty bindings!) and walls of paintings, and even, in many families, the limitation placed upon the number of children—an economic liability from the urban middle-class point of view—are greatly influenced by the felt need to "keep up with the Joneses." If this competitive drive is an important feature of middle-class sentiment, no less strong is the emphasis given to education as a means of permitting the individual to improve his lot (which goes with the suspicion of purely "cultural" education) and the stress upon independence, industriousness, and "drive" (which goes with the suspicion of inherited wealth and of the lack of industriousness). Success in the secular world, in keeping with one aspect of traditional Protestant thought, continues to be an index of intrinsic merit in the middle-class-minded, although, as we shall see, this is less the case today than in earlier years. These various elements of the middle-class outlook are found in different degrees from person to person and from group to group, of course, but the competitive quality of the sentiment remains dominant through the changes of the class attitudes of a large proportion of the people of the United States.[38]

[2] *Competitive sentiment and economic division:* In this country, then, the values associated with the growth of an open-class society and with the rise of the *bourgeoisie* to a high position in the social structure are reflected in the attitudes of the members of most economic sections of the population. On the one hand, the viewpoint of the "honest tradesman"—expressed, for example in the admonitions of Benjamin Franklin and W. G. Sumner and Calvin Coolidge—tends to stamp the outlook of the American toward all of his fellows—he counts no man his superior. On the other hand, he is apt to gain

38. For an earlier vigorous affirmation of "middle-class" thinking, see W. G. Sumner, *What the Social Classes Owe to Each Other* (New York, 1920; originally published in 1883). This viewpoint is graphically described in R. S. and H. M. Lynd, *Middletown in Transition* (New York, 1937), Chap. XII; and R. S. Lynd, *Knowledge For What?* (Princeton, N.J., 1939), Chap. III. For the historical development of some of its aspects, including its reflection in literature, see F. C. Palm, *The Middle Classes, Then and Now* (New York, 1936).

a special social status on the basis of his particular calling, his particular functional niche within the vastly complex occupational division of labor. This, too, supports the competitive sentiment, for in our system status is not fixed; there are almost always some "Joneses" above to set the pace, some with whom to keep up, and some below upon whom to look down.

The United States presents a striking example of the lack of correspondence between economic division and subjective class attitudes. The first, the economic, represents a series of grades, not clearly distinguishable strata, ranging from the small wealthy section of the population at the top to the large group in the lower-income brackets, restricted in consuming power, educational level, and, as we have seen, enjoying a limited opportunity to rise in the economic scale. The sociopsychological divisions, however, in so far as they can be ascertained on the basis of attitude studies, opinion polls, and the like, cut across the economic lines, each principal attitude-group including at least some members of several economic levels. The two types of division and their general relationship to one another are presented in Chart XIV.

CHART XIV **Simplified Figure Suggesting the Relation of Class Attitudes to Economic Divisions in the United States**

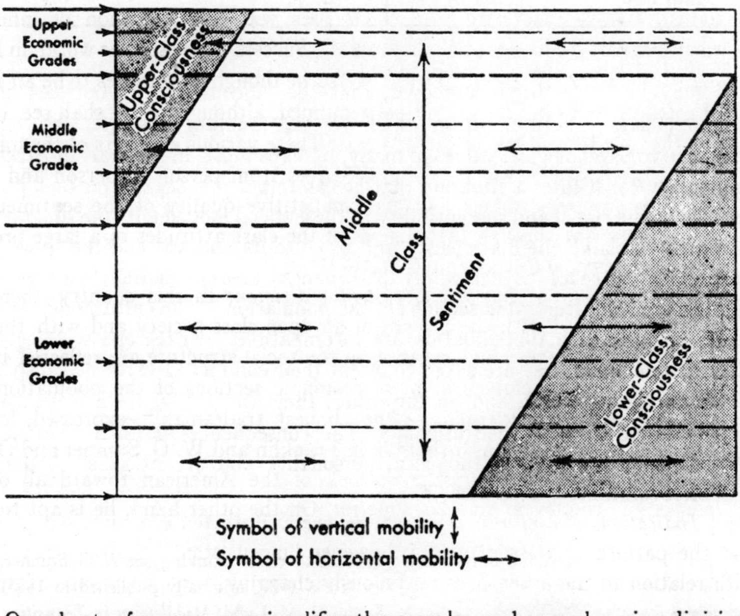

Our chart, of course, oversimplifies the complex and ever-changing divisions and relationships that make up the class structure of the United States. Nevertheless there seem to be grounds for the conclusions that conscious identification with an upper class is made only by a minority of the members of the highest economic grades but is found also among some members of the "middle" economic class; that middle-class sentiment typifies the class attitudes of large proportions of all economic segments; and that lower-class feeling, while largely confined to the lower economic levels, characterizes as well the attitudes of a few persons of higher economic class standing. This situation is suggested, for example, by the responses given to questions asking individuals to identify themselves by "class." The results of one such study are shown in Table XII.

TABLE XII **How Americans Identified Themselves by "Class" in 1940**[39]

Answered	People who are economically classified as			
	Prosperous	Upper middle	Lower middle	Poor
"Upper class"	23.6%	7.9%	4.6%	4.5%
"Middle class"	74.7	89.0	89.4	70.3
"Lower class"	.3	.6	3.1	19.1
"Don't know"	1.4	2.5	2.9	6.1

It may be conjectured, moreover, that the "inconsistency" between the economic-class structure, within which vertical mobility is limited, and the competitive psychological values of many, perhaps most, individuals in American society constitutes a situation that has an important bearing on such phenomena as the rise of and susceptibility to those social movements the programs of which "explain" the discrepancy and promise its removal and the possibly increasing degree of psychological disturbances among middle-class-minded but economically frustrated sections of the population. "The cultural demands made on persons in this situation are incompatible," writes one sociologist. "On the one hand, they are asked to orient their conduct toward the prospect of accumulating wealth and on the other, they are largely denied effective opportunities to do so institutionally. The consequences of such structural inconsistency are psychopathological personality and/or antisocial conduct, and/or revolutionary activities."[40]

[3] *Indications of corporate class consciousness:* Both the economic structure and the pattern of class attitudes, however "inconsistent" the one may be with relation to the other, are continuously changing, though perhaps at dif-

39. Adapted from "Fortune Survey," Feb., 1940.
40. R. K. Merton, "Social Structure and Anomie," *American Sociological Review*, III (1938), 679.

ferent rates. There are, for example, indications that competitive middle-class sentiment, though persistent and pervasive, as we have seen, is being replaced in certain areas by corporate class consciousness. The growth of the latter is particularly evident in two widely separated groups.

The first of these consists of families of long settlement who enjoy a tradition of affluence, often associated with a record of public service or cultivation of the arts and sciences, and who effectively exclude from their informal, if not their formal, associations individuals without the proper credentials of "birth and breeding." Small "aristocracies" of this type, with memberships that frequently include otherwise eligible persons of relatively limited economic means, are characteristic of the older communities in the eastern regions of the United States. Together they make up most of the shaded area to the left in Chart XIV.

Although the degree of corporate unity is not as marked, both the number of persons involved and the potential sociological significance of the change in class attitudes are much greater in the second group, the industrial workers (shaded area to the right in Chart XIV). Competitive class feeling with its stress upon individual attainment has for many decades generally dominated American workers, especially in the skilled crafts, including those organized within the American Federation of Labor and the larger "independent" unions. However, with the enormous growth of mass industries, the increasing organization of employees on an industry-wide basis in both the older unions and the more recent C.I.O., the replacement of skilled artisans by machine operatives in many fields, the substitution of collective bargaining for individual contracting of labor, the expanding union programs stressing *workers'* educational and recreational activities, and the growing political role of organized labor, individualized competitive attitudes are in some degree diminishing. While they are not to any large extent being replaced by the militant socialistically oriented working-class consciousness that Marx envisioned, there is mounting evidence that American workers are becoming more concerned with economic security *as a group* than with individual rise in the social scale. This attitude has become more pronounced as the dislocations of the economic order have grown and as the benefits of social security provisions and collective action have become more apparent to the factory employee. The worker's conception of his own chances of advancement, his conviction that diligence and application will "pay off," his faith in "better times" ahead have at least been shaken. These conclusions are substantiated by polling studies of workers' opinions made in recent years and by more intensive field investigations of the industrial employees of different communities throughout the country.[41]

41. See, for example, the opinion studies cited in note 37 above; for changing class attitudes among industrial workers in New Haven, see E. W. Bakke, *Citizens without Work* (New Haven, 1940), especially Chap. V; in Akron, A. W. Jones, *Life, Liberty, and Property* (Philadelphia, 1941), especially Chaps. XXIII and XXIV; in a small New England city, W. L. Warner and

Class in the local community. The class structure of the local community, the local village or town or city, has preoccupied a number of students in very recent years. Most of the resulting reports have been made by cultural anthropologists or have incorporated their "field" techniques of investigation—the same kind of objective portrayal of the social life of, say, "Middletown" or "Yankee City" or "Plainville" has been attempted as that sought in the study of the Tanala or the Alorese. This approach necessarily emphasizes the interrelatedness of different aspects of the social structure. It considers, for example, not only the objective data reported in statistics of income, occupation, and formal affiliations but also the evidences of class structure revealed in the attitudes, the day-to-day behavior, the informal associations, and the verbal symbols of group differentiation used by the people themselves.

[1] *Some illustrations of class stratification:* This approach seeks, in other words, to put into the more systematic language of social science the indications of social hierarchy that are shown to us in the first instance by the overt and covert behavior, the biases, the formal and informal imposition of restrictions, the gossip of the participants in the community life.[42] Let us consider some specific cases.

ONE: MIDDLETOWN. Although the authors of the well-known surveys of "Middletown," an Indiana city of almost 50,000 population, did not focus their investigations upon the class structure, a part of their second volume, published in 1937, treats of the social hierarchy. Middletown is a multi-functional city, with a well-developed industry, extensive commercial activities, a local college, and other features characteristic of many cities in the Mid-western region. Much of its economic life is directly managed, and its political and cultural life often indirectly controlled, by a small group in the highest economic brackets.[43] But the system of social classes reported in the study is more complex than this economic domination might suggest, for it includes several distinguishable strata. At the top was found the very small local "upper class," setting the cultural standards, made up of larger manufacturers, leading managers and bankers, and a few lawyers, all strategically located in the business life; just below, a slightly larger group of smaller manufacturers, high-salaried employees, merchants, and professionals generally following the lead of the class above; then, "Middletown's own middle class," composed of some employed professionals, small retailers and entrepreneurs, salesmen, and other "white-collar" workers; next, "an aristocracy of local labor," including

---

J. O. Low, *The Social System of the Modern Factory* (New Haven, 1947), especially Chaps. IX and X.

42. For discussions of this approach and some of the techniques involved in the study of class structure see, for example, J. Dollard, *Caste and Class in a Southern Town* (New Haven, 1937), Chap. II; W. L. Warner and P. S. Lunt, *The Social Life of a Modern Community* (New Haven, 1941), Chaps. I–V.

43. Lynd and Lynd, *op. cit.*, Chap. III.

many of the foremen and skilled workers: fifth and by far the largest, the class of semiskilled and unskilled wage earners; and, finally, the smaller "ragged bottom margin," all unskilled, including the newly or temporarily acquired "poor whites" from surrounding states.[44] This structure of six classes profoundly affects and reflects the life of the community. Yet "if the nascent 'class' system . . . appears to follow somewhat the above lines," the authors state significantly, "Middletown itself will turn away from any such picture of the fissures and gullies across the surface of its social life. It is far more congenial to the mood of the city, proud of its traditions of democratic equality, to think of the lines of cleavage within its social system as based not upon class differences but rather upon the entirely spontaneous and completely individual and personal predilections of the 22,500 families who compose its population."[45] Class stratification is an important element of the community's social structure, to be sure, but its members refrain from the use of "class" language—a characteristic phenomenon in this country.

TWO: YANKEE CITY. This small New England city of about 15,000 persons is a coastal community of long establishment with many of its residents claiming "old American" status, but the home also of numerous families of more recent arrival in the United States. In a series of volumes, W. Lloyd Warner and his associates have reported in microscopic detail the results of several years of investigation of this presumably "well-integrated" and partially independent community, stressing particularly its system of social classes and status groups, the associational affiliations, its ethnic composition, the role of its changing industrial structure, and the interrelationships between these various features of its social life. As in Middletown, a hierarchy of six classes is portrayed into which, it is claimed, "individuals were placed by the evaluations of Yankee City itself."[46] The latter do not think of these divisions as "classes," but their differentiating and discriminating behavior justifies, perhaps, the distinctions made by the authors between "upper-upper," "lower-upper," "upper-middle," "lower-middle," "upper-lower," and "lower-lower." The first of these, including less than 1½ per cent of the population, consists of the old families, generally but not always wealthy, who stress lineage and maintain fairly rigidly a closed class. The members of the lower-upper group, a slightly larger class, often lack the birth requisite of top position but nevertheless stress its desirability, and, more significantly, conspicuously display their material affluence. About 10

44. *Ibid.*, pp. 458–460.
45. *Ibid.*, pp. 460–461.
46. *The Social Life of the Modern American Community*, p. 90; in this volume, for the details of Yankee City's class structure, see especially Chaps. V–VIII and XX–XXII; see further W. L. Warner and P. S. Lunt, *The Status System of a Modern Community* (New Haven, 1942), especially Chaps. III and V; W. L. Warner and Leo Srole, *The Social Systems of American Ethnic Groups* (New Haven, 1945), especially Chap. V; *The Social System of the Modern Factory*, especially Chaps. VIII and IX.

per cent of Yankee City is upper-middle, which, like the class above, shows a strong belief in money and material comforts, with most members striving for higher status; and about 28 per cent is lower-middle, with the members adding "morals" to money as the "keys to all their problems." These same values are present in the one third of the population described as the "upper-lower" class, whose material standards are low but whose ambitions, at least for their children with the aid of education, are noticeable. But in the one fourth of Yankee City designated as "lower-lower," where all members are unskilled workers today (though many are descendants of skilled craftsmen) and where the material level is the lowest, little interest is shown in education, and the values of thrift and ambition have clearly diminished. While we may question the "discovery" and separation of *six* social classes (rather than some other number), the evidence clearly indicates the existence of a structure of broad status groups of basic significance in the political and economic and cultural activities of Yankee City. We see, again, more markedly than in Middlewestern Middletown, the tendency of groups at the extremes to solidify and to develop their own customs, a sense of uniqueness, their own class consciousness; while the classes between, from "upper-lower" to "lower-upper" inclusively, tend to share the values associated with competitive middle-class sentiment.[47]

THREE: PLAINVILLE. This Missouri rural village of less than three hundred inhabitants might be assumed to display few signs of class stratification. Its people, when asked, usually deny the existence of classes in their "democratic" community, yet a recent field study reports not only a basic division into two broad groups but a loose hierarchy of possibly five distinct strata, with the "upper-crust" leaders at the top and the nonreligious people "who live like animals" at the bottom. Here there is no such complex system as found in the large cities but there seems little doubt that a class order has developed and that it plays an important role in determining the attitudes, the aspirations, even the child-training techniques of the members of Plainville's different social groups. These conclusions are borne out in a number of similar investigations of the influence of class differentiation in other rural communities.[48]

[2] *Criteria of social class in the local community:* These studies of local communities tell us a great deal about the values in terms of which individuals and families set themselves apart from others and thus upon which are based the barriers of social distance separating class from class. There are several such

47. Among other studies utilizing Warner's approach and reporting a six-class system are A. Davis, B. B. and M. R. Gardner, *Deep South* (Chicago, 1944); and, to a less extent, St. C. Drake and H. K. Cayton, *Black Metropolis* (New York, 1945), Chaps. XIX–XXII.

48. J. West (pseudonym), *Plainville, U.S.A.* (New York, 1945), Chap. III. For other studies of stratification in rural communities see, for example, H. F. Kaufman, *Prestige Classes in a New York Rural Community* (Ithaca, N.Y., 1944); A. D. Edwards, *Beaverdam: A Rural Community in Transition* (Blacksburg, Va., 1942).

differentiating criteria which, although usually interrelated, may be distinguished.[49]

ONE: WEALTH—RESIDENCE—POSSESSIONS. In our relatively open-class society, wealth continues to rule as the principal badge of social position, the basic criterion of status. This is borne out in the investigations we have cited—in each community the great majority of the population rate one another according to the degree of wealth. Estimating the other fellow's affluence is greatly abetted by the customary devices of conspicuous display, making easier "invidious comparisons." Closely associated with wealth and primarily dependent upon it, place of residence or "neighborhood" in Middletown and Yankee City and even in Plainville, and probably in almost every American community, serves as an unmistakable mark of status. Similarly, material possessions, whether the modern agricultural tools that distinguish the "better-class people" from the "scratch-farmers" in Plainville or the array of fashionable goods available in the city, function as an important basis for social ranking in American life.

TWO: LINEAGE—"MANNERS"—"MORALS." If most of the members of local communities are concerned with wealth and its more obvious attributes there are some, nonetheless, who give first place to lineage, to what is often expressed as "good family" or "good American stock." Thus the small "upper-upper" class of Yankee City keeps its ranks almost completely closed to the frequently wealthier aspirants for top position, displaying a pattern repeated in many other communities. (The most extreme example of the use of birth as the determinant of status is seen in the rigid separation of color "castes.") The emphasis on lineage is often associated with the criterion of "manners" as a differentiating index, though expressed in quite a variety of ways, and this index is utilized within and between all but the lowest social ranks in the community.

"Morality," in the sense of behavior in keeping with the conventions, is an especially significant mark of status in "middle-class" groups. Propriety and conventionality are often used to mark off the "better class" of people from others below (and sometimes above) in the social hierarchy. "Low morality," including dishonesty, tendencies toward violence, and departures from the sex code, are attributed, for example, to the "lower-lower" class of Yankee City and to the "lower element" of Plainville by those of higher social position.[50] When the members of the lower classes are of distinct ethnic or racial origin, this attribution of lower "morality" often grows into curious beliefs concerning the immoral practices, even the sexual prowess, of such groups. These beliefs

49. The criteria of social ranking used below are presented in *Plainville, U.S.A.*, pp. 119–126, though in different order and with specific reference to one community.

50. On differential sex mores and practices in the United States see A. C. Kinsey, W. B. Pomeroy, and C. E. Martin, *Sexual Behavior in the Human Male* (Philadelphia, 1948) especially Chap. X.

play an important role in American social life, as we shall see in the following chapter.

[3] *The local community and the larger society:* We have already indicated the major characteristics of the economic and social divisions of the United States as a whole. This broader structure, we must now emphasize, is both a reflection of and, in turn, an influence upon the structure of the local community. The impact of the nation-wide pattern becomes more and more apparent as our economic and political associations become increasingly complex and interdependent and as they develop on a vaster scale and with a greater degree of centralization. A decision made today in New York to build a new industrial plant in "Yankee City" may tomorrow alter the latter's social as well as its economic structure; a decision of the federal government to undertake a river-valley regional plan may change the social features of a whole area. The class structure of the local villages or town or city should not be viewed as a closed system when it is tied in with the greater community by a growing network of communication, when the values and ideas and conflicts of the larger society more and more become those of its smaller divisions. The small town or a segment of a larger city provides, to be sure, a "workable" body of information concerning its social stratification, and, moreover, the attitudes and behavior of its members constitute the basic sociological data in this field. But a local class system in the modern world is never *merely* local: it is a phenomenon that must be understood as a part of a large-scale and changing social order.

The Broader Significance of Class

Class and the character of the community. The class system at any time reflects and also profoundly influences the whole life of a community, whether a small village or a great nation. Its relation to the whole social structure is apparent if we contrast briefly its different manifestations in various countries.

[1] *The class system as a reflection of community values:* In the United States, as we have seen, there is, on the one hand, a lack of formal (though not informal) class distinctions, considerable class mobility, a relative absence of cultural barriers between classes; and, on the other hand, there is some degree of correlation between class lines and nationality or racial distinctions, a high development of wealth prestige or plutocracy, and a comparatively small growth of a hereditary "aristocracy." In England, by contrast, we find still, in spite of the diminished power of wealth and the extension of political democracy, traditionally deep grooves of class superiority and inferiority, an established, if no longer powerful, aristocracy, supported by still prevalent though weakening historically rooted attitudes, as witnessed by the subservience of many groups toward their social "betters." In France, since the Revolution, the

middle or bourgeois class has been dominant, though its position is now seriously challenged, and localized aristocracies have in some degree survived. In Germany occurred the abrupt though long-prepared transition from a feudal military class structure, the collapse under military defeat after World War I of the social prestige of a landowning aristocracy, the subsequent suppression, under Nazi leadership, of the proletarian class movement and the destruction after World War II of the short-lived elite of Hitler's "national socialism." In Russia, we see a class system that constitutes a partial reversal of the traditional Western hierarchy, with the proletariat officially accorded highest prestige and privilege, but with a new ruling group emerging, possessing special status and responsibility and power.

This catalogue, showing the differences of class systems corresponding to general differences in social structures and in predominant values, might be continued indefinitely, but we will conclude it with the remarkable contrast exhibited in this respect by India and China. The vast society of India is deeply permeated by the immemorial tradition of caste, so that every aspect of life, religion, education, occupation, social intercourse, has been governed by its rigid code of distances, though at length national independence and the emergence of new values are showing significant signs of undermining it. In China, on the other hand, we have the contrary spectacle of an enormous society in which class distinctions have traditionally played a very minor role. In theory, and to some extent, in practice, ranking prestige has belonged to the scholar rather than to the man of wealth or power, whatever his background; and, more importantly, so overwhelming has been the value attached to the family as such that loyalty to this organization has outweighed other considerations in determining the respect which a man receives from his fellows. In China, as in all communities, the rise of new values within the society or the impact of values from without inevitably alters, as the changes today illustrate, the character of the social structure and of the class system itself.[51]

[2] *How the class system affects the community life:* The character of a class system, whether it be closed and rigid, whether it make birth or wealth or military prowess or occupation or intellectual attainment the main determinant of social distinction, greatly influences the modes of living, the ideals of the group, and the whole process of social selection. A caste order, for example, discounts intrinsic merits and capacities, and by denying opportunities for advancement to those who belong to the lower castes deprives itself of the potential contributions that might emanate from their ranks. A rigid system of caste, at the same time, *in so far as* it is supported by commonly shared basic values and beliefs, provides a stability in the community and individual life. But we may reasonably infer that whenever a system limits opportunity to

---

51. For a brief comparison of several types of class systems see B. Moore, Jr., "A Comparative Analysis of the Class Struggle," *American Sociological Review*, X (1945), 31-37.

privileged groups within it, the society is needlessly losing the aptitudes and talents that might otherwise be brought to light within the ranks of the unprivileged The fact that more individuals of personal distinction and high social achievement arise in the higher income groups in proportion to their numbers, while sometimes used as an argument for the intrinsic superiority of those groups, might with at least as much logic be made an argument for the expansion of opportunity.[52]

A further serious penalty of a system that limits the use of intrinsic merit is that it establishes other than merit standards, and therefore socially inefficient standards, in the privileged class. This characteristic is not only an aspect of a caste system but also of a competitive plutocratic system. Under the latter a condition peculiarly detachable from personal quality—the amount of one's wealth—is made a ground of esteem, and, moreover, the keeping up of appearances becomes an end of life. "Good form," the conventions and shibboleths of the prestige group, often assumes an importance superior to merit or character. The gain sought by the social climber is a purely relative one, so that the satisfaction of success is speedily dimmed by the new comparisons that each step on the class ladder brings into view. In the middle classes particularly, as we have seen, "respectability" is apt to become a fetish. It becomes the measure, for example, of a "good marriage" or of a "good" political candidate or even of a "sound" economic or political doctrine. Another illustration of the opposition between class standards and intrinsic qualifications is presented by the outmoded system of appointment and promotion in the military and naval hierarchy. Officers, especially in countries with long-established traditions, were apt to form almost a caste, in which ability was subordinated to the considerations of status, so that there was little promotion from the ranks in times of peace. But the necessity created by warfare for technological and leadership skills has greatly altered this situation, giving the man of capacity some opportunity to rise to command, and has revealed the initial weakness of a system that identified the officer with the "gentleman."

Sometimes the social function of an upper class marked off by predetermined status is viewed as beneficial to the community. This type of class system has been defended as a means of protecting and elevating cultural standards, of developing a way of living that stimulates refinement and prevents the encroachment of vulgarity, and of evoking and providing a market for artistic and intellectual abilities. The flowering of the artistic life in fifth-century (B.C.) Athens and, under the patronage of the Medici, in fifteenth-century Florence is cited as evidence of this function. The history of capitalism shows how modern luxury and the arts that administer to it were the offspring of the courtly establishments of the Middle Ages.[53] If a dominant class is itself cultured it will promote, to be sure, those cultural expressions that are not out of

52. See Chapter IV.

53. W. Sombart, *Luxus und Kapitalismus* (Munich, 1913), Chap. IV.

accord with its interests. It will promote, for example, the arts of painting and music and architecture rather than free intellectual activity that tends to question the social status quo.

Moreover, the basis of a class system is the possession, officially or informally, of power, not of culture, and there is no historical evidence that power and cultural attainment must go together.[54] Against the instances cited may be set many other examples of upper classes that did little to promote the development of the arts or actually frustrated their growth. Even the music-loving aristocracies of Central Europe kept Mozart and Beethoven in poverty and allowed Schubert to die in destitution. Patronage, whether that of a money plutocracy or of a hereditary aristocracy or of a new ruling elite, is a precarious stimulant of artistic endeavor. Class power is a close neighbor of class intolerance, and a dominant social group is more apt to dictate cultural conditions than to permit their spontaneous development—whether the conditions demand absence of criticism of capitalistic vested interests, as in the case of professors who are too "liberal" for the trustees, or whether they demand, as in Soviet Russia today, the production of music and literature free of "bourgeois" taint. In countries where the great masses are sunk in poverty, a dominant class will certainly maintain a luxury otherwise impossible, and thus may provide an incentive to the finer arts and crafts, though this will probably involve further depression of the standards of living of the rest of the population. In countries enjoying a wider distribution of economic prosperity and maintaining rights of freedom of expression, the social function sometimes attributed to ruling classes is more adequately performed by the special cultural groups, not necessarily power groups, that arise in a more complex society.[55]

The transformation of class systems. The intimate relationship between the class system and the whole structure of a society is best revealed when we examine the process of social change. Here we may briefly consider one aspect of this subject, one which we shall discuss more thoroughly in Book Three, the final section of this volume.

[1] *Class and revolutionary change:* In the historical process the transformation of classes has accompanied all great revolutionary movements. The governing elements of a society have generally represented a dominant social class, what Pareto calls an *elite.* The conditions on which their dominance rests are subject to change, and their power is threatened and finally overthrown as new elements rise to power. Pareto maintains that the fall of elites is due to their decline in relative numbers and to their decay in quality; the followers of

54. On class and power see R. M. MacIver, *The Web of Government* (New York, 1947), Chap. V.

55. For a discussion of class and art, see A. S. Tomars, *Introduction to the Sociology of Art* (Mexico, 1940), Part II.

Marx insist that the material conditions of a social order inevitably bring about the transformation of class power. Whatever the explanation—a problem we shall face in a later chapter—"history," as Pareto puts it, "is a graveyard of aristocracies."[56] Their fall is at least the sign of important changes in the social structure. In ancient Athens, for example, the reforms of Cleisthenes and of Solon, reducing the political control of the old families, were made in response to deep-seated economic and social changes. In ancient Rome the status of the patricians was gradually undermined in correspondence with the conditions of an empire which, as it grew in extent, profoundly changed the distribution of wealth and poverty. In eighteenth-century France the aristocracy of a luxurious court disregarded the growing unrest of a population driven by economic pressures to an insurgence that at length abruptly destroyed the old order.

The conditions that transformed feudalism into our modern state-systems brought also, both as consequences and as causes of that transformation, the enfranchisement of the serf, the disintegration of old classes, the rise of the burghers, the greater importance of office and function as against predetermined status, and finally that new power of the capital-owning classes that overcame the aristocracy of landownership. The new status of the industrialist and the financier reflected the new social economy, a transformation which broke up old traditions and old thought forms, and which affected every aspect of life—morals, religions, philosophies, no less than the modes of work and leisure.[57] It brought with it also the phenomenon of a class to which the new conditions of industrial employment gave a cohesion and a degree of solidarity and of definite organization hitherto lacking. The industrial proletariat has been unified not only by its discontent with the economic system but, especially in Europe, by the utopian and powerful appeal of the Marxist doctrine, which, for thirty years, has had the strong backing of the governing elite of a vast nation. The rise of leaders of this class, whether within the democratic framework of some European nations or within the authoritarian structure of others, may be the most important factor in the further modification of the class system of Western civilization.[58]

[2] *The case of the United States:* In the United States the process of industrialization and the transformation of classes took a somewhat different form from the European. The period following the Civil War witnessed a vast and sudden access of industrialism, in which an agrarian economy with its

---

56. V. Pareto, *The Mind and Society* (A. Livingston, ed., New York, 1935), Vol. III, §2053.

57. For the history of this class transformation, see, for example, K. Bücher, *Industrial Evolution* (S. M. Wickett, tr., New York, 1901); and for a recent interpretation of some aspects of this change, K. Polanyi, *The Great Transformation* (New York, 1944).

58. For a suggestive analysis of the role and aspirations of the working class in Europe see Briefs, *The Proletariat*, and for an interpretation of the role of Soviet Russia in this connection, E. H. Carr, *The Soviet Impact on the Western World* (New York, 1947).

farmers, traders, and small individual capitalists yielded, though not without a struggle, before a system of "big business" and centralized finance, with its dominating magnates of steel and oil, of mine and railroad. The old traditions, whether of New England Puritan or Southern gentleman, whether of hardy pioneer or thrifty artisan extolled by Franklin, could not resist the tide that carried to power the trust-builder and the political boss. The old "middle-class" conceptions of democracy, of individualism, of Jeffersonian equality, while still significantly reflected in American attitudes, as we have seen, were considerably altered by the new concentration and distribution of power on the one hand and on the other by the new heterogeneity of a population to which successive waves of immigration added workers of alien culture and lower standards of living.[59] The old traditions have not perished but they have lost vitality. And in the process arose the present dominantly competitive and confused class system, with its strongly plutocratic aspects, with its inconsistency between concentrated economic power and equalitarian attitudes. If there are certain contradictions within our complex and changing system of social and economic classes, they are even more manifest in the ethnic and racial divisions of the social structure. These divisions are the subject of the following chapter.

---

59. For discussions of various indications of these changes see, for example, Page, *Class and American Sociology*, Chap. I; and V. L. Parrington, *Main Currents in American Thought*, especially Vol. III, *The Beginnings of Critical Realism in American 1860–1920* (New York, 1930).

15

Ethnic and Racial Groups

Ethnic and Racial Relations in Social Life

Some preliminary precautions. The reader who has followed the present division of Book Two of this volume thus far knows that our primary interest here lies in the delineation of the principal aspects of the social structure. We have been concerned especially with the types of social groups which in their various manifestations and interrelationships make up a large part of the complex pattern of the social order. This remains the focus of our attention in the present chapter. In it we consider those divisions of the community that are often discussed in sociological literature under such headings as "race," "minority groups," and "ethnic groups," with the frequent addition of the term "problems." The use of this term is understandable in view of the fact that these lines of separation over and over again prevent the fulfillment of common interests and frustrate the satisfactory realization of the individual life. Yet, however impatient we are to condemn or to defend the barriers between groups of different national and cultural origins, of different religious practices, or of different physiological characteristics, we must approach this area of social life in the spirit of our science. We must, in other words, view these problems within the context of the social conditions and relationships from which they stem and of which they are a part.

[1] *The complexity of the problem:* In the isolated societies of "primitive" life, solidified by ties of kin and place, the social differentiation is of a relatively simple type, based usually upon sex, age, and such occupational differences as comprise the social division of labor. But in modern complex society each person belongs to one or more divisions of the population set apart from the rest by nationality background or by unique cultural customs or by religious observance or by physical traits or, more commonly, by combinations of these factors. These "ethnic" or "racial" differences not only frequently become the

basis for a distinctive type of social group, as we shall see, but they often mix with or merge into the other types of social group. This greatly complicates the problem of analyzing ethnic and racial groups *as such*. Many communities and semicommunities, for example, are made up entirely or predominantly of the members of one national or racial or religious segment of the larger society, who may or may not possess a consciousness of unity other than community sentiment.

The case of the Jews suggests the complexity of our problem, for many Jews, besides being members of a vaguely defined people, possess a common religion, and many a common national aspiration, while others are marked by neither of these characteristics. At the same time, many of them are race *conscious*, though biologically they are in fact a very mixed population. Or consider the case of the American Negro. Culturally he is American, belonging to one of our earliest immigrations, but economically and politically he constitutes, to a large extent, an exploited class, and, on other counts, a separated and closed "caste," while, biologically, his group is an identifiable though by no means a "pure" race. Yet the American Negro's *social* position stands in striking contrast with that of his racial equivalent in certain other countries, such as Brazil. Or compare the situation of the Irish in the United States in the mid-nineteenth century, when they met the strong hostility of the older residents and were quite rigidly relegated to a "minority group" status, with their situation today wherein their members are spread from the bottom to the top of the social and economic hierarchy.

This list of illustrations, each representing a special case of the general type of grouping under consideration, ethnic and racial divisions, could be greatly extended. But at this point we seek merely to underscore the variety and complexity of social relationships that are involved in this area and the extent to which ethnic and racial groupings overlap or merge with such structural forms as community, class and caste, economic organization and religious division, and, even, as we shall see in the following chapter, with the phenomenon of crowd.[1]

[2] *"Race" as a sociological category:* Another difficulty confronting the student of ethnic and racial relations is the confused and misleading use so frequently made of the term "race." A race is often thought of as a group biologically different because it represents a common and distinctive heredity. But strictly there are no pure races in this sense. The most we can discover are characteristic physical types prevailing in some regions of considerable size. We may call these types "races," but we cannot regard them as the product of an exclusive heredity, since some inmixture of outside stocks is found in every large group and since the physical type itself has environmental

1. We suggest that the reader again examine Chart VII in Chapter X, page 215, and note the position of "Ethnic and Racial Groups" with relation to the other major types of groups in the social structure.

determinants and is certainly subject to environmental selection. Moreover, even the classification into the three great physiological "races," the Caucasian and Mongoloid and Negroid, is criticized by certain authorities, who see the first two as belonging to one biological group; in any event, the dispersion and mixture of peoples during many recent centuries have taken place on such a vast scale that no single region contains in any large degree an "untainted" biological type. Much nonsense, inspired by group egoisms, but frequently giving "scientific" justification to unbelievable human cruelty and sustaining a most dangerous form of social ignorance, has been written on races and race qualities as though races were pure biological categories uninfluenced by environment and underived from a combination of diverse elements. But all these theories ignore or fail to understand the relation between life and environment with which we dealt in Chapter IV.[2]

In what sense, then, may we use the term "race" in the study of social phenomena? Mongoloids, Negroids, Caucasians, and the various subtypes such as "Nordics" or "Alpines" are obviously not found as integral social groups at all. The light-skinned person socially defined as a "Negro" in the United States may be viewed as a "White" in another country; the Caucasian-featured Japanese is an "Oriental" only to those who know him and identify him as such. The term "race," when properly used, signifies a *biological* category. It refers to human stocks that are *genetically* distinguished, to major human types that owe their differences from one another, especially their physiological differences, to a remote separation of ancestry. Such differences, however, often arise from exposure of groups to distinctive environments and from participation in distinctive cultures. Wherever large groups distinguished by any differences of physical features lay claim to superior status or superior power or superior quality, they are apt to develop a *consciousness* of race. Anthropological investigation shows that it is generally, if not always, a false consciousness. The consciousness of race is a sociological phenomenon, one that has an impact on social relationships. The sociologist does not deal with races as such but only with race-conscious groups.

The meaning and significance of ethnic divisions. The race-conscious group, as we have defined it, is but one manifestation of the type of social division with which we are presently concerned. For man is separated from man, not only by real or assumed physiological traits, but by differences of group traditions, national or regional or religious, that may or may not be associated with biological distinctions.

[1] *Ethnic divisions as a type of social group:* An ethnic group is generally conceived to be one whose members share a distinctive social and cultural

2. For criticisms of "racist" theories and of commonly held misconceptions see, for example, R. Benedict, *Race: Science and Politics* (New York, 1945); M. F. A. Montagu, *Man's Most Dangerous Myth: The Fallacy of Race* (New York, 1945).

tradition, maintained within the group from generation to generation, whether as part of a more complex society or in isolation. This mode of social differentiation has its own distinguishing characteristics.[3]

The affiliations that tie the individual with an ethnic group—that identify him in the United States, for example, as an "Old American" or Jew or Negro or Irish Catholic or "Italian" or "Pole"—are not the same as those that bind him to the intimate face-to-face associations, though there are certain similarities here, as we shall see, and much of his primary group life may be confined to the ethnic division to which his parentage assigns him. Nor does his affiliation with the ethnic group have the same meaning as citizenship in the state or membership in the union or political party or some other large association, though in size the former may rival or surpass the latter. The individual's position in the class structure, on the other hand, and especially when that structure contains divisions marked by elements of caste, may be partly determined by and may in some measure correspond with his position in the prevailing system of ethnic groups. But ethnic groups, much more so than great associations and more often than classes (though not castes), are in-groups, maintaining cleavages between the "they" and the "we" in social life. The ethnic group, then, is a nonvoluntary interest-conscious unity, generally without formal organization and relatively unlimited in size, within which the members are linked together by both primary and secondary relationships.

There is an additional characteristic of fundamental significance, for the members of an ethnic division within a community are usually subject to *some measure* of differentiation or of disapproval or of prejudice or of discrimination by the other groups. The distinguishing attitudes range from the mere recognition of difference to the most intense hatreds and revulsions; they may reflect a simple spirit of group unity or they may reveal a blinded and blinding group egoism. Even when mere recognition of difference is all that marks the relationship between groups—an inevitable situation in complex society—there is a necessary antithesis between the "they" and the "we," between in-group and out-group. This antithesis is a characteristic of all group loyalty, of group unity itself. There must be some feeling of warmth toward the "we" that is withheld from the "they." Rarely, however, are the relations between such groups governed by the mere awareness of difference, especially in our contemporary world. The epithets with which we label this group or that, the prejudices we harbor, the groundless attributions of inferior or evil group qualities we accept, the discriminations we practice, are evidence of the deep and dangerous cleavages that separate many ethnic groups. We often call these groups "minorities," not because of their smaller size, but because, on the basis

3. For the meaning of ethnic group and related concepts see, for example, R. M. Williams, Jr., *The Reduction of Intergroup Tensions*, Social Science Research Council Bulletin 57 (New York, 1947), pp. 42-43; W. L. Warner and L. Srole, *The Social Systems of American Ethnic Groups* (New Haven, 1945), Chap. X.

of their physical or cultural characteristics, they "are singled out from the others in the society in which they live for differential and unequal treatment, and . . . therefore regard themselves as objects of collective discrimination."[4]

Wherever there are two or more ethnic groups within the same community there is apt to be a developed *system*, officially or informally sustained, of ethnic superordination and subordination. In such systems the superior or dominant group, which may constitute a majority or only a small proportion of the total population, also meets our definition of an ethnic group, for it possesses its own cultural uniqueness and its own "consciousness of kind," as, for example, the "Old Americans" in our own society or the "Spanish" natives in the Philippines. Ethnic systems vary enormously from region to region, from country to country, and from time to time. They interlock in different ways and in different degrees with structures of class and of caste. But common to all systems is the feeling of each group of belonging to the "us" and the sense of difference from the "others," while in some of them, though not in all, are focused unique social accommodations as well as grave social conflicts.

[2] *The significance of ethnic groups in contemporary life:* In almost every large region of the earth we witness man's efforts to compose, to change, or to destroy ethnic divisions. In India we see a great and often violent conflict between Hindu and Moslem, a conflict complicated by and often conducted with the appeal to the values of nationalism and of religion; in South Africa we see these same values penetrate the relations between the various ethnic groups, the dominant European and the dominated Mohammedan and native, made the more complex by the additional factor of color; in Palestine is daily witnessed the evidence of the significance of ethnic conflict. In contrast, we may cite the relatively peaceful adjustments of diverse racial or religious or nationality groups in China (where conflict is on other than ethnic grounds), in large areas of Latin America, in Hawaii, in Soviet Russia, in much of Southeastern Asia. In Europe, on the other hand, there has taken place on the part of the recent rulers of Nazi Germany the outright destruction of millions of members of one ethnic group in the name of "racial purity," a phenomenon the repercussions of which will no doubt be with us for generations.

This problem has a particular significance and a particular interest in the United States, where vast immigrations and the process of assimilation have been conspicuous features of the community life.[5] No other large modern nation has been as successful in bringing together peoples of different tongues and faiths and different backgrounds and in creating an effective national amalgamation, based upon commonly shared principles of social equality and individual opportunity. Yet today, standing in stark contrast with these principles, at least a third of the total American population is set apart by attitudes

4. L. Wirth, "The Problem of Minority Groups," in *The Science of Man in the World Crisis* (R. Linton, ed., New York, 1945), p. 347. This is an excellent essay on the title subject.
5. For assimilation in the United States see Chapter VI, pages 126 131.

and sentiments often approximating those of caste. Closest to this status are the some thirteen million Negroes, some two million Mexicans and other Latin Americans, perhaps four hundred thousand American Indians, and the somewhat smaller groups of Orientals, mainly Chinese, Japanese, and Filipino. Less socially isolated, but separated by a deep fissure line of a special type, are the some five million Jews—we have here no exact figures. Further barriers detach a considerable number of ethnic groups, including about five million Italians, and smaller groups of Slavs, Poles, Czechs, Slovenes, Hungarians and other Eastern Europeans, totaling about sixteen million persons. If we add all of the individuals in such organizations as the Roman Catholic Church and the Holiness religious sects, whose members in certain regions are likely to sense that they are not fully admitted to the community life, it is probable that as many as fifty million persons in the United States experience all or some of the time the feeling that they are in some measure excluded, that they are in this respect members of "minority groups."[6]

The presence in our nation of these numerous ethnic groups, the fact that they experience different types of prejudice and discrimination of varying intensities, and the inescapable conclusion that in this connection, perhaps more than in any other, there exists a serious and disturbing contradiction between democratic ideal and customary practice, have led in recent years to a large amount of research and organizational activity in this field. Various private antidiscrimination associations, some public agencies, schools, churches, and other organizations have more and more sought the advice and aid of social scientists, many of whom have become specialists in "action research" designed to diagnose and to assist in the adjustment of conflicts and tensions involved in ethnic group relationships.[7] In a later section of this chapter we shall discuss some of these programs and activities, especially as they bear upon the problems of group prejudice and group discrimination. The understanding of and the amelioration of these phenomena, however, require that we first examine the ways in which they reflect basic aspects of the social structure itself.

Variant patterns of ethnic group relationships. The bases of ethnic group differentiation, whether race consciousness or nationality, whether religion or some other cultural factor, vary greatly with the social-historical conditions. So do the nature and intensity of the relationships.

[1] *Illustrations of ethnic systems:* The literature describing the group features

---

6. Cf. R. M. MacIver, *The More Perfect Union* (New York, 1948), Chap. III. For detailed figures on national and racial groups in the United States, see, for example, F. J. Brown and J. S. Roucek, *One America* (New York, 1946), pp. 632-657.

7. For summaries and appraisals of the research and organizational activities in this area see Williams, *The Reduction of Intergroup Tensions;* and G. Watson, *Action for Unity* (New York, 1947). See also the Report of the President's Committee on Civil Rights, *To Secure These Rights* (Washington, D.C., 1947).

of different communities contains an almost endless amount of material on the numerous ethnic arrangements that man has devised at different times and in different places. The multiplicity of these various systems should warn us of the necessity of viewing any particular ethnic structure with relation to the peculiar historical circumstances within which it has emerged. As Professor Wirth puts it:

> In Europe and in America there are today vast differences between the status of different ethnic groups from country to country and from region to region. In pre-war Poland under the Czarist regime the Poles were a distinct ethnic minority. When they gained their independence at the end of the first World War, they lost their minority status but reduced their Jewish fellow Poles to the status of a minority. As immigrants to the United States the Poles again became themselves a minority. During the brief period of Nazi domination the Sudeten Germans of Czechoslovakia reveled in their position of dominance over the Czechs among whom they had only recently been a minority. The European immigrants to the United States from such dominantly Catholic countries as Italy and Poland, for instance, find themselves reduced from a dominant to a minority group in the course of their immigration. It is not the specific characteristics, therefore, whether racial or ethnic, that mark a people as a minority but the relationship of their group to some other group in the society in which they live.[8]

Ethnic group relations are thus the products of historical conditions. The specific characteristics which people find to be of significance in establishing their group loyalties and in determining their group divisions are always relative to the social and cultural context. This is why we cannot attribute to color or other physical traits *as such*, or language *as such*, or religious belief *as such*, any fundamental role in the explanation of ethnic systems, or use any such "factor" as a principal lead in diagnosing tensions between ethnic groups. This point is borne out by the illustrations contained in the above quotation, and the same conclusion is reached if we consider the contrasting positions of ethnic groups in various social structures at the present time.

In colonial countries, for example, we generally find the colored peoples rigidly subordinated to the dominating white minorities, socially and economically and politically. The history of imperialism during the last few centuries, though marked by variations of policy and of strictness from one "mother country" to another, shows the maintenance of a definite color line, imposing upon the native populations, even when a selected few of them are trained for and used in administrative posts, a "caste" status. This has been the case generally, whether the subordinated group is Negroid as in Africa and Australia and Melanesia, or dark-skinned "Aryan" as in India, or highly mixed lighter colored people as in the Polynesian and Micronesian areas of the Pacific. Nor

8. Reprinted from *The Science of Man in the World Crisis*, edited by Ralph Linton. Copyright 1945 by Columbia University Press.

have the vast variations in civilizational attainment, ranging from simple hunting "cultures" in certain preliterate groups to social systems at least as highly developed as the European, brought about until very recently any major departures from the rigid code separating the rulers from the ruled. The same social distinction was maintained in the Philippines during the half-century of American control, though in this unusual case of a colonial possession the United States quite consistently advanced a program leading eventually to independence.[9]

Apart from the more or less naked exploitative features of colonial imperialism, we can observe interesting variations in ethnic systems. In the Philippines, for example, with its mixed population of Mongoloid, Malaysian, Micronesian, and European strains, the "Spanish" mestizos, mostly to be found in the few urban centers, claim a superior status to the majority of the native peasantry; the commercially successful Chinese are set apart (as they are almost throughout Southeastern Asia) by attitudes quite similar to those in Western society which disparage the Jews as a money-seeking and sharp-dealing people; while certain nonliterate groups, such as the Negritos, occupy a social position somewhat comparable to that of the American Indians in the United States or of the Ainu in Japan. In Hawaii, with an even more variegated population—including the native Polynesians, the Portuguese, the Filipinos, the predominantly American "Haole," a small but socially powerful group, the Japanese, and the Chinese—attitudes of social equality are sufficiently prevalent to permit a large amount of vertical mobility for members of all ethnic groups throughout the class structure and to allow a considerable number of intermarriages. However, these phenomena take place much more frequently in the urban areas than in the rural plantation communities, the degree of social intercourse varies markedly from group to group, and economic control is heavily concentrated in a few "Haole" families. Even more fluid, racially and culturally, is the situation in Brazil, a country with a distinctly different history and tradition from the others we have mentioned. Brazil was originally settled by Portuguese and later by Italians, both Catholic peoples, by Germans from Northern Europe, by Japanese, and especially by African Negroes. The emphasis upon the common interest of the Brazilian national community, together, no doubt, with other factors that have not as yet been sufficiently studied, has led to the almost complete obliteration of the color line and the firm execution of a policy of nondiscrimination resulting in the increasing racial and ethnic amalgamation. Not only is there a great deal of biological intermixture in this country but there is an enhancement of communal unity on the one side and of individual

9. For the colonial situation see, for example, R. Kennedy, "The Colonial Crisis and the Future," in *The Science of Man in the World Crisis*, pp. 306–346; and illustrative material is presented in *When Peoples Meet* (A. Locke and B. J. Stern, eds., New York, 1942), especially Chaps. V and XIII.

opportunity unfrustrated by ethnic lines on the other that is not achieved in the ethnic systems of various other countries.[10]

In our own country, although there are fissure lines between racial or ethnic groups that are nationwide, such as those marking off the Negro and the Oriental and the Jew, there are considerable differences from one region to another. Thus the social position of the "Old American" is higher in the East and the Southeast than in more recently developed areas; in most of the Southeast the Negro is almost the only occupant of a rigidly defined "caste," while in the Southwest and Far West the Mexican and the Oriental possess a similar status; in New England the Irish Catholics and the French Canadians, both quite numerous in that section, occupy positions similar to those held by other ethnic groups in other parts of the country. Regional variations such as these, as well as the differences between country and country, bring out once more the role of the special historical circumstances that must be taken into account in explaining each ethnic system.

[2] *The position of ethnic groups in the social structure:* What kinds of circumstance determine the position of ethnic and racial groups in the community structure? Why, for example, is the status of the Portuguese one thing in New England coastal towns and another in Hawaiian seaports; or why have the Jews in China had a history completely different from their experience in Western countries? There are no easy answers to these questions, as our discussion of the variety of ethnic patterns and of the importance of particular conditions indicates. But certain types of circumstance clearly and significantly affect ethnic relationships and the social status of ethnic groups in almost all regions marked by ethnic divisions.

ONE: NUMBER AND SIZE OF ETHNIC GROUPS. When a large number of ethnic groups live within the same community it is probable that the different groups will possess quite different statuses and will experience different degrees of prejudice and discrimination. Thus the Negro in this country "has become the principal shock absorber of the antiminority sentiment of the dominant whites"; he is, in fact, discriminated against by the members of other ethnic minorities, sometimes even more openly than he is by the "Older Americans."[11] Similarly, in pre-Soviet Russia, a country inhabited by innumerable linguistic, cultural, and "national" peoples, the Jews were relegated to the lowest social position and were often the victims of brutal attack in the form of the pogroms, a situation vastly altered under the policy of the Soviet government. Where there

---

10. See, for example, for the Philippines, J. R. Haydon, *The Philippines; A Study in National Development* (New York, 1942), Chap. I; H. W. Krieger, *Peoples of the Philippines* (Washington, D.C., 1942); for Hawaii, S. L. Gulick, *Mixing the Races in Hawaii* (Honolulu, 1937); A. W. Lind, *An Island Community* (Chicago, 1938); E. G. Burrows, *Hawaiian Americans* (New Haven, 1947); for Brazil, D. Pierson, *Negroes in Brazil* (Chicago, 1942); G. Freyre, *Brazil: An Interpretation* (New York, 1945), Chap. IV.

11. Cf. Wirth, "The Problem of Minority Groups," p. 353.

are only two or three basic ethnic divisions, such as that between the Flemings and the Walloons in Belgium or between the European Whites, the Moslems, and the Negroes in parts of South Africa, there are apt to be clear-cut lines of demarcation often combined with a rigid pattern of dominance and subordination.

The size of the ethnic groups also helps to determine its position in the social system. The relatively easy accommodation of one or two "foreign" families in the small American town, for example, or the general social acceptance of the Negro in the urban areas of France, stands in sharp contrast to the aggravated situation that is likely to develop when numerous representatives of the ethnic group enter the community. When the dominant group is matched in size or is outnumbered by a subordinated people, as in sections of the South and in most colonial countries, the latter is frequently believed to be a threat to the ongoing way of life and various official and informal devices are employed to maintain the social status quo. Both the number and the size of "minority" groups affect the group relations, to be sure, but these factors take on their significance only in conjunction with others.

TWO: PHYSIOLOGICAL DIFFERENCES. These differences also function only in relationship with other factors. Considerable experimental evidence tells us that human beings possess no "natural" or inborn antipathy toward others of a different color or appearance. Yet these visible marks of difference assume great importance in a social environment in which a tradition of slavery or some other type of obvious exploitation or of open discrimination has been nourished. The subordinate status of Negroes, Orientals, and Indians, and of white peoples of swarthy appearance in the United States is reinforced by their recognizable physical characteristics, by their deviation in this respect from the stereotyped "Nordic" norm. But we must emphasize again that these differences *as such* play merely a secondary role in determining intergroup relations, though they may assume great importance in the maintenance of relations already established.

THREE: CULTURAL DIFFERENCES. When language, religion, or other cultural traits distinguish "minority" peoples they have a divisive influence. Cultural differences frequently involve different and sometimes irreconcilable contradictions in basic values. The extreme conflicts between Jew and Arab in Palestine and between Moslem and Hindu in India are intensified by the contrasting religious and philosophical viewpoints of the different groups. It would be a mistake, however, to explain these tensions without taking into account such crucial aspects as growing national sentiment and divergent economic and political programs. Religious belief may help to solidify the ethnic group itself and may deepen the demarcation between groups, but it may, if the belief incorporates a system of universalist values, such as the nondogmatic faiths of the Taoist and the Confucian, have the opposite effect of discouraging intergroup controversy.

FOUR: OPPOSING VALUES AND THE SOCIAL STRUCTURE. If the relative absence of ethnic tension in a community like China is closely associated with the inclusive nature of traditional Oriental religious philosophy, its conspicuous presence in our own country is no less related to certain fundamental values in American social life. The doctrines of "fair play," social equality, and equal opportunity should, we might assume, work against the formation of disturbing ethnic divisions—and so they have in many instances, as the history of assimilation shows. But other influences and values, including the individual's drive for material affluence, his zealous guarding of status once gained, his fear of any real or supposed threat to his own social and occupational and political (and even sexual, as we shall see) prerogatives, his traditional but disappearing insularity from cosmopolitan diversities, are forces that powerfully support the imposed barriers between the dominant White-Anglo-Gentile majority and the racial and ethnic minorities. The resulting inconsistency between democratic values, espoused in some measure by all members of the community, and discriminatory restrictions, experienced to some extent by perhaps a third of the population, guarantee an unstable and troublesome disequilibrium in the social structure, which is both a reflection and a cause of the contradictions and frustrations experienced by the individual.

The nature of the social structure and of the prevailing cultural values, then, is of crucial significance in determining the character of ethnic relationships. In a caste society, in which each group is assigned a particular niche, and where throughout the society the system is sanctioned by a suprasocial authority, the whole structure tends to be stable, and alternative group arrangements are not generally sought. In a mobile open-class society, on the other hand, groups set apart as "minorities" nevertheless share the over-all values of opportunity and individual attainment, and their members understandably seek to improve their lot in accordance with the commonly approved procedures. In this effort they are confronted with barriers, sometimes legally imposed, as in the case of "Jim Crow" restrictions, but more often informally maintained, barriers which are frequently described as lines of "caste" in the social structure.

Ethnic and Racial Groups as "Castes"

Are racial and ethnic groups "castes"? Caste, as we explained in Chapter XIV, always rests on differences determined at birth, differences that cannot be changed by individual achievement, economic or professional or political, or by any other means. It would seem, then, that those intracommunal racial and ethnic lines, which constitute social barriers that are wholly unsurmountable, are at the same time marks of caste in the social structure. This conception is central in the approach of a number of investigators who recently have been studying the American Negro-White situation, and is one, we believe, that merits a wider application. In this section we shall discuss this view and examine particularly its usefulness in analyzing ethnic group relationships in the United States.

[1] *Criticisms of the caste approach:* The designation of racial or ethnic groups in an open-class society as "castes" is criticized by certain writers on various grounds. In the first place, it is pointed out, a caste system, such as that in traditional Hindu society, is a stable order in which each group not only has a rigidly defined status and function but one in which the lower castes are not moved to improve their position. So long as the system itself and the values that sustain it are not shaken by the impact of an alternative set of institutions, the individuals within it do not struggle against the caste lines. A contrary situation holds in a mobile society. The Negroes in this country, for example, sense very strongly their lower status, the prejudice and discrimination practiced against them, and, especially, the inconsistency between their social position and democratic equalitarian values. Rather than a stable "caste," they are, we are told to remember, members of an exploited economic class as well as of a race-conscious group. In the second place, their status in this respect is understandable only if we trace the historical pattern of its development, noting that racial prejudice and the attitudes associated with it grew up as a result of the economic exploitation of early capitalism when in various colonial countries, including certain of the American settlements, the Negroes (as well as other non-European peoples) were forced to become a cheap labor supply. Finally, it is claimed that when social scientists treat ethnic or racial groups as "castes," they are not only misconstruing the nature of a "true" stable caste system but they are consciously or unconsciously avoiding the heart of the problem, namely the economic exploitative aspect, the one that must be recognized and remedied if either effective analysis or a genuine alteration of the situation is to be accomplished. Indeed, "caste" betokens a whole system of social organization, so far found only in India, and not an aspect of the quite different type of social organization characteristic of capitalism, runs the argument. These criticisms have been voiced by various writers, including those of Marxist persuasion, and have been expressed vehemently, if not altogether consistently, in the recent volume by O. C. Cox, *Caste, Class, and Race.*[12]

[2] *The utility of the caste approach:* We should not lightly dismiss these arguments. Certainly there are large differences between the status and particularly the aspirations of, say, a lower-caste Hindu and an American Negro. There is, to be sure, an important distinction between a caste-permeated social organization and one in which wealth is the guiding principle of the system, as we explained in Chapter XIV. Again, we would agree that any analysis of the Negro-White relationship that disregarded or underestimated the economic situation, in both its historical and its contemporary aspects, is very apt to be

12. See especially Chaps. XXII-XXIV. A more tempered criticism of the caste approach is found in C. S. Johnson, *Growing Up in the Black Belt* (Washington, D.C., 1941), pp. 325-327.

> fundamental fact of caste is materialized in a great number of political, judicial, and social disabilities imposed upon Negroes somewhat independent of their class, and in the rigid rule that the Negro is not allowed to pass legitimately from the one side to the other.[15]

We should remember, moreover, that diagrammatical presentations cannot avoid the oversimplification of an area of complex group relationships. Not only are there innumerable variations of the caste-class structure in different localities, but this dual mode of stratification, though resistant to change, especially in the South, is continually undergoing alterations as the social and economic conditions themselves change.

[2] *General characteristics of the structure:* While we should not overlook the variant and dynamic nature of this structure of caste and class, we may, on the basis of several recent investigations, sketch the more characteristic social traits of the groups found within it. Most of these studies report a hierarchy of three principal social classes, with each class usually further stratified, in both the Negro and the White castes. In the Southern community the upper-class White emphasizes his lineage, tends to idealize the past, is generally paternalistic in his treatment of lower-class Negroes, and is apt to feel, but not overtly display, an antagonism toward upper- and middle-class Negroes. The middle-class White is more concerned with economic advancement, social conformity, and "morality," his paternalism is less "aristocratic," and he is more likely to reveal his antipathy toward the better-placed Negroes. The lower-class White, economically insecure, less educated, not well integrated in the community life, and not as high in class position as *some* of the colored, is frequently the most extreme and outspoken advocate of "White supremacy"—a traditional antagonism rooted in part in the older plantation system in which the Negro was often identified with the wealthy white owners.

The Negro social classes do not parallel the white divisions, nor are the criteria of status identical. One important mark of prestige within this caste is the degree of acceptance of "white" modes of behavior. This is most apparent in the small Negro upper class, the members of which are usually well educated and often successful businessmen or professional persons, tending to be highly class conscious, but who frequently sense keenly the unsurmountability of the caste line, yet may not show open aggression, and who, as leaders of their race, must often choose between loyalty to caste or to class. The middle-class Negro, including lesser professional persons, smaller owners, and some artisans and "white-collar" workers, similarly stress the desirability of education (itself a significant sign of status in the Negro caste), and, like the Whites, emphasize "manners" and "morality," but more carefully guard against displays of "caste" aggression, although they tend to despise the less successful "poor whites." The Negro lower class, on the other hand, the largest group and one containing

15. *Op. cit.*, I, 692–693.

several subdivisions, permits a greater degree of departure from the "middle-class" norms of morality and a larger amount of open aggression, and considers educational attainment of less significance, while some of its members are quite strongly loyal to upper-class Whites.

There are many deviations from this pattern, and especially in the northern regions of the United States the caste line itself, while clearly present, is less rigidly maintained in certain respects. But these two major types of stratification, class and caste, their interrelationship with one another, and the degree to which they determine the social position and therefore many of the individual problems of the members of the various classes in both castes, must be recognized as essential considerations in any sociologically valid study of the Negro group in this country.[16]

[3] *Special aspects of the structure:* Consideration of the social stratification between and within the Negro and White groups reveals a number of specific problems which are frequently of concern to the citizen as well as of interest to the social scientist. Here we can only briefly indicate a few of the more significant special aspects of the structural pattern of class and caste.

ONE: COLOR AND STATUS. The dominating rôle of "White" evaluations in our society is reflected in the fact that relative lightness of skin is often correlated with social status within the Negro caste. The higher prestige of lighter Negroes stems in part from the pre-Civil War emancipation of many mulattoes and their early separation as an independent "marginal" group. Today the prestige of color is revealed in the social distinctions made in the formal and informal group activities, in school and club and clique, of the Negro, a phenomenon apparently more pronounced in the North and in the cities than in the South and the rural areas. A study of some 400 males in Chicago, for example, shows over 6 per cent of the upper class to be "passable" (physically indistinguishable from the White population) as compared with only 1½ per cent of the lower class; moreover a fairly consistent correlation is reported between class position and lightness of skin in both sexes in this city.[17] In recent years, as race consciousness has increased among some of the Negro

16. For studies of the caste-class structure in communities of the South see Davis, *et al.*, *Deep South;* Johnson, *Growing Up in the Black Belt*; J. Dollard, *Caste and Class in a Southern Town* (New Haven, 1937); H. Powdermaker, *After Freedom* (New York, 1939); A. Davis and J. Dollard, *Children of Bondage* (Washington, D.C., 1940); for those in the Middle states, E. F. Frazier, *Negro Youth at the Crossways* (Washington, D.C., 1940); for the Northern city, W. L. Warner, B. M. Junker, and W. A. Adams, *Color and Human Nature* (Washington, D.C., 1941); St. C. Drake and H. R. Cayton, *Black Metropolis* (New York, 1945), especially Part III; and for a comparative sketch of the North and South, W. L. Warner, *ibid.*, pp. 769–782.

17. Cf. Warner, *et al.*, *Color and Human Nature*, Chap. I. A large part of this volume and briefer sections of the studies cited in note 16 above discuss the relation of color and status; for a summary treatment of the large literature in this field see Myrdal, *An American Dilemma*, I, 675–700.

people, as a larger number of darker-skinned persons have gained positions of prestige and leadership, and, no doubt, as the lack of any objective basis for associating lightness of skin with individual or cultural superiority has become more recognized, public display of color preference has fallen into disfavor and, in some instances, has been strongly condemned as a mark of disloyalty to the Negro race. Nevertheless this historically established factor continues to function, in some degree, as a determinant of social relationships in America's Negro caste.

TWO: CASTE AND PERSONALITY. We are provided with perhaps no better illustration of the fundamental linkage between culture and personality (with which we dealt in Chapter III) than is afforded by several of the recent investigations of the effect of the caste-class structure upon Negro youth. Detailed case studies of individuals of upper-, middle-, and lower-class status in the Negro caste, often psychoanalytically oriented, indicate that an individual's inherited position in the system of stratification is of basic significance in shaping his attitudes, his aspirations and dreams, his overt or restrained aggressiveness, his reaction to the overshadowing fact of the caste line itself. No simple generalizations are possible in this complicated area, made the more complex by such factors as color preference within the Negro group and by the fact that the Negro shares with the White many of the same attitudes and evaluations, including, in certain cases, especially among the middle and upper classes, the attribution of blame to the Negroes themselves for their treatment by the dominant caste. The adjustment of the lower-class individual to the Negro world is often "easier" than that of the higher-placed person, particularly if he is deprived of adequate schooling and other cultural contacts, and the large majority of Negroes are effectively kept in the lower class. But for the member of this group, and even more for the ambitious, the lucky, the talented, whatever his class origins, the ultimate barrier of caste is an ever-present force in the structuring of his own personality. This is the conclusion of Professor R. L. Sutherland, who, in commenting on a series of studies of Negro personality, states:

> The self-attitudes reflecting the shadow of race varied widely. Some persons compensated through humor, others through extreme ambition, others through outright aggressiveness, and still others through reticence and withdrawal. But the presence of the shadow of race in some degree or in some form was the constant in the life experiences of all Negro youth. And as long as the dominant society continues to have stereotyped attitudes toward people of a certain hue, those who are of that hue will continue to rationalize, to conceal, or to shift attention to other matters, but they will never entirely escape psychologically their cultural heritage.[18]

18. *Color, Class and Personality* (Washington, D.C., 1942), p. 75. Reprinted by permission of the American Council on Education. This volume summarizes the findings of a series of studies prepared for the American Youth Commission of the American Council on Education.

THREE: CASTE AND DEVIATIONS FROM THE SOCIAL CODE. The tensions and frustrations experienced by the individual member of the subordinated caste are one reason for certain disparities between the crime and delinquency rates of Negroes and of Whites and for other forms of deviant behavior on the part of Negro groups. For some crimes, such as homicide, Negroes exhibit a higher rate than the population as a whole, though less for others, such as larceny. It should be remembered, however, that the percentage of illiteracy is vastly greater among Negroes than among Whites and that the standard of living is lower. If we take a sample of the White population representing the same amount of illiteracy and of poverty, its crime rate is on a par with that of the Negroes as a whole. (Upper- and middle-class Negroes are at least as law-abiding as the members of the corresponding White strata.) Comparative crime statistics are very apt to be misleading for they include only those cases reported in official police or court records, a fact to keep in mind in considering any variations between classes or between ethnic groups. The unequal administration of justice, more markedly in the South but present also in the North, the much lower standards of living, of education, of health, the blockages to aspiration in the "normal" social channels, and particularly the fact that most Negroes are confined to the lowest social stratum in our society all function to bring about deviational forms of behavior. In spite of these social conditions productive of disorganization, however, a large percentage of crimes committed by Negroes are "petty" violations; mental disease appears to be significantly more prevalent than among Whites only in the Northern migratory groups; and the suicide rate of Negroes is only about one fourth that of the Whites.[19]

Partly the result of the relationship between Negroes and Whites is a phenomenon that has significance for the understanding of the "disorganization" of the former, namely the development of a "shady" social structure in some Negro communities. Here individuals willing to break with the prescribed middle-class norms, including persons of special talents, are able to circumvent, in a degree, the usual barriers of both caste and class. This demiworld of gambling and drug addiction and sexual deviation—in no sense characteristic of Negro community life in general—not only provides economic opportunity for some individuals but has a strong attraction for certain Whites and is one within which the strict caste line is often relaxed. Bordering on the "shady" area is the field of popular entertainment—with the two closely associated in some instances, as, for example, in the early New Orleans period of jazz music—where both opportunity for the talented and reduced discrimination on the basis of color are more apt to be present than in the conventional modes of work. These characteristics of the "shady" structure and of such occupations as music and professional sport explain in large measure their appeal to many

---

19. For more extensive treatment of these phenomena see, for example, Myrdal, *op. cit.*, Vol. II, Chap. XLIV.

Negroes (as well as to members of other racial and ethnic groups). We should not make the mistake, therefore, of attributing the disproportionate number of, say, jazz musicians or of boxers who are Negroes to unique and innate biological traits. For this phenomenon, like the phenomena of crime and delinquency, is essentially the result of the prevailing social conditions.[20]

FOUR: MISCEGENATION AND "PASSING." A large percentage—the exact figure cannot be determined with accuracy—of the racial group designated by American attitudes as "Negro" is made up of persons who, biologically, are of very mixed ancestry, including Caucasian and, to a less extent, Mongoloid (American Indian) strains as well as the Negroid. Miscegenation has a long history in this country, going back to the earliest days of settlement, continued by the sexual prerogatives exercised by the slave-owning White males in the ante bellum South and by the freer sexual relations in the cities of that period, and probably lessening in degree in more recent times. The result today is that American Negroes vary in physical appearance from the "pure" Negroid type to one that cannot be distinguished from the White peoples. A significant comment on the caste nature of the division between Negro and White is that *all* of the former, whatever their biological makeup, are defined by our folk attitudes and folk practices as members of an "inferior" stock and therefore properly subject to discriminatory treatment.

It is hardly surprising that some members of that part of the Negro group physically unidentifiable "pass" into the White population. Various estimates have been made of the numbers involved in "total passing," that is, in becoming permanently and completely identified with the White caste. The calculations range from a few thousand to twenty-five thousand persons yearly. The latter figure is no doubt much too large, and would, we believe, include a large percentage of those who practice, deliberately and oftentimes inadvertently, "partial" or "segmental" passing, on the job, in recreational and other cultural activities, while traveling, and so forth. While the social impositions of the caste barrier lead some light-skinned Negroes, apparently more men and youth than women and older persons, and more city dwellers than rural people, to sever completely their tie with the Negro world—as "Anglos" or Southern Europeans or even as Filipinos or Indians, depending in part on their visible qualifications—and lead a greater number to "pass" temporarily for special reasons, most, perhaps, of the otherwise eligible do not do so. The deterrents to "passing" include the fear of discovery, the problems of adjusting to a somewhat alien "White" social world, sometimes construed as a "cold" way of life, the associated uprooting of habituations formed in the caste-imposed "culture" of our society, and, especially, the implied disloyalty to and desertion from a

20. For unconventional occupations of the Negro, see, for example, *ibid.*, I, pp. 329–332; Drake and Cayton, *op. cit.*, pp. 524 ff.

group which has long been promised but has not, as yet, experienced a common sharing of democratic and equalitarian values.[21]

[4] *Will the caste system persist?* It has been claimed by some writers, including a few leaders of the Negro people, that the social demarcation between the color groups can and should be maintained. Professor Warner's schematic diagram of the caste-class system (Chart XV), for example, suggests that the caste line (*AB*), which has been tilted upward by the development of Negro upper and middle social classes, may continue to rotate until it reaches the vertical position (*de*). This would mean that the Negro class structure would exactly parallel the White, which could be accomplished, presumably, by guaranteeing equal conditions of educational and economic opportunity, while the caste barriers to intermarriage and intimate social contacts would remain. This "possible, and indeed probable," result, according to Warner, seems to us highly unlikely, if not impossible. For we would agree with Warner's own admission that if a complete "parallelism" were established it would necessarily bring about the thorough alteration, no doubt the elimination, of the caste system itself.[22] So long as caste remains, just so long do such of its attributes as unequal education, social discrimination, and economic exploitation remain, and if in any large measure these attributes are removed, there must ultimately follow the elimination of endogamous restrictions and one-sided sex taboos.

The caste element in other ethnic and racial groups. In a population as diverse as ours, and in a society in which the ethnic "norm" is taken to be White-Northern-European-Protestant, there are, of course, several groups other than the Negro set apart by varying degrees of social distance. The attitudes of dissociation and of superiority of the traditionally dominant element in the United States are often sufficiently powerful and the resulting discriminations sufficiently severe that this element maintains a superordinate "caste" status with relation to various minority groups.

[1] *Some lesser "castes":* Among such minorities we may designate as subordinated "castes" the Orientals, most of the Spanish-speaking groups, and the American Indians. The Chinese, for example, originally brought to this country as a "coolie" labor force, numbered over 100,000 in 1890; the figure today is less than 80,000. The Chinese have experienced extreme discrimination, in some instances brutality; have been subject to "exclusion" legislation, resulting in a predominantly male population and preventing naturalization; and have been segregated in the overcrowded "Chinatowns" of a few large

21. On miscegenation and "passing" see, for example, Myrdal, *op. cit.*, Vol. I, Chap. V; L. Wirth and H. Goldenhamer, "The Hybrid and the Problem of Miscegenation," Part V in *Characteristics of the American Negro* (O. Klineberg, ed., New York, 1944).

22. Cf. Warner in *Deep South*, pp. 11–12.

cities. Even more the target for the racist doctrine of the "Yellow Peril" have been the Japanese, totaling over 125,000 persons in 1941. In that year over half of this group inhabited "Little Tokyos" in the urban centers; and almost as large a number were farmers on the West coast, severely restricted in their landowning and production operations by the Alien Land Acts. The story of the peacetime treatment of the Japanese, let alone the "relocation" of four fifths of them during World War II, is, again, the record of a discriminated color-caste. A similar record marks the longer history of the more than 3,000,000 Spanish-speaking people, a majority of whom are the Mexicans of the Southwest. The census designation of this group as "White," no doubt a wise practice, does not mean that its members enjoy "White" privileges, economically or socially or politically—indeed the "caste" status of the Mexican is as conspicuous in such states as Texas and California as is that of the Negro in the Deep South. The American Indians, though they were not regarded as belonging to a "lower" race by the original European arrivals on this continent, in the course of its settlement not only have been relegated to such a status but have, until the important reversal of this trend in recent years, suffered severe losses of population and enforced segregation. This small castelike group, only about one fourth of 1 per cent of the United States population today, has had, in the process of our emergence as a modern nation, an important part in shaping our objectively ungrounded attitudes of superiority toward all colored minorities. We may add to this list of peoples whose physical inheritance almost guarantees, under present social conditions, their designation as in some degree "untouchable," and therefore not eligible for full participation in the community life, the Filipino, the Puerto Rican, the Virgin Islander, and other smaller groups of mixed biological composition.[23]

[2] *The complex case of the Jewish people:* Unlike the physically distinguishable groups that make up the relatively recently formed "color-castes" in American society, the Jewish people has been set apart by a deep fissure line which has a very long history in the Western world. The effects of the centuries-old tradition of exclusion are evident not only in the Jews themselves but, perhaps more significantly, in the various groups that have been responsible for their persecution, their segregation, and the discriminations practiced against them. The religious factor played an important role in the earlier period, to be sure, but in the course of European and American history this factor became highly intermeshed with racialism and with economic, political, and cultural factors; and today it is by no means true that the Jews represent a solidified religious body. Here we cannot examine this historical record, nor even its most horrifying episode, the recent mass murders undertaken by the Nazis, an event which has gone far to unify the Jews in this country. But we

23. For statistical information about these various minorities see Brown and Roucek, *One America*, Chaps. III, X, XI; and for a sympathetic account, C. McWilliams, *Brothers under the Skin* (Boston, 1943).

must emphasize the fact that *in this historical process*, and *not* as a result of any unique "racial" or inherent traits, were patterned the defensive-aggressive responses and the special abilities that enabled the Jews to develop for themselves occupational opportunities not seized upon by others, such as trading and moneylending in the earlier period. Their success in combining a keen speculativeness in economic matters with a strongly conservative socio-religious system brought about new antagonisms and new discriminations. And the latter were stimulated once more when in recent times some Jewish intellectuals found in radical or revolutionary doctrines a solution to the social frustrations imposed upon their people. Add to these circumstances the necessity of the Jews, a necessity enforced by extreme exclusion, to seek psychological and, at times, economic security only within their own people, and the perpetuation of their own cultural ways—which in itself need not be a ground for discrimination—and we have a combination of conditions that places them in certain respects in the situation of a caste.[24]

This conclusion, in the case of the United States, may seem inconsistent with the fact that some individual Jews reach positions of great wealth and prominence. Occupationally and geographically, it is true, the some 5,000,000 Jews are a fairly diffused group. Predominantly urban, they make up almost one third of the population of New York City. Nevertheless all communities of 25,000 or larger have some Jewish people, who compose about 11 per cent of the population of cities of 100,000 and over. They are engaged in a variety of occupations, particularly in trade, merchandising, and light and small-unit types of manufacture, with relatively few in the heavy industries or transportation. Contrary to a popular view, they are poorly represented in the important financial establishments; even in the motion-picture industry the majority of the large companies are controlled by non-Jews. On the other hand, they are well represented in the theatrical and musical world and, in New York City, in the professions of law, medicine, and teaching. Their success in certain fields, such as the clothing industry in which they predominate, is due partly to the trade and craft skills possessed by many of the earlier immigrants, permitting some to reach fairly high economic levels and a large number to become members of the economic middle class. This achievement, in fact, has been accomplished by the Jewish people more rapidly than it has by most immigrant groups, including some of longer residence in this country—a situation in itself that has aroused the jealously and at times the enmity of other ethnic divisions seeking to free themselves of an inferior social status.

The deep fissure line between Jew and non-Jew, then, is drawn more in social than in economic terms. It is revealed most clearly in the exclusion of Jews from the social life of the upper and upper-middle classes, in the taboo, for

---

24. Cf. MacIver, *The More Perfect Union*, pp. 29–33; see also the pertinent discussion of G. DeGré in his *Society and Ideology* (New York, 1943), pp. 13–18.

example, against their use of clubs, hotels, residential areas, apartment houses, resorts, and even hospital wards. The exclusion extends not only to such status-dominated occupations as banking, high finance, and insurance but to many private schools and universities. The competitive-minded upper-middle class takes the lead, often "silently" and informally, in maintaining these discriminatory practices and therefore has a large responsibility for the fact that they permeate all social classes, frequently becoming nakedly overt in the lower status groups. One consequence is the cultural and, to some extent, the occupational segregation of the Jewish people. That they have their own shops and restaurants and resorts, their own charities and hospitals and schools, and even one or two industries almost their own, should be attributed not to any unique "Jewish" characteristics and interests but to the castelike barrier that cuts off this group from the total community.[25]

There are large differences, of course, between the social position of the Jew and that of the Negro in the United States. But there are similarities, as there must be wherever the caste principle is invoked. The economic level of the Jewish group as a whole is far higher, but within it, too, are distinct divisions of social class based upon several interrelated factors, including length of residence in this country, national origin, and degree of religious orthodoxy, as well as economic status. And, as in the case of most ethnic minorities subject to discrimination, a "shady structure" has grown up in Jewish life, linking its participants in some measure with others engaged in illegal or disreputable activities. Another important parallel is found in the frustrations faced by members of this semicaste. It might be assumed that these could be overcome by "passing," a process much more available to the Jew than to the Negro, and many of the former, both completely and segmentally, have, of course, lost their identification with the ethnic group. But most individuals remain Jews, even when severing all religious ties, for much the same reasons that bind the Negro to his people—the possibility of discovery, the need to make new adjustments, and, of tremendous psychological weight, especially today, the increasing in-group solidarity and the consequent loyalty to the group stimulated by the anti-Semitism of the modern world.[26] Anti-Semitism itself involves much of the same complex of attitudes as the anti-Negro stand. Significantly, the same people and the same groups, in many cases, hold these attitudes and practice discrimination against both peoples. For, given the

25. Cf. MacIver, *The More Perfect Union*, p. 33. For the methods of exclusion and the economic pressures on the Jews see C. McWilliams, *A Mask for Privilege* (Boston, 1948), Chaps. V and VI; and for the social position of the Jews in a New England city, Warner and Srole, *The Social Systems of American Ethnic Groups*, Chaps. IV and V.

26. Two novels that treat this problem are B. Schulberg, *What Makes Sammy Run* (New York, 1941) and J. Sinclair, *Wasteland* (New York, 1946), both of which, we believe, are more suggestive sociologically than the more popular one by L. Z. Hobson, *Gentleman's Agreement* (New York, 1947).

conditions, social and economic and cultural, that exist in our complex society, some of its members inevitably benefit—or believe that they benefit—from the maintenance of prejudice and discrimination.

Group Prejudice and Discrimination

The formation and nature of group prejudice. We have reserved for this final division of the chapter the specific consideration of group prejudice and group discrimination because, as we have already emphasized, these phenomena are essentially the product of conditions obtaining in the social structure—a point we must keep in view here. Moreover, our treatment of this subject is necessarily brief. The reader who wishes to examine it in greater detail will find a significant and growing body of research and writing in this area.[27]

[1] *The development of prejudice:* The individual is not born with prejudices any more than he is born with sociological understanding. The way he thinks as a member of a group, especially about other groups, is at bottom the result of social indoctrination, in both its direct and its indirect forms, indoctrination that inculcates beliefs and attitudes, which easily take firm hold in his life through the processes of habituation. This point is borne out in a vast amount of anthropological, sociological, and psychological research; it is substantiated by the experience of educators. Therefore the "natural" antipathies displayed by the members of some groups toward others are "natural" only in the sense that they more or less automatically reflect the particular social and cultural conditions; and the extent to which these conditions are changing or are susceptible to change represents, generally, the extent to which group prejudices themselves are subject to alteration or redefinition or even elimination. In relatively isolated and "static" societies the attitudes toward the out-groups are strongly molded in the individual and are uprooted or changed only when new contacts or new forces in the community life break down the isolation or bring about institutional rearrangements in the social structure. But in the dynamic multigroup society there exist not only the diverse codes of the different groups, themselves in the process of change, but a greater exposure to the variety of beliefs and to the official and unofficial efforts to make predominant one or another set of values.

In our society, nevertheless, "the young child undoubtedly starts his life without prejudice, and during pre-school years seems almost incapable of fixing hostility upon any group *as a whole*."[28] We do not in the least imply

27. Useful publications which contain extensive bibliographical references include Williams, *The Reduction of Intergroup Tensions; The Annals of the American Academy of Political and Social Science*, Vol. CCXLIV (March, 1946); and *Survey Graphic*, Jan., 1947.

28. G. W. Allport and B. M. Kramer, "Some Roots of Prejudice," *Journal of Psychology*, XXII (1946), 22 (italics ours).

that egoistic and aggressive tendencies are not native to the human being; what we are pointing out is that the accentuation of these tendencies and *their direction against particular groups* are socially acquired. The child's acquisition of prejudice is a subtle and gradual development. It is traceable, as we explained in Chapter II, to the same processes of socialization that in the earliest years engender the sense of "we," the sense of identification with family and play group. The process by which "mine" becomes identified with "ours" and in which the child inevitably attributes a superiority to the members of his own primary groups carries over into the widening circles of his associations—in the school, the playground, the gang, and so forth. Thus his feeling of attachment and loyalty, usually first nourished in the family, is extended to include those particular groups that the circumstances of his environment call to his attention. He learns, for example, that he is a Protestant or a Catholic or a Jew, that he is a "Polack" or a "Wop" or an "American," that he is unhappily "colored" or happily a "superior white." He learns to differentiate, but more, he learns, by the time he reaches the elementary or lower high school years, to rate the "others" in terms of the myth-based superiority-inferiority values predominant in his specific circumstances, including his own heritage. He is largely unaware of the process that makes of him, say, an anti-Semite or an advocate of White supremacy, and when he reaches adulthood he rarely can identify the influences that shaped his views in earlier years. These deeply rooted convictions tend to be "true" and "right" for the individual, supported as they are by some established mores. They bolster his sense of self, his ego, by identifying him with those who share them, and they are, as every teacher of sociology knows so well, emotionally adhered to and remarkably persistent even in the face of scientific evidence which, on rational grounds alone, should bring about their diminution or disappearance.

Group prejudice, then, is *learned*. And in some degree, it is universal, existing wherever human society is found, for allegiance to the in-group is, of course, a universal phenomenon. Yet prejudice and hostility toward the out-group vary enormously from group to group and from time to time just as they vary in degree of intensity from individual to individual. Two specialists in this field have underscored their significance in the United States in estimating "that at least four-fifths of the American population lead mental lives in which feelings of group hostility play an appreciable role."[29]

[2] *The ethnic or racial group as a stereotype:* That so many human beings are thus affected is abetted by the fact that the modern multigroup community furnishes its members with simplified and usually prejudicial concepts of its diverse divisions. These "stereotypes," as Walter Lippmann called them,

29. *Ibid.*, p. 9. For the origin and prevalence of group prejudice see also C. Kluckhohn, "Group Tensions: Analysis of a Case History," in *Approaches to National Unity* (L. Bryson, L. Finkelstein, and R. M. MacIver, eds., New York, 1945), pp. 221–241; J. Dollard, "Hostility and Fear in Social Life," *Social Forces*, Vol. XVII (1938).

attribute to the groups *as such* a type character and tend to prevent the judgment of one person by another on the basis of his individual qualities. The process of constructing mental images of out-groups is characteristic of all societies, simple or complex; in the latter, classes and parties and occupations and regions and religions are set apart by stereotyped conceptions. Social participation, in fact, could hardly take place without these "pictures in our heads" to guide us, however misled we may be in following them. In many of these relations where stereotyped thinking is apparent, such as that between the "capitalist" and "worker" or between "Westerner" and "New Englander," the basis of differentiation is a matter of specific interests or of cultural viewpoint. Racial and ethnic groups, however, lend themselves to an especially uncontrolled kind of stereotyping, for here the differences are relatively unspecified and prejudice may function almost without limit in its image-making activity.[30]

We see one illustration of uncontrolled labeling in the derogatory terms of popular speech applied to the Negro, the Chinese, the Mexican, the Pole, the Slav, the Italian, the Jew, and others. "Nigger" suggests to many in this country a race that is dirty, lazy, fun-loving, at times bestial, endowed with a special sex prowess, and generally incapable of assimilation; "Mex" is associated with similar attributes; and so with such names as "Polack," "Wop," and even "Okie." Significantly, the stereotyped image of one group, say the Irish during an earlier period of our history, often fades out, when changes take place in the composition of the population and when the sources of immigration shift, only to reappear as the image of another group—a fact that in itself should guard us against belief in these false generalizations. However, the same elements are not found in all group stereotypes. The "Jew," for example, like the Chinese in the Philippines, and in contrast with the Negro stereotype, "is universally damned, not because he is lazy, but because he is *too* industrious; not because he is incapable of learning, but because he is *too* intelligent—that is, too knowing and cunning."[31] These assumptions provide a neat, though misleading, rationalization of the Jew as taking over positions of great power and give to anti-Semitism a peculiar character.

Ethnic and racial stereotypes, then, are more or less rigidly patterned sets of attitudes, frequently symbolized and summarized by the labels of popular speech, representing the prejudicial misconceptions that prevail in the community life. They may mark a brief stage in the history of this or that group or they may persist and even grow in intensity in time, depending upon the particular social conditions. Generally, in this country, they indicate the

30. Cf. MacIver, *The More Perfect Union*, p. 188; see also the same author's "Group Images and Group Realities," in *Group Relations and Group Antagonisms* (R. M. MacIver, ed., New York, 1944).

31. McWilliams, *A Mask for Privilege*, p. 164.

presumption of a sharp departure from the "White-Anglo-Gentile" "norm"—itself a quite misleading stereotype. Moreover, their widespread diffusion makes it possible for persons having little or no direct contact with the groups in question to develop prejudiced and hostile attitudes toward them, a phenomenon conspicuously present in the more isolated regions of our land.

[3] *Types of prejudice:* Not only is group prejudice universal, as we have seen, but the diversity of its manifestations is as great as the diversity of social conditions, as great, in fact, as the number of personalities who display prejudice. The distinction that we now draw, therefore, should not be taken as exhaustive, and the categories themselves are not mutually exclusive. These two forms, however, help us to throw into sharper relief certain aspects of prejudice and discrimination of considerable significance at the present time.[32]

ONE: PREJUDICE AS CONFORMITY. The first, the more common type, consists of those prejudicial attitudes that indoctrination and habituation give to the individual, who is usually unaware of their absorption. He acquires prejudice as he acquires other elements of his social heritage. "Woven into the very fabric of personality" in perhaps most cases, these attitudes sustain him in the ways of "his own" group. Conformity to the group mores, and therefore integration in group life, often means conformity to prejudice itself. The risk of nonconformity by displaying too much toleration or understanding of the outsider, or by being critical of group-sanctioned intolerance, is a risk relatively few individuals are willing to take. "Brotherhood," as a clergyman has expressed it, "requires bravery." More, it often requires the uprooting of ego-supporting group values and group ways—a very difficult, and psychologically often impossible task for the individual.

TWO: PREJUDICE AS A MANIFESTATION OF PERSONALITY DISTURBANCE. Conformity, however, does not necessarily indicate psychological adjustment. For prejudice, in certain instances, is rooted in the individual's failure to achieve a satisfactory integration in the group. He may, in fact, seize upon the conformity-pattern as a solution for his own inner disturbance. We have considerable evidence that the seriously maladjusted personality, frustrated by the conditions of his own life history, and often experiencing, in early years or later, some particular psychic upheaval, may attach his otherwise "free-floating" hostility to this or that group (though, of course there are many other channels for such expression). Discriminated and "inferior" groups afford a socially sanctioned and therefore a particularly vulnerable target for hostile, aggressive, and sadistic compulsions. The person balked in his own circles may strive to destroy the "enemy" Jews or Negroes or Catholics; the rejected individual may overstate his membership by damning the outsider. Of the many human beings who manifest group prejudice, probably relatively

32. This distinction is presented in MacIver, *The More Perfect Union*, pp. 195–207; for I. Chein's similar formulation, see "Some Considerations in Combating Intergroup Prejudice," *Journal of Educational Sociology*, XIX (1946), 412–419.

few belong to this type, but there is some indication that many of the more extreme promoters of racism and group hatred are among the maladjusted, the frustrated, the insecure.[33]

In many specific cases, no doubt, it is impossible to draw any sharp line of division between these two modes of prejudice. They sometimes shade into one another and there are many variations of each type. Moreover, neither form could develop without the prior existence of prejudice in the social life. Both types illustrate the relationship between prejudice and personality. Personality, as we saw in Chapter III, cannot be divorced from social and cultural conditions—nor can prejudice and discrimination. Here we have an important clue to their persistence in the modern community.

The persistence of prejudice and discrimination. Prejudice, hostility, and their overt and active manifestation, group discrimination, are not indulged in for their own sake, unless we assign end value to complex individual motivations themselves. Prejudice and discrimination are rooted in the folkways of the community or groups within the community, they are woven into the habituations of the individual life, and, of fundamental importance, they render or are thought to render definite advantages to the persons or groups that cling to them. Their persistence, then, is not *simply* a matter of ignorance or irrationality, however large these factors bulk in the maintenance of intergroup hostility.

[1] *Stakes in maintaining the fissure lines:* What benefits does the individual or the group gain in the practice of prejudice? The most apparent of these and the easiest to document is the sheerly economic. The waves of immigrants from abroad as well as the millions of Negroes already in the United States have provided our expanding economy a force of manual labor. These "inferior" peoples entered the bottom rungs of the prestige ladder—they became groups from whom the withholding of equal pay for equal work, equal schooling, equal use of public facilities, equal union privileges, paid economic dividends to employers, large scale and small, and, in some cases, to organized labor as well. Many members of the minority groups, especially the Negroes and Mexicans and Eastern and Southern Europeans, are still low in the status scale and still, in large measure, furnish a supply of cheap labor. Here we see one important reason for the continuation of discrimination in employment, in industrial and commercial enterprise, in the professions and in the professional schools, even in domestic service. The withholding of educational and occupational opportunity is easily justified by the stereotyped view that regards this group or that as "naturally" inferior and therefore as "naturally" less deserving.

Moreover, social discriminations that restrict the practice of certain occupations, such as the professions, to the minority members themselves tend not

33. See, for example, Allport and Kramer, *op. cit.*, p. 38; Williams, *op. cit.*, pp. 52-54.

only to induce a double standard of professional attainment but to establish a more or less closed market for the proportionately few trained persons in the group. This situation is especially evident in the case of the Negroes. Here segregation and discrimination have given rise to a vested occupational interest *within* the colored caste while being at the same time in accord with the economic interests of certain White employers.[34] On the other hand, it is often to the interest of the employer to have the larger supply of skilled and semi-skilled labor that is prevented by policies of discrimination, but in such situations labor unions have not infrequently, though there are important exceptions, insisted on restriction.

But economic interest in discrimination is by no means the only factor, and perhaps not even the most important one, contributing to its persistence. Conformity to the group, as we have seen, frequently means abiding by the practices of active prejudice; nonconformity, in this respect as in others, is a threat to the individual's feeling of security that is maintained by his relations with the group. "We misconceive group prejudice when we think of it as primarily a prejudice *against* some one or more particular groups: as anti-Semitism, anti-Catholicism, anti-Anything-in-particular. It is instead at bottom a prejudice *in favor* of 'My Own Group' as against all others, 'pro-us' prejudice eternal, live, and waiting, ready to be focussed and intensified against *Any* Other Group."[35] The individual's need to identify himself more or less exclusively with the group in which he has been reared or with his "own" intimate associates means, in other words, that he often has a security stake in prejudice and discrimination. This sociopsychological gain takes on a greater significance in an urban society increasingly dominated by impersonal relations and increasingly subject to large-scale changes or threats of changes, conditions that propel many in the direction of their long-known and "dependable" in-groups. The severing or risking the loss of these in-group bonds would mean for many persons the undermining of a kind of temporary psychic support. The feeling of "I" sustained by the sense of "we" is apt to be enhanced by those who band together to maintain Jim Crow, to enforce restrictive covenants, to regulate admissions to school or occupation or church or club or political party on the basis of racial or ethnic group affiliation rather than on the basis of individual qualification.

The persistence of these practices, then, is accountable, in part, to the persistent need for close group ties. But there is a further stake, we believe, in prejudice of a sociopsychological nature. In our society, in which are stressed the themes of individual worth, of broad social equality, and, to some extent, the teachings of the Hebraic-Christian social gospel, it is probable that the

34. See, for example, E. F. Frazier, "Human, All Too Human," *Survey Graphic*, Jan., 1947.
35. K. Llewellyn, "Group Prejudice and Social Education," in *Civilization and Group Relationships* (R. M. MacIver, ed., New York, 1945).

inconsistency between these values and the practices of discrimination stimulates in a considerable number of people an uneasiness, reaching the point of conscious or unconscious guilt feeling. One way to decrease this feeling is found in the stereotyped rationalizations that attribute inherent inferiority or immorality or cupidity to the subordinated groups. For when the stereotypes are deliberately or merely automatically seized upon they become for the practitioners of prejudice a justifiable explanation or defense for their (ethically or democratically) unjustifiable position. So long as an ambivalence exists between democratic precept and discriminatory practice, just so long will some individuals continue to seek and to find a reconciliation in the prejudicial generalizations that mark the community life.

[2] *The "scapegoat" function:* The persistence of prejudice is likewise served by the assignment to minority groups of responsibility or "blame" for social and economic disturbances. Problems as diverse in the United States as those associated with the economic frustrations of the small farmer and of the industrial worker, the instability of the financial market, governmental inefficiency or even malfeasance, economic depressions, international tensions and war itself, various changes taking place in the traditional "middle-class" and "American" way of life, the rise of radicalism, the decline of certain religious values, the "corruption" of art and literature—the list could be extended—have been "explained" on the basis of the attributed characteristics or special interest of various ethnic and racial groups. Blaming the latter for whatever phenomena are construed as maladies in the social order at a given time has taken place at various periods in the history of Western society. But as that society and its problems have become more complex, as the conflict between economic plutocracy on the one side and the demand for and the extension of democratic participation and material security on the other have become more evident, and as the older ways have proved insufficient to meet the demands of new conditions, resort to and susceptibility to the scapegoat explanation have become more pronounced. The most extensive use of this device in modern times was incorporated in the Nazi program in Europe.

In this country the attacks against the Roman Catholics, the Negroes, the Orientals, the Jews, and "foreigners" in general on the part of the extremist nativistic movements utilize the same scapegoat argument. These groups, to be sure, do not have equal availability as targets, as the regional and temporal variations indicate. The Oriental, for example, can hardly be construed as the "cause" of social disorganization, when he represents a tiny minority, save in certain West coast areas. The Negro, much more numerous and often conceived as a "threat" in the Deep South, possesses very low economic and social status generally and attracts the sympathy and incites little envy outside that region. The Jews, on the other hand, though constituting less than 4 per cent of the total population, have become, especially during the last twenty years, in the words of one author, "the residual legatee of the counter-tradition" in American life.[36]

Several factors combine to give the Jews this unique and unhappy distinction. In the first place, the role of tradition itself is significant. For several centuries in Western society many people, including at least a few writers of distinction on other counts, have associated the Jewish stereotype with innovations which they have deemed undesirable, innovations in the economy, in political thought, in the arts, and especially in the social attributes of the *nouveaux riches*—an association hardly warranted by the historical facts. Secondly, in certain European countries but most significantly in the United States, the Jew is the more readily attacked because, as we have seen, many individual Jewish persons have attained higher social and economic status than that gained by members of other minority groups. "Those whom we consider below us," says one authority in this field, "we may despise or pity, but we neither love nor hate them as we do our equals."[37] Thirdly, the Jew is a "*special* kind of immigrant" in the sense that the social pressures do not permit him to pass through the characteristic assimilation process, a point aptly illustrated in the following comparison:

> When the Jugoslav immigrant "assimilates," in the traditional manner, by changing his name from Martinovich to Martin, discarding his native customs, forgetting his native tongue, and joining Rotary, we applaud his agility and, somewhat reluctantly perhaps, make room for the New American. We certainly do not regard Martinovich as either a traitor or a renegade. But the Jewish immigrant who changes his name, joins the Ethical Culture movement or the Christian Science Church, or marries a Gentile, is generally regarded, in both camps, as a social renegade. What is perhaps more important, he often comes to regard himself in much this same light. In some vague way, he is conscious of having betrayed an ennobling impulse of his own nature.[38]

Add to these factors the concern of many people, Jews and non-Jews, over the long absence of a Jewish "homeland," made the more intense by the Palestine difficulties, the paradoxical but potent attribution of financial power and radical belief incorporated in the Jewish stereotype, the imposed segregation and informally operating "conspiracy of silence," the covertly expressed hunch of various citizens that "Hitler may have been right in this instance," the urban concentration of Jews, and the fact that a long tradition of subordination has resulted in oversensitivity or overaggressiveness in specific cases, we then see at least some of the reasons that give them a particular vulnerability as a scapegoat group.

---

36. McWilliams, *A Mask for Privilege*, Chap. IV.
37. J. F. Brown, as quoted in McWilliams, *A Mask for Privilege* (Boston: Little, Brown & Company, 1948), p. 83.
38. *Ibid.*, p. 84.

Fluctuations of intergroup tensions. The phenomena of prejudice, tension, and discrimination between groups are extremely variable; they diminish, increase, or take new directions according to the conditions. Sometimes these fluctuations are remarkably rapid; sometimes there is the slower and broader movement of the culmination or reduction of tensions. The rapidity of change under certain conditions is well illustrated from the international scene. In a brief period, sometimes almost overnight, the mental picture one people has of another may be transformed. In recent times, for example, this transformation has happened repeatedly to the picture of "the Russian" seen through the "mind's eye" of the American.

As an instance of more gradual change we may take the shifting attitudes of the people of the United States to Orientals or, again, to Negroes. The picture has been growing more favorable, with some diminution of the exclusiveness of distance. The change is witnessed to by legislation repealing laws that denied citizenship to the members of various Oriental groups; by the enactment of laws, in a number of states, that prohibit occupational discrimination on the grounds of race, creed, or national origin; by the drastic recommendations for the abolition of discrimination unanimously put forward in 1947 by the President's Committee on Civil Rights; and by the rise of numerous organizations, some of them in the Southern states, devoted to the combating of intergroup discrimination and anti-Negro segregation.[39] Nowhere has the change been more significant than in White-Negro relationships. During World War I, although there was then also a great shortage of labor power, the Negro was unable to break down any of the barriers that denied him access to positions of skill or responsibility. During World War II, several of these barriers were reduced or removed altogether, so that he made fairly substantial gains in occupational status, gains that were increased rather than diminished in the years immediately following the end of the war.[40] The only form of antigroup prejudice that appears to have resisted this trend is anti-Semitism. This ancient and stubborn prejudice, that has swollen and subsided so many times in the history of Western civilization, has, as we have already suggested, different roots and follows different laws—though in saying this we do not imply that it cannot be overcome by appropriate social strategy.

In this connection it is worth recording that social scientists have recently added to their field the investigation of the principles, methods, and techniques whereby intergroup tensions may be most effectively subjected to control. Considerable work to this end has already been done by anthropologists, psychologists, psychiatrists, and sociologists. Concerted efforts are being fostered by special organizations of social scientists, such as the Society for

39. For lists of such organizations see the *Directory of Agencies in Race Relations, National, State, and Local,* Julius Rosenwald Fund, 1945; or G. B. Watson, *op. cit.*, Chap. II.

40. See S. L. Wolfbein, "Post-War Trends in Negro Employment," *Monthly Labor Review*, Bureau of Labor Statistics, Dec., 1947.

the Psychological Study of Social Issues and the Committee (of the Social Science Research Council) on Techniques for Reducing Group Hostility, by national and international committees sponsored by psychiatrists, by research bureaus associated with leading universities, by the team of social scientists who under the offices of UNESCO are studying the conditions of international tensions, and by various other bodies. It lies beyond the scope of this volume to discuss the progress of these efforts. But the investigations already made clearly reveal the need for expert guidance in the treatment of this whole problem.

In this and the preceding chapter we have considered the sociological nature and some of the significant implications of class, racial, and ethnic stratification. These major fissure lines in the social structure are relatively permanent social phenomena. However, they are often the signs of instability, of disequilibrium, in the smaller and the greater community. They also nourish, in many instances, those temporary groupings of social life, some of which have for their purpose the destruction of life itself, that are known as crowds. These are our concern in the following chapter.

16

Herd, Crowd, and Mass Communication

Herd Sentiment

The study of temporary groupings. In this chapter we move from the more or less permanent types of grouping to those manifestations of social life that express themselves sporadically. Community, association, class, and ethnic group, in their various forms and interrelationships, are clearly significant aspects of the social structure. The crowd, the audience, and the "public" are more fleeting phenomena and, on certain counts, more difficult to describe and to interpret. Yet these temporary groups are of permanent interest to the sociologist for they are ever reappearing in one mode or another, and within them are often expressed some of man's keenest interests and his most deeply seated attitudes. Moreover, the crowd, the audience, and the like must be viewed within a context of the more persistent features of the social structure because, as we shall see, the former are not merely an expression of man's nature but reflect, in a large degree, the particular characteristics of the community organization, the institutional arrangements, the mores, the social cleavages, of a given time and place.

Sociologists, social psychologists, and political scientists have long been concerned with the temporary groupings, especially the crowd, and with the sociopsychological processes that operate within them. These phenomena became the chief interest of a "crowd school" of sociology which developed half a century ago, and since that time there have been added to the earlier speculative generalizations a considerable body of verified information and a number of suggestive interpretative leads based upon the theories of modern social science. Nevertheless the field of "collective behavior," as it is sometimes called, is one in which no systematic analysis has been as yet generally acclaimed. Of the many interesting and important aspects of this field, we have selected those that seem appropriate in a general study of social structure and social change and particularly significant in the life of modern complex society.[1]

The herd in social life. Wherever we find society we find gregariousness and conformity bringing men together. One result is the institutionalization of group ways, leading to the more permanent features of the social structure. But there are other indications of man's "consciousness of kind" and of his seeming need to be like other men, indications that may be described as reflections of *herd sentiment.*

[1] *Distinction of the herd from the crowd:* Several writers on the crowd do not distinguish it from the herd. Although the two have resemblances, they differ in important respects. Strictly speaking, human societies are never herds, and when we apply the term to social manifestations we are imputing to them attributes that we find more simply and clearly present in the behavior of the ranging aggregations of animals properly named "herds." The nearest approximation to a true herd in the modern world is perhaps that occasional phenomenon of social disruption, exemplified by the displaced persons in Europe and elsewhere before and after World War II, the "aimless migration of refugees."[2] The herd is, for certain gregarious animals, a permanent mode of life. The herd sentiment, present even in the most modern societies, is also a relatively permanent factor. But the crowd is ephemeral. It is not a mode of life but an incident, an eruption, sometimes a disturbance of an established social pattern. Possibly it is what we here name herd sentiment that is revealed in the sudden concerted action of the crowd, but this takes place only under social and cultural conditions that are absent in the herd proper. We should understand the crowd as an unorganized grouping occurring within a system of social organization. A brief description of the herd sentiment should make clear this difference and may serve as an approach to the distinctive character of the human crowd.

Herd sentiment is the *imitative cohesion* revealed when men conform blindly to the traditions and beliefs and ways of a group, when they approve of these because they are accepted and disapprove simply because they are divergent from the established norms, when they are moved by the slogans, the stereotypes, the conventions, the "idols" of their in-groups. In animal society, herd feeling is the manifestation of the gregarious instinct, the simplest form of socialization. In human society, this feeling is broadened into a sentiment that attaches itself to the socially indoctrinated ways. We think of the herd as moving as one, and we exhibit its sentiment when our conduct is determined by the

---

1. The most extensive treatments of crowd and related phenomena are undertaken by sociologically oriented psychologists or psychologically oriented sociologists; in other words, by "social psychologists." See, for example, K. Young, *Social Psychology* (New York, 1944), Part III; R. T. LaPiere, *Collective Behavior* (New York, 1938), Parts I and V; H. Cantril, *The Psychology of Social Movements* (New York, 1941); N. E. Miller and J. Dollard, *Social Learning and Imitation* (New Haven, 1941), Chaps. XIV and XV.

2. Cf. W. E. Hocking, *Man and State* (New Haven, 1926), Chap. XVIII. On the refugees in this country see, for example, M. R. Davie, *The Refugee Immigrant in the United States* (New York, 1946).

question, What do others think and feel about this, what is the *correct* thing to do? Herd sentiment leads men to follow the band or to "get on the band wagon." It leads them to desert the side with little chance and to flock to the likely winner in political contests and generally in matters of opinion. It leads them to discriminate against or to remove from their society those who do not worship at their own shrines, including frequently those who are more sensitive, more intelligent, more independent, than themselves. Herd sentiment, in a word, identifies mores and morals, conformity and solidarity. All who differ from its opinions are "undermining" the social order, morality, the constitution, the church, the sacred family, or whatever "way of life" they cling to against the menace of change. Herd sentiment, then, is the unthinking response to convention. And, as various writers have pointed out, it tends to pervade the expressions of "public opinion."[3]

[2] *Manifestations of herd sentiment:* Herd sentiment, however, is witnessed not only in the blind resistance to change but also in the gregarious pursuit of some superficial novelty. It operates in the acceptance of fashions as well as of mores, and in this area, as we saw in an earlier chapter, socially accredited leaders can often set the direction for the "herd." Or again there are illustrations of what appears as a simultaneous discovery by the group that some new thing is the vogue, the craze—some song, some expression, some parlor game, or whatever it be. These "crazes" come and go, and while their origin may at times seem mysterious, their departure is not difficult to explain, since the novelty on which their appeal so often depends soon wears off. On the other hand, temporary acceptance of this or that craze is not merely accidental, for the appeal itself, though short-lived, is traceable to the social and cultural conditions of a given time and place.

A more significant manifestation of herd sentiment is the emotional epidemic that sometimes sweeps through a country or even a wider region. These epidemics give vent to emotions that are associated with the beliefs or superstitions of the culture or with the tensions stemming from contradictions in the social order, and are aroused to intensity by some accident, crisis, or conjuncture. They have frequently taken religious forms, as evangelistic revivals, where they occur under the stimulation of some leader who is either fanatical himself or has learned the art of breaking the dams of emotional feeling in his audience. Such epidemics comform to the prevalent tendencies of the communities and periods in which they occur. They are accentuated when superstition is unchecked by science and intellectual discipline and when socially imposed frustrations surround the individual life. The Middle Ages were characterized by the crusades, the persecution of heretics, the flagellant manias (in which people went about whipping one another). Perhaps no epidemic of that epoch rivaled in its release of fears and in its breakdown of inhibitions the

---

3. See, for example, P. Odegard, *The American Public Mind* (New York, 1930), Chap. II; W. Albig, *Public Opinion* (New York, 1939), Chaps. I, II, and IV; H. D. Lasswell, *Democracy through Public Opinion* (Menasha, Wisc., 1941), Chap. II.

dancing delirium that began in Europe late in the fourteenth century; sometimes these ecstatic bacchantic outbursts were inspired by visions of the heavenly host, sometimes they took the form of demoniacal possession, while in Italy the strange belief arose that these dances were the antidote to the deadly bite of the tarantula (a harmless spider), the fear of which became a general delusion.[4] Widespread terror of demons was prevalent in the centuries which followed, and no inhumanity, no torture, it seems, was too fiendish to be used on those who were supposed to be possessed by evil spirits.

In the seventeenth, eighteenth, and nineteenth centuries a quite different type of epidemic developed, expressive of a new social economy and new cultural conditions. This was the speculative contagion or boom phenomenon, represented, for example, by the Dutch tulip mania (bulbs sometimes sold for as much as or more than their weight in gold), the South Sea Bubble, the Mississippi Scheme, and the California and Alaska gold rushes. In somewhat modified forms, these speculative fevers have recurred down to the present, illustrated by extreme stock-market activity, such as the boom that preceded the famous crash of 1929, and by the California and Florida real-estate booms.[5] In these cases, involving intense and widespread activity in the economic area, similar sociopsychological processes are at work as in such noneconomic crazes as crossword puzzles, chain letters, zoot suits, jam and jive sessions, goldfish swallowing, and so forth. The study of the processes themselves, largely the province of social psychology, would be necessary in a complete treatment of what we have called herd sentiment.[6]

Types of interest and herd sentiment. An essentially sociological task faces us, however, when we consider the various manifestations of herd sentiment. For we must draw a distinction between two broad types of mass reaction, a distinction based upon the nature of the interests that motivate men in their different forms of "band-wagon" behavior.

[1] *Herd sentiment and like interest:* Note that most of the examples of herd sentiment we have presented are inspired mainly by *self-regarding* fears and hopes—individual fears of demons, hopes of individual salvation or of individual profits. Certain social epidemics and, more obviously, the economic boom, therefore, fall in our category of like-interest social phenomena.[7] Individual interest is here the primary incentive of social behavior. It is stimulated by suggestion and by imitation and, under appropriate social conditions, whole groups follow herd ways to attain personal safety or personal affluence.

---

4. For an account of this social epidemic and others of this period, see B. Sidis, *The Psychology of Suggestion* (New York, 1911), Chap. XXVIII.

5. For a description of various booms, see M. S. Handman, "Boom," *Encyclopaedia of the Social Sciences* (New York, 1935), II, 638–641.

6. For characteristic statements by social psychologists see, for example, Young, *Social Psychology*, Chap. XVII; R. T. LaPiere and P. R. Farnsworth, *Social Psychology* (New York, 1942), pp. 353–358.

7. For a discussion of like interest and common interest in social life, a distinction we have employed in several areas, see Chapter II.

[2] *Herd sentiment and common interest:* But there is another very significant type of "herd" expression, through which is manifested the sense of common interest, the deep feeling of community. Any occasion that suddenly stirs the community consciousness is apt to touch off an emotional impulse of an epidemic character. This is seen on a smaller scale in the fervor that seizes a group when the school or town or city team is victorious against a rival. It is displayed more broadly when a whole nation is aroused by a national triumph of some spectacular sort, or by a disaster, or by a supposed insult to its honor. The crisis of war, or the threat of war, is peculiarly apt to evoke this tense communicable emotion, which tends to engulf each individual so that his individuality is submerged while at the same time his ego is enlarged. "We" have won, "we" have been insulted, "we" are threatened—in this "we" he is emotionally absorbed and in it, too, his own ego is exalted and liberated from social pressures because its goal is now identified with that of all the rest. This situation involves an immense simplification of thought and feeling; it involves a sudden resolution of the problem of the individual's relation to society. Under these conditions his individuality may be elevated and released from narrow self-seeking aims and self-indulgences, or it may be reduced to a lower level in which all deliberation and reasoning power are lost. The latter manifestation is the typical herd reaction. The individual's pride, his itch for power and glory, his desire to love and to hate, are given a temporary *social* justification. At the same time that he feels at one with his fellows he is free to indulge the passions which society under normal conditions holds most in control. This double release—the mergence with the group and the emergence of drives usually checked—gives a particularly powerful quality to herd sentiment when it expresses the common interest of the tribe or nation or smaller group.[3]

These various epidemics and other manifestations of herd sentiment, involving an appeal to like or common interests, or to both, illustrate the gregarious nature of human beings. In the original "herd" situation, the sensitivity to common danger and the rapid communication of the sense of danger through the suggestible "subconscious" mind are factors of safety. These tendencies, found in all periods of civilized life, may be survivals from a remote past, ill adapted as they often are to the conditions of modern society. They often give rise to the phenomenon of the crowd, but, as we have seen, they occur on a far broader scale.

The Crowd and Crowd Sentiment

The nature and types of crowd. The crowd is the most transitory and unstable of all social groups; yet it exhibits characteristics that not only are highly significant in themselves but also throw light on the fundamental problem of

3. For an account and interpretation of various psychological studies in this area see M. Sherif and H. Cantril, *The Psychology of Ego-Involvements* (New York, 1947), Chap. IV.

the relation of the individual to the whole. Consequently the study of the crowd has been a favorite meeting point of representatives of various disciplines of social science. The crowd belongs to our category of *unorganized* groups. We mean by this not that the crowd exhibits no patterns, no characteristic expressions, but that the units in it are not organized in relation to one another. The crowd may be deliberately instigated, but it falls into no predetermined order. It may be led, but only on the basis of the feelings and views of its members, only on the basis of its own sentiment. The peculiar qualities of the crowd, as we shall see, are in large part attributable to this fact that it arises only in the crevices of social organization.

[1] *The crowd proper:* The crowd proper we distinguish as a physically compact aggregation of human beings brought into direct, temporary, and unorganized contact with one another. It is quickly created and quickly dissolved. It is an unorganized manifestation occurring in a world of organization. There are, of course, myriads of casual meetings of friends, acquaintances, or strangers taking place at all times in every society, on the street, on the house porch, on the train, in the office, in the market place, and so forth. These unorganized meetings differ from crowds because they are, sociologically as well as physically, face-to-face meetings and because they take place on a much smaller scale. *Numbers* are necessary to make a crowd, though there is considerable variation here, and the numbers are only *randomly* thrown together in physical proximity. In the latter respect, the crowd differs from such groups as the assembly, public meeting, reception, and so on, where the participants fall into a predetermined order and are arranged according to some principle of selection. A borderline case between the crowd proper and the *audience* is the group that casually gathers to listen to an orator in a park or public square. Here the organization into which the group falls is reduced to a minimum, that of a circle of listeners around the focus of a speaker. In the crowd, mere conjuncture takes the place of any definite order controlling the physical relation of person to person.[9]

Thus we might speak of the crowd which participates in some organized public demonstration or celebration, referring thereby to those who are merely aggregated in a mass during the occasion. If, instead of being aggregated, they fell into lines and formed a marching procession, they would cease to be a crowd in our sense of the term, though the name would properly apply to the groups of people who from the sidewalks watched the procession march through the streets. On the other hand, an organized audience, such as that brought together in the assembly hall or in the stadium, may, if the pattern of organization is suddenly broken by the impact of events, become a crowd proper.

[2] *Types of crowd:* The two types of manifestation of herd sentiment, which we described in the previous section, provide the basis for our distinction between two principal types of crowd. Compare, for example, the crowd that

9. For a diagrammatic presentation of different types of crowds and audiences, see Young, *Social Psychology*, p. 389.

gathers to watch a fire or accident with the crowd that participates in a popular celebration, in a strike demonstration, in a riot or a lynching.

ONE: THE LIKE-INTEREST CROWD. The former is a like-interest crowd. It is brought together by the curiosity of individuals who happen to be in the vicinity. It has no common purpose. Each person could satisfy his curiosity more easily if he were not incommoded by the presence of the others. The curiosity of each is, to be sure, enhanced by the presence of numbers—there is the possible thrill of being in a crowd as well as the thrill of watching the fire or the flagpole sitter or the victim of an accident. But the immediate object of each does not need the presence of the rest. There is a common external *focus* of interest but not a common interest. This character is still more obvious in crowds composed of persons seeking at the same time, and to the inconvenience of one another, to board some means of transportation, to enter a theater or stadium, or, to cite the extreme case, to escape a danger, such as a fire or flood. The like-interest crowd can do nothing *as a crowd*. If it breaks out in protest against some inconvenience it suffers or some incident it witnesses, it is transformed into a common-interest crowd and its nature is radically changed. If it decides, say, to put out the fire it is watching or to render aid in some accident, it undergoes organization, falls into an order, and thereby ceases to be a crowd.

TWO: THE COMMON-INTEREST CROWD. From the sociological standpoint the common-interest crowd is a more significant phenomenon. If all crowds arise within the crevices of social organization, this type comes into being to do something for which the existing machinery does not provide. The occasion may be a sudden need, a crisis, a spontaneous outburst of group joy or hatred, a festival, the appearance or the death of a hero. Crowds of this sort are not necessarily antagonistic to the established order. But they may break through the regulations of organization. Sometimes they merely manifest a desire to escape the discipline, the pressure of regimentation, seeking release through some common spontaneous activity, as college youths are apt to do under some incitement such as the victory of their team. But sometimes they arise to protest against, to defeat, even to destroy regulation and order. A lynching crowd is an example, or again the crowds that have signalized political revolutions. Such outbursts offer the clearest revelations of the inner characteristics of the crowd itself.

In either type of crowd, the interest may be focused upon a specific object or specific goal or it may be less sharply defined. Moreover, we should remember that crowds, like other social groupings, often, perhaps always, exhibit a mixture or combination of like-interest and common-interest elements. However, because of their short-lived nature and the relative simplicity of their manifestations (but not necessarily of their causation), it is generally evident whether the like or the common interest predominates in them. Thus the reader should easily be able to bring additional illustrations to those listed under each type of crowd, as presented in Chart XVI.

CHART XVI A Classification of Types of Crowds

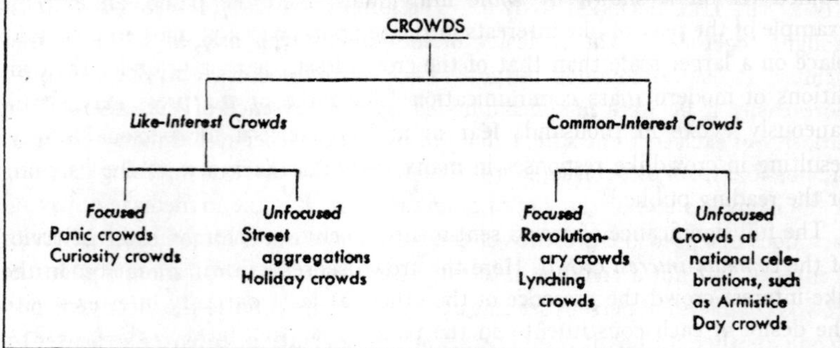

Crowd sentiment. A variety of vivid expressions have been used to indicate the nature of crowd sentiment, such as "herd spirit," "mob feeling," "mass reaction," and so forth. These terms suggest the unique psychological quality that tends to pervade certain types of crowd, to be sure, but at best they are merely descriptive. Sociological analysis requires that we examine, if only briefly, the basic interests and principal processes that are involved and brought into play whenever the temporary crowd comes into existence.

[1] *Interests and crowd sentiment:* In the first place, crowds differ greatly on the psychological level according to the character of the interest which pervades them. If it is a general or vague *like interest*, such as that of the crowds who promenade the streets during intermissions of work or in the evening, most of the psychological characteristics that are usually attributed to the crowd phenomenon may be absent. Some occurrence may focus the like interest of the crowd upon a specific event—a parade or an accident or a fire, for example—and at once an elemental curiosity gives the crowd, or part of it, a focus of attention and thus stimulates its particular attributes. Jostling, excitement, loss of poise, simplification of purpose quickly develop. If the occurrence touches more nearly the vital concerns of the assembled persons, the peculiar quality of crowd sentiment and crowd conduct is intensified. In this situation the crowd may overthrow the standards and the habits which the education and discipline of civilized life have built up in its members: the everyday social controls may falter or break down. The phenomenon of panic reveals how sudden and overwhelming this change from normal behavior may be. With appalling swiftness an orderly audience can, on an alarm of fire, for instance, be transformed into a maddened crowd, heedless to every consideration beyond the individualized impulse of flight. The panic is like the stampede of the herd, demolishing the reserves of reason and the resistances of socialized habituation. It is a situation in which the elementary urge for self-preservation may easily achieve a socially disastrous victory unless the greatest resourcefulness of

trained reason is shown by some individuals. And the panic, an extreme example of the play of like interests in the temporary group, may, in fact, take place on a larger scale than that of the crowd itself, especially under the conditions of modern mass communication. The radio or the press may simultaneously evoke in thousands fear or a deep concern for personal safety, resulting in crowdlike responses in many individual members of the listening or the reading public.[10]

The full significance of crowd sentiment is seen more clearly in the behavior of the *common-interest* crowd. Here the crowd senses its own solidarity. In the like-interest crowd the presence of the others at least partially interferes with the desire of each constituent—in the panic it is often fatal to these desires. But in the common-interest crowd the presence of the others supports the desire of each. Numbers give strength to the protest, to the celebration, to the group-defined revenge, as in the case of lynching; numbers make possible a destructive fury or a joy, the storming of Bastilles or of goal posts. In the common-interest crowd there is always a "cause" that leads each to identify himself with all the rest. The numbers are with him, on his side. The "we" sentiment, the sense of absorption, is intensified, and this feeling of togetherness, temporarily released from the bonds of organization, is apt to run wild.

Without organization, its emotion heightened while the capacity to reflect is lowered, the common-interest crowd can do nothing constructive. It may express tumultuous admiration of its hero of the moment (though it may at the same time remove his clothing, or even injure him with physical adulation, as various celebrities know who have been acclaimed by crowds); it can cheer and wave its banners. But its impulse to action is more likely to find a destructive outlet. To destroy requires neither system nor deliberation. It is easy to cast stones, to trample a man down, to maim and kill Perhaps too, under the conditions of crowd excitement, hatred and revenge are more easily stimulated than love and admiration, though we should not assume, as some writers do, that the crowd is always "a creature of hate."[11] Certainly the crowd easily finds a victim or an enemy and is very open to suggestions of punishment or vengeance. Crowd sentiment sometimes communicates itself to the guardians of order who oppose its excess, so that they on such occasions are also guilty of needless cruelty and violence. The mere suggestion of a victim not infrequently turns a peaceful crowd into a mob, that is, a crowd in motion, offering a common focus to the restless undirected energies let loose within it. And since in organized society the impulse to hate and to destroy is that which is most held in abeyance, the release is all the more violent as well as the more congenial to the unreasoning and no longer restrained spirit of the crowd. Perhaps it is a

10. For a study of the panic reactions to a radio broadcast of H. G. Wells's story of an invasion from Mars, see H. Cantril, *The Invasion from Mars* (Princeton, N.J., 1940).

11. Cf. E. D. Martin, *The Behavior of Crowds* (New York, 1929), Chap. V.

similar release that accounts for the thrill aroused by rumors of war in some normally peaceful and otherwise reasonable persons.[12]

[2] *Processes correlated with crowd feeling:* Not only does the type of interest influence the quality of crowd sentiment, but different processes combine in various ways to bring about the intensified feeling characteristic of the crowd. Three of these processes in particular are of basic significance in stimulating the extreme forms of psychological and overt behavior we witness in the crowd.

ONE: INTERSTIMULATION AND CROWD RHYTHM. Probably every adult has experienced the situation in which a mode of behavior, say a rally cry or a form of applause, becomes more intense, more vivid as it passes from one person to another. Here each individual seems to function as an amplifier of a mood, of a feeling, or merely of a verbal expression. The crowd, with its close physical contacts, provides an ideal setting for this process, an appropriate temporary environment within which its members are more susceptible to the interstimulation of suggestion and of imitation. Once the crowd is assembled, there grows a spontaneous accumulation of excitement and a "sympathetic induction," the symptoms and expressions of emotion coming to each constituent as a collective influence and heightening the feeling in each individual. As the mood of each grows into conformity with that of the others they all tend to exhibit simultaneous and rhythmic gestures. The group sways and surges in unison. (Swaying movements of arms and bodies are frequently used on the stage to convey the effect of crowd emotion.) It is significant in this regard that simpler peoples often employ the reiterated monotonous beat of a drum or other percussion instrument to evoke an orgiastic feeling in the group. Similar devices are used in the more fervent displays of religious emotion that characterize the assemblies of the Shakers or the "Holy Rollers" and other sects, and the "wakes" and "revivals" of certain Negro communities. The religious devotees, like the followers of Orpheus and Dionysus (in earlier times), feel that "the Spirit" or "the God" has taken possession of them. One student of religious groups offers the following "composite and impressionistic picture" of a meeting of certain small sects in North Carolina:

> All the while waves of ecstatic rhythm have been sweeping over the congregation, with the actions of the preacher setting the pace. There are patterns to the rhythmic actions: running around the pulpit, holding trembling hands to the sky, very fast clogging of the feet, swinging the arms in sharp staccato motions. One girl leaps from her seat as though struck by an electric shock, races four times around the aisles of the church, screaming "O God . . . O Jesus . . . O God . . . glory, glory, glory . . . give me more . . . glory, glory, glory"; falling over backward with hands outstretched, her whole body quivering and rhythmically jerking, she collapses at last in a dull heap on the floor. . . . Others rise and shout at the top of their lungs for five minutes, or bang on something in staccato rhythm.

12. On the motivations for rumors, see G. W. Allport and L. Postman, *The Psychology of Rumor* (New York, 1947), especially Chaps. II and IX.

> The same persons respond again and again. . . . Each responds with an individual pattern of motions, but all motions revolve around a few general types. The motions appear to have been culturally conditioned, whether immediately conditioned by the agent or not. One wonders if some form of mass hypnotism is at work.[13]

These cases reveal in an extreme manner the "hypnotic" quality characteristic of the crowd and the degree to which the suggestibility of the individual is enhanced when he becomes one of a physically compact group. Le Bon and his followers have attributed this reduced resistance to suggestion to the submergence of the individual in the group, a process in which intellectual and other differences are thrown off and all find a common level.[14] That this is what *appears* to happen in many crowds there can be no doubt, but the full explanation of crowd behavior cannot be found in such a simple formula as Le Bon's.

TWO: NUMBERS AND RESPONSIBILITY. All students of the crowd have noted the loss of the sense of responsibility, the breakdown of inhibitions, experienced by its individual constituents. The latter find themselves suddenly members of a group in which the normal standards of conduct are temporarily redefined. "The social is twisted around into giving approval of behavior which the culture normally forbids." The college boy does not ordinarily pull down goal posts or derail streetcars; in a victory celebration he does. The American woman does not undress in public; in demonstrations of patriotic fervor she has been known to. The white man does not normally kill and mutilate his fellow citizens of a different color; in lynch mobs he sometimes does. Deviational behavior is momentarily supported by the numbers of the crowd, providing the individual a short-lived social sanction for the acts forbidden in everyday life. This diminution of responsibility takes place in both the like-interest crowd, as in the panic where people may destroy others so as to save themselves, and in the common-interest crowd, as in the "race riot" which not only throws aside the usual orderly procedures but may take heavy tolls of property and of life.[15]

THREE: EMOTIONAL EXPRESSION. The heightened suggestibility and the lowered sense of individual responsibility interact in the crowd situation, each tending to evoke the other, and both serve to stimulate emotional release. The actual conditions under which crowd sentiment develops always include an element that touches some strong basic emotion. In the common-interest crowd a "blinding" emotion often overspreads the sense of group solidarity. In the panic the threat to self-preservation evokes a fundamental fear. In the "run on the bank" and in the crowds that assemble in a stock-market crisis

13. Liston Pope, *Millhands and Preachers* (New Haven: Yale University Press, 1942), pp. 132-133, by permission.

14. See, for example, G. Le Bon, *The Crowd* (Eng. tr., London, 1925), Chap. II.

15. For a detailed account of the riots in Detroit in 1943 see A. M. Lee and N. D. Humphrey, *Race Riot* (New York, 1943).

is aroused the sudden dread of impoverishment. In the harvest festivals and other dance celebrations of primitive peoples sexual emotion is stimulated, as it is in various "carnivals" and in the uninhibited acclamations of folk heroes among ourselves. Sex emotion is also prominent in crowd phenomena that ostensibly arise from quite different motivations. Thus certain types of religious "revival" combine an ardent verbal rejection of the "sins of the flesh" with an orgiastic behavior pattern in which sex feeling is clearly evident. Again, those lynching outbreaks that "uphold the honor of white womanhood" are marked, in some instances, by the sexual mutilation of the victim and by other evidences of deep-seated fears and jealousies in the white group.[16] The fierce vindication of the established norms of sex relationship which characterizes both these types of crowd represents a situation in which socially repressed sex tendencies take their revenge.

The role of crowd leadership. Given the occasions that stimulate these processes and evoke emotion, various devices may be deliberately employed by leaders or "agitators" to enhance crowd sentiment and to focus its attention. The skillful political speaker, the evangelist, the expert cheer leader, the fiery patriot, the advocate of class or racial conflict, the tribal witch doctor, all use similar methods, though the methods may be "unconscious" or "natural" aspects of the crowd leader's makeup.

[1] *Mechanisms of leadership:* In the first place, the speaker may rivet attention on himself with tricks of mannerism, gesture, and voice. Here he shares with the actor the well-known devices of "capturing" the audience. In addition, he may, with reiteration, with the use of "trigger terms" and stereotyped expressions, build up images and ideas that present reality in the colors of the dominant emotion and the intense immediate interest. Some types of political leader, especially certain of those who have come into positions of power or influence in times of stress, emergency, or crisis, depend peculiarly on the ability to sway crowds, to re-excite by various spectacular devices the crowd emotions that first aided in raising them to prominence or place. This ability played an important role, for example, in the political careers of Mussolini and Hitler in Europe and "Huey" Long in the United States. The revivalist preachers and the leaders of such groups as Father Divine's "Angels" depend also, in their own way, on their ability to arouse an intense crowd feeling in their hearers, and the techniques they use, the modes in which they convey vivid visions of hell or of salvation to create the hectic crowd atmosphere they require, are likewise instructive to the student of the mechanisms of propaganda and "mass" leadership.[17]

---

16. For suggestive studies of lynching mobs see Cantril, *The Psychology of Social Movements*, Chap. IV; and Miller and Dollard, *Social Learning and Imitation*, Chap. XV.

17. On these mechanisms see, for example, L. W. Doob, *Propaganda: Its Psychology and Technique* (New York, 1935); A. M. and E. B. Lee, *The Fine Art of Propaganda* (New York, 1939).

[2] *Leadership and the loss of individual judgment:* The "spell" of the effective crowd leader, as of the orator, lies in the fact that he enlists on the side of the prevalent state of feeling the reasoning power which was previously resistant and critical of it. But he usually achieves this end by dulling or, as it were, by "hypnotizing" the reasoning ability itself. He persuades the crowd by arguments that addressed to its individuals in isolation would fail to convince; as members of the crowd they are credulous of statements that in their normal social activities they would more cautiously scrutinize. The wildest rumors are apt to gain credence in a crowd situation in proportion as excitement grows, and in turn they increase the excitement. The clever leader can easily convince the oversuggestible and milling throng that its interests are in danger, that some group or individual is responsible for a calamitous or unwanted event, that the solution for some pressing problem or the appropriate release for a pent-up tension lies in the leader's suggestions. The crowd, like the nation in wartime or other crisis period, is so attuned, so manipulatable, that it tends to accept as truth every charge cast at its real or supposed enemies while convinced of the splendid righteousness of its own cause.

Interpretations of crowd behavior. Neither the sociopsychological processes that take place within the crowd nor the techniques employed by the crowd leader provide, in themselves, an adequate understanding of the peculiarities of crowd behavior. Of the various attempts that have been made to explain crowd phenomena, the following interpretations have received the largest emphasis in the literature of the crowd.

[1] *The "group mind" thesis:* Some writers have maintained that in the crowd, with the loss of individuality, a form of group consciousness develops, a fusion of mind with mind, a sympathetic participation of each with each on the emotional level which is common to all of the participants. According to this theory, the crowd becomes so attuned that it responds only to the appeals, the slogans, the ideas which are conformable to this de-individualized mentality. The notion of a "collective mind" or a "collective representation" is found in the writings of certain of the earlier students of crowd behavior, in the works of Le Bon and McDougall for example, but hardly meets the demands of modern sociology or social psychology. There is no evidence of a "group mind," a mind that exists apart from and controls the minds of the individual members of the crowd (or some other group, such as the "public" or "mass"). The postulation of such a phenomenon provides an easy "explanation" for any mode of collective behavior but one that, at best, is a literary device with which to describe the interstimulation and suggestibility that come about under the influence of crowd excitement. Yet this unprovable and largely rejected thesis is one that continues to have a popular appeal. For the personification of the crowd itself as an actor, with the same or similar attributes as the individual being, however misleading, in its very simplicity is apt to "make

sense" of an otherwise complex and seemingly incomprehensible area of group life.[18]

[2] *Crowd behavior as the release of repressed drives:* A contrasting interpretation of crowd behavior has been stimulated by certain Freudian and near-Freudian theories. Thus some students hold that the removal of inhibitions in the crowd situation brings into play not only the consciously repressed desires of men but also those hidden and unconscious desires that the discipline of normal social life has buried. The suggestibility, the exaltation, the lack of self-consciousness, the egoistic expansion and spontaneity, exhibited by the members of the crowd, are phenomena susceptible of this kind of explanation. What Freud called the "censor" within the individual—a product of socially determined restraints—is temporarily set aside, and the primitive or infantile or "id" impulses, which are normally confined to the inner depths of the personality, come to the surface. The crowd, in the manner of the dream or the reverie, provides a momentary release of otherwise repressed drives.

Most theories of crowd behavior agree that the peculiar manifestations of the crowd are the expressions of impulses repressed or thwarted by the conditions and social controls of everyday life. But the "orthodox" Freudian theory goes farther, for it assumes that it is not merely the thwarted conscious impulse that asserts itself but some deeper-lying elemental urge which the exponents of this view identify with the primal aspect of human nature. This theory, like the "group-mind" doctrine, often makes convincing reading but is not substantiated by factual investigation. "Instincts" or basic "id" impulses, whatever their nature may be, are of very little use in interpreting *group* phenomena unless the social and cultural context within which such psychological forces are revealed is taken into account.[19]

[3] *Social conditions and crowd behavior:* We may think of *the* crowd, then, as a temporary collectivity within which thwarted impulses are afforded an outlet. But if we shift our attention from the crowd as such to the many varieties of crowd expression at different times and places we cannot fail to observe an important relationship between particular social and cultural conditions and particular modes of crowd. Among primitive societies, for example, there are some that encourage frequent expression of emotional outburst; there are others that provide periodic group activities during which the everyday restraints are relaxed or removed; there are still others that impose upon their members as severe restrictions as any found in the traditional New England

18. The group-mind fallacy is inherent in the philosophy of G. W. F. Hegel and his successors; see, for example, *The Phenomenology of Mind* (originally published in 1807, J. B. Baillie, tr., New York, 1910). W. McDougall rejected the hypothesis of a group consciousness while adhering to the formula of a group mind; see *The Group Mind* (New York, 1920), Chap. II. For evaluations of this doctrine see, for example, R. M. MacIver, *Community* (New York, 1920), Book II, Chap. I; LaPiere, *Collective Behavior*, Chap. I.

19. Sigmund Freud's theory is developed, for example, in his *Group Psychology and Analysis of the Ego* (J. Strachey, tr., New York [no date]); it is applied specifically to the crowd by E. D. Martin in *The Behavior of Crowds*, especially in Chap. III.

community. We can observe somewhat similar contrasts in modern cultures—the community-wide celebrations or "festivals" characteristic of the "Latin" countries, the relatively staid and orderly demonstrations found in England and other Northern European nations, the lynching mob indigenous to specific regions in the United States. These examples strongly suggest the close connection between the underlying characteristics of the cultural conditions and the types of crowd that are apt to mark the community life.

Consider specific cases. Why, in recent years, have large gatherings of youths in New York and other large cities been moved to frenzied and orgiastic demonstrations when confronted with the person and the voice of a popular singer? No doubt the techniques of the performer were an essential stimulus and no doubt the "id" impulses were in some measure released. But any complete answer would have to reckon with the conditions of the urban environment, its vicariousness and impersonality, its limited opportunities for spontaneous expression, and the ways in which it endows its celebrities with the quality of "greatness." Why, in 1938, did thousands of Americans become panic-stricken by a radio program that described an invasion from Mars based upon an early novel by H. G. Wells, and why did many of them refuse to believe their neighbors' reassurances that the broadcast was merely a dramatic presentation of a piece of fiction? Certainly the skill of the narrator played a role, as did the appeal to the basic sense of self-protection. But to these factors must be added the widespread concern over the threat of war at that time and, perhaps, the anxieties induced by a depression-ridden era.[20] Again, how are we to explain the fact that the phenomenon of lynching in recent years, though occurring infrequently, has very rarely taken place outside the Southern states? Obviously any satisfactory answer would have to take note of the peculiar characteristics of the social stratification of that region, its value-systems and folk beliefs, and its deep-seated conflicts. We need not extend this list of illustrations in order to underscore the need for a sociology, as well as a psychology, of crowd behavior, for an approach the focus of which is the *relationship* between the individual and the social order.

The crowd and the sense of social solidarity. The manifestations of crowd feeling deserve study not only because they reveal the significance of this transitory form of aggregation, but also because they throw light on other social phenomena. An element of crowd contagion is often present in the more ordered assemblies of men, even though the fact of organization hinders its free expression and development. The audience that listens to a public address, the spectators who watch a game or other spectacle, the members who take part in a parade are all liable to the influence of crowd sentiment; and if anything occurs that suddenly arouses them above the normal pitch they may easily break altogether loose from the bonds of organization and for the moment become a crowd.

20. Cf. Cantril, *The Invasion from Mars*, Chap. IX.

Moreover, the study of the crowd illuminates the principle of solidarity itself. For the crowd exhibits fundamental social impulses as it overflows the channels of custom and habit, and thereby reveals the undifferentiated gregariousness which in more limited, refined, and specialized forms animates all of our *social* contacts. In the crowd we return, as it were, to the primary sense of society, of social relationship, at once simple and profound, wherein differences are submerged, where all act as one man. But it acts as no one man would act in his ordinary senses, for the crowd, punishing its victim or shouting its slogans of praise, is under a "spell." It takes its members into the world of magic, where things happen unaccountably. The very nature of the crowd, as we have seen, renders it unthinking in its love and ruthless in its hate. Thus though it often voices high purposes, it can rarely act to promote the welfare of the group.

Mass Communication

The modern extension of audiences. The crowd, as we have seen, offers a special opportunity for the emergence of herd sentiment. But this phenomenon has other avenues of expression apart from the physical crowd. In this final division of the chapter we shall consider briefly those aspects of modern complex society that have a particular importance in the study of the wider manifestations of herd sentiment.

[1] *The role of communication:* Communication, we know, is an essential process in social life. Throughout history it has operated to bring men together to sense their oneness; and it has functioned also, depending in part as it does on the stereotypes and unreal dichotomies of human thinking, to blind as well as guide men, to increase their susceptibility to suggestion and imitation, to make them subject to the managers and manipulators of communication itself. However, the tremendous increase of the technical facilities of communication in recent times, of the press and radio and motion picture, in conjuncture with other changes, has brought into the modern scene new problems and new potentialities in the area of "collective behavior." Most obviously, the mass media of communication have vastly extended the size of audiences. Where once a political candidate or officeholder addressed a few hundred persons, he now may include as listeners half or more of an entire national population. Certain news analysts and entertainers and others enjoy regular radio audiences of millions. Some magazines and newspapers can count on a sizable percentage of the population at least to scan their pages regularly. And the movies, in the United States and somewhat less so in most other modern countries, are seen by the residents of city, town, and village.

Here we have a situation in which unprecedented numbers of persons are brought into contact with the same objective stimuli, the same ideas, often the same distortions or one-sided interpretations of events of general interest. The reactions of listeners or readers or other audience members are certainly not the same, but depend in large measure on their experiences and attitudes and judgments. Nor are these scattered audiences in any exact sense crowds, spurred by the interstimulation of physical proximity. Nevertheless their size or potential size is itself a temptation for the purveyors of news or opinion or entertainment to standardize their fare in keeping with their own interests or with their own convictions concerning the nature of the public welfare. We witness the extreme case of this standardization in "totalitarian" nations where, as Mussolini was the first to demonstrate, entire peoples can be harangued, cajoled, praised, or persuaded under almost completely controlled conditions. In democratic countries, where the agencies of mass communication are relatively uncontrolled, the tendency toward standardization in some areas, such as the political, is in part checked or limited by the guarantees of free press and free radio, but in others, notably in entertainment, the stereotyped movie, "comic strip," and novel are evidences of a process of standardization largely maintained by commercial interests. (There are exceptions here, of course.)

The great growth of the modern audience, increasingly easy to reach with the advanced techniques of communication, is a trend of enormous interest to the social scientist. For it is a trend of double-edged potentialities. It breaks down the barriers of human intercourse and brings ever larger numbers within the range of knowledge and cultural stimulation: it opens up avenues of social education on a scale hitherto unknown. But it also gives a powerful tool to the propagandist, the salesmen of a particular brand of thought or of goods. And the danger here is enhanced by the very nature of mass communications, with their strictly limited possibility of audience participation. As one writer puts it, "The secondary personal contact with voice and image may increase the amount of mass regimentation, all the more because the opportunity for individual members reacting directly upon the leader [or "opinion manager"] himself, as in a local meeting, become farther and farther removed."[21] Modern urban society, highly specialized and impersonalized, composed of so many more spectators *of* events than immediate participants *in* events, provides exactly the elements for a large-scale susceptibility to the appeals to "mass" sentiment.

[2] *Characteristics of the diffused audience:* The techniques of mass communication have thus helped to shape a new kind of social grouping, which we may refer to as the *diffused audience*. Not a physically compact group like the crowd or assembly (a *physical* audience), it is made up of all the members of a modern community, of a city or region or nation or even larger territory, who can be reached by film or press or radio. Its constituents are to a large extent physically separated individuals, often unaware of the interests or sentiments of one another. Yet, in a degree they are bound together by like or common interests, and by the fact that their attention is focused on some

21. L. Mumford, *Technics and Civilization* (New York, 1934), p. 241.

particular activity or program or idea or grievance. On technological grounds alone there is perhaps no limit to the size of the diffused audience and, on these grounds, there are few barriers to the inclusion of additional members—we can "beam" our programs where we will. The exploitation of this characteristic, when combined with a ruthless and centralized control of the communication media over a sufficient period of time, can quite effectively indoctrinate a single point of view and prevent any reasonable calculation of alternatives. This, of course, is the "totalitarian" pattern, a pattern the prolonged use of which can turn the diffused audience into a crowdlike "mass."

In the democratic countries, however, with their freer interplay between the numerous groups and between the complex variety of attitudes and values, there is less possibility of the growth of *a* "mass" audience. Rather, the population represents an ever-changing area of *specialized* and dispersed audiences. (In political terms, *the* public may be thought of as consisting of several actual or potential specialized "publics."[22]) The specialized audience is, again, not a cohesive social group but a segment of the community loosely linked by a particular interest, and frequently characterized by a particular social or cultural make-up. Its significance lies in the fact that the concerns of its constituents are such that their attention may be easily gained by the appropriate communications appeals. Thus in addition to such widespread groupings as voting and buying or consuming "publics," there are numerous smaller divisions marked by more limited interests or opportunities or by more sharply defined predispositions and susceptibilities. Specialized audiences of this type include, for example, those who follow sports events, those who own radios, those who read the "slick" magazines (or some other type, say the "pulp"), those who are potential buyers of bonds or stocks, those who are reform-minded, those who are status conscious (a sizable element in this country), those who are seeking romance, those who fear radicalism, those who are interested in peace, *ad infinitum*. These are the audience populations for whom the radio program, the publicity campaign, the advertisement, the cartoon, the editorial, the motion picture are designed or are "slanted." The problems involved here are complex and call for the highly developed skills of the communications expert, whose knowledge must include a realistic understanding of the social and psychological traits of his one or several audiences.[23] But these problems involve more than technical skill and knowledge. For the one-sidedness of the audience position in the communication process gives it a peculiar vulnerability as a target for the salesmen of a particular commodity or a special program of action or a particular idea.

---

22. Specialized "publics" are discussed by various sociologists and social psychologists; see, for example, K. Young, *Social Psychology*, Chap. XVIII. In view of the particular usage of the concept "public" followed by many political scientists, we prefer in this context the term "audience."

23. For pertinent discussions of this area, see P. F. Lazarsfeld and G. Knupfer, "Communications Research and International Cooperation," in *The Science of Man in the World Crisis*

The larger problems of mass communication. In recent years the study of mass communications has become one of the most active research fields in the social sciences. Stimulated by the growing significance of propaganda methods and by the investigations of public opinion, governmental agencies, business firms, independent research institutes, and institutes attached to universities (at Columbia and Princeton and at the universities of Chicago, Michigan, and Washington, for example) have employed sociologists, psychologists, and political scientists, among others, to work in this area. These specialists have set about the tasks of analyzing the make-up of audiences to whom communications are addressed, of studying audience responses, of dissecting the content of whatever is said or displayed, and of tracing the sources of various types of communications.[24] We are not here concerned with the specialized problems faced by the communications specialist or with the already considerable accomplishments he has achieved. We may conclude this chapter, however, by indicating certain of the larger issues raised or implied by the mounting preoccupation with the technical aspects of the mass communication process.

[1] *Technical efficiency and social goals:* The communications expert knows or can discover the reactions of various groups to this or that type of advertising, of political speech, of entertainment, of fund-raising device—he can determine with at least a fair degree of accuracy the efficacy of his communications techniques. He utilizes the tools of social science, of psychology and statistics, to sell and to persuade. But the wares he sells or the causes he supports in his role as "expert" are not themselves decided by his proficiency or by his knowledge. Like the engineer's, his occupational task is essentially technological, concerned with the instruments that will produce results. Yet the expert cannot, if his vision carries very far, fail to see that the process in which he is engaged has another and, from a sociological viewpoint, a more significant dimension. For the ends of his effort, the commodity he sells, the idea or program he "puts across," may be of vital import to the social well-being; it may reflect his values and beliefs or it may not. One sociologist, R. K. Merton, who has himself contributed to communications research, has referred to this situation as a "moral dilemma."

> The practitioner in propaganda is at once confronted by a dilemma: he must either forego the use of certain techniques of persuasion which will help him obtain the immediate end-in-view or violate prevailing moral codes. He must choose between being a less than fully effective technician and a scrupulous human being or an effective technician and a less than scrupulous human being. The pressure of the immediate objective tends to push him toward the first of these alternatives. For when effective mass persuasion is sought, and when

(R. Linton, ed., New York, 1945), pp. 463–495; and B. L. Smith, "The Political Communication Specialist of Our Times," in Smith, H. D. Lasswell, and R. D. Casey, *Propaganda-Communication, and Public Opinion* (Princeton, N.J., 1946), pp. 31-73. The latter volume contains an excellent annotated bibliography of studies in communications research.

24. Cf. Lazarsfeld and Knupfer, *op. cit.*, pp. 472 ff.

> "effectiveness" is measured solely by the number of people who can be brought to the desired action or the desired frame of mind, then the choice of techniques of persuasion will be governed by a narrowly technical and amoral criterion. And this criterion exacts a price of the prevailing morality, for it expresses a manipulative attitude toward man and society. It inevitably pushes toward the use of whatsoever techniques "work."[25]

Some men at all times, of course, have been moved by narrow or self-seeking ends and have shown a "manipulative attitude" toward their fellow beings. Propaganda and demagoguery were hardly new in the days of ancient Greece and Rome. But today, with the great increase in the range of communications and in the size of audiences, and with the constant improvement of the techniques of persuasion, the latter have become an instrument of social control of unprecedented possibilities. Men may use these techniques to seek or to retain power or prestige, or to stimulate hatred and conflict. On the other hand, they may be used to enhance and to extend the community life itself.

[2] *The appeal to herd sentiment:* Modern society is multigroup and multistandard. It is crossed by divisions of class and race and nationality. Its huge national communities are struggling to achieve at once an ordered and a free way of life internally and in their external relationships. Modern communications cannot help play a major role in the resolution of these struggles. But the press, radio, and motion picture all too often become agencies for the transmission and development of herd sentiment. They may suggest that a foreign people or an opposing political party or any group, religious, racial, economic, that can be distinguished in some simple way from the group to which they appeal, is essentially inferior, suspicious, evil, designing. The herd emotion coheres around the "consciousness of kind" when the "kind" to which we belong is set in sharp contrast with some other. This deep-rooted feeling, when based on one simple distinction, refuses to make any other, for that would threaten its hold. But social intelligence demands that we make distinctions. Hence the prejudicial quality of undiscerning herd sentiment in modern society, where groups of all kinds are in necessary contact. Hence the peculiar danger of its manifestation in international relations, where it deludes peoples into destructive antagonisms though their fundamental interests are interdependent. Hence, finally, the need for that social education which guards us against the most expert of "practitioners of propaganda," with their techniques of simple stereotype and unreal dichotomy that appeal to the herd sentiment, and which permits us to exercise to the utmost our individual discernment.

---

25. R. K. Merton, *Mass Persuasion* (New York: Harper & Brothers, 1946), p. 185, by permission.

17

Associations and Interests

Interests as the Basis of Organization

The formation of associations. In this chapter we take up the type of social group which, from the sociological viewpoint, is the most characteristic feature of modern complex society—the association organized to promote specific interests. In Chapter I we observed that the association establishes a specifically defined and limited relationship between its members. We become members by virtue of particular attributes or qualifications, corresponding to the particular purposes for which it is organized. We profess a faith or cultivate an art or pursue some kind of knowledge or run some kind of business, and in so doing find it desirable or advantageous to join with others. Practically all associations arise in this way. Our task here is to analyze the relationship between the organized group itself and the nature of the interests around which it is formed.

[1] *The role of interests*: As we pointed out in Chapter II, we must explain the formation and maintenance of associations in terms of interests rather than of attitudes. Attitudes encourage or discourage the process of organizing, but they do not create organizations. Associations develop as means or modes of attaining interests. An association is likely to be formed wherever people recognize a like, complementary, or common interest sufficiently enduring and sufficiently distinct to be capable of more effective promotion through collective action, provided their differences outside the field of this interest are not so strong as to prevent the partial agreement involved in its formation. This principle holds for the formation of a family, a business firm, a church, a union, a club, a professional society, and even, as we shall see, a political state.

A heterogeneous specialized community, it is clear, affords more opportunity for the creation of organized groups than does a simple or primitive community. In the former we are able to distinguish particular interests from the general concerns, and the very fact of specialization makes necessary the organization of these particular interests. Moreover, the constant changes that occur in a specialized community precipitate conditions favorable to the emergence of new groups. In terms of social structure, nothing is more distinctive of modern societies than the multiplicity of organizations they contain.[1]

[2] *The role of leadership*: The mere recognition of an interest that can be promoted by organization is not sufficient to bring about the formation of an association. For inertias, prejudices, and problems of ways and means must be overcome, and here is where the role of leadership is most manifest. Usually the initiative, enthusiasm, and energy of one or a small number of persons prepare the ground for organization. The leaders, whether from sheer devotion to the cause or from a sense of advantage to themselves in the form of status or power or economic gain—usually, in fact, from a combination of these motives—play up the desirability of organization and seek to establish attitudes in the potential members favorable to its formation. Often some precipitant, some crisis or unusual conjuncture of events, stimulates the leaders themselves to action. We cannot here pursue the interesting theme of the social psychology of leadership, about which there is a large literature, but indicate rather the leader's function with relation to the group interest.[2] His tasks in the early stage are to create or to intensify a consciousness of the need for the new organization, or, in other words, the awareness of the interest around which it is organized, to instill confidence in the promoters and thus in the efficiency of the organization they propose, and to harness this heightened sense of need to the practical necessities of financial or other co-operation on the part of the members. In order to organize an interest, it must *first* be presented as such, in detachment from other interests, and then, *in its organized form*, it must somehow be brought into harmony with the other interests of the members. The reader who has organized a club or committee or discussion group can easily illustrate this principle from his own experience.

The nature of the interest to be organized determines in part the specific task of leadership. Where the interest is essentially economic the task is different from what it is when a recreational or educational or religious interest is in question. It is different where the interest is general or vague and where the interest has an intimate and limited appeal. Consider the example of a "peace society." For multitudes of people the promotion of international peace is an interest, though an indefinite one. When a peace organization arises, the interest receives some definition by the group's practical goal that serves to

---

1. The development of this point has been an important feature of a large amount of sociological literature. For two recent and contrasting systematic presentations, see E. T. Hiller, *Social Relations and Structures* (New York, 1947), Part V; and P. A. Sorokin, *Society, Culture, and Personality* (New York, 1947), Chaps. XXI-XXIV.

2. For the social psychology of leadership see, for example, R. T. LaPiere and P. R. Farnsworth, *Social Psychology* (New York, 1942), Chaps. XVIII-XX; and K. Young, *Social Psychology* (New York, 1944), Chap. X.

focus and further the interest. The particular obstacles which in this instance the leaders must overcome in the potential members include the feeling of remoteness from the controlling forces in the situation and thus of the futility of the nascent organization, the danger of cleavages over policy that a project so general and so "ideal" is apt to engender, and the resistance of traditions that tend to identify the advocacy of peace with a lack of patriotism or with "pacifism." This last barrier exemplifies a problem that often arises in the promotion of associations of this type. Most men are reluctant or unable to observe likenesses or unlikenesses that disturb their social attitudes, that break their stereotypes, confounding their established complacencies regarding social values and unsettling the sense of unity and difference which confirms limited group loyalties and maintains "social distances" between themselves and others. "Pacifist" is such a stereotype to many, belonging to the same order as the stereotypes that represent the Catholic to the Protestant and vice versa, the Jew to the Gentile, and so forth. A new organization which evokes these stereotypes, such as the Ku Klux Klan and certain supernationalistic associations, is likely to grow more rapidly, though its foundations may be less secure, than one that opposes the use of these misleading group images.

[3] *Leadership and the type of interest:* The development of appropriate leadership is subject to difficulties which vary with the type of the interest to be organized. Where economic like interests are the main consideration, as in the business corporation or the labor union, a strong competitive struggle for leadership is likely to take place, followed by a process of selection, tending on the whole toward the emergence of leaders with appropriate qualities. Here the chief danger is that the leader will give preference, in guiding the organization, to economic interests of his own that are not in harmony with the economic interests of the group as a whole.[3] Where common interests are the object of organization, other difficulties arise. The leader, *as leader*, has *like* interests. And these may prove too strong for his sincere service to the common cause. This point has been emphasized by Robert Michels and, more recently, by a number of other writers who have used the "life histories" of political leaders and labor leaders to illustrate their tendency to retain power for its own sake—a phenomenon perhaps generally characteristic of bureaucratic structures.[4] Another obstacle to effective leadership of organizations based upon common interests of the more idealistic type is that control tends not infrequently to

3. The success of certain labor leaders in remaining long in office is attributable in large part to the fact that they forward their constituents' like interests, or, as the miners say of John L. Lewis, they "deliver." This point is often neglected by those critics of organized labor in this country who prefer to account for union leaders' lengthy tenure on the basis of "bureaucratic" control.

4. In addition to R. Michels, *Political Parties* (Eng. tr., New York, 1915), see, for example, P. Selznick, "An Approach to a Theory of Bureaucracy," *American Sociological Review*, VII (1943), 47-54, and the same author's "Foundations of a Theory of Organization," *ibid.*, XIII (1948), 25-35.

fall into the hands of narrow-minded enthusiasts who, because of their zeal, are most ready to undertake the onerous tasks of leadership while they are often least conscious of its problems. In the political sphere we see a significant example of how the heavy responsibilities and often the sacrifices leadership involves act as a deterrent to some qualified candidates and thus leave the field more free for those who seek aggrandizement or power or personal gain. In all spheres of organization, socially beneficial leadership involves some reconciliation of like and common interests.

The combination of like and common interests in associations. Since interests generally determine the form and character of associations we shall classify the latter in terms of interests. In the next section our classification is based upon their intrinsic character or content. First, however, we must consider the major types of interests themselves.

[1] *The basic distinction:* Here we are concerned with the modes of relationship exhibited by the interests of *different* individuals. In accordance with the usage established in Chapter II, we shall speak of *like* interest when two or more persons severally or distributively pursue a like object or value, each for himself; we shall speak of *common* interest when two or more persons seek a goal or objective which is one and indivisible for them all, which unites them with one another in a quest that cannot be resolved merely into an aggregate of individual quests. Like interests are individualized; common interests are necessarily shared.

An association may be formed primarily to promote either a like interest or a common interest of the members. An economic association is generally based on like interest. Its main function is usually to provide wages or salaries or profits or dividends for those who belong to it. What we shall call a *cultural* association, such as a peace society, is generally organized around a common interest, though this does not imply that the common interest contains the main motive which inspires the adherence or devotion of its members, but only that apart from the common interest it could not come into existence or be maintained. Moreover, in spite of this initial difference between these two types of association, it should be remembered that, *once established*, nearly all organized groups represent, for at least some of its members, *both* a like and a common interest. This double character of the interest an association sustains is so important for the understanding of the social structure that we must illustrate and explain it more fully.

[2] *Illustrations of how the two types of interest are interwoven:* Let us take first a college society, a team, say, or a fraternity. Obviously the members enjoy an individual or private satisfaction through belonging to it. Membership in the team, for example, satisfies their like interests of recreation and physical exercise, perhaps brings some distinction with it; it also satisfies the like and the complementary interest of companionship. But it has a further interest for its

members. They want the team to succeed not simply because it redounds to their credit as individuals. They want it to succeed also for the credit of the team or for the credit of the college. Their individual interests merge in this inclusive interest. If a player does badly he is still gratified that the team wins; if he shines, he is still distressed that the team loses. Each has in degree the sense of the whole. Each shares a common interest.

Or consider a family group. Again it satisfies certain like and complementary interests of the members. But the family itself is normally an interest to each, a common interest. Each has some concern for the well-being of the others, not *merely* because their well-being is a means to his own, but because also he cares directly for his family. When one of the family distinguishes himself, the gratification of the others cannot be resolved *merely* into a sense of reflected glory. When one member disgraces himself, the others are downcast not *simply* because it affects their own reputations or because it makes the family a less desirable or less efficient agency for the fulfillment of their self-centered interests. The family itself is an interest to each, so that like interest and common interest are for each inextricably combined. In the pride and sorrow which the members share, in their attachment to common traditions and common achievements, in their struggles and sacrifices for the welfare of the whole, in their memory of its past and their hope for its future, they reveal in varying degrees that social solidarity which marks the presence of a common interest. We see one striking evidence of this in the anxiety of members of the family to provide for others in a future beyond their own lives. This sense of responsibility for others can arise only in the presence of a common interest.

Finally, we may take two examples in which the initial dominance of like interests is manifest, as in a business firm and in a labor union. The former is established to provide dividends or profits, but if it endures it tends to mean something more in the lives of the partners or directors. This does not mean merely that in addition to profits they find it the source of power or personal prestige. It is likely to appear in their eyes as a co-operative enterprise, perhaps also as a service to the community. They find some satisfaction in its success, in its tradition, in its institutions, apart from their personal advantage. They will spend money, not wholly for its advertising value, in erecting a beautiful building, a model factory, a templelike bank. A common interest has developed out of a like interest. The same process takes place in the labor union. The employees initially come together to bargain more effectively with the employer, to protect or improve their wages, their conditions of work, and so forth. But as the union gains a tradition, as it extends its activities into new areas, such as education and recreation, as it develops its songs and slogans of brotherhood, the common interest emerges to join with the like interest in binding its members to the organization.[5]

5. The combination of like and common interests in business and labor associations is illustrated in a large literature from these fields. For two pertinent statements, see O. Tead,

[3] *Confusions to avoid:* The existence of common interest, as we have defined it, is sometimes denied because of a psychological confusion. Certain writers have inferred that because we receive individual satisfaction from some situation—in this context, from the associational common interest—we pursue this course in order to gain this sense of satisfaction, and that therefore all interests are at bottom self-centered. This psychological hedonism, as has often been pointed out, is unsound. We would not in fact have the sense of satisfaction, as it is realized, say, in family life or business or political activities, unless the achievement of the interest or the well-being of the group were the *direct* object of our desires. In this connection we should remember that like and common interests cannot be identified respectively with "selfish" and "unselfish" interests. Such ethical terms are misleading and irrelevant in psychological analysis. Confusion also arises, as we pointed out in Chapter II, because we do not always keep in mind the distinction between *interest* and *motivation.* Motivations are often of primary concern to the student of individual behavior. But to the sociologist and social psychologist the group as a whole has a fundamental significance, for it remains a common interest no matter what motives may be discovered in the individual lives of those who entertain it. We must avoid these confusions in considering the relationship of association and types of interest.

[4] *Associational cultivation of common interest:* We shall fail to appreciate the social significance of the association unless we realize that it is held together by the twofold interest of its members in it, by the subtly interwoven bonds of like and common interest. When an association of the economic order brings like interests into co-operative harmony it is at the same time, as we have seen, supplementing the like interest by a common interest and thus enlarging the sphere of common interest. In this way, within the limits of membership, each association sends a taproot down to the deep sources of society. The more enduring the association the stronger this taproot is likely to grow. Within every association there arises also the conflict of dividing interests, of the competitive desires for place and power. These are normally kept within limits because the existence of the association itself becomes a primary condition on which their satisfaction depends. In other words, the like interests must be accommodated to the common interest.

Every organized group, therefore, in seeking its own preservation or expansion, endeavors in various ways to cultivate the common interest. For example, it devises symbols of its unity and keeps them before the attention of its members; it emphasizes the common interest with slogans, appellations of brotherhood, emblems, flags, festivals, parades, processions, initiation rites, rallies, intergroup competition (used in *both* socialistic and capitalistic economic

"The Development of Leadership Power," in *Human Factors in Management* (S. D. Hoslett, ed., Parkville, Mo., 1946), pp. 5-12; and C. S. Golden and H. J. Ruttenberg, "Motives for Union Membership," *ibid.*, pp. 186-202.

associations), and so on, all designed to evoke or sustain the *esprit de corps* of the members, to make them feel their solidarity. The student will find it worth while to compare the various ways in which different associations, according to their kind—unions, business firms, churches, schools, clubs, mystic brotherhoods, political parties, professional societies—make their appeal directly or indirectly, through symbols or through exhortations, to the common interest. For no association can in the long run survive unless its constituents are in some degree bound together by indivisible social bonds.

The Classification of Associations

Associations in a complex society. In a complex society, associations tend to be specialized so that each stands for a particular type of interest or interest complex. In primitive society, where there is less division of labor and where change is slower, there are few associations and they are more inclusive. They are communal or semicommunal in the range of their interest. A newly developed interest does not so often create, as with us, a new association, but is incorporated in the general body of interests pursued by the existing organization. Thus in primitive life, associations lack the specific, limited functional character which our own possess. They take such forms as age-groups, kin-groups, sex-groups, groups for the performance of communal rites and ceremonies, secret societies, rather than the economic or professional or political or cultural varieties familiar to ourselves. This contrast will be shown more fully in Book Three, the final one of this volume, devoted to the subject of social change. Meantime, it may suffice to note that the functional differentiation of modern organized groups makes it possible for us to classify them according to the characteristic interests they severally pursue.

Some specific problems of classification. In classifying associations in terms of the nature of their interests, however, we are confronted with certain difficulties. There are four particularly important precautions we should have in mind in depicting the interest characteristic of any organized group.

[1] *The professed interest not always the determinant interest:* The group's ostensible interest is not always determinant; the professed or formulated aims of an association do not necessarily reveal the full or even the true character of the goal that it chiefly seeks. But at least a part of this difficulty disappears when we take as the basis of classification the immediate field of interest rather than the remote objectives or purposes, when in particular we avoid the confusion of interests and motivations. It would indeed be a hazardous task to classify associations in terms of professed objectives or ulterior aims. For one thing, a disparity not infrequently arises because the association, passing through historical changes, clings traditionally to older formulations—as

religious bodies are particularly apt to do—or because the leaders idealize its aims, in the desire to broaden its appeal, to strengthen its public position, to secure funds, and so forth. Such idealization is seen not only in the platforms of political parties but also in the pronouncements of many other organizations. Often an organization will stress the more altruistic of the objects which lie within the field of its interest. A department store will proclaim that it exists to serve the community. A professional organization will emphasize the necessity of rigid qualifications for membership on the ground that the service of the public must be safeguarded while it is more or less silent on the competitive economic advantage thereby gained.

[2] *Professed interest modified by variant conditions:* We should also observe that we are far from expressing the distinctive character of any individual association when we have placed it in its interest category. The character of an individual association is often very subtle, and it is only in the light of a considerable study of its activities that its actual purpose and proper distinctiveness can be found. Moreover, in every case the interest it pursues is colored or modified by the personalities of the constituents and the social make-up of the community in which it functions. Often certain features of organizations are not brought into the focus of consciousness by the members or even by the leaders. For example, an organization which has gradually abandoned a traditional basis of solidarity may gropingly move in a new direction and gain a new kind of solidarity, related to but different from that which its leaders believe and certainly state that it possesses. This situation is illustrated in the history of certain semireligious organizations such as the Y.M.C.A. and the Y.W.C.A. Shall we classify them as religious or recreational or generally educational or in a broad sense as "social" clubs? What element is focal or dominant in the interest complex? For reasons just suggested it is difficult to answer. The Y.M.C.A. or the Y.W.C.A. is a characteristic association, a certain "kind" of association with its own social "flavor." But it is a different kind in a rural area and in, say, a metropolitan area. In each region it has responded to certain social exigencies, seeking in the face of competing social agencies still to represent something, something in some way different from the rest, for when an organization loses its specific identity it loses its most important reason for existence in our highly organized society.

An associated problem of classification, arising out of the changing relation of associations to interests, is revealed in the struggle to survive of those interests which have fulfilled their original *raison d'être*. Organizations of people, like the individuals themselves, are tenacious of life. They refuse to die when their day is past. New interests are thus sought within them which will justify their existence in a continuing purpose. This organizational "will to live" centers in the officials, in the occupants of the "bureaucratic structure."[6] A political association is organized to achieve some piece of legislation; it is

6. For the development of this point see our earlier discussion in Chapter X.

attained but the association lingers on. Thus a league for the enfranchisement of women turns into a party organization when the women gain the vote; or a reform movement to eliminate the "machine" becomes itself a machine after achieving its initial goal. An ancient guild is rendered obsolete by industrial change, yet it survives as an "honorable company," to perpetuate traditional ceremonies at annual dinners—once an economic organization, it has passed over into another category. This list can be easily extended—patriotic societies, veterans' groups, hooded organizations, and many others have sought and found new interests when the old have disappeared.

[3] *The main interest sometimes hard to determine:* A more important obstacle to a satisfactory classification is presented by those organizations which stand for a variety of different interests in such a way that it is hard to designate any one as dominant. Shall we classify a denominational college as a religious organization? Sometimes religion is the primary interest, sometimes merely the historical matrix. Shall we assign an organization for workers' education as economic or as cultural? It may exist to train union leaders or to inculcate the principles of Marx or to provide a general education—and it may combine all these interests in one. Shall we call a businessmen's club an association for social intercourse or an economic association? One aspect may be dominant at one time, the other at another. These are examples of the difficulty which frequently occurs when we seek to place associations in the categories described below. This difficulty leads up to our final caution.

[4] *Some important interests do not create specific associations:* We are making interests the basis of our classification, but the correspondence of interest and association is not, even in our specialized society, a simple one. There are some strong interests, such as the interest of power and of distinction, which do not normally create specific associations but ramify through associations of every kind. The dynastic state might be termed a "power organization," but the quest of power in some form invades every political system, underlies the interest of wealth which is the direct object of economic association, and in fact is found wherever organization of any kind exists. We might call certain kinds of clubs "prestige organizations," but as the interest of prestige is fostered no less in many other kinds of association, and particularly as men do not pursue prestige except through the medium of other interests, such an attribution would only confuse our classification. Again, the interest of companionship or of social intercourse is so pervasive that it is in some degree satisfied by every association and thus it is often dubious whether or not it is the main determinant. In our classification below, we take the club as the type-form association corresponding to this interest, but social intercourse is not the focus of all bodies called clubs and, on the other hand, there are various groups ostensibly established for other objects, from library associations to spelling bees, from charity leagues to sewing meetings, which are sustained mainly by this interest. The main interest of a group cannot be inferred from the name

we apply to it. A gang, for example, may be little more than a boys' brotherhood, or it may be essentially an economic organization, exploiting a neighborhood by illegal means for economic ends.

Associations classified by interests. We may now turn to the classification as set forth in Chart XVII. We suggest that the reader consult this chart as he considers the following explanation.

[1] *Explanation of our general classification:* We first divide associations into *unspecialized* and *specialized*. Here we refer to the fact that they may stand for the total interests of a group or class or, on the other hand, they may represent either a particular interest or a particular method of pursuing interests. We include the state among specialized associations because, in spite of the vast range of its interests, it works through the special agencies of law and government.[7] As we have already pointed out, unspecialized associations are less characteristic of modern society—and less effective within it—than specialized associations.

The latter are classified in terms of the distinction between *primary* and *secondary* interests. By the former we mean those interests which have for men a final value, which are *ends* in themselves. By the latter we mean those interests which by their intrinsic nature are *means* to other interests. We do *not* mean that primary interests are more pervasive or necessarily even more significant in social life than secondary interests, or that the one or the other type functions in isolation from the other. The fuller significance of this division will appear in Chapter XXI, in which we develop the distinction between *civilization*, as the sphere of secondary interests, and *culture*, as the sphere of primary interests.[8] Here a preliminary statement about these categories is in order.

Our distinction is one of ends and means. One difficulty in applying the distinction lies in the fact that *any* object we seek can become the "end" of our search, so that we look for no utility beyond it. We may seek wealth merely to possess it and not for its ulterior services; we may construct instruments or mechanisms (perhaps even social mechanisms) because we enjoy doing so and not because they will aid us to achieve other objects. But this is a problem of individual motivations, not of social organization. As aspects of the latter, the economic system would not exist but for the interests which underlie it, and technological mechanisms would be idle and soon forgotten toys but for their service as man's instruments. We divide these secondary or *utilitarian* interests into three classes, the *economic*, the *political*, and the *technological*. We have placed another large group of interests, the *educational*, in an inter-

7. For the state as an association see below, Chapter XVIII.

8. For the further development of this distinction see R. M. MacIver, *Social Causation* (Boston, 1942), Chap. X; and for its application to the problems of government in complex society, the same author's *The Web of Government* (New York, 1947), pp. 421–430.

CHART XVII General Classification of Interests and Associations

Interests	*Associations*
A. Unspecialized	Class and caste organizations
	Tribal and quasi-political organization of simpler societies
	Age-groups and sex-groups
	The patriarchal family
	(Perhaps also such organizations as vigilante groups, civic welfare associations, etc.)
B. Specialized	
I. *Secondary* (civilizational or utilitarian)	
(a) Economic interests	Type form: *The business*
	Industrial, financial, and agricultural organizations, including unions
	Occupational and professional associations[a]
	Protective and insurance societies
	Charity and philanthropic societies[b]
	Gangs, "rackets," etc.
(b) Political interests	Type form: *The state*
	Municipal and other territorial divisions of the state
	Parties, lobbies, propagandist groups
(c) Technological interests	Associations for technical research, and for the solution of practical problems of many kinds[c]
II. *Intermediate*	
Educational interests	Type form: *The school*
	Colleges, universities, study groups, reformatories, etc.
III. *Primary* (cultural)	
(a) Social intercourse	Type form: *The club*
	Various organizations ostensibly for the pursuit of other interests
(b) Health and recreation	Associations for sports, games, dancing, gymnastic and other exercises, for diversions and amusements[d]
(c) Sex and reproduction	Type form: *The family*
(d) Religion	Type form: *The church*
	Religious propagandist associations
	Monasteries, etc.[e]
(e) Aesthetic interests, art, music, literature, etc.	Corresponding associations
(f) Science and philosophy	Learned societies

[a]These combine economic and technological interest; where the latter are dominant the associations fall in I (c).

[b]The economic interest is usually, though by no means always, the focus of these associations. The fact that it is the economic welfare of others than the members which is sought does not affect the classification.

[c]The technological interest is generally subordinate to the economic, i.e., it is a means to a means. Hence it is usually pursued through subagencies of the economic order. Sometimes it is organized, under political auspices, through such divisions as a department of agriculture, bureau of standards, atomic commissions, etc.

[d]The interest of health and of recreation may of course be entirely dissociated. The interest of recreation is, on the other hand, often associated with the aesthetic interests, so that various associations could be classified under III (b) or under III (e).

[e]The monastery is a quasi-community, but if religion is the main determinant of its activities as well as the basis of organization, we can retain it under III (d).

mediate position between secondary and primary, since they involve both means and ends, since they are both utilitarian and cultural. All genuine education, elementary or higher, technical or "liberal," is at the same time an instrumental equipment for living and itself a cultural mode of life. We set the cul-

CHART XVIII Associations Classified According to the Durability of the Interest

Interests	*Associations*
(a) Interests realizable once for all—definite temporary objectives	Associations for the achievement of a specific reform, reconstruction, etc., political or other (e.g., anti-slavery); for a celebration, erection of a memorial, etc., for an emergency such as a flood, economic crisis, war
(b) Interests peculiar to a definite number of original or potential members—the "broken plate" situation[a]	Groups composed of the members of a school or college class or year, of army veterans, of the survivors of a shipwreck, etc.
(c) Interests limited to age-periods of a relatively short range	School and college teams, debating societies, etc.; boy scouts, junior leagues, etc.—associations continuous as individual structures but with rapidly successive memberships
(d) Interests limited by the tenure or life span of some original or present members[c]	Partnerships of various kinds; groups of friends; the family—permanent as a social system embodied in successive individual associations[b]
(e) Interests unlimited by a time span	The corporation; most large-scale organizations, state, church, occupational associations, scientific associations, etc.—associations individually continuous through the recruitment and incorporation of new members

[a]The reference here is to an illustration given by G. Simmel in *Soziologie* (Munich, 1923), p. 60. A group of industrialists were seated at a banquet when a plate was dropped and shattered into fragments. It was observed that the number of pieces corresponded to the number of those present. Each received one fragment, and the group agreed that at the death of any member his fragment was to be returned, the plate being thus gradually pieced together until the last surviving member fitted in the last fragment and shattered again the whole plate.

[b]The larger patriarchal family or the "joint family" does not fall within this class, but the modern individual family does. We speak of the family in another sense, as when we say that a person is a member of an "old" family, but in this sense the family is not an association. See Chapter XI.

[c]Observe particularly the difference between the groups under (b) and under (d). The interest which creates an association under (b) is unique, peculiar to the members, and dies with the association. It has therefore little significance for the social structure. The interest under (d) is universal in its appeal and particularizes itself in a multitude of individual associations. The interest under (b) is in fact the social bond itself, whereas the interest under (d) is the perennial source of the social bond.

tural or primary interests over against the secondary interests. We pursue the cultural goals apart from external pressure or necessity. Again, cultural interests may serve us merely as means, but, sociologically, their utilitarian service is incidental to the fact that we, or some of us, pursue them for their own sakes, because, that is, they bring us some *direct* satisfaction.

[2] *Other modes of classification in terms of interests:* While the specific nature of the interest is the main clue to the character of the corresponding associa-

tion, as set out in Chart XVII, there are other ways of classifying interests that throw further light on the relation between them and associations. Thus the direct social interest in *persons* is the distinguishing feature of *primary groups*, whereas the interest in the *impersonal* means and ends of living characterizes the *large-scale association*, as we saw in Chapter X. Again, we can distinguish interests according to their degree of duration in the life history of their members. In terms of this criterion, associations within the same field may be transient, rapidly successive, or permanent. They may be permanent, as established *forms* of social organization like the family, though the individual instances are mortal, or they may be long-lived, potentially immortal, as individual structures, like the corporation. In Chart XVIII we neglect the types of interest in order to classify associations according to their *durability*.

The classification in our first chart (XVII) is meant to serve as an introduction to the organized aspects of the social structure. The task in this study, which we undertake in the concluding four chapters of this division of Book Two, is to reveal the distinctive types of association that enter into the social structure—distinctive with respect to the kinds of social relationship they exhibit—and at the same time to show their place and function in the social order, their relation to one another and to the whole.

Intra-Associational Conflict of Interests

Social cohesion and conflict. The interest for which an association stands is the primary ground of its unity, the basis of its particular cohesion or solidarity. This unity is reinforced by other bonds, by the shared tradition and prestige of the association or the associates, by the sustenance of the general need of social relationships that it may provide, by the particular habituations and attitudes that it supports, by the other common interests the members share in whole or in part. But at the same time forces are generated or revealed within the association that cause tensions and strains in its solidarity.

Conflicts develop in the field of the particular interest the association promotes and conflicts arise from oppositions between that interest and other interests of the members. Like the greater communal manifestations of social cohesion—class, ethnic and racial group, and crowd, as well as the community itself—the unity of the association is imperfect and unstable, representing, while it endures, the victory of integrative over disintegrative processes. A study of the conflicts and harmonies of interest that appear within the life of associations could be for the student an excellent preparation for the investigation of that greater unstable equilibrium which is the social order itself.

Types of interest-conflict within associations. Here we select for brief discussion three main types of interest-conflict. These three types occur persistently in the history of organized groups, especially in the variety of associations that grow up in modern complex society.

[1] *Conflicts within the interest-complex:* The first arises from a lack of harmony between the objectives that fall within the interest-complex. A clear illustration is frequently presented within professional or occupational associations. The economic interest, the maintenance or enhancement of the emoluments of the service they render, is often difficult to reconcile with the professional interest proper, the quality and extent of the professional service.

The medical profession offers a peculiarly interesting situation. If it could achieve its professional ideal, it would thereby reduce to a minimum the need for its therapeutic service while enlarging greatly its preventive service. The former is mainly private practice, the latter is largely socialized, provided through clinics, hospitals, state departments, public and semi-public institutions of various kinds. Here a dilemma is apt to arise not only because private practice is more in accord with the traditions of the profession but also because it tends, under prevailing conditions, to be more remunerative. If economic interest alone determined the policy of a professional organization, whether medical or other, we would have simply a conflict between the associational interest and the public interest. But the members of a medical association, like those of other professional groups, are concerned with the efficacy of the service the group represents. Hence there arises a conflict of interests within the association itself in the attempt to work out a policy that will reconcile or adjust the economic interest and the professional ideal. The problem has a peculiar character in this case, since under competitive conditions the livelihood of the physician depends on the length of treatment, on the seriousness of cases, and generally on the amount of disease prevalent in the community.[9]

Similar problems of the adjustment of interests arise within bar associations, educational organizations, business firms, labor unions, and other bodies. The conflict is seen very clearly in political groups. It is only in the extreme exploitative political organizations, such as that centering round a "boss," that the economic interest drives out almost altogether the professional interest, that of the standard of service. When this happens any "professional" organization becomes an association of another and frequently of a socially detrimental type.[10]

---

9. See, for example, J. Rorty, *American Medicine Mobilizes* (New York, 1937); C. Binger, *The Doctor's Job* (New York, 1945); and for brief reviews of the question, R. H. Shrylock, "Freedom and Interference in Medicine," *The Annals of the American Academy of Political and Social Science*, Nov., 1938; W. T. Foster, *Doctors, Dollars, and Disease*, Public Affairs Pamphlet No. 10 (rev., New York, 1944).

10. The conflict of interests in the professions is stressed in a large literature. Many illustrations may be found, for example, in A. M. Carr-Saunders and P. A. Wilson, *The Professions* (New York, 1933); E. L. Brown, *Lawyers and the Promotion of Justice* (New York, 1938); and L. Wilson, *The Academic Man* (New York, 1942).

[2] *Conflicts between relevant and irrelevant interests:* The second type of conflict arises where the specific interest of the association demands a course of action which is opposed to some other interests not relevant to the association as such but nevertheless entertained by some members of the group. A highly qualified Negro, let us say, seeks admission to a university. He possesses the requisite qualifications, for racial difference is no bar to scholarship. But other considerations that have nothing to do with the express purpose of the association enter in and create within the association a conflict concerning policy. In one form or another such conflicts are constantly occurring. Outside interests prevent the association from pursuing with single-mindedness its stated objectives. Group prejudices modify the devotion of the association to its avowed purpose. Individual jealousies and predilections thwart the interest which is the *raison d'être* of the organization. Thus confusion and disharmony appear within its councils.

We may include in the same general category the conflict which arises owing to the fact that the interests of the officials or leaders are not identical with those of the other members, or cease to be identical once they have enjoyed the fruits of office. The officials may be anxious to enhance their authority, though this course may lead to policies detrimental to the general associational interest. Or they may have an economic interest at variance with the interest, economic or other, of the group. The degree of maladjustment varies not only with the personalities involved, but also with the nature of the interest. A particularly significant illustration is furnished by groups founded on principles of equality, whether economic, political, or religious. Organization is essential to each and hence a bureaucratic structure emerges. It has even been maintained that officials, as soon as they acquire power, are driven by the logic of their position to antidemocratic attitudes, and thus no democratic or socialist organization can ever translate its principles into effective practice.[11] The argument is too sweeping, but the numerous instances adduced by the proponents of this "iron law of oligarchy" sufficiently illustrate the serious conflicts and confusions created by the dilemma of leadership.

[3] *Conflicts between alternative policies in the pursuit of interests:* A third source of conflict is found in the constant necessity of the new adaptation of means to ends. By the end we here understand the provisional basis of agreement regarding the interest of the association, which has to be translated into action by means of a policy. A group meets to decide a course of action in a given situation. The group interest has already been defined and redefined by past decisions, has been canalized in the series of adjustments which the group has undergone. But a new occasion often demands more than a routine following of the channel. Being different, it demands a fresh decision, a new expression of policy. The members meet on the assumption that all are agreed regarding the end—the problem is the appropriate means. A business must decide

11. Michels, *op. cit.*

how to deal with a new competitive threat. A club must raise funds to meet a deficit. A church must decide how to act in the face of a declining membership. A settlement house must adapt itself to a changing neighborhood or to the "competition" of state agencies. A political party, say a revolutionary party, must adjust its strategy to changing historical circumstances.

In these situations, the agreement on ends is implicit, taken for granted. But the agreement on means must be explicit. This necessity inevitably evokes differences of temperament and viewpoint within the group. Shall the club raise the necessary funds by an extension of membership or by a levy on its present members? Shall the church popularize its regular services or undertake additional social activities? Shall the national revolutionary party support a program of military preparedness in its own country or advocate a policy of peace at all costs? Some members answer one way, some another—the interplay of divergent personal factors and divergent policies is very complex. The sense of solidarity may prevail, an adjustment may be reached, and a generally acceptable policy formed. But in the process acute differences may emerge sufficient to disrupt or even to end the life of the association.

The type of association and internal conflict. In conclusion, we may point out that if the association stands for a broad cultural interest or one strongly charged with emotional elements there is greater danger that difference will lead to schism. For here differences on matters of policy are apt to extend down into differences regarding the *implicit end* which the policy is meant to serve. The interest of a business firm is relatively simple. The end to which its policy must be adapted is accepted and understood without dispute. But it is otherwise with the interest of a church, of an artist group, or, in some cases, of a political party. Dissension over means may here reveal the inadequacy of the more basic agreement over ends. The end itself, at some level, is brought into the arena of conflict, and thus the solidarity of the organization may be shaken. When a church faces a declining membership it may be forced to raise the further question concerning its proper mission. When the business faces declining sales, its endeavor to restore profits raises no similar question regarding the appropriate definition of its quest. Such considerations help to explain the tendency to schism exhibited by churches which do not adhere strongly to authoritative interpretations, by left-wing parties generally, by artistic and other bodies united around some cultural conviction. The particular case of the political association we shall discuss in the following chapter.

18

The Great Associations: Political

The State as a Form of Association

Sociology and the great associations. The state is the subject of the science of government, or political science. One of its attributes, lawmaking, is the subject of legal science or, broadly, of jurisprudence. Some other sciences or branches of science, such as public finance, criminology, penology, are concerned primarily with particular activities of the state. Similarly, economic associations are the subject of the many-branched science of economics. In short, the social sciences divide between them the study of the great associations with which we are to be concerned in the next three chapters. In what way, then, do these associations constitute part of the subject matter of sociology? We shall here seek to answer that question with special reference to the state.

[1] *The sociological approach to the state:* Our concern as sociologists is not with constitutions and forms of government, nor with the modes in which states fulfill their various functions. In this chapter we are seeking to discern the character of the state as a distinctive form of association, to discover its sociological type, so to speak, and thereafter to show its typical relationships to the other parts of the social system. We shall proceed in a similar way in the two succeeding chapters. This is a sociological task, in the furtherance of which sociology can and should co-operate with the other social sciences. The great associations have brought into being their own distinctive sciences. Sociology can neither be inclusive of the subject matter of these sciences nor be a substitute for them. To offer a smattering of them would be foolish. But the great associations exhibit significant differences of type, and they are interwrought in the whole structure of a society. For these reasons they are of profound interest to the sociologist.

[2] *The basis of the state in secondary interests:* It should be evident from the argument of the preceding chapter that we can classify the great associations

of modern society according as they are primarily utilitarian or primarily cultural. For example, economic organizations belong obviously to the former category and religious organizations to the latter. Sometimes there may be doubt as to the category in which we should place a particular association, and certain thinkers would claim that the state is no less a cultural than a utilitarian organization. While not denying that the state has an important cultural role, we think it is more appropriately conceived as a part, and indeed a major part, of the apparatus of civilization. The reasons for this view should be apparent in what follows.

In all the more complex societies the organizations of the political and economic order become the comprehensive framework of the social structure. They ramify everywhere, creating an ever wider and ever more intricate scheme of relationships. They link land with land over all the earth, often outstripping in their advance the associations of the cultural order. They link the savage to the civilized man. While particular states may be based on the principle of nationality and while some states claim to stand for a distinctive creed, in their actual operation political as well as economic interests are not bounded by any such considerations. This condition arises out of the peculiar character of these interests. We have already classified them as "secondary interests," constituting, as it were, neutral means to which all other interests of men are related and through which all other interests may be pursued. Consequently, given the means of communication, they are capable of unlimited expansion. In their development they establish great forms of social order which both liberate and limit the expression of all our primary interests.

The state and the community. We pointed out in Chapter I that the state itself is a form of association. Since this conception is of cardinal importance for the understanding of its nature we must here return to it.

[1] *The state as a community agency:* When we call the state an association we mean that it is a specific organization of society. We distinguish it thereby from the country or the nation on the one hand, from the unity of the social structure on the other. The confusion is still a prevalent one. It is encouraged by language, since we use the same terms, "the United States," "England," "Germany," and so forth, to denote both the country and its people or the state and its government. We say "The United States makes a treaty"—and here we mean the state—or we say "The United States has a standard of living"—and here we mean the people. It is fostered by the tradition of old theories which regarded the state, contrary to definite evidences, as a *universal* partnership. It is a mistaken inference from the fact that the state does actually control or regulate a great part of our social activities and relationships and that it is *constitutionally* competent to control a still greater part. It is consequently maintained that if the state lets other aspects of social life alone "it is none the less dealing with them—it only lets them alone in a certain way and on certain

terms."[1] But even if we accepted this position it does not follow that the regulator is to be identified with that which is regulated.

Moreover, there are, as we have seen, various social codes which are distinct from and only in small part controlled by the code of the state. And there are many associations to which we belong which are in no sense merely divisions or branches of the great association of the state. As social beings, we are more than merely citizens of a state. We enter into many relationships, we carry on many social activities, not as members of a state, not as citizens, but as social beings, as friends or lovers, as members of families, of churches, of clubs or other groups. The real problem, that of the relation of the state to the inclusive community, is obscured only if we begin by identifying the two. Most modern constitutions set limits to the things the state can do. Generally, for example, a constitution forbids the state to require the profession of any religion of its citizens or to discriminate between citizens with respect to their religion. We say it forbids the state and not simply the government. For it proclaims—or rather the people proclaim through it—that laws of a certain nature shall not be passed and that certain liberties shall not be abrogated, and to this end it usually provides that a mere majority shall not suffice to alter these constitutional guarantees. Whatever practical difficulties may arise from such provisions, they surely bear witness to the intention of "the people" or the community to set limits to the place and power of the state itself.

[2] *The state as a limited agency:* The state, then, is an essential part, but never the whole, of the social structure. It is best conceived of as an agency of the community with very broad and important functions, but nevertheless limited. It does not, and cannot, take the place of other agencies; these have their own functions, which they alone are fitted to perform. The family has its place, the church has its place, and so forth. How far the state *should* regulate other associations is a question admitting vast experimentation; how far the state *can* take over the functions of certain associations, particularly of the economic order, is another question of great significance. But under no conditions which we can conceive of, and certainly under no conditions which exist anywhere in the civilized world, is the state all-sufficing. If the communistic state, for example, absorbs into itself nearly the whole system of economic organization, it leaves the family more unrestricted than do most capitalistic states. It is true that in recent times a form of state has arisen which claims to be totalitarian, and professes to "co-ordinate" and to control *all* the interests of its citizens. But the claim, in so far as valid, has been realized only by the forceful suppression of those interests and those groups that could not or would not be "co-ordinated." Moreover, in no instance has the end been wholly achieved. Even in the extreme instance, that of Nazi

1. Quotation from a letter to one of the authors by the late Professor Bosanquet, who asserted this point of view in his work, *The Philosophical Theory of the State.*

Germany, "in the Church, and in the Church alone, the Nazi dictatorship has found an insuperable obstacle to its absolutistic pretensions."[2] The state can effectively supervise only the external aspects of life. Beyond all else, it cannot under any conditions be a substitute for those cultural organizations which express the variant beliefs, opinions, interests, and ideals of the diversified groups of a modern society.

The peculiar nature of the state. The reason for this limitation, historically revealed through many a painful struggle and most of all in the great conflicts of church and state, depends on the peculiar nature of the state. The state is an organization with special attributes, special instruments, special powers.

[1] *Coercion and the nationwide reference of political law: The state is distinguished from all other associations by its exclusive investment with the final power of coercion.* Consequently, its law differs from all other social laws in two ways: first, that there is attached to it the peculiar sanction of socialized and unconditional compulsion; second—a corollary from the first—that it applies without exception to everyone within a geographical area. In these respects the legal code has an advantage over all other codes, but it must pay a price for it.

Because its sanction is force, its power of appeal is limited. Other associations, to which men freely belong, can on that very ground use means of persuasion with greater efficacy than can the state. They appeal to the free will which is automatically secured by voluntary membership. The state can appeal to its citizens and above all can control powerful engines of propagandism to influence them, but always behind the appeal there is the threat of compulsion. In other associations the malcontents have the alternative of leaving; if grave differences arise within them, the association itself can dissolve or split. But obviously these alternatives are for practical purposes ruled out in the case of the state. In earlier stages of civilization a group which disapproved the policy of the state might, with hardship and peril, secede and establish a new one, as did the Roman plebeians and the Pilgrim Fathers, but in the modern world this recourse is practically impossible.

The state has thus a compulsive aspect which very definitely limits its control over the spirit of its people. Dictatorial states seek to overcome this limitation by monopolizing and focusing all the agencies of propaganda. The combination of monopoly and compulsion is very formidable, but it suppresses the creative impulses of human beings as well as their inveterate tendency to assert their differences. Hence there are always fear and insecurity behind its seeming strength.

[2] *The changing activities of the state:* It follows that there are certain things which the state can do well, others it can do less well than the free associations,

---

2. F. L. Schuman, *The Nazi Dictatorship* (2nd ed., New York, 1936), p. 385.

and others which it cannot do at all. What actions fall in these various categories depends in part on the particular conditions of individual states. The functions of the state vary greatly at different stages of its history. Sometimes the state has been mainly an exploitative power, controlling the rest of the population in the interest of a dominant class. As the basis of citizenship broadened, it assumed to a larger extent protective functions, and these must always remain an important aspect of its task. In quite recent times another aspect has begun to assume significance, that of the state as a positive agency of social welfare. Thus in some countries of Europe we see old strongholds, the seats of a former exploitative nobility, turned into employment offices and health insurance bureaus. The three aspects of the state exist together, with varying emphasis, in present-day democracy. These considerations raise our next question, that of the functions of the state in modern society.

The Functions of the State in a Complex Society

The limits to the functions of the state. Perennial controversy rages around the functions of the state. They are the issues of party warfare. They vary from state to state, from period to period, even from year to year. The capitalistic and the communistic state seem at opposite poles in their solutions of the question. The liberal state and the fascist state give contradictory answers. The totalitarian state would usurp all functions.

[1] *Why sovereignty is not total authority:* One is tempted to think that the functions of the state are whatever functions the controlling power within any state cares to assume. And this view is supported by the traditional doctrine of state sovereignty. "The sovereign," said a characteristic exponent of this tradition, "has the complete disposal of the life, rights, and duties of the individual."[3] The sovereign, said the jurist Blackstone, is "a supreme, irresistible, uncontrollable authority." But in reality, whatever the legal or constitutional form may be, the state has limits to what it can do. It is limited by the instruments and means which it must use. It is limited also by the resistance offered to political action by the mores of the community. And it is limited by the existence, in any complex society, of other organizations which exercise functions of their own. Practically everyone agrees that there are social functions which the state alone can perform, that there are others which it is more qualified to perform than any other association, that there are others for which it is less qualified, and finally that there are functions which the state is wholly incapable of performing. There are wide divergences of opinion concerning the items that fall in these various categories, but if we examine the categories themselves in the light of the practice of modern states we shall discover that there is nevertheless a substantial amount of agreement.

3. Cornewall Lewis, ***The Use and Abuse of Political Terms*** (Oxford, 1898). Chap. V.

[2] *The problem of state regulation:* Let us take these categories in order, premising that there is no way of determining what the functions of the state are or what they should be other than the test of experience. In other words, the business of the state is to do what it is capable of doing well, provided the citizens of the state want it done. Men differ regarding what the state can do well as they differ regarding what needs doing at all. But social experience has already laid down certain broad lines of the state. Social experience led the state to take over, for example, the administration of justice and the provision of elementary education, and political experience has confirmed the state in the exercise of these functions. As new social situations arise they create new problems regarding the functions of the state. Thus the development of international finance, of industrial monopoly, of inventions such as the radio, and so on, raises constantly new problems of state regulation.

Above all, the vast economic and technological changes associated with capitalistic methods of production and distribution have created profound and still largely unsolved political issues. Different states attempt to meet them in very different ways. The Soviet state presents the extreme instance of centralized political control over the whole area of economic activity. It accepts the principle of the unified planning of a country's economic development. Other states, though animated by social philosophies of an entirely opposite character, have assumed considerable control over economic policies, as did mercantilist France and Fascist Italy.

The great majority of modern states leave many economic concerns in the area of private enterprise but take over the management of numerous others. These states may be described as "sociocapitalistic," since they combine socialistic and capitalistic features. There is a wide range of variation in this respect, from, say, the system now prevailing in Sweden, Denmark, or the United Kingdom to that characteristic of the United States. Here remains the greatest of all political problems, still in the region of controversy and experiment. The success or failure of these experiments will no doubt help to determine still further the main functions of the state, though these must always be subject to variation in accordance with the social and economic development of different communities and the traditions and attitudes which prevail within them.

The relation of state functions to different areas of social life. We may now consider the specific social functions of the state. In modern society there are, at one extreme, some tasks that no other agency can carry out and, at the other, some functions that no state can effectively undertake.

[1] *Functions peculiar to the state:* First, then, there are social functions which the state alone can perform. The state alone can establish an effective and basic order in a complex society. The state can maintain such an order because of the peculiar attributes which we saw that it and it alone possesses.

On the one hand its law is binding on *all* who live within an entire geographical area; on the other hand it possesses the ultimate right of enforcement. The establishment and maintenance of a universal order are thus an essential function of the state, its function par excellence. The state alone can make rules of universal application. It alone can guarantee facilities which shall be equally available to all the members of a community. It alone can establish rights and obligations which admit of no exceptions. It alone can establish conditions of equal opportunity. It alone can ensure the universal validity of units and standards of measurement, weight, quality, and value. It alone can set up minimum standards requisite for decent living with the assurance that none shall be allowed to fall below them. It alone can define the areas and limits of subordinate powers. It alone can co-ordinate within one great social framework the various organizations of a society. The state, in short, is the guarantor and the guardian of the public order.

The immensity of this service, at least in every complex society, is hard to realize. A momentary glimpse of it is provided in the rare crisis of revolution when all legal safeguards are in abeyance and the machinery of society is paralyzed. In a simple society, community-guarded custom suffices to maintain order; in a complex society, order is impossible apart from the state. For here it is necessary to prevent not only the encroachment of individual on individual but also the encroachment of group on group. And these groups in the complex society are not only very diverse but vary endlessly in their range and in their power. But for the restraining influence of the state, the social and economic conflict between them would lead to chaos. But for this influence, ruthless organizations would exercise an intolerable tyranny broken only by equally ruthless uprisings against them. Even within the order of the state, where government is corrupt or ineffective, lawless organizations sometimes emerge. The so-called racket in our present American cities is an example. Moreover, the state is necessary not only to prevent the usurpations of power but also to maintain the vast and elaborate contractual system which a modern society requires. Unless this system is guaranteed under the civil code, the business of the community would be utterly disrupted. Order is the first requirement of the diverse, specialized, interdependent activity of modern man, and this order the state alone can maintain.

But the state cannot be content with the mere establishment of order. The order maintained by a tyranny or by a slave state or by an empire differs vastly from the order of a "free" or democratic state. Order is always based on some principle, and the state is vitally concerned with the broad social policy of which a given order is the expression. Order may rest on privilege and status, or it may be guided by the ideal of equal opportunity. It may be designed to keep the weak in subjection to the strong or to prevent the strong from encroachment on the weak. Some principle of *justice* is inevitably involved, and the attainment of justice is a far more difficult and more controversial function than the attainment of order. It is obviously not secured by the simple "rule of law" which makes everyone equally subject to its dictates, which, as Anatole France remarked, "in its majestic equality forbids the rich as well as the poor to sleep in the streets and to beg bread."[4] One of the fundamentals of any order is a system of property rights, and since such rights are not given by "nature" they must be determined by authority. Justice, in the old phrase, is "to give every man his own" (*suum cuique tribuere*), but how to decide what a man's own may be is an ever-perplexing problem. The old individualistic notion, translated into modern economic terms in the "labor theory of value," that men gain legitimate titles to goods in terms of the toil they expend in transforming them from their natural state, becomes meaningless in the world of economic and social interdependence. Yet the state cannot fulfill its clear and inevitable function of maintaining order without involving itself in the further and infinitely harder task of securing justice. And in the last resort, so far as this end can be achieved, it can be achieved only through the instrumentality of the state. Alone possessing jurisdiction over all the members of a community, it alone can represent the interests common to all of them as against the interests which divide them.

[2] *Functions for which the state is well adapted:* We turn next to those functions which the state, in virtue of the means at its command, is more fitted to perform than any other organization. In this category comes the conservation of natural resources. Against the competitive interests which seek immediate economic gain the state can uphold the interest of the whole and the interest of the future. Reluctantly and often belatedly the state has had to intervene to prevent the wasteful consumption of the community's resources, its forests, its fisheries, its wild life, its irreplaceable mineral assets. The squandering of the oil resources in various lands, and particularly in the United States, offers one of the most recent as well as one of the most remarkable instances of the need for the state with respect to the safeguarding of the economic basis of society against reckless individualistic exploitation. And if the state is needed to control the social dangers of competition, it is also needed to check the domination of private monopoly. Wherever particular interests manifestly infringe the common interest, the state is called upon to uphold the latter, though often the political pressure exerted by those particular interests prevent or even pervert its function. It is not possible within our limits to specify the magnitude and the variety of this task. Only recently has the state come at all to realize its significance. All so-called social legislation, the establishment by law of various forms of industrial protection and insurance, may be regarded as coming within this category.

The conservation and the development of the personal, no less than of the economic, resources of the community devolve in large measure on the state.

4. On this subject cf. G. E. G. Catlin, *A Study of the Principles of Politics* (New York, 1930), Chap. VII, in which the above quotation is applied.

Included in this function is the general provision of education. Every civilized state has found that this essential service cannot be left to private agencies, that to be at all adequate for the needs of the future as well as of the present the endowment and control of general education must be publicly established. Only thus can standards be maintained for the community as a whole, and the more glaring inequalities of opportunity, which more than anything else stand in the way of the discovery, evocation, and utilization of human potentialities, be substantially reduced.

As we have said, there is no predetermined limit to what the state can do for the service of the community. In so far as, with its vast and comprehensive organization, it can support and stimulate other agencies providing non-controversial services, there seems no reason why it should not do so if its aid is not out of proportion to the cost. The case for such support is particularly strong with respect to those cultural services, of which education itself is an example, which do not yield an immediate economic return proportionate to their cost. How far the state can and should go in this direction must depend on the cultural values of the community, but the more enlightened it becomes, the more the state can contribute to the development of science, to the encouragement of art, and in general to the economic equipment of those services which yield to mankind the more enduring and less competitive satisfactions. Here we include the provision of public parks, museums, playgrounds, the protection and enhancement of the amenities of the countryside, the proclamation of public holidays, and so forth. Together with such functions we may include that of the provision of the means and opportunities for the study of the greater and more urgent questions of social policy and for the collection, as in the census, of statistical and other information bearing on the welfare of the people. Other agencies can perform these tasks in part, but none so efficiently and on so great a scale and with such authority as can the state.

[3] *Functions for which the state is ill adapted:* We pass thirdly to those social functions in the performance of which the state is at a disadvantage as compared with other agencies. These again must vary with the conditions, but in all societies there are limits to what the state can effectively do. The multitude of diverse associations in an advanced civilization witnesses to those particular needs and selective purposes which the state cannot adequately satisfy. The state is the agency of the *whole* community. There are more intensive, more specialized, and more limited interests which unite groups within it. There are divergent and conflicting interests which properly create their own associations. There are experimental objectives which are far better pursued by the smaller interested groups. There are also interests which unite men on a great scale, but not as members of the state. To this order belong the broader cultural interests, including the religious. The state is not well adapted, in the light of its nature as already described, to sponsor the more intimate or more personal interests, those which admit a variety of spontaneous and

variant expressions. Voluntary associations have a flexibility, an initiative, a capacity for experiment, a liberation from the heavier responsibility of taking risks that the state rarely, if ever, possesses. They can thus foster, in ways not permissible to the state, the nascent interests of groups, and encourage enterprise, social and economic, at the growing points of a society. Even the role of arbiter is here not within the competence of the state. It is not qualified to decide the merits of artistic, literary, scientific endeavor or to arbitrate, say, religious controversies.

[4] *Functions which the state is incapable of performing:* There is a thin border line between the things which the state is ill qualified to do and those which it cannot do at all. Can the state control people's opinions? Given a sufficient support, it can prevent nonconformist groups from expressing their opinion overtly. But it is not thereby meeting opinion on its own ground; it is using the alien instrument of compulsion. An opinion claims truth, and force is entirely irrelevant to this claim. Often the suppression of belief has been worse than futile; sometimes it has given a secret strength to the persecuted belief, but at all times it has prevented belief from meeting the only true test, that of frank examination and discussion.[5]

Can the state control people's morality? It can, given sufficient support, control the external aspects of conduct, but if morality means a set of attitudes toward our fellows and toward life in general, again we have entered a sphere in which mere enforcement is foolish or futile and in which the appeal to the feelings of men comes with greater efficacy from the free associations which, if they claim authority at all, claim it on grounds to which the compulsive state cannot aspire. The history of the state's attempt to control religion is one of the longest and most tragic chapters in the record of man's stupidity, but at least it has revealed this lesson to those who can read and understand: that there are in social man certain resistances to compulsion which it is beyond the power of tyranny to destroy. Again, when a German minister of education, addressing the universities of the country, declared that science has to be "National Socialist science" and "a specific accomplishment of the national spirit," he was trying in the name of the state to make of science something that is contrary to its very nature and that the scientific spirit can never accept.[6] Nor is it only the deeper, more spiritual impulses which resist this control. There are, as we have seen, codes regulative of conduct which are largely independent of the legal code. Custom sets limits to law, and no less does the seemingly superficial code of fashion. In the latter sphere, men—and women still more—accept dictation from the prestige-owning arbiters of

5. The excellent argument of Mill on this point, in Chapter III of the essay *On Liberty*, still holds good. For a fuller discussion see H. Laski, *Liberty in the Modern State* (New York, 1930).

6. Address of Dr. Bernard Rust, as quoted in *The New York Times*, November 8, 1936.

dress which they would violently reject from the government of the state.[7]

In short, the more intimate details of conduct as well as the more deeply cultural traits claim a freedom from compulsion which places them largely outside the region of state control. The trends of culture, of the arts and the sciences, may be affected by the activity of the state, but they owe their vitality and their direction to forces inherent in the community and beyond the capacity of the state to determine.

The State and the Greater Society

The state and international organization. Every state acts beyond its own borders. It deals with other states. It makes treaties and subscribes to international conventions and arrangements of many kinds. It cannot do otherwise, for the interests of men, their cultural as well as their economic interests, far transcend the borders of their respective states. No state depends on itself alone, even if it shuts itself off by "iron curtains."

[1] *The necessity of an international order:* Hence an international order is needed for two reasons. First, because only under it can the common and the complementary interests of peoples be safeguarded and advanced. Trade and commerce between countries, communications, the incessant interchange of cultural contributions, the protection of peoples against the various diseases that ignore frontiers, the establishment of common standards for international dealings, and numerous other interests require a system of international order. Second, because without agreement, in the last analysis without law, every state, and particularly every great state, is a threat to the security of all others.

Within its borders the state is endowed with force, and this force is the assurance of order, is adjusted to the functions which it serves, and in large measure is safeguarded by the constitutional devices which have made its exercise subject to the control of the community. Beyond its borders the force of the state has an entirely different meaning. It is a mode of settling disputes between states, and once loosed it becomes an engine of destruction, without safeguards and without responsibilities. Consequently we face the paradox that the state is, nationally, the great instrument of social security, but internationally, the greatest menace to that security.

This situation has grown ever more aggravated as technological developments on the one hand increase the range and degree of the interdependence of

7. A government may sometimes, though rarely, prescribe a particular material or type of dress on economic or other national grounds, as Frederick William of Prussia prescribed the wearing of cotton clothes. The Turkish government could proscribe the wearing of the fez and the veil, but these were the insignia of a discarded civilization. In neither of these instances was fashion involved.

nations and on the other hand magnify the destructiveness of the weapons of war. Consequently, various expedients and programs have been resorted to, aiming at the establishment of international security. Among such expedients we may perhaps include alliances of states intended to secure a balance—or rather supremacy—of power such as would deter other states from making war on them. This equivocal method has never for very long been successful. In more recent times many treaties have been signed by various states—a movement in which the United States took a prominent part—for the peaceful settlement of their disputes. This movement may be said to have culminated in the Pact of Paris. The establishment of the League of Nations and of the Permanent Court of International Justice represented a further step in the creation of an international system. During World War II the finally victorious powers gave to the peoples, at Moscow and at Teheran, solemn pledges that they would establish a system of permanent security. The result was the organization of the United Nations.[8] Unfortunately this new creation, for all its promise, has not eliminated the menace of war. The great powers did not covenant to set up a binding system of international law, and each of them retained a veto power that is an assertion of its claim, in the last resort, to independent action. All the great states are still burdened by very heavy expenditures on the means of war.

[2] *Obstacles to an international order:* Various obstacles have stood in the way of a more adequate international system, among them the rival efforts of the greater powers to gain possession or control of the economic resources of the less civilized portions of the earth. Another obstacle has been the nationalistic attitude which thinks of states as inclusive economic entities, so that the interests of each are set in opposition to those of the others. Fostered as this attitude is by the interests which immediately profit by it, it is out of harmony with the realities of economic interdependence. A famine or a boycott in India, a revolution in China, a bank failure in Austria, a depression in the United States, a new tariff system or a devaluation of currency in any important country affects the economic well-being of the whole civilized world. National policies based on a misunderstanding of this interdependence recoil on the peoples who promote them. National sentiments based on ignorance of this interdependence hurt the causes to which they are devoted. There are conflicts of interests between groups large and small, including groups as large as the nation itself, but wherever interdependence exists there is also an underlying harmony of interests, the condition of a common interest to be realized. There are also deep rifts between states corresponding to, though not necessarily created by, ideological differences, between dictatorships and democracies,

8. For the text of the Charter of the United Nations and other modern documents on international order see Sigrid Arne, *United Nations Primer* (New York, 1945). For a general conspectus of the problem see R. M. MacIver, *The Web of Government* (New York, 1947), Chap. XII.

between "capitalistic" and "communistic" states. The use of coercion or armed force for the "settlement" of these differences destroys the common interest which is more fundamental than the conflicting interests. There is a gross discrepancy here between political means and political ends.

Beyond all the other obstacles there lies, however, the traditional right of states to settle their disputes by force, a right supported by the principle that each sovereign state is the sole final arbiter of its own claims. Around this right cling sentiments both noble and ignoble, high devotions and unscrupulous interests. The greatest problem of modern statesmanship is how to conserve the values of the state, alike the devotions which it inspires and the services which it renders, while nevertheless finding a way to safeguard that international order without which our whole civilization is imperiled. How this may be achieved is a question which is beyond our purpose here. But it is not unreasonable to think that, given a sufficiently clear and widespread realization of its necessity, its achievement is then made practicable. The final obstacle is the emotional attitude—the suspicion, prejudice, and fear—which does not apprehend the needs of the civilization we have created.

Modern war and modern civilization. The right claimed by the state to make war implies the absence of an authoritative international order. The enormous transformation of the nature of warfare in our times gives new urgency to a requirement inherent in the kind of civilization we have reached, that of a system which, in the language of the Declaration of Teheran (December 1, 1943), "will command the goodwill of the overwhelming mass of the peoples of the world and banish the scourge and terror of war for many generations." Let us consider some of the broad reasons why war making no longer, whatever may have been the situation in the past, can be regarded as a legitimate function of the state.

[1] *The contrast between the internal and the external use of political force:* There were times when other organizations than the state engaged in war, when families and clans carried on murderous feuds, when feudal barons possessed the right of "private wars," when trading companies extended their operations by force of arms, when individuals fought socially sanctioned duels. All these "rights" have been abolished in most states. It was necessary for the state to abolish them in the name of order and of justice. Now only the state itself claims this right over against other states, and the same necessity for its abolition applies with even greater cogency against this last reservation of uncontrolled force. Force within the state is the enemy of violence and is, usually, the efficient servant of government. Force between states has become such concentrated and unlimited violence that it cannot be trusted to serve any constructive purpose whatever.

[2] *The incongruity of means and ends:* To serve social ends, power should not only be responsible power; it should also be limited in correspondence

with the ends it serves. Since no ends are absolute or unlimited, no exercise of power should be. The right of war making assumes that no other ends of life, no other human interests, weigh anything in the balance against political ends and political interests. War is an instrument of policy, the *ultima ratio regum*, the "barrister of crowns." But it is an instrument greatly disproportionate in its effects to the social significance of the policy which sets it in motion, unloosing incalculable processes of destruction such that the initial "cause" of the war is likely to be entirely forgotten in the issues which the struggle itself creates. The truth of this statement was clearly revealed in the course of World War I. It unleashed such uncontrollable forces that, whatever its initial motivations may have been, they were submerged in a blind struggle first for domination and then for survival. World War II, brought about by the stupid calculations of the military-minded Nazis, revealed the same lesson in the utter desolation it wrought and gave it a final demonstration at the end, when the atomic bomb opened up new prospects of hitherto unimaginable destruction. One eminent scientist, Irving Langmuir, has even gone so far as to suggest that in the course of an atomic war our globe itself might be rendered "permanently uninhabitable."[9]

[3] *The contradiction between war and modern ways of life:* The developments we have been discussing have inspired in the great mass of mankind a revulsion against war far greater than existed ever before. Man is far from being a completely "rational" animal, but nevertheless all his institutions are ways he has devised of achieving some end or satisfying some need. From this point of view war as an institution has broken down. It is doubtful whether, under the new conditions of warfare, there is necessary even a "moral equivalent" for it. For war in its present technical development offers no liberation of those qualities which the social restraints of peace may hold in leash. War is a process more mechanized than the working life of peace. It presents a cataclysm and not a solution. The traditional language of glory and high enterprise becomes meaningless in the presence of the monstrous regimentation, broken by fits of nerve-destroying fever, which it imposes. It subjects the fighters to an intense accumulation of horrors and whole nations to vast miseries. From its inferno no reward can arise which is not insignificant beside its devastation. It ruins the victor as well as the vanquished, if indeed these appellations retain any meaning in their reciprocal demolition of the gains of an interdependent civilization. No high policy seems a recompense for the destruction of the manhood of a whole generation, for the culture-disrupting falsehoods and hatreds without which it cannot be waged, for the jeopardy of civilization itself. If man is not wholly rational, he is not wholly irrational. Perhaps at no time did the actual experience of war generate in those who came into most direct contact with it, the common soldier, the ravaged peasant, the women and

9. On the relation of modern scientific developments to international politics see E. M. Friedwald, *Man's Last Choice: Political Creeds and Scientific Realities* (New York, 1948).

children over whom it swept, that mythology of glory which its captains and its kings entertained and which its historians pictured. Perhaps the foot-soldiers of Menelaus and of Hector never could say that they too had

> drunk delight of battle with their peers
> Far on the ringing plains of windy Troy.

But the "fresh terrors and undreamed of fears" aroused by the annihilating mechanisms of modern war have brought about a situation in which even the most unreflecting can no longer contemplate the coming of war without dismay. The revulsion was witnessed after the World War I, for the significant literature that followed it had no reference to the pomp and circumstance of military triumph and contained no paeans to victory. World War II completed the process. These indications point to a new orientation of man toward an institution which has not been rendered obsolete but which has proved to be tragically incongruous with the changed conditions of human life.

19

The Great Associations: Economic

The Nature of Economic Associations

What we mean by economic organization. As we have seen, certain objectives can be pursued either by economic or by political procedures. Wages, for example, may be determined in one of three ways. One is by the unchecked operation of supply and demand. Here, hypothetically at least, no organization is directly involved. The market controls the price of labor. Another way is through collective bargaining. Here two forms of economic organization are usually involved, trade-unions on the one hand and employers' organizations on the other. Neither of these ways requires, so far, any resort to government. The third way is by *political* action to fix wage rates. Similarly prices, working conditions, industrial disputes, and so forth, may be settled either politically or by economic processes. Within the economic order men seek by means of private savings to provide against the contingencies of life—against unemployment, sickness, accident, and old age. Within the political order the same objective is sought under social legislation.

[1] *The economic association:* By economic associations we mean, then, those that are engaged mainly in economic procedures, the procedures of competing and bargaining in the production, distribution, and exchange of goods and services. The typical economic association is a competitive private enterprise, engaged primarily in "making money." It can be a one-man store or a vast corporation. The economic association is a unit in a large system of private enterprise. Its focus is *the market*, the place of exchange, and the whole system of which the market is the focus we call the economic order.

The distinction between the economic and the political association is not so much a distinction between spheres of activity as between methods of action. Economic *interests* are not the exclusive concern of economic associations—every other kind of organization, and not least the state, has economic interests. Many economic activities depend on the concerted activity of public and private agencies. The credit system itself depends on arrangements in which governments co-operate with public, semipublic, or private banks. The economic and the political order interlock at myriad points, even in the most individualistic society, and the old laissez-faire idea, that each can "mind its own business" without interference by the other, is an outworn illusion.

[2] *The economic method:* Economic associations are typically devoted to the acquisition of wealth, to money-making or at least to the provision of the means of living, without reference to the uses to which these means are subsequently applied. The economic means are their end result; the disposal of these means lies beyond their concern. The method which associations so constituted pursue we may term the economic method. It stands in significant contrast to the political method, and an analysis of the difference will serve as an introduction to the study of the nature of economic association.

The economic method is devoted to the exclusive or private control or possession of wealth. In the economic association men seek wealth in conjunction, but ultimately in order to gain individual control or possession. In the process of acquiring wealth, first the association and then its individual members alienate or appropriate means for exclusive use. The political method, on the other hand, socializes or communizes wealth. Having done so, the state may, of course, return this wealth to the economic system by a process of redistribution, but in so far as the state retains it, it assumes a public character. When, for example, the state establishes a national park, or the municipality a hospital or a school, it withdraws these possessions from the processes of the economic system. They become subject to a new and very different kind of regulation. Socialized or communized goods are removed from the sphere of exchange and of the regulating economic forces of supply and demand. In so far as they are communized they no longer enter the market place, any more than do the winds or the clouds. Communized goods may still be shared unequally, but that will be dependent on political conditions, on the fact that differences of political power mean differences in effective control over the wealth of the community.

The economic method differs therefore from the political in that its principle is ultimately distributive. Political action, no matter what private interests may underlie it, is at least ostensibly in the name of, and for the sake of, the common welfare. It is therefore unicentered within the area of a whole community, whereas economic action is multicentered.[1] No matter how far the integration of economic associations advances through amalgamations, trusts, cartels, and other unions, the economic system, by its very nature, remains an arena of competing forces. But the political method is anticompetitive and assumes a complete unification of interest. It may be mistaken or perverted, and even when it does seek the common well-being it may be opposed or thwarted

1. See R. M. MacIver, *The Modern State* (Oxford, 1926), Chap. IX.

by dissentient economic forces, but at least it preserves the form of unity, the conception of the whole, and thus its intervention is, and always has been, necessary to preserve that unity against the disruptive and partial interests of the economic arena.

The economic association as a unique type of organization. The economic association *as such*, then, is indifferent to the uses of the means which it seeks. Moreover, it reaches its developed form only when these means themselves are entirely detachable from any particular uses.

[1] *The "detachment" of the economic sphere:* When this stage is reached, as under modern systems of currency and credit, the economic method becomes more clearly differentiated from the political method. Its results are expressed in abstract units of exchange. A dollar is a convertible good, and a good only because convertible, convertible at the will of its possessor into any one of innumerable specific goods. The economic method is the pursuit through an elaborate mechanism of production, distribution, and exchange of this free kind of buying power. It is the detachment of this power from specific embodiments in forms of property which has made it so formidable and so pervasive. This situation is an aspect of modern capitalism.

[2] *The particular significance of capitalism:* In previous times landownership was never a purely economic category. It has a special social status and a definite political significance. Land was not bought and sold freely in the market place. It was too closely bound up with sentiments and traditions and privileges to be a mere "economic good." It was the inheritance of a family, with all the personal and social attachments consequent thereon. In the process of industrialization it has lost this earlier significance and has become, for the most part, a form of capital. Labor itself has undergone a similar and no less momentous revolution. It is now, under capitalism, a free contractual good; in other words, it is bought and sold, with certain limitations, on economic terms agreed upon between the buyers and the sellers. It has passed from a condition of status to one of contract. The laborer is no longer attached to the land nor are his work and pay determined by the local traditions of an ancient craft. He offers his labor power in the open market, by the hour or by the "piece." He seeks, through combination with his fellows, to affect in his favor the conditions of labor supply, and that is because his labor is now an economic category, so that his wages, and his employment or lack of employment, are immediately determined by the prevailing conditions of supply and demand.

These illustrations may serve to show how the economic method has grown distinct from the political method. In a capitalistic society, economic power, with its peculiar detachment from social objectives, with its consequent lack of direct responsibility for social consequences, and with its vast power entrenched in the new forms of economic organization, offers a formidable challenge to political power. On this account political power, with its emphasis on unity and its claim on behalf of the common welfare, has in turn been compelled to extend its range, seeking at the least to mitigate certain of the more obvious dangers arising from the inequalities of economic power, and at the most, in the instance of Soviet Russia, to destroy that power altogether.

The Economic System

The economic association and the economic system. To understand the nature of the economic association we must see it in relation to a larger economic system.

[1] *The focus of the market:* We have pointed out that the economic association operates for a market, and that the market is the focus of the economic system. In the market, goods and services are exchanged, usually through the medium of money. The direct objective of every economic association is to increase the surplus of money it acquires through the processes of exchange. The purely economic association is, then, one whose interest is limited to the acquisition and control of wealth through such processes, without reference to the ends to which the acquired wealth is devoted. The members of the association, of course, seek this acquisition or control for various ends. They may be animated by private motives or by considerations of public service, but the economic association as such is constituted without reference to the different and often incompatible goals that its members pursue. The association is the common meeting ground of diverse aims, because the means to them, with which alone it is directly concerned, are common means. In a narrow sense the economic association is one directed by the profit motive, but in a broader sense it includes as participants and beneficiaries the workers no less than the shareholders and officials.

[2] *The growth of the economic system:* The economic system grew to large proportions as Western society passed from a feudalistic order to a capitalist or sociocapitalist order. Various conditions contributed to this growth, prominent among them being the following.

ONE: SPECIALIZATION. With the advance of technology, economic functions became increasingly specialized. Specialization promoted and was accompanied by a more elaborate system of exchange. The more men specialize, the more they become dependent on others for the satisfaction of their various needs—the more, in other words, they must resort to the market place.

TWO: IMPERSONALIZATION OF THE MARKET. As the market is enlarged it takes on a new character. Under simpler conditions men made shoes and chairs and lamps and brooches for particular customers. Supply kept close to immediate demand. General markets were held only at intervals, and once a year a locality might have a special "fair." But the enlarged and continuous market provides its variety of goods and services indifferently to unknown clients, so that therefore it provides these goods and services in anticipation of and not merely in response to demand. The economic association which thus works "for the market" is detached from the personal considerations which limit the economic motive and the economic method under the simpler conditions where men work for their immediate neighbors in response to specific demand. Obviously the wider or less localized the market, the greater can be the detachment or "purity" of the economic method. The wider market means at the same time greater specialization and an opportunity for production on a larger scale, both conditions operating to free the economic method from ulterior social interests.

THREE: INCORPORATION. Another important development has been the application of the principle of incorporation. While associations of all kinds now assume a corporate character, this principle has peculiar significance with respect to the economic association. Incorporation gives to an association a specific legal "personality." It defines and limits the functions of the association and the liabilities of its members. Incorporation turns the association into an agency, acting through appointed officials, such that ownership of capital is distinguished clearly from management. Many of the owners, the shareholders, become passive recipients of dividends, just as the bondholders become passive recipients of interest. Their concern thus becomes limited to the efficiency of the association as a producer of economic gains for themselves. The process by which these are produced is hidden from them. In turn the chief responsibility of the directors and management is to ensure due returns for the owners. Thus again the economic method is liberated from extraneous considerations.

Moreover, through the principle of incorporation the amount of capitalization and the number of shareholders are capable of indefinite expansion. The "billion dollar company" becomes feasible and with it the vast enhancement of the economic power of the directorate. This process in turn accentuates the separation of the financial from the industrial administration, of the pecuniary interest from the technological interest. This is the distinction which Veblen stressed when he contrasted the "instinct of workmanship" and the drive for profits.[2] Incorporation as it expands tends to give dominance to the financial interest, the detached economic interest. Its main concern is with the balance sheet, the surplus of profits over costs. It thinks in terms of *values* rather than of goods, and *values* are mathematical entities, subject to the abstract process of division and multiplication, and capable of many kinds of manipulation. Finally, incorporation conveys a kind of impersonal immortality. The corporation, unlike the partnership, is not limited by the life of its existing members. Before the development of this principle, such immortality belonged only to associations like the state and the church, and perhaps to a few chartered trading or banking companies. Now it is set up everywhere in the flux of the

2. In *The Theory of the Leisure Class*, *The Instinct of Workmanship* (New York, 1922), and other studies.

economic life and serves to entrench more deeply within the community the power of economic association.[3]

Economic interest and social function. The liberation of the economic method reveals the more clearly that antithesis between group interest and social function. This antithesis, which exists everywhere within society, is peculiarly accentuated in the relation of the economic association to the whole social system.

[1] *No necessary harmony between the two:* The specific *interest* of the economic association is the acquisition of wealth for its members. Its specific *function* is to make shoes or houses or steel rails or credit instruments for the community. The assumption that the interest and the function are reconciled through some pre-established harmony belongs to an individualistic creed which is neither proven nor any longer generally acceptable. It was possible for Adam Smith to accept it because of his belief in the beneficent equalizing power of competition. Competition, in his thought, made economic reward correspond to social function by leveling undue advantages, by destroying, because of the eagerness of competitors to seize each opportunity for gain, the increment that is not earned by service.[4] We need not discuss the adequacy of this argument, since the condition he postulated, the free competition of equal individuals, is so totally remote from the reality of the world of unequal economic associations. In this world the guarantees that reward will correspond to service are wholly inadequate, for reasons which every student of economics understands. There is no assurance that in pursuing to the utmost the enrichment of its members the economic association is therefore fulfilling most effectively its function of economic service.

[2] *Checks on economic interest:* It is true that there are certain checks on any excessive divergence of the two. Demand is not so clear-sighted as the classical economists presumed. The public is exposed to the representations of salesmanship and is untrained to discriminate quality with respect to the myriads of specialized commodities. There are few agencies whose function it is to guide the consumer and many which seek to persuade him. Even the co-operative consumers' associations, which have reached such high development in various countries, are, on the whole, designed rather to make the consumer a participant in the profits of trading than to direct him with respect to the quality and serviceableness of his purchases. But within limits, and especially as regards standardized products, some judgment of the value of goods and service is effective. What is harder to determine is the relation of costs and prices, and this is particularly important where the good is produced under monopoly or semimonopoly conditions, such as apply to public utilities. Here

3. See, for example, A. A. Berle and G. C. Means, *The Modern Corporation and Private Property* (New York, 1932), Books I and IV.

4. Cf., for example, *The Wealth of Nations*, Book I, Chap. X, *init.*

there is no safeguard against a gross discrepancy between service and return, except in so far as vigilant scrutiny and regulation are maintained by constituted authority.

Tensions within the economic system. The maladjustment of the specific economic interest and the broader social interest constitutes only one of the tensions to which economic organization is subject. As was pointed out in the preceding section, the economic system is alway an arena of contending forces.

[1] *Competition and bargaining:* This condition is inherent in the very nature of the economic method. For it rests on two premises, competition and bargaining. *Competition* is the simultaneous offer of like or of alternative economic services to the same potential purchaser. *Bargaining* is the process by which the antithetical interests of supply and demand, of buyer and seller, are finally adjusted. The relation to one another of the manufacturers of the same goods or of substitute goods is a competitive one; the relation of the producer of raw materials to the producer of manufactured goods, of wholesaler to retailer, of retailer to consumer, of employer to employee, of lender to borrower, is a bargaining relationship. The two types, though often confused. are entirely distinct. Competitors do not need one another--they seek to oust one another. Bargainers offer complementary not competitive services. Each stands to gain from the transaction, because each wants what the other offers. Bargaining is the process which ends in the act of exchange. Exchange is reciprocal giving and taking, and the giving is the price of the taking. Price is at once cost and reward of service, so that always the antithesis of economic interests is found in every transaction.

[2] *Implications of large-scale growth:* The increase in the scale of economic organization creates larger areas from which the tensions of competition and of bargaining are in part or in whole removed, but these tensions still exist, sometimes in a more acute form, between the larger economic units thus created. For the competition of individual producers there is substituted the competition of large-scale businesses. Instead of the individual bargaining of employer and workman there appears the collective bargaining of the associations of capital and of labor. In fact, the bitter conflicts involved in the bargaining process between organizations of capital and labor reveal the profoundest and most universal of all the tensions which beset capitalistic society. On the other hand the competitive conflict is mitigated by organizations of capital and of labor respectively. In the larger areas created by price agreements or by agreements allotting the proportionate production of the various units (through "cartels") or the respective market territories of the units (as in certain types of "combine"), some forms of competition are removed while others remain active.[5] In the relatively rare instances where monopoly is nearly

5. On cartels and their methods of controlling production, prices, and distribution see Corwin Edwards, *Cartels*, Senate Committee on Military Affairs (Washington, D. C., 1944).

complete, competition—though not bargaining—loses significance, but thereby other tensions are set up, for now the demand of the consumers for protection makes some form of political regulation inevitable.

The economic system as an automatic regulator. The economic system therefore presents itself as an intricate combination of conflict and interdependence between its units large and small. In what sense is this combination a "system"?

[1] *Why the economic order is a system:* It is definitely a system, in spite of these conflicts, because even competitive units are subject to common conditions, to certain rules of the game set up either by themselves or by economic tradition or by political authority. It is a system also because there are forces operative within it as well as without it which reveal a potential common interest, however little recognized or organized, of the whole. The most obvious signs of this potential common interest are the fluctuations of the economic cycle, involving varying levels of prosperity and of adversity over the widest areas. It is a system because, with the development of banking and credit systems, a decision taken by any strategic group has swift repercussions near and far. "A simple rise in the New York bank rate, if it be sudden and steep, may threaten disaster to every struggling industry the world over, bring privation to millions of workers' homes, and change the pulse of life itself."[6] It is a system because there is an *automatic* readjustment of part to part throughout its whole fabric whenever the conditions anywhere change, when the demand for any product rises, when the wage rates of any group fall, when fashions change, when a new law is passed, when a bad harvest occurs. Finally, it is a system because this pervasive interdependence inevitably creates foci of regulation, some within the system, such as central banks, some without it, such as direct government control, some limited by national bounds, some attaining an international character. The slowly ripening experience thereby gained, together with the increasing recognition of the world-wide nexus of economic cause and effect, is an augury pointing toward a vaster future organization.

[2] *Inadequacy of automatic regulation:* We have seen that the economic order, unlike the political, reveals itself in *automatic* adjustments, effected through the price system. But these automatic adjustments are in part, from the point of view of the lives subjected to them, maladjustments. When business activity slackens, wages are depressed—the adjustment of wages to the decline of demand may bring grievous ills to many a worker's family. In a speculative boom the prices of commodities rise—the standard of living will fall for wage and salary earners. The more complex the system is, the more obvious and the more serious become these maladjustments. They are seen in the gross disparities of poverty and of wealth, of power and of helplessness, in the wasteful exploitation of resources, in monopolistic advantage and in the competitive

6. H. N. Brailsford, *Olives of Endless Age* (New York, 1928), Chap. XI.

disadvantage of those whose services or goods are in too free supply, in the excessive production of some types of commodity, as compared with others, in the overexpansion of plants in relation to the demand for their products, and perhaps above all in the persistence of unemployment as well as in those recurrent crises when unemployment becomes acute. The specific description of these economic maladjustments and of the conditions determining them belongs to the study of economics. What we are here concerned to point out is that they are evidence of the automatic working of the economic system and that, because of their vital bearing on the well-being of the community, they form a challenge to the constructive abilities of men which, in so far as it is accepted, may lead —as in degree it has already led—to a greater unification of control within the economic order itself.

Occupational Associations

Types of occupational organization. In the preceding section we distinguished the pure type of economic association. In so designating it we do not imply that its actual pursuit of wealth is not tempered or qualified by any social considerations, but we do imply that its interest, as an association, does not include any social objectives beyond the stage of wealth acquisition and control. Since the economic interest is to some extent involved in practically all association and since many types of association resort to some extent to the economic method, we find all degrees of approximation to the pure type. The way in which the economic interest combines with others is one of the most intricate and significant aspects of social organization. The occupational associations with which we are here concerned exhibit important differences in this respect.

Occupational associations have grown numerous and powerful with the functional specialization and interdependence of modern society. They fall under various types. We may in the first place distinguish those that are based on the performance of a specific function, vocational organizations in the strict sense, whether the vocation be industrial, financial, mercantile, professional, or any other. This category would include trade-unions, organizations of producers, dealers, or traders in any particular line, organizations of schoolteachers, civil servants, doctors, lawyers, scientists, artists, and so forth. From these we distinguish organizations that exist to promote the interests of an inclusive group bound together by similarity of functions or status. Here would fall associations of manufacturers (without distinction of product), chambers of commerce, Rotary Clubs and similar groups, amalgamations or federations of labor unions, veterans' associations, and so forth. Such organizations play very significant roles in present-day society. They are so numerous and various that we cannot concern ourselves with their special manifestations, though the study of these is becoming an important area of sociological investigation. We shall limit ourselves in the discussion that follows to two forms of specific vocational organization, the trade-union and the professional association.

The trade-union. Both the trade-union and the professional association seek to advance the economic interest of their respective members. They differ, however, in that the professional association has a direct interest in the advancement of the science or art or craft of which its members are practitioners and consequently regards itself as having a *definite* social function that lies outside economic considerations. In this respect it is perhaps nearer to the medieval guild than to either the labor union or the typical business association of the modern world. In modern capitalistic society the trade-union is not, like the old guild, the guardian of a craft. It is primarily organized for economic struggle and its objective is determined mainly by this fact. Under some conditions it combines a political objective with a directly economic one. But its essential concern is the strengthening of the economic status of its members and the improvement of their working conditions, through negotiations with employers, collective bargaining, strikes, participation in political movements, the establishment of the "closed shop," and other devices. With the growth of mechanization in industry it has been moving away from the craft basis and tending toward the form of the industrial union in which the various crafts are combined. In so far as this tendency develops there is a greater contrast between the trade-union type of organization and that which characterizes the professions.

The trade-union itself is a phenomenon of an industrialized society, where the wage earner is a hired employee with little or no attachment to the factory or office other than the week-by-week "wage-nexus." The earliest trade-unions were small organizations of workmen seeking some means of mitigating their competitive weakness against the employer, and they had to face the hostility of government as well as the social disesteem that attended their lowly status and blocked their efforts to modify the established order. The economists of the day—in the earlier part of the nineteenth century—held that these efforts must be in vain against the inexorable "law" of the market. The size and number of trade-unions have greatly increased in recent times, so that now in most industrialized countries, through their national confederations or amalgamations, they play a major role in the determination of wage rates, hours, and working conditions, exercising at the same time considerable political influence. The chief source of their power is the weapon of the strike, involving the stoppage of production in order to obtain their demands.[7]

[1] *Types of trade-union:* Trade-unions fall into two main classes, the craft

7. There are many studies of unionism; for a good brief discussion see S. H. Slichter, *The Challenge of Industrial Relations* (Ithaca, N. Y., 1947). C. Wright Mills' *The New Men of Power* (New York, 1948) includes a study of the views of American labor leaders.

unions and the industrial unions. The craft union, or the trade-union in the older sense, is an organization of the workers in a particular craft or occupation, usually a skilled or semiskilled occupation. The industrial union takes the industry itself as the unit of organization, without distinction of craft. The railroad brotherhood, the machinists, the unions of the various building trades belong to the former category; the United Mine Workers and the United Automobile Workers belong to the latter. The American Federation of Labor was originally organized on a craft basis, and the various craft unions are all enrolled in it, though it now contains industrial unions as well. The Congress of Industrial Organizations (C.I.O.) is composed entirely of industrial unions.

We should note in passing that, apart from the more formal organization of the trade-union, the conditions of modern industrial life, bringing workers together in large numbers within the same plant, tend to evoke the informal or spontaneous "getting together" of workers. The sense of their common interest shows itself, for instance, in their attitudes toward the management and expresses itself in concerted behavior.[8]

[2] *The "closed shop" and the "closed union":* One objective of trade-unionism is to obtain the "closed shop," so that a worker must join his union in order to obtain employment and so that union representatives may be able to bargain in the name of the whole working force. The "closed shop" should be distinguished from the "closed union," existing in a few of the skilled crafts, where the union restricts the number of its members or the number of apprentices working in the craft, directly or by setting high initiation dues. This kind of monopoly control has the dangers inherent in other forms of nonpublic monopoly. It has, however, a limited range and is always threatened by technological advances that reduce the need for the specialized expertness characteristic of handicraft production. The exclusion of qualified persons from the practice of a trade or profession is not infrequently sought through racial or ethnic discrimination. In the United States this procedure has been applied particularly, though by no means exclusively, against Negroes. Public attention has in recent years been directed to the consequences of such discrimination, and various measures have been and are being devised to combat it.[9]

The professional association. No hard line can be drawn between professions and other occupations, but the profession implies in the practitioner a broader background of knowledge, the mastery of a specific science or art demanding prolonged study before it can be competently applied, and a relative independence in the performance of his function. He is more on his own, so to speak. He has more scope for initiative. In some professions, the practitioner works

8. F. J. Roethlisberger and William J. Dickson, *Management and the Worker* (Cambridge, Mass., 1939), especially Chap. XXI.

9. See *To Secure These Rights,* The Report of the President's Committee on Civil Rights (Washington, D.C., 1947), and R. M. MacIver, *The More Perfect Union* (New York, 1948).

by himself on his own projects, like the painter, the writer, the musician; in others, he works either independently or with a few associates, as do physicians, dentists, lawyers, and clergymen; in others, his methods are not dictated by the organization of which he is a member, as is true of engineers, teachers, scientific researchers, and social workers. These differences give a certain status to the professional worker.[10]

[1] *The functional aspect of professional organization:* In professional associations the functional concept is explicitly recognized and formulated in specific codes. The latter assume an obligation and an oath of service. "A profession," says the ethical code of the American Medical Association, "has for its prime object the service it can render to humanity; reward or financial gain should be a subordinate consideration," and again it proclaims that the principles laid down for the guidance of the profession "are primarily for the good of the public." Similar statements are contained in the codes of the other distinctively organized professions. "The profession," says the code of the Canadian legal profession, "is a branch of the administration of justice and not a mere money-getting occupation." Such professions as teaching, the ministry, the civil service, and social work by their very nature imply like conceptions of responsibility. They imply that while the profession is of necessity a means of livelihood or of financial reward, the devoted service which it inspires is motivated by other considerations.

The more nearly an association approximates the pure economic type, the less does it present the aspect of a profession. Moreover, in the world of business there is a further obstacle in the cleavage of interest between capital and labor, employer and employee. This internal strife reveals a fundamental conflict of acquisitive interests within the business world and not only accentuates that interest in both parties to the struggle but makes it impossible for the intrinsic "professional" interest to prevail. The professions are in general saved from this conflict. Within the professions there is not, as a rule, the situation where one group habitually employs for gain another group whose function, economic interest, and social position are entirely distinct from its own.

[2] *The problem of the reconciliation of interests:* Once that position is attained, the problem of occupational conduct takes a new form. It was stated clearly long enough ago by Plato in the *Republic*. Each "art," he pointed out, has a special good or service. "Medicine, for example, gives us health; navigation, safety at sea, and so on. . . . Medicine is not the art—or profession—of receiving pay because a man takes fees while he is engaged in healing. . . . The pay is not derived by the several 'artists' from their respective 'arts.' But the truth is, that while the 'art' of medicine gives health, and the 'art' of the builder builds a house, another 'art' attends them which is the 'art' of pay."[11] The ethical

10. On this subject in general, see E. T. Hiller, *Social Relations and Structures* (New York, 1947), Chaps. XXXIII, XXXIV.

11. *Op. cit.*, I, 346 (Jowett's translation).

problem of the profession, then, is to reconcile the two "arts," or, more generally, to fulfill as completely as possible the primary service for which it stands while securing the legitimate economic interest of its members. It is the attempt to effect this reconciliation, to find the due place of the intrinsic and of the extrinsic interest, which gives a profound social significance to professional codes of ethics.

Nevertheless, as was pointed out in Chapter XVII, this reconciliation of the economic interest with professional function is no easy task. We may distinguish, apart from the economic interest, three others which are operative in various degrees in professional associations. Most closely allied with the economic interest is the interest in the authority and the prestige of the group. It generally seeks exclusive privileges, such as the right to limit the entrance to the profession, to exclude from membership those who fall below certain professional standards or do not accept the professional "etiquette," to exclude from the practice of the profession all who are not registered as members of the association and do not possess certain qualifications represented by diplomas, degrees, or other distinctions. These demands, made in the name of the functional requirements of the profession, obviously have also an economic importance, as giving control over the conditions of service and a degree of monopoly to the association itself. Closely bound with this in turn is the technical interest, directed to the art and craft of the profession, to the maintenance and enhancement of its efficiency, to the quest for new and better methods and processes, and to the development of the sciences which underlie its techniques. Finally, we may include a definitely cultural interest.

To illustrate, in the profession of teaching the technical interest in the system of imparting knowledge is one thing, and the cultural interest in the knowledge imparted quite another. The distinction is clear also in the spheres of the sciences and of the fine arts where the interest in truth or beauty may be discerned from the interest in the technique of investigation or of expression. In other professions it may be harder to identify the cultural as distinct from the technical interest, but if we interpret the concept "culture" widely enough to include such aspects as the beauty of workmanship, it may be maintained that the cultural interest belongs to every profession and is in fact one of the criteria by which to determine whether or not a given occupation is to be classed as a profession.

Interwoven as are these strands of interest, nevertheless they are subject to the pulls of opposing forces. Thus better technique may at points be antagonistic to economic advantage. The lawyer may lose a source of profits by the introduction of a simpler and more efficient system of conveyancing. The architect, working on a percentage basis, may find his pecuniary advantage at variance with his professional duty to secure the best service for the least cost. Again, the limitation of membership may be based on the sense of vested right or traditional prestige and may involve irrelevant exclusion, apart from the fitness of the excluded to carry on the professional function. The refusal to admit women to the practice of certain professions, though no longer so prevalent, is an illustration. Likewise, opposition may arise between the economic and the cultural interest. The teacher and the preacher may suffer loss from a wholehearted devotion to the spirit of truth as they conceive it. The artist, the playwright, the author may have to choose between the ideals of their art and the more lucrative devices of popularity. Finally, the technical and the cultural interest may work apart. Routine methods and processes may dominate the professional mind to the obscuration of the ends which they should serve. A concise statement of this opposition appears in an investigation into professional organization in England. The investigation points to "the undisguised contempt in which both solicitors and barristers, notably those who have attained success in their profession and control its organization, hold, and have always held, not only all scholarship or academic learning of a professional kind, but also any theoretic or philosophical or scientific treatment of law."[12]

The main problem which these cases illustrate is once more that of the reconciliation of group interest and social function. The professions generally seek to lay down the lines of reconciliation by the establishment of special codes. Some codes distinguish elaborately between the various types of obligation incumbent on the members of the profession. The lawyer, for example, is declared to have specific duties to his client, to the public, to the court or to the law, to his professional brethren and to himself. It would occupy too much space to consider the interactions, harmonies, and potential conflicts of such various duties. Perhaps the least satisfactory reconciliation is that relating the interest of the client to the interest of the public, not merely in the consideration of the particular cases as they arise but still more in the adaptation of the service to the needs of the public as a whole as distinct from those of the individual clients. Thus the medical profession has incurred to many minds a serious liability, in spite of the development of its service to actual patients, by its failure for so long to apply the preventive side of medicine, in particular to suggest ways and means for the prevention of the needless loss of life and health and happiness caused by the general medical ignorance and helplessness of the poor.[13]

[3] *Social function and professional bias:* The difficulty of harmonizing group interest and social function is increased by the general and the specific bias which a profession, like every other group, exhibits. The general bias may be seen in such attempts to maintain a vested interest as may be found in the undue restriction of entrants to the profession—undue when determined by such professionally irrelevant considerations as high fees and expensive licenses; in the resistance to specialization, whether of tasks or of men, the former cor-

12. *New Statesman*, April 21 and 28, 1917.

13. See, for example, B. J. Stern, *Society and Medical Progress* (Princeton, N. J., 1941), especially Chap. IX.

responding to the resistance to "dilution" in the trade-union field;[14] in the insistence on a too-narrow orthodoxy, which would debar from professional practice men trained in a different school; in the unnecessary multiplication of tasks, of which a flagrant example is the English severance of barrister and solicitor. Another aspect of the general bias is found in the shuffling of responsibility under the cloak of the code. This is most marked in the public services, particularly the civil service and the Army and the Navy—and incidentally it may be noted that the problem of professional ethics is aggravated when the profession as a whole is in the employ of the state. "An official," says M. Faguet in one of his ruthless criticisms of officialdom (*The Dread of Responsibility*), "is a man whose first and almost only duty is to have no will of his own."

This last instance brings us near to what we have called the specific bias of the profession. Each profession has a limited field, a special environment, a group "mentality." Each profession tends to leave its distinctive stamp upon a man. The group environment creates a group bias. The man of law develops respect for property at the risk of his respect for personal rights. The teacher is apt to make his teaching an over-narrow discipline. The priest is apt to underestimate the costs of the maintenance of sanctity. The diplomat may overvalue good form and neglect the penalty of exclusiveness. The civil servant may make a fetish of the principle of seniority, and the soldier may interpret morality as mere *esprit de corps*.[15]

But the bias of the occupational group is subject to a process of correction which is not operative to control the bias of class and other nonfunctional unities. For it is organized in terms of a specific service which its members fulfill, not to themselves but to the community. It must therefore be responsive to the demands of the community. The social function, in the name of which the association exists, is itself capable of continuous development and thus resists the stereotyping of group attitudes around group interests. The great growth of occupational associations is one aspect of social differentiation. We have seen that professional associations represent a unity of service which is not attained in the sphere of business, where dividing interests, and above all those of capital and of labor, are separately organized. Professional associations therefore embody the fullest present attainment of the principle of functional organization, the principle which seeks to modify economic interest by subordinating it, where the two conflict, to social function. Their increase is therefore part of a movement whereby the fulfillment of function appears as

---

14. "Dilution" is a term applied sometimes to the practice of allowing less skilled workers or helpers to do certain tasks of a simple or routine nature which fall within the field of operation of the more skilled workers.

15. For discussions of the relationship between professional organizations and personality see, for example, L. Wilson, *The Academic Man* (New York, 1942), *passim;* R. K. Merton, "Bureaucratic Structure and Personality," *Social Forces*, XVIII (1940), 560–568; C. H. Page, "Bureaucracy's Other Face," *ibid.*, XXV (1946), 88–94.

a definite social force, not only above the sheer drive of economic interest, but also in partial substitution for the principle of nonfunctional organization, for the tradition of birth and race and even of nation. In this process the activity of service becomes a basis of social organization, as distinct from the passivity of status.

20

The Great Associations: Cultural

Some Distinctive Aspects of Cultural Organization

What makes an association cultural? The reader who has followed the argument of the preceding chapters may still have some doubts regarding the classification of associations as respectively cultural and utilitarian. Do not all associations organize means for the pursuit of ends? In so far as they are concerned with means are they not utilitarian; in so far as they promote ends are they not cultural? Is not the state concerned with security and more broadly with social well-being and are these not cultural goals? Do not men enter into economic associations in order to attain as far as possible the good things of life, and are these not also cultural goals? And on the other hand if men join together to promote an art or a faith or for the sake of social intercourse, is not the organization thus created still utilitarian, still a device or a technique directed to ends lying beyond the organization? Admitting then that there is a distinction between culture and utility (or civilization), have we yet any right to classify *associations* as representative of one rather than of the other?

The answer to the above question is implicitly given in our previous discussion and will be more fully presented in the chapter that follows. The distinction depends on a difference of primary objective. We shall, for example, treat the church as a cultural association, and we place in the same category the social club, the reading circle, the association of music lovers, the amateur ball team, the "learned society," and thousands of other organizations devoted to the things in which people find direct personal fulfillment or a satisfying way of spending their leisure time. Sometimes there may be a doubt as to what the primary objective of an organization is. Sometimes objectives are so mixed that an association falls as much in one as in the other category. If, for example, we accept as a proper description of religion the statement that it is "the opium of the people," then the church would doubtfully be admitted as a form of cultural organization. If, on the other hand, we regard religion as having a primary value, then the church, so far as it sustains that value, is clearly a cultural association. Fortunately there are certain more specific criteria that will serve broadly to determine whether or not we should classify a particular association as cultural. They are as follows.

[1] *The mode of participation:* A cultural association is either itself a primary group or else a union of primary groups linked together by a central organization. Unless the members meet as primary groups, the objectives of the cultural association cannot be realized. What, for example, would a church be if its members did not come together for worship and for sustenance in their faith? The central organization might still function, but the church, as a living association, would exist no more. The church is a fellowship, no matter what further organization may be involved. Everywhere the cultural association leads back to the primary focus, the club, the theater, the concert hall, the discussion group, the play group, the family. From that focus it draws not only its vitality but also its meaning. Thus the cultural and the social elements are fused in the cultural association.

This condition is not necessary for the functioning of the utilitarian system. A member can derive all the benefits accruing from an economic association apart from his personal contacts with it. If he is a shareholder of a corporation, his interest, as shareholder, is in the dividends it pays. If he is a member of a mutual insurance company, his interest is in the protection it gives him, and not in anything that accrues from the personal experience of belonging. Even as a member of the state, a man does not attend political meetings, when he attends at all, because he receives the benefits of the state by his presence there, but because he wants by his presence to assure certain benefits that come to him in other ways. In the cultural association the end is achieved, at least in part, in the *process* of meeting with others; in the utilitarian association it is the *product* that is directly significant. The organization of civilization is in this sense more impersonal than that of culture.

[2] *The liberty of alternatives:* By this expression we signify a very important characteristic of cultural associations, though one that is not easy to describe briefly. Let us compare the church with the state. There cannot be more than one state established in a particular area; there can be any number of churches—not different branches of the same church but separate churches with different creeds or even based on quite different principles. There is nothing in the logic of organization to prevent the most diverse, the most conflicting religious associations from existing side by side within the same community. A similar statement holds true of all other kinds of cultural associations. In a well-ordered community every man can worship in his own way without thereby preventing other men from worshiping in different ways or from abstaining altogether from worship. And so it is with diverse modes of thinking and living,

diverse modes of creative activity, diverse modes of social intercourse, diverse modes of recreation, diverse tastes, and diverse hobbies. In short, the differences of cultural expression are in themselves and apart from external coercion not subject to the necessity of co-ordination in a single system. In this sense they are by nature "pluralistic."

We may compare, in this respect, cultural activities and their corresponding associations with economic and technological activities. We can find many variant units of economic organization, many different ways of organizing a business, within the same community. But they all fall within a single framework of economic organization. In the first place there can be only one monetary system—without much confusion and disturbance—in the same territory. Furthermore, the economic is, as we have seen, so closely linked with the political that some similarity of procedure is incumbent on all economic organizations subject to a particular form of government. Again, the nature of economic activity involves a direct causal nexus between the behavior and the success of one agent and of another. Competing manufacturers cannot pay widely different wages in the same city nor can competing storekeepers sell their goods at widely different prices without directly prejudicing some of their numbers and causing some of them to go out of business. There are a great many requirements of the economic system which must be uniform for all concerned (whether the uniformity is achieved by competition or regulation) unless the system is to turn into chaos. But no similar system and no similar imperatives are needed in the freer realm of culture.

The ground of the difference lies in the essential nature of the cultural life, which must be free and creative or else it stagnates and decays, whereas technological activities must be co-ordinated if their objectives are to be adequately attained. In the technological area the criterion of efficiency rules. So far as the basic technology is concerned, one system of techniques, the most up-to-date, inevitably dominates. In short, in the utilitarian order of things the liberty of alternatives that marks the cultural order is not practicable.

Corollary regarding the organization of culture. An important corollary follows from the fact that culture is not subject to the logical necessity of uniformity characteristic of civilization. Cultural activity attains its ends more fully when it is free to organize itself in associations that are not dependent on the organization of the political-economic complex. Otherwise the variety and freedom of direction in which culture manifests itself are checked. The spontaneity of cultural expression—and we have seen that an essential aspect of culture is expression—is stifled. Thus the liberation of cultural association from the control of the political-economic organization is a very significant aspect of social evolution. If the conditions of co-ordination and uniformity appropriate to the technological order are imposed on the cultural life it means that moral, religious, and aesthetic impulses are bound hand and foot by alien restrictions.

It is a rejection of the principle that men can be citizens of the same state and still belong to different churches, cherish different values, and pursue different ideals. This is a principle that in the Western world was born only after enormous travail, and though it is formally recognized in the constitutions of some modern states, it is still far from being fully established. Sometimes the claim for the co-ordination or regimentation of culture has come from the state itself, sometimes from dominant economic powers, and sometimes from a cultural organization identifying itself with a political order, as did the medieval church at certain times. In our own times successive fresh attempts to "co-ordinate" the cultural life have come from the totalitarian state. The results have shown how uncongenial to creative culture such controls invariably are. Even in the area of pure science, which might seem to be somewhat remote from the encroachments of modern ideologies, the results have been detrimental.[1]

The Church as a Cultural Association

The distinctive features of the church. In view of the great variety of cultural associations in modern society it is not possible within our limits to deal with the different sociological types they present and the manifold deviations of social behavior which a study of them would reveal. We shall here confine ourselves to that form of cultural association which has had the most remarkable historic continuity and which in the nearer past has been a preponderant influence over our cultural life. The part played by the church in the evolution of modern society will be discussed at a later stage. Here we are concerned to bring out the distinctive features of the church as a form of association.

[1] *The twofold relationship postulated by the church:* The character of the church, as a religious association, is in one fundamental respect different from that of every other type. For religion implies an attitude of man, not primarily to his fellow man, but to some power beyond his range, a power regarded by every monotheistic religion as supreme. Consequently the church seeks to establish a form of communication or rapport with an invisible and superior being. It is true that certain ethical cults may take the name of religion although they do not directly invoke any such being. It is true also that certain religions of the East, such as Confucianism and Buddhism, do not presume any particularized deity. But *some relation of man to something beyond man* is inherent in the religious attitude. Hence the church postulates a suprasocial form of relationship which within the religious assembly prescribes the social relations

1. Germany, at the time the Nazis came to power, was easily first in this area, if we may judge by its proportion of Nobel prize winners in physics and chemistry, but lost this place during the Nazi regime. Russia, before the advent of Communism, had not been prominent in science but had won two Nobel prizes. Under the Soviet regime, up to the time of writing, it has not had a single prize winner. See E. M. Friedwald, *Man's Last Choice* (New York, 1948), Chap. I.

of the members. The church is a form of association in which men enter into relations with one another ostensibly determined by a prior relationship to a nonhuman being or beings, whether a universal spirit, the mystical "oneness" of all things, a local god, a ghost, a dead ancestor, even a stick or stone regarded as imbued with supernatural might.

[2] *Religion versus magic:* Here, let us note in passing, lies the difference between *religion* and *magic*, closely interwoven as the two have been. For magic is a system of manipulation of the unknown. It is pseudo science, based on a false conception of causality, assuming a control over powers not understood, by means the relation of which to these powers is not subjected to the test of objective exploration. It is magic to sing an incantation over a wound. It is magic to stick a pin in a waxen figure in order to injure the person it represents. Magic pretends to control. Religion acts through communication, imputing control to the higher powers. Its modes of communication, such as worship, intercession, prayer, and hymn, do not imply control. Magic involves no social relationship. Religion involves generally twofold communion, that of man with a nonhuman power and a derivative communion of man with man.

Some sociological implications. The attributes, tendencies, and problems of the church arise mainly out of the twofold relationship above defined. On it depend the distinctive features that throughout history have been manifested by the church as a form of association. Some of them are as follows.

[1] *The church and social restraint:* In the religious assembly there is a restraint on the more familiar and more intimate aspects of behavior. The sense of a higher presence induces in the faithful a reverential attitude which limits their relations to their fellows. The distinction between the "sacred" and the "profane" or "secular" holds sway and introduces an appropriate set of inhibitions, while it may, in certain moments of religious exaltation or ecstasy, dissolve others. These attitudes find expression in characteristic ceremonies and rituals.[2] Every occasion of a solemn character is apt to be celebrated through such devices, which create regular and prescribed channels for the orientation and limitation of social intercourse.

[2] *The church and authority:* Moreover, since the being or power to which the religious attitude is directed cannot be known by the normal modes of perception or by the procedures of scientific investigation, the church becomes in a peculiar way the exponent and repository of a lore. More than other cultural associations it depends on continuity of doctrine. It generally assumes an original revelation, set forth in inspired writings but requiring the interpretation of the leaders in the faith. Consequently a church has usually a strong authoritarian character. If it has endured long, its authority is rooted in the past and is strongly impregnated with the tradition of interpretation.

2. On the nature of ceremony and ritual, see Chapter VIII.

Hence its teaching is essentially deductive. It lays stress on orthodoxy, on the true faith delivered once for all. Its doctrinal problems are problems of exegesis, and since it claims, in its more dogmatic forms, to be "the pillar and foundation of all truth," it seeks the truth through an authoritative interpretation of the inspired word. This orthodoxy is further impressed on the faithful by the supernatural sanctions which it usually associates with the acceptance and rejection of belief. To the social taboos on nonconformist conduct the church adds the formidable taboos based on rewards and punishments in an afterlife.

We are discussing here the nature of the church, not of religion. The church takes a religious faith, often at first inchoate and flexible, and gives it a systematic form. The free expression of the religious sense is canalized in creeds and formulas and edicts and glosses. Such appears to be the history of all the greater faiths. We can follow, for example, the process by which Christianity, in its first manifestation so antiformalist, became institutionalized as a closed system of thought forms, acquiring, through church councils such as that of Nicaea, a precise, dogmatic character. Official interpretation creates a canon of conformity, and this canon is repressive of all new interpretations. It becomes "the will of God," and as such tends to be a profoundly conservative influence on all social thinking. Revelation stands in the way of revaluation. No doubt the trend of civilization in subtle and often unrealized ways affects churchly doctrines and the religious life, but, especially in the days before modern science undermined the basis of many religious dogmas, the claim of supernatural authority has been one of the most powerful of all controls and one most resistant to the spontaneous social expression of the conceptions corresponding to a changing social order. It has been said that "modern social theory, like modern political theory, develops only when society is given a naturalistic instead of a religious interpretation, and a capital fact which presides at the birth of both is a change in the conception held of the nature and functions of a church."[3]

[3] *The church and changing needs:* Numerous illustrations could be offered of the resistance of religious organizations to the social adjustments which new inventions or new conditions seemed to demand. Because of the traditional nature of religious formulations, often derived from a source remote in time, in national character, and in evolutionary stage, the authority of the church has constantly sought to retain practices and conceptions which were growing alien to the changed character of the surrounding culture. Scarcely any new illumination of man's life and destiny or any new means of controlling it, from the knowledge of the starry heavens to that of human evolution, from the establishment of republicanism to the emancipation of women, from anaesthetics to birth control, but has been condemned or proscribed in the name of religion. The retention of Sabbatarian laws in various countries is a good

3. R. H. Tawney, *Religion and the Rise of Capitalism* (New York, 1926), Chap. I.

example of the way in which the authority of the church has clung to prescriptions emanating from the radically different conditions of life under which the code was originally formed. The "day of rest" naturally took, under the conditions of life among an ancient pastoral people like the Jews of Palestine, a form which might be ill adapted to the circumstances of life in a mechanized age and in a modern city.

It is true that traditions resistant to new needs cohere around all established institutions, economic or political as well as religious. But the institutions of the church have generally claimed a unique finality. The church, dealing with ultimates, has regarded its own truth as ultimate, as absolute instead of relative to time and place and the process of knowledge, as sacrosanct and eternal. Consequently it has set up a dichotomy of the sacred and the secular, of the supernatural and the natural. Thus it proclaims a prior standard by which social institutions of the "natural" order are to be judged and to which they should be subjected. The church, in Catholic theory, is a "perfect society of supernatural universal character."[4] The predetermined order which the church assumes makes it more difficult for the social experience generated within the religious group to find expression through a readjustment of its own institutions or of the institutions over which it exercises control. For example, a system of caste is usually supported, as in India, by religious dogmas, and thus exercises a dominance over the mind which prevents the free criticism of its social values and the transition to a more flexible order which changing conditions within and beyond the society would otherwise promote.

Nevertheless, in times of social ferment, the pressure of authoritarian religious prescription is liable to be broken in various ways. In our present age, when large numbers owe no serious allegiance to a church, the ease with which members can withdraw from its communion reduces the internal stresses which characterized those ages when a church affiliation was socially or even politically obligatory. Under the latter conditions insurgent religious movements created schism within the established church and led to the formation of a variety of sects, each claiming to possess the true interpretation of the same original faith. Hence arose two social phenomena peculiarly associated with the history of religion, persecution or attempted conversion of those who espoused other beliefs. A church is rarely exclusive with respect to membership; it is rather in keeping with a church's spirit that it should bring the whole world into a single fold. But the days when this ideal seemed feasible are past, and the claim of universality, so influential in certain historical stages and so markedly in contrast with the exclusive spirit of most other associations, is submerged by the multiplicity of sects, by the tendency in our times for new religions to arise as well as new sects, and by the withdrawal of large

4. Cf. the papal encyclical of January 11, 1930, on the Christian Education of Youth.

numbers from all church connections. The decline of dogma in some of the more "protestant" forms of religion has led, on the other hand, to a movement for their unification.

[4] *The church as an instrument of power:* The twofold relationship postulated by the church is responsible also for an inner conflict, a conflict of purpose, that is liable to appear when the church becomes a far-reaching large-scale organization. The church has considerable concern with the everyday affairs of men—if only because the religion it professes prescribes certain modes of behavior in accordance with a system of ethical values. Not only so, but the church exercises a wide influence over the policies of government. Furthermore, it is a property owner of magnitude. Hence its leaders inevitably have some role as policy makers. Thus arises the conflict to which we refer. Exercising power, it is not unlikely to become engrossed in the problems of power. Regulating mundane affairs, it may be very well become itself mundane. Using political means, it may become immersed in political deals. Its leaders, its hierarchy, are exposed to the temptations of power. But religion draws a distinction between the "sacred" and the "secular." It demands some kind of apartness from the attitudes and practices of the world outside. Hence there is a danger that its primary purpose may be distorted by its preoccupation with the problems of power.

Here, according to various writers on the sociology of religion, is the great dilemma of the church. R. H. Tawney, for example, endeavors to show that the secular claims of the Roman Catholic Church in the fourteenth and fifteenth centuries were incompatible with and indeed perverted its spiritual mission.[5] Other writers, such as Max Weber, Ernst Troeltsch, and Joachim Wach, treat the problem as a general one and have discussed the approaches of different churches and religions to secular affairs.[6] One sociologist, Leopold von Wiese, takes a more extreme position, regarding the dilemma as a hopeless one. "The two sets of values which are here bottled up together are wholly alien to each other and often directly opposed." All that is possible is some compromise between the two.[7]

The complex of interests served by the church. The church, as we have seen, is distinguished from other associations by its suprasocial orientation. This orientation is, of course, the expression of certain human impulses or needs. But the church is at the same time a fellowship, a brotherhood of believers, a basis of social intercourse. Here we see another aspect of the twofold relationship that is so characteristic of the church.

---

5. *Op. cit.*, Chap. XI.
6. For Max Weber, see T. Parsons, *Structure of Social Action*, (New York, 1937), Part III, Chaps. XIII-XIV; E. Troeltsch, *The Social Teachings of the Christian Church* (O. Wyon, tr., New York, 1931); Joachim Wach, *Sociology of Religion* (Chicago, 1944), Chaps. III, VII.
7. *Systematic Sociology* (H. Becker, ed., New York, 1932), Chap. XLIV.

[1] *The suprasocial interest:* In more primitive forms religion may serve the desire to appease the formidable powers which seem to beset the life and determine the lot and fate of men. But this desire may be regarded as the germ of a more inclusive impulse, the essentially religious yearning for cosmic security, for an adjustment of the individual toward the universe as he is able to conceive it. The core of this religious principle is expressed in the famous words of St. Augustine: "Our heart is restless till it finds rest in Thee." It is the esoteric way of escape from those fears and negations and frustrations which surmount ordinary human contrivance. As these change with changing experience, so does, at length, religion. The church stabilizes and, as we have seen, in part checks this process, setting up explicit formulations of the conditions under which the individual can achieve the sense of cosmic unity. It propounds, for example, a schematic doctrine of an afterlife in response to the yearning for immortality. It develops a formula for the expiation of sin or guilt in response to the feeling of imperfection, frailty, or wrongdoing. In short, it elaborates a compensatory thought-system designed to assure those adjustments of the emotional nature of man toward the order of the universe which seem to be contradicted, or at least unattainable, on the level of everyday experience.

[2] *Social interest:* The religious interest, as above distinguished, is too nearly related to the social interests and pressures of the group to find a pure or simple embodiment in social organization. Religion, so understood, could scarcely be expected to emancipate itself from more immediate concerns. Alike its compensations and its penalties are rooted in the mores of the group, past or present. The distinction of the religious and the moral is still a hard one even for the reflective mind. So the church was inevitably a strong agent of social control, the more powerful because of its absolutist claims and the consequent passivity of its lay membership. Being conservative by the very nature of its mission, as we have seen, it was a potent instrument of social submission, and as such was consciously or unconsciously exploited by the dominant forces in the community. The consequent confusion of its aims, and particularly the difficulty of its relationship to the powers of the state, will be considered in a later chapter.

Moreover, the church lives in the assembling of its members in local units of fellowship. Hence for its members and others it is a social rallying point, furnishing in many rural communities the chief occasion for the regular meeting of the folk. Under such conditions the church is less a specific association than a communal institution. It is the focus for the celebration and symbolization of the great occasions and crises of life, a cultural center of the life of the community. It conducts and controls many social activities, political, educational, charitable, recreational. In the more complex society other agencies take over, in part at least, these functions. Hence the church has had to face a problem similar to that which has confronted the family, that of finding its place and role within a more specialized system. With the decline in the hold of dogmatic religion, especially in the large cities, this problem has been for the church one of peculiar difficulty. Its traditional basis becomes uncongenial to a social life which has in other respects abandoned old traditions, and yet it is exceedingly hard for a church to reformulate its basis without losing its distinctive character or with any assurance of thereby fulfilling some function which is not more definitely fulfilled by other organizations.[8]

The manner in which churches have served as a rallying point for cultural interests is well revealed by the strength which they possess among groups which feel their cultural unity but lack adequate political means for its expression. The cultural cohesion of the Jewish people has been in great measure expressed through the synagogue, rabbinical rituals, and religious commemorations. In Catholic Ireland's struggle for independence, the church played an important part. In French Quebec, incorporated within a political area dominated by English traditions, the church has retained an authority which it has lost in France. In other countries, such as Poland, where two peoples of different religions and different traditions are associated, religious affiliations have retained considerable social significance. It has often been observed also that immigrant groups in the United States cling to their traditional church with an added intensity because of their cultural isolation. On the other hand, the militant freethinking of the Czech population was an expression of nationalist opposition to Austrian Catholicism.[9] The church has thus played historically a double role: claiming universality, it has preached the brotherhood of man, but it has also embodied and perpetuated in its different forms the social traditions of diverse and often conflicting groups.

---

8. Cf. H. P. Douglass, *The Church in the Changing City* (New York, 1927) and *The Protestant Church as a Social Institution* (New York, 1935); E. C. Lindeman, *The Church in the Changing Community* (published by The Community Church of New York, 1929).

9. For fuller illustration of these points see H. A. Miller, *Races, Nations, and Classes* (Philadelphia, 1924).

21

Functional Systems

The Institutional Complex

What we mean by functional systems. We have now surveyed the different constituents of the social structure—the inclusive community, the stratifications of class, the various kinds of interest group, the numerous associations, large scale or face to face, ranging from the family to the state. But these structural elements do not merely exist side by side to make up the total structure of a society. There are particular combinations and integrations of particular components. There are particular adaptations of one to another in the service of particular social functions. These we shall call *functional systems.* Here we may use the analogy of the organism. We cannot be content to describe its various organs in terms of their separate structures or functions. We must also show how these organs enter into specific relations in the fulfillment of the organic functions. Thus we have the circulatory system, the nervous system, the digestive system, the excretory system, and so forth.

The structure of a modern society is an elaborate one, more elaborate than we generally realize, and it is harder to conceive than the structure of a physical or biological unity, because the social framework is invisible and intangible. We all *experience* the fact that there is a social order. We perceive its results and point to the evidences that indicate its changes; but the order itself is not of the kind that directly meets the eye or the ear. On that account it is all the more important that the student should try to *understand* it.

In Chapter XVII we explained how interests are focused in associations, and classified the broad types of organized groups according to types of interest (see Chart XVII on page 447); and in the three following chapters we considered respectively the political, economic, and cultural organizations. The functional coherence of interest, however, is not fully brought out by the study of specific associations. Interests create social formations beyond or outside the range of individual associations. They cohere in two principal ways which our earlier classification fails to represent.

[1] *The institutional complex:* For purposes of classification we have distinguished such formally specialized interests as the economic and the political, and the technological and the economic; or, taking a wider range, the political and the religious, and the economic and the sexual. But such interests, though formally distinct, may be closely interwoven. The economic and the political are inevitably bound together; the religious and the political cohere under certain conditions. Economic institutions—the market, the system of "private enterprise," the economic corporation—are interadapted with political institutions—the forms and limits of governmental controls, the rules of contractual rights and obligations, the politically maintained monetary and credit system. Thus is constituted the politico-economic complex. Similarly the state and the church, where one church is dominant, may be closely linked. These unifications we shall speak of as institutional complexes.

[2] *The fundamental orders corresponding to major types of interest:* The major divisions of interest as given in the classification on page 447 are represented by no associations of corresponding range. There is no association broad enough to incorporate all primary interests or all secondary interests. But each of these general types of human interests has characteristic features of its own, present in all the species of the genus. Consequently these species also constitute coherent systems, the great orders of human experience. These orders, corresponding respectively to primary and to secondary interests, we shall distinguish as the *order of culture* and the *order of civilization*. The techniques, the mechanical devices, the whole apparatus of means through which men seek to realize their desires or satisfy their needs, cohere, especially in modern society with its elaborate technology, into one great order, from which we ought to distinguish the manifestations of the cultural order. The patterns, relations, and processes that each of these orders reveals, both within itself and in relation to the antithetical order, are of vast importance for the understanding of social relationships and social unities and, as we shall see in Book Three, are essential determinants of social change.

Modes of the institutional complex. If a perfectly static society were conceivable, it would be one in which all the constituent elements were completely co-ordinated into a single unified scheme. The habits of all men would be fixed and would be completely adjusted to a set of institutions every one of which would be wholly accommodated to all the rest. But in actual life with its incessant change, and particularly under the conditions of a complex society, there is and there can be no such perfect co-ordination. In any large-scale society there are, however, some particular areas within which a high degree of integration is attained. Where this occurs, various factors are interadjusted by institutional arrangements so that they function harmoniously toward the same ends. Contrast, for example, the situation in which church and state form a unified system of social control with that in which the church is relatively separate from and independent of the state. In the former case we have an institutional complex. Again, we find that while the economic systems of different times and of different countries may be very unlike, they all involve a system of government congenial to their respective characters. In fact, when we use terms like "socialism," "capitalism," "sociocapitalism," or "communism," we are not referring to an economic system alone or to a political system alone, but always to an institutional complex.

[1] *The economic-political complex:* Not one or two types of interest, but often many, are combined in an institutional complex. Let us take *capitalism*, or, more strictly, capitalistic organization, as an example. Capitalism is not a single phenomenon or a mere cluster of economic phenomena. It is not merely a set of economic relationships between the owners or managers of producers' goods and those they hire to operate them, not merely a system in which corporate control and private enterprise determine the conditions of production; it is at the same time, and inevitably, also a political phenomenon supported by congenial mores and cultural valuations. Capitalism could not exist unless maintained by the appropriate political and legal institutions, since in the first instance a system involving private property, free contractual relationships, monetary and banking facilities congenial to capitalistic enterprise, corporate rights and powers, and so forth, depends throughout on legal establishment. The specifically economic conditions, the profits system, the wage system, the combination of competition and partial monopoly, the marketing system, and all the rest, are the counterpart of specifically political conditions. And both sets of conditions depend in turn on appropriate mores, such as beliefs concerning the value and social role of competitive struggle, the private inheritance of wealth, individualistic acquisition, the superiority of a "free" to a "planned" economy, and the incentives to effort which arise from the prospect of private gain.

In this list of interadjusted factors of capitalism we have not included the technological conditions of which in a sense capitalism is the product. Without the development of the means of communication, without considerable division of labor or specialization, without the mechanisms of production, without large-scale markets, capitalism as we understand it here could not have developed. These technological factors, however, are detachable from the institutional complex of capitalism. They enter also into alternative institutional complexes, particularly that of socialism, whereas the factors we have mentioned above are necessary coherent elements of the capitalism complex. Again, capitalism, like all institutional complexes, is historically associated with a variety of other conditions, such as monarchical, republican, or dictatorial forms of government, which are not essential to its existence though they may be components of larger complexes of a looser or more temporary character.

[2] *Other types of institutional complex:* We see then that institutional complexes may be more or less inclusive and may vary in magnitude and in the degree of interadjustment between their elements. When, for example, a country changes its constitution or form of government, the change is never confined to its political institutions. Corresponding changes occur or have previously been occurring in economic relationships, in the class structure, in the dominant ways of thinking. Democratic and fascist and communist systems are alike institutional complexes. A democratic order is not intelligible merely as a particular way of choosing a government and of making laws. It cannot function except as part of a more inclusive system, supported by congenial mores. It cannot function—more exactly, it cannot exist—if dominant economic powers prevent the free expression of opinion. It cannot function if, say, a highly organized hierarchical religion directly controls the manner of life of the community. Similarly, a dictatorship or a form of class government must rest on a congenial social order, or if it has seized power in an order based on other principles, it must, to be effective, contrive, by persuasion or by force, to change that order into conformity with its own character. Every political system, in short, is always part of an institutional complex of greater or less range, just as we have seen that every economic system must be.

Complexes of this kind are found everywhere, since social reality is not broken up into compartments corresponding to the distinctions between interests or to the respective subjects of the various social sciences As we shall see later, different types of institutional complex characterize different stages of social evolution. The institutional nexus between cultural institutions (expressive of primary interests) is particularly significant in this respect. For example, the eighteenth-century herald of revolution, Jean Jacques Rousseau, vehemently opposed the dissolution of the political-religious complex and declared that to "separate the religious from the political system" was to "destroy the unity of the state and to cause the intestine divisions which have never ceased to agitate Christian nations."[1] In this he was at one with the conservatives who denounced him, such as the English orator Edmund Burke. But the trend since his time has on the whole been the breakup of this complex. In a modern society the complex of political and economic institutions is as well established as ever, though the mode of co-ordination may be different. But the relations between cultural and utilitarian institutions is far more variable and generally less intimate. The reasons for this will appear in the following section of this chapter.[2]

---

1. *Social Contract*, Book IV, Chap. VIII.
2. Few sociologists have treated the "institutional complex" as such: for a brief statement see E. T. Hiller, *Social Relations and Structures* (New York, 1947), Chap. XVI. The interdependence of institutions is well brought out in J. W. Bennett and M. M. Tumin, *Social Life Structure and Function* (New York, 1948), Chaps. XII–XIII.

Culture and Civilization

What we mean by civilization and culture. Pursuing our classification of interests into primary and secondary, we discover two great areas of human experience and of human activity, those we have named respectively "culture" and "civilization." All the things that man does, all the things he creates—all his artifacts—fall predominantly into one order or the other.

[1] *Civilization:* Take, for example, a typewriter. We observe at once that it belongs to the same order as a printing press, a lathe, a factory, a locomotive, a bank, a currency system. These things are all *utilitarian*. They are conceived, devised, and operated as means to ends. We do not normally want any of them for the satisfaction their existence brings to us; we want them because we can secure certain satisfactions by using them as means. They are useful as equipment, as apparatus. They all belong to the realm of civilization. By civilization, then, we mean the whole mechanism and organization which man has devised in his endeavor to control the conditions of his life. It would include not only our systems of social organization but also our techniques and our material instruments. It would include alike the ballot box and the telephone, the Interstate Commerce Commission and the railroads, our laws as well as our schools, and our banking systems as well as our banks.

Within the order of civilization we can now distinguish what we shall call the *basic technology* from the *social technology*. The basic technology is directed to man's control over natural phenomena. It is the area of the engineer and the mechanic. It applies the laws of physics, chemistry, and biology to the service of human objectives. It rules the processes of production in industry, agriculture, and the extractive industries. It constructs ships and planes and armaments and tractors and elevators and an endless variety of artifacts. It shapes and assembles objects of every scale. It makes the skyscraper and the open-hearth furnace, and also the tinsel for Christmas trees. It plans the modernized city and its parkways, and also the newest design of women's hats. By the social technology, on the other hand, we mean the techniques directed to the regulation of the behavior of human beings. It has two essential divisions, the *economic technology*, which is concerned with economic processes and the immediate relationships of men to one another in the pursuit of economic means, and the *political technology*, which in a broader way, presently to be explained, regulates a wide range of human relationships.

[2] *Culture:* Just as the typewriter belongs to one great order, so the novel which may be written by its aid falls into another. It is in an important respect akin to a picture, a poem, a drama, a motion-picture film, a game, a philosophy, a creed, a cathedral. All these things we bring into existence because we want them as such, because it is their function to give us directly, not merely as intermediaries, something that we crave after or think we need. They all repre-

sent ways in which we express ourselves. They respond to a necessity within us, not to an outer necessity. They belong to the realm of culture. This is the realm of values, of styles, of emotional attachments, of intellectual adventures. Culture, then, is the antithesis of civilization. It is the expression of our nature in our modes of living and of thinking, in our everyday intercourse, in art, in literature, in religion, in recreation and enjoyment.

While, as we shall see, many objects possess both a civilizational and a cultural element, we can often decide the question of their classification by asking: Do we want these things themselves or do we merely use them in order to attain some other thing we want? Do they exist because of some outer necessity or because we seek them as such? Often we make a virtue of necessity and impress on utilitarian objects a cultural quality, as when we build banks to rival temples, but if these objects would not exist at all for the *direct* satisfaction they yield us we may classify them as within the category of civilization. On the other hand, many objects combine both elements so inextricably, for example our clothing and our homes, that we must be content simply to distinguish the two aspects of the service they render.[3]

The two orders compared. In what follows we shall seek to bring out important differences between the characteristics of the two orders. This we must do in some detail, since they are so closely interwoven that it is easy to slur over the distinction. Only when we have grasped the differences they present can we proceed to discuss the ways in which they are related.

[1] *Civilization has a precise standard of measurement, but not culture:* Civilization, or the utilitarian order, is subject to the criterion of efficiency. When comparing the products and processes of civilization we can with confidence impute superiority and inferiority. Since they are means to ends, their degree of efficiency can readily be estimated and, provided the end is clearly postulated, can in fact be measured. The only difficulty lies in our judgment of the value of the ends which they serve, either in themselves or relatively to other ends. No one disputes the superiority of the tractor over the hand plow or of the

---

3. The anthropologist uses the term "culture" in a different and very inclusive sense, as we explained in Chapter III. Thus, for example, A. Goldenweiser makes it inclusive of "our attitudes, beliefs, and ideas, our judgments and values; our institutions, political and legal, religious and economic; our ethical codes and codes of etiquette; our books and machines, our sciences, philosophies and philosophers—all of these things and many other things and beings, both in themselves and in their multiform inter-relations."—*Early Civilization* (New York, 1926), p. 15. For sociological purposes the more limited usage of the text seems more serviceable, especially as it is close to the older and ordinary use of the term. The distinction drawn in the text is akin to that made by Alfred Weber in his study, "Prinzipielles zur Kultursociologie," *Archiv für Sozialwissenschaft und Sozialpolitik*, Vol. 47 (1921). It is developed also in MacIver's *Modern State*, Chap. X, and in his article, "The Historical Pattern of Social Change," in *Authority and the Individual* (Cambridge, Mass., 1937). For a sweeping criticism of it see P. A. Sorokin, *Social and Cultural Dynamics*, Vol. IV, (New York, 1941), Chap. IV.

modern currency and credit system over primitive barter. No one disputes the superiority of the machine gun over the tomahawk, though here the question arises over the wisdom or folly which employs the superior engine of destruction. We dispute concerning "scientific management" and labor unions and trusts and socialistic policies, not so much because we cannot measure the efficiency of these means toward the achievement of particular ends but because we differ regarding the relative value of these ends in the total scheme of life. It is always the cultural aspect that raises the ultimate unarbitrable problem of values. And so with the greater achievements of culture. We have no universal measuring rod by which to assess them. Different ages and different groups vary in their judgments. At best we content ourselves with the slowly gathered wisdom of a succession of "authorities," knowing that this also is precarious. If Shaw claims that he is a better dramatist than Shakespeare, no one can prove—or disprove—his claim; we can only disagree—or agree—with it. Progress, in the absolute sense, which means cultural progress, remains a matter of faith, of the congruity between the facts as we know them and the particular conceptions we entertain as to what is ultimately worth while. And no matter what standards we accept, we find an ebb and flow, a lack of certitude in the movement of culture which stands in marked contrast to the victorious march of civilization.

[2] *Civilization is always advancing, but not culture:* Civilization not only marches, it marches always, provided there is no catastrophic break of social continuity, in the same direction. An achievement of civilization is generally exploited and improved, going on from strength to strength, until it is superseded or rendered obsolete by some new invention. It is true that in past ages some achievements of civilization have again been lost. Men forgot the arts which raised the pyramids of Egypt and which constructed the roads and aqueducts of the Romans. But these losses occurred through catastrophic changes which blotted out the records of civilization. With the widening of the areas of civilization and with superior methods of recording discoveries, any utilitarian or technical gain becomes a permanent possession within the social heritage and the condition of further gains. It is otherwise with cultural achievements. They do not lead assuredly to higher or improved ones. Since man first invented the automobile, it has continuously improved. Our means of transportation grow constantly more swift and more efficient. They are vastly superior to those which the ancient Greeks employed. But can we say the same of our dramas and our sculptures, our conversation and our recreation? Here certitude fails us. There are no automobiles today so comparatively inefficient as the first vehicles of Henry Ford—his work and that of other inventors inevitably prepared the way for better ones. But our plays are not necessarily better today because of the achievements of Shakespeare. There is no "march" of culture. It is subject to retrogression as well as to advance. Its past does not assure its future.

[3] *Civilization is passed on without effort, but not culture:* The transmission of culture within a society follows a different principle from that which determines the transmission of civilization. Culture is communicated only to the like-minded. No one without the quality of the artist can appreciate art, nor without the ear of the musician can one enjoy music. Civilization in general makes no such demand. We can enjoy its products without sharing the capacity which creates them. Moreover, the process of creation itself is different. Lesser minds improve the work of the great inventors, but lesser poets do not improve on Shakespeare. The product of the artist is more revelatory of his personality than is that of the technician, just as the quality of a people is peculiarly expressed in its culture rather than in its civilization. What we acquire of the culture of the present or of the past depends on what we are. We do not inherit it as we inherit civilization. We acquire it selectively, as individuals and as groups. We inherit those aspects of it of which we are ourselves worthy. A new generation cannot enjoy the greater cultural achievements of the past unless they win it afresh for themselves. But the greatest achievements of the civilization around us can be ours to use and to enjoy without any special effort, without any particular qualification on our part. Again, culture, being the immediate expression of the human spirit, can advance only if that spirit is capable of finer efforts, has itself something more to express. Civilization is the vehicle of culture; its improvement is no guarantee of finer quality in that which it conveys. The radio can carry our words to the ends of the earth, but the words need be no wiser on that account.

[4] *Civilization is borrowed without change or loss, but not culture:* The transference of cultural elements from one area of society to another likewise differs in significant respects from the transference or "borrowing" of utilitarian elements. Given adequate means of communication, any improvement in the apparatus of life will quickly spread. In fact, with the modern development of communications, a single system of civilization is already encompassing nearly all the earth. Even the savage is ready to discard his bow and spear and to adopt the rifle. The power machine displaces the hand tool wherever men have the means to acquire it. The corporate form of industry encroaches everywhere on older forms as irresistibly as the factory displaces the domestic system of production. We have pointed out that these techniques are readily comparable, and the relative superiority of one over the other is easily adjudged. Civilization has its objective tests so that it is a simple matter to decide that one mode of hygiene or one method of road building is preferable to another. The advance of civilization is seriously resisted only when the older form is closely associated with the culture of a people. For a people will not freely abandon its culture for another, since to do so would be to sacrifice its intrinsic quality. Even when one civilization covers the globe, great cultural differences, modified as they become under such conditions, will endure, just as they endure today among the industrialized peoples. It is true that cultural "borrowing" occurs, but it

is selective and seemingly wayward, dependent on a degree of affinity, of like-mindedness, in the borrowers and always colored or even distorted by their personality.

The history of religious conversion and proselytism affords sufficient evidences of this selective process. The Geneva of Calvin and the Scotland of Knox and the Massachusetts of Cotton Mather were receptive of certain strains in the multiform tradition of Christianity, selecting ascetic, authoritarian, patriarchal, eschatological elements within it and translating them into a system which they identified with Christianity itself, just as other peoples and other times selected and transmuted other elements to form their creeds. It may also be noted that this selective "borrowing" is not limited to recent or contemporaneous contributions to the stock of culture. In this also it differs from the process by which civilization spreads. Cultural elements may be adopted as readily from the past as from the present, from any epoch of the past no less than from the present hour. Cultural affinity may revert to the legends of Greece or of the German forests, to the art of tenth-century China or of pre-Raphaelite Florence, to the meditations of Job or of Marcus Aurelius. Its range of selection runs from the newest culture-fashion to the myths that linger from the dawn of history.

In the light of these distinctions it should be clear that the expansion of a civilization follows different principles from those which determine cultural development. Where communications admit, the former tends to proceed more rapidly, more simply, less selectively, always spreading outward from the foci of technological and economic advance. The products of civilization are conveyed over every trade route, and they prepare the way for the techniques and systems which created them. People trade with one another before they understand one another. The expansion of civilization has perils on that very account. For the interdependence of peoples within a common civilization outstrips the formation of those cultural attitudes necessary for its maintenance.

The contrasts we have drawn between the two orders are particularly clear when we contrast the *basic technology* with culture. They are not, for the most part, so well illustrated with respect to the *social technology* because the social technology is more dependent on the particular values prevalent where it is applied. Certain ways of organizing men, whether economic or political, certain of the techniques adopted for the regulation of associations of any kind, are limited in their use by the cultural conditions. They can, of course, be borrowed, but they are likely to be misfits unless the cultural conditions are favorable. Take, for example, any system for the governing of men. A democratic constitution cannot be successfully established in a country where the proper cultural preparation is lacking. This consideration brings us to our next subject, the relationship between the two orders.

The two orders related. It is of primary importance for the understanding of social change that we should seek to trace the changing involvements and dependencies of culture and of technology. This subject will occupy us in Book Three. At this point we deal rather with some principles determining the interrelations of the two orders. We shall look first at particular products and processes and then at the orders themselves viewed as total systems.

[1] *How particular artifacts combine cultural and technological aspects:* An object or a practice may be predominantly technological or predominantly cultural, but it usually has both technological and cultural aspects. We are not referring here to the obvious fact that the *same* object may be cultural for one person and utilitarian for another. We are considering rather the fact that any particular object may have embodied in it something of both aspects. More specifically, *the objects that fall mainly in the category of civilization have generally and in different degrees a cultural aspect*, while on the other hand *the objects that fall mainly in the category of culture have invariably a technological or utilitarian medium.*

ONE: THE CULTURAL VARIATIONS OF TECHNOLOGICAL PRODUCTS. Men are seldom content with the purely utilitarian aspect of the instruments they use; they want the utility embellished. They want style in an automobile as well as performance or comfort. The degree in which a cultural character is added to the mere utility varies with the nature of the object and with the social conditions. It is a general rule that what the economists term "consumers' goods" are more "embellished" than "producers' goods." The steam shovel, for example, is less stylized than the automobile. Another interesting point is that the longer an object of civilization endures, the more likely it is to acquire a cultural aspect. When the instruments of production tend to grow rapidly obsolete and to be replaced by more efficient or at least newer types, they are likely to assume more purely utilitarian forms. The culture of the community has not had time to express itself in them. But in more static primitive communities the tool is more than a tool; it is the bearer of tradition, a symbol of culture, on which accordingly the craftsman lavishes his art. Under these conditions the techniques of production as well as the products have a ceremonial, symbolic, in general a cultural quality. When the savage builds a canoe, the technique is associated throughout with a ritual expressive of the folkways. Some relics of this blending of technique and culture remain among ourselves, as in the ceremony of laying a foundation stone or of launching a ship.

What applies to the concrete instruments of civilization applies still more obviously to institutions and organizations. A constitution or a code of laws is not simply a means of government. At the same time it expresses the spirit of a people and as such tends to be treasured for its own sake as the embodiment of tradition. This merging of the cultural with the utilitarian creates a resistance to change. The engineer, dominated by the idea of efficiency, never admires the mechanism of the past or the present so much that it impedes his search for improvements, nor in turn is he impeded by the attachment of his fellow men to antique designs. But men are more apt to admire the social agencies of the political or the economic order, the work of their forefathers hallowed by time, in such a way that they refuse to exercise upon them their own constructive powers or to consider objectively the advantages and disadvantages of proposed changes.

TWO: THE TECHNOLOGICAL MEDIA OF CULTURAL PRODUCTS. Consider next the products and processes that are dominantly cultural. All the phenomena that we classify as cultural expressions depend on some technical medium and technical process. The expression is limited and modified by technical requirements, whether the medium be language or paint or stone or gesture or other external sign. That is why, for example, it is harder to translate a poem into a foreign language than a treatise on engineering. It is impossible really to reproduce the former, to give in another medium the entire significance of the original blending of meaningful sounds and rhythms. Every artist has a constant struggle to master his medium. When we try to communicate to others some experience we have had or some scene we have witnessed, we find ourselves forever hampered by the difficulties of expression even in the most familiar of all media, our own language. We may mean what we say, but it is vastly harder to say what we mean. In a court of law we swear to tell the whole truth, but no one, with the best will in the world, can do so, can present to others a whole situation precisely as he has experienced it. The greater the artist the more he succeeds in making the medium express his thoughts or his purposes. This problem of the technical medium applies not only to the fine arts but also to the art of living, to the pursuit of the everyday satisfactions which are the cultural expressions of the majority of men. These also must be sought and attained under the conditions and the limitations set by the civilization in which we live.

[2] *How the orders themselves are interactive:* We must now think of the whole apparatus of civilization viewed as a system of interdependent devices and instruments, so as to examine some of its broader relations to the cultural life. From what has already been said it is apparent that at every stage technology is (a) a vehicle of culture; (b) a factor determining the degree in which cultural activity, of whatever kind, is released or limited; and (c) an environment of culture to which in some measure culture always adapts itself.

ONE: CIVILIZATION AS A VEHICLE OF CULTURE. The first aspect has already been partially dwelt on. Here we should add that cultural modes are responsive to the stage of technological development. Thus the form as well as the range of appeal of the literary art has been greatly affected by the development of printing. For example, apart from that development we would not have the lengthy novels that are popular today nor the spread of the habit of reading throughout the population. It is obvious in particular that the evolution of the means of communication has had a profound impact on the modes of expression which are so essential to cultural activity. In this sense, as well as in that already mentioned, civilization is the vehicle of culture.

TWO: THE CIVILIZATIONAL FACTOR IN THE RELEASE OF CULTURAL ACTIVITY. But many of the devices of civilization are of minor importance as direct vehicles of our culture—our elaborate mechanisms of production, for example. These mechanisms are more capable of serving our culture indirectly, as a means of exploiting nature and thus of liberating energies which otherwise would be used up in the necessities of mere living. If the whole day were consumed in the struggle to satisfy organic necessities, to secure food and warmth and shelter and protection, then there would be little opportunity for cultural development. The advance of technology has made possible in increasing measure the liberation of energies that otherwise must be devoted to these ends. The degree and the manner in which these liberated energies are utilized may themselves be a criterion of our culture. The elaborate apparatus does not inevitably raise its standard or its quality. Under certain conditions it may even prove an obstacle. The engrossment of energies in the expansion of civilization when conditions are favorable to it may be prejudicial to culture, and this charge is often brought against periods of great mechanical advance such as the United States has experienced in conjunction with a rapidly growing population. The quantitative growth of civilization may check the qualitative growth of culture. It may be claimed, on the other hand, that some peoples have a greater genius for the building up of civilization than for the achievement of culture, a comparison which receives some support from the examples of Greece and Rome and which for these peoples was in fact admitted and proclaimed by the greatest of Roman poets. Other peoples, he said proudly, referring chiefly to the Greeks, may excel us in such arts as the making of figures in bronze and the carving of marble, or in oratory or in astronomy, but the business of the Roman is the practical art of government.[4]

Another important aspect of relationship is here suggested. The art of government is an art of control, and in controlling it constantly exercises power over at least some range of cultural expression. Some forms of government, inspired by the particular cultural valuations of the holders of power, even seek to dominate the whole cultural life. More generally, all possession or organization of utilitarian means, whether economic, technological, or political, places power in the hands of a hierarchy of control, which thereby exercises directly or indirectly a strong influence over cultural activities, limiting or suppressing some and supporting, providing for, and encouraging others.

THREE: CIVILIZATION AS AN ENVIRONMENT OF CULTURE. Civilization does more than provide channels and outlets for culture. The relation between the mind and the environment cannot be summed up in that external way. The instruments we use are the creatures of our desires, but they evoke, modify, and deflect our desires in turn. Mechanisms devised as mere utilities affect our

---

4. Excudent alii spirantia mollius aera.
(credo equidem), vivos ducent de marmore vultus,
orabunt causas melius caelique meatus
describent radio et surgentia sidera dicent,
tu regere imperio populos, Romane, memento.
—Virgil *Aen.* vi, 847–851.

lives, our thoughts, our aims and hopes and fears, in ways entirely beyond our foreknowledge. Our civilization, as it were, takes revenge upon us. Like the work of Frankenstein, it cannot be wholly controlled by its creators. The machine age has stimulated new habits and enjoyments, new philosophies and ethics, as well as new methods of production and means of locomotion. The telescope revises our ideas of the universe, the microscope our ideas about the nature of life, and thus more subtly they influence our religions and our conduct. The power mechanism, inexorably fulfilling immutable if newly discovered laws, instills new conceptions of the nature of authority. If in ancient Egypt or Judaea the wonders of electrical energy had been revealed, the peoples of these lands would also have had a different "revelation" of God which might well have affected the course of history. In the eras of slower change the influence of civilization on culture was less observed, but in our own age, with its rapid technological development, the fact has become a commonplace, though, as we shall see later, the precise nature and limits of that influence are exceedingly hard to diagnose.

Finally, let us look on the other side, the way in which the cultural order affects our civilization. Culture is the realm of final valuations, and human beings must interpret the whole world, including their own devices, techniques, and power, in the light of their valuations.[5] Every people and every age has its characteristic ways of looking at things, its characteristic attitudes, no matter what diversity there may be among them, its own thought-forms and philosophies. The powers it uses and the manner in which it uses them, the inventions it develops and the directions in which they are applied, the means it amasses and the modes of their exploitation, cannot escape altogether from the influence of the creeds and the standards and the styles of the age. We see this more clearly when we survey past stages of civilization, and it is only because we are so wrapped in our own valuations that we have greater difficulty in perceiving it in the movements of our own age. Moreover, it is in the light of our culture that we conceive all the *unities* to which we belong, the unity of people and nation, of family and social class, of an international order, of civilization itself; and every application of means to sustain or advance these various unities is inspired by our culture. In the culture live the valuations that create group loyalties and group unities, that narrow or widen the range of community, and that organize the means and powers of society to the service of all common ends.

5. Cf. the parallel distinction between *techniques* and *myths* in R. M. MacIver, *The Web of Government* (New York, 1947), Chap. I.

BOOK III

Social Change

Foreword: THE SOCIAL STRUCTURE is subject to incessant change, growing, decaying, finding renewal, accommodating itself to extremely variant conditions and suffering vast modifications in the course of time. Its contemporaneous aspect holds and hides the secret of its past. We know its nature, as we know the nature of the living person, only in the comprehension of it through a time-span. Its meaning is never revealed in any moment of its existence, but, finally and fully, only in the whole process through which it passes. To understand the social structure we must therefore view it in the historical process, seeking continuity, observing also how differences emerge. We must, in other words, discover the direction of change, or all is meaningless. That is why the principle of evolution becomes of supreme significance.

In other fields of science the principle of evolution has become the most important clew to the discovery of order in the endless processes of change. Modern sociology has tended to neglect or even to reject this principle, mainly because it was too uncritically applied by an earlier generation of sociologists. We shall try to show, nevertheless, that it has a very significant place in the interpretation of social change.

It is soon apparent that social change is a process responsive to many types of change, to changes in the man-made conditions of living, to changes in the attitudes and beliefs of men, and to changes that go back beyond human control to the biological and the physical nature of things. To understand how social change takes place and why it follows certain trends it is necessary to investigate its relation to the three great orders, the biophysical, the cultural, and the technological. This investigation occupies the central part of this Book. We then proceed to consider social change as such, and particularly in its evolutionary aspects.

22

Society as Process

In What Sense Society Endures

The face of social change. A thousand years ago, in Europe and America, the face of society was vastly different from that with which we are familiar today. A thousand years hence it will assuredly have undergone vast new transformations. What it will be like ten thousand years from now—what shiftings and readjustments, what new groupings and solidarities, what changes in the very foundations of the most fundamental forms such as the family and the state, what permeations of new ideals into social institutions, what social responses to new scientific discoveries, will have taken place—lies beyond the power of the imagination to conceive. Men have in all ages played with social prophecies, but the distantly born future has always outwitted their dreams.

[1] *The rapidity of social change:* A thousand years is but a moment in the history of the earth, in the history of the rocks, of the species of living creatures, of human nature itself. Yet in a moment of that moment, in the course of a mere generation or two, significant changes can and do occur in human society. The society of Russia has been drastically reconstituted in the time that light takes to reach us from the nearest star.

Since the outbreak of World War I numerous countries have passed through profound changes, not only in their political institutions but in their class structures, their economic systems, their mores and modes of living—in short, in all the fundamental relations of man to man. Not a few countries have undergone successive transformations of this sort. These changes are so portentous that no one who lived in the year 1914 could possibly have predicted them. Our own country has been sheltered from the more extreme impacts of this time of troubles, but even so it has experienced far-reaching change, in social legislation, in economic conditions, in the relations of group to group as each seeks opportunity or advantage, in the attitudes of the people toward great social and economic issues, in many new experiences and reactions arising out of the costs and challenges of unprecedented warfare, in the utterly new responsibilities that have come to it as one of the two outstanding powers in a world seething with division, privation, and unrest.

For reasons that we shall discuss later, contemporary society appears to be unusually unstable, but history witnesses to the changefulness that besets all societies. Of all the objects we can study, none changes so rapidly before our very eyes as the works of man, and particularly the social structures which he builds. Of all sciences, none is so dependent upon—and so embarrassed by—its changing historical content as is the science of society. For the astronomer, for the physicist, even for the biologist, the territory he explores has remained essentially the same since men first sought to be scientists. Though here, too, all is process; yet for purposes of study the past stays past even as the present stays present. Even a subject so closely allied to sociology as is psychology has to deal with a human nature which it cannot assume to have been different in important respects a hundred, even a thousand years ago. But the territory which the sociologist explores changes even as he explores it. This fact has an important bearing both on his methods and on his results. Here at least we cannot seek for eternal laws. If we seek for laws, it must be for principles of change. And it is with such that we shall be concerned in this last Book.

[2] *Social science and prediction:* Moreover, these principles are not such that they enable us to forecast with any assurance, even over a brief period, the changes which society will undergo. The reasons for this statement will appear as we proceed. It is sometimes claimed that the power to predict is the hallmark of true science. It is a dubious claim, if prediction means the forecasting of variation, and not of recurrent uniformity or of the persistence of processes where no new factors intervene to change their direction. As we pass from the physical sciences to the biological and then to the social, the conditions are more unstable as well as more complex, and therefore the limits of prediction are increasingly narrow.

We can predict with high probability of accuracy that the beaches will be thronged in summer and empty in winter, that urban means of transportation will be most heavily utilized at particular periods of the day, that there will be a great increase of retail trade in the weeks before Christmas, that employment will be generally slack in the month of January, that the mortality rate will be relatively high in February, and so forth. But we cannot with any assurance predict long-term trends or the particular events of future years. The number of variables is too great and their relation to one another is too uncertain. We can predict in the fullest sense only where certain factors can be isolated so that they form a sufficient system by themselves and where the relation of each factor to the rest follows a precise quantitative formula.[1]

1. On this subject consult Harold A. Phelps, *Principles and Laws of Sociology* (New York, 1936), Chap. XXI.

[3] *Society and the time-process:* Moreover, social phenomena are historical phenomena in a profounder sense than any other. This point is a hard one to grasp, but if the student perceives it he will understand aright why precise and unconditional prediction in sociology is impracticable, not merely on account of our inadequate knowledge but on account of the very nature of our subject matter. Society exists only as a time-sequence. It is a becoming, not a being; a process, not a product. In other words, *as soon as the process ceases, the product disappears.* The product of a machine endures after the machine has been scrapped. The "everlasting hills" are the product of forces that now are spent. The fossil lives on for ages although the life that created it was transitory. In all these instances the product is separable from the process and continues to exist apart altogether from the forces that gave it its form and character. In degree the same is true not only of the material relics of man's past culture but even of his immaterial cultural achievements. They are products that are transmitted down the generations, such as the Homeric poems; and in so far as human nature retains the same capacities, they remain a vehicle by which past generations communicate with the present. The process that created them has vanished, the product endures, and, enduring, has no inner history. But an institution or a class system is a product that endures only in the process that creates it. If people no longer observe a custom, the custom no longer exists on the face of the earth. It has no body that remains after it dies. It exists only as a mode of activity, patterned in the minds of those who follow it. A mode of relationship cannot be abstracted from the life of which it is an expression. A social structure cannot be placed in a museum to save it from the ravages of time. The class system of Homeric days could no more stand still than the age of a living creature. It could not be preserved for later ages in the sense in which the Homeric poems were preserved.

The illustration we have just given will also show the importance of distinguishing the study of society from the study of culture or of civilization. The latter embody themselves in products which persist and exercise an influence by their continued presence, while the society in which they arose lives on only as a *changing equilibrium of present relationships.* Social change is therefore a distinct thing from cultural or civilizational change, entering in a different way into the time process. Once more we must insist that our direct concern as sociologists is with social relationships. It is the change in these which alone we shall regard as social change. When we speak of social evolution we shall not mean human evolution, but only an aspect of it, nor shall we mean cultural evolution, but only a concomitant of it.

How we are to study social change. A social structure is a nexus of *present* relationships. It lives only as it is maintained by the will of social beings in the present. It is upheld from moment to moment, as were the hands of Moses by

Aaron and Hur. It is like a web that exists only as it is newly spun. If it seems to persist through time, it is because the attitudes and interests of social beings persist so that they maintain its continuous existence. The most sacrosanct and seeming-permanent institutions exist by no other right and in no other strength than that which they derive from the social beings who feel and think and act in accord with them. If the conditions of human life were unchanging, then might the social structure be unchanging also. But these conditions are always unstable. There are primitive societies which we think of as stationary, partly because we know less about their past, partly because, owing to the limits of their control over nature, their relative seclusion, their smaller size and therefore greater homogeneity, the changes that occur are slower and less determinate. But it would be unwise to assume that they are really unchanging, and that the crust of custom, on which writers like Maine and Bagehot laid such stress, holds them inexorably. People have similarly spoken of the "unchanging East," but their judgment was biased by their cultural aloofness; and it has been thoroughly refuted by the great social transformations that have more recently been taking place in China, India, Japan, Indonesia, Turkey, and other Eastern lands.

Our theme is the changing ways in which human beings relate themselves to one another, the processes which institutions and organizations undergo, the transformations of the social structure and the forces that bring them about. We shall seek to show how the social system changes in response to the changing conditions on which it depends. We are not undertaking the immense task of tracing the history of mankind or even the history of society. Instead, our object is to suggest and exemplify a method of *interpreting* social change. We are taking one aspect of human history, the sociological aspect, and endeavoring to explain its relation to the main factors in the total human situation. These main factors have their own modes and conditions of change, and for the reasons given in the preceding paragraphs we regard social change as essentially a response to their changes. In accordance with our previous analysis, we shall classify these factors under three main heads: (1) the order of "nature" or of external causality, (2) the utilitarian, and particularly the technological order, and (3) the cultural order. The first of these orders here comprises all those factors of change which exist independently of human or social activity.

The Permanent Conditions of Social Change

Interdepedence of the factors underlying social change. Every change in man's relation to his environment means some change in his relation to his fellows. A new machine, for example, dictates a new division of labor. Men sit side by side on the same assembly line while they previously worked at separate benches. Hundreds of men do different jobs to construct one automobile, whereas one man could fashion a horse-drawn cart. So far the social change is a by-product of man's effort to control his external conditions. But the change does not end there. Child labor laws or labor unions are not a necessary consequence of the use of machinery. Thus in modifying his environment man sets up a double process of social change. Certain social relationships are imposed *on him* by his civilization, others are imposed *by him* on his civilization. Moreover, there are springs of change that lie deeper than either the direct or the indirect results of man's changing relation to his environment. The cultural values of every social group are incessantly at work to adjust the outer environment to their demands; to control, devise, and direct the technological means; and to win in the conflict with opposing cultural values. There are thus instabilities inherent in the very nature of society. We may set out accordingly the following ever-present conditions of social change, passing from the more external to those that are inherent in the conditions of social life.

[1] *The physical environment:* We begin with the physical environment. The surface of our planet is never at rest. There are slow geographical changes as well as the occasional convulsions of nature in storm, earthquake, and flood. Besides the seasonal variations of climate there are longer alternations of weather conditions, secular variations of temperature, humidity, prevailing winds, and beyond these the epochal changes which raise and submerge portions of the earth's surface, which bring ice ages and thaw them out again, and so forth. Since such changes are practically unaffected by human activity, the social changes they initiate may be regarded solely as adaptational responses. Here, and here alone, we find one-way causation.

The difference is clear when we turn to another order of environmental changes. Most of us have seen abandoned lumber towns or mining camps or depopulated farming areas. The natural resources of these regions have been impoverished or exhausted, and the social life has ebbed away. But it was man's activity that initiated these changes. Similar changes on a larger scale have in the past profoundly affected great areas of civilization and changed the whole future of human society. All round the shores of the eastern Mediterranean, in southern Italy, Greece, Palestine, Egypt, and westward toward Morocco, a long process of dessication and soil impoverishment has taken place, changing not only the centers of population, the routes of trade, and the seats of empire, but also the modes of culture and the whole system of social institutions. In the regions where once the power of Arabia, Persia, Babylonia, and Assyria flourished, similar processes have occurred. How far these changes were due to man's ignorance of scientific agriculture, to his destruction of the forests, to his devastation of the land in peace and in war, entailing unforeseen consequences of drought or giving opportunity to insect pests and other injurious influences, and how far to the operation of climatic changes outside man's activity, remains a difficult question.[2] Every civilization is exploitative of the resources of its environment. Its continuance depends, among other things, on its ability to conserve or replace these resources or to find substitutes for them. Our own civilization has reached a stage of control where it can almost maintain the fertility of the soil while satisfying its present agricultural needs, but it has as yet found no adequate means of replenishing the sources of power which it derives from the exhaustible supplies of oil and coal, nor is there an endless stock of the metals, such as iron and copper, which it finds so necessary.

Nevertheless, the advance of science reveals new sources and kinds of power that promise to extend beyond previous conception man's control over his physical environment. The harnessing of atomic energy may well inaugurate an industrial revolution beside which the revolution that was set in motion in the eighteenth century, associated with the harnessing of steam, may shrink to small proportions. And if the earlier revolution provoked vast social changes, this new one may bring more stupendous transformations. For example, it may possibly render obsolete, at length, all our present economic systems, whether we call them socialist or capitalist. All our present modes of organizing production assume a relative scarcity that may no longer exist. This may still seem visionary, and no doubt the road of change, to whatever goals, will be beset by new hazards and new problems. We cannot predict the changes that lie ahead. We can be sure that they will be enormous.[3]

[2] *The biological conditions:* Another source of social change lies in the biological conditions of social continuity; of the perpetuation, growth, or decline of the population, the race, or the stock; of the succession of the generations of men. We have already touched on one aspect of this theme in our discussion of land and population. Here we shall briefly refer to some others. All life, except the very simplest, arises from crossing, from intermixture, so that every new life is a different distribution of qualities and potencies. For mankind, being plastic, not instinct-bound like the lower animals, therefore variable, this mingling and crossing of hereditary factors is a guarantee of change. We tend to think of heredity as a conservative force, but it is also the basis of variation. Moreover, heredity is a selective agency. In the combination of the male and female unit characters, or genes, that determine the innate character of the new life, the biological mechanism, rejecting half of the

2. Some writers place much stress on inevitable climatic and geographical changes, as E. Huntington in *World Power and Evolution* (New Haven, 1919) and other works. V. G. Simkhovitch has, on the other hand, traced the effects on Roman society of soil impoverishment through unscientific agriculture ("Hay and History," *Political Science Quarterly*, XXVIII [1913], 385–403). Another aspect of the unsuccessful "struggle with nature" is suggested in Jones's study of the etiology and consequences of malaria in Greece (W. H. S. Jones, *Malaria and Greek History* [Manchester, 1909]).

3. See, for example, Boris Pregel, "Peacetime Uses of Atomic Energy," *Social Research*, XIV (1947), 27–43.

unit characters of each of the germ cells, allows for a vast amount of diversity between the children of the same parents as well as between parents and children generally. And there are selective processes of various kinds determining who shall be parents, and to what extent. The combined action of intermixture and selection makes it impossible that society should be really static. Because of them no new generation can ever be an exact replica of the old. In a small homogeneous society these principles have less scope, but in a complex society with all its avenues of communication, the range of potential variation is vastly increased.

What makes these biological factors of change so important in human society is that they co-operate with the other factors of change initiated and developed by social beings as such. In this connection we must remember that apart from considerations of intermixture and selection altogether, each new generation is a new beginning. Even were it a replica of what the old once was, it starts with new energies in an altered world. What has already been done furnishes a basis for its own doing. The older generations transmit to the younger, with additions and modifications, the social heritage but, for better or for worse, they do not transmit their *experience* as well. The social heritage is cumulative, though here too there is selection and rejection. The greater the social heritage, the greater, too, the potentiality of change. Herein again human society differs from that of the lower animals. For they, having no accumulated possessions, no instruments they can improve, no culture they can modify, cannot build on the past any more than they can reject it. In human society, with its social heritage, the young cannot do over again just what the old have already done. It is part of the meaning of that heritage that no young life can be content with simple habituation to the conditions which once-young life has established. No matter what the direction, it must go a yet untraveled road.

In another sense, also, the biological conditions change and prepare the way for social change. At all times populations have increased and decreased, but in civilized society a new factor of instability is introduced because of the way the birth rate and the death rate alike respond to the new techniques and the changing valuations of civilized man. In most countries, two centuries ago, five or six or more births per marriage were needed to maintain the population; now in some countries three suffice. With the decline of the death rate and the birth rate the average age of the population has been increasing. The new controls over both birth rate and death rate have constantly been changing the composition of the population. It is not likely that the Western world will again present the phenomenon still witnessed in rural Russia, where an average of seven children per family has been recorded; but the way in which the new controls will work will, like all human controls, be subject to constant change in conformity to new conditions and to the consequences of past changes.

[3] *The technological order:* We turn now to the conditions of social change that are definitely created by man's own activities. In the endeavor to satisfy

his wants man builds up a civilization. In utilizing all manner of techniques he provokes social changes far more extensive and profound than ever he intended. It is as when we build a new house and discover afterward that we must change our settled habits to live in it. Here, then, is another source of social instability. In devising new means to satisfy old wants, we stimulate new wants as well. When only a few generations ago the steam engine was made to work for man, neither the inventors nor the users realized that they were precipitating great social changes which would overturn old customs and institutions, old political systems and even old faiths. When the telephone and the automobile and the radio were made practicable, men did not dream of the ways in which these inventions would influence the life of the family. In a study of the influence of the radio, Professor W. F. Ogburn lists one hundred and fifty "effects" which it has had on social life, ranging from a modest encouragement of "morning exercises" to "cultural diffusion among nations."[4] We should, however, be careful not to assume that the radio, or any other device, has the same "effects" under all conditions. Much depends on the scheme of values already operative in the various social situations into which the new invention is introduced. The radio, for example, can become an agency to promote international goodwill or, if powerful governments so decide, a means of keeping the nations apart, suspicious, and misinformed. Nevertheless, the social repercussions of technological advance are so far reaching and so momentous that some sociologists, such as Veblen, regard them as the main explanation of social change.

Man's utilitarian devices are also in a different way responsible for social change. In order to apply these devices effectively it is often necessary to establish new social relations. A hundred men can work side by side with pick and shovel, but when the steam shovel came along the men required to operate it had to assume their several definite functions in accordance with the specific requirements of the mechanism. Every change in the processes of production, every new attempt to utilize means either for private or for public gains, involves a new alignment of the human beings engaged in it. The nature and disposition of the machinery in a plant determine in degree the tasks and relations of the workers, but the management organizes and reorganizes these tasks and relations, changing the machinery in the process and sometimes preparing the way for the introduction and even the invention of new machines. In the plant the objective of the management is simple and predetermined. In a society a myriad of objectives, concordant and conflicting, are present. Man's desire to control nature is itself directed by his ulterior desire to express his

---

4. *Recent Social Trends* (New York, 1933), I, 152–157. For a critical discussion, see R. M. MacIver, *Social Causation* (Boston, 1942), pp. 358–362. For further illustrations, see W. F. Ogburn, *Social Change* (New York, 1922), Part II; F. S. Chapin, *Cultural Change* (New York, 1928), Chaps. VIII–XI; and particularly Karl Mannheim, *Man and Society in an Age of Reconstruction* (New York, 1940), pp. 243ff.

own nature. Every new invention changes his opportunity to do so and thereby brings about changes in the social system.

There is a further reason why, particularly in modern society, technological change should be a powerful source of social change. As we shall show in Chapter XXIX, one difference between a primitive and a civilized society is that in the latter a great many things become merely or purely utilitarian, merely instruments or means. Now when anything is thought of merely as a means, people try to improve it as a means—they constantly experiment with it to make it more efficient. An automobile engine is such a means, and it is changed almost every year. But a constitution is not regarded in the same way because of its cultural implications; only in times of crisis and then with difficulty is it liable to change in any important respects. The primitive mind regards the techniques and instruments of everyday use in the way that, among ourselves, the majority of people regard the Constitution. But with us, technology has become detached, for the most part, from cultural limitations. It changes very rapidly. One indication is that in the five years ending 1845 the number of patents in the United States was 2,425, whereas in the five years ending 1930 the number was 219,384.[5] One consequence of this free application of inventiveness is, for reasons we have already suggested, a more unstable and changeful social system.

[4] *The cultural order:* As we shall see later, we cannot assume that man's valuations are merely responsive to influences from without or in particular to his own changing techniques. These valuations are themselves intrinsically forces operative to direct social change. Different countries, for example, like the United States, Japan, and Russia, may adopt the same technology, but in so far as their prevalent outlook on life differs, they will apply it in different directions and to different ends. Industrialization and urbanization are only in part a response to the primary necessities of man's organic being under the conditions created by the advance of the arts; they assume a variety of forms and directions determined also by the variety of his cultural interests.

It is in the very nature of culture to undergo change. *In one aspect, culture is valuation; in another, it is expression.* Valuations change with changing experience, whether the experience brings satisfaction or dissatisfaction. Every age has its own valuations, its own appraisement of the things worth while, revealed in its literature, in its thought-forms, in the "social movements" that characterize it. These change with the times. What appeals to the fathers no longer appeals to the children. Moreover, the mode of expression, the *style* of culture, is inherently changeful. The law of style is a law of change, in the fine arts, in philosophies, in ideals, as well as in mere fashions of the popular sort. No mode of expression ever fully or finally attains the goal it seeks; and if for a time it satisfies, there comes a later time, a new generation, when it ceases to satisfy.

5. *Recent Social Trends*, Vol. I, Chap. III.

Moreover, within every complex community there is a great diversity of cultural interests. The valuations, the motivations, the mores, of its constituent groups large and small—families, classes, occupational groups, religious groups, and so forth—are at variance and often in conflict. Each seeks influence, prestige, control, partly at the expense of others. In this conflict of values each group seizes the opportunities of the changing situation to promote its own. Every change of circumstance, every advantage accidental or contrived, changes the status of groups with respect to one another. Trends develop according as conditions favor the relative success of this group or that. The United States affords particularly good illustrations of the changing relations of group to group. Besides the pressures exercised by numerous economic groups and apart from the broader issues that rise between organized workers and organized employers, there are the struggles of subordinated groups seeking greater opportunity or more equal social status—Negroes, Orientals, Latin-Americans, Eastern Europeans, and so forth—over against dominant groups that discriminate against them.[6] On a broader scale, whole communities, even whole civilizations, are, in relation to one another, subject to similar trends. Thus in some periods, ideas of liberty and democracy gain dominance over wide areas, and in others, ideas of discipline and centralized order; in some periods religious orthodc prevails and in others religious nonconformity and the right of the individual "conscience"; in some periods, women are regarded as the equal partners of men, and in others, they are relegated by the dominant mores to the domain of "children, church, and cuisine." These changing valuations are no doubt influenced by the technological factors, but it is a mere assumption that they are wholly determined thus.

The task before us. We have now mentioned the main factors that conspire to make society, the system of social relationships, so incessantly changeful. Viewing these factors together, we see two great questions emerge, to which the rest of this volume will be devoted. First, can we elucidate the role of each of these factors in bringing about social change, together with its relation to the other factors that enter into the total changing situation? Second, can we trace any direction, any continuity of meaning, in the multitude of changes to which society is forever subject? But before we attack these questions it will be well to deal with some preparatory points regarding the various modes or types in which social change presents itself.

6. See *Unity and Difference in American Life* (R. M. MacIver, ed., New York, 1947).

23

The Ways of Social Change

Patterns of Change

Order and change. Since change is so incessant, so hard to predict, and so manifold, we must, if we are to grasp it at all, seek to discover some kind of order in change itself. The first thing to notice is that different subjects of change have their own particular ways of undergoing change. We shall here distinguish three patterns characteristically associated with particular subjects.

[1] *Three types of change:* ONE: Take an invention, for example. It seems to be born suddenly, but before it is announced to the world there is generally a long series of preparatory steps, and once it reaches the stage of practicality and exploitation, there commences another long series of cumulative improvements. This process is illustrated by the history of the telephone, the automobile, the airplane, the radio, and so forth. What is distinctive of this mode of change is not its suddenness but the continuous cumulative development of a utilitarian device, until perhaps it is discarded altogether by some new device that has also undergone a similar process.[1] As we have seen, this continuity of direction is characteristic of technological change in general. Somewhat similar is the type of change which a science undergoes. The area of knowledge constantly increases, and the science tends toward greater coherence and integration, partially disturbed from time to time by revolutionary discoveries or theories that prepare the way for a completer synthesis of its material. The growth of the science of biology in the nineteenth century, for the most part gradual but suddenly accelerated by the theories of Darwin and by the discoveries of Mendel, may serve as an example.

TWO: The mode of change just mentioned can be represented graphically by a line that always slopes upward, though with constantly varying angles of

1. For illustrations see W. F. Ogburn, *Social Change* (New York, 1922), Part II, and F. S. Chapin, *Cultural Change* (New York, 1928), Chaps. VIII–XI.

ascent. Its relative permanence of direction distinguishes it from another mode of change which traces an upward line for a time but which is liable to reversals of direction. This mode of change is characteristic of economic phenomena and over longer periods of the phenomena of population. Cities grow and then decline, international trade advances and falls off, business activity rises, booms, and then slumps. In the first mode of change there is a practical certainty that, at whatever pace, the same direction at least will be maintained, both over long and over short periods. In the second mode there is no such assurance.

THREE: Somewhat similar to the second is a third mode of change. Seeking to represent it we resort to a wavelike curve. Many phenomena, alike of nature and of human society, are thought of as following a cyclical course. The variations of business activity are frequently referred to as the economic cycle. The illustrations offered by nature herself are perhaps more convincing—the orbital motions of atoms and of planets, the regular sequence of the seasons, the precession of the equinoxes, the succession of barometric "highs" and "lows," and so forth. Sometimes the term "cyclical" is applied to the process that the individual organism reveals from birth through to maturity and then to decline and death—and there have been many thinkers who have regarded societies and civilizations as pursuing a similar course. Sometimes it is applied to the rhythm of successive ups and downs that repeats itself without definite beginning or ending, like that of the waves, and this pattern, too, many thinkers have thought they discovered in human affairs, in political movements of conservatism and radicalism, in long-range changes of population, in the tides of fashion, in the mores that are by turns more repressive and more free.[2]

These three types of change may therefore be represented as in Chart XIX.

[2] *Complications of change:* There are, of course, many types of change that cannot be represented by such simple diagrams. There are qualitative changes of various kinds that are not measurable in quantitative units, and these become more important as we pass from technology to culture. Even in the technological field the invasion of the cultural element complicates the processes of change. Thus a new invention mimics at first the older device that it replaces—as the automobile imitated the horse-drawn carriage—and then gradually establishes its own type. If the device belongs to the class of "consumers' goods," then style changes will accompany, and sometimes interfere with, advances in efficiency. Wherever cultural values enter in, the way of change becomes complex and objectively indeterminate. Those parts of our civilization that are remote from final valuations move in a different way from those that are more subject to their influence. The science of electrical engineering has a more direct path to follow than has the art of politics.

---

2. For more detailed examples see P. Sorokin, *Society, Culture, and Personality* (New York, 1947), Part VII.

CHART XIX **Three Types of Change**

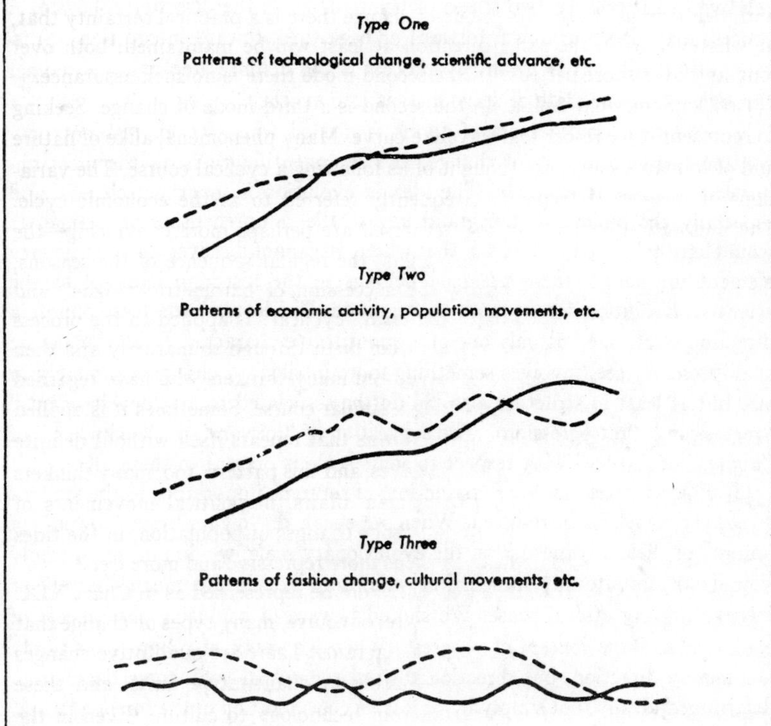

Terms signifying modes of change. We must next distinguish various terms which connote a mode or quality of change. The term "change" itself is wholly neutral, implying nothing but a difference through time in the object to which it is applied. When we speak of "social change," we suggest so far no law, no theory, no direction, even no continuity.

[1] *Process:* The idea of continuity is introduced when we refer to a social change as a *process.* A process means continuous change taking place in a definite manner through the operation of forces present from the first within the situation. Thus we speak of the "group process," or the manner in which the relations of the members of a group, once brought together, acquire a

certain distinctive character. Sociologists are concerned, for example, with such processes as accommodation, integration, disintegration, disorganization, and so forth. In studying a process we observe a series of transitions between one state of being and another. There is no necessary implication as to the relative quality of the two states of being, or as to the direction followed. A process may be up or down, forward or backward, toward integration or disintegration. All that is meant by process is the definite step-by-step manner through which one state or stage merges into another.

[2] *Evolution:* Another set of terms is needed when we express not only continuity but direction of change, and for scientific purposes the most important of these is *evolution*. The idea of evolution is in other sciences, and especially the biological, the grand key to the comprehension of change. It would hardly be too much to say that where we cannot discover an evolutionary element in change, there the past belongs to the historian and not to the scientist. Evolution means more than growth. The latter term does connote a direction of change but only one of a quantitative character. Evolution, as we shall presently see, involves something more intrinsic, a change not merely in size but at least in structure also. So do the associated terms "development," "regression," "retrogression." The suggestion of "forward" or "backward," of "higher" or "lower" with respect to some scale is present in them all.

[3] *Progress:* Here another distinction, of supreme importance to the student of society, must be introduced. When we speak of "higher" and "lower," of "more" or "less advanced," on the evolutionary scale, we do not, or certainly should not, impute any standard of valuation. We do not mean "better" or "worse" in any ethical sense. We should beware of confusing the *concept* of evolution and the *concept* of progress. When we speak of progress we imply not merely direction, but direction toward some final goal, some destination determined ideally, not simply by objective consideration of the forces at work. What defines this goal is the value-judgment of the spectator, not the inevitability of causation. It may be that the evolutionary process moves in accord with our conception of desirable change, but there is no *logical* necessity that it should, and in any event the judgment of final value varies with the mentality and experience of the individual and the group, whereas the process of evolution is objectively given, waiting only to be discovered and understood. If the process so revealed satisfies also *our* sense of values, if the direction of evolutionary change brings also a fuller realization of the values we cherish, then *for us* it is also progress.

[4] *Adaptation, etc.:* There remains a group of terms which signify not the change of one object or system in itself but the changing relation of two or more objects or systems to one another. These terms are often wrongly equated with the terms of the last two groups. They are "adaptation," "adjustment," "accommodation," "assimilation," and their negatives. To these we may add such vaguer terms as "harmony." We have already dwelt on their meaning.

We should note, however, that the positive terms cannot as such *mean* either evolution or progress. They signify merely that the two objects conform to one another within a common process, but whether that process should be named evolution or progress or something else altogether remains thereby undetermined. Adaptation, for example, does not *mean* evolution. There is not the slightest reason to regard the lowest forms of life as less adapted to their environment than are the highest forms. The amoeba can certainly claim to be as well adjusted to its life conditions as is civilized man to his.

We sum up these preliminary distinctions in Chart XX.

CHART XX Terms Signifying Modes of Change

I. Determinate continuous change	***Process*** **Movement, etc.**
II. Determinate continuous change in a specific direction	
(a) quantitatively defined, with respect to size	***Growth*** **Accumulation, etc.**
(b) qualitatively defined, with respect to structural or functional differentiation	***Evolution*** **Development** **Regression** **Retrogression**
(c) qualitatively defined, with respect to its conformity to a standard of value	***Progress*** **Decline** **Decay** **Decadence** **Degeneration**
(d) defined by reference to some other object or system, with respect to their compatibility within a common process	***Adaptation*** **Adjustment** **Accommodation** **Assimilation** **Harmony** **and their contradictories**

Application to Society of Various Concepts of Change

Processes of social change. In every society numerous processes of change are occurring simultaneously. Here adjustment is established and here conflict breaks down adjustment. Here dominance is attained, and here overthrown. Here there is revolution and here quiescence. Here men aspire to new goals, and here they return to old ones. In all this change can we discover any movement of the whole, of society conceived as a unity, whether in terms of a nation, or culture area, or a large civilization? Does society itself, however we define its limits, undergo any processes of change, and if so, have they any specific character or direction? This is a question many thinkers have sought to answer, and we shall here indicate briefly the nature of the answers that have most frequently been offered. Perhaps the oldest is that which conceives social change as following, over sufficiently large periods, a cyclical course.[3]

[1] *Social change as cyclical process:* It is a common reflection that all life, in fact all being, exhibits recurrent rhythmic movement. Many illustrations lie near to us, the beat of the heart, the intake and exhalation of the breath, the recurrent appetites, the succession of the seasons, and the processes of organic growth and decline. Our mechanisms mimic the pulsations of the organism. The skies themselves move in rhythmic periods of the day, the year, and the mightier cycles of the outer cosmos. At the other extreme the scientist conceives the atom as an infinitesimal system of rhythmic motion, electrons forever revolving round a nucleus The pulsations which thus permeate the universe seem to have their counterpart in social phenomena, in the seasonal rhythms of the volume of employment, the frequency of crime, the number of marriages, births, and deaths, and in the longer, less predictable oscillations of prosperity, population growth, fashion trends, political attitudes, and so forth. And if this rhythmic movement affects the particular phenomena of social life, may it not also be revealed in the total being of society?

The most impressive of these rhythms is that which has a definite beginning and ending, the closed cycle of birth and death forever repeated within the life of the species. This theme is renewed on the vast scale of the cosmos.

Worlds on worlds are rolling ever
From creation to decay.

A rhythm so momentous to human beings, themselves manifestations of it, has a peculiar attraction for the interpreter of social change. In all ages men have found a correspondence between the course of the individual life and that of the group, the nation, the empire, the civilization. "Sceptre and crown must tumble down" in fulfillment of the like destiny of all that lives. Generally this principle is merely a form of the inadequate organic analogy, and as such we have dealt with it elsewhere.[4] But sometimes other concepts of a more fruitful nature are combined with it, as we shall see later when we take up the cultural conditions of social change.

[2] *Social change as evolutionary process:* In recent times the evolutionary concept has been applied in diverse ways to the interpretation of social change, sometimes rather superficially and sometimes in a more penetrating and revealing fashion. Even in the ancient world the idea that society evolved occasionally caught the imagination of men, as is witnessed to, for example, by the account of the rise of humanity given in the *Prometheus* of Sophocles and in the remarkable poem by Lucretius, *On the Nature of Things.* But it was after the triumphant advance of evolutionary biology led by Darwin in the middle of

3. For a list of cyclical theories, see Sorokin, *op. cit.*, Chap. XLV.

4. See Chapter III. See also R. M. MacIver, *Community* (New York, 1920). Book III, Chap. II, and Appendix; and the same author's *The Modern State* (Oxford, 1926), Chap. X.

the nineteenth century that the evolutionary clue began to be persistently followed by students of society. Herbert Spencer was a leader in this movement, although his somewhat hasty generalizations have not, for the most part, stood the test of time. This fact has led to a revulsion among sociologists that unduly depreciates the social significance of the evolutionary principle.

Evolution is literally "unrolling," a process in which hidden or latent aspects or characters of a thing reveal themselves. It is an order of change which unfolds the variety of aspects belonging to the nature of the changing object, in which potentialities lying within it are made actual. Evolution cannot properly be predicated of anything whose nature is already completely revealed in the present. Nor can we speak of evolution when an object or system is changed merely by forces acting on it from without. The change must occur within the changing unity, as the manifestation of forces operative within it, so as to constitute a fuller revelation through time of its own capacities. Since, however, nothing is independent of the universe about it, evolution is a process involving at the same time a changing adaptation of the object to its environment and a further manifestation of its own nature. Consequently it is a change permeating the whole character of the object, a sequence in which the equilibrium of its entire structure undergoes modification.

We have not yet stated the primary feature of the evolutionary process, the essential criterion of its presence. The term "evolution" is often loosely used to signify any process of becoming, the series of transitions between two stages of the existence of anything. In more scientific usage it is still applied with somewhat varying significance to different types of object, though with a common core of meaning. Thus we speak of the evolution of an individual organism, of the evolution of a species, and of the evolution of life through different species. We speak also of the evolution of the earth, or the solar system, or the cosmos itself. We speak again of the evolution of any established system, though here the term loses its sharpness, for generally we mean no more than the process by which it has become established.

The distinctive character of the evolutionary process. The concept of evolution gained its wide modern vogue as a result of its successful application in the field of biology. When Charles Darwin wrote of "the evolution of species," he traced a process by which the multiplicity of organic types emerged from earlier, fewer, less differentiated forms of life. The particular mechanistic explanation of this process which Darwin offered may or may not be valid, but the scheme of evolution which he so clearly traced does not stand or fall with any theory of the manner in which it has come about.

[1] *The principle of differentiation:* The scheme itself is corroborated by myriad evidences; the scientific issue is no more the reality of biological evolution but the causal interpretation of it. The basis of the scheme is the correlation of the time-order with the order of appearance of more complex or

more differentiated species. Many divergences occur, many collateral variations which do not exemplify this primary correlation, but it remains the nucleus of the grand plan of organic evolution. It is not, of course, implied that the later in appearance is necessarily the more evolved, but only that the more evolved is later in appearance than the less evolved and proceeds from it by means of the variations somehow emerging in the interplay of heredity and environment. The kernel of organic evolution is therefore ***differentiation***, the process in which latent or rudimentary characters take on distinct and variable forms within the unity of the organism, giving rise to new and more complex types of life. We shall find presently that a similar principle has great significance for the study of society. We shall find, too, that the differentiation of structure must be related to the differentiation of function.

In this quest we shall not follow the dangerous method of analogy. Reliance on this method has impaired the contribution of Herbert Spencer and other sociologists who have followed the evolutionary clew. There are many unities of systems which reveal a process of differentiation, but the process itself varies with the nature of the subject which undergoes it. Thus differentiation occurs:

(a) Where the subject is the whole organic order, life itself as we know it, branching out into its genera and species;

(b) Where the subject is a particular species, as it undergoes further differentiation or as new subspecies or varieties emerge from a single earlier type—we speak, for example, of the evolution of the horse from the eohippos through to the modern forms;

(c) Where the subject is an individual organism, as it develops from the fertilized ovum to the full-grown being;

(d) Where the subject is any unity or system that passes through a series of changes in which it takes on a more articulated form, or variety of forms, in correspondence with greater specificity of function.

Society falls in the last of these groups, and there has been a constant danger of confusing it with one—or all at the same time—of the other three. For example, it is often treated as if it fell at the same time into both group (b) and group (c), a confusion appearing in the pages of Spencer and many other writers. We should observe particularly the difference between these two groups as subjects of evolution. Group (b) exhibits an evolutionary process which has no determinate limits, whereas the process in group (c) is bounded by the life of the individual organism. A species maintains its existence by the reproduction of its members; an individual organism is not self-perpetuating but only a factor in race-perpetuation. An individual organism therefore grows old and is always at some stage in the process from youth to age; its evolution is the expression of an initial life-energy within it. None of these statements can properly be predicated of a species, and it is only a hazardous guess which claims that they are true of other self-perpetuating unities, such as communities or even the social systems which they create.

All organisms grow old and die, and though life has flowed on, some species have become extinct. We have found in differentiation the clew to the evolutionary order, but when the process of decline toward death or extinction sets in, differentiation ceases and some counterprocess takes its place. Or again, a species, once self-maintaining, becomes parasitic, like the duckweeds in the vegetable kindom, and some of its evolved organs degenerate. Shall we then include within the meaning of evolution those reverse tendencies? It seems simpler to do so. Decay and parasitism, whether in a species or in a society, are never simple reversals of a former trend, mere returns to an earlier stage. Age is never, literally, second childhood. From the beginning to the end, new aspects of the nature of the organic being appear. We find in differentiation the clew to evolution and we can therefore also call evolutionary any process which comprises both differentiation and some sequel of differentiation, which includes an "upward" and a consequent "downward" course. When it is desirable to specify an "upward" course only, a process, that is, of increasing differentiation, we can use the appropriate term "development."

[2] *Application to society:* We are now in a position to see what evolution means in its social reference. Wherever in the history of society we find an increasing specialization of organs or units within the system or serving the life of the whole, we can speak of *social evolution*. Observe that such specialization does not mean simply more complexity and is not equivalent to the appearance of mere novelty, for to meet our sense of differentiation such complexity or novelty must be integrated within the social structure, or—what we shall see is here another aspect of the same principle—must contribute to the interrelation of function between the whole and the parts. A diseased condition of the organism may involve additional complexity and introduce new phenomena, but no one would call this an evolutionary process.

Often it is said that evolution is a process of differentiation *and* integration, but the term "differentiation," properly understood, connotes integration. In a society it manifests itself in such ways as the following: (a) a greater division of labor, so that the energy of more individuals is concentrated on more specific tasks and so that thereby a more elaborate system of co-operation, a more intricate nexus of functional relationships, is sustained within the group; (b) an increase in the number and the variety of functional associations and institutions, so that each is more defined or more limited in the range or character of its service; and (c) a greater diversity and refinement in the instruments of social communication, perhaps above all in the medium of language. We may regard the last of these conditions as rather a mark than a mode of differentiation, but as the history of language can often be more accurately traced than the life history of those who spoke it, it is obviously a record of very great importance for the study of the earlier evolution of different peoples and of the same people at different stages.

Various sociologists have laid stress on one or another of these aspects of evolution. Thus Durkheim has insisted on the pre-eminent importance of the social division of labor as a criterion of social development.[5] Other writers have taken the various aspects together and sought to show that society passes through a definite series of evolutionary stages.[6] An extreme example of this procedure is the work of the German sociologist F. Müller-Lyer.[7]

Social change as progress. In the earlier theories of biological evolution the ideas of evolution and of progress were closely associated. This association was emphasized by Darwin's conception of the "survival of the fittest" in the evolutionary process. A similar optimistic note was struck by the majority of the social evolutionists of the nineteenth century, from Comte to Herbert Spencer and Lester Ward. For them social evolution was, in effect, social progress. The rapid technological and industrial advance of the nineteenth century was another consideration that led many philosophers, historians, and sociologists to the position that the major trends of social phenomena made for social progress.

Any of us is free to hold this position—or to deny it—because our view of what constitutes progress depends on our desires and our ideals, and one man's desires and ideals are different from another's. What we are not free to do is to maintain that evolution *means* progress, that because a society is more evolved, *therefore* it is more progressive. It does not follow that the people who maintain the more evolved system are "better" or better fitted to survive, or more moral or more healthy or more happy than those we call primitive. Even if the opposite were true, it would not refute the fact that their society is more evolved. The place of a people on the evolutionary scale does not depend on our ethical judgments. There must be, of course, some relation between the character of the social structure and the kind of life which is lived within it. But this correlation can, and for scientific purposes should, be expressed in terms that do not depend on our particular ideals or sympathies or prejudices.

[1] *Why evolution must be distinguished from progress:* Differentiation, where it occurs, is an evolutionary fact. We can therefore, provided we have the knowledge, classify different societies with entire objectivity as more or less highly evolved. We cannot be accused of arbitrary or subjective valuations when we say that a civilized society is more highly evolved than that of the Eskimos. But if we claim also that civilized life is a better one, the case is different. The Eskimo might deny it—where is the common ground on which we can meet to decide between us? If our life better satisfies our ideals, so does his life his—who then is the arbiter of ideals? Moreover, we do not ourselves agree that civilization is better. Some deny it, and again who is to judge be-

5. *The Division of Labor in Society* (G. Simpson, tr., New York, 1933).

6. For a classification of stage theories see M. Ginsberg, *Studies in Sociology* (London, 1932), Chap. V.

7. *History of Social Development* (Eng. tr., London, 1923).

tween us? If the rest of us affirm it, are these not equally entitled to deny it—as did the young Rousseau or Schopenhauer or Max Nordau or von Hartmann or Tolstoi or Spengler, as do the religious prophets who identify progress with the spread of a faith or with the heyday of a church, as do the hedonists who define progress as more happiness and assert that the savage is happier than the civilized man?

Or let us turn again to our Eskimos, who are very far from being "savages." They might very well claim that their society is superior to ours because, until they are "corrupted" by our civilization, they have better teeth and fewer diseases than we have, because they lead a more "natural" life, because they do not exhibit our "complexes" and our neuroses. On what scales shall we weigh our advantages against their advantages? Does it not appear that the affirmation of evolution depends on our perception of objective evidences, whereas the affirmation or denial of progress depends on our ideals, and therefore on our temperament, on our fortune in life, on our age, perhaps on the state of our liver or our digestion; in short, that evolution is a scientific concept and progress an ethical concept?

[2] *Scientific versus ethical concepts:* Now there is no necessary opposition between the scientific and the ethical attitude, for the one is directed to the comprehension of what is, and the other seeks to determine our relation to what is in such a way that what is and what is good shall so far as practicable coincide. But there is much confusion of the two attitudes, with consequent clashes. For our ethical judgments may rest on misconceptions of the scientific fact and our scientific conclusions may be warped by our ethical preconceptions. The social sciences suffer particularly from this confusion. To avoid it is a profoundly difficult task. The difficulty is twofold. In the first place, we are brought up and constantly indoctrinated in the valuations of our group. The business of living in society makes social valuations of some sort necessary. Unfortunately these vital valuations, owing alike to the prejudices of the group and to our individual misreading of experience, contain ingredients of scientific error. They rationalize the ultimate judgment, "This is good" or "This is bad" (with its corollary, "This is right" or "This is wrong"), into the relative judgment, "This is bad, because such and such results follow from it." Now the latter is a presumptive scientific judgment, in so far as it postulates a causal nexus between two phenomena. But the emotional drive of ethical ideals or social pressures often overrides the cool scientific scrutiny of the alleged causal nexus or forbids it altogether—the rationalization, for example, of the contradictory sex taboos of different cultures affords abundant illustration—and thus our science suffers.

In the second place, we cannot adopt the simpler solution of the physical sciences by keeping outside the realm of ethical valuations altogether. In a very important way these valuations, socially conditioned as they are, enter into our subject matter. Subjective themselves, they determine the objective phenomena of society. As scientists, we must endeavor to keep our own valuations from coloring our perception of social reality, but the reality we perceive is through and through permeated with the valuations of its creators. Ethical concepts have a direct power of moving the world which scientific concepts lack. In some manner they are active in every process of social change. We study, let us say, war or marriage or divorce, but the very existence of any one of these phenomena depends on a sufficient belief or disbelief in its desirability. A like statement can be made of every social organization and institution. In this respect our facts differ markedly from physical facts, and that is why we cannot dismiss valuations—or such concepts as progress—as lightly as can the physical sciences.

It is all the more important for us to distinguish carefully the two types of concept, the scientific and the ethical. It is one thing to recognize value-facts, to trace their operation, to study them as the realities they are; it is quite another to impose our own valuations on them. Democracy, dictatorship, a housing shortage, the segregation of the Negro, laws against discrimination, unemployment, a strike, an increase or a decrease of the birth rate, and so on, exist, where they are found, as objects for scientific study. They are facts, but they are also value-facts, arising out of social valuations. All social change has this double character. We should therefore not define social evolution as though it meant or implied progress. How far we find a correspondence between the direction of social evolution and the direction prescribed by our particular concept of social progress is another matter. We may properly inquire into the relationship between the two. But it is possible to do so only if we define social evolution in ethically neutral terms. Otherwise the confusion we have spoken of will be present from the start.[8]

8. See also Chapter XXVIII.

24

Biological Factors of Social Change

Demographic Change

Scope of the chapter. Since the physical environment changes but slowly except as affected by the ceaseless activity of man, we shall confine our attention, in considering the first of our three main categories of the conditions underlying social change, to the biological processes that determine the numbers, the composition, the selection, and the hereditary quality of the successive generations. These processes may themselves be set in motion by social attitudes and interests, as the latter control sex relations, marriage, racial intermixture, the size of the family, and so forth. Social behavior of various kinds induces biological changes. The population is biologically different, more numerous or less numerous, more healthy or less healthy, more fertile or less fertile, in response to socially determined conditions. Some social arrangements, such as taboos on intermarriage, restrictions on the marriage of the more fit, customs respecting the age at marriage, persecution of minorities, war, tend to lower the biological quality of the population. Others tend to raise it. The biological changes thus induced have their own causality, and in turn bring about new changes on the social level. First we shall look at some of the biological consequences of social behavior, and then we shall consider some of the larger social issues thereby raised.

Changing size of the population. The population of every community is always changing both in numbers and in composition. During the nineteenth century the population of most countries of Western Europe increased with unusual rapidity.[1] Between the period 1871-1875 and the year 1933 the birth rates of the countries of Western Europe fell from a range between 25 and 38 (per

1. For statistics, see R. R. Kuczynski, *The Measurement of Population Growth* (New York, 1936), pp. 230-231.

thousand of the population per annum) to a range between 20 and 14. During the same time the death rates of these countries fell from a range between 18 and 28 to a range between 10 and 16.[2] This double phenomenon is unprecedented in the history of man. Population changes have occurred all through human history, by reason of migration, invasion, war, pestilence, changing food supply, and changing mores. There was depopulation and overpopulation in times past. But where population increased it was not, so far as we know, associated with a decrease in the birth rate. Nor was there ever an increase so great, so rapid, so continuous, and over so great an area. We have no reliable figures for earlier times, but certainly we have no reason to believe that any previous changes were so impressive. There could have been no such doubling of the population of the whole world as happened in the century prior to World War I. There was no such quadrupling of population as took place in England in the nineteenth century. Assuredly there was nothing comparable to the growth of population in the United States since the founding of the Republic—though here immigration rather than natural increase was the major factor.

[1] *Evidences of the transformation:* The swift and steady decline of both the birth rate and the death rate in the past seventy years or so witnesses to a great social transformation. The change was particularly marked in the birth rate, though an earlier change in the death rate probably prepared the way for it. First apparent in France, it began rather abruptly in England in 1878 and in the eighties was markedly revealed in the statistics of Sweden, Denmark, Holland, and Australia. Thence it spread to the countries of Central Europe, and to America, at length including within its range, though in various degrees, every country of Western civilization. This extraordinary development was accompanied by a no less remarkable continuation of the decline of the death rate, more especially of the infant death rate. This double phenomenon is perhaps the most signal instance the world has known of the sudden emergence of new forms of social selection, or as some prefer to put it, of new interferences with natural selection.

There is, of course, a limit to the decline of both rates, and there are some evidences that the limit is in sight in certain countries. The rate of the decline of the birth rate diminishes markedly when a certain level is reached. For example, in the eighties of the last century Germany had a high birth rate (in 1876 it was nearly 41), while France, which led the movement, had what seemed an ominously low one. By 1927 the rates of the two countries were practically equal (19.5 for Germany as against 18.8 for France), but the convergence was due overwhelmingly to the fall of the German rate while the French rate moved very slowly lower. In Germany there was a minor reversion of the trend, the rate moving from 17 in 1931 to over 19 in 1938, but this

2. *Ibid.*, pp. 104–105, 162–163.

modest rise, due to special conditions aided by strong Nazi propaganda, did not signify any return to the old balance of births and deaths.

As for the death rate, the changing composition of the population under a falling birth rate must, for reasons presently to be considered, eventually end its decline, even if the application of medical science and the healthfulness of living conditions continue to advance. The changing composition of the population tends, on the other hand, to lower the birth rate still further, even though the actual fertility, as measured by the number of children born to women of childbearing age, remains constant.[3]

In no country have the changes in size of the population been more significant than in the United States. The increase has, in fact, been quite unprecedented in human history. "From about 2,500,000 in 1776, the population has increased to 122,775,046 in 1930, almost fifty fold in little more than a century and a half."[4] This growth has, of course, been due to a combination of natural increase and immigration. The conditions bringing it about are no longer operative. Net immigration to the United States fell to zero or below during the depression years and it is not likely to become an important population factor in the near future at least, owing to the severe restrictive measures that are in force. At the time of the 1940 census the total population was still increasing, though at a diminished rate. The birth rate for the United States has followed the same course as that of the countries of Western Europe and by 1934 had fallen to 17.1 for the registration area.[5]

[2] *Population problems ahead:* The facts just mentioned have led to a considerable amount of speculation, frequently of a gloomy character, regarding the future. It is rightly pointed out that a continuation of the present rates, not merely of the present trends, would mean for many countries a falling population. The United States and the countries of Western Europe are already producing fewer children than will suffice, if the birth rate does not change its course, to maintain their numbers. A falling population, it is claimed, will place the more advanced countries in a position of economic and political inferiority compared with the more prolific countries. Beyond that threat there is the ominous prospect of "race suicide."

The danger must be recognized, and the responsibility. At the same time it is important to see the problem in proper perspective. The future cannot be mechanically prognosticated by statistical projections of present trends. This method would have led to false conclusions if applied at any earlier

3. For the precise nature of this phenomenon see R. R. Kuczynski, *The Balance of Births and Deaths* (New York, 1928).

4. W. S. Thompson and P. K. Whelpton, "The Population of the Nation," in *Recent Social Trends* (New York, 1933), I, p. 1.

5. On population trends in the United States and their significance, see Frank Lorimer, Ellen Winston, and Louise K. Kiser, *Foundations of American Population Policy* (New York, 1940).

stage of the decline. We should also remember that, throughout the whole period of this decline, the actual increase of the populations of Europe and America has been enormous, and if we take instead the longer period since the decline of the death rate began, the increase has been unprecedented in human history. Since many of the consequences of this growth do not appear until after the lapse of a generation, it is not surprising, particularly in times of large-scale unemployment, that many observers are still impressed with the opposite fear, that of overpopulation. It is surely unreasonable to expect this absolute increase to continue forever. The adjustment of population to changing conditions is itself a changing adjustment and is perhaps more subtle than we generally realize. Only if the total population were seriously dwindling would the fears generated by the present stage of the process seem justified; and if that condition were to appear who can say that it would not in turn set in motion corrective forces? The history of population theories since the eighteenth century shows the precariousness of short-run interpretations and the difficulty—but also the necessity—of the long-run view. Where severe population declines have occurred in past civilizations they have been associated with war and invasion, with pestilence, or with the denudation of the soil. The primal urge of race perpetuation is not necessarily undermined because it accommodates itself to new conditions. The fear of race suicide may sometimes be another form of the ancient majestic terror that "men have become as gods, knowing good and evil."

The changing balance of births and deaths. To gain an adequate understanding of the changes we have been discussing it is essential to remember that the fall of the death rate was not only a sequel but also a precondition of the fall of the birth rate. If the death rate had not fallen, the present birth rate would indeed spell race suicide. On the other hand, under present conditions in Western society, the old birth rate, say between 32 and 45, would involve a multiplication of population such as, over any long period, could scarcely be imagined.

[1] *The positive aspect:* The falling death rate has been a consequence of the advance of science, as scientific knowledge has been applied on the one hand to hygiene, sanitation, and therapeutic and preventive medicine, and on the other hand to the increase of productivity and thus to the raising of the standard of living. Earlier man had little genuine control over disease or over the pestilences that from time to time wiped out large numbers, nor could he "be fruitful and multiply" without pressing disastrously on the means of subsistence. For the vast majority of human beings there was no escape from oppressive poverty, with its concomitants of malnutrition, privation, and exposure to disease.

What, then, has happened in the main is a very remarkable transition from an old balance of births and deaths where both rates were very high, with all the miseries attending this state of affairs, to a balance in which both rates are very considerably lower. This change has proceeded wherever modern civilization has prevailed for any length of time. It has the danger that it puts the balance of population directly under man's control, demanding of social man a new kind of responsibility. But if this responsibility is accepted, the new balance thus attained has very great advantages. It means a higher standard of living, the emancipation of women from endless drudgery, better care for the young, and a greater regard generally for human life and human personality.

[2] *National variations:* Like all great social changes, this transition also has its disturbing features. Since it follows the advance of civilization it spreads gradually from one area to another. It began in the Western countries in which modern civilization first developed. As we have seen, this civilization, with its basic technology, is gradually pervading the globe. The countries that have been later in feeling its impact, those in the earlier stages of the industrial revolution, retain at first their higher birth rate while they are benefiting by a lower death rate. Thus their numbers increase at the same time that their resources increase. This differential gives concern, in a world of power competition, to countries that are reaching a stationary population and fear a falling population. In a previous period the same concern was expressed by England and France regarding Germany, but Germany somewhat abruptly took the same road they did. So, more recently, has Japan been going. Russia, on the other hand, is still in the earliest phase. After the Soviet Revolution, Western technology was hastily imported on a grand scale, with special attention to heavy industry. Before that time Russia was a country with an extremely high birth rate but, owing to heavy mortality, with a relatively low natural increase. Its population was, and still is, overwhelmingly rural. Productivity has been increased, though it is still low by Western standards. In this phase the birth rate remains very high, but now the annual increase is considerable. There can, however, be little doubt that, as the country becomes more urbanized with the advance of technology, the birth rate will drop and Russia, no matter what the policies of its rulers, will gradually move toward the new balance of births and deaths.[6]

Changes in composition of the population. With changes in size go changes in composition. While the birth rate is falling, the proportion of younger people in the population decreases. In the United States the median age of the population rose from 16.7 years in 1820 to 26.4 in 1930.[7] In the period between 1920 and 1930 the numbers in the age-group 45–64 increased by more than a third.[8]

6. For the available facts, see Frank Lorimer, *The Population of the Soviet Union* (Geneva, 1946). For some political implications, R. M. MacIver, *The Web of Government* (New York, 1947), pp. 299–313.

7. Thompson and Whelpton, *loc. cit.*, p. 26.

8. *Ibid.*, p. 28.

Obviously the change in age distribution reacts in turn on the birth rate, since the percentage of the population above childbearing age increases. Less obvious, but probably quite significant, are the social changes responsive to a situation in which the proportion of youths declines and that of elders advances. But the change of age distribution is only one of the many aspects of the changing pattern of population. We have already seen that the proportion of urban to rural dwellers has been steadily increasing. Along with this have gone other processes of recruitment and of redistribution.

[1] *Regional variations:* Birth rates and death rates vary significantly for different areas, different nationality groups, different religious affiliations,

CHART XXI **True Rates of Natural Increase in the United States**[9]

(1930 Census)

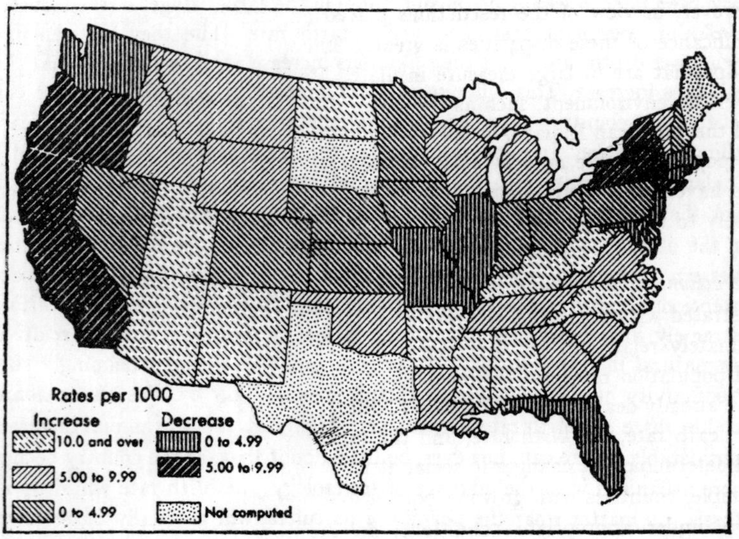

different occupations, and, generally, different modes of living. We shall leave for a later section a discussion of the differential rates for occupations and social classes and look here only on the variations that are exhibited by different parts of the country. The student should, of course, understand that geography itself is no explanation of these differences, but rather the ways of living that are associated with geographical distribution.

A report based on the 1920 census revealed remarkable variations of fertility throughout the United States.[10] Utah had the highest birth rate, twice as high

9. Louis I. Dublin and Alfred J. Lotka, *Length of Life*, p. 258. Copyright 1936, The Ronald Press Company.

10. Census Monograph XI, by Warren S. Thompson (Washington, D.C., 1931).

as the lowest rate, which belonged to California. North Carolina had "over two and two fifths times as many children per 1000 women as California." The agricultural areas everywhere had higher rates than the urban areas. The 1930 census showed similar differences, the lowest fertility being recorded on the Pacific coast, in Florida, and in certain Northeastern states, while the highest fertility was registered in the Southern and Southwestern and Mountain states. Consequently some states of the union were more than maintaining their numbers in the balance of births and deaths, while others had fallen distinctly below the replacement level. These differences are brought out on Chart XXI.

[2] *Other variations:* The birth rate is responsive to certain other conditions. We shall see in a later section how it varies with occupation and with social class. Again, it is higher for the foreign born than for the native born, while at the same time it is lowest for the native born of foreign or mixed parentage. However, in view of the restrictions placed on immigration since 1921, the significance of these disparities is greatly diminishing. We find also that the groups that are in large measure insulated from the cultural impacts of the American environment, such as the Latin Americans, the French Canadians, and the American Indians, usually bring up larger families than do the rest of the population. We note by way of contrast that the birth rate of Negroes, who have no cultural affiliations outside the United States, now corresponds closely to that of Whites.

Interaction of population change and social change. The changes we have illustrated with respect to the size and the composition of the population are intimately related to social changes. It is obvious that economic conditions and population rates are interdependent, and this aspect of the situation we have already dealt with in Chapter V. But it is also clear that the changes in the death rate, the birth rate, and the marriage rate are both responsive to and determinant of changes in social attitudes and in social relationships. For example, countries with growing populations and relatively limited resources have, under appropriate conditions, an incentive to imperialism and to militarism, while these attitudes in turn encourage a further increase of population. Thus in Italy, which is both populous and relatively poor in resources, Mussolini constantly proclaimed that empires cannot be won or defended except by "fecund peoples." On the other hand, increase of population threatens the standard of living and thus inspires a change of attitude. At a certain stage in the unprecedented growth of population in the nineteenth century the practice of birth control took a new development. This practice in turn had many repercussions on family relationships and even on attitudes toward marriage. In the Comstock anti-birth-control law of 1873, contraceptives were designated "immoral." There is strong evidence that a majority of the population no longer holds this view. With the consequent decrease of the size of the individual family the facility of marriage and of divorce, the relations between husband and wife, the relations between children and parents, the mode of upbringing of children, the position of the mother in the house, and the degree of economic self-sufficiency of the family have all been changing. These aspects of the situation we have already brought out in the chapter on the family. Now we shall consider some of the broader social aspects of population change.

The Limitation of Natural Selection

The principle of natural selection. With the changes in the composition of the population and above all with the decline to new levels of both the birth rate and the death rate it becomes necessary to revise our theories of the role that natural selection plays in civilized society. The principle of natural selection, as formulated by Darwin, has been regarded as the great agent of biological evolution and in turn has been given a similar role in the explanation of social evolution.

[1] *The principle stated:* The principle itself can be stated in a few words. Variation is always occurring under the laws of sexual reproduction. These differences from, or rather within, the type may be fluctuating results of transient conditions or they may be distinctive "mutations" capable of hereditary transmission. In either event they are apt to occur in every direction, but they are not equally favorable to the existence of the variant individuals. The less favorable are eliminated in the struggle for existence, the more favorable are encouraged and, if they prove to be mutations, are perpetuated. This is a process which obviously admits a direction of change, through the accumulation of favorable variations, and thus can assume an evolutionary character.

The struggle for existence has various aspects. It includes adaptation to the rigors of nature, to climatic and seasonal changes, to variations in the food supply, and so forth. It includes the resistance to microbic and fungoid infections or the acquisition of specific immunities against them. But it also includes the struggle between the individuals of a species for food, for shelter, for mates. And to this struggle, involving sometimes the preying of individuals on one another, must be added the struggle between species, or, more strictly, the struggle of the preying species to capture their prey and of the latter to avoid capture. It was the pitting of individual against individual, whether of the same or of different species, on which the earlier Darwinian theory placed such emphasis, and it was this picture of nature "red in tooth and claw" which seized the imagination of those social thinkers who made conflict the spur of evolution, though they tended to substitute the conflict of groups for that of individuals.[11]

11. Among proponents of this doctrine of internecine conflict may be mentioned Ratzenhofer and Gumplowicz. See P. Sorokin, *Contemporary Sociological Theories* (New York, 1928), Chap. VI.

[2] *Problems raised by the principle:* From natural selection we should distinguish sexual selection as well as the selection exercised through the differential birth rate. These latter forms, existing in the lower animal world, take on a new significance in human society, within which they are elaborated and intensified. But society itself is in many of its aspects, as a system of co-operation and interdependence, hostile to natural selection, since it sets a limit to the sheer individual struggle for mere existence. Moreover, the principle of natural selection requires not only the continual emergence of biological variations but also a considerable surplus of reproduction above the numbers necessary to maintain the species. The intensity of its operation is limited by the excess of reproduction over survival. Its range is thus more and more limited in human society as the survival rate approximates more and more nearly to the birth rate.

We are not here concerned with the debated question as to the efficacy of natural selection below the level of human society. It should, however, be noted that the term "natural selection" expresses not a fact of observation but an inference. The indisputable fact is natural elimination, which is so adjusted that it tends to preserve the balance of numbers of a species through time and relative to other species. Though this balance is liable to disturbance, it is generally maintained by the greater elimination of the individuals of those species which breed most or fastest. Not even the most extreme Darwinian would maintain that consequently the more prolific species, like the cod or the rabbit, are the most highly selected and therefore the most "fit."[12] Obviously a considerable amount of elimination has no relation to "fitness." The more moderate Darwinian argument is, however, that in the sweep of the eliminative forces the weaklings are destroyed so that the level of the species is maintained, and that among the individuals which escape premature death are likely to be those which vary in a direction advantageous to their survival.

So stated, the principle is a truism. It is not on that account unimportant, but it ceases to be the master key which unlocks all the doors of evolution. It takes on the more modest role of a limiting condition, preventing variation from pursuing unfavorable roads. Nevertheless, the facts show that the favored roads are also numerous. Fitness is always relative to environment, and there are many potential environments as well as many ways of adaptation to them. So far as the principle of natural selection is concerned, it is indifferent whether survival is assured by strength or by cunning, by boldness or by disguise, by speed to pursue or by speed to escape, by native vigor or by high fertility. And it has been sagely remarked that the very existence of the preying animals de-

12. Yet some sociologists seem to reason in a similarly oversimple fashion concerning the intricate question of the efficacy of natural selection within society. Thus, for example, Sorokin (*Contemporary Sociological Theories*, p. 306) approves as follows certain conclusions of the natural-selection school: "A low birth rate, accompanied by a low mortality, means an elimination or weakening of the factor of natural selection; in other words, a survival of the weaklings who would be eliminated under the condition of high mortality which accompanies a high birth rate. Under such conditions, the population of such a society is likely to be composed more and more of the progeny of the weaklings and less 'superior' people."

pends on the existence of the preyed-upon.[13] Moreover, while natural selection may be adduced to explain the maintenance of organic fitness within a species, it certainly does not explain the emergence of variations, especially of mutations, and it further encounters grave difficulties when it attempts to explain the trend of these mutations toward more evolved types or species. The standard of fitness to survive justifies the unevolved amoeba at least as much as it justifies the piece of work called man.

Natural selection and human society. When we turn to consider the operation of natural selection in human society the simplicity of the principle is lost. With respect to the lower animal world it was the term "selection" that created our difficulties; here it is the term "natural."

[1] *Why the principle is less applicable:* The conditions of survival, of success in living and in reproducing, are profoundly modified by society. The struggle for mere existence becomes less individualistic and tends to be converted into struggle on other levels. The cohesion of groups destroys the sheer alternatives of nature under which the individual must wrest his living from her or perish. The struggle of groups with one another becomes more significant than the struggle of individuals, but this new struggle is not of the life-and-death character demanded by natural selection. (Life-and-death struggle survives only in the spasmodic outbreak of war between national groups, in which the fittest *individuals* are *socially* selected for destruction, an entire reversal of the presumptive plan of nature.) The range of co-operation extends more widely, restricting and modifying the action of the eliminative forces. We have seen that this extension of co-operation is a necessary concomitant or part of social evolution, so that there is an actual opposition between social evolution and the principle adduced to explain organic evolution.[14] Above all, the excess of reproduction over survival, the raw material on which natural selection works, grows less and less as the evolution of society proceeds.

Some eliminative forces are intensified under socially created conditions, others are reduced, all are modified. It is only a blind transference of the principle to an alien sphere which could allow us to speak of, as natural selection, the higher death rate of stonecutters from tuberculosis, or the summer mortality from diarrhea of slum-bred infants. If the congestion of cities or the conditions of factory life are unfavorably reflected in the death rate or if, on the contrary, preventive medicine and hygiene applied to these situations lead to a diminution of the death rate, neither can the former be called "natural selection" nor the latter a perilous interference with it. Selection, we have seen, is always relative to the environment, as is the "fitness" which is selected, and now the

13. Cf. Tönnies, *Soziologische Studien und Kritiken*, I, Chap. IX: "If only beasts of prey survived, what animals would remain at all? What would become of the beasts of prey themselves if their prey ceased to exist?"

14. This point was cogently made by Huxley in his *Evolution and Ethics* (New York, 1905).

environment itself has ceased to be, in the particular sense of the term implied by the principle, natural. Man follows his own road, widely diverging from that of all other animals. It is his nature to do so, and he must in doing so meet the demands of the universal nature to which he belongs. If he fails, the eliminative forces are always waiting to destroy him or force him back. In this sense, though in this sense only, he is subject to the limiting conditions of natural selection. But the ways to which natural selection is indifferent, which we have seen to be fairly numerous even in the lower organic world, are now vastly increased.

The social heritage everywhere modifies the stark alternatives of natural selection. The more advanced it is the more are the impulses of men set to other goals than mere survival. It increases the area of indifference within which variant ways of social living are possible and unchecked by natural selection. Society may even reject certain of the ways which natural selection prescribes for those forms of life which have no social heritage. Organic needs, in their raw simplicity, become a smaller part of the whole system of needs which urge men on. A further point is well made in these words of Lloyd Morgan:

> While mental evolution as such is still dependent upon organic evolution, it is no longer wholly subservient to organic needs; nor is it save to a limited extent conditioned and controlled by natural selection. Mind to some extent escapes from its organic thraldom and is free to develop in accordance with the laws of its own proper being, but in relation to a new environment. And although continuity of mental development in the race is still rendered possible by organic heredity, mental progress is mainly due not to inherited increments of mental faculty but to the handing on of the results of human achievement by a vast extension of that which we have seen to be a factor in animal life, namely, tradition.[15]

The conclusion follows, in the words of the same author, that "natural selection is a constantly diminishing factor in the evolution of civilized man." As we shall see, another factor operating in a very different way, social selection, becomes a substitute for it within the increasing area to which natural selection is indifferent.

[2] *Anthropological evidence:* This conclusion is confirmed when we consider the rich variety of folkways revealed by different societies or, in the larger civilizations, by different groups within the same society. If variations are the raw material of natural selection, it is here in abundance. But the rooting-out process is little in evidence. No doubt folkways that are profoundly injurious to the group must be eliminated in time or else they will destroy the group either by their direct effects or, indirectly, by sapping its vitality in the struggle with other groups. But the survival of folkways, even under relatively primitive

15. *Habit and Instinct* (London, 1896), pp. 333–334.

conditions, is no convincing proof of their "fitness." Unfavorable folkways, cherished in ignorance and superstition, may be established, may persist and erect formidable barriers against favorable change. We may take as examples the endless magical devices for controlling disease, the taboos against valuable foods, Indian child-marriage, the celibacy of the more educated orders in the Middle Ages, and such curious practices as that of the Shingu tribes cited by A. G. Keller, where the old men obtain the young women for wives and the young men the old.[16] If even in the primary concern of sex every possible type of relationship is somewhere instituted, it would suggest that as between folkways natural selection does not act very rigorously. Groups have been eliminated in warfare or invasion by other groups, but this rude test is inconclusive since so many factors enter in besides the character of their respective folkways—numbers, economic resources, the possession of superior weapons, leadership, military organization, and so forth. Primitive peoples have been wiped out by the imposition on them of the conditions of an alien civilization, but this again has hardly more claim to be called natural selection than the extinction of animals held in captivity. Depopulation has overcome once-prosperous peoples of the eastern Mediterranean. This has frequently been attributed to their social vices, but without denying that such an explanation may sometimes be tenable, we must observe that the extreme depopulation in question occurred in regions where the conditions of nature became less hospitable to man.

In general, therefore, a survey of the diverse customs and institutions of many peoples leads to the same conclusion as before. There is a certain amount of effective competition, growing as the range of social contacts increases, between the techniques and practical arts of different groups, leading to the elimination of the less effective *methods*. We may, by a stretch of language, speak of this as natural selection. But even this modified form has little application to the folkways. We may quote here the language of a writer who devoted his life to their study.

> In short, as we go upwards from the arts to the mores and from the mores to the philosophies and ethics, we leave behind us the arena on which natural selection produces progressive evolution out of the close competition of forms some of which are more fit to survive than others, and we come into an arena which has no boundaries and no effective competition. The conflicts are freer and freer and the results of the conflicts less and less decisive. The folkways seem to me like a great restless sea of clouds, in which the parts are forever rolling, changing, and jostling, as temperature, wind-currents, and electric discharges

16. *Societal Evolution* (New York, 1915), the reference being to an account of the Shingu tribes by von der Steiner. For numerous other examples, see W. I. Thomas, *Primitive Behavior* (New York, 1937), Chap. X.

> vary. . . . If they conform to the conditions and forces from moment to moment, that is the end of their existence.[17]

But where the eliminative processes are less in evidence, there is another selective process, peculiarly social in its character, which is at work, a process which takes over the area of indifference from which natural selection retreats.

The Range of Social Selection

Some contrasts between natural and social selection. In so far as forces generated within human society and operating through social relationships create conditions which affect the reproduction and survival rates of the population as a whole and differentially of the various groups within it, we can term the process *social selection*. In its modes of operation it stands in marked contrast to natural selection. *Natural selection acts solely through the death rate*, selecting between beings already in existence and only thus determining who shall come into existence. Social selection also acts on the death rate, but its more characteristic action is directly on the birth rate. Natural selection offers only the alternatives of death or successful adaptation; social selection offers many alternatives. It is not merely or mainly eliminative; it is in part preventive and in part creative, determining who are to be born and not only who are to survive. It is concerned with preferences; it makes effective certain out of many possibilities. Consider only one aspect of social selection, that involved in the determination of who shall marry whom. This sexual selection varies endlessly according to the cultural conditions of time and place. There are social standards for mating; there are personal standards themselves responsive to the mores; there are social conditions deciding who shall meet whom and thus limiting the range of choice. Natural selection, on the other hand, demands simply adaptation to a given environment. It has no other standard. It favors equally the scrub of the desert and the tropical forest. Social selection creates its standards in accordance with the society. Natural selection stands on guard outside the increasing area of indifference which the social heritage assures; social selection works within it, turning this indifference into its service. Natural selection limits the directions along which humanity may travel; social selection decides the direction within these limits. Finally, before natural selection the organic being remains passive or merely resistant. It is in no wise an expression of his nature, still less of his desires. But social selection is in large measure volitional, the direct or the indirect result of human purposes or preferences.

17. Quoted in A. G. Keller's *Societal Evolution* (New Haven, Conn.: Yale University Press, 1915), pp. 247–248, from the essay "Evolution and the Mores," by W. G. Sumner.

Two modes of social selection. Social selection functions in two broad and interrelated ways. One way is the mere sequel of social conditions established with different ends in view. The other is the direct result of social planning toward the end thereby achieved. One mode is indirect, the other direct.

[1] *Indirect social selection:* In a great many ways the organization of society, apart from any such intention on the part of its members, alters the balance of reproduction and survival. As an instance of the first mode we may cite the differential mortality from occupational diseases. If stonecutters have a high mortality from tuberculosis or if the children of workers in white lead have a lessened chance of survival, the lethal forces of nature are here implemented by conditions for which society is responsible. If, on the other hand, the child mortality of all classes, though in different degrees, is lessened by better nutrition and hygiene and the various applications of medical science, here the lethal forces of nature are checked by socially created conditions. The social conditions determining the relative success or failure of different groups, the rules regulating economic inheritance, the distribution of occupations responsive to technological advance, the opportunities for the employment of women, the length of the training required for the professions—these are simply a few of the more obvious factors which, as they change, affect also the modes of social selection.

[2] *Direct social selection:* But with these changes *direct* controls of various kinds and degrees emerge. Society directly controls the death rate by rules concerning sanitation and hygiene, by the institution of medical facilities in general, more especially by the application of preventive medicine, and by rules intended to safeguard its members against material hazards endangering life, and in some degree by penalties against homicide, infanticide, and abortion. Society controls the mating relationship partly by definite regulation of the marriage contract, establishing a minimum age limit, proscribing bigamy, permitting or denying divorce, requiring in some states a certificate of health, and so forth; but the control exercised through the mores is far more significant than that exercised through the laws. Society attempts to control the birth rate by prohibiting, permitting, or facilitating the dissemination of knowledge concerning birth control, by mitigating through tax exemptions, wage allowances, and other devices, the costs of raising a family; and by providing for the segregation, and in some instances for the sterilization, of the very "unfit." But here again the controls exercised through the mores of each group and community, controls made effective through individual volition and not through public regulation, are of vastly greater moment.

How social selection operates through the mores. It is well established that economic conditions influence the marriage rate, that they are reflected in the average age at which members of different groups marry, that in times of depression marriages are fewer, that the size of the family varies for different standards of living. But we shall not understand how social selection operates unless we realize that the economic conditions in question do not *as such* cause the various changes with which they are correlated. If, for example, marriages are less numerous in times of depression or if professional groups postpone marriage to a later age than do unskilled workers, it is because of the socially accepted demand for certain prerequisites of marriage. In short, it is the mores of the various groups that are immediately operative. The mores set up the various standards on which mating, the conditions of marriage, and the size of the family depend. The social system establishes the conditions within which these standards operate. Thus in a highly specialized society the members of the same profession or craft are thrown more into one another's company. So teachers are more apt to marry teachers, scientists to marry scientists, musicians to marry musicians, doctors to marry nurses, and so forth. The greater the degree of specialization or of stratification, the greater the tendency to selective mating of this sort.

[1] *Some illustrations:* The selective influence of the mores is revealed in many ways. For example, marriage is less frequent among second-generation than among first-generation immigrants. This fact may be explained as due to the unsettlement of groups who are passing from one set of mores to another. The ways of married life are apt to be more settled ways.[18] Consequently we might expect the less settled, less adjusted groups to be less married. The first-generation immigrant clings the more closely to his traditional usages, but his children, subjected in the formative stage to the clashing demands of the old and the new environment, with family influences on the side of the old and education and generally social prestige on the side of the new, are faced with a different and sometimes insoluble problem of adjustment.

Perhaps a not dissimilar conflict may be present in the change of social environment to which college education introduces in this country so many young men and women, and may be adduced in partial explanation of the low marriage rates of women graduates and even of the peculiarly low birth rates of college graduates as witnessed to by certain studies.[19] No doubt other factors enter in. In the case of women graduates, for example, the argument may be put forward that a larger percentage of those girls who are in any event less likely or less disposed to marry may be expected to carry through a college career. But we are inclined here, as also with respect to certain phenomena of urban life referred to in the discussion of the city, to lay more stress on the influence of the migration from one social status or one set of mores to another

18. Cf. E. R. Groves and W. F. Ogburn, *American Marriage and Family Relationships* (New York, 1928), Chap. X.

19. See, for example, John C. Phillips, "A Study of the Birth Rate in Harvard and Yale Graduates," *Harvard Graduates' Magazine*, Vol. XXV (1907); W. Goodsell, "The Size of Families of College and Non-College Women," *American Journal of Sociology*, XLI (1936), 585–597.

than on the effects of the new condition per se, in this case the effects of a system of education. An examination of this subject would, however, involve too detailed an analysis to be entered upon in this discussion.

The instances we have given may serve to suggest the omnipresent action of the mores as an agency of social selection. Wherever we find a group with a distinctive mode of living we find a group responding also in its own characteristic way to the selective influence of its mores. This fact is shown very clearly if we compare the statistics relating to birth, marriage, and death for different occupational groups. Evidently the processes of social selection are very intricate, as they exhibit the flexible accommodation to the variant conditions of all the distinctive groups within a community. Thus while the influences making for a lower birth rate and a lower death rate have permeated a whole civilization, they show a myriad of differences in their impact and mode of operation. There are, for example, highly significant differences between occupational groups on the same income level. A study of these differences leads us behind the economic fact, behind the standard of living, to the modes of living of each group, in the determination of which the standard of living combines with cultural, occupational, and class differences. It is when we turn to the mode of living that we attain a more adequate understanding of social selection. Some illustrations of these differences will be offered so that we may perceive more fully how the mores operate.

[2] *Occupation and fertility as illustrative of social selection:* The British *Report on the Fertility of Marriage* (Vol. 13 of the Census of England and Wales, 1911, published in 1923) is a landmark in our knowledge of this subject.[20] The *Report* divides the population first into eight classes, five broad social status classes and three classes taken, for reasons which will presently appear, out of the general ranking. These are the textile workers, the miners, and the agricultural workers. The *Report* shows the usual linking of higher child mortality and higher natality with lower economic and social status, but two of the special classes are anomalous in this respect. The textile workers vary unfavorably, having a relatively low birth rate with a high death rate; the agricultural workers show the opposite character of a death rate lower than that of the whole class into which they fall both economically and with respect to the birth rate. The third of the special classes, the miners, differs chiefly in the abnormally high birth rate level which it attains. Already in these broad classifications we see the necessity for taking the mode of living into account.

The *Report* gives statistics for practically every occupational group, showing its crude fertility in terms of children born per one hundred couples, its standardized fertility when allowance is made for the average age of the wives at time of marriage, and its child mortality rate. Some of the correlations which are brought out by the statistics are as follows:

20. Cd. 8678. Part II contains an admirable analysis of the statistics.

(a) The fertility of occupational groups in which the wives engage more generally in "gainful occupations" is lower than that of other groups in the same economic category. The outstanding case is that of the textile workers, who have, compared with any other large group of workers, a markedly low fertility.

(b) The fertility of occupational groups whose work involves considerable change of location or physical mobility is lower than that of other groups in the same economic category. This correlation is illustrated from every position in the social scale. Thus actors, though not given to postponement of marraige, have the lowest fertility in the whole occupational list—note that they fall also under the condition referred to in (a) above. Other groups with relatively low fertility for their respective classes are officers of the Army and the Navy, commercial travelers, and "navvies" or pick-and-shovel laborers who migrate from job to job.

(c) The fertility of occupational groups tends to vary conversely with the length and the expense of the training required for the occupation. Thus while the fertility of the professional groups is throughout lower than that of other occupational groups, the professions which involve the longest preparation, such as those of the barrister and the physician, exhibit a specially low fertility. It is also noteworthy that they postpone marriage till a later age than do the other professions.

(d) The fertility of occupational groups engaged in arduous work requiring much physical exertion is generally higher than that of other groups in the same economic category. Thus the fertility rates of miners, agricultural laborers, and steelworkers head the list for the whole population.

(e) The fertility of those occupational groups whose work brings them into close contact with the members of the "upper classes" is generally lower than that of other groups in the same category. The statistics for such occupations as those of the hairdresser, waiter, and domestic chauffeur bear this out.

The *Report* offers many further evidences of the sensitiveness of fertility to social conditions. One curious indication may be mentioned in conclusion. "The birthplace of the husband," says the *Report*, "has much more influence upon the size of the family than that of the wife." This means that in cases where either the husband or the wife has migrated from areas of higher to those of lower fertility, or vice versa, the family tends to approximate more nearly to the fertility type of the area in which the husband was bred. For example, "rural-born husbands, married to London-born wives in London, return a standardized rate of 266, and rural-born wives, similarly married (i.e. to London-born husbands in London) one of 250, a male excess of 16, while London-born husbands, married to rural-born wives in the rural counties, return a rate of 257, and London-born wives, similarly married, of 273, a female excess of 16." If we accept the hypothesis that the husband exercises the dominant influence—or did in England before 1911—the variation fits in well with our argument. A parallel is found in the English experience of marriages in which either of the contracting parties is an alien. Thus "Irish-born men married to English-born women have considerably larger families than English-born husbands with Irish-born wives, and the same difference applies to Anglo-Russian marriages" (*Report*, Pt. II, p. cliii). It would be extremely interesting to discover how far American experience, with its large proportion of internationality marriages, corroborates this conclusion. but adequate statistics are not available.

Illuminating comparisons can be drawn between these evidences and those provided by the British censuses of 1921 and 1931. During the period between 1911 and 1931 the English birth rate continued to fall, but at different rates for different classes. There was, in consequence, a convergence of the rates of the major classes. By 1931 the birth rate of Class II had fallen below that of Class I, while the white-collar workers, who formed a part of the original Class III, had now become the least fertile of all classes. The most rapid decline in fertility, however, was exhibited by Class IV. Among the miners, also, the rates for the unskilled and the semiskilled showed a sharp drop. The special class of textile workers continued to be marked by its very low birth rate, which by 1931 had fallen below that of their employers. We shall presently examine the significance of these changes.[21]

Such American figures as are available reveal that class and occupational differentials similar to those found in England prevail also in this country.[22] Thus coal miners head the fertility list, closely followed by farmers and farm laborers. Unskilled workers are generally higher than skilled workers. Clerical occupations rate low, being within the same range as the professional groups. Certain contrasts for specific groups between the American and the English figures—for example, the fact that in this country dentists are lower in the fertility list than physicians, whereas in England they are distinctly higher—are probably to be explained by differences of relative income or status. Similar forces are obviously at work in both countries, and indeed everywhere in our modern civilization. The general conclusion that fertility everywhere varies with the conditions and the mores of specific social groups is confirmed by all the researches that have been made in this field.

Social change and biological change. The evidence we have offered strongly suggests that with respect to fertility modern humanity is very sensitive to

21. See J. W. Innes, "Class Birth Rates in England and Wales, 1921–1931," *Milbank Memorial Fund Quarterly*, XIX (1941), 72–96.

22. The most concise presentation will be found in Frank Lorimer and Frederick Osborn, *Dynamics of Population* (New York, 1934), Chap. IV. The subject has been explored chiefly by the investigators of the Milbank Memorial Fund; see, for example, Frank W. Notestein, "Class Differentials in Fertility," *The Annals of the American Academy of Political and Social Science*, Nov., 1936, 26–36.

social influences, as distinct from racial or biological conditions; that whatever biological changes are involved are specifically set in motion by changes within the mores. It is much easier to assume that the conditions of occupation control the variations they reveal than that men select themselves for occupations which discourage fertility, say the occupation of spinner or of bank official, by virtue of a weaker instinct for large families. A like conclusion forces itself upon us when we consider the unprecedented decline in crude fertility which has been in progress throughout the civilized world in recent times, or again when we reflect on both the divergences and the similarities of population rates for different peoples.

[1] *Interpretation of declining fertility:* It is sometimes held that the decline of the birth rate is primarily a biological fact, due, that is, to increasing sterility or infecundity. In support of this conclusion there is some evidence that childless marriages are increasing, at least among the higher social classes.[23] The proportion of childless marriages among the graduates of Harvard and Yale increased somewhat between the period 1861—1870 and the period 1881—1890.[24] Evidences of this kind are susceptible of other interpretations, though it is quite possible that they point to a biological factor. But the differential fertility rates we have been discussing indicate very clearly that the social factor is the predominant one. Only on this hypothesis does it seem possible to explain the various correlations between fertility ratios and socioeconomic conditions, the graded decline of the birth rate from the higher to the lower economic levels, the spread of the decline from the classes and the countries first affected to other classes and to other countries, the concomitance of declining birth rate and declining death rate, and such other statistically established facts as that the disparity in fertility between classes is greatest for early marriages and becomes rapidly smaller for marriages contracted at later age-periods.

The whole situation is far more easily intelligible if we assume that the decline in fertility is due to deliberate control responsive to changing mores and changing conditions. Take, for example, the abruptness with which in some countries the birth rate began to fall. In England the beginning of the continuous decline of the birth rate dates from 1878. It so happened that the previous year witnessed the famous trial of Charles Bradhaugh and Mrs. Annie Besant for their offense in publishing a new edition of an "obscene" book on birth control. Before the trial this book was selling at the rate of 700 copies a year. Because of the great publicity given to the case, 125,000 copies were sold in the three months between the arrest and the trial. In New South Wales a similar trial took place ten years later than the English one, and in the following year

23. A. J. Lotka ("Sterility in American Marriages," *Proceedings*, National Academy of Sciences, XIV [1928], 99-108) found a net sterility rate of 13.1 per cent. Mrs. K. B. Davis, in *Factors in the Sex Life of 2,200 Women* (New York, 1929), concludes that of upper-class marriages generally, 20 per cent are sterile.

24. Phillips, *op. cit.*

the birth rate of that colony dropped sharply.[25] We are not, of course, suggesting that had these trials not taken place the subsequent continuous decline of the birth rate would not have occurred. But it seems a reasonable assumption that these episodes, with their sudden impact on the public mind, helped to precipitate attitudes which more deep-moving forces were fostering.

[2] *The spread of social influences:* In order to interpret these movements it is particularly important to observe the manner in which they spread. Otherwise we may draw false conclusions as to their future course. They have arisen out of the conditions characteristic of modern civlization. First affecting the groups most responsive to these conditions, they have permeated gradually to all other classes. The groups that are semi-isolated from these influences, living by themselves as quasi communities, such as the English agricultural workers and the miners, are those most exempt from the process. And again it is those relatively self-contained communities, with mores strongly opposed to cultural change, such as the French Catholics of Quebec, which retain the old equilibrium of a high birth rate and a high death rate. The power of prestige and the contagion of suggestion, as well as the slower impact of the same cultural influences, all work in the same direction. Nor are there economic obstacles to the spread of these influences such as limit the range of other practices of the well to do. In fact, in an age of compulsory schooling, child-labor laws, and old-age insurance, the former economic obstacles are transformed into economic inducements. The situation out of which this permeation of influences grows is well suggested in the following summary of conditions in a moderate-sized American city.

> The behavior of the community in this matter of the voluntary limitation of parenthood—in this period [1890–1924] of rapidly changing standards of living, irregular employment, the increasing isolation and mobility of the individual family, growing emphasis upon child training and upon education and other long-term family plans such as insurance and enforced home ownership on a time payment basis—presents the appearance of a pyramid. At the top, among most of the business group, the use of relatively efficacious contraceptive methods appears practically universal, while sloping down from the peak is a mixed array of knowledge and ignorance until the base of ignorance is reached. Here fear and worry over pregnancy frequently walk hand in hand with discouragement as to the future of the husband's job and the dreaded lay-off.[26]

The dark problem of social selection. Reviewing the manifold evidences of the activity of social selection, we are impressed by one great difficulty which all investigations along these lines encounter. We find social selection everywhere at work, but we never *see* its results as such. The causes are clear, the results are hidden. How, for example, does the present generation, because of the dis-

25. For these cases see J. A. Field, *Essays on Population* (Chicago, 1931), Chap. VII.
26. R. S. and H. M. Lynd, *Middletown* (New York, 1930 pp. 125–126.

proportionate recruiting of its members from the various economic and social classes of the past generation, differ from the latter? Can we *know* that the particular characteristics which its members display are differences in any degree due to social selection? They have been brought up in a changing social environment, and we can observe their responsiveness to these changes. The selective influences belong within that environment, and we can perceive how these influences affect their conduct, their social relationships. We can perceive how the lower birth rate and lower death rate are factors changing the family, not through selection, however, but through the new situations they create for their *present* members. The results of accommodation to environment we can trace; the results of selection remain a hazardous inference. It is true that many writers speak confidently of the results of selection, writers like Ammon, Lapouge, Karl Pearson, McDougall, and a host of others, but their confidence depends on their various assumptions and not on the demonstrated establishment of a causal nexus. The most disconcerting fact, which they do not face, is that the whole social environment is changing at the same time that selection is taking place. It might be held—though even this assumption is, as we have already seen, somewhat dubious—that physical or biometric traits are withdrawn from the influence of the social environment, and that a study of their changes reveals the specific work of selection. But the conclusions thereby attained, such as Lapouge's "law" that the selective influence of urban life tends to eliminate the short-headed types in favor of the long-headed, are conflicting or contradicted by other evidences. We seem forced to the position that selection is always at work, but what precisely it accomplishes remains unknown. It is certainly far easier to explain the genesis of selective force, such as the differential birth rate, than to interpret the resulting selection.

25

Technological Factors of Social Change

Changing Techniques and Changing Society

A contrast between the biological and the technological factors. We were baffled, in spite of the many evidences that biological selection is always operative, when we sought to trace its more profound effects on society. Social selection decides the hereditary composition of each new generation, but we cannot see *how* it operates, we cannot follow the nexus of biological cause and social effect. Social selection decides which of the endless variety of combinations of genetic elements possible at every moment will be actualized. But with the intricate complications of hereditary transmission, multiplied by the myriad diversely selective pairings which occur in a society, the attempt to learn what difference it would have made if selection had run on different lines is utterly hopeless.

The situation seems different when we turn to the technological factors. A new invention is suddenly introduced and rapidly developed. We can see how it brings about specific social changes. We can see how the radio sets up common standards of speech or how it gives the city a new cultural dominance over the country. We can see how the automobile expands the range of social relationships and reduces the communal character of the neighborhood. We can see how the technical conditions of the modern factory tend to strengthen industrial unionism and to weaken the older type of craft unionism. Moreover, technological advance, as we have seen, moves continually in the same direction, and therefore we can trace its continuous influence over longer periods. At the same time it is concrete, measurable, demonstrable, and therefore the study of its influence on society seems to offer greater prospects to the scientific mind. In so far as we can establish a clear relation between its changes and corresponding social changes we seem to be on scientific ground. In fact it was when sociology began to follow this road that it emerged from the realm of philosophy.

Modern society and the machine age. The approach through technology has on other grounds a particular appeal and significance for our own age. The rapid changes of our society are obviously related to and somehow dependent upon the development of new techniques, new inventions, new modes of production, new standards of living. We live more and more in cities, and "in the city—and particularly in great cities—the external conditions of life are so evidently contrived to meet man's clearly organized needs that the least intellectual . . . are led to think in deterministic and mechanistic terms."[1] *The most novel and pervasive phenomenon of our age is not capitalism but mechanization*, of which modern capitalism may be merely a by-product. We realize now that this mechanization has profoundly altered our modes of life and also of thought.[2]

[1] *Mechanization and social changes:* Attitudes, beliefs, traditions, which once were thought to be the very expression of essential human nature, have crumbled before its advance. Monarchy, the divine ordering of social classes, the prestige of birth, the spirit of craftsmanship, the insulation of the neighborhood, traditions regarding the spheres of the sexes, regarding religion, regarding politics and war, have felt the shock. The process, beginning with the external change and ending with the social response, is easy to follow and to understand. Take, for example, the profound changes which have occurred in the social life and status of women in the industrial age. Industrialism destroyed the domestic system of production, brought women from the home to the factory and the office, differentiated their tasks and distinguished their earnings. Here is the new environment, and the new social life of women is the response. The rapid transitions of modern civilization offer a myriad of other illustrations.

The swift transitions of our industrial mechanized civilization have not only been followed by far-reaching social changes, but very many of these changes are such as appear either necessary accommodations or congenial responses to the world of the machine. In the former category come the higher specialization of all tasks, the exact time-prescribed routine of work, the acceleration of the general tempo of living, the intensification of competition, the obsolescence of the older craftsmanship, the development, on the one hand, of the technician and, on the other, of the machine operative, the expansion of economic frontiers, and the complicated, extending network of political controls. In the latter may be included the various accompaniments of a higher standard of living, the transformation of class structures and of class standards, the undermining of local folkways and the disintegration of the neighborhood, the

1. R. E. Park, chapter on "Magic, Mentality, and City Life," in Park and E. W. Burgess, *The City* (Chicago, 1925).
2. See, for example, L. Mumford, *Technics and Civilization* (New York, 1934); K. Mannheim, *Man and Society in an Age of Reconstruction* (New York, 1940), Part I.

breaking up of the old family system, the building of vast changeful associations in the pursuit of new wealth or power, the increasing dominance of urban ways over those of the country, the spread of fashion, the growth of democracy and of plutocracy, the challenge of industrial organized groups, particularly the organizations of labor, to the older forms of authority.

[2] *Mechanization and changes in values:* With these conditions are bred corresponding attitudes, beliefs, philosophies. A great mass of contemporary social criticism seeks to depict and often to arraign the cultural concomitants of the machine age. Its tenor is generally as follows: Different qualities are now esteemed because the qualities which make for success, for wealth, and for power are different. Success is measured more in pecuniary terms, as possession is more detachable from social and cultural status. A form of democratization has developed which measures everything by units or by quantities and admits no differences in personal values save as they are attached to external goods or are the means of their acquisition. Men grow more devoted to quantity than to quality, to measurement than to appreciation. The desire for speed dominates, for immediate results, for quick speculative advantages, for superficial excitations. The life of reflection, the slow ripening of qualitative judgments, is at a discount. Hence novelty is sought everywhere, and transient interests give a corresponding character to social relationships. The changing interests of civilization absorb men to the relative exclusion of the more permanent interests of culture. Men grow pragmatic in their philosophies. "Things are in the saddle and ride mankind." The mechanistic outlook explains life itself in behavioristic terms, as a series of predetermined responses to successive stimuli. The unity of life is dissipated, since from the mechanistic point of view all things are means to means and to no final ends, functions of functions and of no values beyond.

[3] *Direct and indirect effects of technological change.* That the tendencies thus described are at least accentuated by the mechanization both of work and of the means and conditions of recreation is clearly established by a great mass of evidence. It can scarcely be a mere coincidence that in the periods and in the countries of rapid technological advance there should have developed corresponding or congenial ways of thinking and of living. Nevertheless we should be wary of concluding too hastily that social relations are in all important respects predominantly determined by technological changes. This conclusion would hold only if culture also, the values men set before them as ends for which to live, were essentially the product of technology. But culture in turn seeks to direct technology to its own ends. Man may be the master as well as the slave of the machine. He has already rejected many of the conditions that accompanied and seemed to be imposed by the earlier technology of the industrial revolution. He has taken some steps in all civilized countries to place a variety of controls on factory toil, on the squalor of factory towns, on the shoddiness and ugliness of many factory-made goods, on the risks and fatigues

of many factory operations. Man is a critic as well as a creature of circumstance.

Therefore we should distinguish between the more direct and less direct social consequences of mechanization or other technological process. Certain social consequences are the inevitable results of technological change, such as a new organization of labor, the expansion of the range of social contacts, the specialization of function, and the encroachment of urban influences on rural life. Other concomitants, not being inevitable conditions of the operation of the new techniques, are more provisional or more precarious, such as the increase of unemployment, the intensified distinction between an employing and a wage-earning class, the heightening of competition, and the prevalence of mechanistic creeds. In the remaining sections of this chapter we shall endeavor to show that the deterministic theories which make technological change the dominant or overruling cause of social change are one-sided or misleading. But first it is well to insist on the positive aspect, and show by citing some recent developments how real and how important an agency of social change is the quest of modern man to discover and to utilize new techniques, new and more efficient methods of accomplishing his ends.

How technological advance initiates social change. Every technological advance, by making it possible for men to achieve certain results with less effort or at less cost, at the same time provides new opportunities and establishes new conditions of life. The opportunities, or some of them, are frequently anticipated in the development or exploitation of the new devices; the new conditions of life are in large measure the necessary and unanticipated adjustments to the new opportunities. A few illustrations will bring out the distinction.

[1] *New agricultural techniques and social change:* Take, for example, the advance of agricultural technology. The improvements in the breeds of cattle, in the use of fertilizers, in the varieties of seed, in mechanical laborsaving devices, and so forth, have had as their direct objective the increase in the quantity and quality of agricultural production. But as concomitants of the attainment of this objective there have gone changes in farm economy and in the manner of life of the farming household. And beyond these again there have gone changes in the relation of agriculture to industry, migrations from the farm to the city because of the lessened numbers required to supply the agricultural needs of the whole community, the decay or abandonment of marginal farm lands, tendencies to agricultural depression, new struggles for foreign markets and new tariff barriers. And these changes in turn have stimulated new and difficult economic problems. Thus the achievement of the immediate objective of agricultural technology has led by an inevitable nexus to changes of an entirely different order.

[2] *Advances in communication and social change:* Even more far reaching and complex are the social changes that spring from the development of the

techniques of communication. For communication is at once a primary condition of social relations and a basis of nearly all other forms of technological advance. The course of civilization has been marked by a constant development of the means of communication, but never so rapidly as in our own days, when electricity is not only being adopted as motive power in place of steam, not only is a factor in the improvement of automobile and airplane, not only makes the motion picture a vast commercial enterprise and television a promising adventure, but also, resuming its distance-annihilating range, becomes in the radio a voice that is heard simultaneously by millions over the face of the earth. The impact of these changes on society is too enormous and too multifarious to be dealt with here except by way of incidental illustration.[3] Every step of technological advance inaugurates a series of changes that interact with others emanating from the whole technological system. The radio, for example, affects a family situation already greatly influenced by modern technology, so that its impetus toward the restoration of leisure enjoyment within the home is in part counteracted or limited by opposing tendencies. Again, the radio combines with other technological changes to reduce the cultural differentiation of social classes and of urban and rural communities. On the other hand, by enabling an individual speaker to address great multitudes, it makes possible the rapid rise of new parties or social movements, provided the broadcasting system is not itself politically controlled. In the latter event it tends to produce the opposite result, becoming a most powerful agency of propaganda monopolized by the ruling power. This last illustration should serve to show that what we call the "effects" of invention are in large measure dependent variables of the social situation into which they are introduced.

[3] *The control of atomic energy and social change:* The most spectacular illustration, however, is that afforded by the epoch-making discovery of a way to make atomic energy serviceable to human objectives. Like so many other discoveries of modern science, this new agency is available equally for destructive or for constructive purposes. As an agent of war it forebodes the most appalling annihilation of all the works of man. As an agent of peace it may ultimately bring an unprecedented era of plenty.

The general direction of social change with advancing technology. Bearing in mind the caution contained in the last paragraphs we may still ask whether there is any major direction in which society moves under the continual impact of technological change.

[1] *Specialization:* We have seen that technology itself tends always in the

---

3. For fuller illustration see *Recent Social Trends* (New York, 1933), Chap. III, "The Influence of Invention and Discovery," by W. F. Ogburn and S. C. Gilfillan, and Chap. IV, "The Agencies of Communication," by Malcolm M. Willey and Stuart A. Rice. In reading these chapters the student should bear in mind the distinction made above between direct and indirect effects.

same direction, attaining ever greater efficiency in the performance of *each* of the various functions to which its devices are applied. In doing so it specializes functions more and more, and thus tends to create an ever-increasing division of labor, with whatever social consequences depend thereon. The social significance of this growing division of labor has been given classic treatment by Durkheim, though some of his conclusions, such as that greater liberty and a diminution of class differences are concomitants of specialization, are stated in too sweeping and universal a form.[4] More certain is the correlation between technological advance and a more elaborate social organization with higher interdependence between its parts, greater mobility of the members with respect to location and to occupation, more elaborate systems of laws and of governmental controls, new concentrations both of economic and of political power, greater instability of the institutional order, greater leisure and generally higher standards of living for large numbers. These conditions seem to be directly bound up with growing technological efficiency, and they in turn have further repercussions on every aspect of social life. They also create some extremely important social problems, one being the unbalance of the economic system that accompanies the accelerated processes of technological change. But within our limits we can do no more than suggest some of the immediate social concomitants of technological advance.

[2] *The modern significance of the technological factor:* It is scarcely too much to say that every major problem of modern society is either initiated by or at least strongly affected by technological change. Conflicts between states, as they strive for dominance, for security, or for prosperity, are in no small measure concerned with competing ambitions to secure or control areas rich in oil, coal, or other resources of crucial importance to modern industry. Again, the specialization of functions in a modern economy gives rise to a multitude of organized groups, each of which seeks its own economic advantage and each of which has the power of withholding a service that modern interdependence renders indispensable. On the other hand, these groups are affiliated with or incorporated into massive federations or combinations. These in turn exercise a correspondingly greater power, so that the disputes arising out of their clashing interests sometimes threaten to disrupt the whole social order.

These concomitants are so obvious and so far reaching that they have inspired various doctrines which attach primary importance to technology as the direct or indirect determinant of social change. Since such doctrines tend to minimize the role of the cultural factors which we are presently to consider and since they have attained a great vogue and thus, as beliefs, have themselves become *cultural* conditions of social change, we shall devote the remainder of this chapter to a review of them. For this purpose we shall take up two types of theory, first, the economic-technological interpretation of society which found

4. *The Division of Labor in Society* (G. Simpson, tr., New York, 1933), *passim.*

its most famous exponent in Karl Marx; and second, the specific technological determinism, more congenial to American thought, which is represented by the incisive American sociologist, Thorstein Veblen.

The Marxist Explanation of Social Change

Deterministic theories of society. By deterministic theories we mean here any doctrines that regard human behavior and changes in human behavior as primarily to be explained by environmental, external, or material conditions. Such theories are often implied in explanations of behavior that may at first sight seem to be innocent of any theoretical assumptions. For example, if, with some sociologists and psychologists, we *define* behavior as "response to stimulus" we are thinking in deterministic fashion. For the stimulus is generally conceived as something external to the behaving being and by making behavior merely responsive to it we are in effect assuming the causal priority of environmental factors. No one would deny that these factors are an important part of the explanation of behavior. The question, however, is whether they constitute a total or sufficient explanation.

[1] *The "determining" environment:* This type of explanation has many varieties, according as stress is laid on one or another aspect of the environment. If, for example, climatic or geographical changes are made primary, we are dealing with conditions which man certainly does not bend to his will, and the explanation becomes a very simple (though very inadequate) one. If, however, economic or technological conditions are stressed, the explanation becomes more complex, not only because these are constantly and often rapidly changing but also because they are themselves the expression of human activities and thus the determinism is never absolute. Such explanations can still be called deterministic if they assume that the environmental change is always the initiating or precipitating factor of the social change, or if they make the social change the unintended but necessary result of environmental change, which is indeed the work of man but only as the cumulative consequence of his efforts to satisfy his elemental desires. In one way or another we shall see that these assumptions underlie the important deterministic doctrines which we are presently to examine. In short, for the interpretation of social evolution they make the process of civilization primary, and cultural processes secondary and dependent upon them.

[2] *An initial difficulty:* An initial difficulty of any deterministic theory is that the environment to which we respond is very complex, so that our response to it must be selective. This difficulty is apparent when we try to reconcile the various types of deterministic theory. Suppose, for example, we are seeking to explain the peculiar characteristics of North American society. We cannot at the same time give priority, with Huntington, to the influence of climate

and geography, and with Turner to the influence of the frontier mode of life, and with Marx to the economic system, and with Veblen to the habits engendered by the technique of industry. Any or all of the conditions thus singled out may have significance for the understanding of North American society, but any one of them, if taken as a total explanation, contradicts all the others. The difficulty is that none of them can be established on purely deterministic grounds, for we cannot on these grounds explain why a society responds to some at one time and reacts against them at another. The true nature of this difficulty will be seen when we examine the more explicitly deterministic theories. We shall see that they emphasize factors of large significance in the social process, but that they are inadequate when they postulate the over-simple psychology of stimulus and response which every form of determinism requires.

The materialistic conception of historical change. The social stresses of the industrial revolution led in the nineteenth century to a revival, restatement, and sharper formulation of the theory that the structure of society is an economic creation and its changes essentially the sequel of economic changes. This movement may be said to have culminated in the evolutionary teaching of Karl Marx, particularly in what he called the materialistic conception or construction of history.

[1] *The kernel of the Marxist theory:* In this construction we begin with the power of economic production as the determinant of primary economic relationships—given the stage of productive efficiency, these relationships are "indispensable and independent of men's will."[5] In other words, the stage of technological development determines the mode of production and the relationships and institutions that constitute the economic system. This set of relationships is in turn the chief determinant of the whole social order, or, as Marx puts it in the same work, "the sum total of these relations of production constitutes the economic structure of society—the real foundation, on which rise legal and political superstructures and to which correspond definite forms of social consciousness."[6] The cultural life of man, his intellectual, aesthetic, spiritual life, his creeds and his philosophies, and the social forms which are their vehicles, are the reflection of the economic order. Here is the "material" reality which comes to consciousness in our ideals.

There is some controversy as to whether Marx and his collaborator, Friedrich Engels, really meant to assert that social and cultural phenomena are wholly or only dominantly determined by economic or "material" conditions. Their various statements are not fully reconciled and are susceptible of either interpretation. They are generally put forward dogmatically, without attempted

5. *Critique of Political Economy* (N. I. Stone, tr., New York, 1904), p. 11.
6. *Ibid.*, pp. 11-12.

proof, but the tenor is, with occasional qualifications, deterministic. In their later writings and in their correspondence they several times object to the interpretation of their theories that makes other than economic factors purely derivative and noncausal.[7] But they hold to the position that the economic situation is the foundation of the social order—in fact, it is this position that gives its distinctive character to the whole Marxist system. We are not, however, concerned here with the particular attitudes of individual authors but only with the validity of a mode of social interpretation that happens to be associated with them.

[2] *The lever of social change:* The "material forces of production" are subject to change, and thus a rift arises between the underlying economic factors and the economic relationships built upon them. The productive process demands —and of necessity will secure—a transformation of economic relationships and therewith of the whole social superstructure. But the social and economic order does not conform to the gradual emergence of the economic demand. For the older order has created its "ideologies" and its vested interests. It is those who are fettered by the now obsolescent order who awaken to the consciousness of its decay and accomplish its overthrow. A social revolution thus attends the birth of each new stage of society. The ideology of the dominant economic class opposes itself to the ideology of the class whom that order suppressed and whom the new would liberate. Thus, in the words of the *Communist Manifesto*, "the history of all hitherto existing society is the history of class struggle."

As it was in the past, in the days of ancient slavery and in the feudal age of landowner and serf, so it is today. The stage is different, but the process of evolution is the same—and so it will be until one further stage is reached, which obliterates the "contradictions" latent or open in all preceding stages. The capitalistic order is in this sense penultimate. In it the class struggle is simplified, reducing itself more and more into the clear-cut conflict of two great classes, the *bourgeoisie* and the proletariat. But the underlying processes of economic production are inevitably increasing the numbers of the proletariat in proportion to those of the *bourgeoisie*, preparing for the day when the former shall become the whole and in the last revolution the class struggle shall end and the year of liberation from economic determinism itself shall begin.

How this last revolution will occur—and this is the only aspect of the social process on which Marx lavishes his interest—is as follows. The principle of capitalism is the principle of profit making through the hiring of labor. Labor is the only economic good that produces more than its "cost." It reproduces its "cost," that is, the exchange-value of its own subsistence and maintenance, in so many working hours. This is the price the capitalist pays for it, but his profit is a "surplus-value" that comes from the additional hours during which

7. See, for example, Marx and Engels, *Selected Correspondence* (International Publishers edn., New York, 1934), Letters 213, 214, 229.

he secures for this price the services of labor. "Capital is a monster that is fruitful and multiplies." It is the law of its nature that it must grow in the hands of those who possess most of it. The rich become richer but fewer, the proletariat of wage earners grows ever larger. This process moves to a climax. Capitalism begins with the "expropriation" of the small owner, turning him into a wage earner, then it advances to the "expropriation" of the smaller capitalists. So the situation ripens to its overthrow. At last "the integument is burst asunder" and "the expropriators are expropriated."[8]

We need not here concern ourselves with the scientific quality, on which Marx prided himself, of his economic "laws." His theory of value and its corollary of surplus-value, his theory of the sole productivity of labor as such, and his law of the accumulation of capital are derived from an outmoded, abstract, and narrow doctrine of the equivalence of price and cost which modern economic analysis rejects. The importance of Marx does not rest on his elaborate but uncritical formulations of economic theory. It was as a dramatic and apocalyptic prophet that he stirred the world, appealing to myriads who suffered the hazards and the exploitations which accompanied the growth of capitalism and to whom his dogmatic assurance and his clear-cut, forthright program opened a door of hope or revealed a vision of conquest. From the scientific point of view his significance lies elsewhere. He postulated a theory of economic cause and social effect which became a challenge to later thought. He himself offered no substantiation of this postulate. He and Engels insisted in many works that the legal code, family systems, cultural forms, religious doctrines, and all the rest, are "only" the reflection, expression, or translation of economic relationships, but he attempts no demonstration of any kind. Nowhere does he face the intricate question of social causation.

[3] *The historical "dialectic"*: What Marx does, instead, is to apply the "dialectic" he learned from Hegel, except that he called it materialistic. According to Hegel, evolution proceeds according to a system of three stages, thesis, antithesis, and synthesis. This purely dogmatic assumption was used by Hegel to "reveal" the historical process through which "reason" or "spirit" fulfills itself in society. For Hegel's "spirit" as determinant of change Marx substituted the "material" conditions, that is, the economic factor. His materialism is the counterpart of Hegel's idealism. The principle operates as follows.

Every social and cultural stage is unstable, for Hegel because it is a necessarily inadequate expression of the demand of the spirit for the freedom of fulfillment, for Marx because the economic order depends on productive forces that develop to new forms. Each stage therefore contains the seeds of its own decay, and they ripen into the opposing order of its antithesis, the countermovement which asserts those aspects denied by the former. But the "antithesis" is also a development of what was implicit in the "thesis." It attains a higher level,

8. *Capital* (E. and C. Paul, tr., London, 1929), Chap. XXIV, §7.

and in its supersession the "synthesis" of the two comes into being. Here is the eternal process of evolution, but as Hegel was tempted to discover finality in the synthesis of the nation-state, so Marx, with his vision of a socialist goal itself conceived as an ideal—though like all earthly paradises wisely left by him in visionary outline—ends with the synthesis of socialism. And perhaps the most curious thing in the whole Marxist theory is that at this stage the lever of change that has operated through all past history now ceases to function. With the abolition of classes and of class struggle we enter the realm of liberty, in which material forces no longer control mankind, in which, instead, human beings become "the masters of themselves."[9]

The weakness and strength of Marxism. In both the Hegelian and the Marxist systems social evolution is thought of as advancing through great well-defined stages, not by continuous sequence in the same direction but by the development of opposites. Marx gave a more drastic revolutionary quality to this concept. The Hegelian spiral becomes a kind of zigzag. The established social and cultural superstructure is pulled down in order to be rebuilt.

[1] *The "swing of the pendulum":* It is, of course, a common observation, confirmed by many instances, that modes of thought no less than of external fashion grow stale and breed antithetical modes, that there is a "swing of the pendulum," a critical revulsion of one age or even decade from the philosophies of the preceding, or of the children from the ways of the fathers. Such movements are especially marked in times of crisis, as our own period amply illustrates. On a broader scale of time, puritanism is bred from libertarianism and in turn passes into it again, classicism and romanticism succeed one another, and so forth. But often these changes occur within the same economic framework, and it seems sheer dogmatism to assert that they are necessarily and mainly inspired by *its* changes. There are other causes obviously at work, some on the cultural level itself. The Greek who voted for the ostracism of Aristides because he was tired of hearing him called "the just" was not an abnormal human being. The critical attitude, especially on the freer cultural level, is always present lest "good" customs should corrupt the world or in order that "bad" ones may be reformed.

[2] *Inadequate psychology:* The link between the social change and the economic process is far less direct and simple and sufficient than the Marxian psychology admits. An inadequate psychology is perhaps the fatal weakness of all determinisms. Marx asserted that human beings respond to the changes initiated in the productive system—how initiated, he does not tell us, for he speaks as though the changing technique of production explained itself and were a first cause—in a simple determinate manner. He ignores the complexities of habitua-

9. So Marx, *Critique of Political Economy*, Chap. I; F. Engels, *Socialism Utopian and Scientific* (Kerr edn., Chicago, 1908).

tion on the one hand and of revulsion on the other. He simplifies the attitudes that gather around institutions; the solidarities and loyalties of family, occupation, and nation are wholly subjected to those of economic class. Consequently he proclaims, in the words of the *Communist Manifesto*, that "our epoch has simplified the antagonisms of class" into those of *bourgeoisie* and proletariat, in spite of the fact that class lines are more simple, more demarcated, and fewer in a feudal order than in a developed capitalistic society.

[3] *Economic priority in the causal nexus:* Economic determinism, in other words, does not solve the major problem of social causation. Its attempted solution rules out the influence of too many other factors. Economic influences are certainly powerful and penetrating. There are, for example, many indications that they profoundly affect political activities, and if Marx had merely taken the position that economic relationships are the clew to political relationships he could have offered, as other writers have done, a considerable, though by no means a total, substantiation of this view. Political like economic regulation is a means of control, and we have seen that these two means are directed in large measure to the same ends and are of necessity closely linked. But the relation of the economic to the cultural (and to its social embodiments) is less clear and less conclusive. Our cultural interests are, to be sure, affected by our economic interests. It is not difficult to establish correlations between social changes and economic changes, though it is harder to interpret them.[10] But how do we pass from these indications of interrelationship to the simple causal priority asserted by Marx? There seems no way, and certainly Marx failed to show one.

[4] *The true strength of Marxism:* The strength of Marxism, the power of its appeal to large numbers struggling for bread within capitalist civilization, the drastic revolutionary impetus that enabled it to overthrow in time of crisis the feudal tyranny of Russia and to set up a vast experiment in communism, is the strength of a creed and not the validity of a science. It has created a new society, a form of collectivism radically different from any ever attained before by a great country, but in that society, whatever may be its new contribution to civilization and to culture, the fulfillment predicted by Marx, the inauguration of the realm of liberty, has not been attained. Marx belongs to the order of great prophets who by their predictions change the world but never in such wise that the changed reality corresponds to their predictions.

General grounds for rejecting the deterministic claim. It is characteristic of deterministic theories of social change that they unduly simplify the situations with which they deal. Thus Marx oversimplified the class structure of society, declaring that "in relation to the working class all other classes are only one

10. Cf., for example, Dorothy S. Thomas, *Social Aspects of the Business Cycle* (London, 1925).

reactionary mass." Only under exceptional conditions and strong constraint does the consciousness of class divide mankind wholly or even mainly into a corporate *bourgeoisie* and a corporate proletariat, overriding cultural, religious, racial, and national distinctions. Again, he oversimplified the process of social evolution, accepting the grandiose conception of Hegel that history proceeds by definite stages from "thesis" to "antithesis." He oversimplified the dynamics of social change in giving always the paramount role to the class struggle. He oversimplified the evolution of capitalism by his assumption of the increasing concentration of wealth and the increasing proletariat. He oversimplified the role of the state, as an organization of a dominant class which, with the socialist revolution, would "wither away." The deterministic interpretation of social change is thus too simple.[11]

In passing, we may suggest a general reason for the expectancy that no such simple solution is possible. In one sense economic interests are primary, because they are directed to the means which are a basis for the satisfaction of all other interests. In another sense, however, they are secondary, because they are inspired by interests beyond themselves, ulterior or intrinsic interests of which the economic means are merely the instruments, instruments which, as we have seen, are themselves relatively indifferent with respect to the alternative ends which they can serve.[12] They furnish the necessary equipment for whatever journey, to whatever destination, we undertake. We can agree so far with Marx that our dependence on the economic means determines largely our attitude to the whole social order which yields them to us in scantier or more abundant measure. We can agree that the conservatism or radicalism thus bred is apt to extend to the cultural realm, particularly to the "stabilizing" cultural factors such as religion. We can agree that the mode in which the economic means are acquired influences the nature of the satisfactions we seek through them; that, for example, the competitive spirit engendered in the economic struggle affects our manner of living, our recreations, our philosophies, our ideals. We can agree that the struggle for the means of living, engrossing and perpetual as it is for the vast majority, must color, according to its character, the whole outlook of men. But in so agreeing we are simply admitting that the economic element is one highly important factor in the whole nexus of interactive influences which determine social phenomena. Its relative importance and its relation to other influences, varying according to the conditions, have still to be investigated—as we shall see, an intricate, difficult task. We cannot conclude that, because the painter is absolutely dependent on his paintbox, the nature of its contents explains the picture. No more can we conclude that the struggle of the artist to earn his living explains it. It would indeed be a remarkable conclusion, one certainly needing proofs which Marx never offers,

11. See R. M. MacIver, *Social Causation* (Boston, 1942), Chaps. III and IV.
12. See Chapter XVII above.

that the means we use wholly elucidate the ends to which these means are applied.

On the practical side, the fatal defect of Marxist determinism was the assumption that the abolition of private capital—the private ownership of the means of production—would bring to an end the exploitative rule of man over man. This claim was not only a gross simplification; it was a gross error. Marx and Engels carried it so far as to assert that when the communist society was realized the state would "wither away." It needs, however, only an elementary analysis of society or an elementary knowledge of history to show that the power of man over man has deeper roots than economic advantage and that it can be at least as formidable and as tyrannical under a socialist economy as under any other kind of regime.

Finally, even if we accepted the doctrine that man is the creature of his environment, we would still have no right to make the economic system, the scheme of economic relationships, the supremely determinant factor. Closely bound with the economic are the other aspects of civilization. The economic system, with respect to the distribution of property and the relation of producers to owners, may be revolutionized, as in Russia, while the technological system associated with the former order may endure and develop. We cannot assume that the social phenomena which distinguish a capitalistic civilization are essentially created by capitalism in the economic sense of the term. Within it are other factors, mechanization itself, urbanization, the persistent and ever-swifter contacts of communication and transportation, the development of pure and of applied science, which can never be left out of the reckoning. In fact, other forms of determinism give priority to one or more of these factors. As an example we shall take the doctrine of Veblen.

The Strict Technological Explanation of Social Change

Types of technological explanation. We saw that for Marx the causal series begins with changes in the techniques of production, but he relates these changes indirectly, rather than directly, with the changing social structure. They determine economic relationships, and it is the latter which are crucial in his interpretation. There is indeed considerable obscurity concerning the actual mode in which technical changes function in his system. Other writers have much more explicitly sought to show how social conditions are responsive directly to technological conditions. We may include among them F. J. Turner, who in *The Frontier in American History* depicted along well-known lines the social and cultural attitudes evoked by the life of the pioneer settler—the strong sense of self-determination combined with neighborly helpfulness, the rough practical versatility, the buoyancy and ready optimism, the belief in progress, the leveling spirit toward predetermined social distinctions together with the admiration of the "self-made" man—and proceeded to trace the pervasive influence of these attitudes on American institutions. Many other writers have followed this path or similar ones. Some have carried the method to the deterministic extreme, and as these raise most sharply the issue of social causation we select one of the most thoroughgoing of them for study.

The Veblenian analysis. The many-sided writings of Thorstein Veblen lend themselves to various interpretations and are of interest to students of various fields.[13] On the whole, however, Veblen may be regarded as a technological determinist.

[1] *The guiding principle:* His guiding principle, reiterated insistently in his various writings, may be stated as follows: In human life the great agencies of habituation and mental discipline are those inherent in the kind of work by which men live and particularly in the kind of technique which that work involves. Here, above all, must be sought the influences which shape men's thoughts, their relations with one another, their culture and institutions of control. Habituation is the great molder of the minds as well as of the bodies of men. "The way of habit is the way of thought." Man has certain drives or instincts, and these may be regarded as constants, but the habits to which they prompt vary according to the varying opportunity for expression, according to the material environment. It is thus the difference in environment which explains the difference in the social structure. "A genetic inquiry into institutions will address itself to the growth of habits and conventions as conditioned by material environment, and by innate and persistent propensities of human nature."[14] These propensities are tendencies to act, to achieve, and they are fixed into determinate habits by the conditions of their expression. Man is what he does. "As he acts, so he feels and thinks."[15] The influence of the pragmatic philosophy is evident in Veblen's point of view, and combined with it is the influence of a contemporary mechanistic biology. Thus he tells us that "the forces which have shaped the development of human life and of social structure are no doubt ultimately reducible to terms of living tissue and material environment."[16]

The most explicit statement of Veblen's general viewpoint on social evolution is contained in the following passage:

> Social structure changes, develops, adapts itself to an altered situation, only through a change in the habits of thought of the several classes of the community;

13. For a detailed treatment, see J. Dorfman, *Thorstein Veblen and His America* (New York, 1934); for his "institutional" approach, L. Schneider, *The Freudian Psychology and Veblen's Social Theory* (New York, 1948); and for his ethical convictions and his style, D. Aaron, "Thorstein Veblen: Moralist and Rhetorician," *The Antioch Review*, Fall, 1947.

14. *The Instinct of Workmanship* (New York, 1914), Chap. I.

15. *Ibid.*, p. 192.

16. *The Theory of the Leisure Class* (New York, 1922), p. 189.

or in the last analysis, through a change in the habits of thought of the individuals which make up the community. The evolution of society is substantially a process of mental adaptation on the part of individuals under the stress of circumstances which will no longer tolerate habits of thought formed under and conforming to a different set of circumstances in the past. . . . A readjustment of men's habits of thought to conform with the exigencies of an altered situation is in any case made only tardily and reluctantly, and only under the coercion exercised by a situation which has made the accredited views untenable. The readjustment of institutions and habitual views to an altered environment is made in response to pressure from without; it is of the nature of a response to stimulus. Freedom and facility of readjustment, that is to say capacity for growth in social structure, therefore depends in great measure on the degree of freedom with which the situation at any given time acts on the individual members of the community —the degree of exposure of the individual members to the constraining forces of the environment. If any portion or class of society is sheltered from the action of the environment in any essential respect, that portion of the community, or that class, will adapt its views and its scheme of life more tardily to the altered general situation; it will in so far tend to retard the process of social transformation. The wealthy leisure class is in such a sheltered position with respect to the economic forces that make for change and readjustment. And it may be said that the forces which make for a readjustment of institutions, especially in the case of a modern industrial community, are, in the last analysis, almost entirely of an economic nature.[17]

Veblen explains this last statement further as follows: "Any community may be viewed as an industrial or economic mechanism, the structure of which is made up of what is called its economic institutions. These institutions are habitual methods of carrying on the life process of the community in contact with the material environment in which it lives."

[2] *Application of the principle:* Veblen never tires of showing the correspondence between cultural conditions and underlying techniques. Take the feudal order, for example. Technologically, it represents "a system of trained man power organized on a plan of subordination of man to man." This characterization holds alike of agriculture and of industry. In the cultivation of the soil it prescribes diligent unremitting toil and obedience to the superiors of the land. In industry what counts is, in the language of Adam Smith, the "skill, dexterity, and judgment of the individual worker," since as yet there is no place for the impersonal productivity of the machine and the qualities it evokes. The social structure has a corresponding character. The state is dynastic, based on personal authority and the subordination of class to class. Politics and war are fields of personal exploits, success depending on individual prowess and craft. Religion is personally authoritative, monarchical, hierarch-

17. From *The Theory of the Leisure Class* by Thorstein Veblen, pp. 192–193, by permission of The Viking Press, Inc., New York. The whole chapter (VIII) from which the quotation is taken should be studied.

ical. But gradually the technological basis of this system is transformed, as mechanical power usurps the place of human power. New skills arrive and old skills pass, for the vocations of the designer, the engineer, the machine tender, call for other aptitudes than "dexterity." With habituation to the control of mechanism the idea of power itself changes. The dominating conception is no longer the arbitrary power of personal command, of will over will, but the regulated power of man over man-made mechanisms, obedient to inexorable law.

In this reconstruction of the nature of power is inherent a new attitude, a new logic, which fights a winning battle against feudal preconceptions. The new technology, reinforced by the social necessities it creates, destroys the old organization of society. The institutions which resist the process most are those which are most remote from industrial influences. Thus with respect to high politics, the politics of war and imperialism, the old preconceptions are most tenacious. But the thrones on which they sit are undermined. The ancient virtues of "patriotic animosity and national jealousy" are hard beset by the necessities of international commerce and by the mechanization of warfare. Veblen illustrates this conflict particularly in the book entitled *Imperial Germany and the Industrial Revolution*, a conflict between the patriarchal imperial attitude of the ruling feudal class and the forces of industrialization within the country. The mores of the established order were contradicted by the lessons unconsciously learnt from devotion to technical advance, an advance the ruling class could not oppose because its own prosperity was bound up with it. Thus the system of control became archaic, and when the shock came its hollowness was disclosed. In other lands, as they became industrialized, similar conflicts have occurred.

The peculiar habits of thought of each age are, then, to be traced back to the particular discipline of life which is imposed by its techniques. Moreover, in the more democratic form of society the impact of technique is more unified and therefore more powerful. This idea Velben puts forward in a chapter entitled "Evolution of the Scientific Point of View."[18] Here he points out that under a hierarchical system the technical basis of behavior has a widely different significance for the upper and the lower groups. The institutions of society are chiefly in the keeping of the upper classes, and their social function is the maintenance of the corresponding system of law and order. The discipline to which they are thus themselves subject diverges greatly from the discipline imposed on the subordinate or servile classes, to whom this maintenance of law and order is "at best a wearisome tribulation." Consequently there is a wide cultural difference between the upper and the lower classes. The upper are devoted to social institutions conveying prestige and authority, personal dignity and coercive control. The lower are disciplined by the specific techniques

18. In *The Place of Science in Modern Civilization* (New York, 1919).

of everyday toil. But the spirit of this discipline, the habits of thought and life which their labor imposes, cannot penetrate to the upper classes, who hold themselves aloof from participation in the productive process. Hence there are two cultures instead of one within society. Under the industrial-democratic regime, on the other hand, the influence of technique is more pervasive, and all behavior is more closely related to the same "work-day generalizations." Social attitudes and speculative thought conform more directly to the lessons and impressions derived from the industrial arts. All alike tend to think in terms of mechanism, of geometrical relations, of standardized patterns, of inexorable law.

For Veblen it is the "use and wont" of everyday life, whether it be pastoral, agricultural, or industrial in any of their forms, which is decisive. These habits embody themselves in institutions, and this "fabric of institutions intervenes between the material exigencies of life and the speculative scheme of things." There may, indeed, be a lag in the correspondence of the "speculative scheme" with the "material exigencies," because in times of transition men work in new ways while they still think in the old. The evolutionary process results from the accumulation of technical changes, from the "march of civilization," from the improvement in the industrial arts toward greater efficiency Social evolution is, in short, the process through which our social systems reflect technological advance.

[3] *Contrast of Veblen and Marx:* Here a contrast between Veblen and Marx appears. Marx, in spite of his insistence on the scientific quality of his socialism, cannot conceal his ethical bent. He is an idealist in a deterministic disguise—and to this fact may be attributed the strength of his appeal to large numbers. He projects a goal or consummation of social evolution which, while ascribed to the operation of rigorous laws, will bring about a great liberation of the human spirit and a new social harmony. It is a form of revelation. Veblen, more faithful to the deterministic hypothesis, offers no revelation, no goal. His exposition is, to all appearance, peculiarly matter-of-fact. The process he expounds has no dramatic denouement. "The growth of culture is a cumulative sequence of habituation."[19] If the resulting scheme of life can be called higher, this is merely a way of saying that its technological foundations have become more efficient and more complex, that the pattern of civilization is more elaborate, more subtle, and more diversified.

On these terms Veblen interprets the salient features of the current "scheme of life." Take, for example, the luxury of the leisure class. Its quality of "conspicuous waste" is the expression of the pecuniary estimation of worth which springs from the devotion to detached pecuniary rewards made possible by the financial structure and control of modern business. Take economic unrest. It is the expression, not so much of privation or exploitation as of the spirit

19. *Ibid.*, p. 241.

of emulation and envy which the competitive character of modern economic life engenders. The characteristics of the modern business world are due to the dominance of "pecuniary employments" over industrial activities. In the latter the desire for productive efficiency, a form of the "instinct of workmanship," rules, whereas the former are "predatory" and their spirit is one of "caution, collusion, and chicane."[20]

Some questions regarding the technological explanation. In his description of modern society the matter-of-factness which we have attributed to Veblen is relieved—and perhaps contradicted—by his caustic irony. It appears especially in his attribution of motives—the danger point of all deterministic theories. Is it an adequate explanation which attributes the form of modern luxury to the principle of conspicuous waste? Does it differ in this respect from the luxury of Babylon or of Rome, or is conspicuous waste so much a motivation as a necessary concomitant of all luxurious spending? Is the dog preferred to the cat as a pet because, while he has "nasty" habits compared with the cat, he is also a more wasteful and unprofitable creature?[21] Is ugliness deliberately sought in the realm of fashion so that styles may be discarded more rapidly? Or, to take a more extreme suggestion of our author, was the purpose of the wearing of corsets by women to make them "permanently and obviously unfit" for work?[22]

We are not questioning the value of the contribution which Veblen has made to the study of social evolution. He has revealed with much insight the close relation between the basic arts and the changing structure of society. But we must question the adequacy of his interpretation. Is habituation to changing technique so all-sufficient an explanation? We find marked cultural differences between peoples at the same level of technical advance, especially primitive peoples living in semi-isolation. May there not be grounds of variation inherent in the group itself rather than expressive of its external conditions? Can we be so confident, when we survey the changing trends within a single civilization, that cultural and institutional patterns are not woven from the stuff of ideas and creeds and interests otherwise evolved than as a response to our own material contrivances? What of the borrowing and assimilation of cultural ingredients? What of the reactions against established modes and conditions which are so frequent in the higher expressions of culture? Man is a critic as well as a creature of habit—the irony of Veblen himself is a fine example of contemporary criticism of the social order. Criticism, like all other behavior, is relative to environment, but it is certainly not the expression of habituation. The environment, material and social, offers satisfactions and dissatisfactions,

---

20. *The Higher Learning in America* (New York, 1918), p. 373.
21. *The Theory of the Leisure Class*, Chap. VI.
22. "The Economic Theory of Women's Dress," *Popular Science Monthly*, XLV (1894), 198–205.

pleasures and pains, opportunities and repressions, in endless variety to the differently placed members of every large group. There are habituation and conformity on the one hand; there are stimulus and struggle and liberation and defeat and renewed struggle on the other. Is it not at the meeting points of old civilizations, in the shock of their opposing cultures, that in the past the greater cultures of the greater societies have arisen? And is there not, in the wider ambit of modern civilization, the continuous contact of divergent ways of life and modes of thought to stimulate further changes?

Once more the determinist theory seems too simple, too sweeping, too conclusive. Emphasizing the concrete, perceptual, measurable factors, it would follow the road of physical science to the goal of complete interpretation. But this tempting road does not lead us all the way to the social phenomena. For it does not come to grips with the continual interaction of ends and means, with the way in which cultural values, the beliefs and aspirations and dreams and hopes of men, instigate and direct and limit the search for means and modify and control the whole system of means. If we are adequately to understand the problem of social change, we must look on this interaction from the cultural no less than from the technological or utilitarian side.

From Deterministic to Antideterministic Interpretations

The determinist point of view. The interpretations of social change which we have examined have made it a function, as it were, of environmental change. They have not assumed that human beings and their social relationships are the mere playthings of external forces, but they have regarded them as essentially responsive to the conditions of the outer or material environment. If this position meant simply that with every change of his environment man also changes, it would be, as we have shown in Chapter IV, the most obvious of truths, the mere assertion of the universality of law. When the conditions are different, society is different—a formula of this order is innocuous but unhelpful. But the deterministic theories give priority to one term in the universal correlation. The equally valid converse, when society is different the conditions are different, has little significance for them. But why should the ever-active principle of life, that follows its own determinate lines of development in tree and animal and man and the groupings of men, be regarded as merely formless plasticity poured into the cast of environment? The soil in which the seed is sown and the climatic conditions determine whether the seed will germinate and whether it will grow in strength or be stunted, but the seed itself is a whole cosmos of latent powers and what each seed will become depends not only on its type but also on its individual heredity. Why, then, should the more active factor in the correlation of life and environment be thought of as active only by way of response? So it is in all deterministic theories. Thus, to some, organic adaptation is the key work; to others, conscious adjustment or maladjustment; to others, habituation. To some, the response of life is immediate and semiautomatic; to others, there is a lag before the cultural conditions are adjusted to environmental changes.[23] To all, the environment is the initiating factor in the process of social change.

We have seen that, suggestive as these theories are, they give an unvalidated priority to one factor or set of factors. The exponents of natural selection do not come to terms with the conscious element of control involved in social selection or with the broadening zone of indifference to the operation of natural selection which the social heritage ensures. The economic and technological determinists are too exclusively occupied with the psychology of adjustment or habituation, and, like the behaviorists, are apt to think they have explained a social phenomenon when they indicate that it is a "response" to the "stimulus" of given conditions. Certainly human nature is always responsive to environment, but *how* it responds may depend on its own creative character as well as on the environment it in part creates.

The dogmatic element in deterministic theory. Behind this doctrine of mere responsiveness there is hidden a peculiar dogma. Everywhere else we discover *interactions*, why here *reaction* only? The mind of man is plastic, impressionable, but why plastic only? Why should it alone be subject to no immanent process of change, in which it becomes itself an active source of change within its world? The dogma that human nature does not change (from within) would make it an anomaly in the cosmos. If the configurations of the earth are changeful, if the skies themselves are so changeful that we can discern their inconstancy through abysmal depths of space, if every living thing bears the signs of its own different past, if man's body has evolved from something anthropoid and beyond that from shapes of dim age-buried creatures—how can one share the assurance that his mind, so restless and energetic, so uniquely purposeful, remains miraculously the same, or is so lacking in character, in the quality of development, that it forever merely reflects a changing environment? If no two offspring of the same family are quite alike, if in truth men display remarkable diversities of disposition, why should the race be immutable or reveal no trend of change within itself? If man follows forever his unresting purposes, visioned before they are realized in space and time, why should not these too prepare a path of change and how can they be dismissed as the only inefficacious realities in the whole scheme of things?

To accept a purely deterministic explanation is surely to misunderstand the extreme complexity of relationship between life and environment, and especially the incessant and intricate interaction between man and his social heritage,

23. So W. F. Ogburn, *Social Change* (New York, 1922), and F. S. Chapin, *Introduction to the Study of Social Evolution* (New York, 1923).

that inner environment which is constructed not merely by his arts and his techniques but also by his beliefs, his desires, his fears, and his aspirations. It is here that the antideterminists join issue with the determinists. They insist that human purposes are inherently creative. They insist, for example, that no scrutiny of the environmental conditions of ancient Greece suffices to explain the culture she developed. The old theories which attributed the culture or the social system of the Greeks or other peoples to the work of a few great minds or to the sheer genius of these peoples neglected the environmental factor. So do various modern antideterministic doctrines, those of the racialists and of certain "idealist" schools such as the Hegelian or the Spenglerian. But this contrary one-sidedness should not lead us to dismiss them altogether, any more than we dismiss the one-way theories of the determinists. We cannot thus rule out the cumulative work of human ingenuity, the critical discontent with things as they are, the endless trial and error, the visions baffled or fulfilled, the contagion of ideas. There may be many equally possible ways in which a group can adjust itself to the conditions of its material environment, many ways in which it can respond to its demands. There is room for the directive intelligence of the few. There is room for the play of conjuncture or chance, seized and directed in the unstable flux by the discerning mind. Even the social heritage does not impose one mode of conduct on those who "respond" to it. They respond selectively. There is not one way of writing a novel or building a city or establishing a system of credit. Environment, the total environment, may be only a half-explanation of change. That it is the easier half to deal with in current scientific terms is no scientific reason for making it the whole.

26

Cultural Factors of Social Change

The Hypothesis of Cultural Lag

The current use of the expression "cultural lag." **The concept of cultural lag has become a favorite one with sociologists. The expression has entered into the common vocabulary and has been applied to many and diverse social situations. It is a concept that has a particular appeal in an age in which inventions and discoveries and innovations of many kinds are constantly disturbing and threatening older ways of living. Unfortunately it is often adopted without adequate analysis and consequently it has not been developed in a clear and effective manner. We propose to show that by using the distinction between cultural and technological factors we can free the hypothesis of lag from confusion and give it more fruitful application. In this context it will serve also to introduce the principle that cultural conditions are themselves important agencies in the processes of social change.**

The concept of cultural lag was first given explicit formulation by W. F. Ogburn in his book *Social Change* (Parts IV and V). He distinguishes between "material" and "nonmaterial" culture. When changes occur in the "material" culture, these in turn stimulate changes in the "nonmaterial" culture, particularly in what he terms the "adaptive" culture, or the ways of utilizing, exploiting, or rendering more serviceable the material changes. But this adaptive culture may be slow to respond. The forests of the country may be depleted or destroyed because the art of conservation does not keep pace with industrial or agricultural development. The factory system is well advanced before the need for the protection of workmen from accident and industrial disease and for workmen's compensation acts is realized. The system of political representation may remain unchanged though the character and distribution of the population changes.

[1] *What lags behind what?* Whenever we impute lag we mean that something falls behind or fails to keep pace with something else. What, then, lags behind what? Ogburn, as we have just seen, answered by drawing a distinction between "material" and "nonmaterial" culture. The distinction is not a workable one, as has been pointed out by a number of critics.[1] If, for example, we cling to old-fashioned ways when under new conditions our needs could be better served by changing them we cannot properly say that the lag is between the material and the nonmaterial. Nor again should we assume that it is always the "material" that is in advance of the "nonmaterial" or that the main problem is one of adapting the "nonmaterial" to the "material" culture.

As soon as we face the question, What lags behind what? we perceive that to meet it we must have a standard of measurement applicable alike to the pacemaker and to the laggard. Where no such standard is available we cannot rightly speak of a lag. Wherever one part or aspect of a productive system fails to measure up in efficiency to another part or aspect, the term "lag" is relevant. But wherever the question at issue is not one of comparative efficiency, the use of this term becomes dubious and may convey erroneous implications. The trouble is that the expression "cultural lag" has been applied to all kinds of disequilibrium or maladjustment arising within the processes of social change, instead of being limited to disparities of efficiency within the same system.

In line with our distinction between civilization and culture we find that the term "lag" is appropriate to certain failures of adjustment within the basic technology and the "higher" technological organization, that of the politico-economic order. On the other hand, the term "lag" is not properly applicable to relations between technological factors and the cultural pattern or between the various components of the cultural pattern itself. Following this lead we regard the expression "technological lag" as generally preferable to "cultural lag" and shall employ different terms for the various other types of disequilibrium or maladjustment that have too indiscriminately been lumped together in a single category.

[2] *Why more refined analysis is important:* The complexity of modern social organization gives peculiar significance to the various ways in which the interdependent parts of the inclusive system fail to function harmoniously together, to the discrepancies and disparities of means and ends, to the frictions and checks that impede the working of the system, to the clashes and conflicts that lower its efficiency, disturb its co-ordination, or confound its service. Hence it is important that we assign distinctive names to the very different phenomena with which we have to deal within this broad area.

---

1. See, for example, James W. Woodard, "A New Classification of Culture and a Restatement of the Cultural Lag Theory," *American Sociological Review*, I (1936), 89–104.

A new classification. To this end the following classification is addressed. All the divisions and subdivisions it contains have been included by some writers under the embracing concept of cultural lag.

[1] *Technological lag:* This term is appropriate where any one of the interdependent functions within a technological process fails to achieve or maintain the degree of efficiency requisite for its harmonious co-operation with the rest, so that the productivity of the whole process is impaired, retarded, or blocked at this point. An obvious example is the industrial "bottleneck." Another example is the not infrequent failure of management to maintain over-all efficiency when a corporation expands in scale, particularly when it becomes a part of a combine or trust. An example within the more inclusive system of technology is that offered by Ogburn: we exploit efficiently the products of the forest but fail to apply equal efficiency to the maintenance of the forest itself. The criterion of technological lag depends on our ability to *measure* the relative efficiency of the various interfunctioning factors and thus to show the failure of a particular factor to keep in step.

[2] *Technological restraint:* This term is appropriate where the introduction of more efficient instruments, methods, or agencies, or the utilization of more efficient products is impeded or balked by controls designed to protect some established interest. Many examples can be found in various treatments of the subject.[2] We may distinguish different forms of technological restraint as given below, classified according to the character of the controlling or restraining interest.

ONE: RESTRAINT DETERMINED BY BUREAUCRATIC INTEREST. Here the inertia, tradition, or prestige of an established order opposes the introduction of more efficient methods or techniques. It is claimed, for example, that military hierarchies, at least in time of peace, offer strong resistance to innovations in the art of warfare or retain old concepts of strategy in the face of military developments that render them obsolete. The resistance of governmental departments to the employment of less wasteful and more efficient procedures is an old story. This type of restraint, however, is by no means a prerogative of political office. Many examples have also been cited from the legal profession. It is everywhere a disease of entrenched organization, especially of large-scale organization. Occasional examples that are fully comparable to those exhibited by government bureaus can be found in the behavior of great economic corporations.

TWO: RESTRAINT DETERMINED BY ECONOMIC INTEREST. The typical situation here is that in which some entrenched economic interest, faced with a threat to the profits or other advantages accruing to it, opposes the exploitation of new processes or new methods. It differs from our first type in that the

2. See B. J. Stern, "Resistances to the Adoption of Technological Innovations," in National Resources Board, *Technological Trends and National Policy* (Washington, D.C., 1937); and Corwin Edwards, *Cartels*, Senate Committee on Military Affairs (Washington, D.C., 1944).

opposition stems specifically from economic considerations. No doubt there are instances in which the bureaucratic and the economic determinants combine, but on the other hand there are many instances of resistance that can be explained only by reference to economic interest. A cartel, for example, buys up a patent and puts it "in cold storage." Or a trade-union opposes the use of a laborsaving device. Or a professional organization rejects a change of practice or procedure that may improve its service but interferes with its perquisites or with its economic monopoly.

There is also a rarer kind of economic restraint, where a new device is regarded as threatening, if put into present operation, not to the profits of a group but to the broader conditions of economic well-being, so that it is suppressed either by some authority or even, as in the case of the Rust brothers' cotton-picking invention, by the inventors themselves.

THREE: RESTRAINT DETERMINED BY CULTURAL INTEREST. Our last example might possibly have been included under this third type. Here the main line of opposition to technological developments is determined by the traditions or mores of leaders, groups, or communities or by specific moral or doctrinal considerations. Here, too, there is a wide variety of subtypes. One large and important class is represented by situations where a new technology is imported to areas or countries habituated to a simpler long-established technology. The older technology is thoroughly fused into the prevailing culture in such a way that the introduced technology threatens in part or in whole the cultural life itself.

Since the conflicts arising out of this situation are of great importance in modern society we shall consider it at somewhat greater length. As we look into it we shall see that technological restraint is intimately related to two other phenomena well recognized by sociologists. We can distinguish two main forms in which the conflicts in question have developed under modern conditions.

(a) Sometimes the new technology is introduced from without into a community or country where culture is wedded to a quite different system. The extreme case here is that in which the industrial and other technological methods of an advanced civilization are imposed on a relatively primitive people. We have seen that in primitive society culture and civilization are peculiarly interdependent and inseparable. This harmony is destroyed when an alien technology is imposed on them. It destroys the media through which their native culture expressed itself. Occasionally this may happen through the direct introduction of an alien *culture* possessing higher prestige, as, for example, through missionaries, but generally the native is able to resist this impact, whereas he cannot succeed in resisting the modern methods of trade and commerce and of industrial production that the more advanced civilization demands. So his life is uprooted. The depopulation and disintegration of many of the more primitive peoples in contact with modern civilization, in

North America, in South Africa, in New Zealand and Tasmania, and elsewhere, may be attributable to this process of cultural dissolution.

The situation is different when the alien technology is introduced to or imposed upon peoples of relatively high culture, but here, too, serious disturbances are apt to occur. If the alien technology is deliberately introduced under the control of the government of such a people, as in Japan and to some extent in Turkey, the prevailing culture may be able to readjust itself to or even to dominate the new conditions, though some vehicles of the traditional culture are thereby rendered obsolete. But where outside forces are mainly or largely responsible for the new order of things, as in India and in China, a genuine clash of cultures occurs and brings grave disturbances in its train.[3] In China the permeation of the new technology has been due to a combination of internal and external influences. The abandonment of the classical examination system in 1905, the attack of Chen Tu Hsiu on Confucianism in 1915, the advocacy of Western democracy by Sun Yat Sen, and the introduction of a paper currency in 1935 illustrate the operation of forces of change working from within. But these have been preceded and accompanied by a series of external impacts on the old order. Since Chinese culture has been peculiarly attached to family institutions and since industrial development limits the functions of the family and its social role, there has been strong cultural resistance to the new technology and a danger of cultural disintegration where it has been introduced. This may in large measure explain the slow industrial development of China in the period prior to the Japanese invasion and the long civil war.

In India, on the other hand, the new technology was associated with alien domination and incurred widespread resistance. When Ghandi and his followers clung to the old ways of spinning and weaving and pottery making, it is obvious that their revolt was animated not so much by a love for the older techniques as by a desire to maintain the culture associated with them. An Indian poet painted the contrast between the old order and the new in such words as these:

> I look for the goats coming home in the haze of the evening; I see the trams jerking down the streets crowded with tired workers.
>
> I look for the blue threads of smoke rising from the huts at the cooking of the evening meal; I see the tall chimneys of the factories sending forth black clouds.[4]

But it is the loss of the sentiments and the values regarded by him as belonging to the older ways that he really lamented.

(b) The peoples of the Western world have also been subjected to the sudden impact of a new technology on their older culture, but for them the technology is indigenous and neither imported nor imposed. Hence there has been, on the

3. See, for example, Kuo-Heng-Shih, *China Entering the Machine Age* (Cambridge, Mass., 1944).

4. Quoted from Margaret Read, *The Indian Peasant Uprooted* (London, 1931).

whole, a readiness to adopt and to advance the new devices, though generally without forethought concerning their effect on cultural values. Thus the modern industrial town arose purely in response to immediate utilitarian demands, and its ugliness and lack of amenity, its rows of squalid uniform houses, its smoke and its litter, its devastation of the countryside, were accepted at first with little question, just as were the hazards and the human costs of the labor that operated its unsafeguarded and insanitary factories. A few prophets of the old order, like Ruskin and William Morris and Hilaire Belloc, fulminated vainly against the new system as a whole. It was sufficiently evident that the more effective techniques and the practical applications of advancing science could not be successfully opposed. Only where specific inventions or applications seemed definitely to strike against prevailing moral or religious traditions was there any concerted opposition. In some instances the discoveries of science in the fields of astronomy, geology, and biology were decried by the representatives of traditional beliefs. More obstinate, perhaps, has been the resistance to certain practical controls provided by science which directly conflicted with the earlier mores, such as the use of contraceptives or the prophylaxis of venereal disease. But even here the resistance to indigenous technological advance has been, on the whole, a losing cause. It has become increasingly clear that culture cannot successfully oppose the advance of civilization, but that instead its task is to accept and to direct that advance, controlling it to serve cultural ends. Only thus can the maladjustments of culture and civilization, which must constantly arise in the course of technological advance, be progressively reconciled.[5]

[3] *Culture clash:* The situations we have just been describing, especially those in which the resistance is to an *imported* technology, serve also to illustrate the phenomenon of culture clash. We here use this expression to denote the conflict of opposing value-schemes, creeds, or ways of life, when these are brought into contact inside the same community. The fear of an alien technology is not simply a fear that it will disturb the old values; it is also a fear that with it will be introduced alien values, different standards, different goals. We do not include under culture clash the conflicts of creeds and ideologies so frequent in every modern society. We refer only to conflicts between two entire culture patterns, each of which embraces a whole way of life. Such clashes arise pre-eminently from the coming together within a single community of groups that have been bred in separation before they become thus conjoined. Usually one of the cultures concerned is an imported culture, while the other is indigenous or at least has long been established in its present home.

5. On this subject see L. Mumford, *Technics and Civilization* (New York, 1934), Chap. VII, where he develops the thesis that "our capacity to go beyond the machine rests on our power to assimilate the machine." See also, with special reference to resistance to technological change, the report of the National Resources Committee on *Technological Trends and Their Social Implications* (Washington, D.C., 1937).

The two are brought rather abruptly into contact, and under these conditions one of them appears to be a threat to the very existence of the other, especially if the former is associated with a dominant group.

Culture clash may broadly be said to exist wherever two ways of life or modes of thought within the same community are so opposed that they cannot live side by side, in such wise that the very presence of the one implies the suppression of the other. While it is a very old phenomenon, it has in recent times emerged in an aggravated form. This has been due to the spread of totalitarian philosophies during the crises and tensions created by two world wars and their aftermaths. The consequent culture clash may occur between two different types of totalitarianism, say a fascist and a communist type, or between one type of totalitarianism and any nontotalitarian system, particularly democracy. The most serious of such clashes since World War II is that between the communistic type of totalitarianism and democracy. This culture clash is a sword of division within many countries, both in the East and in the West, provoking civil wars and revolutions.

[4] *Cultural ambivalence:* To complete our main classification we distinguish here between the larger phenomenon of culture clash and a sociopsychological phenomenon that is often connected with it. Sumner spoke of a "trend to consistency" in the mores. A state of culture clash presents a precisely opposite situation. There is also, however, the sense of consistency experienced by the individual who is habituated to and indoctrinated in the mores of his community. The individual makes a selective accommodation to the requirements of the mores—to do so is essential to the unity or integrity of personality. But when the individual is subjected, especially at the formative stage of life, to the counterdemands of clashing culture patterns, he may fail to achieve an adequate *personal* accommodation. He undergoes a process of cultural denudation or, seeking vainly to reconcile in his behavior the opposing demands, he becomes more or less schizophrenic. We have then the phenomenon of cultural ambivalence. Its conditions and characteristics are described in various works, notably in *The Polish Peasant* of Thomas and Znaniecki.

Culture as Determinant of Social Change

Culture as dynamic. Our rejection of the deterministic principle prepares us to look on culture as a dynamic of social change. Everyone acknowledges that there is an intimate connection between our beliefs and our institutions, our valuations and our social relationships. Certainly all cultural change involves social change, for, as we have seen, the social and the cultural are closely interwoven.

[1] *The directional role of culture:* What is less fully realized is that the cultural factor in turn not only is responsive to technological change but also acts back

on it so as to influence its direction and its character. The apparatus of civilization is in a degree indifferent to the use we make of it. The powers we harness for productive purposes stand ready to produce whatever we will. The industrial plant can turn out necessaries or luxuries, the comforts of life or the munitions of war. This increasing indifference of the agencies of production expresses the degree in which our culture is itself a determinant factor. The civilizational means may be represented by a ship which can set sail to various ports. The port we sail to remains a cultural choice. Without the ship we could not sail at all; according to the character of the ship we sail fast or slow, take longer or shorter voyages; our lives are also accommodated to the conditions on shipboard and our experiences vary accordingly. But the direction in which we travel is not predestinated by the design of the ship. The more efficient it is, the more ports lie within the range of our choosing.

[2] *Historical illustrations:* The history of culture offers many confirmatory evidences. We find, for example, cultural types, such as a religious doctrine, which persists with variations throughout many centuries. Even if the variations could be construed as responses to different technological or environmental situations, the type itself, enduring through great diversities of historical circumstance, could not be interpreted in this way. We find, let us say, certain modes of valuation, certain attitudes toward social problems, which develop under one set of circumstances, spread over wide areas, and continue to dominate the thoughts of men under vastly different economic and political conditions. An example of this phenomenon is the view of the role of sex in human life which was formulated by the Church Fathers in the early Middle Ages. Again, the way in which cultural movements spread, the way in which they are associated with the names of great prophets, leaders, and creative minds, and such distinctive features of the cultural process in general as that a cultural style of a long-past age may be revived in the present or that the most primitive and the most advanced cultural elements may live side by side, can hardly be reconciled with any purely responsive or determinist theory.

Curiously enough, the determinist school has provided the supreme illustration of the influence of cultural attitudes on society. It is not possible to explain the Soviet Revolution along the lines of Marx's "materialistic interpretation of history." That revolution was not inspired by the necessity to adjust the culture of Russia to the existing economic situation or to that of the other capitalistic countries. It was the social philosophy of Marxism, wrought into a dynamic evangelism and finding its opportunity in the suffering and disillusionment of a catastrophic war, which gained control of the economic and political order, and by persistent cultural propaganda, aided by the terrorism of the Revolution, transformed it over a vast feudalized territory.

In the quieter processes of industrial evolution the activity and creativeness of cultural forces may also be discerned. We are apt to think of the new industrial civilization as dethroning the old culture, and again there are many evidences which point in that direction. We are apt to fear for the culture of countries which, like Japan or China or Mexico, are threatened by the invasion of machine production. Some among us fervently hope that countries wherein the threat is not yet fulfilled will resist the process to save their souls.[6] But the alternatives are not so simply stated. Every new factor, whether it be a creed or a machine, disturbs an old adjustment. The disturbance created by mechanism was so great that it seemed the enemy of culture, as indeed all revolutions seem. The wealth-bringing machine brought also ugliness, shoddiness, haste, standardization. It brought the meanness of factory towns and mining villages; it brought new hazards, new diseases, industrial fatigue. That was not the fault of the machine and the power plant. It was due to the ruthlessness and greed of those who controlled these great inventions. But human values reasserted themselves against economic exploitation. Culture began, at first very slowly, to redirect the new civilization. It ceased to tolerate the black wretchedness of toil detached from all the purposes of living, which was the early lot of the industrial worker.

At length our culture began to bring the machine also into the world of the imagination and endowed it not only with power but also, often, with beauty. It made the new means of living at length more tractable to the uses of personality, and new arts blossomed on the ruins of the old. The new means became at length means to culture also, nor should we forget, because of the disturbance and the struggle for mastery, that a high culture needs the equipment of civilization.

Max Weber's contribution to the study of culture as determinant. We are justified, therefore, in regarding culture as, no less than civilization, a basic condition of social change. It operates not only directly as a source of social change but also indirectly, by its impact on the utilitarian order.

[1] *Capitalism and Protestantism:* This subject, however, has received comparatively little attention from sociologists. One of the few important contributions to it is that made by Max Weber in his *Sociology of Religion*. The best-known part of this work is the study of the relation between certain forms of Protestantism and early capitalism.[7] Weber saw that there is a direct relation between the practical ethics of a community and the character of its economic system, but he refused to accept the position that the latter determines the former. Each influences the other, and at times the cultural element prepares the way for economic change. Weber was a profound student of scientific method and appreciated the complexity of the problem. He saw that there is a relation between practical ethics and religious beliefs, but also that many factors other than the religious one are involved in the creation of the

6. Cf. Stuart Chase, *Mexico* (New York, 1931).
7. *The Protestant Ethic and the Spirit of Capitalism* (T. Parsons, tr., New York, 1930).

effective forms of conduct. Nevertheless, every period and every group tend to have a typical scheme of beliefs and values, a typical world outlook that find expression in social behavior and in social institutions. The historical correspondence of religious and economic phenomena was studied by him along these lines. He concluded from certain evidences of the historical priority of particular religious forms that they stimulated the economic systems to which their practical ethics were congenial, and in particular that the worldly, ascetic Protestant sects prepared the way for capitalism.

He drew a picture of "the pious bourgeois conducting his business as a calling to which Providence has summoned the elect," and thus by his devotion to the virtues of thrift, saving, assiduous toil, and "worldly asceticism" establishing the conditions appropriate for the development of the earlier phases of capitalism.[8] Guarded and penetrating as is Weber's analysis, it is not wholly conclusive.[9] The institutional complex of certain religious forms and of certain economic procedures can be adequately shown. Thus the interaction of Protestant religious beliefs and of the practical activities characteristic of early capitalism can be demonstrated *within particular historical situations*. But these situations contain so many other elements so variously combined that a clear nexus between the selected factors is exceedingly hard to establish, especially when we find other historical situations, such as that of late-nineteenth-century Japan, in which one of the two develops in the entire absence of the other.

[2] *Concomitance of cultural and social change:* The difficulty, then, does not lie in Weber's approach but in the complex nature of social causation. We saw in Chapter XXII that every social phenomenon is an event belonging to an historical moment. More precisely, it does not endure an instant longer than it is maintained by the contemporary attitudes and activities of social beings. It is a life-expression which must change with the life which it expresses. Not only social relationships themselves but also the modes or formulas in accordance with which they occur, their institutional framework, are subject to this law. Institutions cannot live on like shells within which life is extinct, though, of course, they can endure to the detriment of the life that still upholds them. Social systems are thus directly or indirectly the creations of cultural values, directly in the organization of culture itself and indirectly in the organization of utility. Every change in valuations on the part of social groups registers itself in institutional change. In this respect Max Weber's position is wholly justified. But unfortunately the correspondence, though complete, is

8. From R. H. Tawney's Foreword to Parsons' translation, p. 9.

9. L. Brentano in *Die Anfänge des modernen Kapitalismus* (Munich, 1916) and R. H. Tawney in *Religion and the Rise of Capitalism* (New York, 1926) criticize Weber's argument as being one-sided in its imputation of causes. H. M. Robertson in *Aspects of the Rise of Economic Individualism* (Cambridge, 1933) attacks Weber on historical grounds; see T. Parsons' reply in the *Journal of Political Economy*, XLIII (1935), 688–696.

also complex. The unity of the social structure corresponds to a diversity of social attitudes and interests. These attitudes and interests are not only variant, and variantly influential; they are also in part conflicting as well as in part co-operant—and the social structure is the resultant of them all. To discern how they combine to sustain the structure requires, therefore, a keen and difficult analysis of each changing situation. We may agree with Hobhouse that there is "a broad correlation between the system of institutions and the mentality behind them."[10] But as the system is the same for many divergent minds, the mentality to which it corresponds is, as it were, a composite mentality of various levels.

Yet for the reasons given there must always be a definite relation between changing social forms and changing attitudes, beliefs, and cultural activities. As we have shown, technological change as such does not prescribe the specific direction of cultural change, but instead opens up various alternatives. For example, the economy of effort which is the counterpart of higher technological efficiency means that less toil is needed for the satisfaction of primary organic needs. The organic needs of food, shelter, warmth are relatively satiable. A surplus of energy and of wealth is thus made available, unless the advantage of the higher economy is consumed by a proportionate increase of population, for the satisfaction of various cultural demands. These latter fall into two classes, between which every society strikes some kind of balance. On the one hand there are the expressions of our like competitive interests, seeking forms of possession, luxury, power, distinction, all relative goods because they are valued by comparison. On the other hand there are the expressions of our common interests, absolute goods in the sense that all can share in them without diminution or apportionment, the inclusive cultural or spiritual satisfactions. The *degree in which* one or the other of these alternatives is followed is *culturally* determined.

Specific manifestations of cultural change. In Chapter XXIII we suggested that in so far as cultural processes can be represented graphically they tend to exhibit a rhythmic undulating motion instead of the continuous trend in a single direction characteristic of technological processes. Numerous attempts have in fact been made to show that not only cultural but also economic and political processes are cyclical in character, following a repetitive pattern and possessing a definite periodicity in the succession of their stages.[11] Some writers are even led to postulate for various human phenomena, from fashions to civilizations, a regular order of rise, development, and fall, or else a perfect symmetry of rhythmic recurrence.

---

10. L. T. Hobhouse, *Social Development* (London, 1924), Chap. XII.
11. For lists of such attempts see H. A. Phelps, *Principles and Laws of Sociology* (New York, 1936), Chap. XIX; and P. Sorokin, *Society, Culture, and Personality* (New York, 1947), Part VII.

[1] *Cyclical theories:* This hypothesis, for example, is presented on the scale of world history in the erudite if pretentious volumes of Oswald Spengler on *The Decline of the West*, in which he attempted to show that all cultures go through a regular succession of stages corresponding to spring, summer, autumn, and winter. More recently, in his elaborate review of the great civilizations of the world, Arnold J. Toynbee has sought to trace their rise and decline through a determinate pattern of changes, from their first "response to challenge" to their "time of troubles" and final downfall.[12] In a more matter-of-fact way the principle was used by F. S. Chapin for the interpretation of the synchronous changes of the diverse aspects of human life.[13] And A. L. Kroeber found that the changes in women's clothes from the Civil War to the end of World War I had a wavelike motion and an elaborate periodicity.[14] There is always the danger in these demonstrations—and it is flagrantly illustrated in Spengler's work—that we shall fit the facts to the preconceived symmetry. We are prone to look for the order or balance of simple patterns. The early astronomers found it in the movements of the heavenly bodies. Historians found it in the cycle of history; economists, in the economic cycle. But as knowledge increased, as the intricacy of the changeful world was revealed, these notions had to be discarded. Everywhere nature and history give us intimations of rhythm, but seldom do they follow the pattern of our impatient imaginations.

[2] *The sense in which rhythm is an ever-present aspect of change:* Yet rhythm in some sense is implicit in cultural processes. Culture is life expressing itself in valuations and in styles. It is always selective between the potentialities of expression. Styles are always changeful and valuations always partial. No style can please forever, and no valuations can satisfy the capacities of experience. In those areas where culture is most free from authoritarian controls, as in the fine arts, we have a constant succession of styles, a frequent return with variations to former mores, a supersession of the old by the new and then of the new by the old, presenting something of the pattern of an undulatory rhythm. Even in the more authoritarian and institutionalized areas of culture, even in the fundamental mores, there are aspects of undulation. There are oscillations between conservatism and radicalism, between more asceticism and more libertarianism, between a stronger orthodoxy and a larger tolerance, between self-containedness and expansion. Such oscillations occur in the course of the individual life as well as in the life history of peoples. But in the latter, with the ever-renewed energies and creative impulses of overlapping generations, they repeat themselves without term. It is this fact that gives plausibility to the Hegelian doctrine of social evolution, according to which one historical

12. *A Study of History* (first six vols., London, 1934-1939); one vol. abridgement by D. C. Somervell (New York, 1947).

13. *Cultural Change* (New York, 1928), pp. 211 ff.

14. "On the Principle of Order in Civilization as Exemplified by Changes of Fashion," *American Anthropologist*, N. S., XXI, No. 3 (1919), 235-263.

stage gives place to another that is a revulsion from it, asserting what the former denied. Culture is always in flux, not merely because civilization changes, but because changefulness inheres in it.

[3] *Indices of cultural change:* In order to appreciate how cultural change stimulates social change, it is very desirable that we should develop methods of tracing or measuring cultural trends. This is a harder task than the measurement of technological change, since the latter reveals itself in concrete and comparable embodiments. But many aspects of culture are elusive and intangible. It is relatively easy to trace changes in the arts and in externalized styles, such as those of architecture, decoration, and dress. It is not difficult to trace changes in the range of opinions that register themselves through such devices as voting. It is less easy to study the changes in the ideas that cluster round the everyday life, the popular philosophies, the notions of authority, the doubts and the certitudes, the fears and the hopes of men. Even those larger principles, such as nationalism or socialism, which reveal the character of an age, are seldom intensively studied as *processes of opinion* that emerge and rise to power. We know far more about the rise and fall of institutional systems than about the changing valuations that explain their rise and fall.

In an earlier chapter we discussed the attempts of psychologists and sociologists to "measure" attitudes. To measure *changes* of group attitudes, we should here point out, is a very different thing and not open to the same objections. It is true that we have to depend on a variety of indices, none of them fully revelatory of the subjective change, and all of them therefore requiring careful interpretation. But changes of attitude are indicated in many ways, through their effect on habits, customs, fashions, and modes of living as well as through their expression in art, entertainment, and literature. An example of the way in which popular magazine literature can be used to reveal changes of attitudes is offered in a work to which we have several times referred, *Recent Social Trends.*[15] Among other signs of the somewhat rapid shifts in attitude characteristic of modern society it is there pointed out that the "discussion of sex morals in *Reader's Guide* periodicals was three times as frequent in 1930–1931 as in 1919–1921. . . . In the *New York Times Index*, entries under 'moral,' 'moral conditions,' etc., rose from 0 in 1914, 1915, and 1918, to 92 in 1926 and then sank to 6 in 1931."[16] Another significant indication is that "while popular scientific periodicals increased their proportion of the total circulation about four times, the circulation of Protestant religious periodicals decreased to about one-sixth of what it was in 1900."[17] This last illustration provides an example of the need for the interpretation of indices. In the same work it is pointed out that "the total number of church members in the United States

15. "Changing Social Attitudes and Interests," by Hornell Hart, Vol. I, Chap. VIII.
16. *Ibid.*, p. 417.
17. *Ibid.*, p. 391.

has been growing at virtually the same rate as the population."[18] The one index suggests a stability, the other a weakening, of religious attitudes. We leave it to the student to explain the disparity and to consider in what respects one or the other of the two indices is a better reflection of the changing situation.

18. *Ibid.*, "Changes in Religious Organizations," by Luther Fry, II, p. 1020.

27

The Reality of Social Evolution

Misleading Trails

Skepticism regarding social evolution. Can society or its forms properly be said to have passed through evolutionary stages in the sense in which the species of organism have evolved? It has been fashionable in the last few decades for American anthropologists and sociologists to abandon the concept of social evolution. Some have declared it an advance that sociologists generally speak of social change instead. One school of anthropologists has constantly attacked the doctrine of "unilineal evolution" and tends to disparage the evolutionary method altogether.[1] These tendencies may signify revulsions from oversimple and sweeping formulations of the school of Spencer and Ward and Giddings. With increasing knowledge we learn the endless diversities of social systems. Primitive peoples as well as civilized exhibit many different patterns in their social systems. But it is equally true that there are endless diversities in the species of life, which fact does not prevent the biologist from discovering the evolutionary stages to which they belong. There can be vast differences between societies at the same evolutionary level, and in fact at any of the higher levels there must be—for this itself is part of the significance of evolution—great variations of one from another. If the ambiguous phrase "unilineal evolution" means a sequence in which specific institutions of the simpler societies pass by similar processes into specific institutions of the more advanced societies, then it is certainly to be rejected. But we have no reason to interpret evolution in this way. Differentiation, the emergence of more distinct organs to fulfill more distinct functions, may take a multitude of forms. The system of law differs widely in, say, the United States and in France, but in both

1. Cf. A. Goldenweiser in *The History and Prospects of the Social Sciences* (H. E. Barnes, ed., New York, 1925), pp. 221 ff.

countries it has a character which entitles us to call it more evolved than the corresponding system in Melanesia.

One reason for the neglect of the study of social evolution is that social change is, as we have seen, often confused with technological and cultural change and thus, embracing everything that happens to human beings, is regarded as too complex and many-sided to reveal an evolutionary process. Another reason is that the evolutionary principle is often itself misunderstood. Cats do not evolve from dogs, but both dogs and cats are products of evolution. The patriarchal family may not have evolved from the matriarchal family, but both types have undergone evolutionary change. What we mean by social evolution, which has nothing to do with what is called "unilineal" evolution, should be clear from our earlier discussions. But there is one frequent misunderstanding with which we have not dealt and which deserves some attention. This is the mistaken search for the *origins* of things.

The problem of origins. The question of origins has always been an engrossing one for the human mind, and the mythology of all peoples contains crude answers to it. But the question itself, in most of its forms, belongs to pre-evolutionary thought. People used to ask—and answer—the question, How and when did society begin? That particular question has grown obsolete, and the answers to it, such as that of the "social contract" theory, have been discarded. The seed of society is in the beginnings of life, and if there were such beginnings in any absolute sense we know nothing of them. But we still raise similar questions regarding the family, the state, the church, the law, and other social formations, though the quest for their origins may be as vain as that of the social-contract theorists. It seems at first sight a reasonable enough question. There was certainly a time when there was not a state or a church; therefore, we argue, they must have had a historical beginning. So we have various theories of origin, that the state, for example, was the result of war and conquest and slavery or of the establishment of a dominant class or even of some convention or constitution on which people all at once agreed. But all these theories are misleading because they misconceive the nature of an evolutionary process. There was a time when there was no state, and yet the state has no beginning in time, no point of origin. This is a paradox but not a contradiction, as it would have seemed to pre-evolutionary thought. We recognize now that even salient or revolutionary social changes need have no absolute moment of origination. When, for example, did the "industrial revolution" begin?

[1] ***When and how did the state begin?*** Let us take one theory of the origin of the state to show how such theories mislead us. Franz Oppenheimer in his book, *The State*, gives the following version of the well-known Marxist doctrine of its origin.[2] There are, he points out, two fundamental and fundamentally

2. English translation, New York, 1926. The exploitation theory is not peculiar to Marxist writers; it is also put forward by authors of quite different schools, such as L. Gumplowicz in his *Soziologische Staatsidee* (2nd ed., Innsbruck, 1902).

opposed means whereby man seeks to supply his needs. One is work, the other robbery, or exploitation of the work of others. The former is the economic, the latter the political means, and the state arose when the political means was organized. There are peoples who possess no vestige of the state, primitive grubbers and huntsmen. They have a social structure but no political structure. The latter originates among herdsmen and among vikings, the first groups to exploit others or rob them of the rewards of their toil. Among these arise class distinctions based on wealth and poverty, on privilege and the denial of privilege. The most decisive of these distinctions is that between the slave-owner and the slave. It was the warrior nomad who invented slavery, the seedling of the state. The grubbing peasant who toils for his own would never have discovered it. When he is subjected to the warrior and pays tribute, the land state begins. Similarly, through coastal raids and robberies the vikings created the maritime state.

Now if Oppenheimer had set out to show the importance of the role played by robbery and exploitation in the early making of the state, it would have been a valid enterprise. It would have involved a study of the relation of this factor to other factors and a close and difficult historical investigation which he avoids only by making certain dogmatic assumptions. It is, in the first place, arbitrary to *define* the political means as robbery, from which it follows all too simply that the state, being the organization of the political means, was established in the manner he describes. On this definition a pirate band would be a state, and not because it is organized but because it is organized to rob. Since the organization of the state certainly serves other ends, since it is concerned to establish some principle of internal justice so that the disputes between man and man are settled by a tribunal and not by violence, since the economic factor is only one of its interests, only one of the ways in which from early times the solidarity of the group was maintained by the state, to identify the political means with exploitation is the simplification of an inadequate psychology. Significant as that motive was, it did not work alone. The authority of the elders over the younger kin was not exploitation, but it played a part in the making of the state. The tribal sense of justice evoked agencies of jurisdiction, and they too were conditions of the emerging state. And many factors contributed to create the kind of political loyalty without which the state could never have grown to maturity.

We are thus thrown back on the question, What does the state, *once it has clearly evolved*, mean? It implies, we may say, a territory over which a unified order is maintained by means of law, involving some kind of coercion of those who violate the order and therefore some kind of authority to which appeal can be made. This is the objective fact, the expression, surely, of more than one aspect of human nature. Now, there seems to be no people among which there are not rudiments of this order, a foreshadowing of the state. There may be no settled government, but there are always some elements of organization out of which such government may evolve. There will be elders, or an individual headman or medicine man who wields some sort of authority. This authority will be ostensibly based on age or birth or prowess or religious lore or magical power, but the authority is not wholly without a political aspect. In a small group, say of Andaman Islanders, there is no state as we define the term, but there are already germs of the state organization, custom which prevails by social sanction over a locality, and skilled or aged men who have prestige and win respect and obedience.

[2] *Emergence, not beginning:* We should speak, then, of the emergence of the state rather than of its origin. It is a structure which in a certain process grows more distinct, more elaborate, more permanent. Its organization becomes distinguished from the organization of kinship. Custom passes into law. The patriarch becomes the political chief, the judge becomes the king.[3] Following this process historically, we can better understand the statement that though there was a time before the state was, the state itself has no beginning in time. Its birth is a logical fact, only its evolution belongs to history. The idea of historical origins is here related to that of specific creation, in the pre-evolutionary sense. There is no state among the Yurok Indians or the Andamanese, yet in some degree these are political beings, just as in some degree they are religious beings, though they have no church.

We pointed out in another context that our application to earlier social stages of terms indicative of later and more evolved conditions is apt to confuse our understanding of this fact.[4] Sometimes a term is sufficiently generic to comprehend the less evolved and the more evolved types of the social form referred under it. The term "family" is an example. But in other instances our modern terms denote specializations which did not exist as such in earlier stages. Of these the term "state" and the related terms "sovereignty," "government," and "law" are examples. The specific forms and functions so denoted are lacking not only in primitive tribes such as the Melanesians and the Eskimos, but also under much more advanced conditions. As we shall show presently, specific institutions evolve earlier than specific associations. The people of Athens or of Sparta had no separate term for the state. Their word "polis" did not distinguish the state from the community.[5]

Every community, no matter how primitive, contains germinal elements of the state. We think of primitive communities, in contrast to modern ones, as based on kinship. But this does not mean that the general bases of community, the common living and the common earth, were absent from their consciousness of solidarity. In some degree they were both present and determinative. R. H. Lowie well brings out the point that in the ostensibly kin-based community

3. See R. M. MacIver, *The Modern State* (Oxford, 1926), Chaps. I–IV, and *The Web of Government* (New York, 1947), Chap. II.

4. See pages 141–142.

5. Cf. MacIver, *The Modern State*, Chap. III, §3.

locality also served as a social bond.[6] If the sense of contiguity had not also been active, the social cohesion of the kin-group would have been dissipated. It is in part at least because of this sense of contiguity that the tribe exercises jurisdiction over the differences between families within its area, that it adopts strangers into the kin, and so forth. And other bonds, such as that of religion, merged with the bond of kinship. In fact, under the aegis of kinship were half concealed all the grounds of social relationship, including the rudiments of the state.

What we have shown concerning the state, that the search for specific origins is vain, could also be shown concerning the other significant elements of the social structure. We have already seen how unsatisfactory has been the attempt to find an original specific form of the family.[7] And we shall presently see, when studying the emergence of the church, how that process precludes the idea that it had a specific historical beginning. In this context it is permissible to speak of origins only if we mean thereby a process of formation which itself has no *precise starting point.*

What kinds of social phenomena have definite beginnings and endings? But surely, it may be said, some social phenomena have beginnings and endings. Have not many institutions disappeared and others come into being? Is history not strewn with accounts of the passing of organizations, from empires to outworn sects? We answer that we are dealing with social types, not with individual embodiments of the type which, of course, are always appearing and disappearing. But the type itself is a different category, and is revealed only as process. Here again it may be objected that type-forms also disappear at historical moments. Has not slavery passed away or, if it lingers in some parts of the earth, is not its total abolition practicable? Have not totemism and the classificatory system of kinship disappeared in the more advanced societies? If things have an end, have they not also an origin?

[1] *Totemism and kinship classification:* Let us take the last two cases first. It is not indeed necessary to our argument that no social types should vanish altogether. In the same way the doctrine of the continuity of species is not affected by the disappearance of some forms of life. Nor does the argument hold that what ends in a historical moment also begins in a historical moment. For what ends is a specialized form, and it does not begin as such but only grows into specificity. Even so, the social type-forms which we think of as dead are remarkably persistent. Totemism in its full significance as a basis of social identification and classification is absent in civilized society while characteristic of a wide range of primitive peoples. But the type-form of totemism is present vestigially among ourselves, as Goldenweiser points out, in the use

6. *The Origin of the State*, (New York, 1927), Chap. IV. Cf. also A. Goldenweiser, ***Early Civilization***, (New York, 1929), Chap. XII.

7. Chapter XI, pages 243-246.

of animal mascots, the emblems of political parties, badges and crests and other tokens, in such symbols as the flag and the college colors, in such orders as the Elks, the Lions, and so forth.

> The names and things that are thus used as classifiers and symbols, habitually rest against a background of emotion. In the case of regimental banners, the emotions aroused may reach great violence, while in the instance of animal and bird mascots there arises a complex of attitudes and rites so curiously exotic as to invite an exaggerated analogy with primitive totemism.
>
> The fact remains that the supernaturalistic as well as the social tendencies of totemic days live on in modern society. But in our civilization these tendencies, in the absence of a crystallization point, remain in solution, whereas in primitive communities the same tendencies . . . function as highly distinctive vehicles of culture.[8]

Conversely it may be said that many tendencies which "remain in solution" in primitive society are "crystallized" in our own civilization. Again, the classificatory system which is seemingly so alien to us has its paler analogues among ourselves. We apply the terms "brother" and "sister" to the members of various social orders, and, as Goldenweiser also points out, we even use for classificatory purposes some kinship terms, such as "uncle" and "aunt," which were not so employed in primitive groups.

[2] *Slavery:* Finally, let us take the case of slavery, since it illustrates a further distinction. In the United States, as in various other countries, slavery was abolished at a precise moment of history. It was an ancient institution of mankind. We need not pause to consider whether certain modern applications of the term, in such expressions as "white slave" and "wage slave," are significant or fanciful. The slave economy in the old sense has disappeared. There are still instances to be found, under somewhat disguised appearances, of the relation of master to slave, as, for example, in camps of war prisoners or in the concentration camps of totalitarian countries. As for slavery in general, what has happened is that a once socially accepted system has been legally or constitutionally disestablished. Since slavery involved an essentially coercive relationship, it could exist in a complex society only if legally established. Modes of social regulation can be set up and can be discarded. All specific institutions which depend for their existence on convention or prescriptive law have an hour of birth and may have an hour of death. But the great social forms are more deeply rooted. Regulation may modify them, but it neither creates nor destroys them.

Social relationships are subject to an endless process of transformation, of growth and decay, of fusion and separation. Since they are all expressions of human nature, the social relationships of the present are found in germ at

---

8. From A. Goldenweiser, *Early Civilization*, copyright 1922. Reprinted by permission of the publishers, Alfred A. Knopf, Inc.

least in the past, and those of the past survive, if only as relics, in the present. We distinguish social stages, not by the sheer presence or absence of social factors, but by their prominence, their relation to others, their organizing function.[9] (Even abolished institutions, like slavery, may be present "in solution," ready to "crystallize" again if an opportunity is given.) The most significant social changes are not those which bring an entirely new thing into being, but those which alter the relations of eternal or omnipresent or universal factors. The pattern is always changing but the threads endure. What is new is the emphasis, rather than the factor emphasized. There may remain, for example, some aspects of oligarchy—or even of dictatorship—in a state that is essentially democratic. Elements of contradictory social forms may be present together—what distinguishes different systems is the predominance of one form over the rest.

Continuity, then, is an essential character of the evolutionary process. Continuity is the union of change and permanence, and when in this union we move in the direction of social differentiation we are following the road of evolution. The general nature of this road will occupy us next.

General View of Social Evolution

Primitive society as functionally undifferentiated. The functional interdependence of the groups and organizations of an advanced social system is almost totally lacking in primitive society. The main divisions of the latter—families, clans, exogamous groups, totem groups—are segmentary or compartmental. It may have a fairly elaborate system of ceremonial offices, and a more elaborate system of kin-distinctions than is characteristic of an evolved society. But there are few groupings or categories into which, for the practical purposes of co-operative living, the members fall. The kin-grouping is usually predominant and inclusive. To be a member of the kin is *ipso facto* to share the common and inclusive rights and obligations, the customs, the rituals, the standards, the beliefs of the whole. There are, of course, certain "natural" groupings, particularly those of age and sex. There may be prestige groups, perhaps a simple system of classes or castes, though these latter are not found under the most primitive conditions. There may be some rudimentary occupational distinctions, but the division of labor is narrow and usually follows "natural" lines, such as that between the sexes or between the older and the younger. The great associations do not yet exist. There is no separate organization of religion—still less of religions; there are no schools, no distinct cultural associations; there is little specialization of economic productivity and ex-

9. We may distinguish technological, as distinct from social, stages by the presence or absence of particular devices or inventions, as F. Müller-Lyer, for example, constantly does in his *History of Social Development* (Eng. tr., London, 1923).

change. The only clearly associational groups, other than temporary partnerships in trading ventures and so forth, are usually "secret societies," not specifically functional, and the very fact that they are "secret" is significant, implying that the group has not yet found a way to incorporate them effectively within its unity.[10]

[1] *The undifferentiation of primitive "communism"*: The undifferentiated character of primitive society is seen in the prevalence of a simple form of communism. The kin is a larger family and exhibits something of the communistic character of the family. The tribe devises a system of participation in the booty of the chase and the products of the earth. Where private or family rights are admitted, it is in the right of use, not in the ownership, of the land. Even what are to us the most intimate or personal of rights were then rights pertaining to the blood brotherhood. The lending of wives to tribal guests, common to certain American Indians and many tribes of Africa, Polynesia, and Asia, may be regarded as a mode of admission to the "freedom" of the tribe. It may be, as Julius Lippert interprets it, that thus "the guest enters into all the rights of the tribal members, and the special sanctity of the relationship revives the ancient rights of the latter."[11] The sanctioned license at primitive marriage feasts, the institution among some African peoples of the "bride-hut" where the bride was free to the men of the tribe, the pre-marriage prostitution established as a Babylonian temple rite, may be interpreted as survivals of sexual communism or at least as the assertion, before their alienation through marriage, of rights regarded as belonging intrinsically to the tribe.[12]

Such a communism typifies the simple solidarity of an undifferentiated community. The differentiations as exist are based on the natural distinctions of youth and age, of man and woman, of different aptitudes such as that for leadership, and on a few socially acquired distinctions, such as the inheritance of ceremonial office or of magical lore. The myriad aspects of differentiation belonging to a civilized society are latent. The divergent interests, aptitudes, capacities which may appear in rudimentary forms have no opportunity to develop within the restricted range of the communal life. The social heritage is too rude to afford them selective stimulation. The mores appropriate to that narrow heritage tend to be repressive of such differences, as endangering the

---

10. On primitive secret societies see H. Webster's book so named (New York, 1908); also F. Boas, *The Social Organization and the Secret Societies of the Kwakiutl Indians* (Washington, D. C., 1897).

11. *Evolution of Culture* (P. Murdock, tr., New York, 1931), p. 217.

12. Thus many writers, such as Sir J. G. Frazer (*Golden Bough* [New York, 1935], V, 36 ff.); Sir J. Lubbock (*Origin of Civilization* [New York, 1882], pp. 535 ff.); J. Lippert (*Evolution of Culture* [New York, 1931], pp. 207 ff.); G. E. Howard (*History of Matrimonial Institutions* [Chicago, 1904], I, 50); and R. Briffault (*The Mothers* [New York, 1927], I, Chap. XI) have interpreted these practices. E. Westermarck (*History of Human Marriage* [New York, 1922], I, 218 ff.) takes a different view.

solidarity of like-mindedness, the only solidarity of which the group as a whole is yet capable.

[2] *The modern contrast:* The civilizations of the past and of the present emerged from that early stage. How they emerged, through what blind forces of conquest and subjection and expansion, creating differences of wealth and of class, through what nurture of the arts, through what clashes of customs and faiths leading to some liberation of the mind, through what increments of scientific knowledge and its application, is the main theme of human history. For us here, it is enough to point the contrast. It is characteristic of our own stage that we have a vast multiplicity of organizations of such a nature that to belong to one has no implication of belonging to the rest, that every kind of interest has created its correspondent association, that nearly every kind of attitude can find some social corroboration, and that thus the greater social unity to which we belong is conceived of as multiform, not uniform. This is the necessary intellectual feat demanded of the participants in the "great society," and the many who still cannot achieve it belong to it in form but not in spirit.

Significant forces in social evolution. Long and difficult as the evolutionary process may seem in historical perspective, it has been remarkably rapid if we take the larger perspective of organic evolution. We have already commented on the relative rapidity of social change; we may now add that social evolution has likewise moved at a pace vastly quicker than that of evolution in the biological order. No primitive type of animal evolves into an advanced type in so short a period as that comprised by recorded human history—the very idea seems absurd. But in that period one primitive society after another has moved to a stage that at least by comparison reveals a highly evolved structure.

[1] *The role of diffusion:* Social evolution is liberated in a sense from organic evolution because human beings can use for their purposes instruments that are not part of their own physical structure and because in using them they are in a measure guided by intelligence and not merely by instinct. Thus equipped, they can rapidly increase their social heritage and transmit its evolutionary potentialities to their descendants and communicate them to others over the whole face of the earth.

Sometimes diffusion and evolution are regarded as opposing principles in the interpretation of social change. But in truth there is no need for this opposition. Diffusion should be regarded as one of the most important factors in social evolution. The great societies of the past all reveal, in so far as records remain, the formative and challenging influence of cultural intercourse. The civilization that arose on the Nile penetrated as far as India. The thought-systems of India reached into China and later contributed elements to the awakening civilizations of the West. The Greeks built on the heritage of Mycenae, Crete, and Egypt. Rome from its earliest days began to feel the impact of the cultural forces already full grown in Greece. And so it has been down to our own days.

[2] *Anti-evolutionary influences:* Needless to say, the establishment of this present stage of differentiation was the task of many centuries, and pressures emanating from the older conception of solidarity have been strongly directed against it and are still in some measure operative. In the making of modern society it has usually been the state—though sometimes the church—which has sought to prevent further differentiation by making all other organizations a part of its own structure and subject to the conformity it imposed. Hobbes in the seventeenth century had denounced free associations as being like "worms in the entrails of the natural man," and as late as the end of the eighteenth the French Revolution had sought in the name of liberty to abolish all corporate bodies. Rousseau no less than Burke, the philosopher of revolution as much as the philosopher of reaction—so slowly do our minds perceive the growing social fact—could still not admit the separate organization of state and church, still believed in the "universal partnership" or the "total surrender" which made the membership of a society culturally inclusive. In our own age great societies have been "co-ordinated" back to a less differentiated form of social structure by totalitarian dictatorships, particularly under the Nazi domination of Germany and under the "monolithic" communism of Soviet Russia. But whatever the claims of these opposing principles—and again it should be clear that we are speaking of social evolution and not of social progress—it is significant that the attempts in question have succeeded only in countries which had experienced to a lesser extent or for a shorter period the diversifying conditions of modern industrialism, the cultural variations revealed in divergent faiths, and the conflict over the issue of free association; that they have succeeded only by establishing a coercive control suppressive of the differentiations which would otherwise arise; and that they have occurred as the sudden sequel of catastrophic and abnormal events, not in the more orderly course of social change.

The main line of social evolution. We cannot attempt to trace the historical process by which these various grades of differentiation have come about. But if we turn to our primitive societies we can see the generic lines which that process follows.

[1] *From communal custom to differentiated association:* Before institutions come attitudes and interests. As these grow distinct they become reflected in customs which assume a more and more institutional character. Simple societies are ruled by the all-pervading code of custom. As they grow in size, as they respond to new needs, as the nuclei of one or more special interests become important, or in various other ways, occasions arise for the vesting of particular functions in particular men or subgroups. These men or groups tend to distinguish the rights and privileges of their functions from the general customary

code, to elaborate them, to *institutionalize* them. By slow accretion lores and skills are increased and particular members of the group become their repositories and acknowledged practitioners. Specific modes of procedure, specific taboos, specific approaches to the mysterious powers of nature or to the *sacra* of the tribe, are thus developed—in other words, new institutions are formed.

The formation of institutions usually precedes, and often by a very long interval, the formation of associations. In fact, in relatively primitive societies the step from institutions to associations is seldom taken at all. For the associational phase implies an elasticity of the social structure which primitive conditions and primitive mentality can hardly admit; it implies the more difficult combination of likeness *and* difference. Social evolution must be already well advanced, the scale of society expanded and the pressure of the common mores lightened, the diversification of interests enlarged through the advance of knowledge and the specialization of the economic life, before the right of free association becomes effective. Only under these conditions does the family detach itself sufficiently from the social matrix to become an autonomous unit, dependent for its creation and for its maintenance on the will of the consenting parties. Only under these conditions does the uniformity of communal education break into the variety of particular schools, and other educational associations. And finally the great politico-religious system which claimed to control all the rest reveals the internal disharmonies of its enforced unity, and in their different ways the associations of the state and of the church are formed.

Schematically this process may be presented as follows:

I. Communal Customs
The fusion of political-economic-familial-religious-cultural usages, which pass into

II. Differentiated Communal Institutions
The distinctive forms of political, economic, familial, religious, cultural procedures, which become embodied in

III. Differentiated Associations
The state, the economic corporation, the family, the church, the school, etc.

[2] *The significance of the associational stage:* The passage from the second to the third of these stages means a momentous transformation of the social structure. There may, of course, be some minor incidental associations under primitive social conditions, but the great permanent forms of association, as we define that term, are as yet unthinkable. Primitive solidarity requires that if you belong to the tribe you belong also to—or are adopted into—the kin, that if you share its life you share also its gods. The diversity of institutions, as they unfold themselves, is at first only the diversity of the aspects of communal life. In that growing diversity is hidden the germ of a new order, but it takes ages to develop. For the new order means a new and freer diversity.

In our second stage there is one set of political institutions for the whole community. In our third stage there is still one state, but there are also political organizations embodying diverse ideas concerning the state. In our second stage there is one set of religious institutions recognized by the community, and these are bound up with its political institutions. In our third stage not only have they become detached from the state, culturally autonomous, but they have in consequence created a variety of religious associations. This freedom of association admits an indefinite multiplicity of contingent forms, with endless possibilities of interrelationship and independence, based on the general foundations of a community life, the obligatory aspects of which are now safeguarded by the state.

The differentiation of the great associations from one another is accompanied by vast differentiations within their respective structures, responsive to the same forces which bring about the former. To deal in any detail with this whole process would occupy a large volume in itself. All we can do in the present work is to offer, in rather brief compass, a single illustration of it, so as to bring out more clearly the main principle. For this purpose we shall examine the process by which the organization of religion has evolved.

How the evolutionary clew helps us to understand society. Before we turn to this illustration, it may be well to point out the way in which the evolutionary clew helps us to understand society. While there are many social changes which may seem as undirected and inconsequential as the waves of the sea, there are others which clearly fall within an evolutionary process. And in tracing these the student gets a firmer grip on the social reality and learns that there are great persistent forces underlying many movements which at first he apprehends as mere events in the historical flux. More particularly, the evolutionary clew, where it can be traced, has the following advantages.

[1] *The clarification of distinctions:* In the first place, we see the nature of a system better as it "unfolds" itself. Evolution is a principle of internal growth. It shows us not merely what happens to a thing, but what happens within it. Since in the process latent characters or attributes emerge, we may say that the very nature of the system emerges, that, in Aristotelian phrase, it becomes more fully itself. Suppose, for example, that we are seeking to understand the nature of custom or morality, things we are still very apt to confuse. We understand each the better by seeing how the two, fully merged in primitive society, have grown distinct as the range of conduct over which custom rules has diminished. And so with many another distinction, such as that between religion and magic, or crime and sin, or justice and equity, or right and privilege, or economic and political power.

[2] *The ordering of social types:* Again, the evolutionary clew enables us to set a multitude of facts in significant order, giving them the coherence of successive stages instead of tying them on the purely external thread of chro-

nology. For the historical record presents us with a confusing multitude of events, a mere chaos of change until we find some principle of selection. Inevitably we seek to discover the type or type-situation which these events indicate in a particular frame of time and space, and then to relate that type to earlier and later ones. The latter aim is realized if we discover an evolutionary character in the series of changes. Take, for example, the endless changes of the family. In studying them we discover that within a certain area of modern history the functions of the family have become more limited to those essentially arising out of its foundations in sex; in short, a significant time-succession is revealed. Just as biological science achieved order by following the evolutionary clew, so here at least does social science. And the evolutionary principle, where discernible, is of far-reaching significance because it relates whole successive situations, no matter what their magnitude, to one another and consequently has proved serviceable in every field of science. It is surely a primary order of change that is revealed alike in the history of Rome and of Japan and of America, alike in the record of the snake and of the bird, of the horse and of man, alike in the brief story of each organic being and in the inconceivably immense record of the cosmos itself.

Again, the evolutionary principle provides us with a simple means of classifying and characterizing the most diverse social systems. If we tried to classify all societies on the basis of the kind of customs they followed or creeds they accepted, or of their diverse ways of making pottery or pictures or the like, our classifications would be elaborate, cumbrous, difficult, and limited. When, on the other hand, we classify them according to the degree and mode of differentiation shown by their customs and creeds and techniques, we are taking as our basis a structural character applicable to society everywhere, and one with which the endlessly variant manifestations of customs and creeds are integrally bound.

[3] *An aid in the search for causes:* Finally, the evolutionary clew spurs us to the quest of causes. Where we discover direction in change we know that there are persistent forces cumulatively at work. Some of these are indeed sufficiently obvious. We can trace, for example, the differentiation of the professions, and it is easy to see how the principle of efficiency or economy—which is one form of the expression of intelligence—would, given the conditions for its exercise, such as greater economic resources, a wider market, and better technological equipment, lead to this result. As early as the days of Hesiod it was said of a man that "he had skill in many things, but little skill in any."

The following quotation from an American historian illustrates the condition out of which the differentiated professions arose:

> In the Boston *Gazette*, February 6, 1738, Peter Pelham advertised that he taught "Dancing, Writing, Reading, painting upon Glass, and all kinds of needle work"; he was a painter, an engraver and also gave instruction on the harpsichord and in the elements of psalmody. . . . Really, that society of 1738 did not have sufficient

> occasion for him in all these varied forms of competence to keep him alive and he had to piece out as a merchant of tobacco. Eventually there would be engravers, dancing masters, painters, musicians, various teachers of elementary subjects including manual training, who could trace back the converging lines of their respective developments to such an unforked stem of their general branch.[13]

This particular development is readily explained, but the broader trends of social evolution, like those of organic evolution, raise profoundly interesting and difficult questions of causation.

An Illustration: The Evolution of the Church as a Social Form

Preliminary considerations. It must be premised that in this illustration we are considering not the evolution of religion but the differentiation of a social form through which religion is in part expressed. Religion has other aspects which do not directly concern us here since it is not religion, but society, which we are studying. It should also be observed that in tracing the evolution of the church we are not following a process which has occurred within the limits of any single society or social area. No one society is so permanent and definite, so self-identical through the broad reaches of social evolution, that it could serve for this purpose.

Primitive cults: We are concerned with a series of social transitions, leading at length to the establishment of the church, as a free association within the community. The first step was the formation of specific religious institutions, demarcated though not separated from other social institutions.

[1] *The fusion of religious and other cultural elements:* Under the most primitive conditions of which we know the religious element is wholly fused with others. Primitive mentality has itself less power of, or less exercise in, discrimination. As Lucien Lévy-Bruhl puts it, "the mystic properties with which things and beings are imbued form an integral part of the idea to the primitive, who views it as a synthetic whole."[14] Religion was an aspect of his way of thinking about things, about all significant things. "It was at the first, as it were, a mental atmosphere which enveloped every society, clinging most densely, like mist on the hills, to the salient features and occasions of its life, to sex and birth, to spring and harvest, to death and pestilence, to darkness and to the light that pursues it, to the sudden revelations of natural powers, to the kin-custom, and to the authority of the chief."[15]

13. From an article by Dixon Ryan Fox, "A Synthetic Principle in American Social History," *The American Historical Review*, XXXV (1930), 263.

14. *Primitive Mentality* (L. A. Clare, tr., New York, 1923).

15. MacIver, *The Modern State*, Chap. V, § 2.

Perhaps we should not call this pervasive emotional attitude, so hard for us to appreciate or describe, by the name of religion at all. It is rather the attitude out of which religion grows. Since the primitive mind has no conception of the operation of natural laws, the distinction of the natural and the supernatural, even the disturbing distinction of the physical and the spiritual, is not yet developed. It is not merely that disease and misfortune are attributed to malignant powers against which a system of protection, by the evocation of other powers, may be devised. It is that these powers themselves are both physical and nonphysical, like the *mana* of the Polynesians and other peoples, mysterious properties dwelling in things, combining with the rain and the sunshine to make things grow, combining with the flight of the spear to hurt a man. The "ghost" of a man, even his name or his mark or his painted image, has the same kind of potency as the man himself. Or again the man and his totem are one, identical expressions of the same quality. Even when the gods became distinct, they were but greater men living on the same plane or descending to it. For, as in Genesis, "the sons of God saw the daughters of men that they were fair."

[2] *Cults and magic:* This native response of the primitive mind toward an unknown world becomes, in time, traditionalized in the social heritage, becomes a lore with its rituals and creeds. Guesses at the unknown become formulated, socially accepted, instituted. The mysterious potencies of earth and storm, of animate and inanimate nature, become more definite beings, who must be approached according to prescribed formulas. Priests and interpreters, medicine men and workers in magic arise. The fused religious emotion, thus institutionalized, is gradually narrowed to certain aspects and phenomena of life. Thus cults are formed and are elaborated with accretions from various sources. Among the California Indians, for example, Kroeber sums up this process as "a progressive differentiation during four fairly distinct periods. During these four eras, the most typical cults gradually changed from a personal to a communal aim, ceremonies grew more numerous as well as more elaborate, influences from the outside affected the tribes within California, and local differences increased until the original rather close conformity had been replaced by four quite distinct systems of cults."[16]

These cults are not yet religions in the proper sense of the term. They are hallowed ways of doing things or of celebrating things done, and the sanctity is apt to be transferred from the function or occasion to the rite associated with it. The social is still fused with the suprasocial. There seems to be no clear distinction of quality between the "ghost" which migrates from the body and dwells in some physical object—the form of possession called *fetishism* —and the spirit which pervades inanimate nature. Above all, religion and

16. A. L. Kroeber, *Anthropology* (New York, 1923), Chap. XII. For the broader process of differentiation see Paul Radin, *Primitive Religion* (New York, 1937), Chaps. X, XI; and Joachim Wach, *Sociology of Religion* (Chicago, 1944), Chaps. IV, V.

magic are still closely intertwined. The distinction between them must emerge before we can speak of religion in any adequate sense. For magic is an art based on a pseudo science, translating for purposes of manipulation noncausal association into causal connection. It takes, for example, the parings of a man's nails and by fanciful processes works evil on the man himself, or it makes a waxen image of him and believes that the treatment to which the image is subjected befalls the man also. It stills the storm by incantation and makes the earth produce by a charm. In magic there is no mediation; the act by its inherent virtue produces the result. It has certain elements that belong also to religion—ritual and mystery—but in essentials it is utterly different. For the object to which religion is directed is to be approached in an attitude of reverence, creating relations of worship and of communion as with something high or divine, leading to a rule of life. It is true that even in developed religions the element of magic lingers, such as the belief in the mystic efficacy of ritual or again the belief that a religious ceremony by itself makes something good, such as sex relationship, which apart from it is evil. But in developed religions these are nonessential and even alien elements.

The formation of specifically religious institutions. Such religions could not arise until the human was set in clear contrast to a suprahuman reality regarded as divine and to be worshiped as a first cause. But since life was full of perils and pains, of injustice and violence, the growing moral sense was often compelled to distinguish between suprahuman principles of good and of evil. Demons and devils thus became the counterpart of the gods, and as the issue between them was defined, a new fusion, of great significance for the later development of religion, appeared, that of the moral and the religious principle. In some advanced civilizations, the moral principle becomes so dominant that the religious principle proper grows obsolescent, as in the "religions" of China and India. In others the two remain integrated, leading to many difficult problems of interpretation and preparing the way for the evolution of sects, as the variant moral sense sought to harmonize itself with theological traditions. But that is a much later part of the story.

[1] *Communal deities:* As religion is institutionalized, it becomes in a sense the property of the community. Dead heroes, dead kings, dead ancestors, real or mythical, are translated to the ranks of the gods, and the living kings already possess the attribute of divinity, as in Japan. The nature-powers, not only of native rock and plain and shore, but also of the air and the sky, become localized deities. Among this plethora of divinities, order is achieved by the dominance of one over the rest, and according to the degree of dominance the religion tends either to henotheism or to polytheism. The henotheistic type, waiting to develop into full monotheism, was characteristic of many Semitic peoples, worshipers of Yahweh or Baal or Chemosh or Dagon or Milcom. The Aryans tended to polytheism. Sometimes there were the special gods of the

small community and beyond them the gods of the larger people, as in Attica the local deities were distinct from the Olympians. Localization went still further, down to the presiding deities, the Lares and Penates, of the household.

[2] *Emergence of the "sacred" and "profane":* Religion, thus localized and institutionalized, became the exclusive possession of the group. To leave the community was to leave its gods also. The gods of the tribe watched over its members, rewarded and punished them, gave them victory in battle—an attitude to which civilized peoples also revert in time of war. Religious institutions are then gradually demarcated from other social institutions. Religion itself tends to develop the distinction between the profane and the sacred, its organized mysteries are set apart from the everyday life. Special "religious societies," that is, groups who severally possess certain religious beliefs and "secrets" and practice their own rituals, arise within many communities. Sometimes the distinction takes a curious form. Thus among the Southern Kwakiutl Indians, religious societies alternate seasonally with totemic clans. "In the summer (the *profane* season) the clans constitute the social organization; whereas in the winter (the season of the *secrets*) these are replaced or, more accurately, overshadowed by a system of religious societies."[17] Among more advanced peoples the relation of the priest to the ruler becomes the crucial issue in the process of differentiation. Where the two once coalesced, both the functions and the officials tend to grow distinct. In Israel the people demand a king apart from the sacerdotal judge. In ancient Greece as in Rome the priestly functions of the rulers atrophy and are in part invested in separate officials. In Egypt the conflict for supremacy between priests and kings assumes an age-long character.

From religious institutions to specifically religious associations. The process in which religious and secular institutions become demarcated is too variant and elaborate for examination here. We must pass to the next transition, from the religious institution to the religious association, the church.

[1] *Earlier assaults on socioreligious systems:* The "religious societies" of the primitive world were not at all religious associations in our sense. They were semicommunal, partitioning the community like clans or totem groups; they were not composed of members drawn selectively, by their own adherence, from a whole community. The institutions of religion grew distinct long before the concept of a church arose. The socioreligious organization of each group remained a unity. It was a question of harmonizing religious and other social institutions, more particularly religious and political authority, and the discords that arose were due to the struggle of the two powers exercised over the same community. Sometimes the socioreligious unity was threatened by

---

17. A. Goldenweiser, article "Totemism," in *New International Encyclopedia*, Vol. XXII (New York, 1930).

the introduction of alien religions, not accommodated to the social system, like that of Baal in Judaea or the Orphic and Thracian mysteries in Greece, or the Oriental faiths and finally Christianity in Rome. But either they were driven out or they existed on sufferance, as exotic cults. China presents an interesting contrast here, for the religious principle was so dominated by the ethical that it lost its other-worldly theological characteristics and became a traditionally inspired way of life, admitting without great difficulty the variant interpretations of its prophets, native or introduced. Thus the struggle was far less acute. It is true that sometimes Buddhism was the official religion, sometimes Taoism, that on occasion the one endeavored to suppress the other, while at least once both were officially suppressed in the name of Confucianism. But on the whole these "religions" were able to exist side by side without much disturbance.

In the ancient Western world the greatest assault on the socioreligious unity was that made by Christianity within the Roman Empire. Christianity, perhaps for historical reasons arising out of the situation of the Jews within the Roman Empire, definitely dissociated itself at the outset from the political realm. Its kingdom was "not of this world." It formed a conclave distinct from, in fact separate from, the social order. With the introduction of such a faith the unity of the old socioreligious system was threatened. But the issue never culminated. By a strange reversal, in the disintegrating Roman Empire, Christianity, changing vastly in the process, became the established religion, driving its predecessors underground. In its new form it gained at length an extraordinary control over a social life which had lost its other bonds of unity. The nascent association, with its distinct membership, disappeared, and the socioreligious union is reasserted. Throughout the Middle Ages two sets of institutions, two forms of order, two differently derived authorities, controlled the same society. The communities, themselves simple, relatively passive, predominantly agricultural recipients of a common culture, are subject to strains and stresses arising not within them, but in the unstable hierarchy that ruled them. The favorite medieval conception of the "two swords," the secular and the spiritual, reflects the ultimate conflict of authority. The issue was whether the two powers should be in the same hands, or whether they should be separated, and, if separated, which should dominate the other, or how, in general, they should be related. The idea of two separate memberships, of two associations with distinct spheres and not necessarily the same range, was not yet born.

[2] *Disharmony within continuing socioreligious systems:* In the European Middle Ages the conflicting claims of ecclesiastical and political authorities were never reconciled. The spiritual sword might compel an emperor to do penance in the snow, or the secular sword might send the papacy into exile. But neither Avignon nor Canossa settled the question. Nor did the Reformation establish a new principle in this regard. The claims of Calvinism were at

least as absolute as the claims of *Unam Sanctam*—the bull of Boniface VIII, which roundly proclaimed, as a tenet necessary to salvation, that all the peoples of the earth were the subjects of the Pontiff. The functions of the two authorities, the ecclesiastical and the political, were not delimited with respect to one another. The ecclesiastical authorities exercised political functions through their own courts and councils, and the political authorities exercised religious functions, making religion compulsory, controlling ecclesiastical appointments, and so forth. These conditions prevented the formation of the distinctive religious *association*, the church, having free spiritual authority over its own members only. And we may observe also that it prevented the clarification of the nature of religion also—and more particularly of the religion in the name of which the issue was fought, for it immersed religious institutions in the atmosphere of political intrigue and above all it injected into this religion the alien element of enforcement. The nature neither of church nor of state could be realized until this element was extruded. Hand in hand with the social confusion went an intellectual confusion.

A long process of differentiation was necessary to remove this confusion.

> After, as before the Reformation, the parish continued to be a community in which religious and social obligations were inextricably interwined, and it was as a parishioner, rather than as a subject of the secular authority, that [the villager] bore his share of public burdens and performed such public functions as fell to his lot. The officers of whom he saw most in the routine of his daily life were the church wardens. The place where most public business was transacted, and where news of the doings of the great world came to him, was the parish church. The contributions levied from him were demanded in the name of the parish. Such education as was available for his children was often given by the curate or parish schoolmaster. Such training in co-operation with his fellows as he received sprang from common undertakings maintained by the parish, which owned property, received bequests, let out sheep and cattle, advanced money, made large profits by church sales, and occasionally engaged in trade. Membership of the Church and of the State being co-extensive and equally compulsory, the Government used the ecclesiastical organization of the parish for purposes which, in a later age, when the religious, political, and economic aspects of life were disentangled, were to be regarded as secular.[18]

The ecclesiastical authorities might properly seek, provided they used only "spiritual" means, to make religion permeate the social order, but when they sought to extend their rule over that order they were faced with a hopeless dilemma. They could not grasp the secular sword without losing their proper identity. This was in fact the problem of the later medieval church, torn between the Catholic conception of it as the all-comprehending arbiter of society and the contrary conception of its more spiritually minded members

18. From *Religion and the Rise of Capitalism* by R. H. Tawney, copyright, 1926, by Harcourt, Brace, and Company, Inc.

and groups. The issue was complicated by all manner of more earthly motives on both sides, but without this internal conflict could not have come that final disruption of the "universal church" which was in a measure the unintended result of the teaching of men like Luther, who attacked at the same time the immersion of the "church" in the evils of the social order and the control which it exercised over that order, who protested in the name of "religion pure and undefiled," the religion of the heart—a concept whose far-reaching implications utterly escaped him—who distrusted all institutions and handed them ruthlessly over to the civil power. Within the reformed church the inveterate belief in theocracy arose again to strength with Calvin, who restated the Catholic tradition for a society of burgesses and small traders, and to secure its supremacy translated religion into a tyranny more irresistible than that of any temporal Caesar, in that it rested for popular support on the inculcated superstitution of hell-fire. Its intolerable character was sufficiently revealed in the Geneva of Beza, the Edinburgh of John Knox, and the Boston of Cotton and Endicott.

[3] *The basis of modern differentiation:* These conditions, with their cultural confusions, have been, on the whole though by no means completely, dissolved in Western civilization in the process which from the sixteenth to the nineteenth century led to the establishment of the church on an associational basis and the concomitant differentiation of church and state. This differentiation, now attained in many Western societies, is based on these principles: (1) that the church is a body of believers, a distinctly organized membership, distinct in its offices and services, possessing as a corporate body only cultural means of influencing its members and not claiming to exercise any kind of control over those who are not its members, membership being voluntary and based on fellowship within a faith; and (2) that the state, being an organization exercising compulsion and claiming territorial control, refrains from interference on religious grounds with the members or nonmembers of any church.

The establishment of these principles in Western civilization, subject as they still are to qualifications and exceptions, was the work of centuries of struggle. It was the solution of a problem, the reconciliation of the unity of citizenship with the diversity of belief. But the problem was not solved as problems in engineering are solved, by the deliberate intelligent consideration of its true nature. Politics and religion are too close to human prejudices and passions to admit this method on so crucial an issue. The solution was reached because the old socioreligious unity broke down and every attempt to reassert it was defeated by the underlying conditions. Suppression and persecution and the compromise of "toleration" alike failed.[19] Conditions had arisen under which

19. For the transition from toleration to religious autonomy see MacIver, *The Modern State*, pp. 171–175. For the subsidiary questions of the relationship between church and state see *ibid.*, pp. 175–180. Cf. W. A. Brown, *Church and State in Contemporary America* (New York, 1936); H. P. Van Dusen, *et al.*, *Church and State in the Modern World* (New York, 1937); and

authority could no longer secure religious conformity. Various influences conspired to bring this result—what stress should be laid on one and another of these interactive forces is a much debated question. Certainly among them must be included the advance of science, leading gradually to new conceptions of the universe and disturbing old thought-forms, the more critical and more realistic thinking stimulated by the rediscovery of the Graeco-Roman culture, and the changing attitude toward authority engendered in the political and economic struggles of an age in which nationalisms were forming and the bases of the economic life were shifting.

Under these conditions the great ecclesiastical schisms occurred, and religious sects, hitherto held in check by the suppressive unity of church and state, arose and multiplied. Religion, in short, became to a vastly greater extent a personal affair. The final result was that the organizations of religion lost in many countries much of their social control. The earlier result was that in the countries where anti-authoritarian influences were most in evidence Protestant churches, on a definitely associational basis, grew strong. It has been excellently shown by Max Weber that the spirit of these churches was more favorable to the industrial capitalism which was emerging in the seventeenth and eighteenth centuries.[20] How far that spirit prepared the way for the new economic order and how far it was itself an accommodation to changing economic conditions is again one of the open questions of social causation. Certainly, however, the two were congenial. The variety of economic interests, like the variety of religious interests, expressed itself in a world of manifold associations. This is the evolved character of the social structure in which we live, and it is from this basis that any further changes of an evolutionary character must proceed. Perhaps, for example, we may expect a future development of many varieties of other cultural associations whose seeds were hidden in the once-dominant organization of the church. As we have suggested, the associations of the cultural life are capable of a degree of detachment within the unity of the social order which is not possible for the associations of the economic system.[21] Economy, order, and peace require that men live in a closely integrated politico-economic system, but the system itself, if democratically organized, can equally serve any number of different faiths or different human goals.

The fact that society has evolved is, of course, no guarantee that this evolution will proceed further or even that the reverse process of a return to primitivism will not set in. We have pointed out that anti-evolutionary forces always resist the evolutionary trend. This condition is also manifest in our present world. As regards the relation of church and state, for example, there has been

---

the several articles on "Organized Religion in the United States," *The Annals of the American Academy of Political and Social Science*, March, 1948.

20. Weber, *The Protestant Ethic and the Spirit of Capitalism* (T. Parsons, tr., New York, 1930).

21. Cf. Chapter XX.

in some countries, notably in Germany under Hitler, a drive toward the restoration, in a new form, of the more primitive identification of the two and toward the dissolution of the independent existence of the church. Various totalitarian states have either suppressed the church altogether or, failing in that, sought to turn it into a subservient organ of the government. The latter policy was practiced in Nazi Germany. There the Protestant church was in effect "coordinated," under a dictatorial Minister of Church Affairs, in spite of some resistant elements represented by Pastor Martin Niemoeller and, on one occasion, by ten leaders of the German Evangelical Protestant Church, who told the Führer that the commands of God took precedence over his (July, 1936). The Roman Catholic Church, on the whole, especially as represented by Cardinal Faulhaber of Munich, took a stronger stand against Nazi claims, and political considerations restrained the Nazis from waging outright war against it. In Soviet Russia, on the other hand, the Russian Orthodox Church, which indeed prior to the Revolution had been a mere subsidiary of the state, was divested of opportunities and privileges and allowed to exist on sufferance under conditions that have made it negligible as a social force.

28

Social Evolution and Social Progress

Why Social Progress Cannot Be Identified with Social Evolution

Evolution and progress. That society has evolved is a demonstrable certainty. Can we demonstrate with no less certainty that society has progressed? We may assuredly *believe* in progress, but we cannot demonstrate it to others unless they first accept our valuations. Different people may look on the same social changes, and to some they may spell progress, to others decadence. The evolutionary changes we described in the last chapter are welcomed by some and are opposed by others. Primitivism has always had its champions and it still has them today.[1] Apart from that, many of the conditions on which depend important human values, such as contentment or abiding faith or economic security or freedom from over-heavy stress and strain, are not obviously realized more adequately in the more evolved society—in fact, strong indictments have been drawn against civilization on these counts. Clearly, then, we cannot, without confusion, introduce the idea of progress into our *definition* of evolution.

[1] *The danger of confusion:* Auguste Comte and many of his followers fell into this mistake, which gravely affected the scientific character of their work. The confusion was increased by the writings of Herbert Spencer. It crept also into the formulations of earlier American sociologists, including Lester Ward and F. H. Giddings. It is not absent from the writings of so thoughtful a student of social evolution as L. T. Hobhouse, who defines "social development" in a manner that sways uncertainly between the concept of evolution and that of progress.[2]

1. See, for example, H. O. Lovejoy, *et al.*, *Primitivism and Related Ideas in Antiquity* (Baltimore, 1935).
2. *Social Development* (London, 1924), Chap. IV. Other works in which Hobhouse deals with social evolution include *Morals in Evolution* (New York, 1919) and *Social Evolution and Political Theory* (New York, 1911).

Instead of dwelling on the confusion into which these authors fell, let us look more closely at the need for the distinction. The last of the above-mentioned writers was coauthor of a study in which a considerable number of the simpler peoples were rated on an evolutionary scale. Table XIII is taken from that study.

TABLE XIII **Cases of Peoples Having Certain Institutions Shown as Fractions of Total Number of Peoples in Each Class**[3]

Class	Polygamy general	Nobility	Slavery
Lower Hunters	.29	0	.02
Higher Hunters	.32	.11	.32
Agricultural I	.18	.03	.33
Pastoral I	.53	.20	.37
Agricultural II	.43	.15	.46
Pastoral II	.74	.24	.71
Agricultural III	.64	.23	.78

Observe that the various peoples are listed in the degree of their respective control over nature, as reflected in their arts, the least advanced being placed first. Now, assuming that the order is an evolutionary one, we run against the facts that the more advanced of these peoples are more given to polygamy, are more likely to have an oligarchical structure, and much more frequently have a system of slavery. But would we set down these changes as progress?

[2] *Is progress a "scientific concept*"? The relation of social evolution to social progress is in fact a problem which presents many difficulties, and they arise chiefly because of the variable and inconclusive character of the concept of progress. It has a different significance for different individuals, for different times, and for different social groups. To the eighteenth-century "Enlightenment" progress meant emancipation from the bonds of tradition and the tyranny of power. To late-nineteenth-century America it seemed to be identified with the triumphant expansion of society and the exploitation of the resources of the earth.[4] The concept of progress is a chameleon that takes on the color of

3. L. T. Hobhouse, G. C. Wheeler, and M. Ginsberg, *The Material Culture and the Social Institutions of the Simpler Peoples* (London, 1915), p. 228.

4. "It is a misfortune," said V. L. Parrington in Volume III of his *Main Trends of American Thought* (New York, 1930) (*The Beginnings of Critical Realism in America*, p. 19) "that America has never subjected the abstract idea of progress to critical examination."

the environment when we are adjusted to that environment, and some contrasting color when we feel maladjusted.

It is still sometimes claimed that progress is a "scientific concept," in other words, that it can be so defined as to express an ideal on which all who use the term "scientifically" can agree and one which is itself present in actuality in a degree which can be positively ascertained. Thus one sociologist regards the goal of progress for the individual as "the complete functioning of an integrated personality," and thence proceeds to define social progress as consisting "in those changes in the social structure which release, stimulate, facilitate, and integrate human functioning."[5] But any such solution is apparent, not real. The expressions "complete functioning" and "human functioning," are, like the term "progress" itself, not symbols of definite meaning but verbal brackets which are given different content by different users. Complete functioning, if we try to take the phrase strictly, would turn the plastic human animal into a chimera. All functioning is selective, and everyone defines progress, for himself, in terms not only of the extent but also of the quality of the functioning.

Why the concept of progress can have no universally accepted reference. Can we get no further than this negative result? Although different minds interpret progress differently, is there not a common core of meaning? Are there not fundamental desires common to all mankind, and do they not provide the raw material of the concept of progress, however differently it may be worked up by men of different extraction and circumstances? Do not our psychologists reveal to us the deeper urges of the race, and do not our sociologists tell us of the "four wishes" and other simple formulations of the primary motivations of all men?[6] And if there are perversions and mutilations and aberrations of these, cannot we regard them as deviations from the norm and still find in the norm itself the ground on which to construct a sufficient concept of progress?

[1] *Progress in terms of what?* To answer these questions let us state more explicitly the character of the valuation that the concept of progress involves. When we speak of progress without a qualifying adjective, such as "economic" or "material," we invoke an ultimate, not an intermediate or conditional, standard of value. Economic progress means no more than increase in the economic means to progress. The latter can be measured, but what cannot thereby be measured is the degree in which the measurable increase of the means contributes to the ill-defined and unmeasured end, which is progress itself. On this account we should not, as economists such as Pigou do, speak of eco-

5. Article entitled "Is Progress a Scientific Concept?" by Professor Hornell Hart in *Sociology and Social Research*, XIII (1929), 303-314.

6. The "four wishes" of W. I. Thomas and F. Znaniecki (*The Polish Peasant* [New York, 1918], I, Methodological Note, pp. 72-73, and III, Introduction) are response, recognition, security, and new experience.

nomic welfare as a part of total welfare—it is a condition, not a part.[7] By increasing welfare, or progress per se, we must mean the nearer or fuller realization of a state of being which accords, not even with our desires, but with our sense of the desirable. We are in the realm not only of ultimate values, but of ultimate *ethical* values. In this realm agreement proves nothing except that we agree. If Bornean tribes accept success in head-hunting as progress, it is merely their judgment and may be denied by another people or another civilization. And so with our own social goals. We must go by our own sense of values, for there is no appeal to any higher court.

Moreover, when we leave out the qualifying adjectives, like "economic" or "material," we are then evaluating not this factor or that in the scheme of things but the whole scheme itself. There are so many diverse elements involved that it is hard to comprehend the whole and still harder to evaluate it. In the great movements of social change there is, whatever standard we adopt, loss as well as gain. In what we may designate advance there is assuredly not an equal advance of all the items in our catalogue of goods. Every achievement has its costs, and men often differ as to whether the costs outweigh the values accrued. The "simpler peoples" achieved higher social organization with the aid of slavery—was this progress as it was certainly evolution? Our own civilization has multiplied commodities and services through mechanized, standardized routine. The facilities and stimulations of urbanization go with congestion and the loss of the free contacts with nature. To balance the gain and loss in each total emerging situation is a hazardous personal judgment, and yet such an accounting is involved in every attribution of progress.

[2] *Can we define progress in terms of desire?* It may be said that we ourselves create by our preferences these new social situations, that it is our own devices and techniques which bring them into being, and that therefore they express at least the majority choice, the general estimate of the direction in which progress lies. But the truth is not so simple. Whole situations are not presented to us to choose between. They may be the result of a large number of partial conditioned preferences but they are certainly not the result of an all-round preference. Whatever motives lie behind the inventive spirit, whether the sheer joy of technical mastery or the desire for profit or for fame or for the lightening of toil or the increase of goods, it is certainly not actuated by the desire that more men should live and work in cities and fewer in the country. Yet the chain of causes into which invention enters brings inexorably the last-mentioned result. The various individual items of desire which we pursue—even when they can be co-operatively or harmoniously achieved—do not merge into a whole which is the fullness of our desire. Besides, the distinction between the desired and the desirable here again arises to confute our attempted solution. Mill was surely wrong when he stated that there is no way of knowing what is

7. Cf. A. C. Pigou, *The Economics of Welfare* (London, 1929), Chap. I.

desirable except that men desire it.[8] Our ideals not only stretch further than our desires—sometimes the two are in actual conflict. Creatures of habituation as we are, there are crucial situations when we must say, "I want this, but I know I would be happier or better if I did not want it, or wanted that instead." What we desire and what we feel we ought to desire are here opposed, and it is with the latter and not with the former that we link the idea of good, envisaged as realized or as in process of realization. Even were there universal agreement on the fundamental urges or the "wishes" of mankind, that agreement would not yield an adequate definition of progress.

[3] *Is there any way out?* From these difficulties in the way of a "scientific" concept of progress there seems no escape. Two paths tempt us, but they both lead to the same impasse. We may accept the subjectivity of the concept, and seek a definition in subjective terms. Of these the favorite is "happiness." Suppose, then, we agree that progress means more happiness—though dissent would in fact arise from various quarters—yet happiness has no common reference. The lover and the religious enthusiast, the epicure and the ascetic, do not merely find it in different directions but actually experience it as different subjective states. And if we say, "Be it so, but a precise definition of *social* progress is not on that account barred, for social progress means a change of social conditions such that more people achieve happiness, or more happiness, in their respective ways," then again we are faced with the utilitarian difficulty of the computation and comparability of happiness and with that even more formidable difficulty before which the greatest of the utilitarians yielded when he said that it is better to be Socrates dissatisfied than a fool satisfied.[9]

Finally we may try the other path. Premising that human beings are fundamentally alike, have the same organic natures, the same initial appetites, the same germinal capacities varying in degree of potency or of evocation, we may seek for a common content of progress by setting down those goods or forms of satisfaction which all men seek in the degree of their opportunity. If we examine the actual conduct of men—and all conduct is practical valuation—do we not find a large agreement concerning the things they both desire and find desirable? In this list of goods can we not place health, length of life (given health), assurance of the means of living, sustaining social companionship, the respect of one's fellows, and some degree or kind of power and prestige? And can we not then say that social progress means such change in the conditions of a society that these are provided in greater measure for its members? Observe, however, that our very limited list of common goods already contains two categories, certain minimum requirements of organic well-being and certain desiderata of a social nature. Now the first group contains nothing the desire for which distinguishes the savage from the civilized man or even the man from

---

8. J. S. Mill, *Utilitarianism*, Chap. IV.
9. *Ibid.*, Chap. II.

the lower animal. We should surely regard these fulfillments as elemental conditions of progress rather than as substantial contents of it. The establishment of the social conditions necessary to provide these requirements for the great majority is still far from being attained, and concerning these at least we may agree, concerning this first step on the road of progress. The second category gives us a little more trouble. In it we include one desire that is characteristically, well nigh universally, human, that for distinction, prestige, or power in some direction. But the peculiarity of this desire is that it cannot be translated into a social ideal, for the reason sufficiently summed up in the homely words of the satirist, "when everyone is somebody, then no one's anybody."

Moreover, our minimum list omits certain of the more profoundly human purposes in living. If there is a large measure of agreement concerning its items it is because they are thought of chiefly as means rather than as ends of life. As soon as we try to import into it those cultural items which are more strictly ends, the consensus goes. It is in times of expanding civilization, when men are much preoccupied with means, that whole peoples are most apt to share a common belief and a common confidence in progress, merely because it is falsely identified with the means in which they are engrossed. In short, it is only when civilization and culture are confused that progress is thought of as a "scientific" concept. When that distinction is adequately recognized and people endeavor to express their ideals of the "good life," the difficulties we have already discussed reappear. There is, to begin with, the question of the priority of the goods in our list. The relative importance attached to primary or bodily satisfactions varies greatly. Temperament and education become involved, and the relative, fluctuating, subjective nature of the concept of progress is then apparent.

The Place of the Concept of Progress in Sociology

A crucial question. Should sociology have *anything* to do with such concepts as progress? Should it be concerned at all with the whole great area we call "social problems"? Or should it refuse outright to deal with any subject involving the goals or purposes men pursue? If, for example, the concepts of evolution and of progress belong to such different orders of thought, if the one reveals the emotional neutrality of scientific thinking, and the other the varying coloration of our purposes and of our dreams, is it not the business of sociology, in studying social change, to discard the latter altogether? Is it not one of those alien intrusive concepts that have perturbed, from the days of Plato to the present, the attempt to see society as it is?

[1] *In what sense the social sciences can be "value-free":* It is claimed by writers of various schools of thought that the social sciences should be "value-free." There is an obvious sense in which this claim is correct—when it means

that the social sciences must never let human valuations of any kind or any preconceived doctrines impede, interfere with, or distort the impartiality and neutrality of the scientific method. But sometimes the claim is made in a questionable way. There are those who assert that the social sciences should never even investigate value-facts without denuding them of their valuational elements. For example, they reject, for "scientific" purposes, all such words as "purpose" and they translate the language of values into such terms as "tension or imbalance in an organism."[10]

If values are data of human experience then they are, as such, proper objects of scientific study. The demand of science is simply that we avoid *bias* in our treatment of them. We must always be on guard lest our personal valuations distort the reality we are seeking to understand. We must, as scientists, care more for the truth than for the consequences of the truth. The causal nexus of things must be investigated with scrupulous care for the evidences, whether they confirm or deny our prior beliefs. But if we endeavor to meet the conditions imposed by science we must also reconcile them with the conditions imposed by our subject matter. As has been pointed out, this is no simple task. For human valuations are themselves an aspect of the *subject matter* of the social sciences. These valuations affect and even determine the social relations and institutions with which we deal. They do not affect the realities with which the physical sciences deal. Moreover, these human valuations do not lie objectively before us as the atom or the star lies before the physicist. We discover them only in so far as we ourselves can enter into the experience of other evaluating beings, of the present or of the past. We must apply our own discernment of values if we are to pierce through the confusing layers of overt professions and rationalizations that often conceal the actual valuations of men in society. We must even be able to distinguish between the values actually maintained or fostered by an institution or organization and the values attributed to it by its adherents and its enemies. For unless we know the institution as it is thus set in the antagonisms and harmonies of a social system, we do not know it at all, and we certainly cannot interpret its changes.

In what sense, then, can subjects such as sociology be, in the German phrase, "value-free" (*wertfrei*)? Certainly not in the sense that they leave human values out of account, uninvestigated, unscrutinized. Nor yet in the sense that while they must deal with valuations, or value-facts, they treat them as facts without seeking to comprehend the operative significance of the values they embody. That would be to denude them of their dynamic and essential character. Furthermore, it is doubtful whether sociology can be value-free in the sense that the investigator can or should adopt a standpoint from which all human valuations are to him equally indifferent, for if he attained such a standpoint

10. An extreme exponent of this position is George A. Lundberg. The expression quoted above is from his *Foundations of Sociology* (New York, 1939), p. 272.

then he would probably be unable any longer to *understand* the impulses that control human behavior. The patriot, the religious devotee, the ambitious leader, the lover, the man of affairs, would alike become no more than organisms curiously gesticulating in a social void. We are driven to the conclusion that *the only clear and indubitable sense in which sociology can be value-free is that in dealing with value-facts the sociologist should never suffer his own valuations to intrude into or affect his presentation of the valuations which are registered in the facts themselves.*

[2] *The dilemma of those who make the claim:* Many formulations of the claim that sociology and the other social sciences should entirely abjure the realm of valuations fail to recognize the full significance and the full difficulty of the problem. Even the fine exposition of sociological *Wertfreiheit* by that excellent sociologist, Max Weber, leaves something out of account.[11] The difficulty is illustrated by the writings of those sociologists themselves who make the largest claims for *Wertfreiheit*. Thus Leopold von Wiese ends a discussion of the subject with the words: "Value judgments, adieu."[12] But in the body of the work to which this forms an introduction, he not infrequently admits explicit or implicit value-judgments. Witness the following passage: "The bristling frontiers of such countries as France and Italy, Germany and Poland, China and Russia, the systems of protective tariffs and subsidies, the ever-recurring attempts to monopolize the means of communication, the insatiate expansion of imperialism, the unprecedented growth of war-waging systems, the startling proliferation of technical means of man's destruction . . . can be regarded as advantages only by optimists of the most myopic, resolute, and unwavering stamp."[13] And in a later part of the book he introduces a strong condemnation of modern warfare, which he calls "irrational and absurd."[14] Again, no sociologist has prided himself more on his complete "objectivity" and his exclusive reliance on "logico-experimental" analysis than Vilfredo Pareto. But critical value-judgments abound in his work, and the criticism is directed with particular pungency and more abundant illustration toward certain tendencies or movements, such as socialism, religious nonconformity, pacifism, and sex asceticism.

[3] *The ways in which social science is concerned with values:* One cannot, of course, conclude that a principle is unsound or an ideal false because its proponents fail to live up to it. But the manner in which they do so is illuminating. It suggests the need for a more adequate definition of the sense in which value-

---

11. *Gesammelte Aufsätze zur Wissenschaftslehre* (Tübingen, 1922), pp. 146–214, 451–502. A good survey of the whole problem, with special reference to Max Weber, is given in F. Kaufmann, *Methodenlehre der Sozialwissenschaften* (Vienna, 1936), Part II, Chap. III. See also A. von Schelting, *Max Webers Wissenschaftslehre* (Tübingen, 1934), pp. 58–64.

12. *Systematic Sociology* (New York, 1932), p. 8.

13. *Ibid.*, p. 163. The quotations are taken from the amplified English translation of Howard Becker but are not an interpolation by the translator.

14. *Ibid.*, p. 611.

judgments do not come within the orbit of social science. ***While no science can ever validate any thesis of final values, science nevertheless can and does enter the area of value-judgments along two roads.*** (1) It can test the accuracy, adequacy, and representativeness of the factual evidences adduced in support of a value-judgment. (2) It can test the validity of conclusions concerning what is better or worse in so far as these are supported by reasoning from premises containing statements of fact. It can, for example, prove or disprove such theories as attribute superior moral or intellectual qualities to a particular race or class, such theories as attempt to show the relation to human well-being of a state of peace or a state of war, such evidences of the truth of a religion as consist of historical records or allegations of the occurrence of supernatural phenomena, such views of the beneficence of a system of sex morals as proclaim the social consequences of its establishment or maintenance to be conclusive proof of its value, and so forth. Difficult as some of these matters may be to investigate, they all lie within the potential area of scientific demonstration.

While, then, there remain some controversial issues regarding the manner and degree in which the social sciences are qualified to deal with certain types of value-judgment, there need be no disagreement on the fundamental relation of scientific inquiry to the affirmation of final values. In particular, there should be no dubiety on the following points, which are implicit in the very conception of scientific investigation:

(a) Science is concerned not with the establishment of ultimate ends or values, but only with the relation between means and ends; the ends can never be demonstrated, but only the relevance or adequacy of means to postulated ends.

(b) Science is concerned with what *is*, not with what in the last resort *ought* to be; and it must always avoid the confusion of the *is* and the *ought*, of the fact and the ideal.

(c) Social science has *as part of its subject matter* the valuations operative in social institutions and organizations, but not the valuations of these valuations on the part of those who investigate them.

(d) Social science, in investigating the instrumental character of institutions and organizations, that is, there services and disservices as means to postulated ends, must always guard against the danger that the bias of the investigator will magnify those aspects of service or of disservice which give support to his own valuations.[15] This is the great practical difficulty that faces the student of the value-impregnated processes of society. He must always select from the myriad facets of the presented reality, and is always in peril of selecting in terms of one or another of the various biases to which human beings, whether scientists or laymen, are subject.

---

15. By *bias* we mean a disposition to reject the logic of evidence in favor of a preconceived belief.

The concept of progress in human history. The concept of the desirable, and therefore of that which would be more desirable, or progress, is never absent from human affairs. All conduct implies a consciousness of welfare, of less and greater welfare—we could neither live nor act without it. To live is to act, and to act is to choose, and to choose is to evaluate. Hence as human beings we cannot get rid of the *concept* of progress, though we are of course entitled to deny the reality of progress. The fact that men inevitably differ about it, that we cannot demonstrate the validity of our concept as against theirs, only makes it more indubitably ours. If none can prove it none can refute it. At the least it is a vital myth, ineradicable from the creative strivings of life. What alone is subject to scientific scrutiny is the historical reality of progress, however defined; the manner of the dependence of progress, past or future, on specific means or agencies; and the content of the concept as it is framed by different individuals or groups.

It has been stated that the concept of social progress is a modern one, a birth of Western civilization whose parents were the Darwinian theory and the industrial revolution. It would be truer to say that the confidence in the reality of continuous progress is modern. The *concept* of progress may be as old as mankind. True that often it appeared in the reversed form, so natural to every aging generation, that the world is growing worse, but logically we cannot have the *concept* of "worse" without that of "better." The lamentation for the "good old times" is a commonplace of all literature. We find it in folk myths everywhere. It is present in the third chapter of Genesis, which tells of the loss of Eden and the fall of man. Even thereafter "there were giants in the earth in those days." But sometimes the eyes of the prophets were filled with the vision of future greatness and their minds with the belief in a deliverer who would usher in a new era. In classical literature, as in Jewish, the golden age was generally thought of as lying in the past, but there were dreams of its return, as in the fourth *Eclogue* of Virgil. The belief in achieved progress is not, however, absent. It underlies the *Prometheus* of Sophocles and it rings through the funeral speech of Pericles. On a wider scale, and most notably, it is the theme of the *De Rerum Natura* of Lucretius. Lucretius, who also had remarkable intimations of the modern principle of evolution, implicitly distinguished it from progress and significantly saw the latter as essentially a liberation from the thraldom of superstitious beliefs and practices. After the classical period the dominance of religious authority, with its rigid views of the preordained lot and destiny of mankind, weighted down all interpretations of social progress. Such limited expressions of the principle as did emerge, from Augustine's "City of God" to Dante's *universitas humana*, were conceived in an entirely different spirit.

Many other examples could be given, but these may suffice to show that the concept of progress is not a modern invention. What is modern is the placid assumption, characteristic of groups or peoples living in an expanding industrial economy, that progress is the normal quality of social change. And perhaps no less the assumption that material gain, statistically measured economic increment, is a sufficient indication thereof. But in some sense or another the concept of progress operates as an historical factor in social change and must be reckoned with as such.

Some Problems of the More Evolved Society

The challenge of social change. In a highly differentiated society, modes of living and of social intercourse must obviously differ from those that prevail within a more simple society. But the difference is not merely that between one system of folkways and another, each appropriate to its own time and place. The profounder difference is that between the attitudes of the primitive and those of the civilized being toward the folkways themselves. This difference we have already suggested at various points in the discussion of social change. Here, in concluding, we shall seek to bring out more directly its significance for the problem of living in the more evolved society.

[1] *The need for personal readjustment to changing conditions:* Under all conditions life is a process of continuous readjustment. The changing organism readapts itself to the changing environment. It establishes a moving equilibrium between its needs and the conditions of their attainment. The folkways themselves are built up in this process, not by definite design, as man constructs a machine, but by gradual responses and habituations. They are a solution to various problems of adjustment, both between man and nature and between man and man; and they change in the same gradual responsive undesigned manner in which they were initiated. They assume a world in which change itself is slow and gradual.

But the world of civilization is not that kind of world. With specialization and complexity, and the more rapid tempo of change that accompanies them, new attitudes are required, as a precondition of successful adjustment. In the first place, social institutions can no longer be taken as constant, as a secure system of procedures by the aid of which the individual adjusts himself to the changes in himself, in his fellow men, and in outer nature. Institutions and mores do remain a necessary aid to personal equilibrium, but they no longer assure it, for they themselves have become merged and to them too, as to the rest of his changeful world, the individual must constantly readjust himself. This means a vital difference of attitude, and much of the disorganization and neurosis of modern life may be interpreted as a failure to meet this demand.[16]

16. Different approaches to this problem are represented by S. Freud, *Civilization and Its Discontents* (New York, 1930); Karen Horney, *The Neurotic Personality of Our Time* (New York, 1937); E. Fromm, *Escape from Freedom* (New York, 1941); H. D. Lasswell, *World Politics and Personal Insecurity* (New York, 1935); Karl Mannheim, *Man and Society in an Age of Reconstruction* (New York, 1940).

When people migrate from a rural to an urban area changes occur not only in their customary ways of living but also, unless they have already lost the ability to respond to new conditions, in the underlying attitudes they tend to exhibit toward these customary ways. They are more ready to modify them at need, to regard them as subject to rational reflection concerning their utility. The transition from the old to the new attitudes has its perils, for when men give up the absolute assurance of old certitudes they may never attain the relative assurance of new quests. It is the same problem that frequently faces the young who have been brought up in a home environment where some strong orthodoxy prevails and who move into a world that disregards the indoctrinated ways. Every transition from one social situation to another offers the alternative of readjustment or maladjustment. An obvious index of this is the greater frequency of crime among migrants, whether from one area to another or from one country to another. It has been shown, for example, that the migrants from Canada to the United States have a criminal rate 50 per cent higher than that of the native white population and, conversely, that the migrants from the United States to Canada exhibit a rate nearly twice as high as that of the native Canadian population.[17] While migration from one social environment to another makes a particular and abrupt demand for readjustment, the transitions occurring within every modern society are such that a constant readiness to make readjustment to new situations is now required.

[2] *The need for the redirection of group attitudes:* Just as it is incumbent on individuals to maintain a flexible responsiveness to the challenge of social change, so also is it for groups. In a changeful society each group, in its relations with other groups, must constantly face new conditions that demand a change of attitude or of policy. This holds for groups of every kind and of every scale, from the family to the nation. Here we shall look briefly on only one of the problems that are thus either created or accentuated.

We have seen that in the more evolved society the number of *functionally* differentiated groups tends to increase. At the same time, within the enlarged community, groups that are distinguished by other than functional specialization are also likely to increase in number, set apart in some measure by cultural difference or again by ethnic or racial difference. In this respect most modern societies are multigroup societies.

Let us consider the situation in the United States of America. While other countries have their own problems of intergroup relationships, the United

---

17. This illustration and other interesting ones are offered in the contribution by E. H. Sutherland, "Is There Undue Crime among Immigrants?" *Proceedings* of the National Conference of Social Work, 54th Annual Session (1927), pp. 576–577. It should be recognized, of course, that other factors are involved in the explanation of the higher criminal rate of migrants, in the impulses lying back of migration itself. Furthermore, there is some evidence that the transition to a new social environment may stimulate achievement as well as maladjustment. See also R. M. MacIver, "Maladjustment," *Encyclopaedia of the Social Sciences* (New York, 1935), X, 60–63.

States has to an unusual extent the problem of unifying under a common citizenship many groups of highly diverse origin, with all the complications arising from differences of cultural background, religious affiliation, and economic and social status. These groups are not, as in some other multigroup countries, identified with territorial areas. For the most part their members live together within the same local communities, although there is a concentration of particular groups in various areas.

In the United States there are some thirteen million Negroes, some two million Mexicans and other Latin Americans, some five million Italians and four million Poles, seven millions or more of other East European stocks, about five million Jews, with smaller groups of Japanese, Chinese, Filipinos, American Indians, and others. There are also, of course, many citizens of mixed national origin.[18] Over against these groups, which comprise in all perhaps a third of the total population, there are the older American groups of West European origin, holding a certain dominance and prestige, especially in so far as they have become entrenched through long-established residence, family affiliations, and economic and political controls. The problem is primarily one of the attitudes of dominant groups to subordinate or less privileged groups; usually, though not always, of majority to minority groups. From our present point of view the problem is posed by the processes of social, economic, and political change. Previously established attitudes are out of accord with developing national needs, with the changing position of the groups themselves, and with the conditions of national prosperity.

There is a contradiction between the accepted premises of American democracy and the discrimination and prejudicial treatment suffered by various groups in different degrees, including the racial segregation practiced against Negroes and Orientals.[19] There is a contradiction of no less moment between the international professions of the United States, in a period when it has become one of the greatest world powers, and the domestic mores (and in some areas even the laws) that refuse to extend to many citizens the full enjoyment of citizenship. In other words, old attitudes have failed to respond to new needs. The consequence is a lack of national unity and cohesion, developing intergroup tensions and an unreckoned amount of frustration, embitterment, and psychopathological disorganization. In short, we live in a multigroup society, but our attitudes, as members of groups, are attuned neither to its conditions nor to its needs.[20]

The increasing need for the application of intelligence to social organization. Another and no less challenging demand arises from the rapidity with which

18. For a survey of this situation see F. J. Brown and J. S. Roucek, *One America* (New York, 1946).
19. Cf. G. Myrdal, *An American Dilemma* (New York, 1944), Part I.
20. For an analysis of the problem see R. M. MacIver, *The More Perfect Union* (New York, 1948).

the conditions that underlie the social order, and particularly the technological conditions, undergo change. We can no longer, it would seem, depend on the gradual undesigned adjustment of social institutions to our changing needs. The social system is too intricate, too specialized, too unstable, and its parts are too elaborately and delicately interdependent, for us to trust to the slow "natural" processes of adaptation. The great mechanism is thrown out of balance too easily and does not recover it spontaneously. If the system itself was built up without survey or blueprint, it is becoming more apparent that it cannot be sustained without the introduction of whatever intelligence man can apply to its understanding and control. Nor will it suffice that he apply his intelligence to the individual parts and let the whole take care of itself. The history of world disorganization since 1914 refutes that principle. The readjustment of institutions to meet changing conditions calls for a kind of concerted intelligence that under simpler conditions seemed unnecessary. As Julian Huxley remarks, "This is one of the most remarkable facts of evolution —that consciousness, until a very late period, has played a negligible part," and he goes on to suggest that co-operative intelligence becomes an ever more pressing necessity for the more evolved society.[21] The challenge is indeed so obvious that a few illustrations will suffice to show its nature.

[1] *Problems raised by military and industrial technology:* We are not raising the question whether the old ways are in any absolute sense better or worse than new ones. The point is that our attitudes, our ideas, our mores must change with changing needs and changing conditions *if* we are to satisfy these needs and meet these conditions. Perhaps the most obvious illustration is the transformation of the significance of warfare. Under modern conditions war between great states is tremendously different in its operations and in its consequences from what it was under more simple conditions. Such was already the situation before the world wars of the twentieth century. But the epoch-making discovery of the processes of atomic fission, not to speak of the unfathomed potentialities of bacterial and chemical warfare, has made the lesson simple for all whose minds are not blinded by tradition. Those who still think of war in the old nationalist terms are not facing the realities. The militarist mentality may reasonably be said to be dangerously maladjusted to the world in which we now live, since it fails to comprehend the train of irremediable and overwhelming ruin that modern war involves.

The illustration we have just given owes its cogency to two processes of change: the technological change which has revolutionized the arts of warfare, and that other change, itself technologically derived, in the degree and range of interdependence between nations. The way in which increasing interdependence calls for change of attitudes and of interests may be illustrated from every sphere of economic or of political activity but nowhere more revealingly than in the relations between states. The traditional concept of political sov-

21. *Essays of a Biologist* (London, 1923), p. 41; see also pp. 92 ff.

ereignty dates from a time when countries were more nearly self-sufficient, before large-scale industry and international finance developed, when, therefore, governments could assert that they were absolute powers without obligation to one another, each supreme and unlimited and final. On the line of that tradition economists postulated the "closed national state," determined by its exclusive economic interests. Philosophers proclaimed the state to be "the world the spirit has made for itself" and denied that it had even moral obligations beyond its frontiers.[22] The results of the partial acceptance of these principles in the postwar period are now generally acknowledged to have been grave or even disastrous. The facts of interdependence challenge the old doctrine of sovereignty and raise the problem of its restatement to meet the new conditions. Here as elsewhere it is a question of the transition from absolute to relative unities, from independent to interdependent systems, from exclusive to inclusive loyalties and obligations.

The evolution of modern industry likewise affords many illustrations of the need for a redirection of attitudes and the application of intelligence to social reorganization. The old-time business, conducted as a family affair or by a single craftsman with perhaps an apprentice or two, admitted no great distinction of interests, and therefore no complexity of organization, either within itself or in relation to the business activities of others. But when it changed into a factory or workshop and the owner employed an increasing number of hired men, the interest of the wage earner became more distinct from the interest of the employer. Moreover, the change brought with it a new hazard, the loss of stability, the uncertainty that dogged business enterprise with its general ups and downs and its individual successes and failures. This uncertainty bore with peculiar force on the worker, whose livelihood was now at the mercy of unforeseeable chances. This haunting insecurity, the dread of unemployment, had profound effects on his outlook. His primary need for security is still very inadequately met within the framework of capitalistic enterprise.

As the scale of business increased still further, new distinctions of interest arose. The ownership and management of the business, especially in the corporate form, ceased to be identical and no longer had identical interests.[23] Nor was there any guarantee that the interest of the new class of passive owners, the general body of shareholders, would coincide with the interest of the few active owners, the board of directors. Hence there arose not only the larger issues between labor and capital but also subsidiary conflicts of interests within each category, between skilled labor and unskilled labor, between those whose interest required the distribution of surpluses in the form of

22. Cf., for example, J. G. Fichte, *The Closed Commercial State* (1800), and B. Bosanquet, *Philosophical Theory of the State*, Chap. XI. See R. M. MacIver, *The Web of Government* (New York, 1947), Chap. XII.

23. See, for example, A. A. Berle and G. C. Means, *The Modern Corporation and Private Property* (New York, 1933), Chap. VI.

dividends and those whose interest lay in the accumulation of reserves or in the expansion of the business.

Interest complications similarly arose on the larger scale of industry. The size of the market increased, and with this went an increase in the area and in the intensity of competition. What any one business did began to affect powerfully the interests of other businesses. If it cut prices seriously or if it gained any special advantage in the attempt to reduce costs, it created difficult problems for all its competitors. As a result of these and other developments nearly every industry has come to present a curious combination of agreements and competitive practices, a continually shifting adjustment of harmonious and conflicting like interests.[24] And this situation in turn has intensified the distinction between the interests of the industry and the interest of consumers. Compare with this complex situation that of a simple agricultural community, where every farmer is owner, manager, and worker all in one, where he cultivates the soil with the aid of only his own family, and where he and his family consume a large portion of their own products. The diversity of interests has not arisen, nor has the need for elaborate adjustments to a continually changing situation.

[2] *The needed skills:* This differentiation of interests creates problems on two levels. On one level it demands the skill of the social engineer, and in the last resort of the statesman, whose task it is to maintain and to establish the necessary conditions of the larger co-operation rendered necessary by the extension of interdependence and therefore to reconcile or to regulate the diverse and often conflicting interests of the various special-interest groups and organizations. In the simpler societies the adjustment of interests may not need any special oversight, but in the more evolved society, with its elaborate specialization and far-reaching interdependence, new forms of regulation, demanding high skill and intelligence, become imperative. Those who think in laissez-faire terms, as though these problems solved themselves, fail to understand how the world has changed. Perhaps the greatest and certainly the hardest task that faces cilivized man is to discover how, through the co-operative application of intelligence, he can maintain, advance, and redirect to the service of common ends the elaborate complex of material means and social institutions to which, almost unwittingly, he has fallen heir.

24. See, for example, A. R. Burns, *The Decline of Competition* (New York, 1936), Chaps. I, XI.

29

The Broad Pattern of Social Change

How to Interpret Social Change

The complexity of social change. As we reviewed in previous chapters the basic conditions to which social change is responsive, it became manifest that the latter must be explained as a process contingent on the interaction of numerous factors. Any instance of social change is, in other words, the resultant of a specific and probably unique conjuncture of a considerable diversity of conditions.

[1] *The multiplicity of factors:* Suppose we are seeking to explain a crime wave, an increase of suicide, a new religious movement, an outbreak of class strife. Without a change in attitudes these phenomena could not occur, and thus we must take cognizance of cultural trends in our explanation. But the change of attitude is in some sense responsive to the manner in which the interests and drives of men are affected by changes in the conditions under which they are pursued, and thus we must admit into our explanation the economic and technological and political aspects of the total situation in which the phenomenon occurs. And behind these again may lie changes in the human material—organic changes responsive perhaps to new conditions of work, to new stresses, to variations of diet, to the biological factors affecting energy, vitality, mortality, to varying degrees and types of adjustment to the physical environment. Thus our sociological focus of interest, the particular change of social relationships, involves us in the consideration of a multiplicity of factors, themselves not specifically social, but somehow conspiring to bring the social change into being.

Hence the interpretation of social change is a task beset by great difficulties. For the conspiring factors belong to different orders of reality. How, for example, in studying the causes of the falling birth rate, can we apportion the contribution of such unlike factors as the decline of religious authority, the greater economic independence of women, the increase of social mobility, and the development of contraceptives? On what common scales can these seemingly noncomparable conditions be placed and weighed? What common unit of measurement shall we apply to them? How shall we bring under a common denominator the attitudes and valuations of the cultural order together with the technical devices or the biological adjustments of our second and third orders?

This essential and surely very obvious problem has not received the attention it deserves. Those who have specifically approached the problem have generally followed one of two paths, neither of which leads to the scientific goal they sought.[1] Some have simplified the issue by assuming that all the factors in the situation can be treated as quantitatively measurable forces and thus reduced to terms capable of statistical or mathematical manipulation. The others have equally simplified the issue by regarding one of the orders, or even one factor belonging to one of the orders, as the dominant or primary determinant of all the rest. The latter inadequate method we have already reviewed; concerning the former a few words should be said by way of caution.

[2] *Problems of the quantitative method:* The danger of assuming that the methods of quantitative science are applicable arises from the fact that the problem itself is in an important respect unlike the problems with which physical science deals. We cannot apply a similar experiment to a large number of social instances, as one puts a toxin in the blood of guinea pigs. We cannot isolate a single factor x and then introduce it to a total situation to observe in what degree the total situation is thereby changed. It is quite certain that there is no mechanical solution. By no assiduous collection of instances, by no computation of coefficients of correlation, can we ever measure the contribution of each co-operative factor. Collection and computation serve their own important purposes, but quantitative methods yield only quantitative results. Here we are not dealing with like units of homogeneous forces which combine to produce a total. The service of statistical methods in the study of social causation is to prepare the way, to reveal more precisely the nature of the factors involved, to isolate quantitative indices of aspects of the situation, and to show the degree of their coherence or noncoherence. But these quantitative indices are merely evidences of an interaction which they do not explain; they are not the dynamic factors of which we are in quest. If we appreciate at all the nature of social causation we shall never expect to find that this factor A, presumptively measured by this quantitative unit a, contributes 20 per cent, and so forth. Much ingenuity and still more energy have been lavished on the attempt to reach results which the very nature of the subject matter precludes. Social phenomena are not, like certain physical phenomena, isolable components of a situation. Social phenomena are aspects of a total nonmechanical,

1. See R. M. MacIver, *Social Causation* (Boston, 1942), Chaps. III and IV.

consciously upheld system of relationships. Because the system is nonmechanical, the possible aspects are numerous and dissolve into one another, and we select from among them either by convention or because those selected have a preconceived or discovered significance for us. Behind every social relationship lie social attitudes and interests, which are not separable forces but type-phases of dynamic personality. And even when we pass from the social relationships themselves and deal with their merely tangible products we still remain outside the region where the quantitative contribution of the combining factors can be assessed. We can say that land, labor, capital, and organization—to take the old categories—are all necessary to produce a steel rail, but the question, How much of it does each produce? remains not only unanswerable but meaningless. If a number of factors are alike *necessary* to the production of a result, there can be no quantitative evaluation of their respective contributions. And if this is true of material categories, themselves measurable, and their material products, themselves also measurable, it is more obviously true of the more subtle interactions of personalities, variantly responsive to complex conditions, which determine every social situation.

The search for causes. Like all scientists, the social scientist seeks causes, seeks to explain the "why" of change. His search in the social realm is one that must be guided by the questions, How are the elements related? How do they combine?

[1] *How factors combine to produce social change:* Fear does not "combine" with a gun to explain a case of manslaughter as wind combines with water to produce a storm at sea. The gun is an instrument of the fear in a sense in which the water is not an instrument of the wind. In social causation there is a *logical* order of relationship between the factors that we do not find in physical causation. There is an essential difference, from the standpoint of causation, between a paper flying before the wind and a man flying from a pursuing crowd. The paper knows no fear and the wind no hate, but without fear and hate the man would not fly nor the crowd pursue.[2] If we try to reduce fear to its bodily concomitants we merely substitute the concomitants for the reality experienced as fear. We denude the world of meanings for the sake of a theory, itself a false meaning which deprives us of all the rest. We can interpret experience only on the level of experience. Social changes are phenomena of human experience and in that sense *meaningful*. Hence to explain them we must see not merely how the factors combine, but how they are related within the three orders with which we have already dealt, the order of values or the cultural order, the order of means or the utilitarian order, and the order of nature on which man's valuations and man's devices alike depend.

---

2. The position here advanced is attacked by G. A. Lundberg, *Foundations of Sociology* (New York, 1939), pp. 12-13. The reader is asked to compare the two statements, make his own analysis, and draw his own conclusions.

[2] *How the factors are related in processes of social change:* Let us suppose that the social phenomenon we are seeking to explain is an increase in the amount of crime or, more specifically, of crimes of violence in the United States during a particular period. If we look over the literature we find that some authors lay stress on the lack of home training of youth or the disorganization of family life or the conflict between the mores of the home and the mores of the large community.[3] Other authors find the main explanation in more general cultural conditions, such as the decline of religion or of authoritarianism.[4] But others give prominence to economic factors,[5] or to technological conditions, such as the opportunities for crime in the modern city, the relation between criminals and politicians, the availability of automobiles, firearms, and "hide-outs," the urban development which creates certain favorable areas, sometimes called "interstitial areas."[6] Whereas others again resort to biological explanations, such as "endocrine imbalance" or to neuroses bred in the organism by modern civilization.[7]

At first sight these different modes of explanation seem quite contradictory, and often they are treated as though this were the case. They would be contradictory if we regarded the various "causes" of a social phenomenon as belonging to the same level and therefore combining in a quantitative manner to produce the phenomenon. But if they belong on different levels the problem is of quite another kind. A number of different explanations may be equally justified provided they recognize the true nature of social causation. Observe that we have adduced three distinct modes of explanation, each of which has, of course, many variants. All three may be justified on their respective levels. An increase of crime *may* be the direct reflection of cultural changes, such as a decline of religious authority; and here the problem would be to trace the relation between a general change in the prevailing mores and the particular attitudes that find expression in criminal behavior. The same increase of crime *may* be explained by the new opportunities, conditions, or means of the changing technological order; and here the problem would be to show how this new situation corresponded with or evolved the attitudes that inspire to crime. Finally, the same increase of crime *may* be explained by organic predispositions, hereditary or acquired; and here the problem would be to show how the changing situation either stimulated these conditions or led to their finding to an increasing extent the expression or outlet which we name crime. These various problems, it will be seen, are all aspects of a single problem, since the various

3. For example, Edwin H. Sutherland, *Principles of Criminology* (Philadelphia, 1934).

4. For example, Harry Best, *Crime and the Criminal Law in the United States* (New York, 1930).

5. For example, W. A. Bonger, *Criminality and Economic Conditions* (Boston, 1916).

6. For example, F. M. Thrasher, *The Gang* (Chicago, 1927).

7. For example, M. G. Schlapp and E. H. Smith, *The New Criminology* (New York, 1928). Further examples are given in MacIver, *Social Causation*, Chap. III.

"causes" are all interdependent within the social order which is characterized by an increase in crime.

[3] *The essential task:* Thus in every process of social change we have to deal with *attitudes* dependent on a cultural background and focusing into particular objectives; with a *system of means*, including opportunities, obstacles, and occasions within which the objective shapes (and perhaps is shaped by) its available instrumentalities; and with the *larger environment*, the physical and biological conditions that sustain and prompt the changing objectives and the human nature that pursues them. To understand social causation therefore it is not enough to enumerate factors, to set them side by side, to attribute to them different weights as determinants of change. The first and essential thing is to discover the way in which the various factors are *related* to one another, the logical order within which they fall, the respective modes in which they enter into the causal process. In order to bring out this truth we shall survey the changing relations of our three great orders as they appear in a broad historical perspective.

From Primitive to Civilized Society

A contrast. Many contrasts can, of course, be drawn between primitive and civilized society, but here we shall dwell on one only. We choose it because it throws much light on the manner in which social change, and more particularly social evolution, occurs. It is the contrast between the mode of relationship of the three great orders which characterizes primitive life and that which becomes more and more apparent in evolved society. To grasp its significance the student should bear in mind our previous discussion of the distinction between culture and utility (Chapter XXI) as well as the subject matter of the preceding chapters.

[1] *The primitive fusion:* Primitive societies differ in a multitude of respects from one another, but in certain respects they present in common a contrast to more advanced types of society. Durkheim and others have dwelt on the lesser role of the division of labor in primitive as compared with civilized life. Behind that difference there lies another. In the simpler societies the distinction we have drawn between the cultural and the utilitarian is scarcely discernible. The means of living are not, as so often with us, detached from the ends of living. A modern factory or transportation system is operated purely as a utility, as a means of making profits or earning dividends from the point of view of the shareholders (if it is privately owned), as a means of providing wages from the point of view of the employees, as a means of supplying goods or services from the point of view of the consumer of these utilities. A factory, or a mechanism like the printing press or the ring spindle, does not count among the things that people enjoy or venerate or dance around or sing songs to or

in any sense "live for." It is thought of solely as a productive mechanism. Its efficiency is its sole and sufficient justification. It is controlled and directed under a system of management and of organization which has the definite objective of making it as gainful as possible, except in so far as certain safeguards are applied to limit the human costs of mechanical efficiency.

Turn to a primitive society and the contrast becomes manifest. Read the account of any of the simpler peoples, such as the Kwakiutl Indians or the Trobriand Islanders or the Samoans.[8] Such people hunt and fish and dig and weave and trade, but these utilitarian processes are woven into the social life and are invested with cultural significance. They are surrounded with tradition, with ceremony, with legend, with tribal lore. Scarcely anything is purely utilitarian, and, conversely, there is scarcely anything that is purely cultural. The latter aspect is seen, for example, in primitive art. As Franz Boas has pointed out, this art is mainly decorative. "It consists of designs applied to useful objects. Works of fine art, made for the sake of art alone, are rare."[9] The useful objects themselves, the basket, the mat, the bowl, the spear, the bow, are foci of cultural associations and symbols of cultural values.

Custom and tradition have thus incorporated the simple apparatus of living. Change is not rapid enough to detach the productive techniques and instruments from their cultural setting. Specialization of tasks has not reached the stage where the tasks themselves are too varied and too technical to be clothed with the valuations of a pervading culture. The simplicity of the mode and standard of living makes possible the undisturbed and permanent attachment of sentiment to the objects of daily use. As Malinowski says, "The meager furniture, the hearth, the sleeping bunks, the mats and pegs of a native hut, show a simplicity, even poverty, of form, which, however, becomes immensely significant through the depth and range of sociological and spiritual association."[10] This fusion is revealed in every aspect of primitive life.

> Ritual is as important as craftsmanship in the making of a canoe or in the cultivation of the soil. Prayers are as important as arms in the conduct of war. Religion is compounded with magic and cannot be divorced from the business of living. The dance is as much a means of warding off evil spirits or of inducing fertility as it is a mode of social recreation. The success of a fishing expedition is as much endangered by a woman's touching the fishing tackle as by unfavorable weather. Sickness comes from spells and the breaking of taboos. The people are bound in spirit to the soil, the home of their ancestors and their gods. Everything

---

8. F. Boas, *The Social Organization and Secret Societies of the Kwakiutl Indians* (Washington, D.C., 1897); B. Malinowski, *Argonauts of the Western Pacific* (London, 1922), and *Crime and Custom in Savage Society* (New York, 1926); Margaret Mead, *Coming of Age in Samoa* (New York, 1928); A. R. Radcliffe-Brown, *The Andaman Islanders* (Cambridge, 1933); and Cora Du Bois, *The People of Alor* (Minneapolis, 1944).
9. Article "Anthropology," in the *Encyclopaedia of the Social Sciences*, II, 91.
10. Article "Culture," in the *Encyclopaedia of the Social Sciences*, IV, 632.

> in nature is instinct with social meaning and enshrined in social ceremony. Culture, technique, authority, people, and land are subjectively unified.[11]

The fusion we have been describing helps to explain why modern anthropologists find that each simple people tends to exhibit a strongly prevalent complex of personality traits—what one leader in this field has named a "basic personality structure."[12] Some groups, like the Samoan, seem to possess a high degree of light-heartedness and joy in living; others, like certain Admiralty Island groups, appear suspicious and relatively morose; some, like the Comanche, are self-sufficient and outgoing. We must not assume that the members of these groups are cut to one precise pattern; individuals differ as everywhere else. But each group does seem to have a characteristic outlook and a characteristic set of attitudes, to a degree not found in more complex societies. So far as this is true it is an expression of the more complete fusion of civilization with culture.

[2] *The breakup of the primitive fusion:* In the course of every great civilization this primitive fusion has been in various degrees and in different modes subjected to a process of differentiation, but perhaps never so thoroughly as in the more recent evolution of our Western civilization. The process itself is intricate and we cannot here do more than suggest its nature. The medieval way of life was much nearer to the primitive fusion than is ours today. A strongly authoritarian culture, based on religious orthodoxy, was enthroned and sought to be all-embracing and to control to its purposes the utilitarian aspects of life. But the fusion was incomplete. It proved impossible to weld into one the religious authority and the secular power. Economic activities developed in response to their own impulses, and the church, which for a long time condemned "usury" and laid down rules about just prices, found it increasingly hard to control the direction of economic change. As a money economy replaced a barter economy and as labor became more free to offer itself to any employer, economic organization grew detached from the control of the traditional culture. At length the great technological advance of the later eighteenth century cleft with a new and sharper wedge the unity of culture and utility. The principle of utilitarian efficiency was liberated and built up its own systems devoted exclusively to the means as distinct from the ends of living. We have already seen that technological advance has its own tempo, its own mode of expansion and accumulation, and that culture does not proceed in the same way or at the same pace. The elaborate mechanism of Western civilization is becoming dominant all over the world, in Turkey and in Japan, in India and in Africa, in Russia as well as in the United States. But a thousand differences

11. Quoted from R. M. MacIver's article "The Historical Pattern of Social Change" (*Journal of Social Philosophy*, Vol. II [1936], reprinted in the Harvard Tercentenary volume, *Authority and the Individual* [Cambridge, Mass., 1937]), where the contrast presented in the text is more fully developed and illustrated.

12. A. Kardiner, *The Psychological Frontiers of Society* (New York, 1945).

of tradition, of religion, of national sentiment, and of other cultural valuations strongly divide the groups of the peoples which increasingly share a common civilization. Here arises one of the great problems of the modern world. Groups and peoples with divergent or opposing cultural values are bound together by the conditions and the necessities of a common civilization; they must somehow learn to build a social order that will admit within it these cultural differences.

It could be shown that a similar problem has always arisen wherever civilization developed, as for example in ancient Greece and Rome. We have already had occasion to deal with some aspects of it. Here we are concerned to get a conspectus of the major principle of social differentiation. The student of history can find ample illustration of its operation in the past. The student of contemporary society can find no less illuminating cases of the growing detachment of the cultural and the utilitarian. One intensive form of it, as we have already pointed out, is to be seen in those countries where the more advanced Western civilization is imported or, it may be, imposed, and where the invading technology threatens to disrupt the old cultural life, as it has done in India and in China.

Another aspect of social evolution is the growing distinction or even detachment of the cultural from the biophysical factors. Culture in primitive thought is bound both to the land and to the kin or the blood-group. Religion, for example, is native to and limited to the soil. The gods are tribal gods just as the ways of life are tribal ways. This is again part of the primitive fusion. It is still accepted by many who cling to a traditional culture. "We believe in the absolute oneness of Land and Man," so began the manifesto of a Japanese cultural organization. It went on to say: "In our national classics, which describe in plain but stately words the creed and faith of our forefathers, it is related that in virtue of the creative power of *musubi* the Ruler, Land and People were born in the most natural way from the same divine womb."[13] But growing civilization means wider and more frequent contacts. Science, art, philosophy, literature, technology, as they develop, refuse to be circumscribed within tribal or national boundaries. The scale of community is extended. Petty tribes are merged into great nations. Migration and interbreeding, the concomitants of improved communications, render it no longer plausible to identify the culture and the racial stock. Cultural differences develop within the larger, more heterogeneous peoples, and cultural likenesses unite men beyond the limits of any nation. We showed in an earlier chapter how with the growth of civilization man's dependence on the conditions of locality is reduced.[14] This is true of his culture no less than of his economic dependence. His ideas, his traditions, his valuations are shaped and sustained by influences

---

13. "Manifesto of Nippon Bunka Renmei," *Cultural Nippon*, Vol. IV (1936).
14. Chapter V.

coming from thousands of miles away as well as by those that are bred on his own doorstep. The people are not one blood apart from other bloods and the culture is not that of one people apart from all other peoples. The only uniqueness that a people or a culture can possess any more is the particular combination of the elements it draws from sources common to many peoples and to many cultures.

In short, it is an essential condition of every advancing civilization that it involves the growing demarcation of the three great orders out of that primitive scheme of things which made them one and indivisible.

How social unity is affected. It should be now apparent that in the more evolved society—and generally in periods of rapid changes whether or not they possess an evolutionary character—the type of social solidarity characteristic of a primitive group is no longer attainable. The social being can no longer live entirely in a wholly integrated and all-inclusive community, native to his land and to his blood, marked off by clear-cut bounds from all other communities.

This most significant distinction between primitive and civilized society has been stated in a variety of ways by different sociologists. Thus Ferdinand Tönnies distinguished the "organic" solidarity of what he called *Gemeinschaft* ("community") from the looser, less profound, contractual system of interrelationships that he called *Gesellschaft* ("society").[15] To Tönnies the former was a "natural" solidarity, not deliberately willed but springing from the fundamental social character of man, the unity of those bound by the instinct of the family and the common blood. He regarded the historical process of society as a passage from the solidarity of the "community," so understood, to the more varied, more superficial, and less unified attachments of the civilized life. Another famous statement of the process is that presented by Durkheim, who thought of it as a passage from the solidarity of likeness, in which individual differences are submerged in the homogeneity of the mores, to the solidarity of interdependence, in which functional differences play an increasingly large part in the structure of society.[16] This evolved type of unity Durkheim spoke of as "organic," a term applied by Tönnies to the primitive type. We may perhaps find in this contradiction of usage a warning of the dangers lurking in the sociological application of the concept of organism.

In the more advanced social system, with its specializations, its cultural diversities, its numerous groups and associations, its mingling of many elements into a complex whole, we cannot expect to find the all-embracing solidarity of a simpler society. A nation has inevitably a type of unity different from that of a clan or a tribe. The individual has to choose his cultural loyalties, to main-

15. In his pioneer work, *Gemeinschaft und Gesellschaft* (3rd ed., Berlin, 1920); translated and supplemented by C. P. Loomis as *Fundamental Concepts of Sociology* (New York, 1940).
16. *Division of Labor in Society* (G. Simpson, tr., New York, 1933).

tain his own values, to decide his own attachments, in far greater measure. He must seek for the *common* to which he really belongs, the common to which his individuality responds. The unity of the social group is not to be identified with that of one cultural community. He can share in both kinds, but he has to adjust for himself the one loyalty to the other.[17] *Society no longer integrates all his values for him*—that becomes the task of his own integrating personality. The old unity was "totalitarian," and a great modern society cannot revert to this totalitarianism without repressing the very forces that have built it up to greatness, without retracing the road that society has followed from the dawn of civilization.

17. See Chapter IX.

Notes on Further Reading

These notes are intended to serve two purposes: on the one hand, to indicate representative contributions to the subjects treated in the text and, on the other, to direct the student to works that are specially relevant to the argument presented in the chapters under which they are listed. The readings particularly appropriate for the beginning student are marked with an asterisk. Publication data are given when a work is first listed.

CHAPTER I Primary Concepts

In the present stage of sociology different authors define certain of even the most essential terms in different ways. Many references would therefore be only confusing. The student seeking to find the usage of different authors may consult

E. E. Eubank, *The Concepts of Sociology* (New York, 1932), and the same author's briefer "The Conceptual Approach to Sociology," Chap. III in *Contemporary Social Theory* (ed. H. E. Barnes, H. Becker, and F. B. Becker, New York, 1940).

Attempts to standardize sociological terms include

C. Panunzio, *Major Social Institutions* (New York, 1939), Glossary, pp. 523-568;
**Dictionary of Sociology* (ed. H. P. Fairchild, New York, 1944).

Valuable general works of reference include the monumental

**Encyclopaedia of the Social Sciences* (ed. E. R. A. Seligman and A. Johnson, New York, 1930–1935); and H. E. Barnes, H. Becker, *et al.*, *Social Thought from Lore to Science* (Boston, 1938);
An Introduction to the History of Sociology (ed. H. E. Barnes, Chicago, 1948);
Twentieth Century Sociology (ed. G. Gurvitch and W. E. Moore, New York, 1945).

The definitions presented by the authors are developed also in R. M. MacIver's

Community (London, 1917), Book I, Chap. II;
Elements of Social Science (London, 1921), Chap. I;
The Modern State (Oxford, 1926), Chaps. I, V;
Society: a Textbook of Sociology (New York, 1937), Chap. I.

These definitions are followed in the main in

G. D. H. Cole, *Social Theory* (London, 1923), Chap. I;
E. Jenks, *The State and the Nation* (London, 1935), Chap. I;
E. T. Hiller, *Social Relations and Structures* (New York, 1947), Chaps. I, VI, XV–XIX;
R. M. MacIver, **The Web of Government* (New York, 1947), Chaps. I–III, XIII

The definition of "the social" has been much discussed, particularly by European sociologists. But this issue, as L. von Wiese in *Systematic Sociology* (adapted and amplified by H. Becker, New York, 1932), Chap. I, points out, "belongs not at the beginning but at the end of analysis." In passing we may note that a particularly good statement of the relation of "the social" to "the physical," and of sociology to psychology, is given in the work just mentioned, pp. 64–68.

On folkways and mores consult

W. G. Sumner, **Folkways* (Boston, 1906), pp. 53–64;

W. G. Sumner and A. G. Keller, *The Science of Society* (New Haven, 1927), I, pp. 1–43;

W. I. Thomas, *Primitive Behavior* (New York, 1937).

CHAPTER 2 Interests and Attitudes

Little of the large literature on "attitudes" is satisfactory for sociological purposes. Representative treatments by sociologists and by social psychologists include

Social Attitudes (ed. K. Young, New York, 1931), Chaps. by E. Faris, R. E. Park, L. L. Bernard, and K. Young;

K. Young, **Social Psychology* (New York, 1944), Chaps. VI, IX;

E. T. Hiller, *Social Relations and Structures*, Chap. VII;

M. Sherif and H. Cantril, *The Psychology of Ego-Involvements* (New York, 1947), Chaps. II–IV.

The numerous researches purporting to "measure" attitudes are discussed and given a generally uncritical endorsement in

G. A. Lundberg, *Social Research* (New York, 1942), Chap. VIII;

G. A. Lundberg, *Foundations of Sociology* (New York, 1939), Chap. II.

More temperate discussions of attitude "measurement" include

O. Klineberg, *Social Psychology* (New York, 1940), Chap. XIII;

C. Kirkpatrick, "Assumptions and Methods in Attitude Measurements," *American Sociological Review*, I (1936), 75–88;

R. T. La Piere, "The Sociological Significance of Measurable Attitudes," *American Sociological Review*, III (1938), 175–182.

The logic of measurement and rating is developed in

M. R. Cohen and E. Nagel, **An Introduction to Logic and Scientific Method* (New York, 1934), Chap. XV.

The subject of "interests" was introduced into American sociology mainly in the attempt to derive social phenomena from specific attributes of human nature, a perilous quest. This led to various classifications of interests, or, more vaguely, human wishes or drives. Following G. Ratzenhofer, *Die soziologische Erkenntnis*, came the classification by A. W. Small, *General Sociology* (Chicago, 1905), pp. 197–198. Other social scientists have presented diverse classifications, generally based on no clear or adequate principles. The student will find examples in

E. A. Ross, *Principles of Sociology* (New York, 1938), Chap. VII;

W. I. Thomas and F. Znaniecki, *The Polish Peasant* (New York, 1918) I, pp. 21–23, 72–73;

R. S. Lynd, **Knowledge for What?* (Princeton, 1939), pp. 193–197;

B. Malinowski, **A Scientific Theory of Culture and Other Essays* (Chapel Hill, N.C., 1944), pp. 75–131.

The distinction between types of interest is developed by R. M. MacIver in
Community, Book II, Chap. II; and
*"Interests," *Encyclopaedia of the Social Sciences*, Vol. VIII.

The distinction of like and common interests is suggested also in
M. Ginsberg, *Sociology* (London, 1934), Chap. IV.

The concept of interest, with reference to the discussion contained in the text, is examined in
F. Znaniecki, **Social Actions* (New York, 1936), pp. 54–56.

On motivations, the student should begin by reading the relevant part in some textbook in psychology, such as
G. Murphy, *General Psychology* (New York, 1933), Chap. IV; or E. G. Boring, H. S. Langfeld, H. P. Weld, *et al.*, *Introduction to Psychology* (New York, 1939), Chap. V.

Studies of motivation deserving the attention of the sociologist include

G. Murphy, *Personality* (New York, 1947), Chaps. V, VI;

P. T. Young, *Emotion in Man and Animal* (New York, 1943), Chap. II, and *Motivation of Behavior* (New York, 1936);

A. H. Maslow, *"A Theory of Human Motivation," in *Twentieth Century Psychology* (ed. P. L. Harriman, New York, 1946), pp. 22–48.

CHAPTER 3 Individual and Society

Formulations of the relation between individuality and society will be found in many works, including

J. M. Baldwin, *Social and Ethical Interpretations* (New York, 1906);

C. H. Cooley, **Human Nature and the Social Order* (New York, 1922), Chaps. I–VI, and **Social Organization* (New York, 1929), Part I;

J. Dewey, *Human Nature and Conduct* (New York, 1930), and *"The Social as a Category," *The Monist*, XXXVIII (1928), 161–178;

G. H. Mead, **Mind, Self and Society* (Chicago, 1934), Chaps. III, IV;

E. Faris, *The Nature of Human Nature* (New York, 1937), Part I.

Other aspects of the argument of the text will be found in R. M. MacIver's

**Community*, Book I, Chaps. I–II; Book II, Chap. I; Book III, Chap. III;

The Modern State, Chaps. V, XVI;

**The Web of Government*, Chap. XIII.

The "culture-personality" interrelationship is discussed in several recent works, including

R. Linton, *The Cultural Background of Personality* (New York, 1945);
K. Young, *Personality and Problems of Adjustment* (New York, 1947), Part I;
R. S. Lynd, **Knowledge for What?* Chap. III;
G. Murphy, **Personality*, Part VI;
P. A. Sorokin, *Society, Culture, and Personality* (New York, 1947), Chap. XIX.

This viewpoint is basic to various studies of nonliterate and literate groups in which social anthropology and psychology, including psychoanalysis, have collaborated. For example,

R. Benedict, **Patterns of Culture* (Boston, 1934);
A. Kardiner, *The Individual and His Society* (New York, 1939), and *The Psychological Frontiers of Society* (New York, 1945).

Essentially the same viewpoint is found in such discussions of personality development as

M. Sherif and H. Cantril, *The Psychology of Ego-Involvements*, Chaps. VII–IX;
W. A. Davis and R. J. Havighurst, **Father of the Man* (Boston, 1947).

It is also central in works dealing with broad problems of present-day Western society, including

E. Fromm, *Escape from Freedom* (New York, 1941), and *Man for Himself* (New York, 1947);
K. Mannheim, *Diagnosis of Our Time* (London, 1943).

There is a large literature on social conflict. In fact, it is made the principal datum of some schools of sociology, such as that of L. Gumplowicz and G. Ratzenhofer, that of the racial theorists, and that of the theorists of class struggle. (For references on these schools consult P. A. Sorokin, *Contemporary Sociological Theories* [New York, 1928], pp. 219–356, 480–487, 523–544; and H. E. Barnes, H. Becker, *et al.*, *Social Thought from Lore to Science*, pp. 713–734.)

Among the many works on conflict and co-operation attention should be directed to

G. Simmel, *"The Sociology of Conflict," *American Journal of Sociology*, IX (1903–1904), 490–525;
J. Novicow, *War and Its Alleged Benefits* (New York, 1911);
P. Kropotkin, *Mutual Aid* (London, 1902);
C. H. Cooley, **Social Process* (New York, 1918), Chap. IV;
F. Znaniecki, **Social Actions*, Chaps. VI, XIV–XVIII;
E. T. Hiller, **Social Relations and Structures*, Chaps. VIII–XII;
M. A. May and L. W. Doob, *Competition and Co-operation*, Social Science Research Council Bulletin 25 (New York, 1937).

Co-operation and competition in thirteen primitive societies are reported in

Co-operation and Competition among Primitive Peoples (ed. M. Mead, New York, 1937).

The role of co-operation is emphasized by a group of French writers who uphold a doctrine of organic solidarity, among them C. Gide, L. Bourgeois, and C. Bouglé. In his famous *Division of Labor in Society* (tr. G. Simpson, New York, 1933), E. Durkheim distinguishes different stages of society according to the nature of the social co-operation they exhibit.

CHAPTER 4 Environment and Life

Perhaps the outstanding scientific exponent of the claims of heredity has been Karl Pearson; see

K. Pearson *et al.*, *Eugenics Laboratory Lecture Series* (London, 1911 and later years).

Reviews and criticisms of hereditarian theories are offered in

P. A. Sorokin, *Contemporary Sociological Theories*, Chap. V;

F. H. Hankins, **Introduction to the Study of Society* (New York, 1937), Chaps. VI–VII;

M. Ginsberg, *Sociology*, Chap. III, and **Studies in Sociology* (London, 1932), Chaps. VIII–X.

Heredity is ably discussed in

S. J. Holmes, *Human Genetics and Its Social Import* (New York, 1936);

H. S. Jennings, **The Biological Basis of Human Nature* (New York, 1930), especially Chaps. V, VII, IX;

F. Osborn, *Preface to Eugenics* (New York, 1940);

A. Scheinfeld, **You and Heredity* (New York, 1939).

Good general discussions of heredity and environment are to be found in

G. C. Schwesinger, *Heredity and Environment* (New York, 1933), Chap. VI;

K. Young, **Personality and Problems of Adjustment*, Chap. III;

L. Hogben, *Nature and Nurture* (New York, 1933).

A number of investigations into the relationship of heredity and environment, with useful bibliographies, are reported in

Nature and Nurture, Twenty-seventh Yearbook, National Society for the Study of Education (Bloomington, Ill., 1928);

Intelligence: Its Nature and Nurture, Thirty-ninth Yearbook, National Society for the Study of Education (Bloomington, Ill., 1940);

O. Klineberg, **Social Psychology*, pp. 224–264;

H. H. Newman, F. N. Freeman, and K. J. Holzinger, *Twins: A Study of Heredity and Environment* (Chicago, 1937), especially Chaps. I, II, XIII;

R. S. Woodworth, **Heredity and Environment*, Social Science Research Council Bulletin 47 (New York, 1941).

Among the contributions dealing with race and heredity and environment are

O. Klineberg, **Race Differences* (New York, 1935);

L. C. Dunn and Th. Dobzhansky, *Heredity, Race, and Society* (New York, 1946);

G. Dahlberg, *Race, Reason, and Rubbish* (tr. L. Hogben, New York, 1942);
M. F. Ashley Montagu, **Man's Most Dangerous Myth: The Fallacy of Race* (rev. ed., New York, 1945).

The relation of environment and race is emphasized in
F. Boas, **The Mind of Primitive Man* (rev. ed., New York, 1938), and *Race, Language and Culture* (New York, 1940), pp. 3–195;
F. Hertz, *Race and Civilization* (New York, 1928);
F. H. Hankins, *The Racial Basis of Civilization* (New York, 1926).

CHAPTER 5 Geography and People

The "geographical school" of the last half-century is well represented by
E. Huntington, *Civilization and Climate* (New Haven, 1924), *World Power and Evolution* (New Haven, 1919), and *Mainsprings of Civilization* (New York, 1945);
E. C. Semple, *Influence of Geographic Environment* (New York, 1911), and *American History and Its Geographic Conditions* (New York, 1933);
H. J. Mackinder, *Democratic Ideals and Reality* (London, 1919).

Recent attempts to attribute health and vigor to climate include
C. A. Mills, *Climate Makes the Man* (New York, 1942);
S. F. Markham, *Climate and the Energy of Nations* (New York, 1944).

Among the many works on "geopolitics" are
H. W. Weigert, *Generals and Geographers* (New York, 1942);
R. Strauz-Hupé, *Geopolitics* (New York, 1942);
**Compass of the World* (ed. H. W. Weigert and V. Stefansson, New York, 1944), especially pp. 12–39, 40–52, 74–88, 148–160;
D. Whittlesey, *The Earth and the State* (New York, 1939);
N. J. Spykman, *The Geography of the Peace* (New York, 1944).

Broad surveys of geographical factors are offered from the geographer's point of view in
J. Brunhes, *Human Geography* (New York, 1920);
J. Russell Smith and M. D. Phillips, **North America* (New York, 1940), Chaps. I, XLIX;
G. B. Cressey, *Asia's Lands and People* (New York, 1944);
from a sociological point of view in
P. A. Sorokin, *Contemporary Sociological Theories*, Chap. II;
F. Thomas, "The Role of Anthropogeography in Contemporary Social Theory," in *Contemporary Social Theory* (ed. H. E. Barnes, H. Becker, and F. B. Becker);
R. T. La Piere, **Sociology* (New York, 1946), Chaps. V–VI;
and in terms of a historical perspective in
A. J. Toynbee, **A Study of History* (London, 1934), I, pp. 249 ff. or in the abridgement by D. C. Somervell (New York, 1947), Chaps. V–VIII.

Of the regional studies we mention

H. W. Odum and H. E. Moore, **American Regionalism* (New York, 1938), Chaps. I, XVIII.

On the relation of land to population, the classic is, of course,

T. R. Malthus, *Essay on Population* (various editions);

while the problems he posed are explored in such recent studies as

F. A. Pearson and F. A. Harper, *The World's Hunger* (Ithaca, N.Y., 1945);

R. Mukerjee, *Races, Lands, and Food* (New York, 1946);

and in the stimulating but somewhat overstated

W. Vogt, **Road to Survival* (New York, 1948).

Of the many recent studies on population it may suffice here to mention

W. S. Thompson, *Population Problems* (New York, 1942);

P. H. Landis, *Population Problems* (New York, 1943);

**Compass of the World* (ed. H. W. Weigert and V. Stefansson), Chap. VI;

**World Population in Transition* (ed. K. Davis), issue of *The Annals* of the American Academy of Political and Social Science for Jan., 1945, Vol. CCXXXVII.

CHAPTER 6 The Total Environment and Accommodation

The subject of this chapter is broadly treated in

A. G. A. Balz, **The Basis of Social Theory* (New York, 1924), Chap. II;

R. C. Dexter, *Social Adjustment* (New York, 1927);

R. E. Park and E. W. Burgess, *Introduction to the Science of Sociology* (Chicago, 1924), Chap. X.

Aspects of the subject are dealt with in some textbooks of sociology, such as

E. T. Hiller, *Principles of Sociology* (New York, 1933), Chaps. XX, XXIII–XXIV;

J. L. Gillin and J. P. Gillin, *An Introduction to Sociology* (New York, 1948), Chaps. XXI–XXII;

K. Young, *Sociology* (New York, 1942), Chaps. XXXI–XXXII.

A special aspect of it is discussed in

R. M. MacIver, *Sociology and Social Work* (New York, 1931), Chap. II.

The nature of man's complex environment is suggestively dealt with in

G. Wallas, *The Great Society* (London, 1920), Part II; and **Our Social Heritage* (New Haven, 1921), Chap. I;

R. T. La Piere, **Sociology*, Part II;

L. L. Bernard, *"A Classification of Environments," *American Journal of Sociology*, XXXI (1925), 318–332; "Culture and Environment," *Social Forces*, VIII (1929–1930), 327–334, and IX (1930–1931), 39–48.

Adjustment and maladjustment are discussed in

E. W. Burgess, "Accommodation," *Encyclopaedia of the Social Sciences*, Vol. I;

R. M. MacIver, *"Maladjustment," *Encyclopaedia of the Social Sciences*, Vol. X;
K. Young, *Personality and Problems of Adjustment*, Part II;
A. I. Hallowell, *"Sociopsychological Aspects of Acculturation," in *The Science of Man in the World Crisis* (ed. R. Linton, New York, 1945).

Numerous examples of adjustment problems are offered in
When Peoples Meet (ed. A. Locke and B. J. Stern, New York, 1942).

Among the many studies of the adjustment and maladjustment of immigrants may be mentioned
N. Carpenter, *Immigrants and Their Children* (Washington, D.C., 1927);
L. G. Brown, **Immigration* (New York, 1933), Chap. XII;
R. E. Park and H. A. Miller, *Old World Traits Transplanted* (New York, 1921);
One America (ed. F. J. Brown and J. S. Roucek, New York, 1946);
C. Wittke, *We Who Built America* (New York, 1940).

The classic study of a particular immigrant group is
W. I. Thomas and F. Znaniecki, *The Polish Peasant*,
which is analyzed in detail in
H. Blumer, *Critiques of Research in the Social Sciences: I, An Appraisal of Thomas and Znaniecki's The Polish Peasant in Europe and America*, Social Science Research Council Bulletin 44 (New York, 1939).

Mention should also be made of
L. Wirth, *The Ghetto* (Chicago, 1929);
C. McWilliams, **Brothers under the Skin* (Boston, 1943), and *Prejudice—Japanese Americans* (Boston, 1944);
G. Saenger, *Today's Refugees, Tomorrow's Citizens* (New York, 1941);
M. R. Davie, *The Refugee Immigrant in the United States* (New York, 1946);
W. L. Warner and L. Srole, **The Social Systems of American Ethnic Groups* (New Haven, 1945), Chaps. I, X;
W. F. Whyte, *Street Corner Society* (Chicago, 1943).

For man's adjustment to extraordinarily severe or unusual conditions see, for example,
A. H. Leighton, **The Governing of Men* (Princeton, 1945);
D. S. Thomas and R. S. Nishimoto, *The Spoilage* (Berkeley, Cal., 1946);
and such novels as
A. Koestler, *Scum of the Earth* (New York, 1941);
D. Rousset, *The Other Kingdom* (New York, 1947).

CHAPTER 7 The Mores and Social Control

On the subject of social codes pioneer work of importance was done by earlier sociologists, notably
W. G. Sumner, **Folkways;*
W. Bagehot, *Physics and Politics* (New York, 1906);

Sir Henry Maine, *Ancient Law* (London, 1907);
H. Spencer, *Principles of Sociology* (New York, 1896);
G. Tarde, *The Laws of Imitation* (tr. E. C. Parsons, New York, 1903).

Modern anthropology has thrown a fuller light on the subject, as illustrated by the following works:

B. Malinowski, **Crime and Custom in Savage Society* (New York, 1926), and *Sex and Repression in Savage Society* (New York, 1927);
E. S. Hartland, *Primitive Law* (London, 1924);
K. N. Llewellyn and E. A. Hoebel, **The Cheyenne Way* (Norman, Okla., 1941);
C. Du Bois, **The People of Alor* (Minneapolis, 1944), Part III.

Studies of social control include the pioneer but still significant
E. A. Ross, **Social Control* (New York, 1901);
and such textbooks as
P. H. Landis, *Social Control* (Philadelphia, 1939);
L. L. Bernard, *Social Control in Its Sociological Aspects* (New York, 1939);
J. S. Roucek *et al.*, *Social Control* (New York, 1947).

The last-named volume provides an extensive bibliography on the subject.

On leadership and authority consult
C. H. Cooley, **Human Nature and the Social Order*, Chap. IX;
F. Znaniecki, **Social Actions*, Chaps. VI–X;
E. S. Bogardus, *Leaders and Leadership* (New York, 1934);
R. Michels, "Authority," *Encyclopaedia of the Social Sciences*, Vol. II;
R. M. MacIver, **The Web of Government*, Chap. III;
J. S. Roucek *et al.*, *Social Control*, Chap. XVII.

On political leadership in particular see, for example,
R. Michels, *Political Parties* (New York, 1915);
C. E. Merriam, *Political Power* (New York, 1934), and **Systematic Politics* (Chicago, 1945), Chap. X;
H. D. Lasswell, *Politics: Who Gets What, When, How* (New York, 1936).

On leadership in business and industry see, for example,
C. I. Barnard, **The Functions of the Executive* (Cambridge, Mass., 1939);
F. J. Roethlisberger, *Management and Morale* (Cambridge, Mass., 1943);
W. F. Whyte, *Human Problems of the Restaurant Industry* (New York, 1948), Part IV.

For suggestive studies of the cases of Lenin and Gandhi see, respectively,
S. Hook, *The Hero in History* (New York, 1941); and
K. Shridharani, *War without Violence* (New York, 1939).

On ritual consult
W. G. Sumner and A. G. Keller, *The Science of Society*, II, Chap. XXXII;

R. Benedict, *"Ritual," *Encyclopaedia of the Social Sciences*, Vol. XIII;
L. S. Cressman, *"Ritual the Conserver," *American Journal of Sociology*, XXXV (1930), 564–572.

The place of ritual in primitive life is discussed and illustrated in
E. Durkheim, *Elementary Forms of the Religious Life* (New York, 1926);
J. G. Frazer, *The Golden Bough* (3rd ed., New York, 1935);
B. Malinowski, *Coral Gardens and Their Magic* (2 vols., New York, 1935);
for ritual in secret societies see
N. P. Gist, **Secret Societies: A Cultural Study of Fraternalism in the United States* (Columbia, Mo., 1940), Chap. VII;
J. S. Roucek *et al.*, *Social Control*, Chap. XVIII.

On symbolism and society consult
E. Sapir, *"Symbolism," *Encyclopaedia of the Social Sciences*, Vol. XIV;
G. Coyle, *The Social Process in Organized Groups* (New York, 1930), Chap. VII;
J. S. Roucek *et al.*, *Social Control*, Chaps. XIII and XIV;
C. Wright Mills, "Language, Logic and Culture," *American Sociological Review*, IV (1939), 670–680.

Basic works in the "science of semantics" include
L. K. Ogden and I. A. Richards, *The Meaning of Meaning* (New York, 1938), Chap. X;
A. Korzybski, *Science and Sanity* (Lancaster, Pa., 1941);
and of the popular presentations may be mentioned
S. I. Hayakawa, *Language in Action* (New York, 1941);
H. Walpole, *Semantics* (New York, 1941).

The social role of coercion is brought out in
J. Dewey, **Human Nature and Conduct*, Chap. I;
H. M. Kallen, "Coercion," *Encyclopaedia of the Social Sciences*, Vol. III;
and with relation to power is treated, for example, in
R. M. MacIver, **The Web of Government*, Chap. V;
B. Russell, *Power* (New York, 1938).

Of the many studies of "Utopian" communities those having special relevance for students of sociology include
M. Choukas, *Black Angels of Athos* (Brattleboro, Vt., 1934);
L. E. Deets, **The Hutterites: A Study in Social Cohesion* (Gettysburg, Pa., 1939);
V. F. Calverton, *Where Angels Dared to Tread* (Indianapolis, 1941);
H. F. Infield, **Cooperative Communities at Work* (New York, 1945), Chaps. I–IV.

CHAPTER 8 The Major Social Codes

The great variety of social codes is brought out in the studies of primitive peoples. In addition to the detailed investigations of specific groups, much illustrative material may be found in

W. I. Thomas, *Primitive Behavior;*
A. A. Goldenweiser, *Anthropology: An Introduction to Primitive Culture* (New York, 1937);
R. Linton, *The Study of Man* (New York, 1936).

For different treatments of the relation of religion and morals see
H. Spencer, *Principles of Sociology*, III, pp. 150 ff.;
H. Bergson, *The Two Sources of Morality and Religion* (New York, 1935);
R. Otto, *Das Heilige* (Gotha, 1927);
J. Wach, **Sociology of Religion* (Chicago, 1944), Chap. III;
and for statements by two modern representatives of "naturalism"
S. P. Lamprecht and J. H. Randall, Jr., in *Naturalism and the Human Spirit* (ed. Y. H. Krikorian, New York, 1944).

The views of a French school of sociologists will be found in
E. Durkheim, *Elementary Forms of the Religious Life;*
L. Lévy-Bruhl, *How Natives Think* (London, 1926).

The whole subject is comprehensively explored in
M. Weber, *Gesammelte Aufsätze zur Religionssoziologie* (Tübingen, 1923), of which Volume I is translated by T. Parsons as **The Protestant Ethic and the Spirit of Capitalism* (New York, 1930);
in the last-mentioned volume see also the Introduction by R. H. Tawney. Other works are
**From Max Weber: Essays in Sociology* (tr. and ed. H. H. Gerth and C. W. Mills, New York, 1946), Part III;
J. M. Yinger, *Religion in the Struggle for Power* (Durham, N.C., 1946), Chap. IV.

Brief reviews of the sociology of religion are
J. Wach, Chap. XIV in *Twentieth Century Sociology* (ed. G. Gurvitch and W E. Moore);
M. J. Williams, Chap. XXIII in *Contemporary Social Theory* (ed. H. E. Barnes, H. Becker, and F. B. Becker);
and suggestive material is contained in
E. Troeltsch, *The Social Teaching of the Christian Churches* (New York, 1931);
F. S. C. Northrop. *The Meeting of East and West* (New York, 1946), Chaps. IX–X.

Custom and law are treated in
R. M. MacIver, *The Modern State*, Chaps. V, VII, and **The Web of Government*, Chap. IV;
J. Dickinson, "Social Order and Political Authority," *American Political Science Review*, XXIII (1929), 293–328, 593–632;
R. Pound, *Social Control through Law* (New Haven, 1942);
and with specific reference to primitive societies in
B. Malinowski, *Crime and Custom in Savage Society;*
K. N. Llewellyn and E. A. Hoebel, **The Cheyenne Way.*

General studies of the sociology of law include

N. S. Timasheff, *An Introduction to the Sociology of Law* (Cambridge, Mass., 1939), especially Chap. XII;

G. Gurvitch, *Sociology of Law* (New York, 1942);

briefer discussions are

R. Pound, Chap. XI in *Twentieth Century Sociology* (ed. G. Gurvitch and W. E. Moore);

W. Seagle, Chap. XIX in *Contemporary Social Theory* (ed. H. E. Barnes, H. Becker, and F. B. Becker).

Interesting accounts of law and custom in the army are

M. Berger, *"Law and Custom in the Army," *Social Forces*, XXV (1946), 82–87, and "Cultural Enforcement in the American Army," *Journal of Legal and Political Sociology*, IV (1946), 96–103.

Custom and fashion are treated in

W. G. Sumner, *Folkways*, pp. 184–220;

E. Sapir, *"Fashion," *Encyclopaedia of the Social Sciences*, Vol. VI;

K. Young, **Social Psychology*, Chap. XVII;

R. T. La Piere, *Collective Behavior* (New York, 1938), Chap. IX.

The caustic analysis of Veblen is presented in

T. Veblen, *The Theory of the Leisure Class* (New York, 1922), Chaps. I, III, IV, VII;

and much illustrative material may be found in

J. C. Flügel, *The Psychology of Clothes* (London, 1930);

E. B. Hurlock, *The Psychology of Dress* (New York, 1929);

D. L. Cohn, *The Good Old Days* (New York, 1940).

CHAPTER 9 Social Codes and the Individual Life

The references given under Chapter VIII are, in general, applicable to the present chapter as well.

For the relation of the individual and the mores see also

C. H. Cooley, **Human Nature and the Social Order*, Chap. X;

F. Znaniecki, **Social Actions*, Chap. XIII;

J. Dewey, *Human Nature and Conduct*, Chap. IV;

G. H. Mead, *Mind, Self, and Society*, Part III.

Of the large literature dealing with the problems of the individual in a multi-standard society, mention may be given to

K. Horney, *The Neurotic Personality of Our Time* (New York, 1937), especially Chap. XV, and *New Ways in Psychoanalysis* (New York, 1939), Chap. X;

A. Kardiner, *The Psychological Frontiers of Society*, Chap. XIV;

K. Young, *Personality and Problems of Adjustment*, Chaps. XXVIII–XXX;

K. Mannheim, *Diagnosis of Our Time*, Chaps. II, V;
R. R. Grinker and J. P. Spiegel, **Men under Stress* (Philadelphia, 1945), Part V;
**American Journal of Sociology*, Vol. XLII, No. 6 (1937), articles by F. Alexander, T. Burrow, E. Mayo, P. Schilder, H. S. Sullivan, and E. Sapir.

The relationship between the social codes and individual freedom is brought out in *Freedom: Its Meaning* (ed. R. N. Anshen, New York, 1940), chapters by R. M. MacIver, J. Dewey, J. MacMurray, and P. W. Bridgman;
it poses the central problem for the provocative but inconclusive
E. Fromm, *Man for Himself*.

CHAPTER 10 Types of Social Groups

Systematic analysis of the group was considered the central sociological task by G. Simmel and L. von Wiese. For their treatments see
N. J. Spykman, *The Social Theory of Georg Simmel* (Chicago, 1925), Book II;
L. von Wiese and H. Becker, *Systematic Sociology*.

More recent discussions include
E. T. Hiller, **Social Relations and Structures*, Chaps. XVII–XIX;
G. A. Lundberg, *Foundations of Sociology*, Chap. IX;
D. Sanderson, "Group Description," *Social Forces*, XVI (1938), 309–319, and "A Preliminary Structural Classification of Groups," *ibid.*, XVII (1938), 1–6;
L. Wilson, *"Sociography of Groups," *Twentieth Century Sociology* (ed. G. Gurvitch and W. E. Moore), Chap. VII;
E. Sapir, "Group," *Encyclopaedia of the Social Sciences*, Vol. VII;
American Journal of Sociology, Vol. XLIV (May, 1939), especially the articles by F. Znaniecki, R. S. Woodworth, J. E. Anderson, and B. Malinowski.

The distinction between the small, intimate group and the large-scale group was developed by F. Tönnies in *Gemeinschaft und Gesellschaft* (Leipzig, 1887), which has been translated and amplified in
C. P. Loomis, *Fundamental Concepts of Sociology* (New York, 1940).

On the primary group see
C. H. Cooley, **Social Organization*, Part I;
L. von Wiese and H. Becker, *Systematic Sociology*, Chaps. XXXVIII–XL.

Much material on the primary group in various areas of social life is contained in such studies as
G. Coyle, **The Social Process in Organized Groups;*
F. M. Thrasher, *The Gang* (Chicago, 1929);
J. Piaget, *The Moral Judgment of the Child* (New York, 1932);
H. H. Jennings, *Leadership and Isolation: A Study of Personality in Inter-Personal Relations* (New York, 1943);
J. L. Moreno, *Who Shall Survive?* (Washington, D.C., 1934);

F. J. Roethlisberger and W. J. Dixon, **Management and the Worker* (Cambridge, Mass., 1939);
W. F. Whyte, **Street Corner Society;*
W. L. Warner and P. S. Lunt, *The Social Life of a Modern Community* (New Haven, 1941), Chap. XVI;
A. E. Sheffield, *Social Insight in Case Situations* (New York, 1937);
(Anonymous), "Informal Social Organization in the Army," *American Journal of Sociology,* LI (1946), 365–370; and C. H. Page, "Bureaucracy's Other Face," *Social Forces,* XXV (1946), 88–94.

On the large-scale associations consult the references for Chapters XVIII, XIX, and XX. Here it may suffice to mention the significant contributions of M. Weber, some of which may be found in
From Max Weber: Essays in Sociology (tr. and ed. H. H. Gerth and C. W. Mills), Chap. VIII;
**The Theory of Social and Economic Organization* (tr. and ed. T. Parsons and A. M. Henderson, New York, 1947), pp. 30–86, 136–157, 324–358, 407–423.

CHAPTER 11 The Family

The literature of the family is enormous, the subject forming a part of nearly every anthropological study and of very many sociological studies.

On the early family consult
E. Westermarck, **Short History of Marriage* (London, 1926), especially Chaps. VIII–X, and *History of Human Marriage* (New York, 1922);
and the contrasting account in
R. Briffault, **The Mothers* (New York, 1927), especially Book I, Chaps. III–VI, X.

Histories of the family include
G. E. Howard, *History of Matrimonial Institutions* (Chicago, 1904);
W. Goodsell, *A History of Marriage and the Family* (New York, 1934);
C. C. Zimmerman, *Family and Civilization* (New York, 1947);
A. W. Calhoun, *Social History of the American Family* (Cleveland, 1917–1919).

The great variety of family forms is shown, for example, in
R. Linton, **The Study of Man,* Chaps. X–XI;
W. I. Thomas, *Primitive Behavior,* Chaps. V and X;
M. Mead, *From the South Seas* (New York, 1939);
The Family Past and Present (ed. B. J. Stern, New York, 1938), Parts 1–6;
C. C. Zimmerman and M. E. Frampton, *Family and Society* (New York, 1935).

Of the many textbooks on the family mention may be made of
J. K. Folsom, **The Family and Democratic Society* (New York, 1943);
E. W. Burgess and H. J. Locke, *The Family* (New York, 1945);

M. F. Nimkoff, *Marriage and the Family* (Boston, 1947);

and of those specially concerned with the American family

W. W. Waller, **The Family* (New York, 1938);

A. G. Truxal and F. E. Merrill, **The Family in American Culture* (New York, 1947).

Useful collections of articles on various aspects of the family are

American Sociological Review, Vol. II, No. 5 (Oct., 1937);

American Journal of Sociology, Vol. LII, No. 3 (Nov., 1946), and Vol. LIII, No. 6 (May, 1948).

Family "disorganization" is treated in most textbooks on the family as well as in such studies as

E. R. Mowrer, *Family Disorganization* (rev. ed., Chicago, 1939);

H. R. Mowrer, *Personality Adjustment and Domestic Discord* (New York, 1935);

K. Young, *Personality and Problems of Adjustment*, Chap. XXI;

M. A. Elliott and F. E. Merrill, **Social Disorganization* (rev. ed., New York, 1941), Chaps. XXV–XVII.

The effect of economic depression on family life has been frequently explored, as in

R. C. Angell, *The Family Encounters the Depression* (New York, 1936);

R. S. Cavan and K. H. Ranck, *The Family and the Depression* (Chicago, 1938);

M. Komarovsky, **The Unemployed Man and His Family* (New York, 1940);

and of war, as in

W. W. Waller, *War and the Family* (New York, 1940);

"The American Family in World War II," *The Annals* of the American Academy of Political and Social Science, CCXXIX (1943), 1–175.

On divorce see

J. P. Lichtenberger, *Divorce* (New York, 1931);

A. Cahen, *Statistical Analysis of American Divorce* (New York, 1932);

K. Davis, *"Children of Divorced Parents: A Sociological and Statistical Analysis," *Law and Contemporary Problems*, Vol. X (1944);

W. W. Waller, *The Old Love and the New* (New York, 1930).

The child in the modern family is treated in many works, for example

W. I. and D. S. Thomas, *The Child in America* (New York, 1928);

G. Abbott, *The Child and the State* (New York, 1938);

J. K. Folsom, **Youth, Family, and Education* (Washington, D.C., 1941).

Considerable research has been undertaken in marital adjustment, the most thorough of which is reported in

E. W. Burgess and L. Cottrell, Jr., *Predicting Success or Failure in Marriage* (New York, 1938);

L. Terman *et al.*, *Psychological Factors in Marital Happiness* (New York, 1939).

Innumerable works are published offering advice about marriage, of which good examples are

E. M. Duvall and R. Hill, *When You Marry* (New York, 1945);
T. B. Rice, *Sex, Marriage, and Family* (Philadelphia, 1946).

The literature on sex relations is equally large; for a readable and generally sound presentation see
A. Scheinfeld, **Women and Men* (New York, 1943);
and for the most extensive investigation of sex behavior to date
A. C. Kinsey, W. B. Pomeroy, and C. E. Martin, *Sexual Behavior in the Human Male* (Philadelphia, 1948).

There is no thorough treatment of the relation of the state and family, though considerable information may be found in
S. P. Breckenridge, *The Family and the State* (Chicago, 1934);
A. G. Truxal and F. E. Merrill, **The Family in American Culture*, Chaps. VII–VIII;
N. Fishman, *Marriage: This Business of Living Together* (New York, 1946);
C. C. Zimmerman, *Family and Civilization*, Chap. XXIII.

CHAPTER 12 The Community

On the general concept of the community see
R. M. MacIver, *The Community*, and **Elements of Social Science*, Chap. II;
C. C. Zimmerman, *The Changing Community* (New York, 1938), Chap. I;
J. A. Kinneman, **The Community in American Society* (New York, 1947), Chap. I.

The relation of community and communications is treated in
E. T. Hiller,* *Principles of Sociology*, Chaps. VIII–IX;
and aspects of it in
G. L. Bird and F. E. Merwin, *The Newspaper and Society* (New York, 1942), Chaps. IV, XVII, XXIII.

On the physical aspects of the urban community see, in addition to the works of the ecological school listed under Chapter XIII,
**Building the Future City, The Annals* of the American Academy of Political and Social Science, CCXLII (Nov., 1945), 7–17, 25–78;
W. Firey, *Land Use in Central Boston* (Cambridge, Mass., 1947);
R. D. McKenzie, *The Metropolitan Community* (New York, 1933), Chaps. VII, X, XI, XVI, XIX;
L. Mumford, **The Culture of Cities* (New York, 1938), Chap. III;
and of the rural community
J. H. Kolb and E. de S. Brunner, *A Study of Rural Society* (Boston, 1946), Chap. XIV;
U.S. Department of Agriculture, **Rural Life Series*, 1–5 (1941–1942);
C. P. Loomis, *Studies of Rural Social Organization in the United States, Latin America and Germany* (East Lansing, Mich., 1945).

Of the large literature on community planning, see, for example,

L. Mumford, *City Development* (New York, 1945);

J. Van Sickle, *Planning for the South* (Nashville, Tenn., 1943);

L. L. Lorwin, *Postwar Plans of the United Nations* (New York, 1943), Chap. III;

N. P. Gist and L. A. Halbert, **Urban Society* (New York, 1941), Chap. XXIII;

**Building the Future City, The Annals* of the American Academy of Political and Social Science, CCXLII (Nov., 1945), 79–162.

There are few systematic treatments of community sentiment. However, some of its characteristics are brought out in

P. A. Sorokin and C. C. Zimmerman, *Principles of Rural-Urban Sociology* (New York, 1939), Part III;

J. A. Kinneman, *The Community in American Society*, Chap. XII;

J. H. Kolb and E. de S. Brunner, *A Study of Rural Society*, Chap. V;

W. Firey, **Land Use in Central Boston*, Chap. IV;

S. D. Alinsky, *Reveille for Radicals* (Chicago, 1946).

Innumerable studies have been made of specific communities. Among those of special importance for the student of sociology are

R. S. and H. M. Lynd, **Middletown* (New York, 1929), and **Middletown in Transition* (New York, 1937);

W. L. Warner and P. S. Lunt, **The Social Life of a Modern Community;*

James West (pseudonym), *Plainville, U.S.A.* (New York, 1945);

C. F. Schmid, *Social Saga of Two Cities* (Minneapolis, 1937);

J. F. Embree, **Suye Mura, A Japanese Village* (Chicago, 1939);

C. M. Arensberg and S. T. Kimball, *Family and Community in Ireland* (Cambridge, Mass., 1940).

The nature of national community sentiment is treated in

R. M. MacIver, **The Modern State*, Chap. IV, §2, and **The Web of Government*, pp. 162 ff.

Most books on nationality and nationalism are written from a historical or political viewpoint. See

C. J. H. Hayes, *Essays on Nationalism* (New York, 1926), and *Historical Evolution of Modern Nationalism* (New York, 1931);

H. Kohn, **The Idea of Nationalism* (New York, 1946), especially Chap. I, and **World Order in Historical Perspective* (Cambridge, Mass., 1942), Chap. II.

Works on national traits are apt to be misleading. Those showing sociological insight include

D. W. Brogan, *The American Character* (New York, 1944), *The English People* (New York, 1943), and *French Personalities and Problems* (London, 1946);

K. Shridharani, *My India, My America* (New York, 1941);

R. Benedict, *The Chrysanthemum and the Sword: Patterns of Japanese Culture* (Boston, 1946).

For intracommunal differences see the readings listed under Chapters XIV and XV.

CHAPTER 13 City, Country, and Region

Many of the references listed under Chapter XII are equally relevant for this chapter.

A good basis for the comparison of city and country may be found in the study of the migrating peasant, of which the classic sociological work is

W. I. Thomas and F. Znaniecki, **The Polish Peasant;*

but almost as revealing are the characterizations in such novels as

O. E. Rölvaag, *Giants in the Earth* (New York, 1928);

K. Hamsun, **Growth of the Soil* (New York, 1921);

P. Buck, *The Good Earth* (New York, 1931);

J. Steinbeck, *Grapes of Wrath* (New York, 1939).

A mass of information about rural life is contained in

P. A. Sorokin and C. C. Zimmerman, *Principles of Rural-Urban Sociology;*

P. A. Sorokin, C. C. Zimmerman, and C. J. Galpin, *A Systematic Sourcebook in Rural Sociology* (Minneapolis, 1930);

Rural Sociology (the journal).

The condition of rural life throughout the world is explored in

E. de S. Brunner, I. T. Sanders, and D. Ensminger, *Farmers of the World* (New York, 1945);

K. Brandt, *The Reconstruction of World Agriculture* (New York, 1945)

For the influence of the pioneer economy on North American civilization the classic is

F. J. Turner, *"Significance of the Frontier in American History," *Annual Report of the American Historical Association* (1893), pp. 199–227;

while the transition from pioneer conditions is suggestively treated in

W. H. Wilson, *The Evolution of the Country Community* (rev. ed., Boston, 1923);

J. M. Williams, *Our Rural Heritage* (New York, 1925).

Small communities are discussed, for example, in

A. Blumenthal, *Small Town Stuff* (Chicago, 1932);

E. de S. Brunner, *Village Communities* (New York, 1927);

D. L. Sanderson, *The Rural Community* (Boston, 1932), and **Leadership for Rural Life* (New York, 1940);

C. C. Zimmerman, **The Changing Community;*

and their place in contemporary civilization is well stated in

A. Morgan, **The Small Community* (New York, 1942).

For reasons given in the text it is harder to find comprehensive works dealing with the social life of the city. The socioeconomic aspects of a metropolis were surveyed in the monumental co-operative work

C. Booth *et al.*, *Life and Labor of the People of London* (16 vols., London, 1892), more recently brought up to date in the undertaking sponsored by the London School of Economics and Social Science,

Sir Huber L. Smith (Director), *The New Survey of London Life and Labor* (9 vols., London, 1930–1935);

and an American industrial city is similarly surveyed in

The Pittsburgh Survey (ed. P. U. Kellogg, 6 vols., New York, 1910–1914);

P. Klein, *A Social Study of Pittsburgh* (New York, 1938).

Much information about cities may be found also in

Regional Survey of New York and Its Environs (New York, 1927–1929);

the results of which are presented in briefer form in

R. L. Duffus, **Mastering a Metropolis* (New York, 1930);

and in

National Resources Committee, **Our Cities* (Washington, D.C., 1937), and *Better Cities* (Washington, D.C., 1942);

W. F. Ogburn, *Social Characteristics of Cities* (Chicago, 1937).

Of the textbooks in "urban sociology" mention should be made of

N. Carpenter, *The Sociology of City Life* (New York, 1931);

S. A. Queen and L. F. Thomas, *The City* (New York, 1939);

E. Muntz, *Urban Sociology* (New York, 1938);

N. P. Gist and L. A. Halbert, **Urban Society*.

Significant aspects of urban life are treated in

L. Wirth. *"Urbanism as a Way of Life," *American Journal of Sociology*, XLIV (1938), 1-24;

L. Mumford, *The Culture of Cities*. Chaps. I–VI;

Cities Are Abnormal (ed. E. T. Peterson, Norman, Okla., 1946).

Special urban areas and types have been studied by the ecological school, including, for example,

The Urban Community (ed. E. W. Burgess, Chicago, 1926);

R. E. Park *et al.*, **The City* (Chicago, 1925);

H. W. Zorbaugh, *The Goldcoast and the Slum* (Chicago, 1929);

C. R. Shaw, *Delinquency Areas* (Chicago, 1929);

R. S. Cavan, *Suicide* (Chicago, 1928);

R. E. L. Faris and H. W. Dunham, **Mental Disorders in Urban Areas* (Chicago, 1939);

while a critique of this approach may be found in

M. A. Alihan, *Social Ecology* (New York, 1938).

Certain aspects of the urban environment are revealed in such studies as

J. Addams, *Twenty Years at Hull House* (New York, 1923);

C. F. Ware, *Greenwich Village, 1920–1930* (Boston, 1935).

City growth was earlier ably presented in

A. F. Weber, *The Growth of Cities* (New York, 1899);

and its more recent manifestations are revealed in such statistical reports as

C. Goodrich *et al.*, *Migration and Economic Opportunity* (Philadelphia, 1936);
U.S. Bureau of the Census, *Sixteenth Census of the United States:* 1940, Special Reports, *Internal Migration*, 1935–1940 (4 vols., Washington, D.C., 1943, 1946);

while a good brief treatment is

A. J. Jaffe, *"Population Trends and City Growth," *The Annals* of the American Academy of Political and Social Science, CCXLII (Nov., 1945), 18–29.

The social consequences of urbanization are treated pessimistically in a number of works; extremely so in

O. Spengler, *Decline of the West* (tr. C. F. Atkinson, New York, 1926), Vol. II, Chap. IV;

and somewhat more realistically in

L. Mumford, *The Culture of Cities*, Chap. IV;

see also

E. Saarinen, *The City: Its Growth, Its Decay, Its Future* (New York, 1943).

The position of "regionalism" is stated in

**In Search of the Regional Balance in America* (ed. H. W. Odum and K. Jocher, Chapel Hill, N.C., 1945);
L. Mumford, *The Culture of Cities*, Chaps. VII–IX;

is emphasized in the textbook

H. W. Odum, *Understanding Society* (New York, 1947);

and is basic to the approach of the popular

J. Gunther, *Inside U.S.A.* (New York, 1947).

Among the significant studies of regions in the United States are

H. W. Odum, *Southern Regions* (Chapel Hill, N.C., 1936);
R. P. Vance, *All These People* (Chapel Hill, N.C., 1945);
H. W. Odum and H. E. Moore, **American Regionalism*, especially Part III.

CHAPTER 14 Social Class and Caste

Until recent years the sociology of class was developed largely by European writers, for example,

K. Bucher, *Industrial Revolution* (New York, 1912);
T. Geiger, *Die Masse und ihre Aktion* (Stuttgart, 1926);
W. Sombart, *Der moderne Kapitalismus* (3 vols., Munich, 1924–1927), a large part of which is to be found in
F. L. Nussbaum, **A History of the Economic Institutions of Modern Europe* (New York, 1933).

The views of the earlier American sociologists are presented in

C. H. Page, *Class and American Sociology: From Ward to Ross* (New York, 1940).

The trends of modern classes are discussed in a number of works, such as

T. Veblen, **The Theory of the Leisure Class;*

P. A. Sorokin, *Social Mobility* (New York, 1927);
C. C. North, *Social Differentiation* (Chapel Hill, N.C., 1926);
F. C. Palm, **The Middle Classes, Then and Now* (New York, 1936);
G. A. Briefs, *The Proletariat* (New York, 1937).

The concept of class and the criteria of class are treated in
Class Conflict and Social Stratification (ed. T. H. Marshall, London, 1938), especially the articles by J. Hilton, T. H. Marshall, L. Robbins, M. Dobb, and C. A. Mace;
T. H. Marshall, "Social Class—A Preliminary Analysis," *Sociological Review*, XXVI (1934), 55–76;
P. Mombert, *"Class," *Encyclopaedia of the Social Sciences*, Vol. III;
T. Parsons, "Analytical Approach to the Theory of Social Stratification," *American Journal of Sociology*, LXV (1940), 841–862;
**From Max Weber: Essays in Sociology* (tr. and ed. H. H. Gerth and C. W. Mills), pp. 180–195;
Max Weber, **The Theory of Social and Economic Organization* (tr. T. Parsons and A. M. Henderson), pp. 424–429.

Status in primitive society is discussed in
G. Landtman, **The Origin of the Inequality of the Social Classes* (Chicago, 1938), especially Chap. I;
its complexity in modern society in
E. Benoit-Smullyan, "Status, Status Types, and Status Interrelations." *American Sociological Review*, IX (1944), 151–161;
E. C. Hughes, *"Dilemmas and Contradictions of Status," *American Journal of Sociology*, L (1945), 353–359;
and its relation to occupation in
W. E. Moore, **Industrial Relations and the Social Order* (New York, 1946), Chap. XXII.

For ethnic and racial groups as "castes" see the references listed under Chapter XV. Of the considerable literature on the relation of caste to the social structure may be mentioned
C. Bouglé, *Essais sur le Régime des Castes* (Paris, 1908);
E. Senart, *Caste in India* (London, 1930);
G. S. Ghurye, *Caste and Race in India* (New York, 1932);
**From Max Weber: Essays in Sociology*, pp. 396–415;
O. C. Cox, *Caste, Class, and Race* (New York, 1948), Part One.

The Marxist doctrine of class and class consciousness is expounded in numerous works, including
K. Marx, *Wage-Labour and Capital* (New York, 1933), Chap. IX;
F. Engels, *Anti-Duehring* (New York, 1935), III, Chap. II;
N. Bukharin, **Historical Materialism* (New York, 1925), Chap. VIII;
and is applied to the United States in

L. Corey, *The Crisis of the Middle Class* (New York, 1935), and *The Decline of American Capitalism* (New York, 1934).

Of the many critiques of the Marxist doctrine, see especially

A. D. Lindsay, **Karl Marx's Capital* (London, 1925).

There is no good general study of class in the United States, but various aspects are treated in numerous works. On economic concentration see

A. A. Berle and G. C. Means, *The Modern Corporation and Private Property* (New York, 1933);

D. Lynch, **The Concentration of Economic Power* (New York, 1946);

on occupational structure and trends see

U.S. Bureau of the Census, **Comparative Occupational Statistics for the United States, 1870 to 1940* (Washington, D.C., 1943), especially Chap. XIV;

on social mobility see

P. E. Davidson and H. D. Anderson, *Occupational Mobility in an American Community* (Stanford University, 1937);

R. Canters, *"Occupational Mobility of Urban Occupational Strata," *American Sociological Review*, XIII (1948), 197–203;

and on class attitudes see, for example,

A. W. Kornhauser, "Analysis of 'Class' Structure of Contemporary American Society—Psychological Bases of Class Divisions," in *Industrial Conflict: A Psychological Interpretation* (ed. G. W. Hartmann and T. Newcomb, New York, 1939), Chap. XI;

E. Roper, *"Fortune Survey," *Fortune* (Feb., 1940, and Jan., 1947).

Good studies of class divisions in specific communities include

W. L. Warner and P. S. Lunt, **The Social Life of a Modern Community*, especially Chaps. IV–VIII, XX–XXII, and *The Status System of a Modern Community* (New Haven, 1942);

W. L. Warner and J. O. Low, *The Social System of the Modern Factory* (New Haven, 1947), especially Chaps. VIII–X;

A. W. Jones, *Life, Liberty, and Property* (Philadelphia, 1941), especially Chaps. XXIII–XXIV;

James West (pseudonym), **Plainville, U.S.A.*, Chap. III.

The political significance of class in the United States is treated in

A. N. Holcombe, *The New Party Politics* (New York, 1933), and *The Middle Classes in American Politics* (Cambridge, Mass., 1940);

A. M. Bingham, *Insurgent America* (New York, 1935), Parts I and II.

The broad sociological significance of the subject is brought out in

R. M. MacIver, **The Web of Government*, Chaps. V–VI;

K. Mannheim, *Man and Society in an Age of Reconstruction* (New York, 1940), Parts I and II.

CHAPTER 15 Ethnic and Racial Groups

On the nature of race consult

R. Benedict, **Race: Science and Politics* (New York, 1945);

M. F. Ashley Montagu, *Man's Most Dangerous Myth;*

and on ethnic and "minority" groups see, for example,

W. L. Warner and L. Srole, **The Social Systems of American Ethnic Groups*, Chap. X;

C. F. Ware, "Ethnic Communities," *Encyclopaedia of the Social Sciences*, Vol. V;

L. Wirth, *"The Problem of Minority Groups," in *The Science of Man in the World Crisis* (ed. R. Linton).

Ethnic and racial relationships (as well as other types) are discussed from various viewpoints in the series of studies edited by R. M. MacIver:

Group Relations and Group Antagonisms (New York, 1944);

Civilization and Group Relationships (New York, 1945);

Unity and Difference in American Life (New York, 1947).

Much illustrative material may be found in

When Peoples Meet (ed. A. Locke and B. J. Stern).

There are many works on the American Negro, including

E. R. Embree, *Brown Americans* (New York, 1943);

Characteristics of the American Negro (ed. O. Klineberg, New York, 1944);

and the most comprehensive to date,

G. Myrdal, **An American Dilemma* (2 vols., New York, 1944).

Part VIII, Volume I, of the last-named work incorporates the "caste" approach, which is developed in such studies as

J. Dollard, **Caste and Class in a Southern Town* (New Haven, 1937);

H. Powdermaker, *After Freedom* (New York, 1939);

A. Davis, B. B. and M. R. Gardner, *Deep South* (Chicago, 1941);

St. C. Drake and H. R. Cayton, **Black Metropolis* (New York, 1945), Part III.

The same approach is used in a number of investigations of personality formation among Negroes, several of which are discussed in

R. L. Sutherland, **Color, Class and Personality* (Washington, D.C., 1942).

The use of the concept of "caste" in interpreting race relations is somewhat bitterly attacked in

O. C. Cox, *Caste, Class, and Race*, Part III.

Of the many studies of the Jews, mention should be made of

The American Jew (ed. O. I. Janowsky, New York, 1942);

C. McWilliams, **A Mask for Privilege* (Boston, 1948).

A good source of information on the various "minority" groups in the United States is

F. J. Brown and J. S. Roucek (eds.), *One America.*

Ethnic group relations in two New England communities are reported in

W. L. Warner and L. Srole, **The Social Systems of American Ethnic Groups*, Chaps. I–IX;

E. L. Anderson, **We Americans* (Cambridge, Mass., 1937).

In spite of the large and increasing literature on prejudice and discrimination, few systematic or analytical works are available. Useful sources, which contain bibliographies, include

Controlling Group Prejudice (ed. G. W. Allport), *The Annals* of the American Academy of Political and Social Science, Vol. CCXLIV (March, 1946);

Survey Graphic (Jan., 1947);

R. M. Williams, Jr., *The Reduction of Intergroup Tensions*, Social Science Research Council Bulletin 57 (New York, 1947);

and the Report of the President's Committee on Civil Rights

**To Secure These Rights* (Washington, D.C., and New York, 1947).

Strategy against discrimination is worked out in

R. M. MacIver, **The More Perfect Union* (New York, 1948);

see also

G. Watson, *Action for Unity* (New York, 1947).

Among the popularly written works dealing with this problem may be mentioned

M. Halsey, **Color Blind* (New York, 1946);

and the novels

J. Sinclair, *Wasteland* (New York, 1946);

B. Schulberg, *What Makes Sammy Run* (New York, 1941);

L. Z. Hobson, *Gentlemen's Agreement* (New York, 1947);

S. Lewis, *Kingsblood Royal* (New York, 1947).

CHAPTER 16 Herd, Crowd, and Mass Communication

Earlier influential works specially devoted to the study of crowd behavior and sentiment include

G. Le Bon, *The Crowd* (Eng. tr., London, 1925);

G. Tarde, *L'opinion et la foule* (Paris, 1922);

W. Trotter, *Instincts of the Herd in Peace and War* (London, 1920);

E. D. Martin, *The Behavior of Crowds* (New York, 1929);

and also such studies as

W. McDougall, *The Group Mind* (Cambridge, 1927), Chap. II;

B. Sidis, **The Psychology of Suggestion* (New York, 1921);

G. Wallas, *Human Nature in Politics* (New York, 1924).

Analyses of "collective behavior" are given in

L. von Wiese and H. Becker, *Systematic Sociology*, Chaps. XXXIV–XXXVII;

H. Blumer *"Collective Behavior," in *An Outline of the Principles of Sociology* (ed. A. M. Lee, New York, 1946);

and the subject is dealt with in various books on social psychology, including

K. Young, **Social Psychology*, Part III;

R. T. La Piere, *Collective Behavior*, Parts I and V;

N. E. Miller and J. Dollard, **Social Learning and Imitation* (New Haven, 1941), Chaps. XIV–XV;

M. Sherif and H. Cantril, *The Psychology of Ego-Involvements*, Chap. IV;

and much illustrative material may be found in

K. Young, *Source Book for Social Psychology* (New York, 1930), Chaps. XXII–XXIV.

Special aspects of herd and crowd behavior are treated in

G. W. Allport and L. Postman, *The Psychology of Rumor* (New York, 1947);

H. Cantril, *The Psychology of Social Movements* (New York, 1941), Part I.

Chapter IV of the last-named volume deals with a single type of crowd, as do

W. White, *Rope and Faggot* (New York, 1929);

A. F. Raper, *The Tragedy of Lynching* (Chapel Hill, N.C., 1933);

A. M. Lee and N. D. Humphrey, **Race Riot* (New York, 1943).

Much of the rapidly growing literature in mass communication is listed in

B. L. Smith, H. D. Lasswell, and R. D. Casey, *Propaganda, Communication and Public Opinion* (Princeton, 1946);

see also

W. Albig, *Public Opinion* (New York, 1939);

Print, Radio and Film in a Democracy (ed. D. Waples, Chicago, 1942);

H. Cantril, *Gauging Public Opinion* (Princeton, 1943);

R. T. La Piere, **Sociology*, Chap. X.

Audience and crowd leadership techniques are discussed in

L. W. Doob, *Propaganda: Its Psychology and Technique* (New York, 1935);

A. M. and E. B. Lee, **The Fine Art of Propaganda* (New York, 1939).

Interesting studies of the effect of mass communication in specific instances are

H. Cantril, *The Invasion from Mars* (Princeton, 1940);

R. K. Merton, **Mass Persuasion* (New York, 1946).

Interpretations of the nature and trends of "mass" society include

E. Lederer, *The State of the Masses* (New York, 1940);

S. Neumann, *Permanent Revolution* (New York, 1942), Chaps. IV, VII;

K. Mannheim, *Man and Society in an Age of Reconstruction, passim.*

CHAPTER 17 Associations and Interests

For the nature and classification of interests see references under Chapter II.

An elaborate analysis of the conditions determining the formation of associations is offered in

L. von Wiese and H. Becker, *Systematic Sociology*, Part II;
other treatments include
H. A. Phelps, *Principles and Laws of Sociology* (New York, 1936), Chap. XVI;
P. A. Sorokin, *Society, Culture, and Personality*, Part VI;
E. T. Hiller, *Social Relations and Structures*, Part V.

Suggestive discussions of group leadership and interests may be found in
R. Michels, *Political Parties;*
R. Schmidt, "Leadership," *Encyclopaedia of the Social Sciences*, Vol. IX;
P. Pigors, **Leadership or Domination* (Boston, 1935);
O. Tead, *The Art of Leadership* (New York, 1935);
E. S. Bogardus, *Leaders and Leadership;*
G. L. Coyle, **Studies in Group Behavior* (New York, 1937);
K. Young, **Social Psychology*, Chap. X.

Many works treat intergroup conflict and solidarity. See, for example,
F. Znaniecki, **Social Actions*, Chaps. XI, XIV, XVII;
R. T. La Piere, **Sociology*, Chap. XVI;
G. E. G. Catlin, *A Study of the Principles of Politics* (New York, 1930), Chap. V;
G. L. Coyle, **The Social Process in Organized Groups*.

See also the references on conflict and co-operation listed under Chapter III.

CHAPTER 18 The Great Associations: Political

On the development of political control in society see, for example,
R. H. Lowie, *The Origin of the State* (New York, 1927);
R. M. MacIver, **The Web of Government*, Part I.

The function of the state as an organ of society is the subject of many interpretations. The point of view of the text is more fully developed in R. M. MacIver's
The Modern State, especially Chaps. I, V, XVI;
Leviathan and the People (University, La., 1939), Part I;
**The Web of Government*, especially Chaps. IV, VIII, XIII.

Similar viewpoints will be found in
G. D. H. Cole, *Social Theory;*
E. Jenks, *The State and the Nation;*
A. D. Lindsay, **The Essentials of Democracy* (London, 1945), and **The Modern Democratic State* (London, 1943), Vol. I.

The student of sociology should also refer to
G. E. G. Catlin, *A Study of the Principles of Politics*, Chap. VIII;
W. W. Willoughby, *An Examination of the Nature of the State* (New York, 1928);
R. Pound, *Social Control through Law;*
L. von Wiese and H. Becker, *Systematic Sociology*, Chap. XLIII;

C. E. Merriam, **Systematic Politics*, Chaps. I–III;
J. Marshall, *Swords and Symbols* (New York, 1939).

Reviews of sociological theories of the state will be found in
H. E. Barnes, *Sociology and Political Theory* (New York, 1924), and the same author's *Chap. XVIII in *Contemporary Social Theory* (ed. H. E. Barnes, H. Becker, and F. B. Becker).

The relation of the state to the economic order is discussed in many works, including
A. F. Bentley, *The Process of Government* (Chicago, 1908);
F. Delaisi, *Political Myths and Economic Realities* (New York, 1927), especially Part IV;
H. Laski, *The Grammar of Politics* (New Haven, 1931);
C. Becker, **Modern Democracy* (New York, 1941);
C. A. Beard, *The Economic Basis of Politics* (rev. ed., New York, 1945);
R. M. MacIver, **The Web of Government*, Chap. VI.

On state planning consult
L. L. Lorwin, *Time for Planning* (New York, 1944);
B. Wootton, *Freedom under Planning* (Chapel Hill, N.C., 1945);
K. Mannheim, *Man and Society in an Age of Reconstruction*, Parts IV–VI.

The class theory of the state is given in
F. Oppenheimer, *The State* (New York, 1926);
N. Lenin, *The State and Revolution* (New York, 1927);
H. Laski, *The State in Theory and Practice* (New York, 1935);
and the views of its exponents are ably discussed in
G. Catlin, **The Story of the Political Philosophers* (New York, 1939), Chaps. XVIII–XX.

The inclusive theory of the state is contained in many works, from those of Plato to those of Hitler. See, for example,
B. Bosanquet, *The Philosophical Theory of the State* (London, 1920);
B. Mussolini, *The Political and Social Doctrine of Fascism* (New York, 1935);
and for evaluations of the theory
R. M. MacIver, **Leviathan and the People*, Chaps. IV–V;
B. Russell, *History of Western Philosophy* (New York, 1945), Chap. XXII;
G. Catlin, *The Story of the Political Philosophers*, Chaps. XIV–XVII.

There are many studies of the state in the larger society. Here it may suffice to mention
R. M. MacIver, *Towards an Abiding Peace* (New York, 1943), and **The Web of Government*, Chap. XII;
Human Nature and Enduring Peace (ed. G. Murphy, Boston, 1945).

CHAPTER 19 The Great Associations: Economic

Vast as is the literature of economics, peculiarly little has been done on the sociological problem of distinguishing and characterizing the type-form of economic organization. Among the more significant attempts is W. Sombart's, whose views are presented in

F. L. Nussbaum, *A History of the Economic Institutions of Modern Europe*, especially Part IV;

W. Sombart, *"Capitalism," *Encyclopaedia of the Social Sciences*, Vol. III.

See also

J. R. Commons, *Legal Foundations of Capitalism* (New York, 1934);

R. M. MacIver, *The Modern State*, Chap. IX;

N. J. Spykman, *The Social Theory of Georg Simmel*, pp. 121 ff;

T. Parsons, *The Structure of Social Action* (New York, 1937), especially Chaps. IV, XII–XV;

K. Polanyi, *The Great Transformation* (New York, 1944), especially Chaps. XI–XXI;

and the summary articles

T. Parsons, *Chap. XVII in *Contemporary Social Theory* (ed. H. E. Barnes, H. Becker, and F. B Becker);

W. E. Moore, Chap. XV in *Twentieth Century Sociology* (ed. G. Gurvitch and W. E. Moore).

The beginning student will find particularly useful

W. E. Moore, **Industrial Relations and the Social Order*, Parts I–II;

S. McKee and L. Rosen, *Technology and Society* (New York, 1941), Parts I–II.

The specific character of economic activity and economic organization is incisively brought out in the writings of T. Veblen, particularly

The Instinct of Workmanship (New York, 1922);

**The Theory of Business Enterprise* (New York, 1904);

and in the writings of M. Weber, see

The Theory of Social and Economic Organization (tr. T. Parsons and A. M. Henderson), pp. 30–55, 158–323.

Sociological aspects of modern economic organization are accented in many of the writings in "industrial sociology," for example,

F. J. Roethlisberger and W. J. Dixon, *Management and the Worker;*

E. Mayo, *The Human Problems of an Industrial Civilization* (New York, 1933);

T. N. Whitehead, *The Industrial Worker* (Cambridge, Mass., 1938);

C. I. Barnard, *The Functions of the Executive;*

**Industry and Society* (ed. W. F. Whyte, New York, 1946);

B. B. Gardner, *Human Relations in Industry* (Chicago, 1945);

W. L. Warner and J. O. Low, **The Social System of the Modern Factory.*

There is a large literature on professional and other occupational organizations. The student of sociology will find suggestive material in

A. M. Carr-Saunders and P. A. Wilson, *The Professions* (London, 1933);

L. Wilson, **The Academic Man* (New York, 1942);

F. Znaniecki, *The Social Role of the Man of Knowledge* (New York, 1940);

W. F. Cottrell, **The Railroader* (Stanford University, Cal., 1940);
H. A. Millis and R. E. Montgomery, *Organized Labor* (New York, 1945);
P. K. Crosser, *Ideologies and American Labor* (New York, 1941), Part II;
C. Wright Mills, *The New Men of Power* (New York, 1948).

CHAPTER 20 The Great Associations: Cultural

There is little sociological literature dealing directly with the subject treated in the first section of this chapter. See, however, the references on culture and civilization under Chapter XXI.

On the social form and function of the church see, for example,

L. von Wiese and H. Becker, *Systematic Sociology*, Chap. XLIV;
H. A. Miller, *Races, Nations, and Classes* (Philadelphia, 1924), Chap. V;
R. M. MacIver, **The Modern State*, Chap. V, §2;
J. Wach, *Sociology of Religion*, especially Part II;
J. M. Yinger, **Religion in the Struggle for Power*, Chaps. II, V;
R. E. L. Faris, **Social Disorganization* (New York, 1948), Chap. XI;
P. J. Tillich, *"The Social Functions of the Churches in Europe and America," *Social Research*, III (1936), 90–104;
**Organized Religion in the United States* (ed. R. H. Abrams), *The Annals* of the American Academy of Political and Social Science, CCLVI (Mar., 1948), 1–24, 72–147.

Studies of church organization and activities in different types of communities include

H. P. Douglass and E. de S. Brunner, **The Protestant Church as a Social Institution* (New York, 1935);
E. C. Lindeman, *The Church in the Changing Community* (New York, 1929);
R. C. Smith, *The Church in Our Town* (Nashville, Tenn., 1945);
L. Pope, **Millhands and Preachers* (New Haven, 1942);
R. S. and H. M. Lynd, *Middletown*, Part V, and *Middletown in Transition*, Chap. VIII.

CHAPTER 21 Functional Systems

The "institutional complex" has scarcely been treated as such in works on sociology.

For a brief statement see

E. T. Hiller, *Social Relations and Structures*, Chap. XVI.

The interdependence of social institutions is stressed in many sociological studies, such as

L. von Wiese and H. Becker, *Systematic Sociology*, Chap. XLV;
R. T. La Piere, *Sociology*, Part III;
R. C. Angell, *Integration of American Society* (New York, 1941), especially Chap. II;
R. E. L. Faris, *Social Disorganization*, Chaps. I–II.

There is, of course, much illustrative material, especially in works dealing with the relation of economics and politics, such as

C. A. Beard, *The Economic Basis of Politics;*

C. Becker, *Modern Democracy;*

also in works dealing with the relation of economic and technological factors to other aspects of social life, such as

T. A. Salter, *Modern Mechanization and Its Effects on the Structure of Society* (London, 1933);

S. McKee and L. Rosen, *Technology and Society;*

L. Mumford, *Technics and Civilization* (New York, 1934);

and in works dealing with the relation of church and state, as given in the references under Chapter XX, and such books as

H. P. Van Dusen *et al., Church and State in the Modern World* (New York, 1937).

For the anthropological concept of culture consult

R. Linton, **The Study of Man*, Chaps. V–VI;

C. Wissler, *Man and Culture* (New York, 1938), Chap. XII;

B. Malinowski, "Culture," *Encyclopaedia of the Social Sciences*, Vol. IV;

and for difficulties involved in this usage

C. Kluckhohn and W. H. Kelly, *"The Concept of Culture," in *The Science of Man in the World Crisis* (ed. R. Linton).

The distinction between culture and civilization is developed in R. M. MacIver's *The Modern State*, Chap. V, §2;

"The Historical Pattern of Social Change," *Journal of Social Philosophy*, II (1936), 35–54;

**Social Causation* (Boston, 1942), Chap. X;

and corresponds in the main to the usage of A. Weber (*Archiv für Sozialwissenschaft und Sozialpolitik*, XLVII [1920], 1–49), which is discussed in

S. Neumann, "Alfred Weber's Conception of Historicocultural Sociology," in *An Introduction to the History of Sociology* (ed. H. E. Barnes).

See also the discussions in

J. W. Woodard, "A New Classification of Culture and a Restatement of the Cultural Lag Theory," *American Sociological Review*, I (1936), 89–102;

R. K. Merton, "Civilization and Culture," *Sociology and Social Research*, XXI (1936), 103–113;

and the criticism of the distinction by P. A. Sorokin in

Social and Cultural Dynamics (New York, 1937–1941), IV, pp. 157 ff.

Society, Culture, and Personality, pp. 580–582, 668–673.

CHAPTER 22 Society as Process

The literature interpretative of social change in its larger aspects is far from adequate. Of general works may be mentioned

A. G. Keller, *Societal Evolution* (rev. ed., New York, 1931);

W. F. Ogburn, *Social Change* (New York, 1922),
F. S. Chapin, *Cultural Change* (New York, 1928);
N. L. R. Sims, **The Problem of Social Change* (New York, 1939), Parts I and III.

Various aspects of social change are dealt with in numerous books, for example,
C. H. Cooley, *Social Process;*
R. M. MacIver, *Social Causation;*
K. Mannheim, *Man and Society in an Age of Reconstruction;*
E. Fromm, *Escape from Freedom.*

Useful data for the study of social change are contained in such compilations as
President's Research Committee on Social Trends, *Recent Social Trends* (New York, 1933); see especially the introductory *"Review of Findings," pp. xi-lxxv;
National Resources Committee, *Technological Trends and National Policy* (Washington, D.C., 1937);
American Society in Wartime (ed. W. F. Ogburn, Chicago, 1943);
and in the volume
H. E. Barnes, *Society in Transition* (New York, 1939).

On the prediction of social change see
H. A. Phelps, *Principles and Laws of Sociology*, Chap. XXI;
H. Becker, "Constructive Typology in the Social Sciences," Chap. II in *Contemporary Social Theory* (ed. H. E. Barnes, H. Becker, and F. B. Becker).

On the "three orders" underlying social change see the Introduction to *Recent Social Trends* cited above and the writings of R. M. MacIver referred to under Chapter XXI.

An attempt to grapple with the interpretation of social change is made in the writings of A. J. Toynbee, including
A Study of History, of which the one-volume abridgment by D. C. Somervell will serve the student's purposes;
Civilization on Trial (New York, 1948), especially Chaps. I–III, V, XI.

Another attempt is made in the writings of P. A. Sorokin, including
Social and Cultural Dynamics, especially Vol. IV;
The Crisis of Our Age (New York, 1945);
Society, Culture, and Personality, Parts VI and VII.

It is also a central issue in the suggestive volumes of L. Mumford, including
Technics and Civilization;
The Culture of Cities;
The Condition of Man (New York, 1944).

The views of these and other writers on social change are discussed in
H. Becker, *"Historical Sociology," Chap. XV in *Contemporary Social Theory* (ed. H. E. Barnes, H. Becker, and F. B. Becker);
H. E. Barnes, *Historical Sociology: Its Origins and Development* (New York, 1948).

CHAPTER 23 The Ways of Social Change

For illustrations of the modes of change see the works of Ogburn and Chapin cited under Chapter XXII. See also

E. T. Hiller, **Principles of Sociology*, Chap. XXV;

W. F. Ogburn and M. F. Nimkoff, *Sociology* (Boston, 1946), Chaps. XXIV–XXVII;

P. A. Sorokin, *Society, Culture, and Personality*, Parts V and VI.

The meaning of evolutionary change is treated in many works. See, for example

E. Durkheim, **The Division of Labor in Society;*

M. Ginsberg, *Studies in Sociology*, Chaps. IV and V;

R. M. MacIver, **Community*, Book III;

H. E. Barnes and H. Becker, *Social Thought from Lore to Science*, Chap. XX;

R. H. Lowie, *Social Organization* (New York, 1948), Chap. III;

A. Goldenweiser, *"Evolution, Social," *Encyclopaedia of the Social Sciences*, Vol. V.

For processes of adjustment, assimilation, and so forth, see such a textbook as

J. L. and J. P. Gillin, *An Introduction to Sociology*, Part V.

For brief treatments of the idea of cyclical change see

P. A. Sorokin, *"Sociocultural Dynamics and Evolution," Chap. V in *Twentieth Century Sociology* (ed. G. Gurvitch and W. E. Moore);

H. A. Phelps, *Principles and Laws of Sociology*, Chap. XIX;

N. L. R. Sims, *The Problem of Social Change*, Chap. XIV;

R. M. MacIver, **Social Causation*, pp. 101–107.

On the idea of progress see the references under Chapter XXVIII.

CHAPTER 24 Biological Factors of Social Change

For the facts of world-wide demographic change see

A. M. Carr-Saunders, *World Population* (Oxford, 1936);

D. Glass, *Population Policies and Movements in Europe* (Oxford, 1940);

**World Population in Transition* (ed. K. Davis), issue of *The Annals* of the American Academy of Political and Social Science for Jan., 1945, Vol. CCXXXVII;

and the textbooks in population

W. S. Thompson, *Population Problems;*

P. H. Landis, *Population Problems.*

Extensive data on population trends in the United States may be found in

National Resources Committee, *Problems of a Changing Population* (Washington, D.C., 1938), and *Human Conservation* (Washington, D.C., 1943);

*F. E. Linder and R. D. Grove, *Vital Statistics Rates in the United States, 1900–1940* (Washington, D.C., 1943),

and in the numerous reports of the Milbank Foundation.

On natural selection the classics are, of course, C. Darwin's
**The Descent of Man and Selection in Relation to Sex*, and *The Origin of Species* (both in various editions).

The difference between natural and social selection was clearly stated by various biologists years ago. See
T. H. Huxley, *Evolution and Ethics* (New York, 1905);
C. L. Morgan, *Habit and Instinct* (London, 1896);
J. Huxley, **Essays of a Biologist* (London, 1923), Chap. I.

Few sociologists have adequately studied the subject, but reference may be made to
A. G. Keller, *Societal Evolution;*
H. E. Barnes, *Society in Transition*, Chap. VI;
R. T. La Piere, **Sociology*, Chaps. VI–VII;
H. W. Odum, *Understanding Society*, Chaps. XXI–XXII.

Accounts of the history of birth control are given in
F. H. Hankins, "Birth Control," *Encyclopaedia of the Social Sciences*, Vol. II;
N. E. Himes, *Medical History of Contraception* (Baltimore, 1936).

An entirely different view of the cause of the falling birth rate from that suggested in the text is given in
R. Pearl, *The Biology of Population Growth* (New York, 1930);
and different views of the wider implications of the population trends are in
E. A. Hooton, *Twilight of Man* (New York, 1939);
W. B. Reddaway, *The Economics of a Declining Population* (New York, 1939).

A good brief discussion of the whole problem is
K. Sax *"Population Problems," in *The Science of Man in the World Crisis* (ed. R. Linton), pp. 258–281.

CHAPTER 25 Technological Factors of Social Change

The influence of invention and technological change on society is treated in a large number of works, for example,
Recent Social Trends, Chaps. III and IV;
National Resources Committee, *Technological Trends and National Policy;*
W. F. Ogburn, *Social Change*, and *The Social Effects of Aviation* (Boston, 1946);
S. C. Gilfillan, *The Sociology of Invention* (Chicago, 1935);
S. McKee and L. Rosen, **Technology and Society;*
S. Chase, *Men and Machines* (New York, 1929);
L. Mumford, **Technics and Civilization;*
A. P. Usher, *A History of Mechanical Inventions* (New York, 1929);
S. Giedon, **Mechanization Takes Command* (New York, 1948);
and is accented in the textbook
W. F. Ogburn and M. F. Nimkoff, *Sociology*, Part VII.

For basic contributions to Marxist theory consult

K. Marx, **Contribution to the Critique of Political Economy* (tr. N. I. Stone, New York, 1904), and *Capital* (various editions), I, Part VIII;

K. Marx and F. Engels, **The Communist Manifesto* (tr. S. Moore, New York, 1933);

F. Engels, *Anti-Duehring*, Parts II and III.

For writers in the Marxist tradition a few references out of a vast literature must suffice:

K. Kautsky, *The Class Struggle* (tr. W. E. Bohn, Chicago, 1910);

A. Loria, *The Economic Foundations of Society* (London, 1899);

A. Labriola, *Essays on the Materialistic Conception of History* (tr. C. K. Kerr, Chicago, 1908);

N. Bukharin, *Historical Materialism;*

L. Corey, *The Decline of American Capitalism;*

P. M. Sweezy, *The Theory of Capitalist Development* (New York, 1942), especially Parts III and IV.

Of numerous interpretations and criticisms of Marxism we must limit reference to the following:

A. D. Lindsay, **Karl Marx's Capital;*

M. Beer, *Life and Teachings of Karl Marx* (New York, 1929);

K. Korsch, *Karl Marx* (New York, 1938);

S. Hook, *Towards the Understanding of Karl Marx* (New York, 1933), and **Reason, Social Myths, and Democracy* (New York, 1940), Chaps. VII–XII;

G. D. H. Cole, **What Marx Really Meant* (New York, 1937);

K. Federn, *The Materialist Conception of History* (London, 1939).

Technological determinism is seldom stated as explicitly or definitely as economic determinism is postulated by the Marxists, but it is implied or suggested in such works as those of Ogburn, Chase, and Gilfillan cited above. For the views of Veblen see particularly

T. Veblen, **The Theory of the Leisure Class*, Chap. VIII, and **The Instinct of Workmanship*, Chap. I;

J. Dorfman, *Thorstein Veblen and His America* (New York, 1934), especially Chaps. XII–XIV;

J. A. Hobson, *Veblen* (New York, 1937).

CHAPTER 26 Cultural Factors of Social Change

For the doctrine of "cultural lag" consult

W. F. Ogburn, **Social Change*, pp. 200–265;

F. S. Chapin, *Cultural Change*, Chaps. X and XI;

H. E. Barnes, **Society in Transition*, Chaps. XV and XXI;

and of the several critiques of this doctrine see

J. W. Woodard, "A New Classification of Culture and a Restatement of the Cultural Lag Theory," *American Sociological Review*, I (1936), 89–104;

M. Choukas, "The Concept of Cultural Lag Re-examined," *American Sociological Review*, I (1936), 752–760;

W. D. Wallis, "The Concept of Lag," *Sociology and Social Research*, XX (1935), 403–406;

J. Schneider, *"Cultural Lag: What Is It?" *American Sociological Review*, (1945), 786–791.

The idea that cultural or spiritual forces are dominant in social change has found expression in the theories of various philosophers, such as Hegel, Spengler, and Bergson. But the scholarly attempt to show the actual influence of culture in changing situations is scarcely older than the work of M. Weber. On the latter see

M. Weber, **The Protestant Ethic and the Spirit of Capitalism;*

From Max Weber: Essays in Sociology (tr. H. H. Gerth and C. W. Mills), Part III;

T. Parsons, *The Structure of Social Action*, Part III, and the same author's essay in Max Weber, *The Theory of Social and Economic Organization* (tr. T. Parsons and A. M. Henderson), pp. 8–55;

R. Bendix, "Max Weber's Interpretation of Conduct and History," *American Journal of Sociology*, LI (1946), 518–526.

On the general theme consult

M. R. Cohen, **Reason and Nature* (New York, 1931), Book II, especially Chap. III;

P. A. Sorokin, *Social and Cultural Dynamics*, Vol. IV, Part III;

R. M. MacIver, **Social Causation*, Part IV.

Much is made of cultural factors in social change in

A. J. Toynbee, *A Study of History*, and *Civilization on Trial;*

F. S. C. Northrop, *The Meeting of East and West;*

E. Fromm, *Escape from Freedom.*

These works contain many historical illustrations of the clash of culture and civilization. For illustrations of this clash in Western society see Fromm and

L. Mumford, **Technics and Civilization*, and **The Condition of Man.*

The cultural effects of the introduction of Western civilization into Eastern communities are recorded in many studies of the economic and political changes in China, India, Japan, and other countries. For a general discussion see

E. T. Hiller, **Principles of Sociology*, Chaps. XXI–XXIII;

and for numerous illustrations see

When Peoples Meet (ed. A. Locke and B. J. Stern), especially pp. 56–67, 171–191, 590–597, 601–649.

CHAPTER 27 The Reality of Social Evolution

On the question of origins consult

R. H. Lowie, **The Origin of the State;*

A. M. Tozzer, *Social Origins and Social Continuities* (New York, 1925);
G. Landtman, *The Origin of the Inequality of the Social Classes;*
P. Radin, **Primitive Religion* (New York, 1937);
S. H. Hooke, *The Origins of Early Semitic Ritual* (London, 1938);
W. I. Thomas, *Source Book for Social Origins* (Boston, 1929);

and for the difficulties involved in the quest for origins

R. M. MacIver, **Social Causation*, pp. 107–113.

The student should remember that diffusion and evolution are not incompatible. For diffusion and related processes see, for example,

R. Linton, *The Study of Man*, Chaps. XVIII–XIX;
M. J. Herskovits, *"The Processes of Cultural Change," in *The Science of Man in the World Crisis* (ed. R. Linton);
A. A. Goldenweiser, *"Leading Contributions of Anthropology to Social Theory," Chap. XIV in *Contemporary Social Theory* (ed. H. E. Barnes, H. Becker, and F. B. Becker);
F. Boas, *Race, Language, and Culture*, pp. 290–294, 437–445,

as well as the comparative anthropological studies cited under Chapter XXIX.

On the evolution of the church as a social form consult

R. H. Tawney, **Religion and the Rise of Capitalism* (New York, 1926);
M. Weber, *The Protestant Ethic and the Spirit of Capitalism;*
J. Wach, *Sociology of Religion*, Chaps. IV–VII;
J. M. Yinger, *Religion in the Struggle for Power*, Chaps. III–IV;
Various authors, *"Religious Institutions," *Encyclopaedia of the Social Sciences*, Vol. XIII;
**Organized Religion in the United States* (ed. R. H. Abrams), *The Annals* of the American Academy of Political and Social Science, CCLVI (Mar., 1948), 13–62.

CHAPTER 28 Social Evolution and Social Progress

For various theories of the nature of progress see

J. B. Bury, *The Idea of Progress* (London, 1920);
A. J. Todd, *Theories of Social Progress* (New York, 1926);
J. K. Folsom, *Culture and Social Progress* (New York, 1928);
N. L. R. Sims, **The Problem of Social Change*, Chap. XII;
C. Becker, *"Progress," *Enclyclopaedia of the Social Sciences*, Vol. XII.

Discussions by biologists on the relation between evolution and progress include

C. L. Morgan, *Emergent Evolution* (London, 1923);
J. Huxley, *Essays of a Biologist*, Chaps. I–II, and *"The New Evolution," Chap. XII in *Our Emergent Civilization* (ed. R. Anshen, New York, 1947).

Aspects of the subject are dealt with in most of the contributions to the last-named volume; see especially the chapters by R. N. Anshen, B. Blanshard, W. Jaeger,

F. H. Knight. See also

L. T. Hobhouse, *Development and Purpose* (London, 1919);

C. H. Cooley, *Social Process*, Parts VI and VII;

W. D. Wallis, *Culture and Progress* (New York, 1930);

C. Becker, *Progress and Power* (London, 1936).

These references are relevant also for the discussion of the place of value-concepts in the social sciences. For more explicit treatment of the latter subject consult

L. von Wiese and H. Becker, *Systematic Sociology*, Chap. I, §2;

F. Kaufmann, *Methodology of the Social Sciences* (New York, 1944), Chaps. XIV–XV;

R. S. Lynd, *Knowledge for What?* Chaps. I and V;

G. Myrdal, **An American Dilemma*, Vol. II, Appendix 2;

F. S. C. Northrop, *The Logic of the Sciences and the Humanities* (New York, 1947), Chaps. XVI and XXI;

**Science and Man* (ed. R. Anshen, New York, 1942), the essays by B. Blanshard, C. Becker, F. H. Knight, and R. B. Perry.

Numerous books deal with problems of modern society, such as the textbooks

R. E. L. Faris, *Social Disorganization;*

H. A. Phelps, *Contemporary Social Problems* (New York, 1947);

M. A. Elliott and F. E. Merrill, *Social Disorganization.*

But it should be remembered that the expression "social problems" is usually extended to mean "problems of human well-being," most of which are not merely or specifically *social* in the sense in which the term is used throughout this book.

CHAPTER 29 The Broad Pattern of Social Change

The interpretation of social change involves important and difficult questions of method. In American sociology a major issue has been between those who accept and those who reject a significant difference between the character of social causation and that of physical causation. Representative of the former viewpoint are

C. H. Cooley, **Sociological Theory and Social Research* (New York, 1930), especially Chap. IX;

C. A. Ellwood, *Methods in Sociology* (Durham, N.C., 1933);

R. M. MacIver, **Social Causation;*

W. Waller, "Insight and Scientific Method," *American Journal of Sociology*, XL (1934), 285–297.

The opposing viewpoint is vigorously stated in

G. A. Lundberg, **Foundations of Sociology*, especially Part I;

S. C. Dodd, *Dimensions of Society* (New York, 1942), Part I;

R. Bain, "Trends in American Sociological Theory," Chap. II in G. A. Lundberg *et al.*, *Trends in American Sociology* (New York, 1929);

and is also expressed in the popularly written

G. A. Lundberg, *Can Science Save Us?* (New York, 1947).

The student should endeavor to reach his own conclusion on the subject. To this end he may consult

M. R. Cohen, **Reason and Nature*, Book III, Chap. I;

F. Znaniecki, *The Method of Sociology* (New York, 1934);

F. Kaufmann, *Methodology of the Social Sciences*, Chaps. X–XIII;

M. Weber, **The Theory of Social and Economic Organization* (tr. T. Parsons and A. M. Henderson), pp. 87–123;

T. Parsons, *Structure of Social Action*, Chap. XVI;

P. A. Sorokin, *Social and Cultural Dynamics*, Vol. I, Chap. I, and Vol. IV, Chap. I;

F. S. C. Northrop, *The Logic of the Sciences and the Humanities*, Chap. XIV;

J. Huxley, *"Science, Natural and Social," in *Science and Man* (ed. R. Anshen).

To appreciate the contrast between the social patterns of primitive and civilized societies, respectively, the student should be familiar with the social organization of some primitive peoples. For studies of particular societies see, for example,

B. Malinowski, *Argonauts of the Western Pacific* (London, 1922), and *Coral Gardens and Their Magic;*

H. Powdermaker, *Life in Lesu* (New York, 1933);

W. L. Warner, *A Black Civilization* (New York, 1937);

C. Du Bois, **The People of Alor;*

C. Kluckhohn and D. Leighton, **The Navaho* (Cambridge, Mass., 1946).

Among comparative studies may be mentioned

F. Boas, **The Mind of Primitive Man;*

L. T. Hobhouse, G. C. Wheeler, and M. Ginsberg, *The Material Culture and Social Institutions of the Simpler Peoples* (London, 1915);

R. H. Lowie, *Social Organization*, especially Part IV;

W. I. Thomas, *Primitive Behavior;*

R. Benedict, **Patterns of Culture;*

M. Mead, *From the South Seas;*

R. Linton, **The Study of Man;*

A. Kardiner, *The Psychological Frontiers of Society*, Chaps. III–VI.

The contrast between primitive and civilized society presented in the text should, we believe, help to clarify the student's understanding of the complex problem of social change. We face, in our own world society, no more difficult—or no more crucial—task.

Author and Subject Indexes

Author Index

Subject Index